AND THERE
SHALL BE WARS

WORLD WAR II DIARIES AND MEMOIRS
BY
BUD WAGNER

EDITED
BY
LLOYD WAGNER

AND THERE SHALL BE WARS.
Copyright 2000 by Wilmer A. Wagner and Lloyd E. Wagner

ISBN 0-9754538-0-7

Book design by Lloyd Wagner
Cover photograph by Jeff Frey and Associates

Published by
Wilmer Wagner and Lloyd Wagner Press
P.O. Box 1031
Twig, MN 55791

FIRST EDITION, 2000

AND THERE
SHALL BE WARS

My Grandfather, August Seelig said of World War I, the war that
was supposedly fought to end all wars,
"Germany didn't lose the war; she just stopped to take a rest."

My father, Henry Wagner said of the war to end all wars,
"Ja, it was the end for some."

Dr. James Dobson, Christian leader of **Focus on the Family,** said
of the peace we had fought to restore,
"Peace is just the time it takes us to reload and start again."

Norman Schwarzkopf, the US Commanding General during the
Persian Gulf War said,
"War's a profanity — You've got two opposing sides trying
to settle their differences
by killing as many of each other as they can."

And Jesus, the Prince of Peace foresaw wars in humanity's future,
as he said,
"And when ye shall hear of wars and rumors of wars, be ye not
troubled; for such things must needs be, but the end shall not be
yet." (Mark 13: 7)

**As in every war before this one,
The fighting was done largely by men
Who knew little about why it had started,
Who was to blame, or exactly
What sort of world it would
Leave when it was all over.**

**Written by an ex-soldier who is no writer,
For those who are not necessarily soldiers.
None of these stories have been ruined
by other than an eye witness, Bud Wagner**

CONTENTS

iv

vi

LIST OF ILLUSTRATIONS

Claiborne, April 1941.
Page 19:   *(Top) The rain came. These tents probably were not made ready for the rain until it came. In that case, you went out during the rain and tied down the flaps. It's easy to see how Claiborne was called a "tent city."*
(Bottom) Several batteries of men had to assemble together to hear lectures of the Articles of War, *or whatever else it was they had to lecture us on.*
Page 22:   *Camp Claiborne, May 12, 1941. We were practicing using a winch to pull ourselves out if we got stuck in a pond or swamp. We had to watch the winch cable very closely when pulling another vehicle out of a hole, since if it kinked or didn't wind up right, it was liable to snarl, and it was a hard job to get it straight again. A vehicle could be winched out with the help of another vehicle, even if the wheels weren't turning.*
Page 23:   *This was the one Service Club for the whole camp. There was entertainment here, but it was always too crowded for comfort or enjoyment. Each battalion had it's own Recreation Hall, which suited me better than the Service Club, as it was quiet, and reading and writing material was available.*
Page 28:   *(Top) We needed land mines for training, but we had no genuine mines issued to us. We had to cut down this pine tree and cut off slices about 3 inches thick to make our own "mines." This picture was taken on a 2-day bivouac, June 3, 1941. I am on the right.*
(Bottom) This was an illegal act of our bunch on the way back to Camp Claiborne. Our afternoon ration of 1 canteen of water was soon too hot to drink, so we stopped at this farmer's well and filled up with cool water.
Page 29:   *(Top) Our latrine facilities. We had to wash our clothes in here as well. I would usually wash clothes as late as I could before Taps sounded.*
(Bottom) After a rainstorm. The buildings on the far side of the street were the canteens, recreation halls, mess halls, and latrines. Notice the floating duckwalk.
Page 31:   *Our range guard area. When it was my turn to rest, I would visit a small farm on the other side of the woods away from the firing range.*
Page 36:   *Wooden "machine guns" which I helped make, that we used for practice. Ted Nelson, on the left, facing the camera, was a barber from Le Sueur, Minnesota, a good friend. He taught me to use a straightedge razor in Ireland. He lost a leg during the Salerno invasion in September 1943, and I didn't see him again after that.*
Page 37:   *One of the 5 pumping stations that kept Camp Claiborne in water. We had to have guards posted at these places, as they were manned by civilians and considered subject to sabotage. There were only white people working here. All public places, rest rooms, depots, restaurants, etc., were segregated in Louisiana in 1941.*
Page 39:   *July 2, 1941. 34th Division Review.*
Page 40:   *An outdoor market on the way to St. Charles, Louisiana, July 4, 1941.*
Page 43:   *A row of weapons-carriers at Camp Claiborne, Louisiana.*
Page 44:   *DeQuincy farm — was near where Rieman and I were range*

ix

guards. The civilians treated us with respect, and I don't remember any soldiers behaving disrespectfully to the civilians either.

Page 46:   *Rieman resting during our range guarding. Live ammo was sometimes used on the firing range, and it was our job to keep civilians out of that area.*

Page 47:   *This was infantry drill training. They always had to carry rifles, and many times packs as well. Notice the pumping station behind the column. July 1941.*

Page 53:   *These were 6X6 trucks. This area was called the gun park, and the vehicles were kept here as well.*

Page 54:   *A pop man would stop sometimes, and we were able to buy a bottle of pop. These drivers sometimes would stop and treat some smaller groups of soldiers to a free pop as well.*

Page 56:   *Lyle Ellefson and I chopping up onions where I first started cooking while on maneuvers. There are guys peeling potatoes on the left, and another guy is mixing something on the right. There's a jug of vinegar and a sack of onions by Lyle's feet.*

Page 57:   *One of our better kitchen tents and positions during Louisiana maneuvers. We probably were assured of staying in one position for a few days. August 1941.*

Page 61:   *Serving supper on Louisiana maneuvers. We cooked and served everything out of aluminum pots. I am the server without a hat on, at the end of the table.*

Page 72:   *In Hinkley, Minnesota on my way home on furlough, October 1941.*

Page 73:   *I was helping my brother Ray cut a load of cabbage that we took to Hibbing, Minnesota and sold the next day. On furlough, October 14, 1941.*

Page 75:   *At home in Hermantown on furlough, October 1941. With my sister, Arlene. My brother Ray's car.*

Page 77:   *The mess hall at Camp Claiborne, October 1941. The kitchen was towards the back of the building, and it could be closed off from the main dining room at the serving counter. This room was frequently used for meetings, as there was privacy between the meeting area and the kitchen.*

Page 92:   *Supplies for our 1941 Christmas dinner.*

Page 94:   *Bud Meyers (left) and I (right) were the only 2 cooks for our battalion for our Christmas dinner, as many were gone home on furlough.*

Pages 98, 99, 100:   *Stationery I bought at Camp Claiborne.*

Page 109:   *One of the destroyers that followed us across the Atlantic. January 1942. They seldom looked this big, but were usually farther away, and sometimes nearly out of sight because of the ocean waves.*

Page 110:   *This is where I used to stand by the hour watching the wake.*

Page 117:   *The 151st Field Artillery and the 133rd Infantry disembarking at Belfast, Northern Ireland, January 26, 1942.*

Page 118:   *A postcard my parents received sometime late in February 1942 concerning my safe arrival in Ireland on January 26. It didn't tell them* much about where I was. This was for security reasons.

Page 119:   There was drill training every day, along with all the other training schedules. Cooks were exempt, since we were either working, or had every other day off and could do what we wanted to do on our days off. Sgt. Meagher was First Sergeant, and his drill commands were easily heard. There were about 10 of these Quonset huts encircling a big field, and all partially in under the trees for a natural camouflage.

Page 120:   The patch-quilt pattern of Irish countryside; it was always pretty, and mostly green.

Page 123:   The Presbyterian church about a mile away from Ballerena camp that was built during the 1500's. Bob Vaughn, Don Sternke and I came here sometimes as well, as Eva Auld sang in the choir. The pastor was always hard to understand.

Page 127:   A 2 or 3 day maneuver in Northern Ireland, February 1942. I recognize Cpl. Jolie in front of the truck. He used to be the Battalion Agent at that time. Notice we were still using the 1918 helmets, as well as the old World War I mess kits.

Page 131:   Ready for camp guard, Ballerena Camp, Limavady, Northern Ireland, February 1942. Left to right, front row: Al Weils, Arden Harris, Louie Day and Sgt. Hogfuss. Arden Harris was later Killed in Action. Sgt. Hogfuss was the man in charge of the 50 mm machine guns later in North Africa. Later, in Italy, he was on the Observation Patrol and was captured, but got away the same night.

Page 140:   Don Sternke and I would ride along the coast on our days off. This is me.

Page 144:   (Top) The Estate of Lady Heggetesp at Ballerena. This is near Limavady. We saw the Lady a few times, and she gave us permission to go through the gardens — no chance to go through her castle, though. I don't ever remember seeing any servants, groundskeepers or workers here, except those who were around the kitchen and the horses.
(Bottom) Wilber Anderson (Andy), one of my fellow cooks, in the estate gardens at Ballerena Castle.

Page 147:   (Top) Don Sternke and I at Ballerena Camp, during the summer of 1942.
(Bottom) The same Don Sternke and the same Bud Wagner at Don's place in Marshall Minnesota, 52 years after the last picture was taken. Summer 1994.

Page 151:   Tynan Abbey, one of the nicest shacks I've ever seen.

Page 152:   The back side of Tynan Abbey. The servants' quarters where we lived were behind this area.

Page 153:   Map of Northern Ireland, including locations of our camps.

Page 157:   George Milliken, my caretaker friend. The "hotbed" (greenhouse) held mostly tomatoes. The giant horseshoe on the right was made from concrete blocks.

Page 159:   Hurley Soderlind, a cook from B Battery who became a good friend of mine when we worked together in Ireland. This picture was taken at Camp Claiborne just before we left there.

Page 167: *The George Milliken home on Tynan Abbey Estate. They lived in the left half, and another caretaker had the other half. The road heading south to the Irish Free State was just on the other side of the house. George is picking up the hay. There were no animals on any of these estates, but the grass was mowed (by hand) to keep things neat.*

Page 169: *George, Maggie, Olive, Maureen (in front), and Peggy Milliken. Olive's husband and Maureen's father, "Mack," was away. He was an English soldier.*

Page 171: *Upon our arrival at Castle Coole, our last camp in Ireland on the outskirts of Enniskillen. Arky Vaughn is the one facing the camera. Late August 1942.*

Page 172: *I had my photo taken in Belfast. At that time my only decoration was a good conduct medal. I was a T corporal because I was a second cook.*

Page 175: *Thomas Cooke home and small farm close to Enniskillen Camp. "Through the woods" to get there.*

Page 176: *Father and son team digging potatoes. The father was quick to tell me he had a relative in the Eastern United States, and the son had a few questions, but was shy about talking. Most of the Irish country people had little chance to talk to us American soldiers, but were always willing to if they could. September 18, 1942.*

Page 185: *Mrs. Thomas Cooke with her 5 live-in children from Belfast. The taller boy was Fred. The 2 boys on the right were the ones I would take to see a movie at camp, then walk back through the fields and woods with them after the show. The Cookes were generous to keep these 5 kids, as they weren't all that well-to-do. October 1942.*

Page 186: *Arky Vaughn "writing to Jean," as he did daily. Her picture is up on the stand.*

Page 187: *Arky in the kitchen at Enniskillen, November 1942.*

Page 188: *At Enniskillen Camp. Most of the men washed their own clothes here, as there were not many close neighbors. My bunk was at the other end of the barracks from Bob Vaughn's. The rifle rack was next to my bed. The square cans were 20-pound coffee cans, and made good coal and trash cans when empty. A 20-pound can of coffee didn't last long when feeding 125 men. Notice blackout curtains, and coal stove, right lower center of picture.*

Page 189: *At Enniskillen Camp, November 1942. Left side from front to rear: Joe Gradle, Ken Kramer (who was Killed in Action at Anzio, Italy), Bob McKoy and Larry Coons. Right side from front to rear: Bob Vaughn, Bill Snyder, Thompson and George Pittlekow. These were all kitchen workers except for Ken Kramer. The fellows didn't always sit at the same table this way, but were that evening. Notice the blackout curtain over the window.*

Page 195: *John McGuire, the caretaker and gardener at Castle Coole, in his small lean-to home. I went to see him pretty often. He reminisced a lot, and smoked his pipe always. December 1942.*

Page 206: *(Top) Our first dump-off spot after we were taken from the boat at Oran Harbor to this rocky, open place, and organized to go to Montagnac.*

It rained, and everything was wet, but at least it wasn't muddy. It was so rocky it was practically impossible to put up a pup tent. We had to serve some meals here.

(Middle) Col. Sylvester (left) seems to be in a good mood, with Sgt. Meagher (right) giving him advice. I've seen it just the opposite too. This is at our first stop in the African hill country, January 1943. This picture is closely cropped from much farther away.

(Bottom) Sgt. Meagher, the tall guy in the middle of the picture with his hands in his pockets. The day after our arrival in Montagnac, January 11, 1943.

Page 207:   *(Top) This is the way our camp in the town square of Montagnac looked the first day we arrived. We were drying out our bedding and clothing. January 11, 1943.*

(Middle) The Arab women in Montagnac always used the headboard to carry something.

(Bottom) Arab women washing clothes in the town center at Montagnac. There was a big water tank inside the building, and water was running into the tank from either a spring or a small stream on the other side of the building. None of us Americans bothered these Arab women to get our clothes washed because there were enough French people in the town who were looking for the job — and besides, we had strict instructions to have nothing to do with the Arabs. January 1943.

Page 209:   *Arabs in Montagnac. January 1943.*

Page 210:   *I don't know what these Arabs were talking about, but we used to think they were talking about us. Montagnac, North Africa, January 1943.*

Page 211:   *A common scene at Montagnac, showing a typical building in the town. They were hauling rocks in the horse trailer. North Africa, January 1943.*

Page 212:   *A good picture of the back portion of our kitchen and battery area at Montagnac. Notice the line in front to keep the Arabs and townspeople out. We always had to dig holes to empty out the contents of the garbage cans. It took another 3 big garbage cans of hot water for washing mess kits; 1 with soapy water, and 2 with hot rinse water. An inquisitive Arab can be seen underneath the drying clothes on the right. January 1943.*

Page 214:   *At Montagnac. Sgt. Wombsley was with us for a time, and I got to know him before he was transferred out of our unit. He was later Killed in Action.*

Page 215:   *Ed Dengler. Picture taken in Belfast, Northern Ireland.*

Page 216:   *Natalie and Ann, the 2 French girls who did my washing of clothes at Montagnac. February 1943.*

Page 221:   *Map of the North Coast of Africa.*

Page 227:   *I was still working in the kitchen when I took this picture of a hole made by a German 88. My rifle and gloves help to show the size of the shell hole. This was taken when we saw our first action in Africa.*

Page 231:   *One of the first German graves we saw in Africa. I well remember this one, as the name I read on the marker was "Heinrich (Henry) Seelig,"* xiv

Page 275:   *I was traffic marker at a corner in Constantine, North Africa. Lynn Miller rode with me, and we could change off going away from the corner to see a bit of the town. Kids were always around for a handout of candy and gum.*

Page 281:   *This was after the African Campaign during the time Division Headquarters was 110 miles away from Division Artillery. I had to go back and forth, but not every day. This picture was taken on a Sunday. The church made me lonesome.*

Page 284:   *This was taken on our 3rd 800-mile trip between Oran and Tunis, this time heading again for Tunis. The fellow with me (with helmet and no sunglasses) is Fred Trompeter, a dairyman from North Dakota. The other 2 were not from our 151st Battalion. Our lunch stop would usually bring some other people or French soldiers to our group. Fred and I would change off driving each other's vehicles, mostly to ease our backs and have a change. Fred was one of the first to go home on rotation. He took a big loss during the war in that he ended up losing his dairy. Note our bulging shirt pockets, where we could keep our personal objects. In my case it was mostly my diary. Some guys carried pictures and letters from their family or girlfriend. August 22, 1943.*

Page 285:   *(Top) Wallace Pomerleau, who was our mailman. This picture was taken in a German airplane graveyard close to Bizerte. We drivers were stuck in this area for about 3 days while we waterproofed our vehicles, and we interested ourselves by going through the planes. Pom brought in some of the last mail we were to see for awhile, as we were soon headed for Italy. (Middle) This was a 1940 Volkswagen the Germans had left behind for some reason. Someone had fixed it up, and the fellows drove it for awhile. Probably a German officer's car.*
(Bottom) A German tank that had lost its tracks.

Page 286:   *My peep, waterproofed and ready to load on the LST. The muffler was bypassed, and the vehicle pipe was attached to the exhaust manifold. My German rifle rack is holding my rifle, but later I had to remove it, as I hauled an officer one time, and he told me it was too dangerous to have a rifle in a position like that.*

Page 288:   *Another shot of my peep ready to load. This fellow is the same as the fellow perched up where the Piper Cubs are in the next picture, but I've forgotten his name.*

Page 289:   *The 2 Piper Cubs on their makeshift flight deck above my peep. The 6X6 on the right is a gun truck loaded with the gun-crewmen's equipment: musette bags hanging down the side of the truck. After the landing at Salerno, the gun crews were too busy firing to use their bedrolls, etc.; but when they had a chance, the gun truck was there with their equipment and canned rations. September 1, 1943.*

Pages 292-293:   *Original diary pages from D-day, September 9, 1943, through September 11, 1943. These pages' actual size was 1 3/8" X 3", so my writing had to be pretty tiny.*

Page 298:   *This is a picture I found in a blown-out German tank at Salerno.*

The complete crew was killed. "Some gave all." September 10, 1943.
Page 299:   *A pile of brass 105 mm shell casings. These were picked up afterwards by rear echelon troops and reused. The cows couldn't dig foxholes, and we didn't want them in ours, so they had to fend for themselves. Many farm animals were killed by shellfire, of course.*
Page 305:   *A German cemetery. German crosses were black; ours were white.*
Page 307:   *A 155 mm gun of the 185th Field Artillery. Notice the camouflage net over the top. Powder bags were used without a shell casing. Projectiles were 90 pounds.*
Page 309:   *These boys were hauling gravel or rock. It looks like they stopped to see a tipped-over tank that probably got too close to the edge and lost its balance. The gravel or rock was used to fix the roads, but I usually didn't see many fixed roads until after I was already gone.*
Page 310-311:   *A reduced-sized V-mail, here just a little smaller than actual size, and the envelope it was sent in, also a little smaller than actual size. These were difficult to read even at their best, but the postage was free.*
Page 312:   *This was the first flight of American bombers I saw during the war — a welcome sight, as we were well into Italy before our bombers started to go north from bases in Southern Italy or even Africa. I believe these planes were B-17's or "Flying Fortresses."*
Page 318:   *I can't remember the name of this small town which was completely demolished and deserted, but I went through it many times, almost always at night, and always while under enemy observation. The main roads were heavy with traffic at nights: ammo trucks, wire crew, tanks, and infantry marching forward.*
Page 322:   *This is a picture of the bomb crater where Captain Smith of the 168th Infantry was killed, and others wounded. It was close to the Castle "Old Podrue." Barney Devine and Ribelin went along with me when we looked at this crater on Friday, November 5, 1943.*
Page 324:   *"Old Podrue" is the only name I knew for this old castle. I suppose a person could spend an entire year in history class just on the history of this place, but I got very little information on it during the time I was passing through southern Italy. Barney Devine, Reb and I looked over it pretty well, or as best as we had time for. Our attitude of it was, "Amazing!" If World War II didn't succeed in tearing it down, I imagine it is still standing today.*
Page 326:   *A "sea of mud" north of the Volturno River crossing. Any one of the mud tracks could have been the road. You can see troops trying to build a better road to the right of the picture.*
Page 327:   *This is what the peep and I looked like after a night of trips on the muddy Volturno River banks, and sometimes between the banks as well. Hand-operated windshield wipers gave a small view. Shifting gears, steering, and windshield wiping all at the same time was sometimes tricky. It's a good thing the clutch and gas were foot-operated instead of by hand.*
Page 332:   *I've forgotten the name of this Italian town, but I haven't*

forgotten the blown-out bridge. This part of it had had some shops and maybe dwellings built into it. You can see the by-pass below the blown-out part.

Page 333:   *We 4 messengers stayed under this old viaduct or water main, which was near Colli, from November 28 to December 9, 1943, when we were finally pulled back to Alife for a much needed rest. We closed up the inner wall with shelter halves, had a charcoal stove, and were pretty well protected from artillery fire, though the viaduct was hit several times further up from where we were. We could tell that this viaduct was very old, as the concrete was crumbling where the top part met with the foundation. This area was where Lt. Ross Fleming was killed taking off in an observation plane, and I saw at least 7 men Killed in Action in this vicinity.*

Pages 338-339:   *My diary pages from December 9 to December 12, 1943. This was one of the more intense periods of the war while we were staying under the viaduct.*

Page 340:   *I believe this is a portion of the town of Piedmonte, but I am not totally sure anymore. You can see what was left of the tree after being hit by German and American shellfire — just a trunk and a few branches.*

Page 341:   *(Top) Nate Levy's relatives' home near Piedmonte. The reunion was very emotional, and I considered myself lucky to have been a part of it. Nate is the one wearing a helmet.*

(Bottom) A big city square in Naples when I was on pass there.

Pages 346-347:   *Back to the front after rest in Alife and Naples. It was cold, and rough going, "rough as a cob." January 2 through January 17, 1944.*

Page 348:   *There were two completely shelled and bombed-out towns that were close to each other, and this could have been either one of them. One was San Vittorie, and the other San Pietro.*

Page 358:   *(Top) A picture of an Italian soldier that I picked up from the stamps and papers strewn across the floor in the blown-up Post Office in Cervaro, Italy, February 5, 1944.*

(Bottom) Just before church services in an olive grove on an Italian mountainside. We usually sat on our helmets during the service. The chaplain had a driver to carry his equipment, which included a portable organ.

Page 359:   *Dug into a foxhole for protection against artillery fire. On the left was Ken Kramer, a friend who I met while in Ireland, and on the right, one of the medics who I was somewhat acquainted with, John Keller. Ken was Killed in Action shortly after this picture was taken in February 1944 — by a "friendly" American bomb. John Keller was also Killed in Action a little later during the war.*

Page 360:   *What was left of the town of Cervaro, near Cassino.*

Page 365:   *The 109th Evacuation Hospital.*

Page 366:   *The town of Caserta. (I spelled the name wrong on my original photograph.) This is an example of an Italian town that hadn't been broken up too badly by the war.*

Page 368:   *Our peep convoy after we retreated from the Caserta area and went back to Naples. We were the forward liaison group to help prepare locations and connections for our battalions which followed a few days later to meet at the beachhead at Anzio.*

Casablanca, July 6, 1945. I was pretty proud of it at the time, as not every-one I knew had flown in an airplane — but I suppose people would laugh nowadays.

Pages 522-523:   *A microfilmed copy of my Honorable Discharge from the Army of the United States, July 20, 1945. Unlike my Induction Notice of April 12, 1941, which was sent to me free of charge, I had to pay the Clerk of Records in the County Court House in Duluth several dollars for this paper copy.*

Page 524:   *I'd like to see this plaque corrected somewhat, in that Lt. Ross T. Fleming was actually a member of the Air Observation Patrol, not of Headquarters Battery. I knew nearly every one of these men, and many of them were friends of mine.*

Page 528:   *Me posing by the big sign at the entrance to Camp Claiborne.*

INTRODUCTION

I began keeping a diary when I was quite young. I have many small books with short entries, and at the time I registered for the draft in October 1940 when I was 22, I was closing the 5th year in a leather-bound 5-year diary.

I didn't even consider stopping with my diary because of my draft status, and I decided that in addition, I would keep a small camera with me at all times I possibly could during my Army service. My intention was to keep all my Army time on record to the best of my ability. On the front page of the 5-year diary I had written the Chinese proverb, "The faintest ink is better than the strongest memory."

There were many times during my Army career when I couldn't make my diary entries on the day they occurred. Days and nights would often run together when we were on the move, and dates were unimportant to me at the time.

Another reason I sometimes couldn't make daily entries is that for security reasons, I tried to keep my diary to myself. There were probably only three close friends who knew I was keeping it. I always carried it in my shirt pocket, and towards the end of the war, it was getting to be quite a bulky burden. If I hadn't sent a part of it home before leaving Ireland, I wouldn't have been able to carry it all on my person.

Some of the problems I faced in writing it were: (1) no light at night, (2) difficulty in getting ink and (3) the fact that I didn't even have a real diary at times, but only small notebooks to write in.

There were times when I couldn't get away by myself that I would make believe I was writing a letter — when actually I was trying to recollect and put in writing what had happened to me during the previous days or sometimes the previous week.

After I returned home in July 1945, the diaries were put into a drawer. They moved with me several times and were all but forgotten until about 1977, when our family was all together one Sunday afternoon. The talk turned to my Army life, and when I mentioned the diaries, everyone wanted to see them.

One of our sons-in-law, Ed Newman, a writer, thought there was potential in it for short stories, a journal, or a book. Our other son-in-law Harrold Andresen, a mechanic, was interested in all the mechanical work that had to be done to the vehicles. Our son Lloyd had heard some things about what I had written, and had been studying American and European history including that of the World Wars, so he was very interested as well.

Nevertheless, as I was still too busy raising a family to think about writing up war diaries, they were put back into the desk drawer for 4 more years until 1981. Sylvia, a girl from a Mexican orphanage where Nancy Andresen and Susie Newman, our daughters, had worked for several years, came to live with our family for a year. Not being used to our Minnesota weather, Sylvia felt really cooped up in the house during our long winter. To give her something to do, I asked her if she would type up my diaries.

This was a laborious job for her using an old typewriter and carbons to make 4 copies to distribute to members of my family. It took her most of the winter, as she had to struggle with the miniaturized handwriting in the small notebooks and the abbreviations which were unfamiliar to her. Her native language, of course, was Spanish.

It was very gratifying to me to see the diaries in any sort of printed form, however; and the fact that there were now multiple copies was a relief to me as well, in case something should have happened to the original copy.

Over the years, my son-in-law Ed would sometimes nonchalantly mention that I had some writing to do. I think he actually thought I would never get started on it; and after a while, he even stopped mentioning it.

During the early 1990's, my wife Evelyn's health began to fail, and I had to quit my market-gardening and greenhouse business. As I had to spend a lot more time in the house to help take care of my wife, I began to start to think seriously of writing up the diaries.

For practice, I started by writing up some vacation trip records I had kept. I had to learn to type and print using a computer. I found that the computer was much easier than using a typewriter and carbon paper, which encouraged me to continue.

As the original diary entries were not changed except in the interest of clarity, I also had to write a commentary on the daily entries to help explain the larger world picture, much of which I was not aware of at the time it was happening.

My objective was to show as accurately as possible what Army life was like for me, without in any way taking away any credit from any other soldier who went through similar circumstances. I can make no comparison whatsoever between what I went through and what the infantry and other front-line combat men went through in World War II. They had it immeasurably worse.

The 151st Field Artillery Battalion lost 45 men during the war. I knew them all; many I knew well, and six were close friends of mine. I also lost friends who I had met at basic training at Camp Claiborne, Louisiana, who ended up in different outfits than I did. (I was unexpectedly transferred into the 151st just one day prior to leaving Louisiana on our way towards Northern Ireland.) Some lost brothers, and some families lost every son.

The short lives of those killed were hardly a flicker here on earth. Though most of their names will never appear in history books, they were all heroes. Every battle left heroes: the survivors and the dead. I can have nothing but sad respect for those men who had so few joys and so many miseries, and who gave their lives so others could go on living.

Though temporal suffering clouds our understanding of God's Master Plan, I still hold on to my faith that "Temporal loss can be the price of eternal gain."

CHAPTER 1
Drafted. From the farm to basic training.

Wednesday, October 16, 1940 I went to the [Hermantown] Town Hall this morning and registered for the draft.

I had to listen to some of Pa's grumbling first. He says we should mind our own business and not get involved in another war. He's often said we had no business being over there during the Great War, but maybe if I do have to serve a year now, it just might help to prevent another war.

Anyway, it's the law: "You register today, October 16." I have some idea what might happen if I didn't register today too, and I wonder where I'll end up if I do have to go.

A lady asked lots of questions, like all the vital statistics, then someone who would always know your address if it changed.

They wrote all the information on a white card which they filed away for their future use. Then they gave me a smaller card that I had to carry with me at all times to prove I had registered.

I went through a lot of mixed thoughts and emotions that day as I walked home from the Town Hall.

In 1938, my dad had given me use of about an acre of good garden ground to get me started in the market-gardening business. I really wanted to continue in this business. My brother Ray had joined me in it during the summer of 1939 when he first got out of the Civilian Conservation Corps (CCC's, a work program for low-income young men during the 1930's), and we'd also worked together during the summer of 1940.

During the winters, my brother and I had been cutting wood near Payne, Minnesota, and this was going fairly well for us also.

I had some doubts in my mind, however, as to what I'd be doing during the next year. Since the spring of 1940, President Roosevelt had been publicly denouncing the Nazis' methods, their invasion of Denmark and their invasion of Norway — and telling the American people to "be ready to meet force with force."

The President had also been warning Japan to stay out of The Netherlands East Indies — which was the source of much of America's rubber and tin. Americans were starting to look at the size of their Naval fleet — and of

Japan's, Britain's and Germany's.

Tuesday, October 29, 1940   Have been hauling manure with the horses and cleaning up the fields.

I walked to Dick's tonight to listen to the National Draft Lottery. The low number was 158. Mine's just about that low, so I know what to expect.

My actual draft number was 154. Though there were many more rules and formulas involved in the drafting of men than only "the numbers," I still knew what to expect.

The work on my dad's farm was done by real horsepower, as he refused to own a tractor. He insisted that a tractor's wheels would pack the ground down too hard to raise a good crop. My dad didn't have a radio or electricity either, though power lines had gone by our place since 1936.

My cousin Dick Wagner, a bachelor who had been in the infantry in France during World War I, owned a battery-run radio.

Monday, November 4, 1940   I disked at Rhunke's place north of his barn with the horses.

Ray and I went to town [Duluth] this afternoon and bought all our provisions for the woods this winter.

The Rhunkes owned a farm a half mile north of my dad's place. Mr. Rhunke wanted a new garden behind the barn, so he hired me to break this land.

After the war, my brother Ray and I bought Rhunke's farm, and that's where we raised our families and did our farming.

Tuesday, November 5, 1940   Saddled Bird and rode to the Town Hall to vote in my first presidential election. Voted for Wilkie and straight Republican ticket.

Packed my things together for the woods.

I had listened to the hard-line Isolationist Republicans and had voted that way, but have often wished I'd voted for Roosevelt.

Monday, November 11, 1940   At Payne now. We have our second shack built, and a barn for Bird. Ray went down to get hay.

A record snowstorm hit us on November 11 and almost paralyzed traffic with two feet of snow.

Payne is about 35 miles from my dad's place in Hermantown. My brother left to get hay on November 11 and didn't make it back until Wednesday, the 13th. I had shoveled snow all day on Tuesday so we could get the truck a mile and a quarter down the Lake Nichols Road to our shack from the main road at Payne, but it still took the two of us four more hours on Wednesday to finish the job.

I had a lot of time to read in the woods at Payne, as winter nights are long in Minnesota. I had a subscription to *Life*, and I was starting to take an interest in the world situation, especially since I had registered for the draft.

Hitler (with some help from Mussolini) had already taken over or was in the process of invading Austria, Czechoslovakia, Poland, Hungary, Yugoslavia, France, North Africa, Greece, Crete and Norway. He was bombing England, Northern Ireland and South Wales.

Finland was being invaded as well, by Russia; and, as it later became apparent, the German Planning Committee was at this very time planning a Spring Offensive against Russia. Though Stalin and Hitler had signed a creamy nonaggression pact and had split Poland up between them, Stalin must have sensed the pact was going sour, and he wanted part of Finland as defense against a possible invasion by Germany. Evidently he didn't quite trust Hitler's word.

The Battle of the Atlantic was also in full swing at this time, and unfortunately it was going in Germany's favor.

For the time being, Old Adolph was certainly a man with many fronts.

What is really amazing is the indifference and ignorance towards all this displayed by almost all of the people I knew. As recently as October 1940, one of my uncles had listened to Hitler speak on the radio, and he told us that after hearing this speech, he felt much encouraged about Hitler's attitude towards world conquest. My uncle felt that Hitler would never bother the United States, as long as he got what he wanted in Europe — or in my uncle's opinion, what he was "entitled" to in Europe.

Friday, December 6, 1940   Grandpa Seelig's funeral was today.

Ray and I took a small load of tamarack firewood down and we went to the funeral. Everyone met over home afterwards.

Saturday, February 8, 1941   We cut until 11:00, then I finished skidding out a load of Pa's wood.

Ray left for home at 3:00.

I washed clothes, fried fish for supper, took a sponge bath and washed my hair.

Guess I'll soon be in the Army. Makes me feel blue in a way, and then again not.

We have been cutting posts, cordwood and a few ties, and hauling some down once in a while.

Last month was pretty steady work all month, and got a lot done.

There is news in the paper about conscription, and I'm assuming by my number that I will be among the first to go.

Monday, February 10, 1941   Peeled posts this forenoon; cut this afternoon. Warm, cloudy.

Rode Bird to the Payne Store tonight after the mail. It's a mile and a quarter each way. Full moon and almost as bright as day. Enjoyed the ride.

I wrote to the local Draft Board in Proctor concerning how soon I may be drafted into the service.

Our winter here is growing short; it seems as though we haven't been here as long as we have.

Wednesday, February 12, 1941   Skidded out one load of wood.

L.A. Wagner [no relation] from southern Minnesota came and bought all our fence posts at five cents apiece. We hauled them to the railway car at Payne.

My questionnaire came for service. It must have crossed in the mail with the letter I sent them asking when I'll be going. It came sooner than I expected; sobers me up, and I start thinking a lot about it again.

A letter from George Nash. He and Ethel moved to Canton, Ohio. George is foreman on a government job there.

George Nash, and Ethel's brother, Roy, used to talk about Ger-

many, "The Invader," even a year ago. They both knew well what was going on, and what was going to happen.

George and Roy were pretty sharp. They questioned the alliance between Germany and Russia a long time before most people did. I remember Roy saying more than once, "Why do we keep on sending Japan scrap iron and steel? Just wait and see. We'll get every bit of it back." We sure did get it back. But it took the United States until September 26, 1940, to impose an embargo on the export of scrap to Japan.

Thursday, February 13, 1941   Snowed all night, and kept on until noon. Warm. It quit snowing at noon and turned colder.

I filled out my questionnaire and took it over to Payne Store to have Rask [the postmaster] acknowledge the affidavit.

Didn't do anything this p.m. Made potato pancakes for supper.

Friday, February 14, 1941   Both Eagle and Bird were still laying when I came in the barn this morning. I had to chase them up.

I finished the road I was cutting on by noon, and skidded wood this p.m. It was warmer.

Walked to Payne for the mail. Stopped in at Otto's for an hour. He talked a lot about the old country. He is Swedish, but was brought up in Germany.

Received answer from the local board in Proctor concerning the time I'll be drafted. They say I may be inducted by June 30.

I'm thinking a lot as to what I will be doing in the Army. Would like to get in the cavalry.

I tried to finish reading my Bible through, but won't get it done. I did finish the New Testament, though.

Tuesday, March 4, 1941   We tried to start the truck, but it wouldn't.

Pa and Dick came all day again. Ma always makes a big lunch and sends it along.

I peeled balsam all day, and Ray hauled for Oscar this p.m.

We tried to trim Eagle's hoof on noon, but couldn't do anything with him.

Was 16 degrees below zero this morning, but it warmed up.

Received my summons to appear to have my physical on March 10. This is sooner than I thought. Within the next year, I'm sure many things will change.

Monday, March 10, 1941   Brought a load of cull fence posts home last night. Helped Pa milk.

Went to the Webber Hospital to take my physical at 10 a.m., but the doctor wouldn't be in until 2:00. I went to the Draft Board and raised heck, but it didn't do any good, so I went to see a show. We

didn't get our examination until almost 4:00.

Was snowing some all day. I helped one lady get her car going on a hill. Came home, and Grandma Seelig was there.

I got back to camp at Payne late tonight and was completely tired out.

The other fellow and I should have made some trouble there today because they kept us waiting so long, but we let it pass.

Pa's birthday. He's 59.

Monday, March 24, 1941   Got up early and we hauled the horses down. Then went back to get our junk. It's about 35 miles each way.

Was glad to get out of the shack after all winter, and am sort of glad I'm going in the Army.

Monday, March 31, 1941   We hauled one load of manure with the truck from Anderson's, then had to quit, as the ground was too soft.

We went to Scarlett's, and Ray and I bought a manure spreader there for $169.

After coming back, we hauled a load of shavings from the box factory.

The reason we bought the manure spreader was because I wasn't going to be at home to help Ray haul and spread the manure. We used to haul it from several local dairies besides what my folks had from their own cows.

We used the shavings for bedding.

Monday, April 14, 1941   I've been using both Pa's team of horses and my own to haul manure with the new spreader.

We got 200 baby chicks a few days ago.

My summons to go into the Army came this week. I'm to go on Thursday. I went to the Draft Board to ask for a few more days to

SELECTIVE SERVICE SYSTEM

ST. LOUIS COUNTY
LOCAL BOARD No. 5
PROCTOR, MINN.
(STAMP OF LOCAL BOARD)

April 12, 1941

Dear Sir:

Inclosed you will find Order to Report for Induction.
You will note that you are to bring this order with
you when you report at this office on the Induction
Date.

Please acknowledge this letter by return mail so that
we may depend on your appearance at the Board office.

We are inclosing a list of supplies which you may need.

Very truly yours,

J.A. Dillen, Chairman

finish up some things, but they wouldn't do it.

I haven't made many preparations yet. I did buy a vest-pocket camera, though, for $8.50.

Tuesday, April 15, 1941   Ray, Dick and I finished tearing the old car apart, loaded and took the parts down to the scrap yard.

Ray and I hauled four loads of manure from Jacobson's using both teams of horses.

When we got home, Uncle Carl was here, and he accused me of going into the Army to "slack off" and leave the farm work to Pa and Ray. We had quite a squall about it. I should have slapped him, but then he never was overly smart either drunk or sober, and slapping wouldn't have helped any.

What bothered me most that day was that no one came to my defense. It was hard enough already that I was the one who had to go into the Army without having any idea what was going to happen to me, without having to put up with someone's ignorant remarks besides.

Thoughts and emotions were rushing through my head that day.

My dad had helped me start my gardening business three years before, in 1938, the summer I turned 19. He had suggested we haul manure for my garden from another dairy, a distance of about four miles each way, with horse and wagon. He had helped me every day despite the amount of farm work he had to do for himself, and we had to load the manure with hand-forks onto the wagon, and throw it off the wagon the same way.

We made two trips a day, which took all day, and we did this for two weeks until Pa was satisfied we had hauled enough manure for my garden.

My dad also let me use his 1931 Graham Paige family car to haul the vegetables I raised to the Duluth Farmer's Market, where I sold them for a gross income of $210 for the summer of 1938. He also got me working on the county road crew for a few days that summer, shoveling gravel onto a truck. I made $60 doing this which was a big help in buying  vegetable seeds and a walk-behind push-cultivator, and for paying the market's rent of $10 per six-foot wide booth for the next year.

Pa had done things for me I can never forget. I wasn't going into the Army to leave the work to him and my brother, and it really bothered me that someone should say so. But to Uncle Carl, my going to fight the Fatherland was the act of a traitor, as he felt that Germany could do no wrong.

Wednesday, April 16, 1941   Ray and I hauled two more loads of manure each this morning.

I went to town afterwards with the truck and bought a few things. I went to see Wing Chinn at the cafe, and he fed me a big dinner for free.

Ken and Bob Butts came over home here tonight, and also Aunt Rose, Uncle Louie, Mary Jean, Lavonne, Jack, Carl and Myrtle.

I'm wondering if this is my last night here for awhile, or forever? I leave it to God's will.

Thursday, April 17, 1941   Got up at 6:00, did the usual chores. Pa worked on the county and left early.

I went to Alvin Reinke's early, but he was already gone to work too. I saw Germaine, though, and went to Dick's.

Came home and packed up.

Hank and Evelyn Seelig came, and Grandma Seelig. Aunt Rose Seelig came too, with some sea-foam candy for me.

Ray took me to Proctor at 1:30. One other fellow was there to leave with me, Charlie Jurvelin, from Floodwood, Minnesota.

We got instructions from Dillen, then walked to the Depot from the Village Hall.

Ma, Grandma Seelig, Annie Reinke [my dad's sister], Alvin and Germaine Reinke, Uncle Art Seelig (he gave me a carton of cigarettes), Alice Reinke, Arlene [my almost-five-year-old little sister], Lorraine Reinke, and Aunt Myrtle Seelig were all there to see me off.

Charlie Jurvelin and I were the first ones to be drafted from this local Draft Board. *The Duluth Herald* newspaper had a photographer at the Depot to take our picture.

CHAPTER 1

Got on the train and went to Duluth. Changed trains there, and got on with another half a dozen "slackers." Good-byes were hard to say; but nonetheless, we headed for St. Paul.

We traveled all the way to Fort Snelling without much conversation. They gave us a good supper, and a bunk upstairs in a barracks.

We didn't converse much there either. Everyone was about the same age as me, and we all had about the same attitude, i.e., "Let's get our year in the service over with so we can continue on with our lives."

Friday, April 18, 1941   They woke us up at 5:15. Given chow at 6:00. Waited around until 7:00, had an exam; took until almost noon.

Was sworn in this p.m., given a test, and issued clothes and a new bunk. I am in a lower one.

The food is good, and I'm getting along. Made buddies with Clarence Weigle from Grand Forks, North Dakota.

Saturday, April 19, 1941   Weigle and I got up at 5:00 and caught heck for it. We had to sweep out the orderly room as punishment.

We listened to a talk by 1st Sgt. Christy. Had an interview. Had the *Articles of War* read to us by a captain.

Had some time off, so Weigle and I walked around a bit. Chow at 4:30.

Quite a bunch of us now in this group. All have new Army woolens that fit a little baggy.

A shipment of men went to Camp Claiborne today.

Sunday, April 20, 1941   They got us up at 7:30. Went to church. Good sermon by the chaplain.

Laid around until noon, then Weigle and I walked over to the Minneapolis Airport. About a mile and a half. Lots of planes there.

Back at 3:00. Wrote home.

To church again tonight. Service was good. Four fellows singing in a quartet, and another good sermon.

Called home tonight and talked to everybody.

Cool, windy. Exceptionally good meals.

Monday, April 21, 1941   Up at 6:15. Had a few lectures given us this forenoon.
  This p.m. we were taught a few fundamentals of drill. Tiresome, but it's almost fun.
  Not so cold tonight.
  Life here is much like the CCC's, only I get along better.

Tuesday, April 22, 1941   We were herded together this morning and told we were going to be shipped to the 151st Field Artillery at Camp Claiborne, Louisiana.

Waited around until 2:00, then hiked to the Depot in Minneapolis.
  Left at 3 p.m. Got down to the Iowa line by tonight.
  We are in a Pullman coach. The black porter made up the berths. I had an upper one alone. Slept better than I thought I would.

  This was exciting to me to be going to Louisiana on a Pullman train. I kept telling myself it wasn't my fault I was there, and I didn't expect to mind at all being a year away from home.

Wednesday, April 23, 1941   Got up about 6:00. First thing, I looked out the window. We were in Missouri. Nice country.
  We are about 360 men altogether. Sgt. Peterson is in charge.
  We stopped at Kansas City and got out to stretch.
  Got to Arkansas sometime tonight. Helped out the cooks on K.P. duties.

  I really enjoyed the train ride, though it was dirty. It was nice to hear the hissing of the steam and the sound of the whistles. The engines, of course, were coal-burning steam engines. If you had your window open, and if the train was rounding a curve, and if the locomotive had to chug a bit at the same time, you could expect to get a black face from the smoke.
  I remember noticing that you could tell how high the water had risen on the Missouri River in spring, because there were bunches of dry grass stuck on the fence wires.
  Crossing the "Mighty Mo" was exciting too, and a little scary. Looking

12

down from the train, all we could see was water.

Sgt. Peterson was a big, nice fellow from Duluth who I later got to know better. He had made quite a few trips back and forth getting troops from Minnesota to Louisiana.

Thursday, April 24, 1941   Got up around 5:30. We were in Louisiana. Lots of small shacks, with several Negroes looking out the windows. The country is wet and swampy.

We got out here at Camp Claiborne about 10:00. Marched through some streets. I was assigned to a tent with Bird, Skold, Wold and Berg. Seem like all nice fellows.

Had to do a few things.

These tents are 16' x 16'. Enough room in here. The tents have roll-up sides that they tell me you roll up in a hurry when the sun shines, or down in a hurry when it starts to rain. All pathways are boardwalks. They say when it rains, I'll know why.

It's very hot, and you sweat a lot.

The others in the tent were all National Guardsmen from Minneapolis. They had been at Camp Claiborne since February.

The tents were in five rows of five tents each. There was a latrine on one end of the rows of tents, and the mess hall was on the other end.

In 1967 my wife and kids and I traveled about the same journey to visit Camp Claiborne. There wasn't much left of the camp except for some concrete piers and foundations, but I managed to find where the 151st Field Artillery was, and the mess hall and tents. The main highway ran right through the middle of where the camp had been. The area was planted over in pine trees which were about 15 feet tall.

Friday, April 25, 1941   Up at 5:00. All the fellows in here treat me fine.

We start the day about 7:00. That's after chow and reveille.

Today all of us were given drill training in marching. This afternoon we were put cleaning up some 75 mm artillery pieces. We had to police up the area and scrub out our tent.

For chow, we all stand in line with our mess kits, and the cooks dish it out. Not bad, but word is that the amount of rations aren't up to the battalion strength, which means there's not quite enough to eat.

We had been issued mess kits that were unissued leftovers from World War I. I carried mine with me for the four years I was in the Army. It traveled many miles, and I ate many meals out of it. After the war, it traveled many more miles on many family camping trips, and in 1998, I gave it to my grandson, Micah.

HEADQUARTERS 151st FIELD ARTILLERY
Office of the Chaplain.

Camp Claiborne, La.

Dear Mr. **Wagner:**

This is to advise you that your **son**
Wilmer A. Wagner has been assigned to service
with this regiment and has had an interview with the Chaplain.

The 151st Field Artillery has a long record of History and
citation with the Army of the United States and among its Officers and
men there have been many outstanding citizens in public and political
life. It is a National Guard regiment from Minneapolis, Minnesota, and
is made up of young men who have but recently entered the Service from
civil life. Colonel John F. Robehm, Jr., our Commanding Officer, has a
year's leave of absence from his position as Principal of Vocational
High School in Minneapolis. Most of our senior Officers are men of
business or other civilian occupations and have obtained leave from such
activities for the year's training. I make this explanation so that
you might better understand the fact your boy will be associated with
men of all walks of life who before February 10th, were every day
citizens like yourself, with the same common problems. In like manner
they will be making the same common adjustments as your boy. We therefore, welcome him as one of us and are confident he will enjoy being
associated with this regiment.

He may find the new enviornment and work a little strenuous
at first but there will be time for recreation. Each regiment has a
Recreational Building for shows, pictures, reading and indoor games.
The Camp Theatre shows the latest movies nightly for a small sum and
the Men's Service Club is about ready to open with all kinds of
recreational facilities. Athletic Sports and events of all kinds are
encouraged and everything possible is being done for the welfare of
our men. A guest house is provided for the relatives and friends of
the enlisted men where one can stay overnight, at a very nominal charge,
and visit with the soldier.

Religious services are arranged throughout the camp to meet
the needs of the various denominations, and a non-denominational
Regimental Service is conducted by the Chaplain every Sunday.

Louisiana is very attractive just now and trips are being
arranged for the men so that they might see the Historic spots and meet
the very cordial and hospitable Southerner.

I consider it a privilege to be the friend and counsellor of all
our men, and if at any time I can be of serviceto you and yours, I would
be happy to have you write to me.

Faithfully yours,

Joseph J. Walker

JOSEPH T. WALKER
Chaplain, 151st F.A.

Here at Camp Claiborne, I encountered a different attitude towards the Army than I had seen previously. Here, the men were learning to handle the guns and equipment and were being trained as combat soldiers. I wasn't hearing much talk anymore about "getting our year's service over with so we can get back to normal life."

The men who had been here since February were not draftees as I was. Some had left good jobs and businesses in civilian life to prepare to fight for their country.

They had been volunteer members of the National Guard, of the 125th Field Artillery of the 34th Division, and of the 1st and 2nd Battalions of the 151st Field Artillery. They had been mobilized and activated during February of 1941.

Draftees such as myself didn't start arriving at Camp Claiborne until April. I had been assigned to the 2nd Battalion of the 151st Field Artillery of the 34th Division.

Saturday, April 26, 1941 Got up around 5:00. Inspection today. Took until 10:00.

Had time off since then. Washed a few clothes.

Of course I'm lonely, but I try not to be. It won't be so hard if I can keep my intentions. I read some this afternoon.

Fell in for reveille at 5:00. We had spaghetti for chow. I haven't been getting enough lately.

I had a haircut here at the canteen for 35 cents.

"Reveille" was usually every workday. The bugle sounded, and we'd all form ranks ("fall in") between tent rows by the First Sergeant's tent. Roll call was given, and then maybe an announcement. Then we waited for the chow call. There was another bugle call for work, then another for chow at noon.

In the evening, we'd come in from work, change from our work clothes into our chino's (light tan shirt and pants, summer weight), and then wait for another bugle call that signaled "retreat" or "strategic withdrawal." We'd all form ranks, and the First Sergeant would make a formal presentation to the Commanding Officer, then the soldiers would "fall out."

Chow call would come right after this. After eating, we were free until 10:00, when taps sounded and it was time to go to sleep.

All the bugle calls were distinct and different, and we had to know each one.

If we were on K.P., guard duty or on some other special duty, the bugle calls didn't apply to us.

Sunday, April 27, 1941 Slept until 7:00. Wrote some cards and letters. Attended church services at the rec hall.

Bird and I walked over to the carnival, about a mile and a half.

Watched the fellows play ball here at camp.

Wrote some more letters tonight. Made a few more acquaintances again today.

We have a Recreation Hall only about a block from here for gatherings, a canteen where you can buy almost anything, and a Service Club further north for the whole camp, which is a really nice two-story building.

I've been taking a lot of pictures, some on the way down, and many around here.

Monday, April 28, 1941   Up at 5:15. Reveille at about 5:40, mess at about 6:15. We start the day at about 7:00. We always have to march in military formation whenever we go somewhere.

Went to the gun park. Had drilling this a.m. We were given fundamentals of truck driving and basic instructions on the gun crew.

Hot. Had headache all day.

Had the best chow tonight that we had since we've been here, and enough of it. Even ice cream.

Got new packs tonight. Raining now.

Tuesday, April 29, 1941 Up at 5:15. We went out in the field. Sgt. Wold drilled us, then we listened to some talks beneath some pine trees.

Rained this p.m. We were taken in the mess hall and asked what we preferred in lines of work. I took truck driving, and/or cooking.

Walked over to the carnival. Bought some handkerchiefs for Ma and Arlene, and sunglasses.

Warm tonight, skies are clear. Letter from Ray.

There was a lot of area east of the camp itself — sort of waste land, lots of pine trees, small clearings, and low brush, as well.

We were marched out to these areas in military formation, across the railroad tracks, and usually were allowed to find a spot under a tree in the shade from the sun if there was room for us to be together enough. Then we'd hear a talk by an officer, usually about some military subject.

This was always a lonesome, homesick walk for me, especially going out in the afternoon with one canteen of water that would soon be almost hot.

Wednesday, April 30, 1941   Drilling this forenoon, and listened to some lectures this p.m.

We had cannoneers' instructions, and we each had a chance to drive truck a short ways. I drove a new Dodge 4X4. It was hard to shift, but otherwise OK.

Payday for the older fellows tonight.

We had late mess, about 7:00. Took a cold shower.

Sent a letter to Alice Reinke.

Hot and sultry. We had to go to the mess hall and listen to a lecture by the captain.

I usually shower in the morning, or at night, or both; no restrictions so far.

Our First Sergeant is Gareys. An older fellow, about 50; he's nice to me. He saw me in the latrine once alone and said I was smart to keep my mouth shut.

One of the highlights of the day during this training schedule was to drink iced tea at night.

Thursday, May 1, 1941   We drilled again this forenoon in the usual place. Got a letter from Ma this forenoon.

We had truck-driving this p.m. again. I drove a GMC 6X6 and a Dodge 4-wheel-drive. I like to drive the big trucks.

Got another letter from home tonight, and from Grandma.

Real hot today. Sweating all the time. We have our blue denim pants and jackets on, and you sweat so much that your skin is blue. The blue pants and jacket look black because you sweat so much.

Friday, May 2, 1941   Drilled this forenoon again. Hot.

We got paid $9.10 this p.m.

Washed trucks. Had my last shot. Scrubbed out the tent.

Got my guitar from home today. Postage $1.45.

Our wages were $21.00 per month.

The shot was probably a tetanus shot.

Saturday, May 3rd, 1941   Up at 4:30. Showered, shaved. Prepared for inspection. I got through OK. We have to be sure to know our Army serial number and stand at attention. When the colonel comes along and grabs your chain with the dog tags on it, jerks it out from under your shirt and asks, "What's your name, rank, and serial number, Soldier?" what you answer had better match what it says on the dog tag. Otherwise, he tells you, "Report to your First Sergeant after this formation." That means extra duty, when you'd have time off otherwise.

We were off after 1:00. Washed some clothes. Straightened up some of my things. Read. Got acquainted with George Dahlgren. He lives close to Fish Lake [about 20 miles north of Duluth]. He knows Violet and Floyd Hanson from the [Duluth Farmer's] Market, and says Floyd is in this regiment now.

Skold, Berg and Wold went on an Army trip to Shreveport. Bird went to town. I'm all alone in here. Payday always does this to fellows.

Sunday, May 4, 1941   We can sleep until 7:30 on Sunday, but I get up around 6:30. Mess at 8:00.

Went to church. Chaplain Walker conducted services.

Played the guitar. A fellow from Battery C came over here. He can play the guitar a little.

Wrote home, read my Bible. Raining all afternoon.

I like playing the guitar — a bunch of fellows came in tonight, and I played the guitar and mouth organ. Another guitar player came from some place too. I didn't know him.

Sunday afternoon never failed to be the most lonesome time at camp. The Service Club was a good place to go, but it was still lonesome. Suppers Sunday nights were always cold cuts of sausage, cheese, bread, and maybe a cold salad.

A letter I wrote home dated May 4th said I had seen Charlie Jurvelin, the fellow I left Proctor with. I told them that Camp Claiborne covered 3,100 acres besides the training grounds, that we had 181 mess halls, and that each would have room for 170 men. I wrote that the officers had smaller mess halls than we enlisted men did, and that they stayed in tents half the size of ours, two officers to each tent. There was an infirmary for each regiment, and a camp hospital that had 1,320 beds. The tent theater held 2,200, and had shows every night. I also told them that we were getting more food, since they had upped the rations to correspond to more men.

Monday, May 5, 1941   Heard Berg and Wold come in last night about 11:30.

It was raining all night. We had to stand reveille in it this morning.

We had classes in the mess hall and Recreation Hall on the *Articles of War*, sex and first aid.

At 10:30 a report came in that a 60 m.p.h. wind was coming in, so we were all sent out to tie down the tent flaps. They are boarded up about 4 feet and are pretty sturdy.

We had classes in the mess hall this p.m. too. Rained steady until 5:00. Ed Wold loaned me a pair of his rubbers.

Got a letter from Al and Germaine.

Van Sloan and I went to a floor show at the Service Club.

When it rains, in just a few minutes there are several inches of water on the ground. Everything is pretty level, and the water has no place to drain away very fast, the reason for the duckwalks. The area is pretty well covered with sea shells and gravel, but it still gets really muddy.

Tuesday, May 6, 1941   We drilled for awhile in camp, then went to the gun park and had physical exercise. It rained some; we were in the mess hall during the time it rained.

This p.m. we had motor maintenance and cannoneer's practice. Warm this p.m. We got summer clothes this p.m. after mess.

Wrote a pen letter. Checked out two books from the sergeant's tent on reading maps and motor maintenance.

Wednesday, May 7, 1941   We spent the forenoon drilling and listening to some lectures by Clark, Wold, Gareys, Pankony and Burns. (All sergeants.)

It was foggy this morning. Turned hot later. Hottest day we've had so far.

Sgt. Burns gave us cannoneer's instruction and motor maintenance.

The boys are not back from bivouac yet. We were issued gas masks tonight.

I washed a few clothes. Sweat runs over my glasses. I'm alone in the tent tonight. I was expecting a letter from someone, but didn't get it.

It's 6:45. They are going in the barn at home to do chores now.

Thursday, May 8, 1941   Went to our usual training place this forenoon, and in the gun park this afternoon.

I drove a '32 Chev station wagon for about two miles. Helped wash trucks. The fellows came back from bivouac tonight.

No mail today either. I'm lonesome now.

Ice cream for supper. The whole meal was pretty good.

Real hot. I always remove my hat when we're not in formation, and am acquiring a dark tan. Also sunburn on my arms.

Ed, Berg and I walked to the carnival tonight. Went in nearly every place, had ice cream, pop and candy. Had a good time.

The carnival is outside of camp on the main highway. Lots of ways to gamble and things to buy.

Friday, May 9, 1941   We had the usual training this forenoon.

This p.m. I didn't do much. I scrubbed out the tent myself, and Moline and I had to scrub out the colonel's tent. Took a shower.

Another fellow came over from Able Battery with his guitar, and also a fellow from another battery, and we all played and sang.

Ed, Berg and Skold went to New Orleans on an excursion trip sponsored by the Army. George and I went to the canteen and had pop.

Hot. 110 degrees today.

Saturday, May 10, 1941   Up at 5:00. I volunteered for K.P. today with Van and two others. Washed tables and mopped the dining room.

Rained this forenoon. Hot this p.m.

I like K.P. I wouldn't mind being on steady if I don't get on truck driving.

Got through about 7:00 tonight. Reents came over with his guitar, and we sang and played.

I'd volunteer for K.P. on Saturdays to get out of having to stand formation for inspection. It was worth it. We'd always get a little extra to eat too, and it felt like a day off to me.

Sunday, May 11, 1941   Got up at 5:45. Took an early shower. It was chilly.

Washed clothes and changed to summer issue. Went to church with George Dahlgren.

George and I went to see Floyd Hanson, Violet's cousin. We had some pop, came back here.

Played the guitar. Lonesome today, not enough to do. When we play, some fellows always come in and listen.

Hot.

A letter I wrote home on May 11 told them I had finished with basic training, and I told my mother not to send me any more papers or magazines. I told them I didn't know for sure what detail I'd be working on.

There were over 30,000 men at Claiborne, and more were coming every day.

CHAPTER 2
Training. Wooden guns.

Monday, May 12, 1941   Up as usual. We all went on a truck convoy today. There were about 25 trucks. I was with Sgt.'s Peterson and

Braham, and Cpl.'s Armquist, Sleigh, Brown and Tracy. I drove a Dodge, and a Chev station wagon. Got along fine with the Dodge and Chev, but we got behind and I really had to go to catch up.

This p.m. we drilled some and were showed again how to pull out trucks with the aid of a winch.

Warm. Got a letter from Ray tonight. Will write him and shower.

Tuesday, May 13, 1941   Up at 5:15. We all marched up to the tent theater and saw a movie on sex hygiene. March back to the gun park.

Had the usual training this p.m. I drove a '40 GMC for about a mile. Got along fine. Had cannoneer instruction and listened to a lecture on driving.

Hot, but not so bad.

Got another shirt tonight. Washed it and some other clothes. Will take a shower and read.

Wednesday, May 14, 1941   Up as usual. I was detailed on anti-tank and anti-aircraft. We were giving instructions concerning 75 mm guns. I had hoped to get on driving truck, but this way may turn out better in the end.

George and I walked to A Battery and saw Hanson.

The captain talked to all of us in the mess hall tonight. We are going on a two day maneuver tomorrow. Packed up all my things.

Thursday, May 15, 1941   Someone changed his mind, and the anti-tank crew isn't going on the bivouac. We worked and studied on the 75 mm's all day.

A bunch of fellows were in here again. I played.

Letter from home tonight. I got pictures back, but they didn't turn out so good.

Friday, May 16, 1941   On the guns all day. We drew a hat on noon; nice, like a western hat. I also got new shoes, pants and dress socks.

Tonight the captain talked to us about maneuvers. We cleaned the tent.

We didn't have to stand in line tonight for chow. Everything was on the table, but we used mess kits to eat out of.

I ironed my pants, and Berg showed me how to iron my shirt.

I got *Life* magazine tonight.

Saturday, May 17, 1941   Fell in for reveille. Cleaned up my things. Another fellow and I had to move Lt. Karlson to another tent.

This p.m. I straightened up my suitcase, wrote up some notes and washed clothes.

After supper, George was over here for awhile. Walked over to see Jurvelin and Hanson, but neither one was in. Hot. Sweating steady.

Arlene's birthday. She is five. I sent her a silk handkerchief.

Sunday, May 18, 1941   Got up around 6:00. Showered. Van and I went for a walk this morning around the woods close to camp.

Went to church.

Wrote letters to Wing Chinn, Dick and home.

Really hot this p.m., about 105 degrees. Slept a little.

I really stow away the food now that I can have all that I want. I guess I'm fairly well satisfied here now.

George and I went for a long walk tonight and ended up at the Service Club. It's a beautiful place. It's nice and cool, and some guys take their girlfriends there.

Monday, May 19, 1941   We had cannoneer instruction all forenoon and part of this p.m.

Got off early tonight. Took a radio aptitude test with Tunning, Nelson and Red.

Warm. Storming tonight and raining hard.

The chaplain kept us in after mess tonight, gave us a talk and had us sing. His talk was inspiring.

I'm learning part of the Morse Code.

The cannoneer instructions were really dry, especially since we didn't have the guns there with us. The radio detail seemed more interesting to me, and I wouldn't have minded being assigned to it.

Wednesday, May 21, 1941   We were officially turned back to the battery today. Everybody went in the field. We anti-tank men took apart a 30 Browning automatic rifle, and put it together again.

A letter from home tonight. Mrs. Young died last Wednesday.

Hot. Have a headache. Talked to George awhile. Wrote a letter to Al and Germaine.

Lt. Darwin got married tonight in the Recreation Hall. Some of us fellows had to go there afterwards and move the benches around.

Thursday, May 22, 1941   On K.P. today with Anderson, Moline, Brandall and Van Sloan. Anderson and I took care of the dining room. This noon we all went out and took grub to the fellows in the field. I dished out tomatoes, sauce and coffee. I dropped a plank on my foot. We came back about 1:00, and got through in the kitchen about 2:15.

Anderson came over to my tent and we were looking at some of my things.

I went to the medics with my foot. The doc put me on quarters. The foot is swollen a lot, and it hurts. I didn't have to stand retreat tonight. It doesn't hurt as much now as it did.

Friday, May 23, 1941   My foot was better, but still sore. I went on sick call, and the doc put me back on duty.

I fixed up some duckwalks in the battery street, then helped the Supply Sergeant count some things. Cleaned the tent, washed clothes.

This p.m. I went out in the field with the rest.

Came in at 3:00. Cleaned the 30 caliber rifle. Packed my blanket roll and bag for tomorrow.

Got a letter from Ma and a *Life* magazine. Listened to the Bare and Louis fight. Will take a shower.

Saturday, May 24, 1941   We all dressed in chinos and went out in the field. I was put on the radio detail temporarily and had to handle a telephone. Had about 6 calls.

This p.m. we had off. Andy and I took a long walk in the woods. We saw a road blockade. It was really built well. Saw a blacksnake about four feet long, close up.

Got a letter from Wing tonight. Wrote one to Alice and answered Wing's. Played guitar in Baker's tent until 10:00.

Sunday, May 25, 1941   Up at 6:45. Dressed in new chinos.

Van and I went to early Mass this morning. It seemed odd to me. Later we went to Protestant services here.

Read. Wrote up notes. Sent a letter home. Andy and I went to the Service Club this p.m.

Slept a little. When I woke up, I was soaking wet with sweat — it's hot as heck. Played a little ball. Played music with Bird for awhile.

Stormed tonight and rained. It looks as though I won't get on radio. Probably just as good.

The crystal broke on my watch while it was in the suitcase.

Monday, May 26, 1941   Everybody went in the field west of here. We anti-tank men went separately, and they read to us. We ate out there.

This p.m. I was posted as a guard. Stood around in one spot. Came in at 3:30.

After mess, the captain talked to us about the shortage of water. Bird and I went to the Service Club.

My letter home dated May 26 told them another fellow and I had talked to a worker at a water pumping station. He'd told us that this station had pumped over a million gallons of water on Friday and that there were three pumps like it in camp. This well was 500 feet deep with a 30-inch casing. (More water got used on Fridays than normally, however, as all trucks and tents were washed for Saturday's inspection.)

I told them I had to dig a hole for garbage one day the past week while I was on K.P. duty, and that the first foot down was sand, and then the soil was red clay.

Tuesday, May 27, 1941   We went in to the usual place, but across the road today.

AND THERE SHALL BE WARS

Didn't do much of anything this forenoon but lay on a tarp and rest.

This p.m. we moved out further and had mess in a beautiful place. Took several pictures.

Got a letter from Ray, and answered it. George was over for awhile.

Wednesday, May 28, 1941　　Got up at 4:15 to go to the latrine. Couldn't go back to sleep afterwards.

Nelson and I went with Culbertson today with other fellows from other batteries to a river west of camp. We are going to convert it into a swimming pool. Started to clear the brush. Dragged out stumps and logs with the winch on the truck. Went back there this p.m. It was raining all the time; we got soaked.

Because of this I didn't have to go on a bivouac, as the other fellows did.

Bird is here in the tent. We few fellows ate at Battery C mess hall tonight. There's too much water in the sewers. I was on C.O. [Camp Orderly] and had to watch so no one used excess water.

Thursday, May 29, 1941　　At the swimming hole all day. Raining all day. Got soaked. Changed clothes on noon, and managed to stay dry. Ripped my raincoat yesterday. Jolie and I worked together.

Got a sore throat out of the mess and a bad cold. Played guitar a little.

Got a letter from Grandma.

There was a water moccasin in one corner of the pool today. Only their head is out of the water. Their body is straight down as they swim.

Friday, May 30, 1941　　Memorial Day. I thought I'd have the day off, but Sgt. Gareys told me while I was eating that I'd be on K.P. today. Urban, Novak, Nelson and Johnson were with me.

Rained steady all day.

Some drivers went to Mississippi today.

The water situation is still serious.

It was good I was on K.P. today. I like being in the kitchen. It's no fun being in the tent all day when it's raining. Besides, it's a good chance to get better acquainted with fellows you don't know so well.

Saturday, May 31, 1941　　Inspection at 9:30. Lasted until almost 11:00.

CHAPTER 2

Payday. I got the $21. Bought a trunk from the canteen for $6. Bought stationery and soap. I won't send any money home, but will try to hang on to some so I won't be broke all the time hereafter. Nearly everybody is out of camp.

By this time, the inspections didn't worry me much anymore. We just had to be ready to answer any questions asked, and not to forget to end it with a "Sir." The CCC's actually had stricter inspections than we had at Camp Claiborne, especially inside the tents. We had to be able to bounce a coin off our blanket in the CCC's, but not much was said here about beds not being perfectly smooth. The 34th Division was part of the National Guard, and that was a factor in the inspections being a little more lax.

I still have the trunk. It was well worth the $6. Just about everyone had one like it.

Sunday, June 1, 1941   Slept until 7:00. Went to church. Washed some clothes. Ironed my chinos.

Went on guard duty tonight on first relief. Cpl. Chandler was in charge. Jurvelin, Felix, Weniss, Shiparo, Shep and Topel. We sleep in the guard house. I went on duty at 5:00.

I challenged Capt. Hanson. I had post 4. Jurvelin was next to me. Cool and nice.

Guard duty didn't come too often. It lasted for 24 hours, but it was on and off for 4 hours at a time. The guard posts were at the pump houses, camp entrances, or any place where there could be sabotage.

Monday, June 2, 1941   On guard all day. Dressed in denims this a.m. Cleaned up. On duty 45 minutes this p.m. Laid around the guard house. Stopped a fellow from taking out a motorcycle. Was through at 5:30.

Got a letters from Ma and Dick. Bought 11 rolls of film for $1.60 tonight from a fellow in the 185th.

Nice today. Reents came over for awhile.

Tuesday, June 3, 1941   We all went on bivouac today. Left around 8:00, and got there around 11:00. We went past Pitman, about 40 miles, all told.

Fralim, Pan, Rieman and I tried to cut some "land mines," but the saw didn't have any set and we broke the handle, so we quit.

Rieman and I pitched tent together. We had a bonfire. We laid down soon after we were through, about 8:00, and talked until 11:00. Enjoyed it. Went to sleep right after, and didn't wake up until Bill shook me.

They killed a blacksnake here, and another one was between two fellows this morning.

We used wood "land mines" for training.

Blacksnakes aren't poisonous, but there were some coral snakes and timber rattlers in this area which are poisonous.

Wednesday, June 4, 1941 We anti-tank men were on range guard today. Rieman and I were together. We were stationed a long way from the others. We had to watch so nobody went into the firing field, as they were firing 75 mm's today.

We took pictures and talked a lot.

At 3:30 we were packed up and sent to a fire. After much effort in getting there, the fire was out.

We started back and got here at 8:00. Rode in Woodworth's weapons carrier. Dusty and dry.

Had a good time. We stopped at Pitman for water. I bought pop. Woodworth sneaked off with us, and we went to a farm and got cold water.

No mail. Played guitar a little.

This was a different day, to be allowed to just sit and talk. We all told each other our whole pre-army life. Rieman had been a garbage man and had owned his own truck.

There was a small farm just across the road. I walked over there. They had a few cows. The barn and house were shacks, but even the barn and manure smelled good to me and reminded me of home.

The store we stopped in was very rustic; you could see through the cracks in the walls to the outside.

Thursday, June 5, 1941
I was latrine orderly to-
day with Bird. We
cleaned the place, then
took turns watching so no
one would use too much
water.

Finished reading *By
Way of the Silver Thorns*,
and started on *River Rat.*

Ma wrote and sent along a letter from George Nash, which was a
nice surprise. Answered both tonight.

Friday, June 6, 1941   Went out in the field and to a gravel pit. Lt.
Darwin gave us some talks. We picked blueberries during rest periods. There are a lot of them, and they are sweet.

This p.m. we anti-tank men went with Woodworth way out in the
woods and cut fake land mines from logs.

Tonight I had to help wash the truck.

Van and I went to the Post Office. I took my suitcase, but couldn't
send it home as I had it locked. This is for security reasons.

Took a shower. One letter from home. Was also a letter from
Norma [a pen-pal from Louisiana].

Saturday, June 7, 1941   Got ready for inspection out in the field. Sat
around a tree. We were all lined up awaiting inspection when it started
to rain. Came in around 11:30.

Really rained hard until this p.m., the heaviest rain I've ever seen.
I slept from 1:00 until almost 4:00.

The leader of our mess table treated us with root beer tonight.

Walked to the car-
nival looking for a photo
album, but didn't like
them.

Finished *River Rat.*
Packed over my trunk.

The rain at Camp
Claiborne came down in
torrents, but usually the
sun would come back out

shortly, with a rainbow.

The leader of our mess table must have been a sergeant. A private couldn't have afforded to buy anyone else root beer at $21 a month.

The canteen had a lot of souvenirs, photo albums, etc, but they were higher in price than elsewhere. The place was always full of soldiers, though, because the clerks were all girls.

Sunday, June 8, 1941   Slept until 7:00. Washed clothes. Went to church. Wrote a letter to Dick and to home.

Andy and I went to the Service Club.

Read a little. It rained tonight; it was hot today.

George and I went to the carnival tonight. Had our pictures taken. I saw Harry Bronk, a fellow I was in the CCC's with. He is in the 125th Headquarters. I was surprised to see him.

A year ago June 8 while German tanks were rolling towards Paris, Detroit started gearing up to build tanks. By the last week of April 1941, Chrysler had finished their new $20,000,000 building and had produced the first pilot model of the M3 Medium 28-ton tank. Full production was expected by the coming fall.

Monday, June 9, 1941   On K.P. today with Galkie Nelson, Randall and Felix. Tonight I took pots and pans. It reminded me of the CCC's.

Got my swim suit tonight. After I was through, I walked over to the 109th Ordnance. I'd heard from Ma that Harvey Olson is in there. We had a nice talk, and we were both glad to see each other. Harvey's brother George is in the 125th. Harvey walked part of the way back with me.

Hot today. Changed sheets. Marion was over for awhile. Ed is in the hospital. He had his tonsils taken out.

Tuesday, June 10, 1941   We went for a long ride this morning. Finally ended up at our old training grounds. I acted as runner of information. Didn't do much. Had mess out in the field. Came in at 4:00.

Parade tonight.

Raining. Washed a few clothes. Am losing my ambition. It's tiresome to not have regular work. No mail for quite a while either.

President Roosevelt spoke from the East Room of the White House on June 9, 1941. He said that Hitler definitely intended to conquer the Western Hemisphere, and that to forestall attack, the US had to and would take military action without further notice, to prevent Germany from acquiring bases in Greenland, Iceland, Dakar, the Azores and Cape Verde.

He said further that all measures necessary to ensure delivery of US goods to Britain would be taken.

He said it was the duty of all American citizens to take logical part in the common defense from that moment forward, and that the US Government would use all its powers to see that neither capital nor labor interfered with arms production.

The President said that the US would not accept a Hitler-dominated world, and neither would we accept a world like the postwar world of the 1920's, in which the seeds of Hitlerism could again be planted and allowed to grow.

He ended his speech by announcing that he had proclaimed a state of unlimited national emergency.

Wednesday, June 11, 1941   Didn't do much this forenoon, except ride. Had some semaphore exercises. This p.m. we had more of it in the gun park, and marching. We signed the payroll tonight.

Thursday, June 12, 1941   Out in the field until 12:30.

Came in, and left at 3:00 on bivouac. Went to Kiskatchi National Forest close to Leesville. Rieman and I pitched together again.

I took my mouth organ along and played a little. We talked until 10:30.

Warm. A school bus full of pop and candy came to sell things there to us soldiers.

Soldiers were all over this part of Louisiana, as Camp Polk and Camp Livingston weren't far from here either.

Friday, June 13, 1941
We got up at 5:00. We were on range guard all day in the usual place.

I went for a walk west, and saw the water tanks of Leesville. I almost stepped on a coral snake.

Rieman and I practiced the semaphore code. Am getting on to it.

We were packed up at 3:00. While going back, Churney noticed he forgot his mussette bag. We went back another way and missed the convoy. We stopped at Pitken and had pop, and got back to camp at 6:00.

Saturday, June 14, 1941   Up at 5:20. Prepared for inspection. As we were all in line, it started to rain, so we didn't have any inspection. Lt. Darwin inspected our tent, though.

Practiced the semaphore code. Washed clothes, laid around.

Tonight I got a cake from home, cupcakes from Aunt Rose, and stationery from the kids.

After mess I took out a canteen book.

Bird and I went to the hospital to visit Skold, Ed, and Ken Baker. Came back at 8:00. Washed chinos and overalls. Very few fellows in camp.

I thought little about my birthday. I am 22 today.

Sunday, June 15, 1941   Up at 6:45. Took an early shower. Bird got his golf clubs yesterday and left early this morning to go to Pineville to play.

Chow was at 8:00. Still had some cake left.

Wrote two letters: home, and to Norma. My pictures came today. They turned out good.

Bought a polo shirt for 70 cents, a lock for 46 cents, a handkerchief holder for 50 cents and a photo album for 35 cents.

Monday, June 16, 1941   About 30 of us were detailed for camp guard. Received instructions this a.m. On until 9:00, off until 11:00. Shaved, dressed. Rained hard until 12:30.

We marched to the stockade. I was put on post 26 at the hospital gas heating plant and had to inspect the workers' passes. It was something to see the big furnaces. One civilian gave me a lunch. I had live ammo for my rifle. I disobeyed general orders and took pictures.

Had to report every hour to the stockade. Was on from 2 to 6 p.m.

Came back to camp around 8:00 and had mess. Back to the stockade. Slept on cots.

Tuesday, June 17, 1941   Got up at 1:30. On post about 2:15. There were only two guards at the meter station. It gets light about 4:30. Was off at 6:30. Came back to camp at 8 a.m. Ate, then went back to the stockade at 9:30. Laid around. Saw some prisoners. Ate at camp, back to the stockade at 12:30.

Left for the firing range at 2:15. Received instructions on how to fire on targets.

It took until 5:30 before we got back to camp. Ate. Walked to the Post Office. Sent my suitcase. $1.66. Bought some stamps.

Ed and Skold are back today.

Warm. No mail.

Wednesday, June 18, 1943   All of us went through a tear gas chamber this morning with our gas masks on. Felt a burning sensation on my skin, but otherwise OK. After that, we had dismounted drill.

This p.m. Lt. Darwin read the *Articles of War* again. At 3:00 we left for the firing range. Each fired 10 rounds. Raining steady. Hit one bulls-eye. The others were poor. Got score of 31.

The *Articles of War* were read to us many, many times. Most were quickly forgotten. One that they tried especially hard to impress on us was that if you were taken prisoner and interrogated, the only thing you could tell them was your name, rank and serial number. And if they continued to ask you questions, you continue answering — and only with your name, rank and serial number.

I later wondered about soldiers in the German Army. One thing for certain was, they hadn't had our *Articles of War* read to them, or their own German *Articles of War*, or else they had forgotten them. At least this was true of any German prisoners who I had anything to do with; they all seemed quite talkative and glad to be out of the fighting.

I never did become a very good shot. I always felt better when I was authorized to carry a .45 pistol rather than a rifle.

Thursday, June 19, 1941   All went out in the field. We anti-tank fellows laid around a lot. Hot.

Bill, Wold, Jim and I came back to camp for the land mines. We were about eight miles out. We ate out there on noon.

This p.m. we practiced judging distances. Came in at 4:00.

Most of the fellows had to move to different tents. I didn't have to, but all the others are different. Now I'm with Sergeant Pankony, Alton, Lucas, Amundson and Topel. All National Guardsmen except for me.

Went to see Reents for awhile. He showed me his pictures, and I showed him mine.

These new fellows are more talkative than in the other tent. Both Pankony and Topel are young and intelligent. Like to talk too. Amundson is always talking about his experiences with women. Lucas is a real quiet studious fellow. He has a brother in this battery, as well.

Friday, June 20, 1941   Had dismount of drill until 8:00. Went in the old training area. Cleaned our pistols.

Practiced semaphore code with Lucas and Shermack. Came in at noon.

Spent the p.m. in care of materiel.

Saw a show outside by the medics about anti-tank. Also *Here Come the Marines* at the Recreation Hall. It took until 10:30.

Saturday, June 21, 1941   Inspection at 10:30. Cleaned up. Hot. While we were at attention, sweat was running down my legs and soaked through the chino pants. It looks black. It's odd the old colonel didn't chew us out for sweating.

Washed clothes. Rained some this p.m. Pan and Topel were out, and came back feeling good.

The usual supper tonight of cold meats, salad and fig bars.

Nelson cut my hair. Weniss, Nelson and I went to the canteen. Had pop. Played in Nelson's tent. Fellows are playing cards in here tonight. I'm looking over my things.

The Battle of Germany started on June 15. Beginning on that day, six days before the German invasion of Russia, the British began to bomb Germany and the occupied countries in force. As many as 500 British planes a night crossed the English Channel, probably as many as the Germans ever sent against England at a time. In one month the RAF dropped about 4,000 tons of bombs on the Continent.

There was criticism from Americans because the British didn't concentrate their bombing on one city at a time. But still, 4000 tons of bombs couldn't help hurting something or somebody.

The German Luftwaffe couldn't knock Britain out of the war, but it had left a lot of corpses and rubble behind it.

Now it was Germany's turn. The British bombing was quite a contrast to Goering's prewar boast that "We will not expose the Ruhr to a single bomb dropped by enemy aircraft."

Sunday, June 22, 1941   On K.P. today with Nelson, Urban, Shermack and Smith. Had a lot of milk to drink, and oranges.

Had a little time off. Wrote to Uncle Louie and home. Went and talked to George awhile.

Real hot, but a little rain tonight cooled things off.

Pan and Topel are arguing about the war and conditions in general. Germany invaded Russia a short time ago, and some of the boys are talking about it.

Both Pankony and Topel were intelligent fellows, and it was good to hear them discuss the war situation. My opinion was still somewhat biased, as I was leaning towards — or from a pro-German family.

Russian armies were fighting desperately at the German supply lines. Oddly, Germany claimed capture of only a few thousand troops during this battle, and not the hundreds of thousands of past campaigns. Then came the German boast that the invincible German armies were just "holding." Though, according to German reports, the Russian Air Force had been repeatedly destroyed, it somehow came back to life again. Within a week from the German invasion of June 22, the Russians were attacking using troops that supposedly did not exist.

Monday, June 23, 1941   All out in the field today. Practiced the semaphore code. Don Gareys said I was the best sender of the new fellows.

This p.m. we went close to the trucks, as it was raining. I sat in the cab of a 6X6 and read my prayer book.

Ironed two sets of chinos tonight. Washed a few clothes. Read.

It was extra hot today. Cooler tonight. No mail for some time.

Don Gareys is the First Sergeant's son, probably a few years older than me. He's married. His wife comes on Sundays or holidays.

My letters home during June were pretty boring. I told of being on guard several times, of field trips, and the fact that we'd had two little pigs around our tent for some time, but the captain made us take them out in the woods.

Tuesday, June 24, 1941   We were all set to go out in the field, and were in the gun park when I heard Col. Lindberg give the officers heck.

Later, he called us anti-tank men together and told us we had to make something out of wood to resemble a 37 mm gun.

We went back to camp, and some of us were sent out to look for lumber. I helped a very little to make three 37 mm guns — out of wood.

Laid around a lot. Hot. Wrote a letter to Otto.

A fellow from Eagle Battery drove a motorcycle into the latrine. He smashed down the door and knocked over Shermack. He got banged up a bit.

Parade and review tonight.

I took out good insurance tonight.

The war effort was gearing up at other places besides Camp Claiborne.

Fort Bragg, North Carolina was over twice the size of Claiborne, with over twice the number of soldiers. On September 30, 1940, Fort Bragg had 376 assorted buildings, and 5466 officers and men. By the middle of June 1941, there were 3,135 buildings, and 67,000 officers and men. A crew of 23,500 men and $30 million made the difference.

New roads, power lines and other facilities were also added, making it North Carolina's third largest city.

Wednesday, June 25, 1941   Finished the wooden guns this p.m. I didn't help much.

Had the p.m. off. Played baseball. Went to the Service Club last night with George. It was talent night.

Got a welcome letter from George and Ethel Nash today, and one from Ray tonight.

Went with a few other fellows to Alexandria tonight to see a wrestling match. Joe Pasendeck won one of the bouts. Don't like to see them take so much punishment. Nice town, and I enjoyed the ride.

On the way back, Golke was going fast to get us in on time. We made it in time for bed check.

Watching my first wresting match was an experience. Joe Pasendeck was from Minneapolis and in our battalion, but I didn't know him.

I'd thought that all the punishment the wrestlers took was genuine, until the other guys set me straight on it.

Thursday, June 26, 1941   Out in the field all day. Was on panel station all day, but didn't do a thing.

Pankony and Wold were caught sleeping today. Got confined to quarters and extra duty. Don Gareys and Gerkie came in after 11:00 last night, and got the same dose.

Wrote to Ray tonight.

Chiggers are bad on my ankles and legs. Went to the medics yesterday and had them fixed.

Bought a cigarette lighter tonight.

Parade and Review tonight. It always gives me a big thrill, especially when marching past the reviewing stand, and marked time.

"Marked time" is when you're standing still, but lifting your legs as if you are marching. Everyone is in step, of course.

Friday, June 27, 1941   Anti-tank men stayed in today and were supposed to paint the guns, but I had to go and help level the shoulder of the road by the officers' quarters. It started to rain about 10:30, and we quit then.

Got ready for camp guard duty. Left at 11:00. I was on first relief. The O.D. [Officer of the Day] came and tested me on post. I had guard post no. 17, a pumping station and water reservoir. A big pump went on and off automatically.

Came back at 6:30. Ate, and went back to the stockade and slept until 1:30.

These buildings for electricity, water supply, etc., never shut down, of course. They had civilian workers; therefore the necessity for guard duty. I never minded the guard duty, as I rather liked the strict procedure with no toleration for foolishness.

Saturday, June 28, 1941   Went on post from 2 a.m. until 6:00. It started to get light at 4:00, but not very light. I was relieved at 6:30. Went back to the stockade, swept out the tents and policed the grounds. We were all through at 1:30.

Most of the prisoners at the stockade are black or Southerners.

Washed clothes.

Don Gareys got busted because he came in late one night. Two fellows fell asleep on guard last night, and they will be Court Martialled.

There was a dance at the Service Club for our regiment. I didn't go. Read in a biographical novel until 10:00. Showered and cleaned up.

The Army is serious business. Don Gareys was our First Sergeant's son and a real serious fellow, but no leniency was shown him because of this.

The two who were caught sleeping on guard duty had heard often enough from the *Articles of War* what would happen to them. Being Court Martialed could end up in a Dishonorable Discharge, which was an easy way to get out of the Army. It would not be easy in civilian life to find a job or to hold your head up, with a D.D. on your record, though.

Sunday, June 29, 1941   Up at 7:15. Mess at 8:00. Went to church again, and it was a good service.

Read before church and after. Went swimming this p.m. to Castor's Plunge. Was in the water for awhile. Nice place.

Came back at 5:30. Wrote a letter home.

Went to the Service Club. I turned in *Calvary Men*, and checked out *Wheels in the Timber*. Read it nearly half through, then came back here. The tent was full, and the fellows were squabbling. Wrote up some notes, and will read for a while.

Castor's Plunge pool was not the one that I had helped Culbertson build. Maybe that creek dried up, or the water moccasin scared people away. Anyway, as far as I knew, it was never finished, or at least never used.

There were times I wished I could have gone back to a quieter tent, but I really liked the type of conversation they stuck to in my tent, and if it ever did get out of hand, there was Lucas to straighten things out.

Monday, June 30, 1941   Went in the field this a.m. Don and I were together on one of our wooden guns. Didn't do a thing.

Had drilling for an hour this p.m. The rest of the time we spent finishing the guns. Was real hot.

At the last minute, I was told to go on guard. I go on at 8:10 to 6:45.

Now as I think back on one year ago, I just don't know what to think. I wonder what it will be like a year from today.

CHAPTER 3

Sick spell. Preparing for maneuvers.

Tuesday, July 1, 1941   I went on guard post no. 7. It was the same one I had last time, but the number was changed. Was on from 8:30 until 1:30, then again from 2:30 until 4:30. Had to change guards by so-called "guardmount."

Got paid $21. Had to give $7 back for insurance, and $2 for boots.

The boys are having a heck of a time tonight. A concertina is going full blast in the next tent. Fellows are drumming on the stove with tent pins. Pan, Lucas and others are leaving tonight on furlough.

Real hot. Someone said 109 degrees.

Wednesday, July 2, 1941   Dressed in chinos. Went to the gun park and sat in the trucks for over an hour. After that was the mounted parade. All the trucks drove in double file along the highway. We sat with arms crossed when we went past the re-viewing stand. A lot of citizens were lined up along the road watching. We were through at 10:30.

Had a real heavy rain this p.m.

I took my picture of the battalion around to the tents and had the fellows sign their names on the back.

Finished *Wheels in the Timber* and *Biography.*

The reviewing stand held a lot of "Brass," i.e., majors, colonels, generals, and maybe the captains and lieutenants too. We performed mostly to show our patriotic duty in being a part of the United States Army, and in celebration of July 4, Independence Day.

Thursday, July 3, 1941   Slept until nearly 5:30. It's the same every day. I wash, brush my teeth, make my bunk. We fall in, police the area. Fall in again, and exercise until 6:00. Mess at 6:15, and fall in again at 6:50.

Today we all went in the mess hall until 8:00. Capt. Hanson gave us a lecture on a new setup for maneuvers.

After that, we anti-tank fellows went to Area F and got five long pine poles. I chopped from 10:00 to 11:00.

Then the lt. colonel gave us another lecture on the coming maneuvers.

Off this p.m. I sorted over my trunk. Read my Bible. Amy and Topel went to town and left me all alone in the tent. Was cool this p.m. Had Pepsi-Cola with our supper. Talked with George.

Friday, July 4, 1941   Got up at 5:45. Left for Lake Charles at 7:45. I rode in Dahlgren's 6X6. There were about 25 of the 6X6's and several station wagons. I had a seat in front of the box.

We followed a railroad track part of the way. Lots of marshland. I got an idea what prairie land might look like.

Got there at 10:00. Our headquarters was in a school.

Walked around town in the a.m., then came back to eat. In the p.m. we went to the beach of the lake and looked around. Pettengale and I went to the YMCA. Read. Walked around town some more. Found a few book matches. Bought *Return of the Native* and two papers.

Left at 8:00, got back at 11:00. I had a headache and felt tough. I slept on the floor of the truck on the way home.

Saturday, July 5, 1941   Up at 7:30. Was on K.P. I washed everything. Johnson, Brown, Randall and Ledwig were with me.

I felt tough, with a headache, cold, and a cough. Was sore and stiff.

Got through at 7:00. Washed clothes, took a shower, and went to the medics. I had a temperature of 102. They made me stay here over night. Talked with another fellow for a while who is in here with a sprained knee.

A letter from Norma. Cool today.

Sunday, July 6, 1941   Up about 5:00. Washed, then lay down again for awhile, then went back to eat.

Came back here at 9:00, and the colonel doctor put me on quarters and made me stay all day. My temperature is still a little over 100.

Wrote a letter to Norma and to home. Still feel tough. Eat at the mess hall. Rested a lot.

Friday I saw two semi-trailers, one full of cattle, the other with horses.

My temperature this p.m. was 102. Was hot today.

To be "on quarters" meant no work. You'd either be ordered to stay in the medics' tent, or in your own tent. Usually you could eat in your own mess hall. If you abused the privilege of being on quarters, the hospital would be next.

Monday, July 7, 1941   Woke up about 5:00. At 6:00 I came back to eat. Everybody was through at 7:30. The medics took my temperature. It had gone down, and I was allowed to come to my tent.

I changed to denims, washed, and read in the Bible. Slept and rested. Feel far from well.

Awful hot, but not bad in the tent. I always manage to eat something, but I'm not feeling hungry.

I talked to George Bowers. He used to work in Duluth. Went to see Charlie Jurvelin. Feel better.

On July 7, 1941, President Roosevelt announced that US Naval Forces had occupied Iceland. There had been some dispute whether Iceland was in the Western Hemisphere and subject to the Monroe Doctrine.

But there had already been fighting in Iceland, in February 1941, when Nazi planes machine-gunned the airport at Reykjavik, and Iceland lay well within the war zone of counter blockade already laid down by Germany.

The announcement made the war seem closer to us, though US and

German gunners had not yet officially exchanged first shots.

Tuesday, July 8, 1941   On quarters today again. Still have a fever and a bad hacking cough. No appetite at all. Laid around. Makes a long day, and no mail either.

Most of the other fellows are on bivouac. Am all alone in the tent. My fever is worse tonight. Hot today.

We may have to stay in the Army until the world crisis is over.

We were always kicking around the conversation piece if we'd be in the Army for just a year, or for "the duration."

I think it was pretty much a fact that we all expected our service life to last longer than a year, but we didn't want to believe it true.

We were somewhat like the captain of a sinking ship; until the last moment, he no doubt hopes some miracle will still happen.

Wednesday, July 9, 1941   Still on quarters. My temperature is 100.8. Laid on my bunk all forenoon.

The fellows came in on noon.

Read a little this p.m. It's hot, but I feel fairly good. My appetite is much better.

Thursday, July 10, 1941   Went to the medics again. Still have a temperature, and was put on quarters. Didn't do much. Not feeling so good again. Cough is bad at times.

The fellows went on another bivouac.

Shermack has been on quarters as long as I have, but with his legs.

No mail.

Friday, July 11, 1941   Bye came in here after 11:00 last night with two letters, one from home and one from Ray. Made me feel better. Everything is OK at home.

Have a temperature of 100.2. On quarters again. I am tired of laying around. The fellows came in around noon.

Lucas came back from furlough tonight. It's raining.

Saturday, July 12, 1941   My temperature is 99.6. I feel OK, but my cough is awful bad. Still on quarters.

We all overslept this a.m. and only woke up when the captain called the battery to attention. The fellows have their bunks displayed for inspection. They have all left with the infantry on a hike.

It was raining all night, and still is. I thought about Saturday market days in Duluth and about home. I read my Bible. I enjoy being alone today, now that I feel a lot better.

A letter from Ma. She said Old Man Hurty has died.

George came over, and I went to see him.

Sunday, July 13, 1941   Got up about 6:45. Shaved and showered. Ate, then went to the medics. I still have a temperature, but feel good except for the cough.

Attended church services. Read some in the Bible. Talked with George. Sold my guitar to Tony for $6 the first part of this week.

Hot. I am sick and tired of laying around.

Monday, July 14, 1941   Still on quarters. It makes me mad.

Wrote to George and Ethel, read, and laid around. Got a letter from Ray, and one from Grandma. It rained this p.m.

Tuesday, July 15, 1941   Up as usual. Early breakfast, then Kiedler and I went to the medics.

I was put on duty and am glad of it. I hope I never have to go back there again so many times in succession. It feels like I'm pretty deaf in my left ear.

Read the Bible, wrote up my notebook, washed and shaved. Got ready and went out with the mess truck at 5:00. I was to take it easy, but the doc said I could go out tonight.

We went quite a ways northwest of Elmer's Point. We ate at 7:00, and I was put with Sgt. Erickson helping the telephone detail. We drove around a lot with a weapons carrier, trying to find some of the fellows.

Wednesday, July 16, 1941   Last night at 9:00 we walked our way out. Most of the trucks were stuck in soft, wet ground. We started picking up telephone wire. I followed it a long ways, and then tore it.

It took until 2 a.m. to get the wire truck out to the main road. Rode in a blackout until 3:15. Then the "war" was over.

Came back to camp at 5 a.m. Tried to sleep awhile. Have the forenoon off. Slept a little, but it was too hot.

This p.m. I washed clothes. Took a shower. Andy and I went to the Service Club at 4:30. Rained during this time.

I stood retreat the first time in 13 days. Got a letter from home. I'm deaf in my left ear. I hope it doesn't last.

Some of this training didn't mean much to us as we went through it at Camp Claiborne, but it did teach us things we'd later have to go through in action, especially laying and picking up telephone wire, getting vehicles out of the mud and traveling in blackout. "Blackout" meant headlights taped over, with just a narrow strip of light pointing downward. A driver could see maybe 20 feet in front of him, unless it was foggy or raining -- then he couldn't see at all.

If at any time there was a definitely depressing season while I was at Camp Claiborne, it had been the previous month or so. At the time, it seemed I would be stuck on the anti-tank detail, which I didn't like. It had been almost unbearably hot every day, and I'd been on quarters with a really bad cold and high fever for two weeks.

The reality that I would probably be stuck in the Army for two years instead of one was beginning to sink in as well, and that was a sickening thought. I was feeling lonesome for home and the gardening business. It was the time of year to begin selling vegetables at the Farmer's Market, and I think the hardest thing for me was not being able to be there.

Thursday, July 17, 1941   Got up at the usual time. Mounted in the trucks. It took until about 10:00 before we really started. We went somewhere around Le Compte. Shermack and I were put on a wooden gun from 2 until 11 p.m. We took turns sleeping.

We were close to a store. We had cake and candy. We were close to where a family lived in a tent. Two small kids came and played with our gun.

We ate about 7:00. The mess truck was in back of the store in a farmyard, under a tree. The farm reminded me of Grandpa Seelig's old place [in Adolph, Minnesota]. Unpainted shacks, old tools, and a few cows around the barn.

After eating, I went to Swede's and Frank's gun so they could go eat. There was a guard there from the 136th Medics who was from Missouri. I talked with him, then came back to Shermack.

Friday, July 18, 1941   When we pulled out last night, (actually this morning), I was put on the wire truck with Frank, Pint (the concertinist) and Paulson. We laid a line of wire to "Hong Kong" and to "fire direction." Came back to our position in blackout. Took until about 3:30 a.m.

Slept until 4:45. Ed woke me up, and I went to eat. Came back to Clark's truck. Slept until about 8:00, moved out at 10:00.

Got to camp at 11:00. Washed. I've grown a little beard during the past few days.

Slept a little this p.m. I cleaned up my things. We scrubbed out the tent. After that I went to the Service Club, checked out *The Virginian*. Read a part of it there, then bought a candy bar and walked around our battalion while I ate it.

Saturday, July 19, 1941   Woke up at 5:20 and thought if I'd been at home, I'd be leaving for the Farmer's Market right now.

Got ready for inspection that was at 10:15. I caught heck for a missing button and a dirty gun belt. For punishment, I had to go to the gun park and stand inspection with another detail's equipment.

Got a letter from Norma in Northfield where she now works. Got a wooden beer mug as a souvenir. Took out a canteen book. Got a short haircut. Bought a scarf for Ma's birthday, and a towel with the 34th Division insignia on it from the canteen for 20 cents.

Straightened up my trunk. Wrote home. It's now 3:30 and raining hard.

Had a good supper. Listened to Pint on the concertina. Talked with Nelson.

Sunday, July 20th, 1941   Got up at 7:20. On K.P. today with Smith, Van Sloan, Ledwig and Idamoe. Meyers is on as cook.

I had no time off at all this morning, but was off from 2:30 to 5:00 tonight. It was awful hot in the kitchen. Sweat poured off me. I washed everything in the kitchen: pots, pans and dishes.

Washed clothes. Tonight I took a shower, shaved and changed clothes. I wrote home and will write to Norma. It's cooled off a lot now. A beautiful sunset tonight, the prettiest I've ever seen. It's almost dark now at 7:30. Cloudy and looked like rain this p.m.

I bought a good-luck charm with key ring yesterday, and had my name and address engraved on it today at the canteen for 20 cents.

Monday, July 21, 1941   As usual, until after we fell in. We fell out again, and didn't have to do anything.

Wrote to Norma, and a card to Carl and Myrtle. Was cloudy all day, looked like rain, and it did rain a little.

I laid around until 4:00. Helped Cosette pile some lumber and then got ready to leave.

It got almost dark, and then the sun came out again and there was a beautiful sunset.

We left about 7:30 from here, and 8:30 from the gun park. I was with West [our driver], Pan, Yoursek and Rieman. I slept nearly all the way out there on one of the seats. The trip was 42 miles. It was raining on the way out. We went through Oakdale, Elizabeth and Union Hill.

Rieman and I were together on a gun. I slept most of the time until 6 a.m., then ate, and then Rieman slept.

Tuesday, July 22, 1941 Sat with Rieman until 11:30. Then we pulled out. Took a long time to get started. I sat in the front seat with West while the boys played cards. The truck hit a bump and spilled some of the cards. The deck was new, so Rieman threw the rest away.

Started raining at Oakdale, and we put the sides down while still on the move.

Got into camp about 3:00. Had a headache.

Had a good supper. Talked with George for about an hour.

"SOLDIERS AND GIRLS HAVE FUN AT AN ARMY RECREATION CAMP IN LOUISIANA."

This was the headline of an article in *Life* magazine of July 21, 1941. This article nearly got me mobbed by fellows trying to take the magazine to find out where this camp was.

The article went on to say that July is "furlough month" for much of the US Army, and that during the past week thousands of soldiers were leaving their big Southern camps for 10-day visits at home. For those who were spending the summer at camp, the Army had provided 12 recreational camps throughout the country at lakes, mountains, etc. The purpose of these was to give the soldiers some fun.

The article said that these [lucky] solders knocked off work Friday noon and boarded a motor convoy ride to the recreation areas. Once there, they were on their own, with no formations, no roll-call and no special time to go to bed or get up in the morning. Expenses were small, as the tents cost them nothing, and food for the weekend only cost them about $2. For small additional sums, they could go to dances, amusement parks, play golf or tennis, swim or fish.

The fellows were really excited when I told them about this place. The only trouble was, there weren't any soldiers from Camp Claiborne going on furlough during July. And we couldn't figure out how we could knock off on Friday noon, when we could hardly get ready for Saturday inspection by noon that day. Not a one of us had heard of this camp, and if we had, we didn't think we would have been able to afford to go there even with "small expenses," since we were still only earning $21 a month, and that was hardly enough to get through the month right there at Camp Claiborne.

Well, we couldn't deny that the *Life* magazine article sure made the evening more exciting than it would have been otherwise. But about all we could hope for as far as recreation went was a pass after Saturday inspection, and then we had had to be back Sunday night. That was if we didn't have any special duty such as guard duty or K.P.

Wednesday, July 23, 1941   Were off until 9:45, then we marched to the vicinity of the big tent with the 168th Infantry. We listened to some big shots give us both heck and praise on our last maneuver.

Came back at 11:45. Rained, and we got a little wet.

This p.m. I finished *The Virginian.* Got *Smokey, the Cow-Horse* from George. Got a letter from Dick and Mom. Washed clothes after mess. Read. Cool day.

Ma says they are still making hay at Rhunke's. My life at home seems almost like that of a dream. I think seldom of my horses, and most the time only lightly at that. I guess we are stuck here for the duration of the war.

Thursday, July 24, 1941   This morning, Urban and I helped Bird with the latrine until 9:00. Then Lt. Karlson gave us a lecture on camouflage. Then we had a half hour lesson on our gas masks.

After that, we sat in Shermack's tent, and Sgt. Wold read to us. Retreat as usual. Washed my gun belt after mess. Shaved as I do nearly every night. Showered. George came over for awhile. Read in *Smokey*.

Hot as usual. We have had rain for 44 consecutive days. Where we last bivouacked was 127 feet above sea level.

Friday, July 25, 1941   Fall in after mess. Rieman and I were detailed to help our Supply Sergeant [Lamonte].

First, we loaded a bunch of clothes on the kitchen truck, and took it back to the warehouse no. 22. We had to wait until they opened, then we carried it in. Then we came back here.

Lamonte went to town. I had charge of the supply tents while he was gone. Cleaned up the place this p.m. We had to wash the supply truck. Afterwards, I washed my musette bag, gas mask, case, canteen cup, and mess kit.

After retreat, I washed my gun belt again and at last got it clean. Finished *Smokey*. Good book, the life of a horse. Took a shower, and to bed as usual, around 10:00.

Saturday, July 26, 1941   Woke up earlier than the bugle blew first call or the band played — but this a.m. I had some time to myself.

Had to help in the kitchen until 8:00. Got ready for inspection, which came at 10:00 and lasted until 12:00. I passed in fine shape. Worst heat we have ever had here.

Had a good dinner. Washed clothes this p.m. Spent an enjoyable hour packing over everything I own.

Two new fellows came in our battery yesterday from a camp in California. One is from Oregon, the other from Montana.

It rained after 2 p.m. and cooled off. Just got a letter from Ray. Rhunke is driving my team making hay now. Ray is loading the pulp wood we cut this past winter.

CHAPTER 3

The pulp wood we had cut at Payne the past winter had been hauled to the main road, then peeled and left to dry for several months. Then it was loaded on flat railroad cars and shipped to the paper company in Cloquet.

Sunday, July 27, 1941   Up at 7:00. Cleaned up the tent. Went to church with Elton. A small congregation.
Looked over my things. Real hot. Sweat runs off me. Wrote home this p.m.
Got ready for guard duty at 5:00. Went down there. Was put on 3rd relief, under Cpl. Faran.
Came back here, and have to report back to the guard base at 8:15. Talked to George.
Thought a lot of home. No doubt they were making hay today.
Some rumors are going around here now that we are going to be transferred to Camp Ripley after maneuvers. Hope it's true.

Elton was my tent-mate Lucas' brother, who had been visiting Lucas that morning and decided to go with me to church.

Monday, July 28, 1941   Had my usual post in the gun park last night and this morning: number 7. Faran was my corporal, and he let me come back to my tent to pack over some of my things.
This p.m. after mess, the captain called us into the mess hall and put a crimp in our thoughts. He said that after maneuvers, we are definitely not coming back to Claiborne, and that we are to send all personal equipment home. It put me in a turmoil. I hate to part with my things, especially my trunk.
Had formal guardmount at 5:30. After mess we had to wash trucks until almost 8:00. Talked to Nelson.
Hot today. A letter from Grandma.

Tuesday, July 29, 1941   I usually wake up just before first call. As always, I'm the first up in the tent. Luke is next.
This a.m. we anti-tank men went north of here and listened to Lt. Hanson talk about gun procedures and the coming alert. This p.m. we fellows had an equipment check.
McCullough has been AWOL [Absent Without Official Leave] for about a week now. Real serious thing in the Army. Someone said they caught him in Minneapolis.
A few of us had to listen to the *Articles of War* again, as we'd missed them on Friday. After mess there was a short meeting.

I walked over to see George Olson. Didn't stay long, but came back here. Then went to 109th Ordnance, but couldn't find Harvey. Went to the Recreation Hall and saw a stunt show by all of the batteries. Parts of it were good.

It's starting to get boring again. I'm anxious for maneuvers to start.

Wednesday, July 30, 1941   Amy was up first this morning. I followed a close second.

Shotmiller and I helped the Supply Sergeant for awhile this forenoon. All of us had to turn in our wool blouses, shirt and pants. We had to pack them in boxes.

Got my things together. At 10:00 we had a practice alert. We took our barracks bags and mounted the trucks, but didn't go any place.

This p.m. we had off. I wrote all the fellows' names in my notebook. My ear is OK now. Makes me feel better all around.

At the time we were going through these practice alerts, it was hard for us to realize what good they'd do us in combat ... and we knew that many of our "teachers" in these drills were only teaching us what they themselves had been taught, as they'd never been in combat either. We had a lot of chances during the next three years, though, to benefit from our having learned to pack up and move quickly,

It was my mother's birthday July 30, but I must not have thought of it at all, or I would have mentioned it in my diary. She was 45.

Thursday, July 31, 1941   Up at about 5:20. We got ready for an alert that took place at about 8:00. A few of us had to set tables on top of one another in the mess hall. We were through at 2:00 and came back here and straightened things up.

Went to the Service Club last night. Checked out *Resurrection River*. Finished it tonight.

Hot. I had a bad spell from something this morning and almost fainted from it.

Friday, August 1, 1941   Only we anti-tank fellows went out this morning. We went a short ways from camp. All of the Headquarters Batteries from our regiment, 185th and 125th, will soon form a battery of our own. Had some drill on the guns and foot-drill. I feel better now and enjoy the work a little better. Had mess out in the field.

When we came in tonight, everybody was gone. Ten of us had to eat with Service and Ammunition. I think this was the best meal I've had in the Army. Pankony got a big package of food from home tonight. He gave me some cake.

I got sunburned today.

Saturday, August 2, 1941 We left for the field at 7:00. We all gathered around a big shady tree. Lt. Hanson was giving orders. Part of the 125th, 185th, and we are going to form a battalion of our own, and we got organized.

Practiced a little cannoneering. Came back to camp on noon. Ma sent a big package of cookies, cake, dates and bismarks. We eat at Service and Ammunition morning and noon.

Harvey Olson came over with his car, a '37 Chev, and gave me a ride to Forrest Hill.

Washed a few clothes. Read. After mess I took a long walk around camp. First Saturday since I've been here that we have had no inspection. Was really glad to get the package.

I'd really enjoyed the ride with Harvey that afternoon. Forrest Hill was a spot for the soldiers with entertainment of all kinds. We didn't stay long, though, as on a Saturday afternoon the place was filled with soldiers.

Sunday, August 3, 1941 Woke up this morning at 7:30. After breakfast I was set on having a day off, but Hurbut told me I was on K.P.

Mackensie and I took care of the dining room. He got out of the [Knife River, Minnesota] CCC 1751 just before I got there, but we still had a lot to talk about.

Went to a show tonight. Was fairly good. I wrote a short letter home, and got one from Norma.

Monday, August 4, 1941 Had a short lecture this morning. Left camp around 1:00. Went somewhere around Matter. I was on a 37 mm gun with two fellows from the 185th, and with Frank.

Moved out tonight to another place, and all five of us spent the night in the back of a weapons carrier.

Tuesday, August 5, 1941 Had mess out in the open. Moved alongside of a road. Took turns, then came back to our bivouac area. I put up a hammock from a shelter half. It rained some, and I got wet, but it was better than last night jammed in the back of that small weapons carrier. Then there are the mosquitoes.

Later someone asked me what kind of "dope" we used for mosquitoes, and I said, "Mister, you're the 'dope.' This was 1941."

After several nights of this kind of training, we began to think that the war itself could hardly be any worse than the preparing for it.

Wednesday, August 6, 1941   Moved to a new location this morning, or p.m., whichever it was.

Had to go on duty tonight along the road. Frank and I were together. Slept some. Had sandwiches. Had to dig foxholes.

Thursday, August 7, 1941   Same position all day. Tonight I got a letter from Ma. She sent pictures of the kids and the horses.

At 9:00 we left and went back to our bivouac area. Slept on a tarp.

Friday, August 8, 1941   We were woke up at 4:15. Had mess and pulled out at 8:00. Got to camp around 10:30.

First thing I did was to shave, shower and change clothes. Had the rest of the day off. Got paid this p.m. Bought a few things. Hot. Was going to call home, but were too many ahead of me. It rained. Topel went to the medics. The others are in town.

Since January of 1941, the Army had been building up its ability to make 600,000 pounds of smokeless powder every day, as it was estimated an Army of 1,200,000 men would use that much daily.

The Army's program of national defense-building was moving ahead, in spite of delays and blunders. The United States government had put up $74,000,000 for a powder plant at Charleston. DuPont had agreed to build such a plant on a cost-plus fixed-fee basis, and to operate it for the government.

Saturday, August 9, 1941   Had regular Saturday morning inspection. Washed clothes.

At 1:00 Nelson, Anderson and I went to Alexandria. Got a ride in with one of our trucks. It was crowded with soldiers. Went to a Gene Autry show. Took the bus back.

Between August 9 and 12, at a secret location "somewhere off the coast of Maine," Franklin Roosevelt and Winston Churchill met for the first time. They gave a formal pronouncement to the world, an outline of eight points for peace. They pledged to the "final destruction of the Nazi Tyranny."

Soon after these conversations, an invitation was made to Soviet Premier Stalin to meet with British and American representatives in Moscow to discuss long-term triangular collaboration against Hitler. Josef Stalin quickly accepted.

Sunday, August 10, 1941   Packed my things. Wrote to Norma and Ray. We anti-tankers had to turn our things in tonight. We'll have to sleep on bare springs.

Hot. This will be my last night here for some time, I hope for good.

A letter from George and Ethel.

This is what the fellows have been talking about since I've been here: maneuvers, and the time has finally arrived. The National Guardsmen have gone through this before at Camp Ripley, and to hear them talk, it's more exciting than our daily camp life.

CHAPTER 4

Maneuvers. Starting in the kitchen.

Friday, August 11, 1941　Left at 4:30. Got to our new camp at 9:30. We pitched tents. Frank and I are together at the end of the second row. I helped him with Lt. Hanson's things.

Had a scant dinner of cheese sandwiches and coffee. Walked to a creek and washed.

Farmer close by with 200 cows.

Fair supper tonight. Am sitting outside of our pup tent, writing, and sitting on my barracks bag.

We get to see Louisiana this way, and we had a good start today. I like to hear the Southerners talk. You can hardly understand some of them, though.

The 200 cow herd were all Holsteins, but I couldn't find a way to get close to the buildings or to talk to anyone but a young boy — and all he knew was that there were about 200 cows "at that place."

Tuesday, August 12, 1941　Got to sleep about 10:00. Slept good until Frank woke me up. I had to help put up a supply tent and put some things in it.

Some fellows caught frogs last night for frog legs. They are big, over a foot long.

Helped chop out stumps and police up.

Got a letter from home. After 4:00, Frank and I walked about a half mile from here. Took a bath and washed a few clothes. The water holes are from dynamite.

Fair supper. I went to the farm house after mess, but they were all

54

out milking cows. I just couldn't get to see their operation. Probably, "No soldiers welcome."

President Roosevelt at this time had sent a message to Congress urging the extension of all draftees' and Guardsmens' one-year terms.

There seemed to be a morale problem of the "frustration of inaction," as America was training its first-ever conscript Army in peacetime. It was speculated that this morale problem would be easily solved the instant the first shots of war were fired.

Life magazine of August 4 had the following headline on the featured article: *"America Bares its Weapons of Attack as the Time for Action Draws Nearer."*

The article explained, and showed pictures of the oversized-looking landing craft with a ramp that could go right up onto a beach to discharge its load of one light tank and crew.

Wednesday, August 13, 1941 Woke myself this morning. Had dismounted drill for awhile, then gas mask drill. After that, we went in the trucks for a ride. Got out and marched and watched. Able Battery set up a mock 75 mm gun.

We came back on noon. Went to where they have the field showers and had a cold shower. Went back to the farm house with Wold. Had some cold water and cooking pears. Read a little, laid in the shade. Hot.

Formal retreat tonight. Before we fell out, Lt. Hanson asked if there was anyone in the battery who could cook. My hand shot up in a hurry, and Lt. Hanson told me to stay there, that he wanted to talk to me after the formation was dismissed.

He just asked me a few questions, like what experience I had. I told him we had a camp in the woods, and I've always liked to cook.

So he told me to go and eat, then report to the Mess Sergeant. I did. Then I got to help the other cooks until 8:00.

Thursday, August 14, 1941 Got up at 3 a.m. this morning and helped where I could. I served bacon for breakfast. Had to clean up the kitchen after mess. There are five cooks and a Mess Sergeant. I helped serve this noon as well.

I am off now until tomorrow noon. Walked to the water holes. Washed, shaved, looked at my pictures and Bible in the woods. Am thankful to be on as cook.

I was really excited about getting the cook job. I was up in the clouds, and the anti-tank crew could easily do without me.

I really wanted to get back in the 151st Headquarters Battery where I had a lot of friends. I wasn't positive this new job would do this, but it was certainly a step in the right direction. The fellows seemed nice too. They didn't seem pushy, and anyway, I was willing to do anything.

Lyle Ellefson, one of the cooks, told me several things. First, cooking in camp would be better than cooking in the field (as we were doing). He told me that the cooks got every other day off, and didn't have to stand guard, reveille, retreat, or any other details. He told me that when in action, though, I might not like the fact that there would be a lot of complaining about poor meals — and that in action, the job wouldn't be much more than opening cans.

I was satisfied for the time being, though, and my hopes were that I could stay in the 151st.

Friday, August 15, 1941   Slept through reveille. Ate a late breakfast. Walked in the woods. Slept a little.

Went on duty this p.m. The usual work, except we prepared for

March Order. After supper we started packing. Everything was taken.

We left about 10:00. Six others and I rode in a ration truck. Cramped, hard riding. Came about 30 miles northwest. Are within 3 miles of Texas.

I was put slicing bread for supper. Got a blister on my hand from all the cutting. Am getting better acquainted with Lyle Ellefson. Nice to talk to and not bossy, but helpful.

The every other day off was unexpected to me when I took this job, but Lyle says it isn't always adhered to in the field. But he says the day on isn't much more than what the average soldier puts in every day. I won't mind some exceptions.

I still don't know the Mess Sergeant's name, but he hardly seems to be the boss — but still, everything seems to go smoothly.

August 15 was D-day for our maneuvers. The 2nd Army began to "fight" the 3rd Army in Louisiana. Details were still lacking, but the war starting this day was not between the "Reds" and "Blues," as we had previously been told it would be, but between one group of Southern States called "States of Kotmk" against another group of Southern States known as "Almet."

I figured that the kitchen crew's only obligation was to move when we were told to and to get out a hot meal on time, if possible.

We found out we could cook while on the march, although doing this put the old saying, "All things are possible, but some things are highly improbable," right into focus.

Saturday, August 16, 1941   We got to our new place about 2 a.m. I'm glad it's well organized when we move. Helped put things in shape. Breakfast at about 6:00. I'm on duty, but still had time to write home.

Slept this p.m. Helped put up the kitchen fly, and we took it down this afternoon again. Expected to move again soon.

The country looks about the same, except fires are burning at night in the oil fields. Hot today.

The kitchen fly was a canvas with open sides we cooked and served under. It gave protection from the elements.

Each kitchen truck was a 6X6 fitted with higher-than-normal sides and enclosed top, with three gas stoves lined up against the front end. There were steady K.P.s, and a stove man to keep the stoves in top working condition -- otherwise meals were late, or cold, or C rations [see May 7, 1943 commentary]. The stove man was considered a VIP by everyone.

We also pulled a two-wheel trailer with food and supplies, and a ration truck came every day as well.

Dick Brooks, another cook from Duluth, liked to sing. It was the first time I'd heard some of the songs, like "Don't Sit Under the Apple Tree With Anyone Else but Me" and "Hey, Daddy." His favorite was "Amor, Amor," and he would put one foot up on something, look towards Duluth, and sing away to his girlfriend.

Sunday, August 17, 1941   Got up about 6:00, though I didn't have to. Went to see Frank and started to write to Ray.

At 10:00 we were given March Order, loaded everything, and they changed their minds. We made dinner and supper in the same place.

We moved about 11 p.m., came to one place and stayed there until 5 a.m.

All this moving or not moving, of course had to do with how the battles were going between the armies, who was advancing, and who was retreating.

Some of it didn't seem real crystal-clear to me at the time, but actual war didn't either. These maneuvers were probably the best they could do with training, other than actual war.

Monday, August 18, 1941   Got here about 6 a.m. I broke one case of eggs for pancakes and used two cases of milk. Had a late breakfast at 9:00.

Off this afternoon. Went to a creek with the other cooks and the Mess Sergeant. Nice clear running water, and a sandy bottom.

Tonight I talked to a new cook on our shift. He is from California.

Hot summer day. Some loads of pine logs were going past here today. A lot of black 1940 Ford 1 ½ ton trucks going steady. They have the cabs mostly cut off, and pull a pipe trailer.

Lyle Ellefson showed me how to crack a case of eggs. You put the empty pan that receives the cracked eggs in front of you, with half a case of eggs on each side of you and the pan. Then, take an egg in each hand, crack it, and keep in the shell in one piece, but make it hinge open with your 3rd finger. Throw the shells, and grab two more eggs.

Tuesday, August 19, 1941   Got up around 6:00. Just laid on the ground last night on my shelter half. Warm and not much dew.

The new cook and I went to the creek again, took a bath, and picked some cotton. I sent a half ball of it to Ray.

Cloudy, cool. Just had a "gas attack." Took a picture of a load of logs. The driver stopped when he saw me taking the picture.

Johnson and I cut 16 hams and bread for supper. It wasn't so hot tonight. I drank a lot of canned milk, and we divided a can of pineapple. I'm sure glad I got this job. Gives me something to do that I like. We get through about 8:30.

A "gas attack" began with a pre-announced alarm. No matter what you were doing when you heard it, you'd grab your mask, take it out of the case, put it on, and take it off only when the all-clear sounded.

My letter home of August 19 told a little of maneuvers, but mostly I told them I'd gotten on as cook and that I hoped it would get me out of the anti-tank battalion. I told them that the talk was we wouldn't be going back to Claiborne after maneuvers, but, who knew? Letters had 3 cent stamps on them.

Other news was that we still had some fellows believing that we'd finish up our year in service and then go home, though Congress had now passed the draft extension bill by one vote.

The Nazis were at this time pushing further into the Ukraine, and France was sinking deeper into the quicksands of Hitler's New Order.

Wednesday, August 20, 1941   Ben woke us up at 3:30 this a.m. Johnson and I slept close by. I didn't have any covering at all, all night.

We sliced bread for two meals. I cooked two pans of sausage for dinner, and Holmberg showed me how to handle the stoves. Johnson and I went to the creek and took a bath.

This p.m. we moved to here. Whole trip was about 6 miles.

Laid around, went back with the water truck.

Tonight I talked quite a while to Gertsma, Frank and West. Fairly hot. Johnson and I laid out our blankets and put up our mosquito bar.

Gertsma and Bud Meyers were close friends. They came from the same small town in one of the Dakotas. I liked Gertsma a lot myself, and he was glad to see me get out of anti-tank.

Bud Meyers and I cooked together temporarily later when we got back to Camp Claiborne, but he stayed in anti-tank with Gertsma and was later Killed In Action.

Thursday, August 21, 1941   Was supposed to be off, but Johnson and I had to help load, and make sandwiches.

We left at 11 a.m., went across the Sabine into Texas. The roads are better, and the houses are painted.

Came back to Louisiana and camped close to Merryville. Had to put up tents and unload everything in the dark.

Hot. Johnson and I pitched together.

There are no lights for the kitchen either.

Mack or Max Johnson was from California, and was older than me. He was married. His wife followed along our maneuvers, and somehow they kept pretty much in touch, and they got together at times besides.

He had owned a restaurant somewhere and was pretty well posted on world affairs. We talked a lot at night before we went to sleep — he talked, that is, but I enjoyed listening and profited from it.

Friday, August 22, 1941   We moved about two miles this morning. The kitchens were split in two today. Our shift took half. Wayne, McKeron and I are together. Was supposed to be off this p.m., but we started the new shift, so I was on steady for two days.

Sliced 45 pounds of bacon myself tonight after supper. Took till 9:00. We finally got two gasoline lanterns tonight which help a lot, and will be even more appreciated in the mornings.

Saturday, August 23, 1941   Woke up at 4 a.m. Helped fry the hot cakes and other parts of the breakfast. If everything goes well, we can fry the cakes and serve them right off the griddle as the serving line moves slowly along. It takes two burners, two pans about 16" X 24," and two cooks not missing many moves to do it.

A big problem is the gas stoves. If they act up, it slows you down right away. We feed 219 men.

The other half shift has 197, and officers.

We were supposed to have an inspection, so we cleaned the kitchen, but didn't have any inspection.

This p.m. I was off. Went to the shower, washed clothes, changed into new chinos, wrote home, rested.

Johnson and I are still pitching together, but he is on the other shift.

Sunday, August 24, 1941   Slept a little later. Finished writing home. Read the Bible, looked at my pictures.

Capt. Walker came and gave us a good sermon. The congregation was pitifully small, though.

On duty this p.m. Got through early. The Mess Sergeant, Mack and I went to take a shower.

Laid under the tall pines for awhile.

Mack and I talked for a long time tonight.

Didn't seem as much like Sunday as I would have liked it to.

Monday, August 25, 1941   Mack and Wayne were up about 1:30 and woke me at 2 a.m. We had the bacon sliced last night; had to serve breakfast at 4 a.m.

Hamburger patties for dinner. Mashed potatoes, on my suggestion. Real good meal.

Off this p.m. Slept some. Am anxious for fresh news from home.

Cool this p.m., hot this morning.

An interesting article in this week's *Life* magazine said that there was a steel shortage that assumed greater proportions in the light of the high sea's conference of President Roosevelt and Prime Minister Churchill in the past week's *Life*.

With 67% of the industry capacity already effected to the armament program, it was now under strict rationing. The OPA (Office of Price Administration) admitted that steel production for 1941 would be 11,000,000 tons short.

Open hearth furnaces, which produced of 90% of our steel, required a priming charge of at least one ton of scrap steel for every two tons of pig iron. To produce 87,000,000 tons of steel, the mills needed at least 30,000,000 tons of scrap. They picked up half of this as leftovers in their own plants. The other 15,000,000 tons came from sources such as retail junkers, railroads, factories, auto graveyards, town dumps and back yards.

"Maybe we shouldn't have sent so much of our scrap to Japan in the recent past," I thought as I read this article, remembering what one of my neighbors at home had said over a year ago: "We stand a good chance of getting it all back."

Tuesday, August 26, 1941   Picked up everything and were ready to move by 8 p.m., but sat in the trucks until 3 a.m. before we pulled out. Only one other fellow in the truck that I was in, but there was a lot of junk.

I laid on the floor and slept a little. Dreamed of home. Came quite a way to a railroad track and Camp Polk. Got here after 5:00. Slept a little.

On duty this p.m. Wayne and I worked together a lot and did all the cooking. We made pancake batter.

Put my raincoat on the truck floor and went to sleep.

Wednesday, August 27, 1941   At 12:00 midnight we had March Order. Wayne woke me up. We loaded, sat in the truck and waited until 4 a.m. Moved about 10 miles, went through Leesville, and got here at 6:00.

Wayne and I fried some pancakes. It took until 9:00. Made hamburger patties for dinner.

Went to a small creek and washed. Slept a little.

Started raining at 4:00. Got a package from home, a letter and a card. Went to sleep in one of the 6X6's on a bench.

At 9:00 we were given March Order, left, got to one place. I slept a little more. Went through Leesville.

Thursday, August 28, 1941   Had breakfast and moved one quarter mile. We're supposed to stay here for awhile.
   Put up the fly. Hot. I pitched our tent myself.
   Put out a good supper of roast beef, mashed potatoes, gravy, celery, spinach, bread, pears and coffee.
   One truck took some of the cooks about 5 miles to a swimming hole. There were an awful lot of fellows there, so I didn't go in.
   Back at 8:30. I'm completely worn out.

   K.P.s peeled all potatoes by hand with paring knives. I can't remember any peelers.

Friday, August 29, 1941   The guard woke me at 4:00. Fried eggs and bacon for breakfast; sandwiches and cake for dinner.
   After dinner I washed clothes, took a sponge bath, read, wrote. I got the book I sent for on anti-tank guns.
   Frank came over and brought me two letters from home. Mack and I talked a lot until after 10:00. Hot.
   Read some in Meeks' Army cook book.

Saturday, August 30, 1941   Slept, or laid in the tent until 7 a.m. Had an orange and a slice of bread for breakfast. I eat too much; I've already gained some weight back.
   Wrote a short letter home. Mack gave me 3 airmail stamps.
   On duty this p.m. Through early tonight. Talked a long time with Mack.

Sunday, August 31, 1941   Up about 4:00. Had pancakes. Wayne and I fried them.
   Letter from Ray. Off at noon, but Mack went to Lake Charles to see his wife, so I just kept working for him.
   Got paid. Had to go to our old battery for it. Seen and talked to George Anderson and Ed.
   Got through fairly early. I drew $23.58. Hot. Rained a little. Answered Ray's letter.

Monday, September 1, 1941   Slept fairly late. Laid around, slept a little. Had cured beef for supper. Rained a little.
   Mack and I got to fooling around and broke the tent pole. Had our raincoats over the front, and a candle in here.

Tuesday, September 2, 1941　　Pancakes for breakfast. Mack woke me at 4:00. Five K.P.s instead of three today. Everything had to be spick and span.

Slept this p.m. My brother Rod goes back to school today. Must be the 3rd or 4th grade. Cool and nice. Rained a little last night.

After supper, I went to Battery B. A letter from Ma. Went to the 151st to see the fellows.

A lieutenant didn't know how to find Battery D, so I walked back with him.

Wednesday, September 3, 1941　　Slept late. Raining a little all forenoon.

Put out a good supper: baked ham, sweet potatoes, chocolate pudding, string beans, bread, butter and coffee.

Van was on guard. Talked with him awhile. Went to bed early.

Thursday, September 4, 1941　　Van woke me at 3 a.m. I woke the others. Fried eggs and spuds.

Washed a few pieces of clothes.

Were given March Order at 8:00, but had to make dinner in the same place.

Sat in the Supply until 3:00, then left, and got here at 5:30. Went through Sugartown.

Friday, September 5, 1941　　We were supposed to move at 12:00 last night, but didn't. Slept in the kitchen truck until 5 a.m., then went on top of the trailer.

Moved out at 1:30 p.m. Mack, Wayne and I took supplies for supper and rode with the stoves. Started supper on the way. I opened tomatoes, and it was quite a job.

Went through Pitken and are 16 miles from Camp Claiborne. Had an early supper at 5:00; were through by dark. A nice place here.

A farmer came for the garbage.

Saturday, September 6, 1941　　Up at 3:30. Wayne and I fried pancakes. Couldn't use a light, as it was a "tactical situation."

Had baked ham for dinner, with spuds and united vegetables.

This p.m. I took a sponge bath. Emil Lang cut my hair. Shaved, came out here in a pasture close by the kitchen.

Letter from home and Norma. Will answer Ma's.

Hot. Cool in the shade. Cut my hand on a can. Slept a little. Lit a candle tonight and looked at my pictures. Mack went swimming.

Sunday, September 7, 1941 Up about 6:30. Rolled my pack. Slept this forenoon.

Potato sandwiches for supper, and a salad. I sliced bacon for breakfast.

Hot. Rained just a little. A farmer's boy that comes over every day, about my brother Rod's age, always says "Yes, Sir," or "No, Sir," to me when I talk to him.

Mack and I slept in the usual place.

Monday, September 8, 1941 Up at 3:00. Had fried eggs, bacon and spuds for breakfast.

March Order at 10:30, moved about 6 miles. Same kind of country. Rained a little. Slept on the icebox with Mack.

It turned nice after 4:00; I spread out my bedroll.

We were supposed to have March Order at 12:00, so Mack and I talked until then, but we didn't move.

Tuesday, September 9, 1941 Didn't sleep late. Was too close to the kitchen.

March Order at 11:00. Rode all the way in the cab of the water truck with Corban. Came 48 miles, and we got here south of Oakdale at 6:00. Lots of stops and waiting. Some batteries didn't come in until 9:00.

Got through at 10:00 and slept in the kitchen truck on a table.

Wednesday, September 10, 1941 Up at 4:30. Breakfast was an hour late. Pancakes and bacon.

After mess, the supply tent and fly were set up. Everything was cleaned up and straightened up. Mack put up our tent close in back of the kitchen. All eleven tents of the kitchen force are in one row.

Off this p.m. Laid around.

Thursday, September 11, 1941 Slept late. Dull and cool this forenoon. Laid in the tent. Got letters from Ma and Ray.

At 6:00 we had supper; had roast ham.

Max went to Lake Charles again to see his wife. Took a bath in a G.C. can. Washed clothes. Heard Roosevelt make a speech tonight.

Friday, September 12, 1941 Up at 3:30. Pancakes and bacon for breakfast. Mack came in at 5:00. Had a big cleanup.

Special dinner of a dozen things.

Had to listen to a short lecture from Capt. Smith. Had to move our tent to Headquarters row.

Saturday, September 13, 1941   Didn't sleep very late. Had a big inspection this forenoon. On duty this p.m.

Sunday, September 14, 1941   Up at 5:00. Fried spuds and bacon. A brigadier general came through this morning.

It rained a little. Had to take down the tents and get ready to move.

I slept on my raincoat, and my bag was a pillow.

Monday, September 15, 1941   Was ready to move since 10:00. Pulled out at 11:00.

Got here somewhere north of camp about 5 p.m. Started supper on the road. I rode in both the kitchen and the icebox truck. Raining most of the way. Blackout. I had to slice bacon in blackout. Slept on the kitchen table in the mess truck.

Tuesday, September 16, 1941   Got up at 2 a.m. Were supposed to feed at 4 a.m., but didn't until 6:00. Bacon and scrambled eggs.

Made sandwiches for dinner. Got through at 10:00. Off after that. We got ready to move at 10:00, but didn't until 1:00.

I rode on top of the icebox again. Came about 8 miles.

The kitchen is under several cedars. Laid around. Mack and I had our tent together, as usual. Quite a few planes flying around.

Wednesday, September 17, 1941   Sgt. Hubby woke me at around 5:30. Walter Hunter and I found a blood vine. I cut a piece of it to save.

On this p.m. We put out a big supper.

Played 6-handed smear in the icebox truck until 7:30.

Capt. Schultze woke us up at 11:00. March Order to go at 12:00. Wayne and I were alone in the kitchen truck. I slept on the cutting board on three GI five gallon gas cans. We left at 2 a.m. Was cold riding, but I slept some.

Thursday, September 18, 1941   Wayne and I started frying bacon at about 5:00. Started on pancakes, but there was too much movement on the truck. Aldridge rammed into a truck; it gave us a jolt, and we spilled a lot of syrup.

Stopped in one place for breakfast.

Moved again. Came 59 miles all told.

Took a sponge bath this p.m. Was awful dirty. Have a bad foot from a little scalding this morning.

Somewhat cooler. A lot of planes flying around.

Friday, September 19, 1941   Slept on the icebox last night with Mack. Up early. Slept a little this forenoon.

No K.P.s until tonight. Moved about 1 p.m., about 30 miles. The worst ride I've ever had. Rode on top of a stove. Had clear sight, though. Lots of dust and a black night. A lot of dirt came in here.

Up at 8:00, mess at 9:00. Through at 10:00. Fairly nice place. A gallon of mustard broke in the truck.

Saturday, September 20, 1941   Up at 3:30. Ham and scrambled eggs for breakfast. A lot of boys have been going without grub, or at least without good meals on time. We sent some out tonight.

C rations were available, though, unless some men were "taken prisoner," or lost or isolated for awhile.

Went to a small creek, took a bath and washed a few clothes. When I got back, they were ready to leave.

We came 59 miles. Got here at 2:15. We really came fast. Dusty half the way, and blacktop road the other half.

Got a package and letter from Ma and Ray. Lots of tall pines here, and fairly big.

Sunday, September 21, 1941   Talked quite a bit with Rieman last night. Gave him a few things from the kitchen.

Got up at 7:00. Got ready to move, but didn't. Wrote home. Laid under the tall pines.

Had a fairly easy supper: Jello, fried wieners, ice cream. Loaded up everything tonight. Was going to go to a show, but didn't stay at all. Rieman came over. Gave him a gallon jar of mayonnaise.

My letter home of the 21st told of the moves and of the weather (hot). I told them it was hard to keep stamps from sticking together.

Most of the letters I wrote while out in the field are of pencil. It was hard to keep a sharp point on it. The envelopes and paper are well-yellowed after these 59 years, too.

I usually wrote once a week, even while on maneuvers. I'd tell them, "It was hot yesterday, hotter today, and will be hotter yet tomorrow." We would only consider it hot if was 100 degrees or over.

Rieman liked mayonnaise out of the jar as much as I like canned milk — and I sure got enough of that while I was cooking.

Monday, September 22, 1941   Wayne woke me up at 1:30. Left at 2 a.m. Got here, south of Oakdale. Came 80 miles. Got here at 7:30 a.m. Finished breakfast at 10:00.

Dried beef for dinner, with a few other things. I had my fill of dried beef. If you don't like that, though, it's a mighty skimpy meal.

This p.m. I put up our tent, washed clothes, shaved, wrote up my diary. Rained some this p.m. Cloudy, cool all day.

Rieman came over and talked quite awhile. When Mack got off shift we talked for quite awhile too.

Tuesday, September 23, 1941   Slept until 7:00. Coffee and bread for breakfast.

Some fellows have found and picked up coral snakes and timber rattlers, and put them in jars.

Wednesday, September 24, 1941   Slept on the stoves last night. Got up at 3:00. Raining quite hard some of the night. Hot cakes, bacon for breakfast. Served out of the truck. Cut my thumb while sharpening a knife on the steel; it bled a lot.

Moved out about 11:00. Lots of waiting. Came through Bunkie.

All trucks stopped on the road except ours. We pulled into a farmer's yard to make supper. Two little girls there about my sister Arlene's age: Barbara and Mary Ann.

Thursday, September 25, 1941   Moved out at 9:00. Came quite a ways. I slept part of the time. Got here at 2 a.m.

Slept a little again this morning.

March Order at 10:00; didn't come very far.

Had my bandage changed. Nearly passed out.

Nice and warm after the rain. Got my clothes soaked. Took a sponge bath. Washed and changed clothes.

We are close to Hiway 65. Watched the cars go by tonight. Slept alongside Sweedeen on the ground by the kitchen truck.

Friday, September 26, 1941   Up at 8:00. Fried potatoes and bacon for breakfast. Was real chilly, and coffee went good.

Meat loaf for dinner.

Came beneath the pines and slept a little. A letter from Ma, and *Country Gentleman.* Sat by the highway and watched the cars go by.

Saturday, September 27, 1941   Slept until about 7:00. Can of milk and orange juice for breakfast.

Rieman brought me a letter from Ray. Wrote several short letters today. Got some clippings about maneuvers from Ma.

On duty this p.m. Meat loaf, mashed spuds for supper. Through fairly early.

Sunday, September 28, 1941   Up at 3:30. Mack and I made breakfast and let Wayne sleep. Fried eggs and ham.

Roast beef, pears, spuds and spinach for dinner.

Cool and cloudy this p.m. I slept a little. Read. Am laying watching the cars go by about 100 feet from Hiway 65. Nemoe came over for awhile.

Monday, September 29, 1941   Nemoe and I walked over to Camp Beauregard after mess. It reminded me of our CCC camp. It's used mostly as a school for cooks and bakers.

Came back just as it was getting dark. Rolled out my pack with Sweedeen. March Order about 5:00. Loaded all and headed for Camp Claiborne.

Got to camp about 11:00. Brooks, Swede and I had to walk back from the 185th. Lots of details.

It was really wonderful to get back, especially to get into my trunk again. I really enjoyed maneuvers, though. The main thing, of course, is that I got to start cooking. It was tough at times, but really worth it.

Letters from Rod, home and Wing Chinn. The kitchens were from the 185th and that's why we had to walk back here.

To bed about 2 a.m.

CHAPTER 5

Back at Claiborne. Furlough home. Last days of peace.

Tuesday, September 30, 1941   Chandler woke me at 5:00. Was on guard and had the Recreation Hall. It was opened and cleaned by reveille time. On guard there all day, except for meals. The officers had a meeting this a.m. I had to put out benches.

Wrapped up a knife for Rod and a hankie for Arlene tonight. Also my films.

Hot. Washed some clothes after mess, showered and shaved. Really is nice to be back, but I still liked it better out on maneuvers cooking.

Wrote a letter home.

Wednesday, October 1, 1941   Up at 5:30, as usual. Worked this forenoon with West on the trucks cleaning.

Off this p.m. Washed more equipment. I'm nearly up to normal again now.

Frank and I walked to the Post Office tonight. Sent the knife to Rod and the hankie holder for Sister. Bought stamps. Went to see Brooks, but couldn't find him.

Went to see Sweedeen. He played his violin. Real good playing, and I enjoyed it.

Thursday, October 2, 1941   Fell in as usual, but Tony came and called me out of ranks to go and help him in the kitchen cooking. Had chili, lettuce and salad.

Tony and I would be on cooking together, but some trucks are going to haul troops to Florida, and he went along as cook. So they put Otto and Cajune on with me. Cleaned everything up. Got through at 8:00 tonight.

Really was glad to get on steady with the battery as cook. Makes things a lot brighter for me. Moved into the cook's tent tonight with Herman Persell, Mess Sergeant Tarman, George Bowers, Bud Meyers and Tony.

A letter home told we had got back to Claiborne on Sunday night and had to work most of the night unloading trucks and cleaning up.

There now was a small recreation hall for each battery, and some tents had to be moved. There was also a new church for each regiment.

I told them I hadn't been cooking for a few days, but got back into the kitchen in a hurry when they needed me. I also mentioned that I had moved into the cooks' tent, which made me a *bona fide* 151st cook. I told them of the big walk-in pantry we had that held enough food for our battery of 130 men for a long time, and that new rations seemed to come in two or three times a week. I told them that we had three big gas stoves, and we had three big Coolerator iceboxes, made in Duluth. I said the ice truck came once in awhile.

I said that one of our cooks, Otto, liked to drink the lemon extract, so our Mess Sergeant was now keeping it locked up in his trunk.

Friday, October 3, 1941   Up at 4:00. Woke Otto and two of the other cooks, as we had some extra troops to feed and a lot of the kitchen things were still dirty, and a mess. We had hot cakes and bacon.

I was on all day and enjoyed it. Had spuds and salmon for dinner.

Meat balls and lettuce salad for supper. Through at 8:00.

Showered. Will write home. Awful hot frying hot cakes. Have to change clothes every day.

Tarman, the Mess Sergeant, told me that I came with a high recommendation from the Mess Sergeant on maneuvers.

He said he hated to tell me, but there might be a few days that I wouldn't be able to cook, because though two or three of the older cooks were getting out of the service because of their age, all of their paperwork wasn't finished yet.

I told him that if that was the worst he would ever have to tell me, not to let it worry him, as I could easily understand that I was the youngest cook.

Saturday, October 4, 1941   Brooks came over and showed me some pictures from home and some he took this summer.

I cleaned the tent. Inspection today, and I'm glad that I don't have to stand it. Had a headache. Slept a little.

Got paid $28.68, with $1.38 off for insurance. Looked over all my letters. Threw some away. Bought an alarm clock for $2.15. Got my $5.00 back from Brooks. Fairly warm. The battery street is quite empty tonight; most of the fellows are out spending their money.

Packed over my whole trunk again this afternoon.

Sunday, October 5, 1941   Up at 6:00.

Otto was still drunk, so Tarman got Cajune to help me, though I could have done it myself. A lot of fellows came in for just ice water this morning.

Cajune is good at cooking; he helped with the dinner too, and then some on the supper to get it all lined up. He had planned to go out in the afternoon, so I did all the rest by myself.

We had meat loaf, mashed potatoes, fruit salad, bread, butter, gravy and ice water. I couldn't believe all the compliments I got for it.

Otto was still sick, but he did come in after mess was all over.

Got through at 7:30. Took a shower and shaved. It was hot in the kitchen.

Usually, Sunday nights' dinners were real light, like cold cuts and salad.

I don't know why I went all out as I did that Sunday, but anyway, it turned out to be a break for me. The fellows got all they could eat. It was obvious to everybody I had done the meal myself, so they really thought I could cook.

This was a weekend after payday as well, so camp strength was down. The rations we cooked were always according to the number of men on the roster, not the number we thought might still be in camp on Sunday after payday — so everybody had more than they could eat at mess that day.

Monday, October 6, 1941   Got up around 7:00. Made myself some fried eggs for breakfast.

We went to town with Cajune. He is using someone's '34 Plymouth. Bought a few things, went to a show, came back about 1:30 and washed some clothes.

Tonight we had a chance to hear a report from the captain on how we did on maneuvers. Overall, it was a good report. The statistics were given in authentic terms as if it was real war: e.g., "35 enlisted men and 20 officers out of action," and "All the men from such-and-such a platoon are either dead, wounded or captured."

What had been most authentic to us cooks during maneuvers was the sound of the planes and the long lines of trucks and infantrymen on the highways at times. Generally speaking, we were aware of the fact that the maneuvers involved a lot of effort on everybody's part to give us an idea just what actual war might be like.

It was always the privilege of off-duty cooks to sleep late and to go in the kitchen and make your own breakfast; usually fried eggs and toast. There was one condition, however: Don't bother the on-duty cooks.

This was my day off. Sometimes the on-off schedule was noon to noon; then again it would change, and be morning to morning. We always preferred the full day on and off.

Tuesday, October 7, 1941   Up at 3:45. While I was washing up, Otto came in drunk again, so I had to make breakfast myself. It wasn't too hard, as we only had hot cakes and syrup. When in camp, we fry the cakes ahead and keep them hot in the ovens.

After breakfast, Herman got Antonio to help me. I don't mind him, but he is Filipino and hard for me to understand.

I could go on furlough, but I'm not sure if I want to or not. Will have to decide by tomorrow for sure.

Wednesday, October 8, 1941   Slept until 7:00. Day off. Walked over to the 185th. Saw and talked to Walker.

Went to the carnival. Bought a garrison belt. Nothing much going on.

Decided to go on furlough. Am a little excited about going home. Packed up a few things.

Thursday, October 9, 1941   On duty all day.

Got my furlough papers at 6:00 and left with Shermack and Vulker. Got a ride to Alex in a '37 Ford. Went to a show and the depot.

Wore my woolens. Didn't take many things along.

Friday, October 10, 1941   All the fellows in this coach are from our battery. Left at 12:01 a.m.

Quite comfortable riding. No Pullman this time, but no charge either. I have an extra seat for my feet and can stretch out pretty good. Am close to a window and had it open.

Made slow time. Stopped in Oklahoma. We went through the Ozarks about 6:30 p.m.

Saturday, October 11, 1941   Went through Kansas City about 5:30 this morning. Went through Des Moines and Mason City.

Got into Minneapolis at 5:45. Walked to the bus depot. Caught the

6:15 bus for Duluth.

Got there at 9:45. Went to Wing's; got home about 12:00.

Before I went in, I walked in the vegetable bunching shed and in the barn, but the horses were out. I looked Ray's truck over and looked outside at some of the things.

Ma and everyone else was really surprised. We talked until about 2 a.m.

I had taken the bus up to the corner of Hermantown and Haines Roads, and walked the last 3 miles home. It was a nice, cool evening, and I had plenty of time to relax and think as I walked. The Minnesota air was entirely different: cool, and not humid and sticky like in Louisiana.

Sunday, October 12, 1941   Slept until 10:00.

Ate and went with Rod and Arlene to see Bird and Eagle. Ray, Dick and Pa were digging the last of the potatoes. Aunt Myrtle and Grandma came over. I rode over to Louie's and Hank's on Eagle. Took the truck and looked at the cucumber patch at Paul's. Went to Al's. Seen the twins and Ken.

Nice today. Thankful to be home.

Monday, October 13, 1941   Rod stayed home from school. I rode Bird over to Rhunke's fields, and then went to see him.

Went to Uncle Art's tonight. Enjoyed seeing him.

I remember telling everyone how hot it is in Louisiana both day and night, and my dad said, "Ja, ja. It was hot here this summer too."

Tuesday, October 14, 1941   Helped Ray cut cabbage all day. Hank came over.

Went to Dick's and Green Gables tavern tonight.

Wednesday, October 15, 1941 Helped Ray cut cabbage and get 25 dozen bunches of carrots.

We all went to Aunt Evelyn's for supper tonight.

Thursday, October 16, 1941   Went with Rod and Ray to Hibbing with a

load of cabbage. Had it sold by 1:30.
Stopped at Payne and looked the camp over. Was home at 5:00.

Friday, October 17, 1941   Helped Ray with the market vegetables.
Took all day. I got tired.

Saturday, October 18, 1941   Went with Ray to the Market. Seen
most of the people that were there before. Drove around town with
Ray's truck for awhile, then went back to Market. We stayed at the
Market until 11:00.
Ray bought a '35 Ford coupe at Sterling Motors. I drove the
truck home. Took Nig and Dan and hauled the rutabagas home.

Sunday, October 19, 1941   Didn't do much this forenoon. This p.m.
Ray and I went to Payne. Seen Otto. Went to Carl's and Grandma's
tonight. Louie came.

Monday, October 20, 1941   Walked in the woods. Raining mostly
all day. Went to Al's tonight, but he wasn't home.

Tuesday, October 21, 1941   Helped Ray get up some carrots. Carl
came, and we went with Ray to Proctor for a pint for Carl.
I took Ray's car and went to Gronlund's. Drove over to Homecroft,
and then to Woodland. Stopped at the fire hall and saw Cousin Otto.
Drove around Duluth and stopped at Carl's. Orville came tonight, so
did Witticks.
I took Ray's car and went to Wing's. Went to the Far East Cafe.
Came home about 12:30.

Wednesday, October 22, 1941   Hooked up my team. Went to Johnny's
and got our sulky plow home. Helped Ray and Winton dig parsnips.
Helped Ray haul some wood to Grandma's.
This p.m. went to Carl's for supper. Dick and Paul came.

Thursday, October 23, 1941   Pa worked for Martin on the town
roads. Helped Ray bunch some carrots. Took Ma and the kids to Proctor with Ray's car on noon. Hank and Evelyn came this p.m. So did
Herb and Al.
Helped haul in some cabbage tonight. Dick, Carl and Myrtle came
tonight, and so did Louie and family.
Went to bed about 9:00.

Friday, October 24, 1941 Up at 6:00. Ray took me down to the bus station. Hank and Evelyn came to see me off.

Got to St. Paul at 11:30. Train pulled out at 12:00. Same ride. Tiresome. We are still in Iowa tonight.

Furlough had been kind of depressing. I almost wished I hadn't come, as everything at home looked the same or improved, and no one seemed to show much interest in what I had done over the past summer. It was especially hard for me to have lost my gardening business.

There wasn't much talk about the war at home, though it was obvious to us all that we'd soon be in it, as the draft had been extended 18 more months, or "for the duration." No one wanted to talk too much about the war because there was a pro-German attitude in my family that could never be erased.

Saturday, October 25, 1941 Riding all day. Sat close to the window. Ma sent along a lunch.

Got to Alexandria about 11 p.m. Army trucks there to take us to camp. Got here about 12:30. Had some coffee. Tony is back from Florida.

Sunday, October 26, 1941 Was about 2 a.m. before I got to bed. Up about 7:00, showered.

Off today. Cleaned up my trunk and belongings. Things are more strict since we left, but most of the rules don't pertain to me. Talked to George tonight.

Monday, October 27, 1941 Up at 4:20. On with George Bowers and Bud Meyers. Bowers is one of the three who's leaving soon. They sure don't need three cooks on a shift here. Tried to do something all day.

The captain talked to us in the mess hall tonight, mostly about passes. Took a shower. Quite cool. Have the stove going and tent flaps down.

Tuesday, October 28, 1941 Slept until about 7:00. Straightened up my things and wrote up in here. Wrote to Norma. Have the flaps down and stove going. Wrote 6 letters all told. Took Lyle's pants back tonight, talked with him for awhile.

Wednesday, October 29, 1941   On duty all day. Meyers and I on this p.m. Hamburger steaks for supper.

Some latecomers in tonight after we were through, who I had to make supper for.

Thursday, October 30, 1941   Got up about 7:30. Sent in my laundry, went in the kitchen, made my breakfast. Sgt. Tarman came back from Camp Beauregard today. Herman was acting Mess Sergeant, but is now a cook again. Camp guard out late tonight. Fed them late again. Raining most the day.

Saturday, November 1, 1941   Slept until 8:00. Washed, shaved, helped clean up the tent. Woolens are the official uniform now.

Meyers and I went to the Service Club to miss inspection. Read magazines. Came back here at 11:30.

Cut out some things this afternoon. Slept a little. Brooks came over for awhile. Read my Bible. Seemed so much like Sunday. Listened to the radio. Went to bed at 9:00.

Sunday, November 2, 1941   Up at 6:00. French toast for breakfast with pork sausage. Didn't seem like Sunday.

Fairly warm. Meat balls and french fries for supper. Through at 7:30.

Ed Wold and Bill had their wives here for supper. Usually, wives will come up to the cooks after the meal and compliment and thank us for the meal. These two did.

Monday, November 3, 1941   Off today. Did some reading and writing. Laid around. Didn't do much of importance.

Tuesday, November 4, 1941   On with George and Meyers. This afternoon off. This p.m. had to take a Wassermann blood test, required of all those who handle food in the kitchen.

We got paid $28.68. Meyers, Gertsma, Red and I went to the carnival. We all got tattooed. Hurt quite a bit. Came back at 10:30.

I'd always wanted a tattoo on my arm. My dad's blacksmith, Harold Moe, had a horse's head tattooed on his arm. Every time he'd come to shoe our horses when I was young, I could hardly wait until he was through —

76

because then he'd come in to eat with us, roll up his shirt sleeves to wash, and I'd see his tattoo again.

Now I had my own horse's head with a horseshoe around it. Gertsma didn't want a tattoo. Both Bud Meyers and Red got a bird on their arm.

Wednesday, November 5, 1941   Up at 4:30. On with Tony again now. He slept a good part of the forenoon. Stew for dinner. Spanish rice for supper. Cold. Some of the fellows are going on furlough tonight. Showered and shaved. Went to bed and listened to the radio.

Thursday, November 6, 1941   Was going to sleep late, but Tarman came in and said I'd have to go on K.P. for awhile until Tony or George are discharged. Helped in the dining room. Have some time off too, so I don't mind at all.

A party tonight. They had three half-barrels of beer, pop, peanuts and chips. Pint and Crandall were discharged tonight. Shook hands with them.

Friday, November 7, 1941   K.P. again today. Showered and shaved tonight. Cool.

Saturday, November 8, 1941   K.P. again. Inspection. The colonel came through.

Had to work this afternoon. Was supposed to have it off. Very few in camp. Some went to Shreveport, others on camp guard.

Letter from John Vamachka. He is in Fort Lewis, Washington in the field artillery. His brother is down here in the 125th Infantry.

John Vamachka was a woods-worker at Payne, just across the old road that went to our camp. He and another worker would speak Bohemian as they worked, and I would stop often at their shack at night when I would go to Payne for the daily paper.

I saw him once on a visit to another friend's place after the war, so I know he survived the war. He never wrote again, and I never met his brother.

Sunday, November 9, 1941   Slept until 9:00. Made cinnamon toast for myself. Went to church, read my Bible, brushed up on the Morse code.

Bought a 15-jewel Elgin watch from Tony for $5.00, a ring from Red for $3.00. Wrote home. Have the tent flaps down and stove going all the time.

Monday, November 10, 1941   K.P. again. Washed the dishes after dinner and supper. The colonel was supposed to inspect, but didn't come. We had to stay here and wait.

It warmed up a little. Got newspapers from home tonight. An article in the paper about the Peytons [bankers from Duluth].

Tuesday, November 11, 1941   Veterans Day, and it's a legal holiday for the Army, but not for the kitchen crew. The men still want to eat. I still had all the time off that I needed.

Wednesday, November 12, 1941   Same thing today with K.P. and had to clean 3 field ranges and carry them into the dining room. Got a card of thanks from Pat for the book matches. Cool. Ordered 3 pictures of myself that they took some time ago.

Pat (or Patsy) Honstein was a pen-pal from Baker, Montana. I'd started writing to her from a pen-pal list at Claiborne.

Thursday, November 13, 1941   K.P. again. Had to stay in the kitchen until 8:30 tonight. Seems like a lot of extra work always.

Gave Bud Meyers Lorraine's address so he could write to her. He saw her picture and thought she was cute. She is my first cousin, and hope she writes back to him.

The best news of the day, though, came real late tonight when Tarman came in and said, "Tomorrow you go cooking steady, Wag. Be in the kitchen at five."

Needless to say, I was there on time, all right. I think the others were happy to see me back too. Tony was to leave the next day, George in less than a week. Otto was already gone, and so was Cajune.

Sgt. Tarman told me later that he had a topnotch bunch of cooks now.

Friday, November 14, 1941   Up at 4:30. Cooked all day with George; made most of the dinner myself. We had meat loaf. It really turned out good.

Letter from home. Aunt Anna, Sam and Jack have been there

[from Lewistown, Montana] since Sunday. Merton Fillmore died this week. He was in an iron lung since September. Ray Dahlgren was killed in an auto accident.

Had to stay in the kitchen until 8:45. Capt. DeMurray came through. Really tired.

George Bowers was a nice fellow to work with. He had all the good qualities you could hope for in a fellow worker. He would glance at me if I started to make a big part of the menu on my own — but only to see if I knew what I was doing, then never try to boss.

Ray Dahlgren was a cousin of the George Dahlgren I knew at Claiborne, but I'd never met him.

Saturday, November 15, 1941   Slept until 8:00. Tony came in drunk and fell over my trunk last night.

Ate, then helped George clean the tent. Then we went to the Service Club to miss inspection. I wrote three letters.

Tony, Finsted and Cisette got their discharge papers this morning. They left after supper. Will always remember Tony.

Read the Bible and straightened my trunk. Shermack and I went to the Service Club. Warm tonight and all day.

It was really funny last night when Tony came in the tent. When we go to bed, we pull out our trunks from in under our beds; otherwise, when you lie down on the bed, the springs hit the trunk. Then the last fellow to go to bed puts the night light on so you can see a little, as there is always somebody getting up or going to bed. But last night no one put the night light on, and with all 5 trunks in the middle of the floor, poor Tony just kept falling as fast as he got up. We couldn't stop laughing, but as soon as I could, I turned the light on in the middle of the tent, and Tony flopped on his bed and quieted down.

Sunday, November 16, 1941   George and I on again today. Made bread pudding on my own account this morning. Got off enough time to go to church.

Made lemon pie (just for the cooks) this afternoon. Turned out good. Went to the Service Club tonight. Checked out four books.

Warm and nice. The leaves are starting to turn color and fall. Sat on the mess hall steps and watched the traffic (Army, mostly) go by.

Am pretty well satisfied now with the way things are going. War is inevitable, but I just take it one day at a time. My worst fear was to have been an anti-tanker for the duration.

Monday, November 17, 1941   Slept a little late. Read in one of the books. Laid around. Anderson and I walked to No. 9 Canteen tonight. Took my watch there for a crystal. Stopped at the Service Club. Read quite late.

Tuesday, November 18, 1941   On with George again. Easy meals today. Read between meal-making times. Had to stay in until 8:30 tonight.
Showered, shaved.

Wednesday, November 19,1941   My day off. Woke up with a headache. Still have it.
Read. Slept this p.m., wrote a card to Ray.
Got my three pictures today. Got letters from Ray, and pictures that he took at Payne and home.
Went to the tent theater and saw *Caught in the Draft.*
Came back, and George, Sgt. Tarman and I worked until 10:00 cleaning turkeys and making mincemeat pies.
It was almost fun last night starting the Thanksgiving dinner. The other cooks didn't show up at all to help. Tarman is real appreciative of when we know there is extra work, and we do it without being told to do it when it isn't necessarily our shift.

Thursday, November 20, 1941   Up at 4:00. Got the turkeys in by 6:00. Breakfast at 8:00. Kept us going to get dinner out on time, but we made it. Had everything — too much to mention.
The captain and his family were here, and we got lots of compliments from him.
Made turkey sandwiches for supper. First Sgt. Gareys washed the dishes. He gave us each a package of cigarettes and wine.

We had to switch dates for our Thanksgiving meal from the 27th of November to the 20th, so we also had to switch the menus.

Friday, November 21, 1941   Slept until 8:00. Washed and helped clean the tent. Finished *Nomads of the North.* Cold, windy.
George Bowers is leaving today. Shook hands with him, and he left at noon.
Went to the Service Club and checked out another four books. Raining some. Moved over to where George was. I like a side bunk much better.

Saturday, November 22, 1941   Meyers and I on this a.m. Antonio and I on this p.m. Herman and Dahlgren came back from furlough this morning, and Pankony this p.m.

I had a bad day. Burned the potatoes. Made pumpkin pie and put in too much ginger.

Showered and went to bed early.

We had pumpkin pie left because of the too much ginger I put in — but Rieman liked it that way and kept on coming back for more. As far as I remember, it was all gone when we cleaned up that night.

Sunday, November 23, 1941   Got up at 8:30. Felt swell. Made my breakfast.

Went and got George, and we went to church. The new chapel is open today for the first time. Beautiful building for an Army camp. Real good service.

Played smear and ping-pong with George. Slept a little.

Monday, November 24, 1941   Tony and I on again.

Got letters from home, Otto, Norma. Also an Army cookbook and a package of candy and pictures from Ma.

Tuesday, November 25, 1941   We had an alert today. Things were all balled up as usual. We went 20 miles, then came back here at 8:00. Supper was late. Headache, cold.

A postcard from home said Governor Stassen was in camp to dedicate our new chapel last week. I could see them from the kitchen, but couldn't go over there, as I was on duty.

Wednesday, November 26, 1941   On with Antonio. Chocolate pie for dinner. I made apple turnovers with leftover crust.

Lt. Shuendinger inspected while I was in the kitchen alone.

Got papers from home tonight.

Thursday, November 27, 1941   Slept until 7:00. Changed sheets and turned in laundry. Cut my knuckle last night. Strained my wrist yesterday. Wrote to Norma. Showered.

This p.m. Tarman, Antonio and I went to Alexandria with Service Battery. Tarman bought a few supplies, came back about 3:30.

Had my last shot. Played my guitar. Cajune has it now. Will read the Bible yet.

Friday, November 28, 1941   Antonio and I on today. Got ready for a bivouac. Left at 1:30. All the battery went, except anti-tank. Went 60 miles, all told. West of Pitken.

Had mess ready by 5:30, moved a short way again.

I made the pancake batter and rolled my blankets out. Slept, just on the ground. All the snakes are supposed to leave when there is a lot of activity, and I guess they do.

Saturday, November 29, 1941   Up at 2 a.m. Cold, close to freezing at 4:00. Wasn't through with breakfast until 8:00. Had hot cakes and coffee. Went real good.

Started back at 9:00. Came in at 12:00.

Washed, shaved, straightened up my things. Letter from Ma yesterday.

Sunday, November 30, 1941   Antonio and I on today. Made apple turnovers for dinner. Got off enough time to go to church tonight and this morning.

Monday, December 1, 1941   Off. Sleep late, as a rule, on my day off. Went to town with Tarman. Wrote three letters tonight.

Tarman is a heavy fellow, mostly a happy, nice guy. He has a habit of sort of shaking his head when he talks. He is probably several years older than I am.

I go to Alexandria every time I have a chance to. We haul some of our own rations, but I'm not a part of that, right now at least.

Tuesday, December 2, 1941   On today again. Had to take dinner out in the field. Poor supper tonight. Everybody blamed us.

I had to make a late supper for Hanson and McCollan tonight. Took a hot shower, and went to bed around 9:00.

Whenever I had to make an extra late meal for officers, unless I was told what to make, I'd make up a fast meal of good leftovers (if there were any), or fry some bacon or sausage with eggs. They'd always thank me a lot for it.

Wednesday. December 3. 1941   Slept until 9:00. Washed, ate. Took a shot for something or other, probably tetanus. Went to church tonight with Red. Seven of us there.

Thursday, December 4, 1941   Cooking again with Antonio. Left for the field at 11:15. Went about 50 miles west. Made supper. Situation not "tactical," so we had a big bonfire. Warm. Seemed like a show or a story. Radio was playing.

Friday, December 5, 1941   Up at 5:00. Hot cakes and syrup. Slept good. Always dream when I sleep out.

Came back to camp at 10:00. This p.m. Ceno and I scrubbed out the tent.

Got a letter from Pat tonight and answered it. Will read my Bible. Cool.

A letter from Ma last night in the field. Said Old Man Janzig died in Hermantown — he was the assessor, and played the violin.

Saturday, December 6, 1941   On duty. French toast for breakfast. Stew for dinner. Some fellows that were on detached service came back today. A few more to feed.

After duty, Anderson and I walked up to the theater and saw *Henry Aldridge for President.* Pretty good.

A letter from Ray saying he isn't coming down here for Christmas. Will be lonesome here over the holidays, but I had told him not to come.

Our summer maneuvers called for a lot of backtracking work, settling with land owners, the Brass getting together with other groups in Camp Livingston and Camp Polk, with many other details to work out. Someone was always gone on detached service for one of a multitude of reasons.

My brother Ray was going to come down for Christmas, but we all knew that the United States would soon be in the war.

Sunday, December 7, 1941   Slept until 9:00. Made my own breakfast, which was fried eggs, bacon and toast.

Went to church in the Service Club. Good service by Chaplain Walker. By the time church was out, so was the news of the Japanese bombing of Pearl Harbor. Probably this will affect my life very much in the future. Will go to the Service Club and to church again.

Chaplain Walker gave a real good sermon tonight as well. There were only 8 of us there. I got both of the Lucas brothers to go, and Sheppard.

Undoubtedly, we will be on the alert or affected in some way. Some discharged fellows are to report back to their local boards.

Off today, and nice weather. Talked and listened to a lot of the fellows' ideas as to how this will affect us in the future. There haven't been any specific radio reports on the Pearl Harbor attack that I've heard, but some information comes now and then.

Our first question is, "Just where is it?" Of course, in the Hawaiians, and from all accounts so far, it was bad. It puts all of us in a much more sober mood.

CHAPTER 6

Packing up, getting ready to go. Hurry up and wait.

Monday, December 8, 1941 The United States declares war on Japan. We hear the news on noon. I am on duty with Ceno.

We have an alert tonight at 5:00. The 125th Field Artillery of our Division is starting to pull out of Claiborne. I'm wondering what the folks at home are thinking. I bought another diary book tonight.

I'm still the newest cook in the kitchen, but Tarman likes me pretty well. I do my job and somewhat more, so there are no complaints.

I don't care too much for the Filipino cook.

He seems he might be a bit tricky, but then it might just be a strong desire for a drink. All our bottles of extract are taken care of by the Mess Sergeant, but the Filipino seems to find something to drink.

An alert is always a lot of work, but Tarman told me later that he caught the captain's wink, only loaded a few things of the kitchen, formed a convoy, drove a few miles, then came back to camp.

The Filipino will drink lemon extract as readily as Otto did.

Tuesday, December 9, 1941 Another alert at 12:30 a.m. Hard to get up, but off-duty cooks always have to help load. Most of our personal things go along as well, except for our foot lockers.

Had a bad headache. My things are in a mess. We left at 1:30. Got somewhere around Leesville to the firing range at 4:00.

Tarman and I put up our tent together. The situation is non-tactical, so we built a big bonfire tonight.

As we gathered together around our fire, and after, we had a rip-roaring talk by Capt. Genung. Some of the things he said were, "This is it, Men. We go for the duration. You will learn to bayonet the Japs and Germans as they sleep in their tents. It's all-out war now. Be prepared to go and do what you are told."

After that, we wondered if the Germans could see our big fire and maybe come and bayonet us.

The United States and Great Britain had both declared war on Japan. In his address to Congress, President Roosevelt described the events at Pearl Harbor as the forming part of a "date that will live in infamy." Roosevelt did not ask Congress to declare war on Germany or Italy. Australia, New Zealand, The Netherlands, the Free French, Yugoslavia and several South American countries all declared war on Japan. Also, China declared war on Germany, Italy and Japan.

Some sobering facts had come in since Sunday's attack on Pearl Harbor. At 07:55 local time, Japanese carrier aircraft attacked the main base of the US Pacific Fleet at Pearl Harbor. There was complete tactical and strategic surprise.

Six Japanese carriers were sent with a total of 423 planes. Two waves of attacks were sent in. All eight US battleships in port were damaged; five of them were sunk. Also, three cruisers and three destroyers were sunk. We lost 188 aircraft to the Japanese 29.

Words and accusations were flying. The admiral in charge of the Pacific Fleet would be dismissed because of having all antiaircraft guns locked in peacetime. Then it was Sunday, and many officers and crews from ships were ashore.

We had a lot to talk about, and we wondered at how many more mistakes we would be going through for the "duration?" There were some. And those who made the mistakes were sure to try to cover them.

All in all, we were able to say, as we would many times in the future, "Error is error, and truth is truth."

Wednesday, December 10, 1941   Ceno, Tarman and I got up at 5:00. Hot cakes for breakfast.

Nice weather. Fellows are firing the big guns. Steve, Shermack and I take dinner out to them.

A casual statement as "hot cakes for breakfast' sounds pretty simple, and it was when we were in camp; but this was field cooking in the back of a 6X6 kitchen truck. Everything was piled on top of everything else, and pancakes were always made from scratch.

The batter was made the night before; the syrup was cooked in a dixie pan. Coffee water was ready and on the stove. All three gasoline stoves were filled and ready to go. The stove man always lit them for us if we had problems, and we had one extra burner. The stove man didn't have to get up as early as the cooks did, but it didn't take him long to come if we needed him.

When we took dinner out to the gun crews, we would split the food, and each 2 or 3 cooks would take hot food to the different gun crew positions. They couldn't leave their gun positions to come to eat with the other men.

Most of the food was carried in the canvas-covered trailer pulled by the 6X6 kitchen truck and always parked nearby. Being the youngest cook (in seniority), it was usually my job to go to the trailer for anything that was needed.

When back at camp, the stove man went back to his job of K. P. and kitchen maintenance man. All K.P. help was recruited daily in the regular kitchen from a daily roster, or recruited to help as an incentive not to do again what you did wrong.

Thursday, December 11, 1941   I slept until 9:00. Washed up in the creek.

We hear that Germany and Italy have declared war on the United States. Makes me more concerned of those at home. I spent most of my day in thought, laying in my pup tent, reading my Bible and singing hymns. Raining lightly all day. Cold, damp and wet.

Wasn't needed today until later after chow to help pack some of the things, so I rested and kept my mind busy.

I was sort of glad that the United States hadn't first declared war on Germany and Italy, but that it was the other way around.

Congress replied with a Declaration of War, and agreed that US Forces may be dispatched to any part of the world.

The term of service of those enlisted under the Selective Service Act was extended from "the war's duration" to "six months after the war's end."

The German declaration of war against the United States can be regarded as one of Hitler's greatest mistakes. Without it, US participation in the European war had still been somewhat in doubt.

I was glad too because I always admired Roosevelt, and it sort of took him off the hook from having said during his 1940 campaign, "Our boys will not be sent to fight in any foreign war." He had no choice in the matter this way.

Japan was progressing in the Islands. We had been greatly weakened in that area. News was sketchy, however, and hard to follow. Most of us were most concerned about the war's effect in the United States and how we were going to fare concerning it.

I was really glad I'd taken the furlough in October. My hope now was that we would be sent east (of Louisiana) instead of west.

Friday, December 12, 1941   Tarman and I slept little last night. He, as Mess Sergeant, has to be there almost all the time to supervise, and I was on duty. So it was a double-duty job with making breakfast, and getting ready to move out at 8:00. We had oatmeal and fried eggs for breakfast. Packed up, pulled out at 8:00 sharp. 35 miles to camp, and here at 10:30.

The war is sweeping like wildfire. I'm waiting for the next *Life* magazine.

I made my first cake tonight. A big single layer one in a large, flat cake pan. A real small piece for all. The men appreciate even the small piece. Sgt. Tarman stood there smiling and sort of moving his head up and down as is his habit when the fellows said, "The sample was good, now when do we get a piece of cake?"

We always had extra flour, dried eggs, sugar and canned milk, and it wasn't much extra work to bake a cake once in awhile, but it was over and above the call of duty on my part.

As far as the war went, there were some interesting attitudes some of the fellows had, like, "I want to get into action. They'll get everything I can give them!" The feeling was pretty strong that we wouldn't have to spend much more time in war games and practice. Then we felt that war couldn't be much worse than the practice for it, or so we thought.

Saturday, December 13, 1941   Awoke with a headache. Ceno and I went to the Service Club during inspection. Got a letter from Ma and Grandma. Turned in surplus clothing this p.m. Packed my trunk; it's ready to send home. Sent watch for Rod, bracelet for Sis. Got a long letter from Pat tonight. Sent her a diary. Walked to the PO and No. 9 Canteen. Answered Pat's letter. Cool.

Reports from the East with Japan are not good.

We hear the news in part, as there is no radio in the cooks' tent, and they are not too common in camp. My trunk left today by express for home. Had it about full of things I can't take with me. I saved a lot of letters from Ma and Ray.

Sunday, December 14, 1941   Ceno and I on today. Bacon and toast for breakfast. Cold supper of cold-cuts of sausage and a few trimmings. Not a hard day in a cook's life. Tarman doesn't show himself much when things go well. Through at 6:30 tonight. Showered and went to church with Pettengale. We were the only two there, so we just talked to Chaplain Rogeness and were a guest of his.

Beautiful day. Services on Sunday night are in the chapel just across the street from 1st Battalion's mess hall.

My letter to home said my trunk was sent home yesterday, that everything was in preparation to moving out soon. Most of the furloughs were canceled, and I was sure glad I went when I did.

Monday, December 15, 1941   Off today. Slept until 7:30. Washed some clothes. Sent out the balance of my Christmas cards. Went to the Post Office this p.m. Had 22 money orders made out for fellows who had money to send home. Had $260 on me.

The P.O. is about a half mile west on the main street of camp, close to the hospital.

I took out $8,000 more life insurance on myself. Had to pay 2 months in advance.

Went to organ recital tonight at the Service Club. Wish we would move and have it over with. I will shower yet.

Tuesday, December 16, 1941 Up at 4:30 with Ceno. Roast beef for dinner. Packed away all plates and utensils that mess kits and canteen cups can replace. Kitchen is about ready to move out. We may tonight.

Beautiful day. We feed the men tonight in lines and out of mess kits.

It was much easier to feed tactical style. Few K.P.s were needed, as there were no tables to set. Pots still had to be washed, but several kettles of hot, soapy water and a rinse were what the men washed their own mess kits in. All had 1918 style mess kits, as mine.

Life magazine of December 15, 1941 commented on Pearl Harbor. The writer compared the surprise bombing to an act of "national *hara-kari*" on the part of Japan.

The United States was now united. Senator Wheeler, who until Pearl Harbor was the leader of the die-hard Isolationists, spoke for all when he said, "The only thing now is to do our best to lick hell out of them."

Wednesday, December 17, 1941 Slept until 9:00. Go in the kitchen right after for a bite to eat and some canned milk to drink. There's plenty of food except when it comes to pork chops or roast beef. Then you give out only one piece, and that's it.

Had to fall in for four inspections with field equipment. Tarman was busted down to cook today. Herman is now Mess Sergeant.

Letter from Mother. Answered it. It's a mess around here, though it's a beautiful day.

Pettengale and I are going to church. The atmosphere is tight and tense. We may move out tonight.

Have no idea why Sergeant Tarman was broken down to cook. Makes me feel bad as we got along good, and I hardly know Herman, but so far I've had no trouble getting along with anyone.

Pettengale and I were the only ones again at prayer meeting.

Thursday, December 18, 1941

At 1:30 we woke up to the call of arms. "I think this is it," I thought, but this is the Army. Hurry up and wait. We loaded everything to go, then went to the gun park parking lot and sat for an hour. We came back at 4:30.

Sgt. Herman had Ceno and I go back to bed for awhile while the others unloaded. He got us up at 6:00 to make breakfast and that was "Hot cakes only," he said. Some grumbling, but Herman knows the work there is to pack all the kitchen things up, unload it again, then make breakfast.

Pork chops for dinner, liver and onions for supper. All out of mess kits. Some time off, but really needed it.

Another showdown inspection of all personal things, but no inspectors came. Talked to George Dahlgren. Wrote to Pat. Beautiful summer day.

Hot cakes was an easy breakfast, as we fed them as we fried them. The big gas ranges were ideal for this, and when we had to contend with an alert, "Hot cakes only," saved the day. The Mess Sergeants were allowed to do this if we had extra rations, and we usually did.

If someone had something stolen, a "showdown inspection" was held to try to recover the item. If we had a showdown inspection while we were on duty, we just had to put our things out in the cooks' tent, but didn't have to wait for the officers to come through.

Friday, December 19, 1941 Slept until 8:00. Washed clothes. Copied some recipes from Antonio.

Fellows had to load everything on the trucks again tonight. This time, though, the kitchen was left alone. A good day off for a change.

Got a package from home tonight. A scrapbook and package of eats. Also a card from Aunt Rose.

I used a weapons carrier to get rations tonight myself.

Saturday, December 20, 1941 Mess an hour early. We got up at 3:30. Parade and inspection. Glad I was on duty. Almost had to go on camp guard, but Bud Meyers went instead. Guard came in late tonight. Had to feed them.

Letter from Ray. He is at Payne with Dick. Ray has bought the ash forty southeast of our other camp.

Tarman and Tony are going on furlough. Meyers and I will be here alone. Very few in camp tonight. Passes aren't restricted, and everybody wants one before we pull out.

The "ash forty" is forty acres of land with a lot of ash trees growing on it. After the war I cut ash logs and had them sawed into lumber out of which I built much of my house.

CHAPTER 6

Sunday, December 21, 1941   Tarman and I on today. Last time I'll work with him. He is good, quiet, and does his fair share of the work with no grumbling. Camp guards were coming all day to eat at different times.

Package from Aunt Rose and Hulda Mehling. Cards from Rod, Arlene, Al, Germaine, and Herb and Edith Reinke. Letters from home. Pettengale and I will go to church yet.

We went to church and were the only two there again. Sang some hymns, and we talked. Went over to the 109th Ordnance to see Harvey or George Olson, but they weren't there. A card from Pat tonight.

Monday, December 22, 1941   I slept until 6:30, but was on with Meyers. Raining all forenoon. Fellows were supposed to go on a 20 mile hike, but it was canceled. We had to make sandwiches.

Tarman, Antonio and Herman left tonight on furlough. It's doubtful if I ever see them again.

I went to organ recital at the Service Club tonight at 7:30. A letter from Pat tonight that I answered. To bed at 10:00.

Tuesday, December 23, 1941   Bud Meyers and I on. Up at 4:30. A tough breakfast. Nothing is really normal with Christmas coming up. Key men from the kitchen are gone. Many fellows from the National Guard have their wives here. They're not staying in camp, but in Alexandria, and are here for part of the day and some meals.

Had to wait for rations until 9:00. A whole load came. I was all alone but enjoyed it. We got 8 big turkeys. I cleaned them. Got through at 11:00.

George came in for awhile.

Bud Meyers came to Camp Claiborne the same time as I did in April, but got in the kitchen right away, so he was 1st cook, and I was 2nd cook. Because of Christmas furloughs, and the advanced details leaving, we were the only two men of the kitchen crew.

Ralph Clark was acting Mess Sergeant, but only because he was a sergeant, and about all he did was to see that we got along with our work. Lt. Darwin would stop once in awhile too, to see how we were doing. He said his folks used to have a restaurant in Minneapolis. He was spread pretty thin as the officer in charge of the food division of the battery (or the whole battalion?) and without a Mess Sergeant, Bud Meyers and I were it.

I kept the two monthly menus for November and December 1941. The menu for December 23 says we had the following for breakfast: fresh fruit, fresh milk, corn muffins, pork sausage, bread, butter and coffee.

DELIVERY ORDER AND RECEIPT

Delivery Order No. _____

Work Order No. _____

Camp Claiborne   *12-23* _____, 19*41*
(Post, camp, or station)   (Date)

Deliver to *Hq. Btry* _____ the following supplies.
(Name of individual organization)

For _____
(Building No., shop, plant, or system)

RDERED	DE-LIVERED	STOCK NO.	ARTICLES	UNIT	SPACE FOR ACCOUNTING	
					UNIT COST	TOTAL COST
	2		*Lunch*			
	2		*Pickles Sour*			
	2		*Olive Stuffed*			
	1		*Cracker #2½*			
	3		*Gr. Peppers*			
	4		*apple #10*			
	5		*Mushrooms*			
	6		*Celery*			
	6		*Peas #2*			
	13		*Butter*			
	16		*Gr. Cran Berries*			
	99		*Grapes*			
	64		*Potatoe Sweet*			

Articles listed in column "Delivered" have been received.   19____

_____   _____   _____
(Name)   (Rank)   (Organization)

ORDER TAKEN BY   ISSUED BY   POSTED BY

DATE _____   DATE _____   DATE _____

ORIGINAL   16—12995

One cook had to check the rations when they came in and sign for them. Tonight it was Meyers' turn. But he soon went somewhere, and I couldn't seem to get caught up in the kitchen. The turkeys were about ready, but there was still a lot more to get ready for the big Christmas dinner coming up.

The cooks' tent sure seemed empty with just the two of us in it.

Wednesday, December 24, 1941   I heard the alarm go off at 4:30, but dropped off to sleep again until 5:30. Meyers and I had to hurry to get breakfast out on time.

I had a headache again, so I laid down again after for awhile.

Meyers went to town, so I made dinner and supper. Kolar helped a little. After mess tonight, we made cranberry sauce and did some more things for tomorrow.

Showered and went to the party, but didn't like it.

It's now 10:30. Dahlgren, Meyers and I will go to church tonight at the 11:30 service. Doesn't seem much like Christmas Eve. Some have been decorating the mess hall. A few of the fellows' wives and others have been in there evenings. They don't bother us, as the dining room can be closed off from the kitchen.

We had three big meals today. Some help is available from the K.P.s. Bud Meyers didn't come back from Alexandria.

This is my first Christmas away from home. No snow, and I really miss Roger and Arlene. I'm really thankful to have gotten in the kitchen though, or I really would be depressed tonight.

A real busy day with an important meal tomorrow. The ones in charge really trust Meyers and myself to get it all done with no extra cooks — and some guests to be there tomorrow as well.

Thursday, December 25, 1941   George and I went to church last night. Got to bed at 1:00, and up again at 4:00.

A tough day and everything didn't go automatically. The fellows thanked us a lot. I was really glad I was an integral part of it all.

Meyers got back all right, so I had a chance to sleep from 8:30 to 10:30. We cheated a bit, though, and only had sandwiches for supper.

I was off since 3:00. Wrote to Pat. Looked over my few personal things. Am listening to the radio. I thought how I've spent other Christmas days, and I'm both happy and sad, but very thankful.

We were busy and tired cooks today. The breakfast was more than average, and we followed it almost to the letter. There were several officers and their wives, and Sergeant Garey's wife was there along with some others. There was no checking on us or complaining, only a lot of thanks for the two Buds.

Bud Meyers is a regular guy, my age and size, but maybe a bit more inclined to let loose and have a good time. Because he wasn't there all the time yesterday, he had me go and rest at 8:30, and he finished the sandwiches after the big dinner too.

As I said before, Bud Meyers was later Killed In Action. He had so much to live for, and yet I knew little about his past except that he was from North Dakota.

All the dishes were unpacked again for this Christmas meal, and the tables were set like before Pearl Harbor. Dinner was the 8 turkeys with stuffing. The ration list for December 25 included 175 pounds of turkey, 45 pounds of mashed potatoes peeled by the K.P.s, and 45 pounds of bread. The bread was always white, in one-pound loaves that had to be sliced. It was my self-appointed task to keep the knives razor sharp. The test we had to see if they were sharp enough was to see if you could shave hair off your arm.

Meyers and I did the turkey carving and actual touching of the food. The K.P.s weren't allowed to do that, as they hadn't had the blood tests which were required for the cooks. Everything was sanitary in 1941.

Friday, December 26, 1941   Went to a movie last night. *Saw One Foot in Heaven.* Liked it.

Am getting tired of working every day. The suspense is getting to us. Not quite so hectic today. Fried ham for breakfast. Only 20 pounds of it, but with cinnamon rolls, syrup, and all the bread they wanted, it was all we could come up with.

Dinner was hash brown potatoes with fish (haddock), creamed peas and salad.

Supper was swiss steak, 45 pounds cut to serving size, browned and roasted with our own made gravy.

We are still drawing rations for 100 men right along, and probably feeding only about 75. Our battery strength is 125, but a lot are still on Christmas furlough. We are all eating well.

Doughnuts for supper and cinnamon rolls for breakfast were issued along with the bread. We did no baking here, except for our own crew.

Saturday, December 27, 1941   Inspection this morning. Inspections are always hectic for the kitchen crew, especially the cooks. The colonel found dust BEHIND the kitchen stoves this morning on his white glove, then he puts it right up close to your face, but doesn't say anything. I don't think they even went in the cooks' tent, though, and cooks don't stand formation in the battery on Saturday or have to be in parade dress [pressed chinos, shirt and pants, leggings and shined shoes], so we still don't have it so bad.

Had a headache. Slept for a little while this p.m.

Word is out that cooks can go to a cooks' and bakers' school right here at Claiborne after January 1. All I can say to that is, "Hard to say where I'll be by that time."

They had a dance at the Service Club tonight. I went up there, but came right back.

Sunday, December 28, 1941   Meyers and I on as usual. Had an easy breakfast: creamed dried beef on toast. A favorite of mine in the CCC's and it still is.

This p.m. we started loading for tomorrow. At 5:30, I left with Cajune and we went roller skating in Alexandria. Took me awhile to get used to skates again, but I really enjoyed myself.

Came back to camp about 11:00. Cold. The weather is chilly now at night. Sometimes we start the gas stove, and always roll down all four sides of the tent.

There were several ways to get to town: on the bus, some fellows had cars, or sometimes on weekends, the battery would send in a truck.

Monday, December 29, 1941   We were supposed to serve at 5:30. The alarm clock had stopped, and the guard woke us at 5:05. Finished packing and left at about 6:30.

Came to the firing range. Cold. Watched them fire the 37's from a distance.

Two letters from home.

Breakfast was not always as punctual as dinner or supper. When we had it ready, we'd tell the bugler, and he would blow the chow call. The men would come running, form a line, and come in. They would grab a plate off the table, come up to the counter, and cooks would put food on their plate. They'd then go back to the tables and eat. Some staple foods were already on the tables. It was noisy.

Tuesday, December 30, 1941   I slept with Brink, Haggarth and Cajune. Up at 6:00. Clark is still acting Mess Sergeant.

Fried eggs for breakfast, ham for dinner. It warmed up some. Left for camp at 1:00. Got in at 3:00. Had chili for supper. Got through at 7:00.

Got 10 cigars from Ray, cookies and candy from home, and a package of papers from home. And a letter from Pat with a bookmark shaped as a cross.

These days on the firing range were always tough. There were all the things to load, and making the meals on the back of the kitchen truck was messy. It was hard to keep things washed and your own hands clean. Things weren't always perfectly antiseptic-clean.

It was always nice to get the things back in place, have a supper made, and get the place in shape for the next morning. Then to the shower, and hit the sack.

Wednesday, December 31, 1941   Creamed beef for breakfast. Meyers slept all forenoon. I made dinner. Wrote a few letters. My turn to sleep some this afternoon.

First Battalion has been preparing to move out all day. Tonight we get the order that six of us from 2nd Battalion are being transferred to 1st and will be moving with them. We are being transferred to their battalion to take the place of those still on furlough. "Be prepared to move at once."

It's 8 p.m. now, and I am ready and waiting for further orders.

Brink, Jim Johnson, Sgt. Wyman Revels, Felix and I were the final ones to go to 1st Battalion. This was not our battalion's chance to get rid of us, but a necessary move to replace the men who were still on furlough. My job was to replace Grittsmacher who was 2nd cook not yet back from furlough. Both Johnson and Revels were key men and hard for 2nd Battalion to replace, but a move was immanent, and 1st Battalion's needs had to be met.

Orders came from the First Sergeant at 9:00 that I was to make breakfast here in the morning and await further orders.

My main thoughts were that at least this would finalize my transfer out of the anti-tank battalion, and I was ready to go where they told me to. With my trunk sent home, about all I had to do was unroll my bedroll and lie down, even if sleep might be slow in coming. About all the personal articles I had left were toilet articles, camera and diary.

Well, I remember thinking a lot that night, and I hoped that others were having a HAPPY NEW YEAR!

Thursday, January 1, 1942   Didn't have to help Meyers much, but mostly to serve breakfast. Washed a few clothes, changed, turned in my cook's uniforms.

Good-byes weren't too hard to say. Meyers and some of the fellows were good working partners in this mess together, but I'm thinking this move might be all for my good.

1st Battalion was just across the street from us, identical in about every thing. I took my barracks bag, musette bag and bedroll, and was told to report to the Mess Sergeant at 1st Battalion Headquarters Battery.

I did so, threw my things in a corner with the other guys' bags, and helped clean up the kitchen.

I got there at 1 p.m., and we finally left Camp Claiborne at 6:00. They took us to the station, we got in a cook coach, then to a Pullman coach. I'm in a lower berth, we're a little out of Alex, and we're headed east.

What a day! I didn't know a soul in the 1st Battalion, but I soon got acquainted. I had to report to the Mess Sergeant, Robert Vaughn. His wife, Jean, was there too, spending the last little time with him. Then there were George Pittlekow and Cloyce Rose, the two 1st cooks, and Bob Passow and now me, the two 2nd cooks.

There was no real welcome with handshakes; it took me a while to get to know everyone's names. I hit it off good with R.C. (Arky) Vaughn. Right from the start, Bob Passow treated me right — a real nice guy, and we got to know each other pretty well, as we were together a long time.

The kitchen was still a mess when I reported in, but we had it cleaned up before we left. The attitude of everyone here was completely different from the other kitchen that I just left; there was a lot of loud hollering and excitable actions. A lot of the blame belonged to the First Sergeant, Bob Meagher. He was a tall guy, and mouthy. He swore like a sailor, and he and the Mess Sergeant Arky were always at odds over something. Meagher later became Mess Sergeant himself.

First Battalion was led by Lt. Col. George Sylvester, who had been reassigned from Regimental Executive to resume command of the battalion.

The fellows said good bye to their wives, and we left camp Claiborne heading north from Bringhurst station in late afternoon. The eight and a half months I spent at Claiborne were mostly with good memories. I had a job that I liked with little chance of losing it, unless I got tired of it. I'd learned a lot in how to mix with people. I felt that my future was open, no matter how it might end.

There was one thing I couldn't change whatsoever: New Year's Day 1942 had been an eventful one.

CHAPTER 7

Train ride east. Fort Dix. Crossing the Big Pond. Arrival in Ireland

.

Friday, January 2, 1942 Went to sleep right away. All this traveling in the back of trucks, and long days, and hard, hectic moves, and hard work — I could sleep standing up.

Someone from the kitchen crew woke Passow and me up at 3:45. I thought we were still in Alexandria, but we were in Arkansas, heading northeast.

Cooked all day and served as well. Slept with Passow last night with not much chance to get acquainted.

No snow yet, but there is ice along the tracks. We stopped at Jonesboro, Arkansas for exercise, and we had a chance to buy a few things at the station. Made friends with Hurley Soderlind from Baker Battery, who is a cook as well.

Helped fry steaks for dinner. We are feeding about 580 men. We have 14 gas stoves in here. Lots of cooks and work and supplies.

The Brass let out to us that we are heading for Fort Dix, New Jersey, but nothing about where to after being processed there. The fellows are talking a lot. Places mentioned are British Isles, France or Africa. France has a familiar sound to it — [my cousin] Dick was there in World War I, and I heard plenty of war stories about that.

The fellows don't seem too low on morale, even those who had to leave their wives behind.

We were feeding the entire 151st Field Artillery Battalion (called the "1st Battalion" at Camp Claiborne) which was composed of Headquarters, A, B, C, and Service Batteries. Except for Service Battery, each battery was up to full battle strength of 120 men. Service Battery had less, but there were some additional men such as medics and officers who brought the total number up to about 580 men.

The cooks and Mess Sergeants were working remarkably well together. I figured someone must have been in charge of the whole cooking operation, but I didn't know who he was.

I was doing a lot of serving. This suited me OK, since as I didn't know anyone, it was a good way to get acquainted. It was exciting and a lot of exercise as well. Two of us would take a kettle or pan of whatever we had to serve and go through the whole train. The men would stay in their seats, and as we went by, we'd put the food into their mess kits.

There was an average of 5 teams of servers. We all tried to leave the kitchen at the same time to minimize any meeting of other servers. If we did have to meet for some reason, one set would have to go to the rear or front of the coach to pass. All food was hot. Kettles were 10 or 15 gallons, and the coffee pot was 30 gallons.

After serving, we would take two more kettles of hot water through to wash out mess kits. One 30-gallon kettle was soapy water, and the other, a hot rinse. Each man would slosh his mess kit in the water, but I'm not too sure how clean anything got after the dish water and rinse got through even half the men.

Passing through from coach to coach was interesting, as we had a chance to see where we were and get some fresh air. We could see the couplings that held the coaches together working back and forth. There was an attempt to enclose the open space between the coaches with curtains, but it didn't really do the job that well. Successfully opening and closing both coach doors with a large kettle of hot food, and maneuvering our way between the coaches with it, were quickly-learned skills we were thankful for and proud of. After the kettle was empty, then came the chore of going back to the kitchen coach for more.

There were actually two cook coaches. One had 14 stoves and some work space, and the other was for food preparation and storage. There were 20 cooks altogether, so we got some time off. I spent a lot of time I could have had off in the kitchen coaches helping when I could, though, and getting all I wanted to eat.

I met Hurley Soderlind and Don Sternke, and I got to be good friends with both of them in a hurry as we traveled east and worked together. We remained friends after the war as well. I was glad to have been transferred to 1st Battalion.

Saturday, January 3, 1942   Off today, and I relaxed. Still helped out several times, though.

We went through St. Louis sometime last night and through Indianapolis about 10 a.m. today. We got out and walked around — felt good. The engine has to stop for coal and water, and change crews, and no doubt, locomotives.

An error to say we "walked around." We were marched through part of the town for about a mile — just maybe we would have been short a man or two if we would have had the liberty to walk around on our own.

Still no snow, but all is brown, not green. I can't find my musette bag. Not surprising though, with all the junk and the way we have to travel. The air is cold. Feel pretty good, and seeing the country and it's all new, so it's sort of enjoyable.

Just went through Columbus, Ohio at 4:25 EST. Country is level. Some fields with farms.

Now it's 8:30 p.m. We are going through Pittsburgh, Penn. Hurley came over to talk tonight. It's started to snow. The ground is white.

It's really started to sink into us now: we're going farther away from home; east, and not north. The nostalgic feeling is hard to throw off, when you stop and meditate on it.

We still have our Pullman sleeper. The steady click of the wheels and roll of the car puts you to sleep in a hurry. The washing facilities are not the best, no better than for an "emergency" basis. The fellows are restless.

Sunday, January 4, 1942   Passow and I on, so it's up at 3 a.m. Just left Harrisburg at 5:00, and are in Philadelphia. Much easier to make breakfast when we are stopped or going slow.

Got to Fort Dix about 8 a.m., but was 12:00 before we got off and unloaded. Some Army trucks took us to Dix.

Full of snow and mud. Cold. Everything is dirty. Mess hall is for the whole battalion. All stoves are coal. I was on duty all day, which was long and tough. We finally got out a stew supper for the men at 8:00.

I am in a tent with Pittlekow, Passow and 2 others. Only a small coal stove in it, and I'm probably the only one who knows how to burn coal. We do have cots and blankets, but of course no sheets.

Finally had a chance to shower and clean up right. Only drawback is, the latrine is a long ways from here.

Monday, January 5, 1942   Slept until 9:00. Wrote up the account in here for the past several days. Cold, even with the stove going. It's below zero. We are supposed to go by boat soon to a northern base. Right now, I really don't care what we do. Wrote home and to Patsy.

We are cleaning up the area. There are group meetings, and inspection, which I don't have to stand.

We got Springfield rifles today. All had to turn in their cameras, except me, of course. I started carrying it in my back pocket wrapped up in my handkerchief.

I had just bought my 828 Kodak camera before I left home, and I wasn't entertaining the idea of turning it in. This was really the only rule I had turned my back on, and I refused to obey it for the duration.

I had a few rolls of film, and my brother Ray would send me a few rolls, hidden in one of my mother's packages. Prince Albert Tobacco tins held a few rolls of film along with part of the tobacco that was originally in the can. 828 film rolls were small, only 8-exposure. They came in metal cans the diameter of a penny and 1 ½" long. The negative size was 1 ½ X 1 ¼ inches, but they enlarged nicely.

I was beginning to get to know some of the fellows by name and their rank, and the First Sergeant by his big mouth. We had to stand in ranks one day and answer roll call by a "Yes." Hank Lane answered "Yo!" instead and started Meagher on a blue streak I thought would never end.

Tuesday, January 6, 1942   Up at 3:00. Worked hard all day. Ham for dinner, beans for supper.

Cold this morning. About zero. Our fire was out. Had to walk quite a ways to the mess hall. It was cold on the face. Reminded me of home.

Had our pictures taken for passports. Soderlind went to the canteen tonight. Warmer in the tent. Wrote several letters home.

The men were on different duties, mainly standing inspections, going to classes and still cleaning the area. The officers were receiving instructions. They had to live in tents, as did the enlisted men.

The transition between the mild Louisiana climate and the snow and cold at Fort Dix was not pleasant to take. We were issued seven suits of long underwear. We turned in all khakis and thought for sure we would be heading for Iceland.

Wednesday, January 7, 1942   Overslept until 9:30. Washed clothes and showered at the same time. Changed clothes.

Talked to Hurley a lot. I made out an allotment for $20.00 a month. Had a tooth inspection. Wrote a lot of letters. Mounted things in my scrapbook. It's 10:00 now. Will wash up and go to the latrine. It's a long way.

One advantage of being a cook: I go over to the kitchen and eat when and what I want.

Multiple Mess Sergeants were here, but there was some system among them that worked so that all weren't bossing at the same time. The Mess Sergeants were: Headquarters Battery, Bob Vaughn; Able Battery, Bud Bailey; Baker Battery, Earl Noble; Charlie Battery, Jack McCalaster; and I don't believe Service Battery had a Mess Sergeant at that time.

It was nice to just stand in a corner of the kitchen out of the way, eating, enjoying talk of the past and speculating of the future. Jack McCalaster and Bud Bailey were both great talkers with lots of experience and nice to listen to. Both were older married fellows from Minneapolis. I kept my mouth shut and was considered a good kid.

Don Sternke and Hurley Soderlind were both from B Battery. We worked the same days, though, so we got to know each other better all the time.

Thursday, January 8, 1942   The guard woke me at 3:00. The fire was out again. I started it, and didn't get to the kitchen until 4:00, which was OK. On duty all day. Got two new pairs of denims and socks.

Hurley and I went to the canteen. Talked to him in his tent, which was cold.

Got my woolens back from the cleaners.

I'm ready to leave this place soon. So is everybody else. The war is not going to end any sooner with us just sitting here.

Pretty much a routine day. Some fellows that I know pretty well now call me "Bud," but to most of them, it's "Wag." I'm getting ribbed a lot for drinking canned milk by the cupful. I don't care that much for coffee.

Friday, January 9th, 1942   Woke at 6:00 to see two holes burning in our tent. Lucky I woke up in time. Someone left the draft wide open, and the pipe got too hot.

Got up at 10:00, showered, cleaned up. Sewed my pants and a button on my shirt, and it was 12:00.

Read over old letters. Wrote to Ray, home and Patsy.

Still fairly cold, especially when the fire goes down. Hurley and I went to the Service Club. Met some friends of his from the 109th Signal Corps. Wrote a long letter to Pat.

Saturday, January 10, 1942   Up at 4:00. Snowed 2 inches overnight. Had planned on going to Trenton, but all passes are canceled. Cold water, so no shower. Wrote two last letters, one to Ray and one to the folks and the kids.

I'm a tired soldier tonight. Meat loaf the main dish for supper.

Two cooks feeding 125 men is easier than eight or ten cooks feeding 580, though; it seems there is always one or two who will push some of the work onto the other ones when they can.

Sunday, January 11, 1942   Slept until 10:00. Packed over my things, the little I have. Pittlekow and I walked over to 2nd Battalion. They are over a mile from here. Saw Shermack, Tarman and others. Was good to see them. Fairly warm. Had my X-rays tonight. Had to walk to the hospital for them. Drew more equipment.

Had an awful headache.

The old outfit, 2nd Battalion, was now the 175th Field Artillery Battalion, as my 1st Battalion was now the 151st Field Artillery Battalion. I was glad they didn't try to transfer us back to our old outfit, now that we were in the same place for a few days. I had no desire to go back to it. Hurley, Sternke, Vaughn and I were getting to be good friends, and besides that, I wanted to get going — we'd heard we'd be moving the next day.

Monday, January 12, 1942   Still here at 4:00. A letter from home and one from Grandma. Worked as usual and still had to pack. Had my bedroll made. Bought a mouth organ from Hurley for $1.00. Wrote two letters, to home and to Patsy.

The kitchen crew was a little upset most of the day, as we had to feed the men and still be ready to leave at any time. Glad I'm not in charge of anything. Hurley and I went to the Service Club. I sent a few things home to Ray.

Tuesday, January 13, 1942   Slept until 9:00. Shaved, washed. Looked over my things again. Got a long letter from Patsy with pictures of her. Letter from home. Had to fall in several times for roll call, etc., and to sign the payroll.

Hurley and I went to the Service Club again tonight.

It was a long, boring day. There was no chance to call home or communicate with loved ones in any way, though it was the last chance for those who never made it back.

Wednesday, January 14, 1942   On duty today. Up real early. Started preparations for moving right away. Everything cluttered up for dinner and for pulling out. Changed clothes. Fell in about 4:00. Walked to the station and left at 8:00. We detrained at Hoboken, New Jersey, January 15, 1942.

The moving out of Fort Dix was quite an adventure that I don't like to remember. It really was an acid test for a simple farm boy like me.

From the time we got on the train we carried all our luggage which consisted of our barracks bag, (a big blue one, containing mostly clothes), the musette bag, about 14 inches square and as thick as how much stuff you had jammed into it (mostly personal and toilet articles), your bedroll which consisted of several blankets and half of a pup tent (another soldier would have the other half, as two men always made one tent), your Springfield rifle, full uniform including helmet, your mess kit snapped onto your musette bag, your canteen cup, canteen, and ammo clips (all a part of your ammunition belt which was around your waist), your two feet that were dragging, and a heavy heart.

The ferry ride was in an open old boat of some kind. There was a big open area they herded us all onto; we sat on the deck leaning our backs against the big barracks bags, and across the Hudson we went.

During the time we were heading northeast on the train from Claiborne to Fort Dix, and while we were at Fort Dix, some of the men's wives had been having their own adventure. After the war, Bob Vaughn and his wife Jean became very good friends with my wife Evelyn and myself. Jean wrote me during 1998 and told me some of an Army wife's experience.

Jean and Almay Edwards, another fellow's wife, had rented a little tourist cabin about a mile from Camp Claiborne, just 2 small rooms with a bed in each room. One room had a stove, sink, some cupboards and a refrigerator.

One morning as the two ladies were eating breakfast, a car pulled up, and someone rapped on the door. One of the fellows had sneaked out of camp to tell them that the men were getting ready to pull out. Jean and Almay hurried to camp. They had a pass to get in, though none of the men were supposed to get out.

Bob Vaughn, as Mess Sergeant, was going through bedlam for the next couple of days. They'd tell him to serve lunch and then to pack everything up to move. As soon as everything was packed up, they'd tell him to unpack and serve supper. Jean said they really never even had a chance to talk together, but she just sat over in the corner and watched him peel potatoes as fast as he could go.

The wives would stay as late as they could at night, then walk back to their cabin; but the last night, the officers turned their backs and let them stay all night. Jean said they must have looked as though they had been out all night the next day, because they didn't get much sleep.

After all the men left for Fort Dix, Jean and Almay returned to their cabin. Her room had a canopy bed, one window pane broken with rags stuffed in it, and it was cold. There was a tiny, inadequate gas heater in the room, but plenty of blankets. Sometimes they would stay in bed in the day time just to keep warm. There was a train track a couple hundred feet away, and Jean said that every time a train went by it seemed as though the bed canopy would fall, though it never did. The water froze, as the pipes were all out in the open, so they couldn't take a bath or flush the toilet.

Then two or three of the husbands called, and of course wanted their wives to go to Fort Dix.

So they packed up and got on the Greyhound bus. They went up the East Coast, taking about 2 days and 2 nights to get there. Jean said Virginia was really pretty, with horse farms with miles of white picket fences. They changed buses in Washington, D.C., then found a hotel near Fort Dix.

Jean last saw Bob on the Wednesday we left Fort Dix, marching down the street with his barracks bag over his shoulder.

The women then went to New York City, hoping the men might get a leave there before getting on the ship, but no one got any leaves.

Jean's suitcase had been lost by Greyhound, so she had to wear the same clothes the whole time she was in New York. After a few days the women decided their husbands must have been out at sea (as they had been for two or three days already), and they headed home.

Jean kept calling Greyhound and gave descriptions of the contents of her suitcase. It was finally located in Cleveland, Ohio in June. She was mostly concerned with a picture of Bob and a music box he had given her.

Jean moved in with her mother in an apartment (with its own bathroom) in Minneapolis, and stayed there for the duration of the war. She got a job at a small arms plant in New Brighton, Minnesota called Twin Cities Ordnance, where they made 50 caliber bullets for machine guns. She worked on a large machine where they filled them with powder. When it would storm or thunder, they'd shut that section down for safety. She earned $45 a week, which was good money back then.

The years dragged on for Jean as slowly as it did for us overseas. She said she wrote to Bob every day, and I'll always remember Bob whenever he was in the hut, he'd be perched on his cot with a board on his lap, "Writing to Jean."

Thursday, January 15, 1942   Well, this is it, the Port of Embarkation: New York, New York. The ship, a peninsular and Oriental line steamer; the time, 12:15 a.m. My heart sank. First ocean I've seen, and the first ship.

Walking up the gangplank was something I've heard and read about, but this was my experience. Partially carrying and partially dragging all equipment was an integral part of it.

The ship looked as high as our big round-roofed barn at home, and sounded like a big Malley locomotive in Proctor. You could hear steam coming out of her, and water was trickling down her sides. I saw my first portholes. She looked dirty, but the one part of her character that stood out above all else is that she is big.

We were herded down to H deck which is a ways down, as F deck is even with the water line. The whole battery was put in one large room of this deck, which is a part of the hold. There are about a dozen long tables with dishes put behind slats on an angle so they can't fall out when the ship rolls.

Not sure if she is coal or oil fired. Lots of the fellows threw their belongings on the tables and then slept on them as well. I threw mine off in a corner and was glad to have a corner on the floor to sleep.

Had to help carry food tonight; the ship's galley-crew had slopped it together. It was nothing fancy.

The *Strathaird* is an English ship run by Greeks. I'm assigned to table no. 196. Explored part of the ship. We don't have too many restrictions so far, except for smoking on deck. Guards are to shoot anyone exposing any light at night — which includes a lit cigarette butt.

Besides having been one of the first two draftees from St. Louis County, Minnesota, now I was also on the first convoy of World War II to cross the Atlantic to Europe.

Eventually, it ended up to be an overseas service of 3 years, and 3 days short of 6 months.

None of us thought it would take that long — Germany had almost quit bombing England and Ireland by this time and was fighting on many fronts, so we mistakenly thought we could end the war in a hurry.

Friday, January 16, 1942   Slept on the floor last night with everything on. Cold on H deck. We are in a convoy. The sea is quite calm, except for tonight. Will sleep on the floor again. Dark on deck. Explored the ship again today. Interesting. Helped carry food tonight, and that was confusing. Talked a little to Hurley and Don, about the only two I know well enough to talk to. I can find back to our hole in H deck now, though.

I've been walking the ship almost constantly, or watching the wake, or beginning to stand on the side of the ship and inhaling deeply on the up roll of the ship, then exhaling deeply when she comes back down. This helps somewhat for keeping your stomach settled and guards against seasickness.

We get two meals a day, if you can call them that. Today I ate only one of them. I still watch the planes taking off and landing on the carrier, but there aren't many flying at one time now. The destroyers are still bobbing up and down amongst the waves all day long.

The excitement was still with me — just of being on the ship, the size of it, and the constant roll and creak of her. The creaking seemed more constant at night, but I suppose it was just easier to hear it then. It changed pitch, and the propellers all blended together to make a steady, droning, monotonous groan, except for when a depth charge went off.

Whenever some kind of detector sensed an underwater object, it triggered a large blasting depth charge. These were designed to target German submarines, of course. Judging from the amount of charges that we dropped on our 10-day trip, we had company across the Atlantic.

Our convoy consisted of our ship, another troop ship, an aircraft carrier and two small destroyers. It was considered a small convoy.

It was most interesting to watch the planes take off and land on the carrier. Some of them made up to three attempts before finally landing.

The sea was not very rough, just rolling a little, but still the waves were big. They reminded me of large hills constantly moving and changing in size. The two small destroy-

ers were in and out of sight because of the waves.

I would stand for long periods of time watching the wake, just looking and meditating, and watching that churning, rolling frenzy of foaming water. Members of the crew would put their dirty clothes in a heavy mesh bag and throw it in the wake of the ship for some time and get their washing done that way. The wake shows for a long way. I took some snapshots of it with my forbidden Kodak 828. I didn't let anyone see me take a picture, but would hold the camera up to my chest and snap the shutter without using the viewfinder.

We were carrying many British Army, Navy, and RAF personnel back to England. They had been in the Middle East. We spent time talking to them and beginning to learn the English monetary system and their insignia of rank, and trying to tolerate their cocky attitudes and bragging tongues.

We had life preservers on constantly, and after they started dropping the depth charges, we didn't think it was such a bad idea. German U-boats were busy in the Atlantic.

There were wooden life rafts piled up on the deck and tied down with a big rope. There was a sign that said something like this, "If this ship is sinking, break the glass in the box that holds the ax, and cut the rope." This would set the rafts free so they could float off the ship. These rafts reminded me of wood pallets, but were larger.

None of us could come up with a comfortable thought as to where even half of the soldiers on board could have found enough room on the life rafts in a sinking. We learned later that the only possible chance we'd have had for survival would have been to hang onto the side ropes and let yourself hang in the sea. The too-few life boats would have soon been filled with officers and crew. Long after the war, Don Sternke and I talked about the life boat situation on the *Strathaird* and found we had shared the same fears.

CHAPTER 7

We were soon told that our destination was Belfast, Northern Ireland, and that our advanced task force consisted of two battalions of the 133rd Infantry Regiment, the 1st Battalion of the 151st Field Artillery Regiment, plus attached Quartermaster troops and engineer and other service troops. We were the advanced elements of the new Allied Expedition Force (AEF).

Saturday, January 17, 1942   Started writing a poem to Patsy today. Wrote several others as well.

The latrine is pretty crude. All cold water — cold sea water, that is. The showers aren't very popular. First thing I did was to taste the water to see if it was salty. It was. Lathering up is a problem. Soap doesn't work well in cold, salty sea water. Then standing up is another thing in a rocking ship. It helps if you can be satisfied staying a little dirty until we get to Ireland.

Sunday, January 18, 1942   Up about 7:00 or 8:00. Don't know just what time it is now. Have passed into several time zones. Saw Hurley, and we talked and walked together.

B Battery is in another part of the ship. Didn't eat at all yesterday or today, but lots of fellows are a lot more seasick than I am. Activity is way down on the part of most of the men.

The top deck starts with A and down to the waterline is F, and we are in H. I'm not sure how far down it goes. Lots of places are off limits for the enlisted men. All the garbage is stacked on F Deck and the crew throws it overboard once in awhile. I'm sure the fish don't eat it up so fast that the German U-boats couldn't see some of it and torpedo us.

Monday, January 19, 1942   We had a big disappointment today. We were watching the aircraft carrier, when she slowly started turning around and headed back for New York City. The destroyers stayed with us, though.

Felt a lot better today — I bought some pop and potato chips from the canteen, and it really revived me. Wrote more on the poem for Patsy. I was going to sleep on deck last night, but everybody had to go below to their own stinky holes.

I had a bottle of cream soda today, the very first cream soda I've ever tasted. Seems like the weather is pretty warm, much warmer than at New Jersey, I'm sure.

The canteen is only open once in awhile, the line is long, and no effort is made to hurry along those who have more money and want to buy a lot. So, often, many have to do without.

Tuesday, January 20, 1942   The boat was rocking more today than ever. Drank soda pop to keep my stomach feeling good.

Slept in the elevator way again last night. Some decks have narrow staircases; others have small, vertical stairways that accommodate only one man at a time. There's a round hole cut in the floor for the ladder and man to get through, not unlike that in a fire hall. All in all, space is saved wherever it can be.

Dreamed of home and the woods last night. Slept good, considering the creaking of this old scow all night. The fresh, salty air helped, I'm sure.

Had to help carry food and wash dishes. This is lots harder than serving on a train. Washing dishes wasn't too bad, but all the help were strangers (one from every battery), and the crew in the galley doesn't seem very friendly, and I don't know any Greek.

Wednesday, January 21, 1942   We get up at 6:00. It's 9 a.m. now, and should be 4 p.m. at home. Write this on deck. I spend most of my time on E deck. Finished my poem. Wrote home and to Ray. We hand in the letters to the captain, unsealed. We can still say what we want to in a letter, except our destination.

The sea is rough tonight. Eat most of my meals from the ship's canteen. They consist of pop and potato chips. My money is running out, though, and this morning it looked like worms in the oatmeal. I went without again, as most of the fellows did. We weren't quite that hungry.

My letter home written on the boat, January 21, Wednesday, said little except that it was chilly, and that I was out on deck as much as I could be. I said we exercise several times a day. The letter arrived home March 2, 1942.

Anticipation

Tonight I'm going to try my ability at rhyme,
Because right now I have a lot of time.
We've been floating all day,
But where we are going, no one will say.

We are bound for a port a long way from here,
But when we get there we'll go into high gear,
We are going to fight for greed and for hate,
Only God knows what will be our fate.

I've been out on deck thinking of home,
And just wondering how far we will roam.
The waves are quite big, but yet not so high;
It's so dark out on deck, not a star in the sky.

Way back west, they are sitting at home,
And me out here just thinking alone,
On the Atlantic with very few friends;
I hope it's not long till I go back again.

As I stood gazing out at the sea,
It looked awful deep and so blue to me,
I thought and I thought till my mind seemed to stop,
I was hoping and praying, yet life looks so dark.

Our ship is swaying a little more now
than this morning, before we had chow;
Some boys are dizzy, and I feel the same.
We hope we don't get seasick; they say it's no game.

As I write now, way below deck,
Trying to think of what I'll say next,
Our quarters are below the sea,
But the wood and steel will protect me.

We are very crowded, but the boys don't squawk;
They will do their high-flying when we dock.
Our tables are for mess, are also our beds.
"No smoking below deck," the captain said.

As for me I don't smoke, but think of the things,
Mostly the past and then what the future will bring.
I think of you too, all of my friends,
I'll see you again, but only God knows when.

I've said before, I'm bound for a fate
That is filled with lust, greed and hate.
What it will bring, no one knows;
But now that we've started, on we shall go.

I'll try this again, as its four days now,
That we've been floating along on this old scow.
The ship is pitching; I walk up hill,
Then down, and she stands still.

AND THERE SHALL BE WARS

I go on the deck and lean over the rail,
I cough and cough, but to no avail;
Seasickness has got me, as it has others;
I try not to think of it, but still it bothers.

I've been to the galley, but don't have to cook.
I'm glad of that though, I don't want to look
At the food out there, I know I can't eat;
And I'm not the least fussy, and it's not from the heat.

It's five days now that I've been out to sea.
Seven more to go, or so they tell me.
I'm over my seasickness, sure glad of that.
I hope I don't get it on the way back.

Last nite I was going to sleep out on deck,
But they chased me off, said "Down below quick."
I don't like to be so far below there,
Where the talk is so thick and so is the air.

I'd rather be here where the sea's salty spray
Comes over the rail as I back away,
Where the air is so pure, altho there's no land;
I'd rather be here when it does come at hand.

Today is a week we've been sailing along;
As it is yet, nothing's went wrong.
But the sooner we get there, it will suit me better,
As I'm anxious to get some of your letters.

I've been faring quite good as conditions permit,
But I hope it's not long before I get off this ship.
I hope it's not long before we hit land.
I'm sick and tired of not lending a hand.

So I think I will end this and go up for air.
I'll write you a letter when we get there.
When this is censored, I hope none is cut out.
It was written in truth, nothing in doubt.

May God bless you and keep you as he does me,
Out here on the ocean, sailing the sea.
Don't lose your nerve, and keep up your chin;
God is with us all, so we are sure to win.

Wilmer Wagner, 1942

114

CHAPTER 7

Thursday, January 22, 1942   Up at 6:00 again. I come up on one of the higher decks as soon as I eat. Bob Vaughn and I walked around the ship a little last night. Still hardly know him, but seems like a nice guy to have as Mess Sergeant. He writes some every day to his wife, Jean.

Washed and shaved last night. Have been sleeping in the elevator shaft the last three nights. It's more room and better air. Body smells and not much ventilation really go against me.

Watching the sides of the ship at night was interesting, with all the phosphorous fish. It seemed as though the ship itself caused all the luminous sparks. The fish follow the ship, and the sparks sure look to be genuine.

One thing for certain was that the wake was genuine, and it was a constant reminder that we were steadily heading east. The wake is dark in color, and it was amazing how far back we could see it. I stood there watching the bags of the crew's clothes rolling in the water; the action was great.

The destroyers looked so small, and sometimes they were hard to see at all because of the waves. It seemed that they couldn't have been much help in time of trouble.

The ships didn't travel straight, but zigzagged from side to side as a man trying to escape being hit by lightning. This was to spoil a U-boat's aim.

It was hard for me to realize that I was actually this far away from home, on the Atlantic heading for war. I was really depressed when I dreamed of home. I remember thinking that all those war stories that my cousin Dick had told us would probably soon become a reality for me. But he was in the infantry in France, and this was artillery … but I really hardly knew the difference between the two.

Friday, January 23, 1942   Was really "rough as a cob" last night. A kitchen stove broke loose. One cook got a broken leg. We got no cooked breakfast, but had some kind of dry ration, hardly edible. It is really a rough sea. This part of the North Atlantic is supposed to be the roughest it ever gets in January.

I was sleeping in the elevator shaft when water started to come in, so I had to go in the hole for the rest of the night. It's so rough the waves are coming up to E and D decks at times.

A life boat drill again, and calisthenics, which I always like, then it's talk, walk with someone you know, write, watch the waves and reminisce. I talked to Floyd Hanson from Arnold. I know him a little, as his sister went to the Farmer's Market for awhile.

My money is gone now, so I eat with the bunch. Walked through the kitchen. Had ice water, which was good.

The crew stand around when they have nothing to do. They fold their arms in back of their chest instead of in front like we do. Then they change off standing on one foot while resting the other one, in a crooked fashion.

Saturday, January 24, 1942   Another rough day, but no enemy action as yet, so it's bearable. It's supposed to be almost over. The worn out joke is, "Don't worry, we are only a mile from land, now -- Straight down."

We've been told that the ship changes course constantly, as it is almost impossible for a submarine to torpedo a ship that does so.

Sunday, January 25, 1942   The old ship really rocked last night again. The fear of going down hasn't bothered me for awhile, but I'm not getting to love sailing under these conditions.

I was in the hatchway and made quite a few moves all at the same time — I grabbed my blankets, jumped for the ladder hatch the very same moment a few buckets of water came in, I squeezed into the part of the ship where our battery was quartered, and I spent the rest of the night there.

If it hadn't been quite as bad as it was, I would have just gone up on F deck and laid by the door. No one would have bothered me -- but last night, water was coming over F deck again. There had been a big pile of garbage stacked, but the waves saved the crew some work. This morning it was all gone.

We could sight land about 9:00 this morning. We could see it all day, and it looked good, but no one knew for sure what it was. It appeared to be mountains of rock.

We are in the North Channel tonight. Scotland on portside, North Ireland on starboard. The sea has calmed a lot.

Some RAF planes are giving us cover now, and our destroyers were replaced several days ago by two British corvettes. The submarine activity was heavy, judging by the depth charges.

Monday, January 26, 1942   We were standing still, ready to dock at Belfast this morning.

The whole dock area is covered with balloons. They are anchored down with cables. The reason is to keep German dive bombers at a distance. One of those cables could easily slice off an airplane wing if the plane got too low. Some of the balloons can move with their base, and can be lowered or raised as well.

We sat in the harbor until late afternoon. I suppose we were waiting for

H.M.T. STRATHAIRD

151st F.A. BN. AND 133rd INF. REG. DISEMBARKING
AT BELFAST, NORTH IRELAND, JANUARY 26, 1942.

PHOTO BY OLIVER C. STIVERS ("C" BTRY. 151st F.A. BN.)

high tide before we disembarked in the Belfast Harbor. We got off the ship very willingly. We had to march, of course.

The Irish cheered us from both sides as we marched through, and were singing, "Over There, Over There!" and "The Yanks are Coming, The Yanks are Coming!" The Irish band was playing, and the goose bumps were many on all of us. It was very emotional — they gave us a real welcome. Northern Ireland had already suffered a lot from bomb damage (we could see it), and we were the first of the AEF in World War II.

We had a hot meal from the British, some kind of a meat pie that was some of the best tasting food I've ever eaten. It was probably mutton. We also had a canteen cup of coffee that tasted awful good after having been on that ship for 10 days.

I felt so thankful that day, I'll never forget it. The voyage had proven safe and uneventful, and here we were in Ireland. It took some concentration to steady ourselves as we started walking on land again, as it seemed the ground wouldn't stop rolling either.

Soon it was dark, and we boarded a train headed for Limavady, County Londonderry. There were stops along the way, and people were at the depots, cheering and welcoming us all the way. Though all the windows of the train had blackout curtains (the first we had seen) so no light could shine through, we could move them aside a little to look at the people who were cheering us. The British had done a bang-up job to welcome us, and we couldn't have appreciated it more.

We had to go through Ballymena, and Coleraine, where British lorries (trucks) picked us up and took us to the British Camp at Ballerena. Here

WAR DEPARTMENT

OFFICIAL BUSINESS

PENALTY FOR PRIVATE USE TO AVOID
PAYMENT OF POSTAGE $300

BUY
DEFENSE SAVINGS
BONDS AND STAMPS

Mr. H. G. Wagner

Rt. 2 # 192
Duluth, Minn.

I HAVE ARRIVED SAFELY AT MY DESTINATION.

MY NEW ADDRESS IS:-

APO 813 c/o POSTMASTER. NEW YORK, N. Y.

NORMAL SIGNATURE *Wilmer A. Wagner*

TYPE Pvt	Wagner	Wilmar	A.	37026777
	(Last Name)	(First Name)	(Initial)	(Serial No.)

again the British had a hot meal waiting for us. It was now in the wee hours of the morning, and really appreciated.

We were assigned to Nissen Quonset huts, about 20 men to a building. There was a stove in each hut with a coal fire already burning in it, a real welcome compared to the reception we'd gotten at Fort Dix a month before. The camp was situated between the south shore of Lough Foyle, and Mount Benevenagh, on the estate of Lady Heggetesp.

We each had our own cot with board springs, but a decent straw tick for a mattress which was much better than we had on the *Strathaird*. We didn't feel it would be too hard to get used to the blackout and British food. We were looking forward to meeting the Irish people and experiencing the country. The weather was damp and chilly.

Tuesday, January 27, 1942   Had a few hours of real rest for a change, but we had to get up early and get assigned to our work and get started. Our teachers are all British, mostly noncoms. These fellows had to stay behind to get us used to the British way, while the main part of their battalion moved to another camp.

Bob Vaughn and I made cookies. Got through at 7:10. Cold in the hut, but actually not so bad, as it is already spring here. The grass is green in places, and other colors are showing as well.

One-horse carts instead of teams and wagons. There is a castle on this estate owned by Lady Heggetesp and taken over by the British Army for the duration.

The kitchen is old. Coal ranges for cooking and other things we are not used to. Our biggest problem now is being on British rations, but we have promises of having our own soon.

McKoy, our fireman is sure doing his bit of cussing in his slow Iowa drawl, trying to get enough heat out of these old dogs to satisfy the cooks. Everything to him is "rough as a cob." Guess they use corn cobs instead of old Sears and Roebuck catalogs in their outhouses down in Iowa.

Bob Passow and I made four kidney pies today for the cooks — under strict supervision of Sergeant Major Clarke. We are cooking for the five batteries of the 151st. Lots of cooks are on at one time.

They'll split us up though, as soon as things settle down. Now Bob
Passow and I are the daytime bakers.

The country so far is beautiful, different. Can see some of the
patch-quilt areas in the fields or gardens separated from the next one
with a wall of rock about
three feet high, or by a
row of hedge grown so
thick hardly a dog could
get through.

There are some Irish
workers around, and our
boys have already picked
up common phrases such
as, "Aye, laddie, that it
is," or "Nay" for "No,"
and "The wee one."
The Irish all have a question about America, and a good percent-
age of them have a distant relative in the US that they want to tell you
about.

A lot of Irish came to the United States during the 1840's because of
the great Irish potato famine of 1846.

It didn't take long for the Yankee cooks to start frustrations going with
the British cooks. No one knows as much as an Englishman, except for
another Englishman. Rations were vastly different too. There was tea instead of coffee, and meat was mostly mutton, and biscuits called "scours."

Wednesday, January 28, 1942   Slept until 9:00. Showered with hot,
non-sea water. What a comfort, what a privilege. I've never appreciated a shower like I did this morning.

Another blessing is that we start today on our regular shift of a
day on and a day off.

George Pittlekow and I went for a walk. Leaves are on the bushes,
and the grass is green. Rained some. This isn't quite spring, though.
One Irishman says they plant potatoes in March.

We had to move all around today. The object is to get all men
from the same work details together as much as possible. All the
kitchen crew is in hut no. 32, and I got the one corner by the door,
which I wanted. The end wall affords some extra room for hanging
up clothes on nails. Packed over all my things, which is only what I
have in my musette bag. Hope I can keep my diary as long as I'm
overseas. We start a pay raise now: 20% because of overseas duty.

This camp is mixed government troops and private. The castle and garden is towards one side. We can go into the garden. It's nice, a fountain and pool, greenhouse and stone walks taken care of by gardeners whom I haven't met as yet. A family lives in the big stone house, with several draft horses and carts in a 3-sided shed.

Thursday, January 29, 1942   Up at 5:00. We are getting somewhat used to the British way of doing things. Bob Passow and I made baking powder biscuits or scours again. Took nearly all day. We made the coffee tonight too.

Beautiful day, like spring at home. No snow. Grass is green. Enjoy my work. I like baking better than cooking. Probably because there are more cooks than needed, and only 2 bakers on each day. They seem to want the bakers to work at night, because better use can be made of the coal stoves which have been a bottleneck many times now. When American rations come in, we expect more and better rations for pastries.

Bob Passow was a nice guy to work with. He'd sing a lot and was never grumpy, but sometimes he'd do things without thinking. One day we made oatmeal cookies, he cooked the oatmeal before mixing it in the batter. What a mess.

Our mess hall and cooking area was much different than the one we had at Camp Claiborne. The kitchen area was small, and the attached mess hall was barely adequate. Some of the men from our battalion ate in "the Barn," about 100 feet away. This building was also used for movies. The hay storage portion of the barn was what we used. This was level with the road, and was built into a side-hill with a cattle area on the lower floor.

Friday, January 30, 1942   Have to get up at 6:00 even on my day off. Slept some after that, though.

Inspections are real easy. Someone walks through every day, but as long as beds are made and the floor is swept, there aren't any complaints. It would be pretty hard to make a smooth bed with a straw tick.

There are 14 fellows in here. The ones from the kitchen are Passow, Pittlekow, myself, George Sefscik, Tony Sermguard and Bob Engleson. Bob keeps our spirits up. He has many interesting stories to tell. He's about 30, and a good-sized fellow. He's taken a liking to me, and always calls me Wag.

Saturday, January 31, 1942   Up at 5:00. Worked hard all day, both cooking and baking. The English sergeants are still with us.

On Wednesday, only three days after arriving here, all gun crews, survey crews and others in work related with the guns, started training on the British 25-pounder, so called, of course, because it fired a 25-pound projectile. All instructors were from the Royal Artillery. This training kept the men busy for the next 4 weeks, and morale was high. Some formations and inspections were still held daily and pretty much hated, but the fact that we were preparing for a second front was encouraging.

Schools for officers and noncoms were held each evening, in addition to the full day's training schedule. These were necessary to prepare men for the service practice to take place in 3 weeks. These schools were a success that satisfied the British instructors.

Our official battalion history said that the men and officers of our 151st Field Artillery Battalion were happy and proud to learn that while 2nd Battalion had been redesignated as the 175th Field Artillery Battalion, our 1st Battalion was retaining the original number of the old regiment that was a part of the Rainbow Division in World War I.

CHAPTER 8

Ballerena Camp, Ireland. Preparing for maneuvers.

Sunday, February 1, 1942   Up at 8:30. Have to fall in with the battery for mess on my day off, if I want to eat, that is. The British majors are always there, and they would never stand for off-duty cooks to come in any time they wanted to and eat.

Tried shaving with Kasper's straightedge razor. Nelson, our barber honed it for me and gave me some good pointers on how to use it.

Bob Vaughn and I walked to church this morning. The church is about a mile down the main road and up the hill almost to the top. Houses are along the whole way. One group of houses are all exactly the same. The church was built in the 1500's out of bluestone. The windows had been filled in with stone because of some war long ago, and never taken out again.

A different church service than I'm used to. Not many there. I couldn't understand much of what he said. After the service several ladies invited us to their homes for tea, but we were told not to accept invitations, as the Irish don't have enough for themselves.

Monday, February 2, 1942   Up at 4:30. Helped fry bacon and sausage. Passow and I made cake. The English sergeant gave me what he said was a valued recipe for cake, as follows: 1 lb. margarine, 1 ½ lb. flour, 2 oz. baking power, ½ pint milk essence to taste, 4 eggs, ½ lb. fruit, and 1 lb. sugar. Cream the margarine and sugar, add the flour and baking powder, add fruit and milk. Bake.

Raining all day. Washed a few clothes tonight.

I look forward to the evenings after mess when I am off-duty. Bob Engleson leads the bunch in conversation. George Pittlekow talks a lot too, but he's not at all interesting. Tony Sermguard and George Sefscik are the intellectuals of the group, and they're real interesting as well.

Tuesday, February 3, 1942   Slept until 9:30. Washed more clothes. Have to do it by hand in the latrine, which is pretty crude. A crew of several men comes every day with a nearly new Ford tractor to clean the toilets.

Shaved with the straightedge and slept more this p.m. Felt tough all day; sore, stiff, and a headache. Tonight some of us walked to the Barn and saw a free show. It was Deana Durban in *It's a Date*. The Barn is not far from the kitchen.

I don't get breakfast when I sleep late on my day off, but working in the kitchen compensates for that nicely. Then, I'm not a big eater to start with and already am filled up after the starvation diet we went through on the *Strathaird*.

Wednesday, February 4, 1942   Up at 5:00. Fried sausage, made coffee for breakfast and dinner. Don Sternke and I made cocoa for supper. Shifts will be changed again, so I work tomorrow too. Walked over to B Battery to talk to Ted Nelson, the barber.

Thursday, February 5, 1942   Headquarters, Able, and Baker Batteries will have our own kitchen mess now, with Charlie and Service Batteries serving their own.

I worked with Don Sternke and got to know him a little better. He's from B Battery and comes from a large farm at Marshall, Minnesota. He has been a cook longer than I. He's nice to talk to, about my age and size.

The others on with me are Jack McCalaster, Wilber Anderson, another Anderson from A Battery, with Jack or "Bud" Bailey from A Battery as Mess Sergeant. All are good cooks and good natured fellows.

Each man got a 30 caliber rifle today packed in cosmolene that he has to clean. What a mess. Cosmolene is only a glorified name for axle grease. They're packed that way when shipped to keep them from rusting in the salt air.

Friday, February 6, 1942   Slept until 10:00. Cleaned on the rifle until 1:00 and got most of the grease off it. Showered and shaved, write in my diary.

Saturday, February 7, 1942   On again. Had headache mostly all day. Got paid. I got 3 p-8 shillings, or about $13.00. Most of the fellows are gone tonight. Washed clothes. Cleaned up. Nice day.

Sunday, February 8, 1942   Had to work again. It's taking some adjustments with the other kitchen, but I don't mind. I don't have to eat with the battery, and I never tire walking back and forth from the kitchen. The people, their horses, how they dress and talk, and just being here is like an Irish storybook to me. I want to enjoy it as long as I can.

Misting. Wrote to Wing Chinn. Started another poem for Patsy. Shaved and cleaned up tonight. Bought some ink. My original diary was written in pencil and is faded now.

Monday, February 9, 1942   Worked again. Fairly nice. McKoy and Bennet aren't back yet from Saturday night. Both of them like to talk about their drinking, so they probably had too many Irish spirits. Don wakes me up in the mornings. Through at 7:00 tonight. Stage show tonight, but I didn't go. I'd rather stay here where it's nice and quiet.

Tuesday, February 10, 1942   Slept until 10:00. Showered, changed clothes. Wrote to Pat. Raining again. Went to an Army show. Don and I worked in the kitchen tonight. I made hot cake batter. Through at 9:30. Quite cold.

Wednesday, February 11, 1942   Up at 5:00 again. Got better acquainted with Andy. He was hauling wood around Grand Rapids, Minnesota, and had Ford trucks.

Our crew had it easy. Nothing much to do. Cloudy, sort of cool. Tired. Hard to realize that I haven't heard from home in a month.

Thursday, February 12, 1942   Went to the free stage show tonight. Had a lunch at the kitchen. Off today. Slept until 9:00. Washed, shaved, slept some more this p.m.

Andy, Don and I walked up the mountain. Was steeper and harder to climb than I thought. Saw an old, abandoned rock house. Had a rutabaga, saw a sick ram and 2 farm houses. One fellow was plowing. We saw a small road and went that way on the way down.

Friday, February 13, 1942   Up at 4:00. Bacon, liver, porridge for breakfast. The other meals were easy.

Cool as usual. An Irish fellow finished cleaning my rifle for 5 shillings. Bought 2 bars of Lifebuoy soap for 6 pence.

It's starting to get lonesome around here now. The newness has worn off. Haven't had a chance to go anywhere. No mail.

Saturday, February 14, 1942   Was in the kitchen awhile when our kitchen was inspected. I slept until 9:00.

Don, Andy and I got a pass. Went to Limavady. The bus goes right by the gate. Sent a telegram home. Cost 10 shillings and 7 pence.

At 5:00 we went to Coleraine. Cost 1-6 round trip on the bus, about 26 cents. Bought some souvenirs, handkerchiefs. We went to the town hall dance.

Was a nice change. People don't hesitate to talk to you. I got acquainted with a Noreen, and we talked a lot.

On one of our first trips to Limavady, the conductor on the bus couldn't make the change for what the soldier gave him, so he said, "Oh, that's quite all right, Laddie; just pay me next time." Well, I don't suppose that next time ever came, as I never heard of any good offers from the Irish conductor again.

We were well liked, generally speaking, though, and our troubles were few. It was really nice to get to town. The stores and shops were usually smaller, and there was something quaint about them. It was probably mostly the Irish people themselves who seemed so different. They must have felt the same way about us. Anyway, they seemed to be just waiting for you to talk to them.

Sunday, February 15, 1942   Slept until about 10:00. Most of the fellows from our battery went to Belfast. Don and I weren't needed in the kitchen, so Sgt. Bailey gave us the day off. We always work extra time when needed, so it's appreciated.

Don and I went to church. A beautiful day. Nice walking. Talked to one old fellow after church, and he said it was built about 1790.

Wrote to Pat and home.

Monday, February 16, 1942   Passow wasn't feeling good, so I took his place today. Don't like to work on that shift as well as my regular one, but wanted to help out Passow. There's a lot of loud, loose talk, without any serious sharing of experiences like on our shift.

Tuesday, February 17, 1942   Up at 4:30. Usual work. Gen. Hartle came through the kitchen, also the US Ambassador to Britain.

To bed early. Cool tonight.

When these fellows go through our kitchen here, l can't help but compare this to the nice kitchen we left at Camp Claiborne. It's a good thing they weren't inspecting this one, only looking, and probably enjoying themselves.

Wednesday, February 18, 1942   Slept until 10:00. Washed clothes, showered, shaved. Went to the kitchen to eat. Read a little. Changed clothes.

There was supposed to be a show at the Barn, but the entertainers didn't come. We sat around and some fellows played the piano.

Thursday, February 19, 1942   Up at 5:00. The night fireman went to sleep, and we had a hard time to get the stoves hot so we could make breakfast.

Felt disgusted with myself all day. Nothing much to do, but standing around mostly. Showered, shaved, changed clothes all around.

It wasn't really Bob McKoy's fault that the fires were almost out that morning, though he was the one who did all the cussing about it.

The British always had a fat kettle on the back of the stove, where every drop of excess fat was supposed to be collected and used for explosives. When the stoves weren't burning too hot, McKoy would pour a dipper full of fat on the coal fire, and it would really go. But the British sergeant caught him doing it one time. It really caused a rumpus and temporarily stopped his Yankee ingenuity.

Friday, February 20, 1942   Up at 8:00. Rolled my pack, laid around until noon. We of the kitchen crew left at 2:00, came about 40 miles south. Beautiful drive, mountainous country.

Are quartered in Darrowstown in an old courthouse. The mess hall is below. The cook house is close.

Harry took us to a dance tonight. Others left early, but Kraft and I stayed longer. It was within walking distance.

It was really nice to get out and see a part of Ireland. It is just a quaint, pretty country, and as interesting as we have heard it would be. There are very few cars on the road. All the cars that they have are inside of their barns or garages for the duration, for lack of petrol. All traffic drives on the left side of the road.

Harry was British, not a part of the kitchen crew, but sort of a jack-of-all-trades who was needed sometimes to help coordinate between the British and ourselves. He was a likable guy who knew quite a bit about Ireland.

We had been on a service practice in the Sperrin Mountains. Sometimes the anti-tank battalion would practice at Hogspark Point at Lough Neagh. Some of these groups would go out on day trips. They'd use C rations, so part of the battalion would not have to go.

Saturday, February 21, 1942   I slept until noon, as it was 3:00 this morning when Kraft and I got back here from the dance. I walked around a lot today.

Tonight Harry took us to another dance at Maraha. We just sat around. I only danced once. Went because Harry offered to take us and it was a chance to see something new. Were back at 12:00.

Sunday, February 22, 1942   Kraft and I were on all day. Up at 4:00. Worked steady, but not hard. Fried a steak for an English soldier. Got through at 11:00.

More English moved up here. Talked with one tonight.

Sgt. Noble is the Mess Sergeant from B Battery and is in charge here. He went out tonight, so Kraft and I stayed in to watch things. Someone has to be around the kitchen all the time as it really can't be completely shut down.

Monday, February 23, 1942   Slept until 11:30. Cold. Bought some postcards. Slept again. Got a haircut, 9 pence. Saw the girl I danced with at the Post Office where she works.

After mess, Harry took us to Maraha again. Saw *Fighting 69th*. We got acquainted with Margaret and Jean. All the girls like to talk to us and look at our pictures.

Back to camp at 12:30. Kraft and I go together, and we get along good.

Tuesday, February 24, 1942   Up at 3:30. Kraft and I on duty. After mess we cleaned the kitchen. Rolled our packs and left Draperstown at 10:00. Snow on the way back.

Showered, changed clothes, shaved. Colder. Made pancake batter tonight, and puttered around in the kitchen until almost 11:00.

My letter to home of February 25 had the word "Draperstown" cut out of it by the censor.

Wednesday, February 25, 1942   Up at 4:30. Hot cakes and bacon. Jack was sick today. Cold.

Fried Harry a kidney for his supper. I made it German-style like my mother makes it: sweet and sour, and Harry liked it. There would never be enough kidney for the whole battalion, but this one was still in a quarter of beef.

To bed at 10:00.

Thursday, February 26, 1942   Inspection while we were still in bed. Stropped my razor, shaved, cleaned my things again. Fire is out. Cold in the hut.

Friday, February 27, 1942   Slept late. Washed all of my equipment this afternoon.

Saturday, February 28, 1942   Worked this forenoon. Had inspection. Had to carry our bunks outside and display equipment.

Off this p.m. Got paid, about 6 pounds. George Sefscik and I left for Coleraine at 8:00. Went to the dance. Didn't stay long. Noreen or the girl George knew weren't there. Came back to camp at 11:30.

Sunday, March 1, 1942   Up at 5.00. Worked until noon.

This p.m. Andy and I walked to church. Came back and caught a ride to Limavady in a '40 Chevrolet. We ate in a NAAFI. Went to an organ recital. Came back on the bus. We had a good time.

Monday, March 2, 1942   Up at 5:00. Worked until noon. Washed clothes this p.m.

Baked a cake for our hut tonight that everybody liked and appreciated.

Tuesday, March 3, 1942   Off this p.m. Tried to bake a bigger cake in a flat pan for the battery tonight, but the sides burned and the center was raw.

Wednesday, March 4, 1942   Up at 5:00. Usual work. Mail came in today. I got 24 letters and postcards from Mom, Ray, Rod, Patsy,

Norma and Grandma. Answered Ray's. Got an issue of candy. Spent an enjoyable 3 hours reading all the mail.

Thursday, March 5,1942   Slept until 11:00. Had a religious discussion last night. Started to answer the letters. Worked this p.m. Have a cold. Feel tough.

Friday, March 6, 1942   Worked this a.m. Slept this p.m. Have a bad cold. There seems to be a lot of fog and dampness. We are real close to the Atlantic.

Saturday, March 7, 1942   Slept until 9:00. Straightened out my things for inspection. Andy and I worked alone this p.m. Don is sick and quartered. Went to see him tonight. I feel good, but have a sore throat and hoarse voice. Wrote home and to Patsy.

Sunday, March 8, 1942   Andy and I on all alone today. Got along fine, but there's not much time for visiting when there's only 2 cooks on. It's usually easier on Sundays, though: cold cuts and salad and coffee.

Sgt. Noble took over tonight, so both Andy and I got passes and went to Limavady.

Got talking to 2 boys who reminded me of Rod. Came back on the 11:00 bus. Had a good time, and went to the kitchen after and had a lunch. Feel real good today.

Monday, March 9, 1942   Off this a.m. On this p.m. Don still on quarters. Made pancake batter tonight.

Tuesday, March 10, 1942   Hot cakes for breakfast. Washed clothes, cleaned up. Passow and I went to Limavady. Didn't do much. It's just a break to go to an Irish town to walk and look around. The movie houses all have bicycle racks by the front doors, and they are full of them too. Very few civilian cars to be seen.

Pa's birthday. He's 60.

Wednesday, March 11,1942   Don came back to work today for this p.m. shift. Show tonight. I went, but didn't enjoy it. *Dancing on a Dime.*

Thursday, March 12, 1942   Up at 5:00. French toast for breakfast. Slept this p.m. Will write a letter or two yet.

Friday, March 13, 1942   Off this p.m. Up at 9:00. Washed clothes. Read my Bible as I usually do. Learned the 23rd Psalm and a part of a hymn.

Jack and Andy were on again this p.m. Don and I went to a church program tonight about 2 miles north of here. Lots of civilians there, but we were very welcome. Had more fun than I ever have here before. Played games. Got acquainted with Eva Auld. The 3 of us walked home together.

One of the games they played was "Sweet Maria."

Saturday, March 14, 1942   Up at 5:00. Didn't sleep well. Easy meal: braised beef again. They had inspection, but I didn't have to lay out anything.

Slept 2 hours this p.m. Don came over tonight, and we talked a long time.

Sunday, March 15, 1942   Up at 8:30. Showered and shaved. George Sefscik, Don and I went to church. Eva was there. She sings in the choir. Walked home with her. Came back to camp at 2:00.

Don and I left again. Eva's cousin came along with Don. Walked. We had a good time talking a lot with them. Came back to camp at 11:00. Tired out from walking.

Monday, March 16, 1942   Up at 5:00. Tired and stiff from yester-day. Battery gun crews were out firing today. We took grub out at noon. Off this p.m. Wrote to Ray.

Tuesday, March 17, 1942   Up at 7:30. Prepared to go firing. Went about 6 miles north. We all had to go through this. Fired my 45 rounds. Scored 148 out of a possible 225. Average.

Worked this p.m. My ears ring, and shoulder is sore.

American rations came in tonight. More than a 6X6 load. Don and I unpacked and cut pork chops. Was thankful to see all our own grub again.

Will remember tonight. Got in grub that we hadn't seen in two months. The British food wasn't too bad really, for what that country has gone through, also the Irish.

We got apples, other fruit, canned vegetables, lots of pork, bacon, dried eggs, etc., and a lot of my favorite: canned milk. It's just going to be more enjoyable cooking it up.

Saint Patrick's Day as well. All the Irish were looking for 4-leaf clovers — I mean shamrocks. All ages of people were looking.

I walked down to the small Post Office north of camp to mail some letters. One of my letters going home had a genuine Irish shamrock in it.

Wednesday, March 18, 1942   Don and I worked until 3 a.m. Slept until 9:00. Fried chops all morning.

Off this p.m. Washed clothes. Went to see Don. Saw *Gambling on the High Seas.* Wrote to Ray and home.

Thursday, March 19, 1942   Up at 8:30. Washed clothes. On this p.m. We got in 40 chickens. I cleaned them and cut them up. Was up all night.

Don came in at 11:30 and helped. He had seen Eva. We tried to bake cookies, but they didn't turn out.

Friday, March 20, 1942   Through at 6:20 a.m. Awful tired. Slept until 8:30. Cleaned my gun. Checked out candy and things. Slept until 3:00.

Went to see Don. Sgt. Meagher talked to me.

Fairly nice today. Sgt. Vaughn and I baked apple pie tonight. I left at 12:00 midnight and went to bed.

Saturday, March 21, 1942   Up at 7:30. Cleaned up my corner for inspection.

On this afternoon. Tonight Don and I baked cherry pies. Made 57 of them.

We just had to thicken the cherries, as they were canned and already pitted; but the pies were all individual 9-inchers with top and bottom crust all made by hand with flour and lard. The hardest part was for the night fireman to keep the stoves hot enough to bake the pies. English coal and/or the stoves many times would fail us. We were feeding about 225 men, so by cutting each pie into 5 pieces, we came out OK and would have a few extra pieces left over for samples. Our pies were in big demand as a special treat, since the boys had no chance to go out just any time they wanted to and get something for that "sweet tooth."

Sunday, March 22, 1942   Don and I were up most the night. Finished the pies at 3:30, but stayed in the kitchen and made the hot cakes as well. We stayed in the kitchen until 8:00. Showered, shaved, got ready for church. Larry came with me. Came back at two. We had gone to Eva's home.

We slept until 5:00, ate a little, then went to see Don.

I nearly went to sleep in church.

Monday, March 23, 1942   Slept quite late. On this p.m. Tonight, Don and I baked apple pies, 54 of them. Went with a fellow tonight to look at a bicycle up the road.

I really wanted that bicycle. I had never had one in my whole life. I thought it would really be nice to have one to ride around on, on my days off. I didn't have the 5 pounds that the Irishman wanted for it, though, as I was sending most of my money home. Smitty, another steady K. P., said he would lend me the money.

Tuesday, March 24, 1942   Finished the pies at 4 a.m.

Slept until 10:00, then Don and I went to the farmer's place and bought the bicycle for 5 pounds.

Got a pass. Rode by Eva's. She couldn't go riding, so we just talked at her place.

Sent for $30.00 by cable to home. Met Beaver, who also has a bike, and we rode to Limavady. Went out riding again tonight. Tired, but had a lot of fun.

The bike cost $20.00 and was in good shape. Beaver was an officers' orderly, so he got time off during the day when he finished his work.

Eva and my mother had been writing to one another, so we always had something to talk about. Her family were poor people. They were really nice to talk to and they treated me nice. Her dad worked for someone nearby his own farm, but I can't remember where.

Having a bicycle was really fun. It broke that dull monotonous feeling that settled over me at times, and I spent many happy hours riding along the beach with Eva, and around her parents' place. Then later, Don got a bike too, and we went out riding together.

Wednesday, March 25. 1942   Up at 9:00. Washed, shaved. Rode to Don's and around camp. On this p.m.

Show tonight, *Hit Parade of Hill.*

Don and I wouldn't bake every night; the rations wouldn't stand that much baking.

We were still busy most of the time while in the kitchen, but it was easier than cooking in the field. We were still feeding over 225 men.

Beef and mutton came in by the quarter or half, as did lamb. They called everything "lamb," but if it was over 85 pounds, it was definitely mutton. If you couldn't tell by the weight, you could tell by the stronger smell of the meat.

I cut many quarters and halves by myself. Usually we just cut it into pieces for stew or braised beef. It would have been nice to have steaks or pork chops once in awhile, but we could never get enough of one kind of a cut from a half of beef for everyone.

Besides cutting the meat, we also had to slice the bread, open a lot of cans, and make salads. We had to peel and cook potatoes too, and try to get it done on time and serve it to everyone.

The officers' orderlies would come and take enough food for the officers before we would start serving the men. Either a cook or the Mess Sergeant would put the food in the officer's plate, though, so there was no chance for unfairness.

Some of the officers would buy steaks on their own and bring them in for us to fry them. This was my first experience at frying steaks, or of even knowing that a beef had any special cuts to its carcass. When my parents butchered at home, the meat was just cut into chunks.

Thursday, March 26, 1942   Up at 4:30. On until noon. Washed clothes this p.m. Showered, shaved, drew rations of candy, etc.

Rode around again tonight. Came back at 9:30. Had 2 letters from Ray and another from Mother. Also, church papers and Duluth papers. Got 5 shillings from Arnt for use of my bike.

Friday, March 27, 1942   Up about 9:00. Don came over. Andy, Don and I played ball this a.m. Went to see Kraft in C Battery. Washed Passow's jacket for him. On this p.m.

I let Cloyce Rose use my bike, and he broke off the pedal. Don and I are making sweet potato pie tonight.

Some fellows just didn't want to wash their own clothes, or their outer ones, at least. Some people used to come and get laundry and do it for the men, but you had to pay for it yourself. The Army did not.

There were no white cooks' uniforms for the cooks either, not even white aprons.

Sweet potato pie never went over too well, but it was a little better than no pie at all.

Saturday, March 28, 1942   Jack, Andrew and I made breakfast and dinner. Fried eggs and pork chops. Slept a little this p.m. Read. Don came over, and we talked as usual about home. He showed me a letter from his girl.

Sunday, March 29, 1942   Slept until 9:00. Read in the Duluth Herald, and religious paper from Andy. Went to outside church services this noon at Charlie Battery. Short service, but real good. Slept this p.m. Wrote to Roger.

    Went to Eva's tonight. She had been to see her aunt in another town. I didn't stay long. Don came over, and we went back to his hut together.

Monday, March 30, 1942   On this forenoon. Real good dinner. Made fruit salad with whipped cream.

    Off this p.m. Slept a little. Washed a suit of denims, showered, changed clothes, shaved, read. Don came over. Wrote to Ray, Mother and Grandma.

    Got my bike fixed tonight by the power plant operator. He only charged me 3 shillings, but somehow, Rose got out of paying it. Rode to Eva's tonight. Gave her stamps and post cards. She had just got another letter from my mother.

    Got a registered letter from home tonight with two $5.00 bills in it. Good to see United States money again.

Tuesday, March 31, 1942   Washed a few clothes. Went to see Don. Read.

    On this p.m. Got paid 16/5. My bill was 1 pound 8 shillings.

    Got 8 letters from home tonight. One from Ray, and a package of papers. Cool. Raining. Had my blankets out to air. Rations were issued tonight. I was one of the first, and got a flashlight.

Wednesday, April 1. 1942   Air raid alarm this a.m. at 1:00. To bed at 2:00 and up again at 4:00.

    Hot cakes for breakfast, ham for dinner. Have a headache. Boys let me sleep for awhile. Slept again this p.m. Feel a little better now tonight.

Thursday, April 2, 1942   Up at 8:00. Went to see Don.

    Got a pass. Went to Ballerena. Sent Patsy an Easter cable, and one home. Cost about 21 d. Rode around quite a lot.

On this p.m.

Don and I went to the games night at church. Gordon and Ecklund rode along. Don bought a bike for 4 pounds. Back about 12:00.

Friday, April 3, 1942   Up at 5:00. Fried eggs for breakfast. Chicken *a la king* for dinner. Cleaned my equipment. Slept a little tonight. Don and I went to church at the little school, just down the road. Good sermon. We rode nearly to Limavady. Enjoy it a lot. Nice today.

Saturday, April 4, 1942   Our time goes ahead an hour today. Fixed my things for inspection. Stayed around the kitchen until it was over. Went to work at 1:00. Easy afternoon. Cold meal, corn and cocoa.

Don and I made cherry pies tonight. Made 54. Got through about 1 a.m.

I can't imagine us making that many pies in that amount of time. It's a full evening now for me to make only several of them. But we had a good system going, and it was teamwork

Harvey Swanson and Blackie Arnold always stopped to talk. They were with the medics, and someone of them was always on duty, as they had some kind of a system where they had the whole camp covered with their presence all the time. Harvey or Blackie never held us back in our work, but were nice to talk to, and we would give them a whole pie once in a while for their group.

Sunday, April 5, 1942   Easter today. Boiled eggs for breakfast. Roast veal for dinner.

We rode a lot today. Don and I got through at 1:30, slept until 8:00, showered, changed clothes. Went to church with Don. They had Holy Communion.

This p.m. Don and I rode to Limavady. Rained a little. Rode back with some girls. Bikes are common transportation. The girls' names were Ruby Scull and Eileen Boydl.

Monday, April 6, 1942   Up at 8:30. All day off. Mail again last night. Washed clothes.

On duty this p.m. Easy supper.

Had a flat tire tonight. Raining. Andy is making cake. Wrote some letters.

Tuesday, April 7, 1942   On this forenoon. Andy baked cake last night. He will be on the other shift now, taking Pittlekow's place, who landed in the guardhouse.

Slept, washed clothes, shaved. This Mr. Craig fixed the flat on my bike. Raining on and off. Our time has gone ahead one hour.

Mr. Craig was one of the head workers of the estate. He was always around, and a nice fellow to know. I don't think he charged me for fixing the bike tire.

Pittlekow had gotten picked up in one of the towns for drunkenness, unruly conduct, and AWOL.

Wednesday, April 8, 1942 Slept until 10:00. Showered, read a little. On this p.m.

Had another flat on the bike. Borrowed Gordon's bike. Don and I went to see Eileen and Agnes. Rode with them on their bikes. Gave Eileen gum, candy, apple, and an orange. She hasn't had them for a long time. Came back at 11:00.

Thursday, April 9, 1942 Up at 4:30. French toast and sausage for breakfast. Fried pork chops for dinner.

Slept until 5:00 this p.m. Washed clothes. Straightened up my things. It doesn't get dark until 10:00 now. Cloudy, rainy. Mail came in tonight about 11 p.m. I got a lot of mail and a prayer book from church.

Friday, April 10, 1942 Reread all my mail. Ray is still in the woods.

Passow and I go out in the field on Sunday. Loaded the water bead ons and kitchen stoves this p.m. Easy supper.

I'm in charge of this maneuver, for the cooking, that is. I wish Passow was. He is a better cook than I, but he is so jumpy and change-able in his actions and decisions that he can't be trusted with it.

Got my bike back tonight. Gave Mr. Craig 2 pence for fixing the flat.

We hauled all the water in 5-gallon bead ons. I always wondered why these cans were called by that name. Long after the war, Don Sternke told me they had first been designed and used by the German Army. They were designed flat for ease in carrying and loading without wasting space. They had three hollow handles which allowed for expansion when they got warm, and to let in air as the cans were being drained. The United States copied the German idea, and all our trucks had racks to carry them, both gas bead ons and water bead ons.

Saturday, April 11, 1942   Up at 4:20. Hot cakes for breakfast. Had to get or borrow some things for the field tomorrow. Inspection in the kitchen this morning.

This p.m. I showered, changed clothes, got a few things ready. At 3:00 drew rations for the field, also gas and coal from S-4, and condiments from our mess hall. Took until 5:00 before I was all through.

Packed more of my things. Am a tired boy tonight. Pete is the kitchen truck driver tomorrow.

CHAPTER 9

Field exercises. Officers' mess. Leaving Ballerena Camp

.

Sunday April 12, 1942   Up at 5:00. Ready to roll at 6:00. We ate a little before leaving. These extra trips sure are tough on the cooks by breaking up the crews, and they still need just as many cooks back in camp.

I ride in the cab of the 6X6. Passow, Jewell and Ceedsma in back. We got to Glendry about 10:00. 80 miles.

Took our equipment in a room of a hall in town. A lady is staying in a room next door. Took dinner out to the fellows on the firing range on noon.

Steak for supper. Bob and I slept on the floor by the kitchen stoves. Started to walk to Crumlin, but turned back. Too tired after today.

I remember this trip very well. We got along good with our work.

This town was pretty small. Arrangements were always made ahead of time as to where the men would stay, and where we would be cooking. We didn't have much room, but Bob Passow got along real well with the lady who lived next door.

Monday, April 13, 1942   Up at 5:30. Hot cakes for breakfast. We have to take the grub upstairs to the men's quarters. Good dinner. Bought postcards, cuff links and socks for 6 pence.

Started to load at 1:30. I have the cab again. Back at 6:00. Took several wrong roads. Went through Crumlin, Antrim, Ballavina and Coleraine.

Tuesday, April 14, 1942   Up at 8:30. Vaughn and I unloaded the kitchen truck. Shaved, showered, changed clothes, packed over my things again.

We have to wear white undershirt, clean denims and shined shoes while on duty now. They are expecting high-ranking officials to visit. Worked this p.m. Got some new clothes last night. Jack and I started on pies at 8:30.

Wednesday, April 15,1942   We made 55 apple pies last night. Got through after 3:00. Slept until 11:00.

Read, slept some more this afternoon. Then Don and I went bike riding along the Atlantic coast. We do this as often as we can. The beach must not be very popular, as it's chilly. Lots of small rocks and no houses nearby, but we like it a lot.

My letters home didn't give much news. I told them of the bike and riding along the coast. It had a shift with several speeds, I said, and gave me something to do on my time off.

Thursday, April 16, 1942   Up at 8:30. Washed a lot of clothes. Showered, shaved.

On this p.m. Ham, corn and carrots.

Don, Andy and I made pies. Got through about 8:00.

Beautiful day. Warm like a perfect summer day back home. It's after 9:00 now and the sun is still up. The mountains can be seen nicely. A leg show tonight in the barn, but I didn't go.

Friday, April 17, 1942   On this forenoon. Easy meal.

Off this p.m. Got a pass. Went to Limavady on the bike. Took in dry cleaning, films, bought a razor strap, 5-6, a razor, 13-6, and a razor hone, 3-6.

Came back about 5:00. Met Agnes; we talked awhile. Saw a little boy who had a broken leg from a runaway horse. They were waiting for help, and there was nothing I could do. Went riding again tonight. Bought some souvenirs and cards. Beautiful day.

Agnes works someplace and was on her way home. She lives practically in town. I'm not sure about her friend Eileen who we have met before. It's about 2 ½ miles to Limavady, about the same distance to Proctor at home. Only this is all level and pretty Irish countryside to go through, and it would be hard to ride that distance without talking to more than just a few people.

Saturday, April 18, 1942   Up at 5:30. Had to clean the hut. Off duty, but went and helped in the kitchen. I ground meat.

Gen. Marshall and Harry Hopkins were here for the parade with a lot of other big shots.

Took a few pictures. On this p.m. Easy meal.

Sgt. Meagher was shooting dice all p.m. with the boys in our hut.

Tokyo was bombed on April 18 by American bombers in a surprise attack. The Japanese people had been told that this would be an impossibility.

Gen. James Doolittle had 16 modified B-25 Mitchell bombers crowded on the aircraft carrier *Hornet*. Each plane had 1,000 gallons of gas, two 500-lb. bombs and 1,000 pounds of incendiaries. There were crews of 5 men, survival equipment and small ammunition.

They had 467 feet of flight deck in front of them. Two white lines were painted on the deck; one for the nose wheel, the other for the left wheel. If the pilots kept those wheels on those lines, they would miss the superstructure of the ship by 6 feet. All planes made it off. Landings were 16 different stories.

Bombs were dropped on Tokyo, Yokohama, Kobe, and Nagoya, center of Japan's plane industry. The attack was so unbelievable to the Japanese that at first they ignored the air raid sirens.

It was announced that "The Imperial Family is safe," and it was claimed that 9 of the bombers were shot down.

Sunday, April 19, 1942   Up at 4:00. Don and I made hot cake batter. Others came in later. Mack and Don went out in the field.

I cut up a quarter of beef and took off the rest of the forenoon. Only 9 messes for dinner. Roast beef with gravy, mashed potatoes and corn.

29 messes for supper. Helped Passow make sandwiches. Cold all day. Have the sniffles.

It was easy to make an old-fashioned meal for the men when there were only a few; otherwise there would never have been enough roast beef to go around, and it would have had to been made into stew.

Monday, April 20, 1942   Slept until 10:00. Feel tough with my cold. Was going to work, but the other cooks said to lay down, so I did.

The Master Sergeant from officers' mess wanted to see me tonight. I am to take Rose's place cooking at the officers' mess starting tomorrow.

Still feel tough. Letters from home, cookies and handkerchiefs, and a bar of soap from Aunt Rose.

I didn't want to refuse the different cooking job. It would be a change, and I liked to work with Hurley Soderlind. I had talked to Hurley, and he liked the job there. He didn't care much about working with Rose, though, and really wanted me to take the job with him.

Tuesday, April 21, 1942   Didn't sleep well last night. Up at 8:00. Feel better. Had my blankets out all day.

Nothing much to do. Went riding. Came back early. Got a lot of candy from Mom tonight.

Hurley and I start at officers' mess tomorrow.

Wednesday, April 22, 1942   Up at 5:00. Hurley had the batter made already. Had hot cakes, duck eggs, prunes and coffee. Feed about 30 to 33 officers. Orderlies serve the meals. Two K.P.s do the dirty work. Hurley and I see nothing of the officers. Macaroni and cheese for dinner. Nice and quiet there compared to the battery kitchen.

Washed clothes, feel better, wrote letters. What a snap. We still will have quite a bit time off.

Thursday, April 23, 1942   Woke up at 9:00. Washed clothes, showered. Beans for supper with fried spuds. Russ is the Mess Sergeant, but is on pass.

Friday, April 24, 1942   Up at 5:00. French toast and pork sausage for breakfast. A fellow's horse was caught in the stall this morning.

I made chocolate cake for dinner. Turned out good. Slept a little this p.m.

Washed clothes, showered, changed clothes, shaved. Sent off some letters. Fairly nice.

The officers sent word that "The cake was very good." They were a good bunch to cook for. I can't remember if Hurley and I would take turns, or if we just worked according as to how much there was on the menu. Anyway, it was a snap. I really didn't mind being in the kitchen most of the time, and Hurley felt the same.

The fellow's horse wasn't really caught, but had stepped over his rope. One fellow just couldn't release him by himself. Most of the horses here were big, close to 2,000 pounds.

There were several potato fields planted in the area, but they weren't very big fields.

They'd been planted the past month. One horse did the field work (instead of a team, as at home), and the potatoes were planted by hand. It seemed there were enough gardens to meet the people's needs.

Saturday, April 25, 1942   Up at 8:00. Put my things away for inspection. Hung around both kitchens until 12:00.

Went to work this p.m. Made doughnuts and oatmeal cookies. Nice today. Got through about 7:30 tonight.

Sunday, April 26, 1942   On all day. Hot cakes for breakfast. Steak for dinner, ham for supper. Made 9 cherry pies. Hurley left early. I stayed until 9:00. Don came and kept me company. Fairly nice today. Will shower, shave and change clothes yet. Had my blankets out all day.

Monday, April 27, 1942   Made butterscotch pie this afternoon. Went back later and read. Fairly nice.

Tuesday, April 28, 1942   Fried potatoes for breakfast. I made a cake for dinner. Had stew.

Got a pass, then went to Limavady with Hurley on bikes. Got my pictures. Rode back myself at 8:00. Had a headache.

Wednesday, April 29, 1942   Slept until 10:00. Looked things over. Wrote in here.

Worked this p.m. Hurley made hot rolls. Turned out swell. I made pork chops, gravy and mashed potatoes. Col. Sylvester came back to the kitchen and said it was the best meal the officers had since they had been in Ireland.

Stayed there until almost 11:00. Read, wrote letters. Got 4 letters tonight and cookies from Hank and Evelyn.

I was getting into the habit of going to the kitchen to read and write when I knew no one was there. There was more light than in the hut, and it was very quiet.

Thursday, April 30, 1942   Up at 5:00. Hot cakes for breakfast with bacon. Easy dinner. Stew and spinach. Showered and shaved this p.m. Sent a letter to Otto, home, and to Hank and Evelyn.

Jack and Don are baking cherry pies tonight. Watched them awhile in their kitchen, then went to the hut and went to bed.

I was glad I'd taken the different cook's job. I never had made doughnuts before, and learned it here, and I'd learned how to make other new things as well. I sort of missed working with Don, but we still were together a lot on our days off.

Friday, May 1, 1942   Up at 9:00. Cleaned up. Nelson cut my hair. Read for awhile.
   Went on duty this p.m. Potatoes, salad, beets and bread pudding. My turn to leave early tonight. Cleaned up. Went riding by the river on the bike. Came back to the kitchen. Read. Dick and I were to the estate today. Took pictures, and some tonight.

This was Dickson, who we called Dick. He was a steady K.P. with the officers' mess as long as I was with them.
   I had taken quite a few pictures of the garden, pool and greenhouses with Andy and Hurley, but don't remember just when it was.

Saturday, May 2, 1942
Hot cakes for breakfast. Chocolate pie, spaghetti and meat balls for dinner. Capt. Surdyck came back to the kitchen and complimented us on the meal.
   Washed clothes this p.m. Showered. Changed. Hurley, Andy and I went to the big garden again and took pictures. Beautiful place.

Went by the river again tonight for awhile. Slept a bit. We saw Lady Hagen in the garden. We talked a bit, but didn't want to be too bold. She did say we could come again, though.
   Changed clothes. Got some pictures back.

Sunday, May 3, 1942
Got a pass. Went to church. Saw Eva. Good service.
   Andy and I went to Downhill. Took pictures. Went to the beach. Tasted of the Atlantic for the 1st time.

Came back to Limavady and saw a show. Came back. Rode by Agnes' place. Saw her, and we talked a lot. Back at camp at 10:00. Tired.

Monday, May 4, 1942 Up at 5:00. Hot cakes for breakfast. Got new straw for our ticks today. Slept this p.m. Did a little cleaning. Have a headache. Dreamed of Eagle and Bird. This p.m. I got my bike fixed, with new fenders and brakes.

Tuesday, May 5, 1942 Up at 9:00. Washed. Saddle-soaped my shoes, read.
Baked beans, potatoes, salad, eggnog, coffee. Very good supper. Went riding again by the river. Met the colonel. Read some on the beach. Washed up. Nice day. I'm sure not lonesome anymore.

I can't remember if the colonel greeted me or not. He probably did. If I was riding the bike, it wouldn't have been required that I salute him, though.

Wednesday, May 6, 1942 Hot cakes again. Stew for dinner.
Got a pass. Rode to Limavady. Got my dry cleaning. Came back in 1 ½ hours.
Tonight I saw *Double Date*. Came back about 11:00.
Drew canteen supplies. Traded off my beer and cigarettes.

Thursday, May 7, 1942 Slept until 11:00. Washed up, read a little.
On this p.m. Big supper. Hurley left early. Jake helped me serve.
Don came. We went together to the show. Seen *Silver on the Sage*. Pretty good. Enjoyed seeing the horses in it.

Friday, May 8, 1942 Up at 5:30. Hot cakes again. Easy dinner. Had the fellows clean up the pantries and storeroom.
Washed clothes this p.m. Cleaned up. Don went to see Margaret and send a cable for me for Mothers' Day. Cool. A letter from home. Started a savings account here in camp.

Saturday, May 9, 1942 Up at 8:00. Fixed my things for inspection. Took Don's bike and went by the river. Looked at my pictures. Finished learning *Abide With Me*. Went on duty at 7:00. Washed a few clothes. Changed, showered, shaved.

Sunday, May 10, 1942 Hurley and I got up at 5:00. Listened to the radio in the officers' lounge. Hot cakes for breakfast. Steak for dinner. We got mail again. Got letters from home, Ray and Patsy, and 12 candy bars from Carl and Myrtle. Don and I went to church. Ham for supper. To bed at 11:00.

Most of the church services that we attended now were right at camp. It was easier, and we hadn't seen Eva for awhile anyway.

Monday, May 11, 1942   Overslept until 6:00. French toast and creamed beef for breakfast. Braised beef for dinner. Now am on the same days that Don is. Slept this p.m.
Got paid 7 pounds and 10 shillings. Put 2 pounds in Soldier's Bank. Showered, shaved. Changed clothes. Raining nearly all day.

Tuesday, May 12, 1942   Washed clothes this morning. Had to have our gas masks on for an hour this morning. Read a little. Hurley and I on this p.m.
Stage show tonight, but didn't like it. Got tired and disgusted. Cold and windy today.

Wednesday, May 13, 1942   Up at 5:00. Scrambled eggs for breakfast. Gen. Hartle was here for dinner. Also several English generals. Had hamburger steak, mashed potatoes, macaroni salad, corn fritters, gravy and apple pie.
Changed clothes, showered, shaved. Went riding. Wrote to Eileen, Patsy and Ray. Cool.
2nd Battalion of the 151st, or what now is the 175th, is now in Ireland too. Also the 185th. 65 new replacements came into our camp. They just arrived in Ireland from the United States.

Thursday, May 14, 1942   I slept until 8:30. Read a lot in *Time* magazine.
On this p.m. Made cake. Hurley made cherry pie.
Was supposed to be a show, but the motor went dead. To bed fairly early. Cool. 3 letters tonight from home and Patsy.

Friday, May 15, 1942   Up at 5:00. French toast for breakfast. Macaroni for dinner. Slept a little this p.m. Showered, shaved, changed clothes.
5 letters: 2 from Mother, 1 from Ray and 2 from Patsy with 3 handkerchiefs with "Bud" embroidered on them.

Saturday, May 16, 1942   Up at 8:00. Straightened my things for

inspection. Went on the bike by the river and in a new place in a little wooded spot.

On this p.m. Hurley was to Antrim and didn't come back until 4:00. All cooks, steady K.P.s and firemen moved together.

In hut 34. I still have my usual place in the corner. Nice. Will go to a show yet.

Sunday, May 17, 1942   Up at 6:00. Fried eggs for breakfast. Steak and french fries for dinner.

Off this p.m. Went to church. Started raining. Got back just in time. Slept a little. Got a haircut from Nelson.

Monday, May 18, 1942   Don't remember much, except tonight I started to pack my things for tomorrow.

Tuesday, May 19, 1942   On this morning. We all left for the field this p.m. I rode in the cab with Hawk.

Got to Deragnoyd house about 4:00. We cooks have a room to ourselves. It has a fireplace. Sleep on the concrete floor.

Went to Draperstown. Didn't stay. Nice day. The place is an old hunting lodge. Went for a walk in the woods by myself.

Wednesday, May 20, 1942   Nick and I went to Draperstown. Came back at 11:30. Bought some souvenirs. Nick is the K.P. on with me this afternoon.

A family lives here. They have a 4-year-old little girl, Phyllis, who reminds me a lot of Arlene. Took her picture.

Fairly good kitchen. Up late. Went for my solitary walk again.

Thursday, May 21, 1942   Up at 1:00. Served coffee at 1:30. They went out on a problem. I stayed up. Got the fire going. Breakfast ready at 6:00. Took it out to the field. Back at 9:00. Ham for dinner.

Gave Phyllis an apple and orange. Saw Anderson from 2nd Battalion [175th F.A. Bn]. Off this p.m. Shaved, cleaned up, slept a little. Went for a longer walk. To bed at 10:00.

Friday, May 22, 1942   McKoy came in with B Battery at 11:00. Others came in at 6:00 tonight. Hurley and I on this p.m. Hamburger.

Through at 8:00. Took until 10:00 to get my things in order again. Got canteen supplies. Fairly nice. Sold my bicycle to Hurley. It will be a bother when we move. Got 4 p for it.

Saturday, May 23, 1942   On until noon. No inspection today. Off this p.m. Slept some, washed a few clothes. Nothing much to do.

Sunday, May 24, 1942   Tried to write letters, but got disgusted. Can't think of anything to write about. Off all day. Slept until 8:00. Shaved. Went to church here in camp. Chaplain Walker gave the sermon. Very good.

Changed back to my green twills. Makes me feel more at home. Felt lonesome this p.m. Had a vivid imagination of home, something I can seldom do anymore.

Don came over for a little while. Washed more things.

Monday, May 25, 1942   Hurley and I on this morning. Macaroni and cheese. I made cookies.

Got a 24-hour pass and planned on going up the mountain and staying overnight, but it was raining this afternoon.

I borrowed a bicycle, and Hurley and I went to Limavady. Hurley's girlfriend, Nancy, went with us on the bus to Londonderry. We met her sister, Dorothy. Took some pictures. We talked over some ice cream. Showed them some pictures I had. Dorothy had a 25 pound note. I gave them each a penny, nickel and dime.

Both Nancy and Dorothy were pharmacists. Nancy worked in Limavady, and Dorothy in Armagh. Dorothy had a boyfriend in the British Army. She was older than me, but we soldiers were all lonesome and enjoyed talking. The 25 pound note really impressed me, like seeing a $1000 bill today -- or even more, like seeing several months' pay all at once in one bill. (The only way I see that nowadays is when the tax bill comes.)

Tuesday, May 26, 1942   Washed some clothes this forenoon. Hurley and I on this p.m., though fairly easy.

Wednesday, May 27, 1942   On again this forenoon. Raining on and off. Hurley and I went to Limavady. Got a ride in with an Army truck. Went to several places until 7:30, then we took Nancy and Dorothy to a show, *Toppers Return*. A fantastic story, but enjoyed the picture. Left the girls at 11:30 and walked to camp. Two letters today.

Dorothy had been staying with Nancy a few days on vacation. They came from Belfast. Both were well educated with high standards, and real nice to talk to. Hurley kept in contact with Nancy the whole time we were in Ireland.

Irish girls like these two would never think of inviting boyfriends to their apartment after a movie. Dorothy and I weren't excited about each other, but I was a good fill-in once in a while, and she gave me a good reason to go to town instead of just to walk around.

Thursday, May 28, 1942 Slept until 9:30. Read a little. Hurley and I were on together this p.m. We hurried through tonight.

We each got a pass, I borrowed Don's bike, and we went to Limavady again. We went for a walk with Nancy and Dorothy, across the river and in a park. Dorothy took pictures. She can get film. We just talked a lot, and I had a *Time* magazine that we discussed. We walked back again. To camp at midnight.

Friday, May 29, 1942 Didn't get to sleep until 1:30. Hurley overslept. I really had to move on the double to get breakfast out on time. We had fried potatoes and french toast. Braised beef for dinner.

Off this p.m. Had to load all our things and the kitchen truck and leave the kitchen and our hut real clean. Hurley wanted me to go with him to Limavady again, but lucky for me, no passes were given out. I'm just getting tired out.

CHAPTER 10

Tynan Abbey. The Millikens. Officers' mess.

Saturday, May 30, 1942   Up at 4:00. A hurried breakfast, then loading, cleaning. Get in line with your detail, when all present and accounted for, we leave at 6:30. A long convoy, the first I can remember since Camp Claiborne. I couldn't estimate the number of trucks. The tarp was rolled back on the kitchen truck, but it was cold and windy. I enjoyed the scenery a lot.

We got here at noon at Tynan Abbey. A huge place with a huge

castle where the officers are going to stay, and Hurley and I are still going to be their cooks.

It's a surprise for me, but we are not too far south of Armagh, where Dorothy is a pharmacist in her uncle's drug store. I'm not really excited, but find myself feeling sorry for Hurley. He will be much farther away from Nancy, who is still in Limavady.

We are not far south of Tynan — a little town, but the passenger train goes through every day.

Hurley and I are quartered in the servants' quarters of the castle. It's on the west side and has the kitchen, a real long hallway to the

officers' quarters, with many small rooms on the way on both sides of the hall. Then, on the other side of the kitchen are the servants' quarters. Hurley and I have one room together, our choice. Russ, the Mess Sergeant, has a room of his own, and the officers' orderlies have their own rooms as well.

The battery is a quarter mile away in a large field, but they have enough buildings for cooking and eating. This castle must have been quite a place at one time. It's practically vacant now, except for a few "Lords" in the castle itself.

Sunday, May 31, 1942   Hurley and I on all day. Up at 5:30. Slept good. Was really tired. The kitchen is large and spacious. The stoves are the usual big coal stoves that need a lot of coaxing to get enough heat out of for a meal. We had a lot of unpacking, cleaning and extra work to get out three meals, but all went pretty good.

We had a lot of unpacking and cleaning to do in our room tonight too after work. We have a room almost like we were at home. Table, chairs and cots.

We do have to go outside to go to the kitchen. It's real quiet being away from the battery. Nice day.

Monday, June 1, 1942   Slept until 9:30. Hurley and I showered and changed clothes. Have to walk to the battery to shower.

On this p.m. Easy supper. Found an old cupboard of books, mostly religious. Am reading one. Rainy and cool. Through at 7:00.

It doesn't get dark here in Northern Ireland until about midnight. It seems odd and hard to get used to. It still gets light about the same time in the morning as at home, though.

Tuesday, June 2, 1942   Up at 4:30. Hot cakes for breakfast. Sort of in the blues today.

Through at 1:00. Got paid 9 p 13 d. Got a package of papers

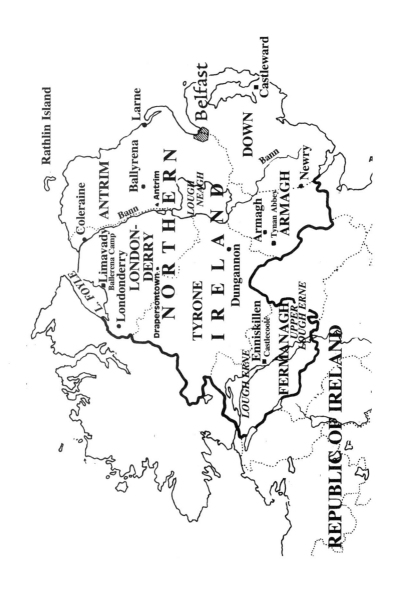

from home tonight. Slept a little, wrote to home, Pat and Myrtle. Hurley's birthday. He is 23.

Wednesday, June 3, 1942 Up at 5:00. Creamed beef, boiled eggs and french toast for breakfast. Macaroni for dinner. Showered after. Hurley and I got passes. Went to Armagh. Took the train back. Bought some souvenirs, had my watch fixed. Came back at 10:00. Saw the drug store where Dorothy works, but she is still in Limavady. A letter from Mom sent May 21st.

We have to walk to the Tynan Railroad Station, only a mile or less, then take the train to Armagh, which doesn't cost much and is not too far.

Thursday, June 4, 1942 Slept until 9:00. Read the *Duluth Herald* from home. Easy supper. Nice and quiet. Our K.P. had been with us, but he found an empty room and moved out. Hurley and I are alone in here now.

Friday, June 5, 1942 Slept until 9:00. Turned in 2 pairs of shoes to be fixed. Changed my board cot for a canvas one. Had to carry it back to the battery, though.

Hot this p.m. On duty. Fried potatoes, chili for supper. To bed about 10:00. Hurley got pictures from Nancy and some of Dorothy.

We have one of the caretakers of the estate who stops in, and I always give him a cup of coffee and something to go with it — he appreciates it so much. His name is George Milliken, and he wants to take me to his house some night to meet his family. I'm more than willing to go.

Saturday, June 6, 1942 Up at 4:30. French toast for breakfast. Hash, spaghetti for dinner.

Off this p.m. Slept until 2:30, washed, showered. Slept a little more. Looked over all my personal things. Cool all day. It never gets hot here. Any temperature over 80 is hardly known.

Sunday, June 7, 1942 Up at 9:00. Off all day. Read this p.m. I went for a walk back of the castle. Nice paths and beautiful trees. Had a nice, quiet, meditating Sunday. No church service that I knew of.

Came back at 4:00. Wrote more letters. Washed clothes. Chilly all day. Hurley and I juggle our work around and arrange it so we can enjoy a full day off instead of changing at noon time.

CHAPTER 10

Monday, June 8, 1942   Worked this forenoon. Got a pass. Showered, cleaned up. Went to Armagh on the 3:15 train. Saw Dorothy in the drug store — I was interested to see her as she looked when she was working.

Got a room in a boarding house. Went and saw *Hell's Angels*. Came back to the room at 11:00. Have a Professor Clyde in another bed in my room, a likable fellow.

Tuesday, June 9, 1942   Up at 6:15. The first time I've slept between sheets since in Camp Claiborne on New Year's Eve.

Breakfast at 8:00, consisting of eggs, fried bread, dark bread and tea. Caught the train back to camp at 9:45.

Package of papers and letters from home, Ray, George and Ethel Nash. Tonight there was a package from Ray: 12 rolls of film, 6 packs of cigarettes.

Worked this p.m.

Wednesday, June 10, 1942   Hurley and I on this forenoon. Easy dinner. Slept a little. This p.m. I drew my rations. Wrote to Ray and Mom. Read, slept a little more. Read. Walked to the battery. Burned my arm this morning cooking, and cut my thumb on a can. Cloudy, cool.

Thursday, June 11, 1942   Slept until 8:30. Read a little. George Milliken, the caretaker, came over and talked awhile. Went with him in the garden. Packed over some of my things.

Worked this p.m. Tried to bake a cake in the Dutch oven, but it didn't turn out. Disgusting.

Four letters tonight.

George Milliken, along with two other men, took care of all the bushes, hedges, and the greenhouses, which were mostly planted to tomatoes.

George stopped a lot, as it was on his way home from work. He lived to the south of the castle across some fields and a pond, in a house that was owned by and part of the estate.

Friday, June 12, 1942   Up at 4:30. Hot cakes for breakfast. Salmon for dinner. Slept from 1:00 to 6:00. Letter from Eileen. More letters tonight, and a package of papers.

Saturday, June 13, 1942   Up at 8:00. Read most of the forenoon. Made a cake, but not quite good enough to serve the officers. Washed out a few clothes. Showered tonight, shaved and cleaned up. Russ went to town.

Sunday, June 14, 1942   Up at 5:30. The fireman woke me at 4:30 instead, so I just laid awake for an hour. Hot cakes for breakfast. Off this p.m. Read a little. Steak for dinner. Cooked luncheon meat for supper with cherry pie. Through at 7:30.

Wrote to Arlene, Patsy, and a friend of Hurley's, Helen Grees. Washed before I write this, and to bed at about 10:00. Hurley took some pictures of me.

One of my least exciting birthdays, but so far, the most historic. Thought of how I've spent others. Cool all day. Rained a little.

Monday, June 15, 1942   Off this a.m. Didn't do much. On this p.m. Felt down in the blues again. Helped Russ make raised doughnuts.

Heard President Roosevelt tonight at 11:15. Letters from home again.

Tuesday, June 16, 1942   On until 1:00 today. Officers came in late. Hurley left at 11:30, probably to go to Limavady to see Nancy. Actually, I was on all day.

Box of candy from home. Papers and letters as well.

Wednesday, June 17, 1942   Changed things around in the kitchen after breakfast. Built a fire in the fireplace, cleaned things up. Hurley came back about noon. Butterscotch pie for supper with whipped cream. Tired tonight. Drew my rations.

Thursday, June 18, 1942   On this forenoon. Russ came back at noon. Showered, shaved.

Niemi and I went for a walk in back of here, went quite a ways. Came back at 4:30. Tired, but enjoyed the walk. Washed clothes tonight.

We had been warned not to go beyond a certain road south of the Abbey, as that it was close to the Irish Free State line, and we could get picked up for it and arrested and possibly shot for spying.

I had asked George Milliken just where the line was. He told me that if we walked a mile we'd be able to see the road that was the state line. Then he told me just how to get to where there was a large culvert, and that if we went through that, we'd be in the Irish Free State.

We just had to say we had been in the Irish Free State, so we crossed through the culvert and had a most uncomfortable feeling — so we went right back to Ulster again. As far as I know, Niemi and I were the only two Yanks who went into the Free State during the time we were in Ireland.

Friday, June 19, 1942 Slept until 8:00. George took me around the garden. A beautiful place. Something like the one at Ballerena. Wrote to Ray.

On this p.m. Potato salad, fruit, hash for supper. Washed my field jacket and gas mask cover. Beautiful day.

Saturday, June 20, 1942 On this forenoon. Fairly easy dinner. Went for a walk this afternoon along the river and canal. Slept a little in the woods.

Hurley went to Larne. Sang with the boys in the kitchen, with Voges at the yuke.

Sunday, June 21, 1942
Up at 8:30. Washed, shaved. George showed me more around the estate. Walked around a lot. He showed me the greenhouses. They are not factory made, but mostly with greenhouse sash. He showed me the canal where they used to haul freight on the water, pulled by horses. It's pretty well grown up now, though.

George took me to his place. Met his wife and daughter, Margaret or Peggy. She is 16, real small, and seems nice. She works at a doctor's home in Tynan. They made tea for me and a little something to eat.

Came back to camp about 4:00. Wrote to George and Ethel Nash. Slept a little, read some. Beautiful day. Don came over and we went for a walk together.

Peggy gave me a bouquet of flowers: roses and sweet williams. I have them on our table.

Monday, June 22, 1942 On this a.m. Slept a little. Went to Milliken's.

Mowed a patch of grass for George. Enjoyed being there. Peggy has a sister who is at home now too, Olive. She is married to an English soldier, Mack, who is away somewhere. They have a little girl, Maureen. One year old. Had tea again and talked a lot.

Back to camp at 12:00. I can go to the Milliken's without getting a pass, as it's just within walking distance behind the castle.

Tuesday, June 23, 1942   Off this p.m. Didn't do much of anything. Worked this p.m. Drew my rations tonight. Played catch.

Wednesday, June 24, 1942   On this p.m. Easy dinner. Showered this p.m. Cleaned up. Went to Milliken's again. Finished mowing the grass. Olive showed me some of her pictures. Peggy was working tonight.

Came back here at 12:00. Beautiful walk coming back here. It's so quiet and peaceful, especially going around the pond. Then it's still about as light as day.

Thursday, June 25, 1942   Slept until 8:00. Busied myself around the room.

On the p.m. Russ made dough. Hurley and I fried the doughnuts tonight. It took until 10:00.

Went for a walk again. Nice today.

Friday, June 26, 1942   Up at 4:30. Pork chops for dinner. Slept this p.m. for awhile. Was going to shower, but water was turned off.

Left at 3:00. Went to the Milliken's. Was going to file a saw, but the file was too big and dull. Russ came later. Olive and Margaret gave me some flowers. Took some pictures, and came back at 12:00.

Saturday, June 27, 1942   Up at 7:45. Cleaned up things. Wrote a few letters. Busied myself until noon. On this p.m. Showered tonight. Went for a walk. Letters from home.

Sunday, June 28, 1942   On all day. Felt good — until tonight when I got a bawling out from Col. Sylvester through no fault of my own. Beautiful day. Write at 9:00.

The colonel had sent down for a sandwich, as he had a lady friend there visiting. Hurley was there, and had just put some peanut butter on dry bread and sent it back to him.

The colonel came down, mad as heck, and bawled me out just because

I was a cook and happened to be in the kitchen when he came. He threatened to take me out of the kitchen and put me into the infantry carrying a rifle on my shoulder for the duration. I had no chance to say anything.

Lt. Jenks, who was kind of a go-between for the officers' mess and the officers, came in later and apologized for him. Old Sly was drunk.

Hurley thought it was funny.

Monday, June 29, 1942   Felt blue all day, even though everything went all right.

Mail from Grandma, Pat and Mom. Two more snapshots of Roger and Arlene.

Tuesday, June 30, 1942   On this morning. Off this p.m. Got paid. Packed all my things. Got paid 8 pounds, 13 shillings.

Wednesday, July 1 - July 10, 1942   These were the infamous maneuvers, also referred to as the "Ten-day Scheme," or the "Atlantic Maneuvers," involving the British 61st and 59th Divisions, and our 1st Armored Division.

We were in and around Antrim in the County of Antrim.

It rained most of the time, it was bone-chilling cold, and whatever contact we had with the Limeys (English) was always agitating. There was some mixing up of rations, which didn't help matters either.

I am only putting this short account of the maneuvers in here to keep my diary complete, not for any enjoyment of reading or remembering it.

Friday, July 10, 1942   We finally got back last night, unloaded, and were ready to work after a fair night's rest. Showered this p.m. Changed clothes. Cleaned my gun. Got pictures back. Went to the Milliken's, back at midnight.

Going without a shower for 10 days isn't the longest I've ever been without being able to take a decent shower, but the whole maneuvers had been disagreeable even without that inconvenience.

I was glad to get back to see the Milliken's. We always had so much to talk about. I really liked when Mrs. Milliken put the tea on and either started the turf fire or stoked it up. The smell of the fire was so much like the peat-fire smell in the woods at Payne.

It was easy to see that they thought of America as a place to dream of living, especially Peggy, who was so wide-eyed when I'd mention some things of home. I wasn't trying to brag up America, only to tell them about it.

Saturday, July 11, 1942   Up at 8:00. Cleaned up the room. Worked this p.m. Wrote a few letters. To bed early.

Sunday, July 12, 1942   On all day. Warm this forenoon. Made most of the supper myself. Went for a walk tonight.
Humphreys caught a large fish. I fried it for him.

This may have been the Sunday afternoon we suddenly heard a shot ring out from the officers' quarters. We kept on cooking, but we were wondering what was going on.
Lt. Jenks soon came over and told us everything was under control.
It seems the officers were enjoying their Sunday by drinking around a table in an ornate room with gilt carvings on the ceiling. Someone suggested it would be almost like a safari to shoot out one of the lions' heads carved on the ceiling, and Capt. Grant had taken out his .45, and shot him "right between the eyes."

Monday, July 13, 1944   Slept until 10:30. Cleaned up things. On this afternoon again.
Got letters from Al and Germaine, and Jack. Answered them.

Tuesday, July 14, 1942   On this forenoon.
Got a pass and was going to go to Armagh, but then couldn't figure out what I wanted to go there for. So I went for a walk, took a short nap and, after I ate, went to Milliken's. Peggy was working, but the others are always glad to see me. I try to always bring them a bit from the kitchen or from one of my packages from home, which they appreciate so much. Hurley went to Belfast.

Wednesday, July 15, 1942   On all day by myself, but no problems at all. Don't remember more.

Thursday, July 16, 1942   Hurley came back last night. We were both on today, or at least in the kitchen together most the time. Hurley and I never have as much to talk about as Don and I do because of our shared farm experiences, but we are very good friends.
Hurley came with me to Milliken's tonight. He'd never been there before. Margaret was there, though she had to work. We stayed as long as I would have, had I gone alone.

Friday, July 17, 1942   On this p.m. Easy supper. Went to see Don tonight. He walked back with me. To bed at 10:00.

Saturday, July 18, 1942   On until noon. Hard dinner. Steak for all, but I like the experience of frying it.
  Slept some. Packed over my things. Showered, cleaned up. Saw a show at the battery, *Ride On, Cowboys*. Sort of a fantastic picture with no sense to it.
  Got letters from Ray, kids, and Mom. Niemi and I took some pictures, mostly of myself.

Sunday, July 19, 1942   Off all day again. We must have lost our pastor. Haven't even heard of churches here.
  Went to Milliken's this afternoon for a short time. Margaret had gone to Tynan, as she didn't know I was coming. Got a few papers. Went to see Don. Took a few pictures.

Monday, July 20, 1942   Up at 3:30. Got very little sleep, as Hurley came in at 1:00. Rolled my bedroll and carried all my things to the battery. Helped with breakfast. Loaded up and left at 7:30. Came close here to a camp at Draperstown at 11:00. Cooks have a hut of their own. Through at 2:00. Slept until 5:00.
  Went for a little walk. Cool, cloudy.
  Talked with Cajune — my old outfit from Claiborne is a mile down the road, but I couldn't leave to see any of them. Went past George Olson's convoy as it was stopped.

Life magazine of the above date showed many pictures of what the English called "The Horrors," the bombed out buildings of London. It's hard to describe without pictures, but the following statistics help: The bombers from Germany had damaged 2,500,000 homes and destroyed 130,000; killed 43,000 men, women and children, and left about 450,000 homeless. The property loss to private persons was estimated to have been about $1,000,000,000.

Tuesday, July 21, 1942   Up at 9:30. Read in *Time*. On this p.m. with Vaughn. Drew rations. To bed at midnight. Saw a show, but it wasn't much good.

Wednesday, July 22, 1942   Up at 4:30. Just made it in time for breakfast. Hamburger for dinner.

Raining nearly all day. Had a terrific headache. Slept until 6:00. This p.m. Vaughn, Sweet, Passow and I went to the 175th F.A. Saw lots of the old fellows. Went to a small town. Got a haircut. Back at 10:00. A letter from home.

Thursday, July 23, 1942   Slept until 10:00. Things went well this afternoon. Worked until 9:00, then went to the show *Dangerously We Live*. Fairly good. Card from Mary Jean today.

Friday, July 24, 1942   Up at 4:30. Fried corn mush, sausage for breakfast. Ham for dinner. Things went well this forenoon. Shaved, cleaned myself up, and my things.
    Didn't do much this p.m. Slept a little. Went to see Don. We came back and went to the show *Courtesy for Andy Hardy*.

Saturday, July 25, 1942   Went for a walk. Took a few pictures. On this p.m. Through at 10:00. Went to see the same show again for something to do. Raining.

Sunday, July 26, 1942   Up at 4:30. Things went smoothly this forenoon. Steak for dinner this p.m. I washed clothes at the creek. Took a bath. Water is cold.
    Changed clothes, put my leggings on and went for a long walk up the mountain road. No traffic, no pedestrians, quiet and peaceful. Took pictures. A little cloudy this p.m., but the sun shone once in awhile. Warm. Enjoyed myself for a change.
    Church in camp tonight. Wrote to Ray.
    Still in the field in Draperstown. The gun crews are doing a lot of firing. We are still close to the 175th, and we wonder always how long it will be before we actually get going after the Krauts.

Monday, July 27, 1942   Slept until 9:30. Started supper early. Had blueberry cobbler. Went to a show. Not much good. Vaughn and I made sandwiches for the whole battery. Took until 11:00. Don came over for awhile. Really nice this p.m. The show was disgusting.
    Bob Meagher is Mess Sergeant now, and Bob Vaughn is first cook. Meagher is not liked too well anywhere he's at. He can be very nice, but it's usually on the surface, and you never know when he will turn on you.

Tuesday, July 28, 1942   Up at 4:00. French toast for breakfast. I made coffee and soup. Bob Vaughn and I took it out with Sgt. Meagher in the field. Came back at 4:00. Raining. Went to see Don awhile. Turned nice later.

Wednesday, July 29, 1942   Slept until 9:30. Went for a walk. Sat by a hay stack and read my Bible and a magazine. Came back at 12:15. On this afternoon. Easy supper. Took a bath in the creek, washed some clothes. Saw *Woman Has Plans*, a pretty good show, but a little corny. Made sandwiches for 90 men. Nice afternoon.

Thursday, July 30, 1942   Up at 3:00. Took mess out in the field. Came back at 9:30. Fed for 3 hours.
  Made dinner. Took it out to the gun crews. Came in at 2:00 with a bad headache. Slept until 6:00.
  Took a bath in the creek. Washed my field jacket. Went for a walk. Back at 10:00. Read my Bible.
  Mom's birthday. Thought of her.

Friday, July 31, 1942   Up at 8:15. Straightened up my things. Cleaned up, dressed in O.D.'s and leggings. Went to the hay stacks to sit, smell the hay, read and relax.
  On this p.m. I took supper out to the boys.
  I wish we would soon leave here, but it won't be until next week.

Saturday, August 1, 1942   Up at 3:00. Started breakfast. Took it out at 4:00. Hot cakes. Back here at 6:30. Hash for dinner.
  Got paid 6 pounds; will keep it as an emergency. Left at 4:00. Went to Mahara; stayed there until 8:00. Took the train to Port Rush. Went around with Vaughn and Passow. Took a taxi home. One shilling each.

Sunday, August 2, 1942   Slept until 11:00. Took supper out to the men. Two shows, but didn't enjoy either one. No mention of any church services that I heard of.

Monday, August 3, 1942   Up at 3:00. Hot cakes. Took breakfast to the field. Sandwiches for dinner. Took them out too. Washed some clothes, changed, cleaned up my things. Got letters from Ethel and Patsy.
  Raining. Went for a walk. Saw a young fellow. Talked to him, and he brought me to his place. He's going to write to my brother Rod.

The Irish were always hungry for an American contact, and Robert Hamilton, the boy I'd met, did correspond with my brother Roger, and wrote to me during the war as well.

Life magazine had another comment on the coming Western Front, calling us the "shock troops" of Gen. Eisenhower. They said we'd been in Northern Ireland for 5 months (excuse me, but I've got to go on the pity pot and say the 151st F.A. Battalion had been in Northern Ireland a wee bit more than **6** months already), reaching our peak by "relentless training and maneuvering."

Life described a show that had been put on for the British King and Queen, where tanks smashed past, followed by fast-moving guns. The 28 ton tanks fired their 75's while still charging across the gorse (a short, prickly, Irish shrub), and hit their target, while motorized troops "screamed past at amazing speed."

Life called our "golden hour of preparation" "impressive fun," but pointed out that the "ultimate job of these troops is to knife the German Army in the back, if possible while they are still busy with the Russian Army."

Tuesday, August 4, 1942   Slept late. On this p.m. Started packing the kitchen supplies. Don came over for awhile. Made sandwiches until 12:00.

Wednesday, August 5, 1942   Up at 3:00. Hot cakes. Finally got loaded. Pulled out for camp at 11:30. Got back about 2:00.

Got straightened out, and my things down here at 2:30. Slept an hour. Making supper is a pleasure again, and nice to get back with Hurley. We went to Milliken's after supper. Olive and I went to Tynan to where Peggy works. Was nice to see her again, but didn't stay long because she actually was working. Olive had a lot to say about the whole family on the way back. She called herself the "wayward" one of the family, and expects to have to move to England after the war with her husband Mack.

It turned out that the whole family moved to England after the war, and as far as I know, Olive and Mack made a go of it. The little girl, Maureen, was loved so much by all.

Thursday, August 6, 1942   Slept until 9:30, cleaned up a little. Went on duty this p.m. Long, tiresome afternoon. Got 2 letters, from Mom and Ray. Felt low and depressed all day.

By this date the United States had already lost — by death, by wounds, by capture or unknown fate, Missing in Action, or Prisoners of War — the Army: 1,381 killed, 2,167 wounded, and 28,452 missing — the Navy: 342

killed, 1,051 wounded, 7,672 missing and 1,022 prisoners.

Friday, August 7, 1942   Up at 4:30. Hot cakes for breakfast. Long, drawn-out forenoon. Slept until 2:30. Showered, cleaned up.

Went for a long walk along the canal, enjoyed it. Ate a good supper. Wrote 5 letters. Will wash clothes yet and get a fresh carrot and a rutabaga this p.m.

The canal was the one that George had showed me in June, the day I met Peggy. George told me he could still remember when horses were used to walk along the bank of the canal pulling rafts or barges loaded with almost anything from one place to another. George was about 50 years old when I was in Ireland. The canal's sides were still pretty straight and uncluttered.

I can't remember whose garden I got the carrot or rutabaga out of, but I never missed a chance to help myself.

Saturday, August 8, 1942   Washed clothes until midnight. Had coffee. Read until 1 a.m.

Up at 8:30. Washed, cleaned up the room. Also my things. Went for another walk or run. Back at 11:45.

On this p.m. Cleaned up after supper. Read a little. Sgt. Meagher came over, mostly to visit, not to complain.

Sunday, August 9, 1942   Our time went back an hour at midnight. Hot cakes for breakfast. Pie for dinner, with roast pork. Slept 3 hours this p.m. Cold supper, practically.

Letter from Eileen this morning. Answered it. Showered tonight, then went for a long walk. Back at 11:30. Dark.

Monday, August 10, 1942   Off this morning. On this afternoon. Letter from home tonight. Also a carton of cigarettes from Uncle Art. They were sent Air Mail. $1.49 for stamps, quite a bit more than the cigarettes cost.

Felt blue tonight. Then I walked to the Milliken's. Only George and Mrs. there, but I felt a lot better when I got back.

Tuesday, August 11, 1942   On this a.m.

Got ready at 10:00. Scheely and I went to Belfast. Bought some postcards, a pipe for Ray. Came back to Armagh. Back to camp at 12:00.

I didn't really care to go to Belfast, but Scheely was a nice guy and hadn't been there before. This was a chance to go with him and show him some of the places so he could find his way back again. He was a steady K.P. of ours.

Wednesday, August 12, 1942   Up at 8:00. Cleaned up my things. Read.
On this p.m.
Washed clothes tonight. Pressed my pants. Through at 11:30. Nice, raining a little.

Thursday, August 13, 1942   Woke up at 1:00. Couldn't get back to sleep, so I got up and shaved, washed and made 3 double-layer chocolate cakes.
I started breakfast for Hurley. Woke him at 6:00. He left at 10:00. I put out dinner. Roast ham.
Lt. Jenks complimented me personally on the cakes.
Showered, went for a walk. It was raining tonight, or I would have gone to Milliken's.

Friday, August 14, 1942   Slept until 10:30. Washed up. The Army's Sunday today. Got a package from Ray with films, Scotch Tape and 2 notebooks.
On this p.m. Hurley came back at 2:00. He was to Limavady.
Showered tonight and shaved.

I can't remember why sometimes I called a day an "Army's Sunday."

Saturday, August 15, 1942   On this forenoon. Off this p.m. Went to see Don. Turned in my Coke bottles, got some new socks.
Saw *All Through the Night*, a mystery. Got 3 rolls of film, 2 letters from Ray, one from Mom, 2 from Patsy.

Sunday, August 16, 1942   Slept until 9:00. Wrote some letters. Don came over this p.m., and we went for a walk over the estate. Came back at 4:00, read a little.
Hurley and I went to Milliken's. Had a good time talking, and we have lots of fun when both Olive and Peggy are there. George and Mrs. both mostly listen and enjoy having us there.
The house is very small. Just the kitchen and one bedroom downstairs and two small bedrooms upstairs. Then the other half of the house is the same thing, with another family from the estate living there.
The highlight of the visit is when Mrs. Milliken stokes up the

"turf" fire and puts the teapot on. The smell of that brings me back to Payne and the woods in a hurry.

It gets completely dark now about 10:00, which seems more like home.

Sunday was top on my list for the most lonesome day of the week. I don't think we ever had the chaplain here at Tynan Abbey, and I don't think the Millikens went to church (though Peggy was always singing or humming gospel tunes). I don't remember any churches in the Tynan area.

Monday, August 17, 1942   Up at 4:30. We have lights on all the time now. Takes the bore out of making breakfast. Ham for dinner.

Off this p.m. Read, showered, changed clothes.

Tuesday, August 18, 1942   Slept late. Went for a walk.

On this p.m. Cinnamon rolls tonight. They turned out swell. Took until after midnight.

Wednesday, August 19, 1942   To bed at 1:00. Up at 4:30. Fried bread. Sausage for dinner.

Slept until 3:00. This p.m. Bob Vaughn came to visit me until 5:00. Washed clothes, went to Milliken's myself. It gets dark now at 9:30, and it was well after that when I got back.

Some bad news is that we are going to be moving in a few days to Enniskillen to the northeast. Both Peggy and I don't like the idea at all. The 175th is moving out, probably to combat in Africa, so things are beginning to change.

Peggy said I could come to visit her from Enniskillen, that the train connections are good.

CHAPTER 11

Leaving Tynan. Enniskillen. Road march.

Thursday, August 20, 1942   Up at 8:00. The news of moving is now an order. So, get ready.

I packed and am ready to go. Wrote to Mary Jean and Arlene. Cool.

Hurley went to Belfast yesterday, then today had to go on advanced detail to the new camp. Don came down to help me with the supper and breakfast.

Friday, August 21, 1942   Slept until 9:00. Packed all my things. Came and helped the battery with dinner.

Got a jeep this afternoon and hauled my things down here to the battery.

Then Bob Vaughn and I went to Armagh with Olive and Peggy. Went to a show. Came back on the 8:30 train. Had tea at Milliken's. Peggy gave me a framed photograph of herself. She must have had it taken to give to me.

This was the end of my job of officers' mess at Tynan Abbey. It was past history now, but it was really nice while it lasted. It was really a valuable lesson for me to learn how two fellows could get along as good as Hurley and I did. I think our Mess Sergeants had it easier than any in the US Army ever did. We shared the work, and either of us was always glad to do a part of the work for the next shift, or even to help through the entire shift, if necessary. The Mess Sergeants were usually around if we ever did need them, though.

Bob and I went to Milliken's, then the four of us walked to Tynan and took the train to Armagh. (Peggy had hardly ever been there, though it wasn't that far.) I don't remember much about the show, but I do remember that it was on the train where Peggy gave me the photograph of herself.

We walked back again from the depot afterwards, and Mrs. Milliken made tea and crumpets. Bob and I had a real good time, and we talked about it many years later.

Walking through the Abbey's back fields and grounds was always illegal. I'd done it all the time, but I never was stopped. Even George walked around and came in the front way, as he was supposed to do …but most of the time he used a bicycle.

My stay at Tynan Abbey in the County of Armagh has always lived in my memory as one of the happiest experiences in my life. I have always wanted to go back to Northern Ireland to visit. During the winter of 1999 - 2000, I began making preparations for a trip there in the fall of 2000. I sent for travel information from the town of Armagh and inquired about the Abbey.

I was informed to my shock that the owners of the estate, Sir Norman Stronge and his son had been shot in 1981, and the "house," as the writer of the travel letter called it, had been virtually burned to the ground. Sir Norman, as he was called while I was at Tynan Abbey, had been a senior member of the Ulster Unionist Party and was also the last Speaker in the old Stormont Parliament, which was dissolved in the early 1970's. I was told that some wartime shelters are still in evidence on the estate, while the farmyard and stables stand derelict. The house was completely demolished about 1998.

"The Troubles" of Northern Ireland were not much in evidence during World War II, as it seemed that even those Irish who hated their arrogant masters, hated the Germans who were indiscriminately bombing Belfast and

other cities in Northern Ireland even more. The Millikens and I never discussed the subject, though Peggy made it clear to me that she didn't like having to curtsey to Sir Norman when she saw him, and that she resented his coming to inspect the house that they lived in. George was a very easy-going person, and nothing seemed to bother him. Perhaps the Millikens themselves were resented by those who didn't have even as good a situation as they did. I don't know. I didn't have any dealings with Sir Norman myself, though I recall seeing him walking his estate, and later got a short letter from him in answer to an inquiry I sent about the Millikens during the 1960's. His stationery had a coat of arms on it, calling him "Her Majesty's Deputy, Sir Norman Stronge."

Saturday, August 22, 1942   We didn't get back here until 11:30. Slept next to Bob Vaughn. Up at 9:30. Showered, cleaned up my things.

On this p.m. with Vaughn. Battery came in late. Through at 9:00. All cooks are back with their own batteries now, and we move in a few days.

Sunday, August 23, 1942   On until noon. Beautiful day. Showered, cleaned up. Will write letters. Left about 4:00. Went walking. Read my Bible. Looked at pictures.

Went to the Milliken's again. Peggy came at nine, but had to go back again to stay at the doctor's. Olive and I walked there with her, and I walked back with Olive. She is the hardest of the family to understand. She always feels free to tell me all her troubles and problems.

Monday, August 24, 1942   Didn't do much this forenoon. Washed and cleaned up.

On this p.m. Quite easy. Got off at 7:00 tonight. Changed clothes. Took my time walking. Got to Milliken's almost 9:00. Peggy was home.

Sgt. Meagher and Ramsey surprised us all when they came late and wanted to give us a ride to the doctor's, mostly because they thought Peggy would like a jeep ride.

I went back to camp with them. I really hated to say good bye to Peggy. I left some money for Maureen.

It was really nice of Sgt. Meagher to get Ramsey and the jeep to give us a ride to Tynan. They had planned it beforehand. Sgt. Meagher didn't have anything to worry about, asking Ramsey, an officers' driver, to take us somewhere at night in an Army jeep in Ireland. Mess Sergeants had a pretty fair amount of say-so. And Ramsey didn't have a whole lot to worry about either, as he was just a driver doing as we all did in the Army: "As told."

The back seat of a jeep isn't very wide, but Peggy and I fit into it all right. Maybe I just imagined it, but I thought she held my hand tighter than she had before.

Tuesday, August 25, 1942   Up at 3:00. Hot cakes for breakfast. Loaded up and ready to roll at 7:30. Left at 8:00.

I rode alone in back of the kitchen truck. Got here to Enniskillen at about 11:30. The place doesn't look so bad, but is muddy and dreary-looking.

Slept a little. Off-duty. Wrote to Peggy and Mary Jean. Lonesome. Canteen supplies to-night.

We had to use part of the castle there at Enniskillen as our kitchen for a few days. We used part of the back entryway. It was no more than a protection from the elements, and was almost like cooking in the field. The men had to use their mess kits, and we had to use field equipment, i.e., gas stoves and all our field cooking utensils.

Wednesday, August 26, 1942   Up at 9:00. Had a headache. Washed some clothes.

On this p.m. Not such a bad kitchen. We started moving in today. It wasn't properly cleaned out. This is the kitchen that 2nd Battalion [the 175th F.A.] had been using. Had a big supper.

Letters from Helen and Ray tonight. He is planning on buying land. Answered both.

Don't mind being in the hut with the rest of the crew, but it's pretty noisy.

This camp is laid out somewhat different than the other two we were in. This one is really stretched out. Headquarters kitchen is just across the road from our kitchen crew hut, and the recreation hall is just a little ways from there. The latrine and showers are at least two blocks up the road though, and the main road of camp runs between the kitchen and our hut. There seems to be a steady stream of men coming or going to the latrine.

I'm glad they abolished the officers' mess as an extra unit. It's nice to be with these guys too. The time goes faster when the bunch is together. Bob Vaughn and I are on shift together. Bob Passow is the baker, I think. We seem to have 5 cooks. George Pittlekow and Rose are on the other shift. And Bob Meagher is the Mess Sergeant. We all fit in the hut, including the steady K.P. and all the cooking crew, and maybe a few more. I have the corner bunk again like I wanted. Most of the fellows don't want it, as the rifles are in my corner. But there is extra room on the wall to hang a few things as well, so I like it.

There is a coal stove in the middle of the hut in case it gets chilly.

One Irishman here said it will freeze a little at night here starting pretty soon, but it will never get very cold in the day time.

Thursday, August 27, 1942 Up at 6:00. Army's Sunday.

Off this p.m. Showered. Went to see Hurley and Don tonight. Got the proofs from the photographer in Belfast. Turned out good.

Nice to work with Bob Vaughn again. He knows a lot about cooking and has done it in restaurants, etc.

B Battery is between here and the castle.

Friday, August 28, 1942 Inspection day. I laid out my equipment. Went in the woods until the inspection was all over.

On this p.m. Easy meal. Washed clothes.

Took C.Q. ["Command of Quarters," an extra detail] voluntarily for Czuik. Answered phone calls. Dressed up in field uniform. Practiced up on my typing in the C.P. [Command Post] hut. To bed at 11:30.

Some of the cooks didn't like it when I voluntarily took someone's duty. They said, "Next, we'll all have to do it too." But sometimes I was bored, and it broke the monotony. I'm glad I kept up on my typing. C.P. had the only typewriter around.

Saturday, August 29, 1942 Up at 4:00. Scrambled eggs for breakfast. I collected necessary equipment for a field kitchen. McKoy and I went using the battery weapons carrier as mess truck. We set the road markers on the way out. We served coffee, soup and sandwiches.

Left at 5:30 with the extra 6X6 truck. I rode in the cab. We picked up markers. Last in the convoy. About 40 miles. Seen Deny tonight.

Sunday, August 30, 1942   Wrote several letters, read some.
   On this p.m. Chili for supper.
   Read in my psychology magazine. Cleaned up tonight. Read in *Country Gentleman*. Feel good all around.
   Our steady K.P.s are Bill Snyder, Ed Dengler, Thompson, Bob McKoy and Nicholas.

Monday, August 31, 1942   Up at 5:00. Scrambled eggs for breakfast. Roast beef for dinner. Slept a little. Got paid. Showered and read.

Tuesday, September 1, 1942   Slept until 9:00. Went for a walk in the woods.
   On this p.m. I got a good start on the supper myself. Vaughn and Passow didn't get back until 3:30. Went to a show tonight.

   "The Movies" were really handy at this place, just across the street, and there were always new ones playing, as well.
   This place is where I really got into the coffee-drinking habit. Just as soon as Bob Vaughn would get in the kitchen, he'd put a small pot of coffee on the stove and have his first cup for the day. It didn't take long before I was drinking as much coffee as Vaughn was, plus all the canned milk I wanted to drink.
   I remember also that someone here had told me to throw a small handful of salt into a 15 gallon pot of coffee to help settle the grounds — but whenever I did that, Bob could taste the salt, and he'd bawl me out for putting it in.

Wednesday, September 2, 1942   Up at 5:00. Mess at 7:30. Easy dinner.
   Washed up this p.m. Sent off a few cards. Read, went for a walk outside of camp. 4 letters from Mom tonight.

Thursday, September 3, 1942   Slept until 9:30. Cleaned up, read. Vienna patties for supper.
   Was going to take a shower, but no water. 3 letters tonight. Grandma, Mom, and Pat, with snaps of her. Baked apple cake tonight. Wrote to Ray.

Friday, September 4, 1942   Got to bed at 3:45. Up at 11:00. Cleaned up. Went for a long walk.

Saturday, September 5, 1942   On this p.m. The usual thing.

Sunday, September 6, 1942   Vaughn, Meagher, Blanton and I went horseback riding this afternoon. There is a place outside of Enniskillen that has them. Meagher got a jeep, and we went. Not all that much fun or too much fun, but it was a little different. Came back here to eat, then we went to Enniskillen to a show. Back at 11:30.

Meagher always had enough nerve to get a jeep or whatever else he wanted, and sometimes I got to go along.

Monday, September 7, 1942   Slept until 11:00. Packed a few things. Vaughn and I went back after our field jackets. Alert for the battery this p.m., but the kitchen stayed in. 2 letters from Mom tonight, one from Ray. Lights are out. Don came over tonight.

Tuesday, September 8, 1942   Up at 4:00. On until noon. Showered this p.m. Changed clothes, wrote some letters, went to a show. Not much good.
7 letters tonight: 3 from Mom, one from Ray, 2 from Pat.

Wednesday September 9, 1942   Army's Sunday today. Slept until 10:30. On this p.m.

Thursday, September 10, 1942   Worked until almost noon. Got a pass and headed for Enniskillen. Took bus to Tynan. Got to Milliken's at 3:45.
My good luck. Peggy's afternoon off. Olive's husband is on leave. Peggy, Maureen and I went for a walk. After we got back, I went in the pasture to talk with the horses for awhile. Nice to be back and see them all. I walked back with Peggy to the doc's place.
We talked after I got back from dropping Peggy off, and I didn't get to bed until after 12:00.

Friday, September 11, 1942   George woke me at 7:30. I had a swell night's sleep. Soft mattress and sheets. Olive was up. Left at 9:30. Bus left at 10:00.
Got back at 12:00. Headache this afternoon. Letter from Helen. Wrote to Ray and Helen.

Saturday, September 12, 1942   Up at 4:30. Felt tough all day. Cold. Joints are sore. Still have a headache. Slept this p.m. Wrote letters. Read a little. May go to see Don yet. Hurley came and we went to Cooke's.

Mr. Cooke was Nancy and Dorothy's uncle, and I'd gone to visit there with Hurley Soderlind a few times. We didn't need a pass to go there either, as it was within walking distance — follow the leader through woods and fields until we got there.

The Cookes didn't have any connection with the estate, but kept several cows and a horse. Mrs. Cooke reminded me a lot of my mother. She churned her own butter, and would always give me a cupful of homemade buttermilk that she kept in a big crock covered with a cloth. It seemed pretty thick at times, but I always liked buttermilk. Hurley would never touch the stuff.

We were never offered a lunch or sandwich or anything. The family was on tight rations, as they were taking care of two boys from Belfast who were staying in the country to escape the German bombing. Cookes had a daughter who was in nursing school in Belfast.

Mr. Cooke wasn't real talkative. He'd talk a little with us and then go out to work again.

Sunday, September 13, 1942   Don't remember much. Have a cold. Don't feel so good.

Monday, September 14, 1942   Same as yesterday, except Andy and I walked to Enniskillen. Sent cables. Back at 5:00.

Tuesday, September 15, 1942   My brother Rod's birthday. He's 10. Inspection day for us. All the officers eat of the food that we cook, but the officers' orderlies are waiting, and just before we serve the men we have to give them a dish of everything that we have for the officers.

Our mess hall here is part of the kitchen, which I like. It's quite a lot like at Camp Claiborne. The stoves are still coal-fired here, but our stove men know pretty well now how to handle English coal, and the cooks are used to the stoves too.

Wednesday, September 16, 1942   Up at 4:00. Hot cakes for breakfast. Took dinner out in the field. Passow went along.
I showered, read, and went over all my things that I own. Mail tonight. 3 from Mom, 1 from Ray, 1 from Ethel, and 1 from Pat. Also a package of films and sky filter from Ray.
The battery came in late, and I volunteered to feed them. A part of the supper was already made, and I didn't do much today except breakfast.

Thursday, September 17, 1942   Up at 8:00. Cleaned up, ate. On this p.m. Not much doing. Wrote to Ray.

Friday, September 18, 1942   On this a.m. Took off an hour and went to church here in camp. The Army's Sunday.
Went for a walk this p.m. Lots to see when one gets out. I followed the RR tracks from town and soon got into the country. A fellow was digging potatoes alongside of the tracks, so I climbed the fence and went and talked to him and his son. They were putting about 5 bushels of potatoes in each pile and covering the piles with earth. They asked me some questions. The father told me he has a relative in one of the Eastern states.

The rails were closer together than tracks in the United States, and the locomotives were much smaller. I had to be careful of trains as I walked the tracks, as in places, there wasn't any room on the side, and there was a steep bank below. I never met any trains, though.

Saturday, September 19, 1942   Picked some blackberries. Had them with my cereal. Went for a long walk past Cooke's place along the road.

On this p.m. Passow is on pass. One letter from Mom, one from Pat, one from Mary Jean and one from Robert Hamilton. Will read awhile yet.

The blackberries were really a treat. Sgt. Meagher allowed us to come in and eat late on our mornings off, so I could have all the canned milk I wanted with my cereal.

Normally, Bob Vaughn and I did all the cooking ourselves. Passow must have been assigned to us at the time as an extra cook because we were cooking for some 30 officers plus the battery of 125 men. Passow also did extra baking and helped out when needed.

Sunday, September 20, 1942   On until noon.

Slept until 6:00 tonight. Went to see Don. Then Hurley, Jerry Colton and I walked over to Cooke's. Came back at 12:00. Read a little. I was the only one again who wanted a glass of Mrs. Cooke's buttermilk.

Monday, September 21, 1942   Up at 7:30. Had to lay out for showdown inspection.

Tuesday, September 22, 1942   Had to lay out for showdown inspection. Don't remember any more.

Wednesday, September 23, 1942   Inspection again this morning. Displayed all my equipment. Somewhere along the way here, something got stolen, but the three inspections haven't brought it to the surface yet.

Took off on a hike right after the inspection. Beautiful morning like fall at home. Enjoyed it. On this p.m. Sewed some corporal T stripes on my shirt.

Thursday, September 24, 1942   On this a.m. A hectic day. Nervous strain.

Supposedly off this p.m., but the off crew had to wash the kitchen truck. Took until 6:00. Cold, wet.

Went for a walk after supper. Wrote home. Got my photographs. Sewed on some stripes.

This must have been when my first rating went through. Second cooks had a rating called a "Corporal Technician," with 2 stripes and a "T" under the stripes. (I'd sewn some stripes on early for my photo in Belfast.)

The pay was much better. With my overseas increase, I was making about $80.00 a month.

Friday, September 25, 1942   Took my rifle and went to Cooke's. Fired 4 rounds. It makes a loud report. Got up early, a cool, fresh fall day. Pressed clothes after I came back.

Able Battery party tonight. We had to make sandwiches. The party was in the show house across the street, and it turned into a mad house — I left when I could. To bed at 12:00. Two letters tonight.

Saturday, September 26, 1942   Up at 4:30. Took dinner out to the firing range. Most of the battery is out there. I had to fire a hundred rounds myself. Got 63 out of it without enjoying it much.

Off this p.m. and slept most of it, or until 9:30. Then I cleaned my rifle, and that took until 12:00.

Sunday, September 27, 1942   Went for a long walk this forenoon. Left at 12:00. Andy stopped in this a.m. Worked until late.

No church that I was aware of. I try to read my Bible at least a little and, with meditation, hang onto what faith I have.

Monday, September 28, 1942   On this forenoon. A hectic one. Slept this p.m. Showered, cleaned up my rifle some more, so now I have it to perfection. Canteen rations tonight.

Letter from Mom.

Meagher could easily make an ordinary day into a hectic one. He had a strange liking for making a fool out of a person for little or no reason, and he had his big size and mouth as an advantage over everyone else. Just waking him up in the morning was an unpleasant task, which I only did once. After he carried on in his usual way just from being woken up, I simply refused to do it again, and Bill Snyder had to take over the job.

No one would turn me in for refusing to wake him up, because it would have exposed him as well. The 151st was a National Guard outfit, and some things were overlooked. We got by with things that maybe wouldn't have been tolerated in the regular Army.

Tuesday, September 29, 1942   Up at 7:00. Wrote letters. Vaughn, Dengler and I went to the garden.

On this p.m. Washed a few clothes. The band leader cooked for the officers — had a hard afternoon.

Reversed a shirt collar for Meagher. A letter from Pat.

This Italian band master wanted to show off to our officers how he could cook, so he practically took over our kitchen for the afternoon. All he made was some meat balls and spaghetti, and we still had our own supper to put out after he got out of our way.

The garden on this estate wasn't as big or fancy as on some of the other places I'd seen. John, the gardener here was a really nice old man who would sit in his chair cross-legged, smoking his pipe, and tell me stories of Ireland. He lived in a lean-to shack attached to one of the greenhouses. Other fellows used to stop to talk with him too.

John told me some of the history of Castle Coole. It had been built between 1790 and 1820 for an estimated $300,000. It belonged to the Earl of Belmore. The stone was imported from Portland, England or Scotland, brought by sea to Ballyshannon, then overland to Lough Erne. The huge blocks were shipped to Enniskillen, and the last two miles by bullock cart to the building site. The cut stone was finished on all sides and the back, as well as the front.

The grounds, including a lake and large park, was taken over by the British government for the duration of the war.

I never even got a peek inside the castle, but the pictures I've seen are beautiful. The staircases are huge; the ceilings are high. The handmade furniture is still in the rooms as built.

I had a hard time imagining how those huge blocks of stone could have been worked into such a beautiful castle, and all over 200 years ago.

After the war the castle was taken over by the National Trust and is maintained by them, though the family still owns the contents and has the right to live there.

Wednesday, September 30, 1942   On until noon. Not such a bad forenoon.

Slept this p.m. Showered. 9 fellows left on furlough tonight. I took a jeep and drove them to the gun park. Went to the ration dump and got 100 pounds of spuds for the kitchen. Went to see Don afterwards. Hurley came back with me and we went to the show.

I hauled all 9 men and furlough packings in one trip. I've seen more than that too, when the top was down, and the driver allowed a couple more fellows to ride on the hood.

Thursday, October 1, 1942   At 8:00 I took my rifle, went to Cooke's and fired 44 rounds. Enjoyed it. Back at noon. Easy supper. Mail tonight from Mom, Ray and Pat. Made coffee cake tonight and rolls for the guards (voluntarily).

Payday was yesterday. Drew the equivalent of $12.60.

Friday, October 2, 1942   Got through with my coffee cake at 3 a.m. Turned out good under the circumstances. Slept until 4:35. Helped Vaughn put out breakfast. Laid down again until 11:00. Inspection for the battery. Through at 8:00. Dengler and I took some time exposures.

My letters home must have been a disappointment to get, as they only told of the letters I'd received from them or of what they could send me. I told them I hadn't seen any cucumbers raised in Ireland except for a few in the greenhouses. I told them I had a 15 gallon pot of sweet dough to work into coffee cake that night.

Saturday, October 3, 1942   Don't remember much. Worked this p.m.

Sunday, October 4, 1942   Worked this morning. Slept this afternoon. No ambition.

Monday, October 5, 1942   Slept late. Had an alert. I went in the woods for a walk.
On this p.m. We made sandwiches tonight. Took until 11:00. Tired out. Tomorrow is road march.

For some reason, Col. Sly had gotten angered up a bit that day in camp. It may have been due to the liquid diet he'd go on at times, but anyway, he'd ordered a 30-mile hike for the next day with packs and gas masks. The hike was to include all men, cooks and all.

I thought to myself that this might be OK for us, but I didn't dare say anything, because the others were all complaining. It was a lot of extra work for the cooks, as we had sandwiches to make and get the kitchen cleaned up, and then get a good start on the next night's supper as well.

Meagher was pretty good for figuring out things like that. I was on duty that morning for breakfast, and I was glad when Larry Koons volunteered to help put it out.

I felt sorry for Ed Dengler. He was such a good dependable worker, but he wasn't the type to walk anywhere unless he had to.

Tuesday, October 6, 1942   Larry and I up at 4:30. Put out breakfast for the battery. Cleaned up the kitchen a bit, then dressed for the march.

Fell in at 8:00 with the whole battalion, headed by Col. Sly himself, and we took off. Only two guards were left in camp. We went good until noon, then a weapons carrier came and took all the cooks in.

I showered and helped in the kitchen. The battery came in at

4:00. All are very tired and footsore. Col. Sylvester was reported "feeling good."

Sgt. Shurke from Service Battery, one of the oldest men in the battalion, made the entire march and tonight walked up to the showers besides. (Service Battery is the farthest from the showers.)

I was disappointed when they came to haul the cooks in. I was already planning on how we could work supper out after the march, but they cut it short for us cooks. The march was cut from 30 miles to 25, and I had been looking forward to finishing it.

Some of the cooks and K.P.s were really sore and stiff. Larry and I went and showered, and then put out the supper.

All the walking I'd done around Ireland put me in good stead.

CHAPTER 12

Enniskillen. Cookes. John McGuire. The 175th F.A. invades North Africa.

Wednesday, October 7, 1942 Slept until 10:00. Did a few odd jobs. On this p.m. Still working with Larry. Chili for supper. Worked late.

I don't remember the circumstances why Larry Koons and I were working together for this period, but I remember we got along good, and that he was always willing to do more than he had to.

Thursday, October 8, 1942 Hot cakes for breakfast. Fried nearly 15 gallons of batter. Deng and I took dinner out for the anti-tank crew. Back at 3:00. Larry, Snyder, Dengler and I went to town. Walked around. Got a room. Larry and I went to the dance. Didn't stay long.

Friday, October 9, 1942 Slept until 10:00. Breakfast at the hotel. Bought a pair of rubber boots. Back to camp at noon. Fried ham for supper. Got gas and potatoes again. Raining slightly all day. Will write to Ray and Pat.

Saturday, October 10, 1942 Fairly easy dinner. Shined all my shoes. Wrote home asking for an air mattress. Showered, talked to Don.

I had asked for some flannel sheets and an air mattress. I told them we had straw ticks, but I wasn't using mine anymore. The sheets never did come, but the air mattress did quite a while later.

I also told them at home that whenever a box of cookies arrived they'd be mostly crumbs.

Sunday, October 11, 1942 Went for a short walk. Loaded up and moved out at 10:00. Got to Draperstown at 2:00. Supper ready by 6:00. Vaughn, Dengler, Nick and I slept together. Sort of nice to be in the open again.

I remember that day Meagher had me grind up a lot of corned beef hash and mix it with ground Spam. Fried lightly as patties, they were an extra item on the menu to give the men and officers a little more variety when the menu was a little lean.

There were some patties left that day, and Meagher told me to throw them out. We didn't want to carry leftovers with us, as we would be leaving the next day and had plenty of beef for dinner. So out in the garbage they went.

About 2 minutes later I heard Meagher's sort-of excited under-his-breath call, "Bud! Go out and get one of those hash burgers you threw out for the colonel, right away!"

I was almost laughing, but I obeyed and got the meat out of the garbage can. Bob took it, made Old Sly a burger and, no doubt, got in a few points as well.

Monday, October 12, 1942   Up at 4:30. Dark as yet. Fed until 9:00. Roast beef for dinner, which was late. Raining all forenoon. Got wet, packed after dinner. Left at 3:00. To camp at 9:00. Batteries got lost, and just got in and situated at 10:00. I had to go to Service Battery and draw rations.

Another 2-meal day, like yesterday. There's always some griping about that, but it's not our fault. Actually, these days are much harder on us than when we serve three meals.

Tuesday, October 13, 1942   Slept quite late. Went to Cooke's with my rifle. Shot 15 rounds. Beautiful day. Went walking around the countryside. On this p.m. with Vaughn.

The Cooke's had given both Hurley and I permission to target practice there whenever we wanted to, so long as we were careful. Mr. Cooke had showed us where not to shoot because of the cows.

Wednesday, October 14, 1942   On this a.m. This p.m. I slept a little. Showered. Didn't do much of anything else. Cleaned my equipment tonight, mostly my rifle.

Thursday, October 15, 1942   Inspection this morning. Laid out my things. Did the disappearing act for two hours. Went walking.

Hard meal tonight. I baked bran muffins. They turned out good.

Friday, October 16, 1942   Vaughn and I on this forenoon. Swiss steak.

Chaplain's orderly ran over a dog here in camp. I buried him.

Showered, changed clothes. Honed both razors. Went walking for 3 hours. Followed the railroad tracks again, the other way this time. Enjoyed myself a lot. Warm, but cloudy. Misting occasionally.

Saturday, October 17, 1942   Up at 8:30. Went walking until 11:30. Went past the place where I saw the father and son digging potatoes some time ago, but they were through. I walked over there, but there weren't even any little potatoes laying around. They had quite a few piles of potatoes covered with dirt.

Got a lot of exercise today. On this p.m. Tonight Sgt. Meagher and I went to John McGuire's. Like the Irish say, he is an interesting "old chap."

Raining, cool. Letters from Mom, Myrtle, Ray and Peggy. Wrote home last night and to Pat. Saw the show *Friendly Enemies*. Interesting.

Sunday, October 17, 1942   Vaughn and I on this forenoon. This p.m. I cleaned up, got a pass and went to Tynan on the bus. Got there at 8:30. Was glad to see the Millikens again.

Peggy asked me to come in the letter I just got yesterday. We talked a lot. Olive, Mack and Maureen were at Mack's camp somewhere in England. We talked until midnight.

Mrs. Milliken kept the turf fire going all the time now. It was all they had to cook on, and also was the only source of heat in the house.

This was the last time I saw the Millikens. I was really thankful I got acquainted with this family. I spent many happy hours with them, and received many letters from Peggy over the next 3 years.

Monday, October 19, 1942   George woke me at 7:30. Ate breakfast at the Milliken's, a cooked cereal which was really good.

Left at 8:30. Walked back to Tynan, about 2 miles, and took the train back to camp at noon.

Sauerkraut for supper. One of the meals that doesn't go over very well, but it's in cans and easy to heat.

Meagher and I went to John McGuire's. Took several time exposures. The Cooke boys came to see a show, so I walked home with them.

My letter home had more news for the folks than usual. I told them of my long walks, and how they keep potatoes over winter. I told them we had shows almost every night, and that Mr. Irons, our Master Sergeant (warrant officer) got the Cooke boys over here one night to see a show, and I walked home with them through the woods. The boys were about 12, not related to Cookes, but staying there for safety for the duration of the war. I told them about Mrs. Cooke's buttermilk, and I told them the last time we were out firing at Draperstown we didn't get in until after 9:00 and still had to unload everything and make supper for the men.

Tuesday, October 20, 1942   Up at 6:00. Spaghetti for dinner. Vaughn left early on pass. Helped Larry cut pork chops for supper. Played the guitar for a while. Cleaned up. Wrote to Ray. Read.

Show tonight. I went after the Cooke boys. Saw *The Spilers.* Good.

Walked home with the boys. Joyce [Cookes' daughter] goes back to nursing school on Thursday. It was nice I could meet her at least once.

I thought that if Mr. Irons could bring the boys to a show, so could I. I suppose, though, he had someone pick them up in a jeep. Being a warrant officer, next best to being a 2nd lieutenant, no one would ask him any questions.

It was quite a walk both on the road and through the woods to Cooke's place, but I always enjoyed every foot of it. Besides the two boys, there were also two little girls from Belfast staying with the Cooke's, and also an older boy, Freddy.

Many years later I received a package from Toronto, Canada and couldn't guess who could have sent it. I had left some of my things at Cooke's when I left Ireland, and Freddy had mailed them from Toronto to my parents' place. My parents' address had changed, but someone in the Post Office knew how to use a phone book. He called around to the Wagners in the book and after some confusion and not a Wagner knowing anyone in Toronto, the pre-computerized Post Office still succeeded in getting the mail through to the addressee, myself. Mice had gotten to the letters, however, and they were ruined.

Wednesday, October 21, 1942   Slept until noon. On this p.m. Tonight Vaughn and I went and listened to White and Stacy play the guitar and fiddle. Took some more time exposures.

Thursday, October 22, 1942   Up at 6:00. Roast beef for dinner. Alert this p.m. Everybody had to pack, but we didn't have to leave the camp. Vaughn and I cleaned a fire unit. Played guitar tonight. Raining and cool.

Friday, October 23, 1942   Up at 8:00. Dressed in O.D.s. Went with Sgt. Pomerleau to Omagh for mail in a jeep. Cold trip. Probably 30 miles each way, north of camp, about a third of the way back to our first camp at Limavady. I got a letter from Patsy. Back at noon.
   Roast beef for supper. Went to the show *Juke Box Jenny*. Beautiful moonlit night. Went for a walk along the tracks.

Saturday, October 24, 1942   On this forenoon. Took dinner out in the field. The gun crews are out about 15 miles. Back at 4:00. Showered and cleaned up.

Sunday, October 25, 1942   Up at 9:00. Laid around until noon. On again this p.m. No church services that I could find. There are no Irish churches that I know of around here either. Boredom has set in for the most of us. Even the hut is too quiet to suit me.

Monday, October 26, 1942   On until noon. Easy dinner.
   Alert this afternoon.
   Arky and I packed up and walked to town. I had a tooth filled by an Irish dentist.
   Back at 6:00. Box of candy from Mom. The tooth I had filled ached terribly tonight. Canteen supplies tonight: 16 candy bars.

   The Irish dentist was an old man and nice to talk to. He apologized for not having silver to use for the filling because of war shortages, but he said he was using aluminum, which was just as good. So he took it out of an old kettle he had there and somehow put it in my tooth.

The tooth seemed to ache more than usual afterwards, but that filling was still in the tooth when it was pulled years later.

Tuesday, October 27, 1942 Slept until 10:00. Didn't do much. Baked beans for supper. Packed over my things. Will read yet.

Wednesday, October 28, 1942 On this a.m. Inspection. Went for a long walk this afternoon. Enjoyed myself and relaxed a lot. The weather feels like fall, but is really nice.

Thursday, October 29, 1942 Slept late. On duty this afternoon.

Friday, October 30, 1942 On this a.m. Alert this afternoon. Packed everything including the kitchen. Didn't have to move, though.

Packed over all my things. Am down to rock bottom. Finished at 11:00.

Talk is starting to be that of moving out soon. We don't hear much about the 175th, except they are in combat training in England.

Saturday, October 31, 1942 Cold. Froze pretty hard last night. Walked to Cooke's and around. This will be my last writing in this diary, but will be resumed in the black notebook.

Sunday, November 1, 1942 Lamb for dinner, or stew, that is — and correction — it really was mutton. I know it was mutton, as I cut it all up.

Up at 4:30. I didn't help much with the breakfast. Bob Vaughn and Larry made it while I cut the mutton.

Dengler came along on my walk this p.m., so I didn't go as far. Back at 6:00. Went to Cooke's myself tonight. 5 letters from home. Wrote to Ray.

No church again. The only clergy I've seen around here is an Irish priest who walks on the road past here.

Monday, November 2, 1942   Up early. On this p.m. Usual routine.

Tuesday, November 3, 1942   French toast, bacon for breakfast. Roast beef for dinner.

Bob and I went to Belfast this p.m. and stayed at the Red Cross. There was no cost to stay or eat here, and it was a nice place to stay. We walked around a lot and went into a restaurant, but there wasn't much food to choose from.

Lots and lots of bomb damage. Some places whole city blocks are nothing but rubble. No rebuilding has been started yet that I could see.

The change and relaxation this trip gave us was worth a lot.

Wednesday, November 3, 1942   Up at 7:00. Breakfast at the Red Cross. Thought a lot of when we first came here last January. Took the train back to camp and got here about 1:00.

I suppose it's about 100 miles, as it's just about across Ulster east to west. The train was a little crowded, and a young couple sat facing us. They were very quiet. We found out that they were just married the night before.

Thursday, November 5, 1942   Up at 4:00. Creamed beef. Meat loaf for dinner. Vaughn took the dinner to the battery in the field. I still had 40 men to feed here in camp.

Showered, changed clothes. 2 letters from Patsy. Damp, cloudy.

Fried a dozen steaks for McGee. Meagher is on pass, but we manage nicely without him.

Friday, November 6, 1942   Slept until 11:00. Washed clothes.

Alert this p.m. Packed everything. Took until 4:00.

Tired tonight. To bed early.

Saturday, November 7, 1942   Up at 9:00. Went for a walk down the road along the tracks. Back across the field.

Beans, vienna sausage for supper.

Letters from Mom, Al and Germaine. Show tonight, *Remember*

Pearl Harbor. Good. Wrote several letters.

Meagher got the idea that all the fellows should move their beds around. We did, but everybody complained so much that we moved back again.

Sunday, November 8, 1942 Up at 4:30. Hot cakes. Lamb for dinner. Alert this p.m. Everything went OK, but it sure is a lot of work. Through at 5:00.

Then the other crew had to make supper for the men. Read. Rainy and cool.

Monday, November 9, 1942 Bob and I on. Early before 5:00 Col. Sylvester came in and had coffee with us and said that US troops had landed in Morocco, Algiers. We asked him a few questions, but all he seemed to know was that the 175th was attached to an infantry division and had to be a part of the assault troops. He told us there would be much more to follow.

If the fellows in the 175th could have heard Capt. Genung that day, he probably would be saying, "This is it, Men." My former 2nd Battalion of the 34th Division had been a part of the invasion force of assault troops attached to the 9th Infantry Division and 1st Armored Division, with 33,000 soldiers and 52 warships. They were led by Gen. Ryder and Admiral Burrough. The British also had forces attached to this invasion.

Also attached to this invasion force were about 35,000 troops from the US 2nd Armored and 3rd Infantry Divisions, besides the Western Task Force that sailed directly from the United States.

I had a lot of thoughts when I heard that my old outfit, the 175th F.A. was involved in the invasion, since I'd spent about 9 months with them, getting used to being away from home, going through training and maneuvers, learning Army discipline, going through endless marching and inspections that seemed ridiculous at the time, and learning to humble myself and blind myself to almost unimaginable personalities and situations.

Some of the fellows were a little jealous that it was the 175th who spearheaded the attack on French North Africa. After all, it was the 151st who had gotten overseas to Ireland first, and they thought we should also have been the ones selected to be the first troops in combat. Personally, I was nothing but excited, though I was convinced that now we would soon be heading in that direction ourselves.

The invasion was considered successful. Beachheads were established, and Algiers was soon taken. Oran was tougher, and 2 destroyers were lost there, but by nightfall the town was secure. Also, an airfield was now in Allied hands manned by Spitfires, one of the planes that had been important in the air defense of Britain.

Fighting at Casablanca was the worst. "Blood and Guts" Patton was in command of ground troops. Admiral Cunningham of Britain wanted to make landings as far east as Bizerte, but this idea was vetoed by the American Chiefs of Staff.

What a mess power can lead to. The unoccupied French government in Vichy was pro-Nazi, and their leader, Marshall Petain was strongly opposed to the Allied landings, and secretly encouraged Admiral Darlan to resist the landings. Darlan was Commander of the French Navy, and was a traitor to France in many peoples' minds. He got what he had coming in a short time, however: a hole in his head by an assassin on Christmas Eve, 1942.

There always seemed to be challenges of command, and every commander seemed to want to dim the other commander's light so his own could shine brighter.

Though there were "only" 1800 casualties, these casualties were mangled human bodies — or perhaps not mangled at all, but just dead from a single bullet wound. They were sons of typical American families who maybe could have been spared, if only national leaders could have got their minds in the right order, or used more humility, or given another person credit where credit was due. But the kettle has always had to call the pot black.

That is the attitude that gave me the title of this book, and it will endure until the end. Man will always war against man until the Prince of Peace himself comes, and warmongers can never use his name for that blasphemous purpose again.

Well, I remember thinking that soon enough, I would have my own first combat lesson, as the 175th had already had theirs.

Tuesday, November 10, 1942   Up at 10:00. Raining. Read until 1:00. Battery's day off. Chili for supper. Made hot cake batter.

Made hot cakes and tried out the batter for myself. Perfect. Read. To bed at 11:30.

Wednesday, November 11, 1942   Up at 4:30. Hot cakes. Steaks for dinner. Another hectic forenoon. Andy stopped in for a change.

Cleaned up this p.m. Went to the medics to get my teeth fixed.

Thursday, November 12, 1942   Slept late. On this p.m. Don't remember much more.

Some news is coming through about the landings in Africa. Some coastal towns have been taken, but there are problems with the unconquered pro-Nazi Vichy government.

Wonder how the 175th came out. We had some men and equipment taken from us awhile back at Castle Coole, but I don't think they were from our battalion. Probably new recruits and equipment from other parts of the Division.

Friday, November 13, 1942   Hot cakes for breakfast. I had to fry them at the officers' mess. Macaroni for dinner.

Vaughn went to Belfast. I went for a long walk this p.m. across fields. Back at 5:30. Tired. Show tonight. *Crossroads.* Fair.

Saturday, November 14, 1942   Up late. Headache. Hamburgers. Fried spuds for supper. Made salad for officers' dance. Cut pork chops for supper. Cool. Raining.

Sunday, November 15, 1942   Up at 5:30. French toast for breakfast. Very few got up. The battery's day off.

Slept this p.m. Showered, changed clothes. Went for a walk. Back at 5:30. Washed clothes. Went to Cooke's with Hurley and Jerry Colton. Nice, but cold. Had my usual buttermilk.

Monday, November 16,1942   Up at 7:30. Cleaned up. Painted my bags.

Went with the medics to 109th Ordnance to get my teeth fixed, but the dentist didn't get to me.

Walked back. Pork chops for supper. Some time off. Warm.

"Painting my bags" meant I was stenciling names and numbers on them in preparation for a move.

Tuesday, November 17, 1942   Creamed beef on toast for breakfast. Meagher on pass. Meat loaf for dinner.

Went to B's kitchen. Talked an hour with Don and Andy. Went for a walk. Slept a little. Went back to see Don. He was baking cobbler.

Nice day.

Wednesday, November 18, 1942   To the dentist. Filled 3.

On this p.m. Meat balls.
Got the battery guitar and played. Wrote to Ray. Made hot cake batter.

Thursday, November 19, 1942   Up at 4:30. Fried cakes at officers' mess.
Off this p.m. Went to town with Rose. Met some friends of his. The most memorable is Eileen, Molly's daughter, a girl of Arlene's size and age..
Back at 11:45. Got 6 letters.

Friday, November 20, 1942   Up at 10:00. Battery out in field. They took dinner out. Salmon loaf supper.
Don came tonight. We went to show together. He stopped at the kitchen afterwards, had a bit to eat.

Saturday, November 21, 1942   Up at 4:30. Creamed beef on toast. Started cutting 3 lambs in quarters.
Left at 8:30. Went to dentist at 10:00. 3 filled. Took Novocain. Back at 2:00.
Showered, read. Wrote 2 letters. One to Mom. Got one from her a few days ago with a school paper with my name in it.

Sunday, November 22, 1942   Off this a.m. Can't remember much. Got a carton of cigarettes from Uncle Art.

Monday, November 23, 1942   Off this p.m. Sgt. Meagher bought 2 chickens for us tonight. Had a nice feed for the whole kitchen crew.

Tuesday, November 24, 1942   All of us up at 4:00. Started loading early and left at 10:00. Went to Draperstown, saw the little girl Phyllis.
We are in our regular old hunting camp area and buildings.

We had steaks, and Bob Vaughn and I were frying them for dinner, using the top of the middle stove to hold the fried steak, as we each fried on a stove on either side. All of a sudden something gave way, and the big pan of steaks fell on the floor. The concrete floor wasn't too dirty, and there was a water hose there. We just grabbed that, turned it on, and in a big hurry got the pan of steaks back where it belonged.
The hurry, of course, was to get it back before Sgt. Meagher saw it. Luckily, he didn't.
Bob and I fried ourselves a couple of eggs each for dinner, instead of steak.

Wednesday, November 25, 1942   Bob and I on until noon. Took dinner out.

Cleaned up this p.m. Mail tonight.

Thursday, November 26, 1942   Up at 10:00. Went for a walk.

On this p.m. Thanksgiving. Doesn't seem like it. A good dinner, but I had little or even nothing to do with it.

Friday, November 27, 1942   Up at 4:30. Loaded by 9:30. Back to camp by 1:30.

Showered, washed clothes, got mail. Letters from Ethel, Mom, Pat and Ray. Box of cigars from my dad, and snuff from Dick.

Drove the kitchen truck back to the gun park. Wrote 6 letters tonight.

Saturday, November 28, 1942   Up at 9:00. Checked over my things. Read. Wrote 3 letters.

On this p.m. I baked 450 buns, 5 chocolate cobblers. Made dressing. Have 16 turkeys that I got almost ready. Took almost until 2 a.m.

Sunday, November 29, 1942   Up at 4:00. Creamed beef for breakfast. Put the turkeys on right away. A hectic forenoon. Heavy dinner. Some fellows left today.

Through at 3:00. Showered. Went over my things again. Wrote a few more letters. Am packed, ready to go. Nice day.

Our Thanksgiving dinner had been postponed because of the trip to Draperstown.

Orders were to be ready to leave on short notice. Some advanced details were already ready to go.

I had two different things to think about at the same time: (1) another trip on the sea, which I knew for sure I wasn't looking forward to and (2) combat, which I didn't think I was looking forward to either. On the other hand, the combat was going after the Krauts [Germans], and that was the point of our being there.

It seemed as though there wasn't much talk or rumors going on about where we'd be going, as we just kind of assumed we'd be following the 175th to North Africa.

Monday, November 30, 1942   Up at 10:00. Headache all afternoon. Easy supper tonight. Spanish rice. Cool, cloudy. Got paid today. 3 p, 2S.

Tuesday, December 1, 1942   Hot cakes. More men left on advanced detail with loaded trucks.
Roast beef for dinner. Packed over all my things again.
Went to Cooke's tonight for a short time. Went to see Andy and Don. Back at 11:00. Cool and cloudy all day. One letter from home.

Wednesday, December 2, 1942   Slept late. On this p.m. Don't remember much. We wonder when and where or how the route will be.

Thursday, December 3, 1942   Don't remember a thing.

Friday, December 4, 1942   On this p.m. Carton of cigarettes from Aunt Anna. Also one from the Defense Council of the [Proctor] School Board. 10 candy bars from Mary Jean, 4 bars of soap.
Some screen stars in town tonight. I didn't go.

Saturday, December 5, 1942   Up at 3:30. All batteries are in the field firing range. Vaughn and I are alone. We made a bite for ourselves to eat, and then Hurley and I went to Cooke's.

Sunday, December 6, 1942   Off this a.m. Slept until 11:30.
Easy supper.
Card from Jean Vaughn. Wrote her a letter of thanks. Also to Pat and home.

Monday, December 7, 1942   Up at 4:30. Hot cakes. Stoves were on the blink. Meat loaf for dinner.
Cleaned up this p.m. Read quite a bit. Packed over my things. Cool and windy.
Pearl Harbor a year ago today. Have moved on since then, and am ready to go to Africa.

Tuesday, December 8, 1942   Up at 9:30. Read a little.
On this p.m. Easy supper.
Went to John's again.

Wednesday, December 9, 1942   Up at 6:15. Battery's day off. Steak for dinner.
Slept a little this p.m. Read, and it's raining.

Thursday, December 10, 1942   Meagher put his hand against a window in the kitchen for some reason, with some of his weight against it. It broke, and he cut his arm badly.

There were a lot of cries for "Medics!!" They came running, but before they got there, Meagher had swallowed his tongue. Bill Snyder probably saved his life by clearing his throat with his finger before the medics arrived.

Bob Vaughn went to the dentist. George Pittlekow and I worked for supper.

Friday, December 11, 1942   Up at 4:30. Hot cakes for breakfast. Pork for dinner.

Showered this p.m.

Have to bake cinnamon rolls.

Saturday, December 12, 1942   Up at 8:00. Packed all things. Said good-bye to Cookes and John.

Bob and I on this p.m. Cooked supper on coal stoves. Laid around until 12:00. Had to do a lot of cleaning. Gas stoves and most equipment was gone today.

The Cookes were good to me. I had lots of buttermilk and company as if I were at home. It was this night I left the box of personal things with Mrs. Cooke, as I thought there might be a possibility I would come back to see Peggy after the war or send for the box.

The box that Freddy later sent me from Toronto contained mostly small things: lots of letters from Patsy and souvenirs from Ireland.

John McGuire wished me well and said as his parting words, "Keep yourself clean here," and indicated the area of his heart with his big hands.

I remember John as he sat in his corner chair smoking his pipe, resting from a hard day's work in the garden or as caretaker. He was always dressed in black, and the only home he knew was that of the garden shed attached to one of the estate's greenhouse.

CHAPTER 13

England. The Princess Maude. *The* Empress of Australia. *An accident at sea. Arrival in Africa. Montagnac.*

Sunday, December 13, 1942   English lorries picked us up sometime after midnight, and it was a long ride to Belfast until about 7 a.m. Marched to Hotel Lehare in Larne and left our equipment there. Walked to a Limey camp for breakfast. Consisted of stew, dry bread and tea. Marched to Doeli.

Got on *The Princess Maude*. A rough sea for 2 hour trip to Scotland. Got there at 3:30. Left at 4:00 by train from Newton Stewart. I was excited to be going through Scotland. Buildings along the track were very common-looking, but now I can say I've been to Scotland too. We got to Chester, England about midnight.

The sailors on the *Maude* said the Irish Sea is always rough. It sure was that day. Many of us were on the verge of being sick. The *Maude* was a small scuttle ship, and the waves were small and choppy.

We didn't see many people cheering us on, nothing at all like when we came almost a year ago. The country wasn't as nice as Ireland, either. Mostly though, we went through the edges of small towns instead of countryside. I don't remember how many men were on the ship or on the train.

Monday, December 14, 1942   Ate a meal prepared by Limeys, then slept until 11 a.m. Another large camp. It's cloudy.

Worked this p.m. All our cooks on one shift. Things didn't go too bad. Through about 8:00. We are 40 miles east of Liverpool.

I remember the kitchen. It was big. Many English people, mostly civilians, were around wanting to trade or buy American cigarettes from us. Most of our equipment was already there, which explained the trucks leaving Enniskillen and the advanced details.

Tuesday, December 15, 1942   Up at 5:00. Easy breakfast. I made coffee in boilers. All meals are cooked on one stove in the kitchen. Off at noon, showered, cleaned up my things.

Service Battery is moving out of our kitchen tonight. Had to prepare things for breakfast.

Wednesday, December 16, 1942   Passow came back yesterday from pass to Chester. He and I on this forenoon. Up at 4:00. A rat-race to get dinner out on time. Slept this p.m.

I have a boil on my back that hurts a lot. Cleaned up.

Have no idea of England yet, as I've only seen this camp. Will write home. It's cool and cloudy.

A short letter home dated December 16 said that I was "somewhere in England." Bob Passow was continually singing "I'm Dreaming of a White Christmas." The mess hall had tables for the men to eat at, but they had to stand in line to get the food in mess-kits.

Bob Passow's cheerful singing was always appreciated. He sang all the new songs, like "Don't Sit Under the Apple Tree, With Anyone Else But Me," "Chatanooga Choo Choo," "I'll Be Seeing You," "I Wonder Who's Kissing Her Now," "I'm Sending You a Big Bouquet of Roses" and many, many more.

After I left the kitchen, there was nobody to keep up the singing; and after we got into combat, things were still quieter as far as joy was concerned.

Thursday, December 17, 1942   Slept late this morning. Not such a hard supper.

I have a headache tonight. Sliced bacon for the morning.

Friday, December 18, 1942   Up at 5:30. Easy dinner.

Off this p.m. Washed clothes, talked to Don and Hurley. The boil hurts a lot. It's on my hip right on the belt-line. Everybody is getting passes, and I couldn't force myself to go.

Saturday, December 19, 1942   Slept until 10:00. On this p.m.

There's plenty of work here with everything strange and the future uncertain. I would like to go to London, but this boil is quite a determent. Lots of fellows are going to Chester. Quite a few Englishmen around here as well, always trying to buy American cigarettes from us.

No mail or Christmas packages, and probably won't be for some time.

I hadn't seen any turf-cutters since leaving Ireland, and I missed them. Usually it was an old Irish man out in a turf bog with his burro, cutting squares of peat and piling them on the animal somehow. Many times my mind has gone back to the Millikens and the tea and the good times that I had there, plus that peat smell that I never tire of.

Here, there was plenty of work for everyone. There were several road marches. We received more clothing and equipment. There were lots of letters to write and mail. In short, the attitude was, "This is really it. Let's go and get it over with."

We weren't all that well informed on world events, but the situation seemed better to us than it had before. The Russians were doing better than before, pushing the Germans back on the Eastern Front. The Japanese were on the retreat. Allied air operations were increasing. There were reports of American bombers bombing Naples, Italy (though we didn't see much evidence of any bombing in that area when we arrived there in the fall of 1943).

The Tunisian Front interested us the most, of course. Our morale was good, because we figured that with our experience and determination, the 34th Division would leave its mark.

. There was talk about a Second Front on the West Coast of Europe. We didn't imagine this Second Front would still be over a year and a half away — though when it did come, it was even harder to imagine our people could perform and succeed as well as they did.

Draft age was now lowered to age 18. America was really gearing up for war.

Sunday, December 20, 1942   On this p.m. Took Larry's place (reluctantly) until 3:00.

Don came over tonight. Blackie Arnold from the medics came too, and he practically made me go to the medical room where the doctor took out the boil. It was hurting so bad I could hardly buckle my belt anymore. Then Blackie poured me a drink of whiskey, but I refused it. They thought that was pretty stupid of me, and I have to admit that the pain did leave me pretty weak for a little while.

In all my time in Ireland I had never even been in an Irish pub or tasted their beer. The company I kept with just didn't care for that, and we got along fine without it. From outward appearances, at least, it seemed to ruin more good times for the fellows when they went on pass if they drank than if they didn't.

Monday, December 21, 1942   Up at 8:00. Went to the medics. The sore is better. I didn't want to be put on quarters.

On this p.m. Simple meals. Enough cooks on duty here to spoil the soup.

Lecture on general principles for noncom's tonight.

My only gripe now is that I'm getting tired of Passow's continually singing of "White Christmas." We get along first rate, but he makes me more lonesome than ever. He is the only one of the crew who will break out with a Christmas carol or an old time gospel song.

I think just about all the trucks and equipment are loaded, but being in the kitchen sort of separates me from the other details, and I can only surmise what's going on. But I do know now that breakfast is the last meal served here.

Tuesday, December 22, 1942　　Up at 2:00, showered and made breakfast. Cleaned up the kitchen every bit as good as we found it.

Left Oulton Park at 8 a.m. in trucks. Got on the train in Chester and got to Liverpool at noon.

Rode on the train to the dock and got on board the *Empress of Australia*. Supper at 5:00. Good.

Passow and I sleep together.

What a contrast the *Empress of Australia* was to crossing the Atlantic on the old *Strathaird*. This was a decent Australian ship designed mostly for passengers. It was run by Canadians, I think, as well as Australians. The canteen was pretty well stocked, and latrine and shower facilities were adequate. I don't remember if there was hot water or not, but it was almost a pleasure to be on it instead of the *Strathaird*.

Don Sternke told me later that he'd found out that the *Empress of Australia* had been built by Germany and called the *Tirpitz*, but had been taken over by the British during World War I.

Wednesday, December 23, 1942　　On board ship in dock all day. Roamed over the ship from bow to stern. Out on deck awhile tonight. This one has some life rafts stacked up on the bow, and also more lifeboats that are already over the side of the ship ready to be lowered down.

I've forgotten any special activity of the crew members on this ship, as everything worked so smoothly that I didn't notice or remember. I even sort of forgot my fear of being on another ship in wartime.

Thursday, December 24, 1942　　Up at 6:00. Still in dock. Walked around the deck dozens of times. Lifeboat drill this morning. Walked around some more this afternoon. See quite a bit of Don. Nothing much around me tonight to remind me of Christmas or of home.

Our battalion furnished crews to man the ship's anti-aircraft gun, and signal men to operate the blinkers on the bridge. We had "Action-Station

Drills" every day.

There was lots of talk around, but I missed it if there was anything about Christmas or the birth of Jesus. My thoughts went far and wide, mostly concerning where I'd been on other Christmas Eves.

The 7-hour time shift made it confusing to figure out what time it was anywhere.

Friday, December 25, 1942   Up at 5:30. Shaved. On C.Q. until noon. Tough job to get things organized.

Turkey for dinner.

Started moving this noon. Tonight we are in the Irish Sea. Waters are unusually calm. Five ships in the convoy so far. Cool, but I am comfortable with only a field jacket on.

No one who I knew or was close to felt like talking about what we used to do at Christmas time at home, and I didn't hear anyone singing "I'm Dreaming of a White Christmas," though most of us were. No mail of any kind, of course, made it doubly a blue Christmas.

Saturday, December 26, 1942   Moving ahead all day, and we survived yesterday. The sea is a little rougher, but real bearable.

I don't remember watching the wake on this trip. I credit that to a freer spirit, higher morale, and just being more contented. We had already put in the lion's share of 2 full years in the Army, and we thought it would soon be over — after we got Rommel out of Africa.

I did plenty of walking the deck, gazing into space and thinking. We got all 3 meals a day on this ship.

There wasn't any U-boat action, and the trip which lasted until January 3 was uneventful and routine until almost the last day.

Sunday, December 27, 1942   Forgot all about it being the Sabbath. Just a usual day, but colder. Where are the chaplains? No one knows.

A service would have been great yesterday or today, or many times in Enniskillen too. The only camp we had regular services in was at Ballerena.

Monday, December 28, 1942   Slept in the hatchway. A little more room, and I felt a little woozy or seasick. The fresh air felt a lot better.

There are about 15 ships in our convoy. No aircraft carriers, though, but it looks like there are some destroyers. I feel much better with all these ships around me than when we were almost all alone on the Atlantic on the *Strathaird*.

Tuesday, December 29, 1942   Don and I together here all forenoon. Exercise every day.

We are bound for North Africa. It's official now. We should be southwest of Ireland now, they think.

Don and I went to a show last night, *Sinners' Paradise*. Good, but hot and stuffy in the room.

On C.Q. from 4 a.m. to 8 a.m. Real quiet. The boys were content.

The *Empress* is real quiet compared to the *Strathaird*. I think of the giant props and motors and whatever is all in the different compartments.

There are all different kinds of fish that follow a ship for meals of the garbage, though the *Empress* doesn't throw out anything much in comparison to the *Strathaird* where they just heaped it up on F deck to let it wash overboard in rough seas.

Wednesday, December 30, 1942   Up at the usual time. No details. Routine throughout the day. Maybe a little rougher, windier and cooler.

Thursday, December 31, 1942, New Year's Eve   Got up at 4:00 to go to the latrine. Slept a little more.

Usual day, though a bit rougher. Up on the deck a lot. A lot of walking, looking, watching the waves and thinking. Meet Don somewhere every day and we talk.

Haven't seen Hurley hardly since Castle Coole, and I wonder why I haven't seen him around on the *Empress*.

Friday, January 1, 1943   Walked the deck before breakfast. Usual day. We are close to the Rock of Gibraltar tonight. We can see a lot of lights in Spain; it looks like Duluth in summer. Being used to blackout for a year, this is a welcome sight.

A quiet day, and it gave me a good chance to think over what I did a year ago. It was more hectic that last day at Claiborne.

Saturday, January 2, 1943   Are in the Mediterranean this morning. Can see Africa on the south side. A little more exciting today because of the fact that we are in sight of land at least.

Tonight got to be real exciting though. We were having chow when we felt a thud that jarred the whole ship. My first thought was TORPEDO! but there was no explosion. We soon found out that another big ship hit us. Several compartments on E and F decks were under several feet of water.

I was on C.Q. until midnight, then sneaked up to F deck towards the bow and mostly just laid alongside some junk hoping I wouldn't slide down if the list got worse.

If we had been further out at sea, it could have been disastrous. All lights and ventilating systems went out immediately. The ship took on a sharp list which changed from starboard to port, as the water in the flooded compartment shifted.

Later in the evening they were able to stabilize the angle to almost keep the hole out of the ocean. She still listed at an uncomfortable angle, though, and I didn't really entertain any notion about walking the deck.

The crew carried through as they had the entire trip, and they managed to get enough power to limp into Oran Harbor the next day.

Sunday, January 3, 1943   I slept quite a bit at that last night after 12:00, as no one bothered anyone who was sleeping, too stupid to be scared. I liked the fresh air compared to what was down in our quarters, especially with the ventilating system hardly functioning.

Were in Oran Harbor all day waiting to get off. We finally did tonight at 6:00. I could see the gash we had in the starboard side amidships.

One of the officers said the hole was 14 feet below the waterline and 15 feet above the waterline, and probably 10 feet wide. You could have easily driven a truck through it.

You could see into the damaged compartments which were filled with barracks bags and other equipment — laying in water on the bottom layers, and only soaking wet on the upper layers. Lucky for me my fears were unfounded, and my bags were dry.

We got off the ship at the port Mors-el-Kebir near Oran, Algeria, North Africa, and marched about 3 miles to Sainte Andre. We got in trucks there, and they took us to a bivouac area near Assi-ban-okba about 12 miles east of Oran.

We arrived at the area about 9:00; a scrub-oak, rock-studded hillside, which looked good to us for what we had been through. It hadn't taken my legs as long to change from sea to land legs this time, as the 3 mile hike helped.

The menu was pretty slim, though. As near as I can remember, we each had a can of C ration hash, the stuff that always gave me heartburn.

We got our bedrolls that the Quartermaster trucks had hauled, and got bedded down on the rocks by 10 p.m.

I thought our arrival in Ireland had been much more exciting than our arrival in Africa, though.

Monday, January 4, 1943   Cold last night. Up at 7:00.

There was no way we could have even been forced to pitch pup tents on this rock pile full of small brush last night. I was in charge of digging a garbage hole, and that was almost impossible.

The area is away from any "real" civilization, but there are plenty of Arabs, ragged and dirty-looking with some oranges to sell.

We have some Limey rations, but no chance to cook them, so we unhappily settled for C rations. I'm not really excited about Africa as yet.

Tuesday, January 5, 1943   Helped around the kitchen this morning cleaning a spot. We are eating Limey rations. Our own stoves came today. We have our kitchen fly set up, which seems to be a temporary headquarters for the whole of Headquarters Battery. Other batteries are in the area too, but I didn't see any of the other cooks.

Raining tonight, miserable weather. We did get our pup tents up; I'm with Casperson. The officers didn't fare as well as the men, as their bedrolls and equipment haven't caught up with them as yet.

I know some mail came in, as I saw them sorting it.

I hoped the German Air Force wasn't flying too much in this area, as we would have really been sitting ducks.

Rations were the British compo E which weren't too bad or too good, but you could get used to them. The tea came premixed with sugar and powdered milk, so at least there wasn't much problem deciding how you would like your tea to be served.

Wednesday, January 6, 1943   Bob and I up at 5:00. Sausage and tea was all for breakfast.

Cleared around the kitchen again to make more room. The fellows are busy enough, and our officers are still doing pretty good in spite of the area and equipment.

We started to get US rations tonight. Also, some mail trickled in. Papers from home and one Christmas card from Pat.

Beautiful day today. Cool at night.

Thursday, January 7, 1943   Raining nearly all day. Stayed in the tent until noon. Cold working. Got soaked cooking in the open — had to do most of the cooking work outside, as there isn't much room under the canvas. The kitchen fly is filled with food and equipment to keep it dry. Talk about miserable.

Go to bed — or lay down on the rocks practically soaked and shivering.

Friday, January 8, 1943   Up at 5:00. Sausage (Limey, mostly arti-ficial; the guys say it's sawdust) and oatmeal for breakfast. Hash for dinner.

Sun out at times, but cold and windy. Off this p.m. and got myself dried out by walking. Some things in my tent I laid out to dry.

I got chewed out by some of my cook buddies for doing calisthenics with the battery when I was off duty. Cooks, even off-duty ones didn't have to fall in for any formation. Some of the cooks were afraid that when I started doing calisthenics, the procedure would be changed so all would have to exercise.

I didn't argue, but I thought of the saying that "Who laughs last, laughs best." I was laughing to myself, and hoping the exercise would help me to "last."

Working as a cook was starting to irritate me about this time. It was mostly opening cans, heating the food, and then listening to the guys gripe about it.

I hadn't been trained for any specific job with the Army, though, and about all I could do besides cook was to drive trucks. Headquarters Battery didn't have any guns to pull, and so only had a few 6X6s. Driving was a coveted job, as you could always be inside in bad or cold weather and have more room to keep your things.

Driving commanded no rating, though. Now that I was a corporal or T-5, I didn't want to lose the extra pay, unless offered a much better job.

Saturday, January 9, 1943   Up early. Don and I went for a walk.

On this p.m. Supper at 4:00. Packed up everything in kitchen equipment.

I slept without my tent up, so I would be ready to go in case we had to break out a stove and feed somebody or make hot food. I'm always ready to feed someone in an emergency.

Don and I walked around a lot until noon. I didn't understand the area at all. Towards the bottom of the hill were unused irrigation ditches or ca-nals. The hills we were on seemed worthless for raising food, with all the sage brush and litteroy covered with small rock.

This area may have been used for sheep, camel or goat pasture, or maybe this was just the wrong season for growing anything green. As I didn't know any of the language, no one could tell me anything about it either. Anyway, I felt satisfied to have walked around a lot of it.

We were buying oranges from the Arabs, so now the English compos were a little more bearable.

Sunday, January 10, 1943   Up at 4:00. No breakfast. On trucks, and headed for Sainte-Barbe-du-Tielat, and boarded the Chemin de for

Algeria.

We boarded the train at 8:05 a.m., official railroad time, and arrived in Tlemcen, 8 miles away at 9 p.m. I repeat 8 miles.

Then, Quartermaster trucks picked us up at Tlemcen and took us to Montagnac, arriving 2 a.m., January 11.

This had to have been the longest lasting train trip in the history of the 151st Field Artillery Battalion. Thirteen hours for 8 miles.

It was a small train, and so crowded in there, you couldn't stretch out at all. We couldn't get off the train the whole time, as it was backing and switching, and the doors were shut.

It got unbearably hot as well, and of course the tempers of the boys were constantly rising besides.

The old expression, "My stomach thinks my throat's been cut," really told the story of our hunger and thirst. If it would have happened a few days later, we could have imagined ourselves headed for a German concentration camp.

Why did all these creamy things have to happen to us on Sundays? And I was still wondering where the chaplains were.

Monday, January 11, 1943   I worked all night. We finally got a kitchen fly up, and the stoves up and going for coffee and whatever we could feed the men, as it went on all night.

The men were all gentlemen, and didn't complain that it was over 24 hours since we'd left the other camp without having anything for our digestive tracts.

We had enough cooks, and with everyone's cooperation, we were finally the victors.

As it started to get light in Montagnac, I noticed the sight was much more interesting than where we had come from. It was a little town of mixed French, Spanish and Arab population in a valley between the North and Central ranges of the Atlas Mountains.

Our Headquarters Battery was quartered in our pup tents in a square block or so in the town's park. There were fair sized trees, and a road or path on the edges of the park, with the typical cement- or plaster-covered homes, barns or other buildings surrounding us.

The Arabs were standing around the area where we were staying, looking at us.

The Arab women, teenage and up, had a white fabric wrapped around them and over their faces and most of their heads. You could see their eyes and a small, dark mark that resembled a birthmark in the lower part of their foreheads. They'd give us a kind of shy, shifty-eyed look as we looked at them, and then look down at the ground and go on their way.

Some girls who seemed younger than teenagers wore the traditional

white garb as the women did. We didn't know if it was purity of religion that enabled them to dress in white, or if it was the choice of their mothers, or the requirement of reaching a certain age.

The women carried bundles on top of their heads. Across the road from our camp area was a concrete watering trough with a roof overhead where the women would come to wash clothes. They would wet the clothes, pound the wet mass with their fists or an object, then rinse and wring it out.

This had been a long drawn-out day, night, and next day. The officers didn't rate much better than we did, as their belongings hadn't caught up with them this night.

Capt. Genung came in for something to eat and hot coffee, and he griped to me about the lack of his bedroll. I pointed to a pile of bedrolls and said, "You're welcome to use mine, Sir; I don't know when I'm going to get to use it." He just smiled a little and seemed to think I'd given him a pretty good answer to his gripe.

George Pittlekow worked with me that night. I had to take back all the bad things I'd thought of him, because he worked just as hard as I did, and deserved a lot of credit. We'd both been up for days and nights, and after feeding men all night long, had to make breakfast as well.

We finally got to put up our tent and took a short nap, but we were soon up again — because this was the first French town we had ever been in, and we wanted to see it ourselves. So we walked around town, which was full of soldiers. (All the other line batteries were in the proximity of Montagnac, but weren't so lucky to be quartered right in the town, as we were.) George wasn't much of a drinker and wasn't thirsty that night — but he had another weakness, so we parted and went our separate ways.

I soon met some other fellows from our battery, and some French people invited us in and offered us wine. We were able to talk to them a little, at least in sign language.

Tuesday, January 12, 1943   I wasn't out late last night, but saw Vaughn and Passow in town. Came home with them after being invited into another French home for more wine. None of us drank much, though it was OK.

Lucky that George and I didn't have to work this morning, not until this p.m. He did all right last night and came in pretty late.

The kitchens broke up that night, with Able Battery and Headquarters Battery staying together.

Baker, Charlie and Service Batteries joined close to the east side of town, where houses were on one side of them and open African country on the other. "Careful where you pitch your pup tents, Men; this is also open outhouse area for some of the townspeople."

George Pittlekow, Bob Vaughn, Bob Passow and I were the cooks from Headquarters Battery, with Bob Meagher as Mess Sergeant.

Jack McCalaster, Andy Larson and another person I can't remember were cooks for Able Battery, with Bud Bailey as Mess Sergeant.

Wednesday, January 13, 1943   Up at 4:15. We start cooking together with A Battery. Bud Bailey is Mess Sergeant. Andy Larson, George and I are the cooks on our shift. We're on sometimes half a day at a time, or sometimes noon to noon.

Washed a few clothes at the town tank. The Arabs kept an eagle eye on me and a couple other GIs.

Changed clothes. Nice today for January — like summer. Many Arabs and French standing around like people at home would stand around watching a circus troupe coming to town to set up camp.

I haven't yet seen an Arab family walking around together, man, wife and children. There are many Arab men, though, dressed in flowing white robes. Their heads are not covered.

Went to town tonight again looking for fruit, nuts and souvenirs. Ed Dengler and I are together in a tent now. I like him. He's clean all around, doesn't drink or smoke. Talks with a slight German accent.

We went together. Walked all over. Most shops have open sides and have fruit to sell. I bought oranges and almonds, besides a big bag of fresh dates.

Was well after dark when we came back, and I ate fresh dates until I was full.

Payday tonight as well. We were paid in specially printed French money. I got 900 francs.

Thursday, January 14, 1943   Off this morning. Still hungry, so I thought I'd finish my fresh dates. I started breaking them open, and ate them by pieces — that is, until I looked at what I was eating. When I did, I saw they were filled with little white worms. No wonder they tasted so good. The battery hadn't finished eating yet, so I grabbed my mess kit, got in line ... and had some hot cakes to top off my breakfast of fresh dates.

Friday, January 15, 1943   On this morning. Up at 4:00. A crap game on all night in our kitchen tent. Payday yesterday brought that on. They had to move out when we came in.
Egg omelet, cereal for breakfast. Easy dinner. Stew.
Cleaned up this p.m., took some pictures. Went to see Don tonight. They are not far from us. Two V-mails from home. Sewing kit from George and Ethel. Don and I walked around. I bought nuts, and we looked in lots of shops.

I sent my first letter home from Africa dated January 15. I told them about the nice weather here compared to January at home. I told them I'd bought oranges, tangerines, dates and figs. I didn't mention the fresh wormy dates.

Saturday, January 16, 1943   Up at 7:30. Took a steam bath. We had to go in groups. It felt really good. Wrote to Ray.
On this p.m. Easy supper. Done at 7:30. Washed a few clothes. Read *How Green Was My Valley.*

Curfew was at 9:00 every night, but there were exceptions for those on pass.

We never ceased to be a wonder for the Arabs and French, though I don't recall any trouble — except for Hank Lane, when he taught some of the natives some off-color words to say in greeting a soldier, such as "Good morning, you censoredxxxcensoredxxx." It was real funny until Capt. Genung found out about it.

We each got a hot bath weekly, which was really appreciated after a long difficult voyage. Things were worse when we first got to Africa than on the ship. At the bivouac area at Assi-ben-Okba, we were rationed a quart of water per man per day.

All officers ranking captain and above were billeted in private homes and had it pretty good. There was plenty of training, exercising, and schooling everyone in alternative duties — except for the Personnel Section and the cooks. Here again I felt left out by not being able to learn something else in Army duties, as I was getting more and more tired of cooking.

Arab children followed us continually with requests for "shoongom," "shawkalat," and "bisquee." Capt. Constant, who was fluent in French, taught a class in French for officers. My total French at this time consisted of "Wee, Wee."

Sunday, January 17, 1943   Up at 5:45. Eggs, hash and cereal for breakfast. Mail came in, and I got 14 letters from Mom, Pat and Ray.
     Took it easy this p.m. A drunk bunch came in tonight. Don came over. Started writing home and to Patsy.

My letter home said I'd tried to send almonds home, but they weren't acceptable to send; that there weren't that many places to buy souvenirs in this town, and that I'd seen a rope factory that looked kind of primitive.

Monday, January 18, 1943   Up early. Capt. Genung bawled all of us out. We are all confined because of drunks coming in late and disturbing people. Read.
     Gen. Stanford was here, and he asked me what my duties were. I answered, "I am a 2nd cook, Sir," with the temptation to say, "As told, Sir," instead. He may not have thought that proper, though.
     On this p.m. Played catch. Sent my watch home.
     Two French teen-age girls, Ann and Natalie, pick up my clothes and take them home and bring them back washed for not much money. Then they stand by the fence close by our tent, and Ann knits as they watch us.
     I go walking some around here, but right outside of town it's rough country; open, rocky, and land that's not interesting at all. The town isn't that nice either.
     I'm pretty well sat-isfied to just sit out by my tent outside when off duty and watch the out-side activities. There are always Arabs coming and going with a horse and cart, or Arab ladies carrying something on their heads, usually clothes, on their way to the watering trough to wash.

Tuesday, January 19, 1943   Hot cakes, boiled eggs. Easy dinner. Cleaned up this p.m. Finished the letters. Played catch, read.

Wednesday, January 20, 1943   Up early. Played catch. 3 letters.

Thursday, January 21, 1943   Up at 5:00. Eggs and bacon for breakfast. Corned beef for dinner.
        Windy this p.m. Two Christmas cards today, but not one package so far.

Friday, January 22, 1943   Woke up after breakfast, but I have enough food of my own in fruit and nuts. On this p.m. Easy meal.

Saturday, January 23, 1943   On for breakfast. Eggs and bacon. Easy dinner.
        Am usually on with George and Andy. George does most of the talking, but I kind of like his ways now. Andy is good, really quiet. Don't know where he's from in the States.
        Bud Bailey doesn't have to be around much. We sweep around

the kitchen. The ground is hard-packed from all the traffic.
        I'm pretty well satisfied now. The camp curfew is off, and the two French sisters take my clothes to wash them. I don't get bored staying in camp all the time anyway, as there's enough activity going on in view around outside of it.
        It's not supposed to be long now before we roll east and contact Jerry [the Germans].

Sunday, January 24, 1943   Rained this morning. Got soaked. The tent leaks, and water runs in the bottom. Laid in the tent until noon.

Mail came in. I got my air mattress, fountain pen, wool socks, ink, dentifrice and shaving cream. Also a letter from Sister.

On this p.m. Dried up a little.

Monday, January 25, 1943   Slept on air last night. Really swell. Woke at 4:00. Raining hard. Puddle of water in the middle of the tent. Wet all forenoon. Nice this p.m. Dried out all my things. Changed clothes. Have them laid out on my air mattress. Waiting for them to dry as I write.

The older French girl comes every day, stands and knits, and watches us.

Tuesday, January 26, 1943   Up at 8:00. 5 letters, all old. Got more laundry back today. Beautiful day. On this p.m. Easy supper. Usual thing tonight. After meal is over, to bed.

Wednesday, January 27, 1943   Up at 4:30. French toast and dried eggs. Big dinner, though. Quite busy.

Package from Hulda today. Jam, candy, nuts. Letter from Mom dated January 18. Snow and cold at home.

Off this p.m., but we have an alert with no time off. I cleaned stoves. Helped with rations. All had to move tents. Dengler and I still together. To bed fairly early.

Thursday, January 28, 1943   Slept until 9:00. Cold in the morning. Moved our tent again. Close to the road. Now it's perfect, and a little higher up. On this p.m. Went to see George and Tom tonight. To bed early.

Friday, January 29, 1943   Air raid alert at 1 a.m. Went in trucks out of town. Up again at 4:45. Hot cakes for breakfast. Chili for dinner.

Hot today, although it was cold this morning. Showdown this p.m. Cleaned all my things. We didn't have to load any equipment or stay out very long this morning.

Saturday, January 30, 1943   Up early. Fixed my things for inspection. Swept up around the kitchen. Easy supper.

Sunday, January 31, 1943   Busy all forenoon. Went over all my things. Don and Jerry came over. Went for a walk around town. Got paid 945 francs.

My letter home of January 31 said I had sent a package home of some extra things, such as several straightedge razors and a sweater from Ireland.

Monday, February 1, 1943   Up at 8:00. Got a package of soap, one sheet, and hair-oil, not very practical things for here. Wrote 3 letters. On this p.m. About the usual thing.

Life went on in this sleepy African town, with not much that would indicate a world war was raging in other parts of the world. Ann and Natalie were by the fence knitting constantly. Arabs came and went steadily; there were always groups of kids around.

Personnel of the other batteries were mostly busy in the daytime. There were more men around in the daytime at Headquarters Battery where I was at, because of 24-hour jobs that gave the men every other day off.

The Arab women continued to wash clothes, and it was almost entertaining to see them carry heavy loads of wet clothing on a large board on their heads. Before they put the square board on their heads, they rolled up something in cloth, made a circle out of it, and placed it on their heads for padding. Then they lifted the board up, and lastly, the load, usually clothes or jugs of water. They walked with a different step than when walking without a load, and one hand was either up there to help balance, or was on ready to help balance.

We noticed no air activity. Any would have been that of the enemy, and not our own yet, which at that time was nearly all concentrated on Germany's mainland and against the Japs in the Pacific.

I heard one report that said, "Inexperienced American forces were given a vicious lesson around Sidebouzid." Von Arnin's and Rommel's attacks were also making good progress. The German Northern Wing was now approaching Sbeitla, having practically destroyed 2/3 of the American's 1st Armored Division, including 2 tank battalions.

We knew we were supposed to be leaving for the Tunisian Front very soon. Most of us still didn't know anything about how we would react to actual combat, but it seemed to be revealing itself to us slowly …

CHAPTER 14

Heading for combat. Headed east. Combat.

Tuesday, February 2, 1943   Up at 4:30. Eggs and oatmeal for breakfast. Meagher was in the guard house. I was acting Mess Sergeant until he came back today. Don't know what he did.

Bud Bailey from the other crew could have taken over just as well as I could have, but cooking has lost its need for special services and experience. Only expertise in can opening is necessary. Only a watchful eye is necessary for things to go along smoothly.

Off this p.m. Didn't do anything of importance. Got 16 letters tonight. Most from Mom and Ray. Marion LeGault is married. To bed early as usual.

Wednesday, February 3, 1943   Up at 8:00. 3 more letters, and magazines. Warm every day, but almost cold at night.

On this p.m. The usual thing.

Dengler always complains he is cold at night, especially his feet. I give him one of my O.D. blankets some nights, especially when I get up early. Dengler, a steady K.P. doesn't get up with the cooks, but only has to be in the kitchen a few minutes before we serve breakfast. Then when they are through cleaning pots and pans, they are through until just before the next meal, unless we have to take a meal out in the field. Our K.P.s are steady good workers. Most are from farms and Iowa country.

Thursday, February 4, 1943   Up at 5:00. French toast. Easy dinner.

Cleaned up this p.m. Went to B Battery with Larry. Wrote to Patsy and Arlene.

Friday, February 5, 1943   Up at 8:00. Read in *Life*. Wrote to Ray. On this p.m. Lots of mail tonight, all old. I got 9 November and December letters.

Saturday, February 6, 1943   Up at 5:00. Eggs, oatmeal. Hard dinner.

Shower this p.m. Getting more ready to pull out. Warm this p.m. Cold this morning. Bought a billfold for 200 francs.

Ann and Natalie came and got me tonight. Went to their home and had a taste of vino. Their family seemed nice, but there wasn't much conversation. I didn't stay long, but walked around the town afterwards.

The girls' home would be hard to describe, but "fair-sized and nothing fancy." There were several rows of them south of where we stayed. It was a just a shame I didn't know some French so I could have gotten to know the family better, but it was still nice to get to know them as well as I did.

Sunday, February 7, 1943   Up at 3:00. Packed up everything after breakfast, and was ready to roll east at 10:00. Ann was knitting as usual, and seemed to not want us to leave.

We made about 70 miles and camped outside of Sidi-bel Abbes. We had a rough job to put out supper, but we had the kitchen truck to work out of. Of course, we weren't trying to serve a banquet.

I rode in the back of a supply truck with extra equipment piled almost to the top. I burrowed a hole in the contents and stretched out to sleep, rest and think. We stopped once in awhile for latrine call and stretch, then go again.

Once again, we had to start on a Sunday. No passes were given, but some guys went to town anyway.

Well, this was really it, heading for combat. Were we really too stupid to bother to be scared, or what?

The kitchen 6X6 held our 3 gas ranges side by side in front. The side-benches were in back, and we had a folding table to set up in back to work on and serve from. We pulled a regular 2-wheeled trailer, canvas-covered, to hold quite a lot of groceries, and there were supply trucks to haul rations and equipment.

All 6X6 trucks were canvas-covered, and "6X6" meant there were 6 wheels driving when all were engaged, that is, the two rear axles, and front wheels drive as well. The only time they couldn't drive is when they were stuck in mud deeper than the height of the transmissions and differentials.

Monday, February 8, 1943   Up at 2 a.m. Frost on my blankets as I slept by the side of the 6X6 — safer than up on top in case there was an air raid.

George and I put out breakfast: powdered eggs with canned milk, and cutup bacon mixed in the eggs.

The old kitchen truck sure felt good this morning. The 3 burners threw off plenty of heat to warm up the truck, also enough light.

Rose and I rode all day in the medics' truck. Slept a little. Hot dinner, but I only had to help serve it.

Came 130 miles today. Parked in a large park tonight. The convoy is really stretched out with 100 yards between each vehicle, so if Jerry bombs or strafes, he won't get more than one of us at a time.

The powdered eggs were always mixed up the night before, and the cutup bacon and coffee water were ready to go too. Mack, our stove man, always had the burners ready to light, and many times he lit them also.

Coffee was made in a 15 gallon aluminum pot, using the burner in the bottom position. The middle stove was in top position, frying the scrambled eggs.

The K.P.s had plenty to do as well. There had to be 2 kettles of boiling water ready for the men to wash their mess kits, and so we could rinse and wash out the egg-baking pan.

George and I really had to move too. The kitchen truck had to be ready to roll at 6 a.m. (sharp). There were enough cooks on a move like this. The problem was the move, and that we practically had to cook on the run. We had strict warning that we had to be on time to move.

Tuesday, February 9, 1943   Rolled all day. Rode in the kitchen truck. Didn't help much, but would have if needed. Scenery is not too bad, but not green either.

A ride was not hard to come by, and we'd kind of pick out our own place. If the kitchen truck had room, then sometimes I would go there. It was always pretty noisy, though, and there wasn't much chance to rest. All the loose talk was enough to get on my nerves. I preferred the medics' truck or a supply truck. I rode in back, of course, as the cab was only available for the driver and the noncom in charge to ride in.

I didn't have any record in my diary of the place where we stayed that night. When we were on the move like this, I couldn't always write up my diary every night. Sometimes I was too tired, sometimes there wasn't enough light, sometimes there just wasn't a place to sit down and write, and sometimes I didn't want others to see what I was doing.

So, by the time I got a chance to write up the diary, many times I would have forgotten some of what had happened, or it just didn't seem important enough to write down.

Wednesday, February 10, 1943   Lots of Arabs around, but mostly adults who would steal the pants off you, if given a chance.

Two inches of snow on the ground. We are parked in a mud-hole tonight. Worst ordeal I've ever been through wading in mud.

Up all night, impossible to sleep. We are about 30 miles east of Setif. Made 136 miles today. Went quite a ways through snowcapped mountains, the first mountains I've ever seen.

The First Sergeant was sad and comical tonight. He [Pete Rettinger] was full of mud and cold like the rest of us, with lots of responsibility on his shoulders besides. When fellows would come into the kitchen truck to talk, get warm and drink coffee (if there was any left), he was looking at his girlfriend's picture, saying, "Your Daddy is mighty sad tonight, Honey," and then kiss her picture.

Pete was tops for a First Sergeant, and later helped me get the Battalion Agent's job that I liked much better than cooking.

I don't remember what we did for cooking that day, and I didn't write anything down. It could have been we were just on C rations.

I do remember that the cooks' job was not the worst to be on when on the move, as there was extra coffee, some heat, and a place to dry out when muddy and wet.

Thursday, February 11, 1943   Rose and I rode in the medics' truck all day and got dried out a bit. Didn't have much to do. In this kind of weather no one goes far from a vehicle. It rained all day, and again, sleep was next to impossible. I had a fair spot in back of the medics' truck, though it was cold and wet.

Reports came in that the ambulance was full — but there were no casualties among them.

In Ain-Abid tonight, or close to it. By the time we could start resting, it turned colder, and there was a foot of snow in places.

Friday, February 12, 1943   Getting ready to roll this morning at 7:00 or earlier, when Sgt. Wyman Revels shot an Arab fatally with his .45 when he caught him stealing equipment from a trailer, and he ignored his order to halt.

Wyman was a trustworthy man held in high regards by everyone. He wasn't trigger-happy at all, but a dedicated soldier. He was a staff sergeant in the Personnel Department. He was real dark and lean and reminded me of a panther, as he always walked in kind of a crouch and with quick motions. He was from Minneapolis and a friend of Bob Vaughn's.

Still don't remember as to how or when we ate, or to any of the day's trip's details.

Saturday, February 13, 1943   The schedule changed slightly today. Up at 8:00 with George and me on to make breakfast.

Because of the close proximity to the front and due to our lack of sleep, we were juggling our position and time of travel to get into position under cover of darkness. So we left at 4 p.m. and got to this wooded area at about midnight.

Between Souk-Arhas and Sakiet. We came through LeKef, where the Personnel Section remained with the Division rear echelon. The remainder of the battalion continued on to an area about 10 miles east of Maktar.

Enemy air activity near the front reported as brisk and especially on the alert for convoys. We are 10 miles from the front, and tension is mounting.

Our motor-march had been about 800 miles over poor, mostly mountainous roads, and through mostly bad weather.

The drivers and Service Battery deserved a high mark in seeing that we got through. If a vehicle did have to stop for any reason, they would have to wait for the Service Battery 6X6 maintenance truck which was the last truck in the convoy. After repairs were made, they would have to catch the convoy; or if they couldn't, they would have to come in and find the bivouac area. Sometimes that would leave them with little time to rest. We weren't outfitted with any 2-way radios, 2-way phones, or cell phones at this time.

Sunday, February 14, 1943   George and I on this morning, when we heard shots at 5:30. It was the guard trying to wake up the men, as Service Battery's kitchen truck caught fire and burned along with its trailer and some personal equipment. Fellows tried to get it out, but it burned to a total loss.

Write this about 2 p.m. Jolie was ran over by a 6X6 last night

somewhere.
Another active Sunday, and no chaplains.

Jolie was the Battalion Agent. I later got his job.
I remember being afraid the fire would attract enemy action, as the gas from the gas stoves and the gasoline from the truck itself made for some big flames — but we were lucky. We were some 14 miles from the front.
From our position we could hear the distant artillery fire, probably from the 125th Field Artillery.

Monday, February 15, 1943   Slept by myself. Used my air mattress. Moonlit night. Up at 7:30. On duty all day, and are just sort of waiting. We are all camouflaged. Have to wear helmets, gun and gun-belt all the time, and seek cover when planes are spotted.
Beautiful day. Our 125th is in the front lines now. Saw my first dogfight. Actually, it was a crippled Mitchell bomber of ours forced out of formation. Then a Jerry fighter plane went after one of the 2 gunners who were parachuting down, and machine gunned him. The Mitchell was shot down as well by the 2 Heinkel 113's.
Loaded up and left at 6:30 p.m. Abandoned equipment along the way. We tipped over our trailer on a bad turn and hole or obstruction that we hit. What a mess to put everything back into it without enough time to really straighten it out until later. Got way to the rear of the convoy because of it.
Saw the burnt Mitchell. Got to our location about midnight. Several air raid alarms.

Tuesday, February 16, 1943   Up at 1:30. Broke down rations. Slept again until 5:30. Lots of cactus; got one in my knee; made it stiff.
No action today. Heard some fire, a few air raids. Off duty. Deng and I put up our tent. I inscribed a horse's head like my tattoo on the stock of my rifle.
Cool. Have a foxhole. Got in bed by 7:00, and right after that, we were alerted. Packed up everything, but the kitchen doesn't move. The other boys head for the front. Jerry is in back of the next mountain.
Got to bed at midnight and was able to stretch out, but it didn't last.

We were about 1 mile east, and placed in Corps reserve in anticipation of a German tank attack expected from the direction of Pichon.
There was some action; enemy strength opposing us was a Panzer Division, so no wonder we were ordered to withdraw that night to positions west

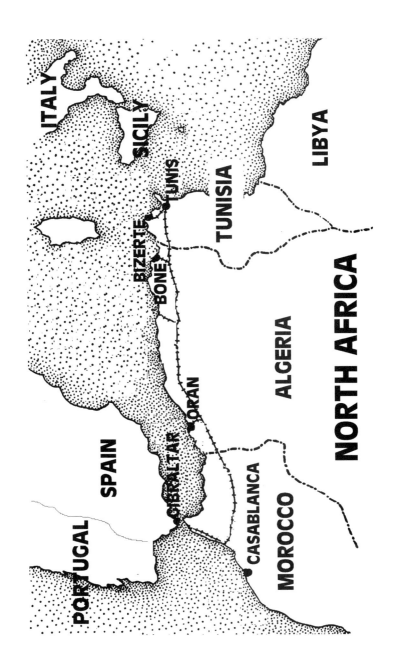

and close to Kef-el-Ahmar.

Both Capt. Surdyk and Capt. Grant were pinned down for a time while they were directing fire. Their lines were cut, and they were in under a 20-minute shelling.

Wednesday, February 17, 1943   Up at 3:30. Helped load breakfast, while George took it out. Slept again until 10:00.

Usually Meagher goes with the fellows who take the food out in the morning. That is, if Snyder can get him up. Bill Snyder is the only one of us that Meagher won't practically slap down when he is awakened in the morning.

A Limey Spitfire went over today, and we thought it was German.

We packed up and pulled out at 6:00. Came 30 miles or so. Are in an open spot. Cactus galore. Saw an abandoned French tank and looked over some Jerry scout cars that our Division got.

Thursday, February 18, 1943   Slept a little. Are close to action. Lines are quiet, though. One of our trucks ran into a mine. Blowed off a wheel, but no casualties. The truck is out of service.

Loaded up about 4:00. I rode in cargo truck. Picked up some infantry stragglers, passed a lot of them.

Convoy was real slow. Cold. Got here in a sandy place with ravines at 10:30. Deng and I pitched our tent. They call the ravines "waddis."

Friday, February 19, 1943   Raining. George and I on all day. Lots of heavy artillery fire all day. We were credited with getting 10 German tanks.

Saturday, February 20, 1943   Off. Up at 8:00. Cleaned up. We are close to a creek. Fairly nice.

Heavy fire most of the day. Some artillery landing pretty close to us.

Andy, Hurley and I walked along the creek. Fired 20 rounds with my rifle. Took a partial bath. We start feeding 2 meals a day, one at 10:00, the other at 4:00.

Sunday, February 21, 1943   George and I on all day. Got our new cargo truck. Changed equipment around. Heavy artillery fire all day. The 185th had some casualties.

The 185th Field Artillery Battalion had 155 mm guns capable of shooting a 90 pound projectile much farther than our 105 Howitzers could shoot.
They were usually behind us, all men from Iowa originally, and I knew no one in the whole battalion.

Monday, February 22, 1943   Up early. Washed a pair of pants and field jacket in the creek. Cleaned my rifle.
One fellow in B Battery shot himself in the shoulder supposedly on accident.
Laid around most the day. Went for a short walk. Pulled out at about 6:00. Came about 15 miles.

On February 22, the battalion withdrew to positions in the vicinity of Rohia, about 10 miles north of Sbiba. However, we failed to inform the enemy we were withdrawing, and he also retreated south, towards Sboitla.

Tuesday, February 23, 1943   Got to sleep about 11 p.m. Put out breakfast (which wasn't fancy), then had to move several more miles. Helped take food out to the battery.
Tonight Deng and I put up our tent. Quiet so far today.

Wednesday, February 24, 1943   Awoke with a terrific headache. Lasted most the day. Got some mail today from Pat, Mom and Ray.
Experienced our first bombing tonight about a mile away. Lots of ack-ack fire went after them. Cool and rain.

"Ack-ack" was the British name for anti-aircraft fire in World War I. It was called "flak" in World War II. Then there were "tracers," a flammable material that burns when fired so the gunner can see where he's shooting, an automatic sighting device. Americans used red tracers; Germans used silver.
A reconnaissance was conducted, and the enemy was encountered looking for us.
C Battery was left at Rohia, while A and B Batteries moved into positions a thousand yards north of Sbiba.
Considerable enemy 10 cm and 88 mm fire dropped on the batteries who had hit their positions in a "crash action" in daylight.
Three anti-tank men, Bressel, Tesch and Shepard, who had been attached to B Battery, were severely wounded and their weapons carrier immobilized, when a shell burst within 20 feet of them.
French light tanks, followed by our infantry, and preceded by our supporting artillery fire, soon dispersed the enemy and gave us our first respite, and an opportunity to lick our wounds and get some much needed sleep.

Thursday, February 25, 1943   Up at 7:00. Still getting English rations. I took breakfast out. Steak and pudding for supper. Through at 7:00. Everything was quiet today.

It was last night that Shepard lost a foot.

Friday, February 26, 1943   Up at 7:00. My day off. Cool. Don't sleep well nights anymore. Wake up often, have bad dreams.

Started to write letters, but got disgusted and tore them up again. Cleaned my rifle. Dug my foxhole deeper. Several air raids, otherwise everything was quiet.

Loaded up and ready to pull out by 7:00, but didn't move until 10:00.

We were mostly in defensive position from about this time until April 4th. We were east of Sbiba and north of Sbeitla.

Part of B Battery accompanied the lst Battalion of the 133rd on a reconnaissance. Five officers and 63 enlisted men of the 133rd were captured by the Germans, as well as Lt. Cullen, Cpl. Waddington and Pfc. Anderson of B Battery.

Saturday, February 27, 1943   Got here to our old place by the creek about 1 a.m. To bed by 2:00. Had rained, and everything is mud.

Up at 6:00. Usual day. I took out supper. It warmed up.

Sunday, February 28, 1943   We put up our tent.

Awoke early and laid and thought what I'd be doing if I was home.

Ate, and washed a few clothes. Didn't accomplish much for the day.

From my letter to home of February 28: "We think the African Campaign won't last much longer. I'm still cooking, but all we do is open cans. Have seen some camels now, and lots of cactus. The oranges have disappeared, though, as we are higher up now than when we landed in January."

Monday, March 1, 1943   Up at 5:00. Stoves didn't work very well. Meal wasn't hot enough for the colonel. I took breakfast out.

I got Bill Snyder's skull cap. Meagher thought he should have it, and bawled me out. I talked back to him, as I didn't think I had done anything wrong. I could have pushed it, but didn't. Meagher is always talking back to the officers, and he always gets by with it.

This was it. I decided to get out of the kitchen for sure now, and as soon as I could. I had always tried to do my best and a little more, but Meagher was impossible.

Tuesday, March 2, 1943   Gave away my overcoat. Got an extra field jacket. Up early. Ate, washed, shaved, and washed a lot of clothes. Did nothing but work all day on something to benefit myself.
Beautiful day, a little windy. Wrote to Ray and Pat.

We were on and off full days now again. I liked it better, but the work was disgusting.
K.P.s had to take turns being on guard duty at night, and though there was griping, it was duty that had to be done. Cooks were exempted from this, and I didn't think it was fair to the K.P.s. I wanted to do my shift as well, but then there would be griping from the cooks.

Wednesday, March 3, 1943   Up at 5:00. I am acting 1st cook now for a few days, as George is on nights. Stoves worked rotten. Not Mack's fault. Some parts aren't available, and all gas comes in 5-gallon bead ons and sometimes has dirt in it.
Rose, the other cook, volunteered to take out the food tonight. Still getting English compos.
Like home tonight after work is done. Warm, sunshine, took a bath at the creek.
We heard via the grape vine that some rear units are receiving US rations.

Thursday, March 4, 1943   Took Dengler's guard from 12 to 1 a.m. Enjoyed it. Deng needs the rest more than I do. He is just slow in his ways, and I enjoy helping him out.
All we have to do is guard the kitchen area and challenge anyone we don't recognize. Then you say the password like "Stop," and if the right answer is "Go," he'd better know it. Your rifle is always ready now and with you.
The password is always given out to every detail every day, and all heads of that detail make sure everyone knows it.
Up at 7:00. Read my Bible. Took a bath. Had my shirt off. Don came over for quite a while. Wrote home.
Everything has quieted down. A few planes over this morning, unidentified. As far as I know, we are holding the western flank.

Friday, March 5, 1943   Up at 5:00. Rose went out this morning with mess, and I tonight.
Started raining about 7:00. Made a mess.

Was on guard 9:00 to 10:00.

The battalion had been on British compo E rations for two months now, and we were thoroughly sick of mutton stew and hard biscuits. After hearing reports that some rear outfits were drawing US rations, all 5 of the Mess Sergeants and Service Battery's Master Sgt. Fred Schurke took a truck and went to the Quartermaster's Depot and managed to draw enough US rations so that every kitchen truck had enough to make hot cakes with the flour, sugar and other small items needed.

Hot cakes were always appreciated by the men. They were always served hot by having the 10-gallon batter pan in the middle stove, and two cooks frying on the side stoves. You had to move to keep frying them fast enough so the line could keep moving right along.

Meagher or a K.P. would grab the man's mess kit from back of the truck, and hold it out to the cook — who would put about 3 hot ones on it, and at the same time, be turning a few and putting more batter on. The other cook would be doing the same.

Hot, melted sugar-water was made beforehand, and was on the ground ready to serve as syrup. There was always a kettle of hot coffee.

We would keep serving and frying for second servings until the batter was gone. Sometimes when it looked like the batter was gone, someone would say, "Come on, Wag, I'll bet you can scrape enough batter out of that pan for a couple more." Usually I could, too.

Saturday, March 6, 1943   Up at 7:00. Rained in our tent. Everything is wet. Sun came out a little. Dried out. Mail came in. I got *Life* magazine, the only mail for the whole kitchen crew.

We have a Piper Cub observation plane with us now. Went to see Don for awhile. Rained some tonight.

Sunday, March 7, 1943   Up at 4:00. Class C rations today. Hash for breakfast with a can of solubles. I went without breakfast.

Back at 10:30. Right now we are hearing a church program from Scotland.

Frank Cajune came over to see me today. He is still in the 175th.

On guard from 8:00 to 9:00. Fairly nice today. Everyone has anticipation of early victory in Africa.

Monday, March 8, 1943   Up at 7:00. English rations again. Cleaned up. Cloudy this morning. Dull, dreary day.

Went for a walk this p.m. Found several shell holes from German 88's. Picked up several pieces of shrapnel. Layed my rifle across a shell hole and took a picture.

To bed early.

Deng and I usually talk about home before going to sleep. He left his farm home when real young and worked as a farm hand on big farms in Iowa. I'm sure he was never in want of a job, being as good a worker as he is, and dependable.

I'd still give him one of my blankets when I'd get up, or even all night sometimes, as he was always complaining about being cold.

Tuesday, March 9, 1943   On guard from 4:00 to 5:00. Breakfast the same as always: sausage.

Corned beef stew for supper. I went out with it. Everything is pretty quiet on the front. Cool, cloudy. Rained last night.

This was a trying time for everyone. The suspense was great; I felt a great sort of a tight feeling. Nobody thought that Rommel was really entertaining the idea of going back home without a big fight.

Rations were another problem. We didn't care that the infantry was getting K rations which were much better than C rations, but we suspected that others were getting US rations destined for us. There were no Arabs around selling fresh fruit, nuts or dates either. Also, packages from home were scarce at this time.

Wednesday, March 10, 1943   Up at 7:00. Shaved. Washed some clothes. Had to take rations out to the liaison. I went through a minefield (marked).

Didn't do much of importance otherwise. Don't really enjoy going up that far towards the front, but just had to unload canned C's and K's.

The liaison crew was the forward Observation Patrol crew who stayed in contact with Headquarters Battery, and were the closest ones in the field artillery to the front. Liaison's basic job was to observe enemy action, and observe firing accuracy of artillery shellfire, then to fire "for effect" when they came close to or on target.

The survey crew was about at the same level as liaison, as they were there observing enemy action looking for new gun positions before anyone else in the battalion.

Thursday, March 11, 1943   On guard from 2:00 from 3:00. Wrote letters to Ray and Ethel.
Opened cans the rest of the time. Had to use the kitchen truck to take the mess out this noon, but the battery came in tonight.
Fairly nice weather.

Friday, March 12, 1943   Up at 7:00. Slept pretty good last night for a change. Rained some again. Washed a pair of O.D.s.
Got letters from Mary Jean and LaVonne. Wrote to Mom and Mary Jean.
Some fellows were hauling American rations somewhere and brought some for us. Opened the canned bacon, sliced it, and made hot cake batter.

I'm not at all sure how we got these rations, but there always was the lurking idea that somewhere some rascals were switching English rations to us, and doing something else with ours. Some were caught, and some were not. None of us could position himself to be a detective and find out either.
A letter home dated the 12th said I had received the news that Uncle Reinke died. I said there had been no more oranges or tangerines for some time. I said that no incoming mail had been censored for over a month. I hadn't seen Harvey or George Olson, but I had seen their unit's (109th Ordnance) markings on some vehicles.

Saturday, March 13, 1943   On guard 12 to 1 a.m. Up again at 4:00.
Rose and I made coffee and oatmeal here, fried the cakes in the field. Everybody appreciated the meal. Back at 10:00.
Limey rations for supper. 3 fellows captured from B Battery; 68 of 133rd Infantry were killed. Quiet on our front. I went out tonight with the food. Saw Don. Raining a little.

I'm not sure how we could have made hot cakes unless we'd taken the kitchen truck out to the front where the men were. B Battery's kitchen was always up front with the men, as most of the men were on the gun crews, and it was easier to give them hot food that way. The objection however, was that it was always another vehicle to have in a dangerous position and to camouflage.
Rommel had left Africa for good. On his way home he met Mussolini in Rome and Hitler in East Prussia, but was not able to persuade either of them to withdraw from Africa.
At home, Americans were extending Lend-Lease agreements for another year. (We thought we would surely be home by then.)
The cost up until February to keep the Battle of the Atlantic going was

almost ten billion dollars.

The Roosevelt Administration made the decree that workers were not to change their jobs in some industries, unless this could be shown to be beneficial to the war effort.

Sunday, March 14, 1943   Woke up at 7:00. Was raining. Still is at 10:00. Got 2 *Life* magazines and *Farmer* yesterday. Letter from Ray, Mom. Laid in tent almost all day. Read Bible, other material. Sunday makes me more lonesome than ever. On guard 10:00.

We wonder more and more: Where are the chaplains? Some of us reason that if he is having services of some kind elsewhere on Sundays, there are another 6 days in the week that he could come to other places. I haven't seen one for months.

Monday, March 15, 1943   Up at 4:30. I went out with the usual poor breakfast for the men.

For supper, the usual poor supper for the men: English steak and kidney, with some leftover luncheon meat and pears. Rose took it out. Andy came over for a little while. Through early.

People at home think we are getting all we want to eat, and that it's the choicest food. Well, maybe it's earmarked for us, but it's not coming through. Anyone who has seen the Quartermaster supply dumps say it's a wonder more of it isn't going to the wrong places.

Tuesday, March 16, 1943   On guard 2:00 to 3:00. Capt. Fischer is O.D. [Officer of the Day]. The password tonight is "Check." The response is "Them."

Up at 7:00, washed some clothes, changed. Got new suit of greens. Read *Life*, *Farmer*. Rained hard. Took sponge bath. Cool.

Wednesday, March 17, 1943   Up at 4:00. Went out with the supper. Raining, wet, miserable.

Went to see Don. Got a *Life* magazine, and a long letter and poem from Ethel Nash.

What We Are Fighting For

From Park Avenue to the Golden West, 'tis a glorious sight to see
Life with sorrows, tears, apprehension, fears; yet above all, free.
It's worth our while to keep such things within our hearts today,
To protect our work, worship, laughter; each one of us must pay.

AND THERE SHALL BE WARS

The sacrifice is high, you say, but have you given it a thought?
The life we have and what's to come, once the battle's fought?
Stop and think. Look about you at the life we have today,
Like a glorious book, you're free to look before deciding it's worth the pay.

Ski tracks in fresh snow, the air so calm and still,
The stars overhead, and a moon casting shadows on the hill,
The crunch of snow beneath your boots as you step briskly along,
Click of skaters on a nearby lake, sleigh bells tinkling like a song.

The first trace of spring, the smell of warm moist ground,
Fresh green, green grass, a dandelion, and the first flowers to be found.
The smell of new buds after a warm spring rain.
Newly plowed fields along the country lanes.

Children in the city, skipping gaily home from school,
Their carefree hearts and laughter will not be silenced by a rule.
Theaters and parks, museums, the penthouses and tenements;
They are all ours, and for each they carry sentiments.

The newsboy on the corner shouts politics to the crowd.
The criticisms of Washington are long and very loud.
We are free to send our choice to that lawmaker's land.
To speak, to vote; they are the rights we all demand.

From cathedrals on the avenue to the parish in the hills,
Come aristocrats, middle classes, the people from the mills,
With bowed heads in humbleness, thank God for all this.
We are free to go to Him, when life is happy or amiss.

The sunrise over a mountain is a blessing to behold,
As the world of beauty about us, before our eyes unfolds.
Pale shadows in the valley to the blaze upon the peak.
The splendor hushes the world, makes the strong feel meek.

A herd of cattle strolling home from mountain pasturelands,
Stiff-legged calves, like mechanical toys, prancing in the sand.
Winding roads up mountain sides with pastel shades galore,
The fertile valley just beyond, as flat as any floor.

The smile on an infant's face as he begins to walk,
The jumble of words, the glorious day, when he begins to talk,
The happy mothers smile, as the father silently vows,
Their son is born in a free land; his head will not be bowed.

Our hearts are heavy for dear ones fighting to protect this life.
May God watch o'er them, lessening their pain and strife.
May we at home stand by and do our rightful share,
Help them and share when we can; this burden is ours to bear.

The Home Front has a battle to fight; we must not relent,
Take it like our soldiers do — let our heads and backs be bent.
The climb is long, with a heavy load; we'll get to the top.
We'll face our soldiers when they come home, with eyes that need not drop.

Ethel K. Nash   (1910 - 1996)

Thursday, March 18, 1943   Up at 7:00. Raining. 3 letters, 2 from Ray and 1 from Mom. Off. Laid in my tent all day. Read, wrote to Ethel and Ray. I can do that all day too, rest and read.

Friday, March 19, 1943   Up at 5:00. On guard, 11:00 - 1:00, before 5 a.m., that is.
George is with me again. They took off the night cook, as there are mostly only the kitchen detail here.
Lucky to have had this place so long, and it's not a bad spot. Raining a little, but dryed out considerably. To bed early.

Saturday, March 20, 1943   Up at 6:30. Washed clothes, shaved, took sponge bath. Changed, packed over my things. Took the tent apart, dried it out. Beautiful day. Seen Don, read quite a bit.
Letters tonight from Mom, Pat and Alice Reinke.
George Pittlekow got word his brother was killed at home.

In the first V-mail I sent home from Africa, I told them the country was mountainous and hilly with not much vegetation, and the letter ends with the sentence, "I'm still opening cans, and we're still on English rations."

Sunday, March 21, 1943   Up at 5:00. I took food out this a.m. with Sgt. Sanders. Started filling in the garbage hole tonight.
On guard 9:00 to 11:00.

Being on guard on a real dark night was no fun when you were alone while everyone else was sleeping. It was best you had your gun on and ready. It was hard to keep awake too, and you had better not get caught sitting down or even leaning against something. After the war, I never could stand the dark again, and I always had a ready light on around the house.

Monday, March 22, 1943   Up at 7:00. Shaved. The air mattress has a leak. Read some, went to see Don. Nothing eventful.

Tuesday, March 23, 1943   Up at 5:00. George went out this morning, I tonight. Hot. Got magazines.

Wednesday, March 24, 1943   On guard 1:00 to 3:00. Shaved. Took a sponge bath. Read *Life*. Took a bath in the creek, too. Another hot day. Got sunburned. Some Jerry planes over this a.m. early while on guard, and also this morning.

Thursday, March 25, 1943   Up at 3:00. Hot cakes. Hard job to put them out. Stew for supper. I went out alone tonight. Had a headache all day. To bed early.

This one fellow came through the line for his ladle of Limey mutton stew, and he said real loud, "Hi, Wag, I see you guys flushed out the kitchen truck today." He said that to Sgt. Meagher one time, and Bob was mad enough to put a bullet in his head.

Well, the poor guys sure had a solid gripe coming, though the cooks had little choice in the matter.

The Cooks Life

We are just crummy cooks that slave every day,
From two in the morning till nine p.m., with little more pay.
No one appreciates whatever we cook;
"Stew and beans again!" they holler, with just one look.

I wish some would starve or start eating hay,
It would lessen our work and shorten our day.
They think we will bake cake; what will be next?
For the appreciation we get, what do they expect?

They come around crying for a bite to eat,
It's between meals now, don't try to cheat.
The Quartermaster is stingy about a man's ration,
So we dish it out after that fashion.

Stew and beans is what they gave us,
So please don't make such a big fuss.
Eat it and like it, or starve on the way,
Because that's what's on the menu today.

Wilmer Wagner, 1943 -- Algeria

Friday, March 26, 1943 Up at 7:00. Busy all day. Got another *Life*. Washed, shaved, took a bath. Packed over my things. Wrote to Rod.

The infantry moved out last night. I walked over there tonight. Took pictures of shells, picked up some souvenirs. Packed up ready to leave tonight.

Waited until 1:00. Came about 30 miles. Slept a little.

Saturday, March 27, 1943 Got here at 4:30. Close to Sbeitla, closer to front. On all day. I went out tonight with the food, saw a demolished jeep. Got the speedometer needle from it.

Deng and I fixed up the tent. Tired. Nice in here. Have candle for light. Mattress holds air again. Are in an old hospital spot. They have it made of gas bead ons.

Some planes in the air. Charlie Battery lost a jeep today. Blowed up by a mine. None killed, but casualties.

Sunday, March 28, 1943 Up at 6:30. Cleaned up. Thankful it's the Sabbath and I'm off. Fried hot cakes for fellows here. Went over my things. Got 7 letters. 3 from Mom, 1 from Pat, 1 from Ray, 2 from Art and 1 from Jean. Another *Life* and *Farmer*.

Got a new shelter half. Put it up in place of Deng's old one. Fairly nice, but windy. Wrote to Arlene and Ray.

Dug slit trench and part of foxhole. A lot of aircraft, mostly friendly, but there was some firing.

Monday, March 29, 1943 Up at 5:00. Corned beef, sausage, coffee. Was nice this morning. Rained, cool, windy the rest of the day. Went to see Don tonight. Sure nice that we don't have to take food out.

Tuesday, March 30, 1943 Up at 7:00. Ate. Showed Hoteck my pictures. He showed me his. He knows Duluth.
Don and I went to Sbeitia with water truck. Saw 4 graves, some old buildings that were falling down, and French garrison that had been bombed.

Back at 11:00. Got paid 630 francs. Read some, cool and cloudy. Got into an interesting conversation with Ed Hoteck on taxidermy and photography.

I can't remember a thing about who Ed Hoteck is, or how I met him.

Wednesday, March 31, 1943   On guard 9:00 to 11:00. Up at 4:00. Hot cakes, eggs. Fried hot cakes in the field. An easy day.

Thursday, April 1, 1943   Up at 7:00. Ate. Fixed the sides of my tent with cardboard. Took a sponge bath. Put my map together in Day's truck. Reading and writing in same place. Washed some clothes tonight. Went to see Don a little while.

Friday, April 2, 1943   Up at 5:00. Hash for breakfast, classics for supper. Got ready to move, but didn't. Had to put our tent back up again tonight. On guard, 9:00 to 11:00.

Saturday, April 3, 1943   Up at 6:00. My day off. Shaved, cleaned up. Got 3 letters from Mom and Sis. Started writing home in cab of 6X6 that we move with us.
   Loaded, left at 10:00. I drove the old truck. Muffler is off, makes a lot of noise. Came about 5 miles. Set up again. Put up our tent. Finished writing my letter in truck. The band and A Battery are close by.

Sunday, April 4, 1943   George and I on all day. Warm. Take food out with a jeep and trailer.

A letter that I wrote home on April 3rd didn't say much except that I had a good place to write in the cab of the truck. I wrote a lot of little things to make a longer letter, and the letter had a "6 cents due" stamp on it.

Monday, April 5, 1943   Cleaned up some things. Write in cab of the truck. Did nothing of importance. Don came tonight.
   Loaded up. Pulled out at 6:30. Arrived at 10:00. I drove the extra 6X6. George rode along in the cab. Not easy to drive in blackout, too hard to see.
   On guard until 11:00.

We had now turned over our defensive position at Sbeitia to a battery of self-propelled 105 tanks and gone into assembly area west of Fondouk.

Reconnaissance was made by battery commanders and the Battalion S-2. Position area was a spot with heights to the east occupied by the enemy. There was no good observation available to use except Djebel Trozza to our left rear. An Observation Post there would put us fifteen thousand yards from the first objective, too far to be of any use.

We were now a part of a groupment in general support, commanded by Gen. Hess of the 36th F.A. Regiment.

CHAPTER 15

Assembly area west of Fondouk. Hill 609. Quit cooking.
Machine gunner. New job, Battalion Agent

Tuesday, April 6, 1943   Up at 3:00. Corn fritters, scrambled eggs for breakfast. Slept in the cab of truck last night. My knee bothers a lot, though, when I'm cramped.

Served 3 meals today instead of the usual two. Hot. Have a headache. Rations today while in cactus patch. Through at 7:00.

Wednesday April 7, 1943   Up at 6:40. Washed clothes. Nice, but windy. 7 letters. Picture of Mom and Arlene. Write in the cab of the 6X6. Sleep close to it for protection. Tech came back from the hospital tonight, and he is the regular driver of it.

I never got to know Tech much. I'd enjoyed driving the 6X6 for awhile, and I enjoyed writing letters in the cab.

The battalion moved (without the kitchen) into position with misgivings. We were the largest concentration of artillery used to date in the II Corps sector.

The following battalions were involved: the 125th F.A., the 175th F.A. and the 185th F.A., all part of the 34th Division, and the 178th F.A. of the 36th Division. There was also support by a heavy concentration of British artillery — with the mission of clearing the heights to the north of the pass at Fondouk and to all the French in front of Pichon.

Thursday, April 8, 1943   Up at 12:30 a.m. Ready with 2 meals: one for here, and one to go out to the front.

At 3:30 I followed 1st Sgt. Deutchens out. We got lost, went 16 miles and found our battery. The attack started at 5 a.m., and we had to come back through it all. Then we had to move up a ways ourselves. Dug the truck in.

Supper not until 11 p.m. Dead tired, and we didn't count the close ones.

At 6 a.m. our infantry requested artillery fire. Fire was delivered, then

lifted to allow the infantry to proceed. There was tough fighting most of the day.
.

Friday, April 9, 1943   Slept until 12:00. Cleaned up. Slept some more. Guard 9:00 to 11:00. There was plenty of fire in and out, but no real close ones. I was thankful for the day off and rest.

Saturday, April 10, 1943   Up at 12:30. Left with breakfast and dinner at 3:30. Back at 6:00. Our battery was shelled last night. No casualties.

Left with supper that George and Rose made, and came back at 10:00. 3 letters. The Germans have retreated some.

It was a mixed-up day, mostly due to us having been under fire, and changing locations.

At 1 a.m. several German 88's came in, and our position was hit. Col. Sylvester's trailer was hit twice, and the colonel was hit during the shelling.

I usually headed for under the kitchen truck for shelter rather than a foxhole, as the truck seemed to offer more protection. A direct hit from an 88 would get you no matter where you were.

We were learning that in addition to blowing as many bridges and blocking as many roads as they could to slow our advance, the Germans had the habit of sending a "parting shot" of artillery shelling prior to a withdrawal. This seemed to be it, as the Germans soon withdrew, and both the British and ourselves secured our objectives.

Life got pretty hectic for the cooks, especially when we had to take hot food to the men near the front. It was always a chore to go out with the meals. Usually there would be a special driver, and several K. P.s went along — but I've gone out with only one helper and had to drive myself as well. Coming back in daylight under observation was no fun either.

B Battery's kitchen was usually up front, within walking distance of the 105 mm guns. There was no problem to provide hot food for the men. A skeleton crew always had to be on duty, so the men had to eat at staggered times.

Our Headquarters Battery was different in that a lot of our details could function a little to the rear just as well as near the front. There were some obvious reasons why no more than the necessary vehicles should be closer to the front.

Sunday, April 11, 1943   Up at 6:00. Shaved, cleaned up all my things. Was really a mess. Have my own tent set up.

Went for one of my solitary walks. Enjoyed it. Level land, but went far enough away to be alone. Read my Bible. Felt lonesome and blue. Such a nice day. Wrote home.

Went twice to see Don, but not there either time. Probably out with a meal.

There was some air activity, including a lone Jerry fighter that brought 3 Junker 87 bombers over our lines. Four bombs were dropped, one close to Battery C of the 175th (no casualties), and one near the O. P. of our battalion.

The JU-87 was a dive bomber or Stuka. We taught the Germans that diving wasn't always the best policy, because our 50 caliber machine guns made them more vulnerable to attack than if they just flew overhead, and left when they were done bombing.

The area the Germans had just evacuated was really devastated. We were given the credit for covering that area thoroughly with our shellfire.

This area also showed that the Krauts had prepared this position for comfort as well as defense. Nearby houses had bunks and eating arrangements, even chickens, so they could have fresh eggs.

Prisoners who were captured appeared to be well fed and equipped, and they commented on the devastating effect of the American artillery fire.

We Americans would have had things set up just as comfortably as the Germans did, but at this stage of the war, we were advancing and changing positions too quickly to allow this. But during the coming winter months of 1943 - 44 and 1944 - 45 in Italy, we weren't advancing, and we set up our quarters as fancy as the Germans could.

Monday, April 12, 1943   Up at 3:00. Hot cakes. Was heck frying them.

Bill and I got rations with the jeep and trailer. I went along with dinner. Back at 2 p.m. We moved up close to the battery. I went along with supper too.

Fourteen recruits came in to fill up our battery strength. Was dead tired. On guard tonight 11:00 to 1:00. Made a real decision today to be transferred to anti-tank as a machine gunner.

Even though we were finally back on all-American rations, my mind was made up. I wanted out of the kitchen. We were already hearing rumors of invading Sicily and Italy, and I wanted more action in the future than in the past.

I had been on the anti-tank crew in Camp Claiborne, although this was similar only in name to anti-tank here. Here the 50 caliber machine gun was mounted on the back of a weapons carrier.

Tuesday, April 13, 1943   An exciting day. Finally got to leave the kitchen. Slept in the open last night. Washed all my clothes. Took a

sponge bath. Shaved, washed my hair. Got paid 630 francs. Told Sgt. Meagher, First Sgt. Deutchens and Sgt. Agness that I wanted to leave. Turned in my stripes. Went to see Don. Together we went and looked at the smashed P-38.

Had to go talk and ask Capt. Genung if I could leave the kitchen. He wanted me to stay and even offered me a T-4 rating, which is like a sergeant, and is a first cook. I thanked him, but said I'd rather not, so he said, "All right, but remember, you're going to be my next Mess Sergeant if you want to be or not."

I think I smiled a bit when I said "Yes, Sir," but I thought to myself, "Not out here supervising someone opening cans with shells falling around us."

Sgt. Agness came after me in a peep. I rolled my bedroll, went with him to Cpl. Bradley's truck and got more acquainted with the 50 caliber machine gun.

I had been a T corporal with 2 stripes as a 2nd cook, and Genung offered me a T-4 rating, or sergeant with 3 stripes. More pay as a first cook — but then someone else would have had to been broken down to a second cook, and that wasn't what I was after.

Wednesday, April 14, 1943   Slept in the open, alone. Up at 5:30.

Sgt. Hogfuss is in charge of our two 37's, and my 50 is in the first section.

"Objective," Brad says, "is to hit what you shoot at." He showed me how to take apart the gun.

We moved up a short ways. No problem moving up with this outfit. I man the gun on moves and am on the ready when we do move. The gun is mounted on a weapons carrier.

Mess at 12:00 and 6:00. Are close to the battery now. Read some, slept, wrote home. Got acquainted with the fellows.

Thursday, April 15, 1943   On guard 2:30 - 4:00. Up at 5:30. Chow at 6:00. Rolled up my bedroll. Did nothing much all day.

The big difference here is that you are already ready to move when the order comes, much unlike the kitchen where it takes all kinds of preparation.

We were now in a bivouac area near Mantra, and we engaged in a service practice. There was much firing of our guns, and some practice was done every day. To prove we could shoot with accuracy, the Division Artillery Commander had the barrage followed by artillery men playing the role of infantry.

Guns were calibrated, and in general, we settled down to a spit-and-polish routine. Cleanliness of men and material was emphasized, and you had better not neglect to salute all officers.

We were all supposed to be seasoned veterans, and most of us didn't like it at all that we were back to a training schedule.

Friday, April 16, 1943   Up at 4:00. Left at 5:00. Came about 40 miles north. Are in a spot with lots of shrubbery. Put up my tent. Cleaned the 50. Played catch. I went to see Don.

Saturday, April 17, 1943   Up at 6:00. Policed the area. Cleaned the 50. Ag showed me a few more things about it. Road hike this a.m. Not so bad, exercising, and I enjoy it.

Wrote to Arlene and Ray. Good meals, get plenty to eat, and finally it's all American rations. Hot all day.

We never had the problem of not enough water. The water detail would find a source river, spring or well, and set up their pumps with gas motors. They'd purify the water, then it would go into 5 gallon bead ons and most of it was hauled to the kitchen.

The Brass knew they had better keep a close eye on the water supply to be sure it was close, and that it was clean and pure. Otherwise they would have ended up with a lot of sick soldiers on their hands. There were always plenty of water holes to pick from, but some weren't the best.

Sunday, April 18, 1943   Up at 6:00. Mess is usually around 6:30. Some shouts and hollering at the approximate time always tells you it's chow time. Guys come running from all over. You're taking your mess kit apart as you're running to the chow line.

Calisthenics for half an hour.

Went to church with a rifle on my back and helmet on my head. Chaplain Walker gave the sermon.

Road march this p.m. Cross country, good exercise. Five rolls of film tonight from Ray. I see Bye and Cajune now once in awhile. Got ahold of some boxing mitts. We are not in a combat zone now, with the Germans heading north in retreat, so we have the training schedule in force.

Monday, April 19, 1943   Up at 5:30. Raining. Haven't much appetite. Not much duty or training today.

Read some. Got *Life* and *The Farmer*. Some Iowa boys usually want *The Farmer* when I'm through with it, and the *Life* magazine is always in big demand. Very few other fellows get any magazines, and I think I get more letters than anyone.

Mail call is always an exciting time when Pomerleau brings it back. The fellows gather around, and he calls the name. If the person isn't there, someone always takes it and puts it in his tent or vehicle for him. If he is on duty in Message Center or cooking, someone brings it to his area, and the fellow shoves it into a pocket until he has a chance to read it.

The sad part was when Pom got through calling names for the mail, and you didn't get a letter, and someone else got a lot of them. Some fellows rarely got mail.

Tuesday, April 20, 1943   Got all ready for inspection. Read *Life* magazine.

Had an inspection like we used to have at Camp Claiborne this p.m. The first I've stood with a rifle.

Off, and all through after 3:00. Read, played ball, ate. Cool and cloudy.

Wednesday, April 21, 1943   The only order today was, "Be ready to roll." I then went to see Don. Their kitchen truck is not far away. Played ball with the bunch. We left about 11:00.

Thursday, April 22, 1943   Traveled all night. Got here about noon. Stopped occasionally, slept very little.

Went through beautiful country, canyons and gullies. Lots of trees, mostly cork. The bark of cork is real thick, and there are many piles and bales of it.

Went through one town, was a sight to see again: white people, pretty girls nicely dressed, two little kids and cute.

Hot. Are in a fair spot with lots of scrub brush. Wrote to Pat. Fixed my mattress again. Played catch with my undershirt off. To bed early.

We were close to Roun-es-Souk, just a few miles inside the Algerian border. This was about a 120 mile move. We got 78 replacements for the whole battalion. We were finally up to full battle strength for the first time in a year.

Morale was considerably higher then what it was at Sbiba and Sbeitla. American rations were regular issue, and we were very thankful for that.

Friday, April 23, 1943   On guard from 3:00 to 4:00. Up at 6:00. Chow at 6:30. Good Friday.

We had to start taking Atebrin tablets for malaria. They are small, yellow tablets, and one of the medics was at the end of the chow line making sure you put the tablet in your mouth and swallowed it.

Brad and I boxed some. Beautiful out last night, also today. Jewell and I boxed. He showed me a lot of tricks. Hot until 4:00, then it cooled off some.

It's a good thing Brad and Elmer Jewell took it easy on me with their boxing. Both were pretty good and about my size. Sometimes I came away from them with a sore nose or sore in other places.

One of the first things I learned was that a round took longer to get through than I had thought, and that you would really have to be a professional to go the whole limit of 15 rounds.

Saturday, April 24, 1943
Up at 6:00. Was a little late for chow, but my old buddies wouldn't say anything. Rained some. Jewell and I boxed. We made coffee for ourselves. Read my Bible.

Went for a walk over the hill. Saw a pile of cork and trees, some large fruit that looked

like an onion. To bed early. On guard 10:00 to 11:00. Still raining a little.

Sunday, April 25, 1943, Easter   Up at 6:00. Had class V eggs and ham, wheat cereal, grapefruit, coffee. Sun came out a little, dried out all my things. Changed into clean clothes. Washed, shaved, cleaned my rifle and the 50.

Went to church. Saw George Niemi; he is the one who gave me 5 rolls of film.

Jewell and I boxed a little ... I'm learning. To bed early.

Monday, April 26, 1943   Up at 4:00. Chow. Packed up, ready to roll now at 5:30. Left at 7:00.

One hour for dinner. Class E's for that.

Came here at 3:00, in open grain field. Hot, dusty ride, but I enjoyed it. Saw beautiful viaduct, must be 100 feet high. Lots of pillars to it. Came down a narrow mountain road, winding roads, breathtaking sights.

Supper at 6:00. Left at 6:30. Came here to the front at 7:30. Germans are within 8,000 yards. Heavy artillery fire all night. Lots of German equipment along the road. Many tanks blowed up, trucks and ammo, and Mark VI tanks.

The entire II Corps was now moved up and on the left of the British First Army, putting an end to the questions of radio commentators and newspapers as to the whereabouts of the II Corps.

Our forward observers, Capt.'s Smith, Grant and Houle, and the O.P. crews stayed at their posts continually and fired the battalion. We drove the Germans back from the hills west of Sidi-Nsir to well-prepared positions on Djebel Tahent -- which was better known to us as Hill 609.

We weren't up against one of the average German units we had previously fought with, but with one of the best in North Africa. Their orders were to hold to the last.

Tuesday, April 27, 1943   On guard 11:00 - 12:00 last night. I could see shell bursts, then hear them.

Up at 4:00. Chow at 6:00. I always get enough. Cleaned up, shaved. Hot. Jewell and I went for a walk.

Some fire nearly all day. Fellow in B Battery shot himself. Not fatal. Cooled off. The cooks made dinner today. Slept some. Very little air activity from either side. I eat very little. I'm losing weight. Just don't have an appetite.

We packed and rolled out. Left at 8:00. Came about 5 miles. Rough road. Are 25 miles from Bizerte, behind the mountain that the Germans held yesterday.

Last night our infantry lost 32 men and several officers. Pvt. Ruben of Service Battery was blown up tampering with Jerry explosives.

The anti-malaria Atebrin dosage started a few days previously had started many cases of diarrhea and milk sickness, which did not help to make our situation any more pleasant. After a few days it was decided to suspend the use of Atebrin until after the campaign..

Thursday, April 29, 1943   Didn't get to bed until 1:00, and that was lying in the foxhole I had to chop out of the hard ground. Brad and Agness don't approve of my just lying under the weapons carrier when being shelled or sleeping. Then guard was 2:00 to 3:00, and up again at 5:00. Plenty of artillery shells coming in. Some landing close enough, but don't think we are under observation.

The flies are thick. Got *Life* magazine and *The Farmer*. Read while on gun duty. We have no special hours for that, but Brad is the corporal, and we have no trouble in keeping one or the other of us on gun duty at all times.

This p.m. Hawk [our driver], Pop Bratton and I went up the mountain that the Germans evacuated yesterday. A regular battlefield. Half of a dead German lying on top of the ground, killed by artillery fire. Blotch of blood by the body. Dead horse. A grave with an American helmet and 3 British. We didn't get too close, as Jerry has a habit of leaving that "parting shot" in the form of booby-trapping their own dead buddies.

Lots of machine gun belts full of ammo. Pop Bratton put several around his neck for a picture. Gas masks and lots of potato masher hand grenades, called "potato mashers" because the grenade is a can-like knob on the end of an eight-inch wooden handle. Much easier to throw, but a lot harder to carry than our "pineapple" grenades.

The area was full of shell holes: 88's, 105's, 155's, 240's and, of

CHAPTER 15

247

course, still the British 25-pounder. Memorable sight. Hard climb.
Took pictures.
    Awful hot. Mail. I took a bath in the creek after we got back.
Artillery fire all day long. Our battery is doing good work. Jerry
dropped some short and wide ones. Enemy planes over this p.m. Our
ack-ack opened up. Pretty, but a dangerous sight.
    Picked up some souvenirs. Supper at dark tonight. Laid down
early. I always wonder if we got in a lucky shot with the 50, or not.
    Brad has a personal reason now to fire the 50. His brother is
Missing In Action in the Philippines. I don't argue with him if he
wants to man the gun. After all, he is the corporal in charge, and
maybe he's a better shot than I am. I'm thankful to be here so it can be
manned at all times.

His Work To Do

You're a machine gunner now, with a job to do,
Shooting down planes, will be something new.
Your lips won't smile, you sing no song,
A machine gunner's life is usually not very long.

You sit there and wait for the enemy to come,
Maybe write letters, or daydream along.
Or think of your home, that you left behind,
And all of the things that you've seen sometime.

You dream of the girl who loves you too,
Wondering if she will remain forever true.
You might name your gun after a friend,
As it's your very best; on it your life depends.

You clean and shine it, keep it on half load,
At an instant's notice it must be ready to go.
You have to get him, before he gets you.
It's a hell of a job, but it's your work to do.

Your ears are trained to catch every sound,
Of a plane in the air, or a man on the ground.
You have to distinguish each kind of a plane,
Stuka, Fortress, Spitfire or whatever the name.

You hope it's friendly in a vague sort of way,
Yet your fingers are itchy, you must make him pay.
He's starting to dive, his belly opens up,
A bomb drops out, so you give him your stuff.

Your breath comes fast, as you aim with your tracer,
You have to be quick; he's coming like a racer.
Your gun is chattering, but you don't hear the noise.
You're far too busy getting him out of the sky.

He's trailing black smoke, you got in a lucky shot.
There he goes down, and you cut your first notch.
It's exciting as heck, but you don't feel right,
You wonder how you look in God's Holy Sight.

It's a hell of a job, but then this is war too.
You're a machine gunner now; that's your work to do.

Wilmer Wagner 1943 — Algeria

Friday, April 30, 1943 On guard last night 10:00 to 11:00. Up again at 5:00. Brad cleaned the machine gun. Nice guy, clean-minded. Has a lady friend back home. He's real sober, not much on talking, but sensible.

Washed clothes, played checkers with Jewell. Ate.

Went for a walk. I caught a mine wire with my pants. Saw the mine, also another one like it. We don't count the close ones. Back at 4:00.

Took another bath. Washed my greens. Supper at dark. Brad and I change off going first to eat, so someone is always at the 50. Two letters from home, one with a photograph of Rod and Arlene. They have changed so much.

On guard from 9:00 to 11:00. Artillery fire all day.

Saturday, May 1, 1943 Up at 5:00. Raining, chow.

We were dive bombed at 5:35. No damage right here. The 50 put out some rounds, then jammed. Have to take it apart or partly so, and put it back as fast as you can. I can do it in the dark now.

Our battery fired some last night close by. Makes a bright light. More going out than coming in, but you still cringe a little every time. We sum up the fear always by saying, "We don't know the real danger — or refuse to believe it."

The close firing shakes both the air and the ground. Instead of the British 25-pounders, we have all 105 Howitzers now that fire a 33 pound projectile

Dive bombed again by Me's. Our 50 did pretty well, but isn't quite right. Sgt. Agness checked it after, and found the head space was off.

Real good meals now with the American rations. We moved our truck to the top of the hill. Better vision for firing at planes. Are close to a bunch of Arab huts. Interesting, looked them over. Found some paper with Arabic writing on it, and baskets woven of rope.

Lots of German mortar ammo.

Mortars are a light weapon carried by the infantry, and fired by dropping the shell into the end of the tube. As it drops down, it fires on contact. A shell comes out with a short range, but designed to break up and soften enemy lines.

Sunday, May 2, 1943   On guard 3 - 4 a.m. Chow at 5:30. Cleaned my rifle, read some. Wrote home. Was badly bitten last night by chiggers.

Capt. Genung wanted to see me. I reported to him, and he offered me the job of Mess Sergeant. I thanked him and said, "I'd rather not, Sir." He wanted reasons, but I just said, "I'd rather not, Sir," again, and he let it go at that.

Lots of money and rank to let slip through my fingers, but I don't think I'll be sorry for it. Sgt. Meagher is talking back to officers and hard to get along with.

Read my Bible. Can't believe it's Sunday. Brad, Roy and I boxed for two hours. Elmer Jewell is driving the liaison truck.

Another exciting thing that happened on a Sunday. I'm glad I had the offer of becoming a staff sergeant, but there wouldn't be any challenge to it at all out here in the field. I sure would have taken it at a place like Claiborne, though.

Monday, May 3, 1943   Chow at 5:00. Finished reading Psalms. Went for a walk around the area. Saw caves made in solid rock, hewed out square. Boxed again with Jewell. Arabs are starting to move back into the area again, with all their belongings packed on horses, driving their cattle ahead of them. Hot this p.m.

The capture of Hill 609 was official by May 1, and we were holding it now. It was a major victory, as we had to take it before we could take Mateur.

It took the steady pounding of our artillery, and the infantry practically had to dig the Krauts out of the rock-hard foxholes.

Again, the captured Prisoners of War stated that our artillery fire had been extremely devastating, leading to their defeat. Enemy casualties from our artillery fire had been heavier than from any other cause.

Lt. Feinburg of the Air O.P. was a big help in using his flying skill in observing enemy positions. Battery D of the 107th anti-aircraft attached to our battalion was credited with downing two enemy planes, but there was no mention of Cpl. Wagner or Cpl. Bradley in downing any enemy planes with their 50 caliber machine gun.

Casualties were suffered on both sides. The only one in our battalion was Pvt. Ruben, who was killed when a German booby trap exploded in his hand.

On May 3rd we finished exchanging our British 25-pounders for American 105's. We had been promised them for 18 months. The fellows in the gun batteries were glad to have them, but of course now they had new things to learn about them, with the elevations and range settings. The trail was split, which made for a much more solid gun when it fired.

The British gun had bags of powder, and the American had brass shell cases. The 25-pounder was a good artillery piece, but about everybody agreed that the 105 was the better one of the two.

Tuesday, May 4, 1943   Cool this forenoon. Slept some this p.m.

Arky Vaughn came out and spent the afternoon with me. Everyone thought me foolish for turning down the staff sergeant rating. Bob and I went for a walk around. Saw the caves and graves again.

We were practically through in North Africa. The American 1st Division was given credit for taking Mateur, and that was the last German stronghold.

Wednesday, May 5, 1943   Stand about 35 minutes guard every night. The kitchen moved in here this morning.

Took a bath at the creek and shaved. Washed a few clothes. Got paid 600 francs.

Went to B Battery's kitchen. Stayed all afternoon. Had supper with Don. Andy is just as optimistic about going home this summer as always.

Traded an old shirt to an old Arab for 10 eggs. Cooked and ate 6 of them myself. Brad has a small stove for cooking coffee and small things.

Rolled up, left at 8:00. Got here at 11:30. Rough trip. Slept some.

Thursday, May 6, 1943   Up at 6:00. Looked over German plane that crashed. Ate dinner, moved a short ways. Waiting to go further. Had supper here. Pulled out about 7:00. Didn't come very far. Are in a valley. Guard from 9:00 to 10:00.

Friday, May 7, 1943   Rained last night. Got a little wet. Up at 5:00. Chow at 6:00. Jerry dropping in some shells. Our artillery firing most the night and this morning. Are 50 kilometers from Tunis. Much less that that from Bizerte. 1st Sgt. Deutchens went out of his mind this morning, or is suffering shell shock. Pete Rettinger took his place.

Ellis rolled the messenger jeep over last night and got a little hurt, so Pete asked me if I wanted the job.

Did I want the job? I jumped at it. Pomerleau and I took the "peep" to Service Battery, had a few things fixed on it. Came to Division Artillery. Dick Johnson is the messenger from the 175th. Headache. At 9:30 I had to take a message back to our battery. Made it OK. Dark, hard driving. Raining most of the day.

I had hardly known this job existed in our battery, but the "Liaison Agent," or "Battalion Agent," or "messenger" from Headquarters Battery

stayed at Division Artillery. When there was something to deliver, be it daily reports, or papers or firing orders, it was all given to the Battalion Agent, and he took it to his Message Center in his "peep," our nickname for a jeep.

Each battalion, the 175th, the 151st, the 125th and the 185th had a Battalion Agent staying at Division Artillery. We were the brains (or nerves) of the 4 artillery battalions and were always in the area just back of the gun positions.

I soon found out that the driving was mostly at night under blackout.

The wire crews would lay wires on the side of the road to all gun crews, but if they were cut by shellfire or by anything else, there was no way to communicate with the guns to change orders. I don't think firing orders were often given by radio, because it could be intercepted. At any rate, we did carry firing orders at times, and our packet that we got from our Message Center was considered "top priority."

We were on duty 24 hours a day and had to be in the proximity of Division Artillery's Message Center's staff sergeant, and Joe Staniger, the Message Center's corporal. They had to know just where we were sleeping at night as well, so they could get us up and going. We hardly ever knew what we carried, unless it was the daily report or a bundle of the US Army's newspaper, *Stars and Stripes*.

I got some C rations from Supply that I carried constantly, as I wasn't always able to be at the kitchen truck for meal time, or get up in time to eat if I came in late. I knew what it was to have to save food for someone or make something special for one man when he came in late, so I seldom bothered the kitchen crew for a late meal.

A flattering description of canned C rations was that "They are as appetizing as they are nourishing. They are light, easily carried, and offer plenty of variety. One day's ration of type C, the basic emergency ration, consists of meat and beans, meat and vegetable, hash meat and vegetable stew, biscuits, sugar, soluble coffee, and 5 different kinds of candy for dessert."

The Army had 30,000,000 cans of this ration which most soldiers carried. Other specialized types of rations used by parachute and armored troops contained as many calories in even smaller space. The Army was making certain that the soldiers would be well fed.

When we were on canned rations, they were almost always C's, except for a few exceptions when we had K's. The C's were never well liked, and they weren't agreeable to me, except for the can with the biscuits, soluble coffee and sugar. A day's ration consisted of 3 cans of the biscuits, one of hash, one of beans, and one of meat and vegetable stew.

I could usually add something to the can of biscuits and get by. The hash and beans and stew would always give me heartburn, though I ate enough of it anyway. In the summer I usually managed to eat off the land when I couldn't make it in for regular chow time.

Saturday, May 8, 1943   Up at 6:00. I stay at Division Artillery. Chow is good. Seems to be more of it. I like this job a lot already.

Finished writing my poem. Made one run this morning to the 151st. About 15 miles. Got my water can filled. The peep runs good despite its being turned over the other night. Dried out my things. Fixed the peep up in some ways to suit myself. Packed up all of Ellis' things. There still is a chance he may get this job back after he comes back from the hospital.

Cleaned up. Dressed in O.D.s. Put up my tent. Am very well satisfied with everything. Hope there's not too many night runs.

Will write to Ray. Wrote a poem, *Battalion Agent*, and another,

The Cook's Life.
   Supper here at 4:30. Good meals so far. The kitchen is better run than ours. Gassed up with this maintenance. To bed fairly early.

   Ellis did come back, as he wasn't hurt very badly, but they didn't put him back on the job. He was from Arkansas, a nice likable fellow, but not really suited for a job where you had to be quick and a good driver.
   I used to say I was better qualified than Ellis, because I had less brains and more nerve than he had. Our motto as messengers was, "Either drive it, or park it." (And I've always held to that motto since, and have taught my son the same, and he's passed it on to his children and grandchildren.)
   The four of us agents hung out together quite a bit, as we were always on duty. I had known Dick Johnson from the 175th in Camp Claiborne, but I hadn't seen him since. We were glad to see each other again, and be together for the duration. Floyd Johnson from the 125th was from Duluth and a real pleasant fellow. Scotty from the 185th always did his job, but we didn't associate as much with him. Joe Staniger (from Hibbing, Minnesota) and Jack Salzer, both working in Division Artillery Message Center, were together with the two Johnsons and me a lot as well.

A Battalion Agent

He works at night, in rain and grime,
Moonlight or not, he tries to find
His battalion's position; it's quite a game.
Good roads or bad, it's all the same.

He's tired as heck when he lays down at night,
Then someone wakes him; he's in for a fight.
He's given a message; what, he doesn't know.
He starts for his peep; he's off to the show.

The road is rough, and it might be wet,
But he's rough and tough, he's always set.
His peep will respond at the slightest touch.
For he's bound to get there; it matters much.

If the road is under shellfire, or being strafed by a plane,
Through wheat or minefield, it's still the same.
His faithful peep must take him through.
It's his very best friend; he keeps it like new.

He can use lights, but he'd rather not;
Perhaps they would get him on the spot.
He travels along at a pretty good clip,
In spite of the roads, with all those dips.

He's wide awake now, for he has to be.
There's a truck stalled on the road, so hard to see.
He slams on his brakes, missed it by an inch,
Turns to his left, off again; this job is no cinch.

It's still the right road; seems he tells by the smell;
With all these turns and trails, it's hard to tell.
He gets through the bomb craters, lucky as yet —
Lucky this African Campaign hasn't cost him his neck.

There's the road that he takes to the right,
But what meets his eyes is an awful sight:
A bridge blown out where the water is deep,
But nothing can stick his faithful peep.

He throws it in low; the motor roars,
Shoves the front wheels in gear, as he nears the shore;
Puts the transfer in low range, tramps down the gas,
He's going through, and he's going fast.

Now where is the place where this officer lives?
He has a sealed message to him he must give.
There's his pup tent, but he's sound asleep.
How can he do it, with the noise of that peep?

The message is taken, and he starts back;
It's cold and raining, the night is still black;
So again he goes through; it's the same either way.
Oh, why can't he do this during the day?

He finally gets back; his nerves are on edge,
Turns off his peep, heads for his bed,
Drops on the ground and prepares for a snooze,
Leaves on his clothes. He's too tired to move.

He awakes in a daze; someone has yelled his name.
"You have a message to deliver; don't mind the rain."
He jumps in his peep; his mind is still hazy,
For he's a Battalion Agent, and it's driving him crazy.

Wilmer Wagner 1943 -- Algeria

CHAPTER 16

R.R.R. Tunis runs. Officers' rotations. Visit to Hill 609. Orders
back to Oran.

Sunday, May 9, 1943   Made a run at 2:30 this morning. Dick came
with me, then went to both Battalion Headquarters Message Centers.
This is permissible so long as the material we have to take isn't top
priority.
    The Message Center at the 151st has Sgt. Tom McGee and Cpl.
Lynn Miller running it.
    Looked for our old kitchen [where I was cook], but couldn't find
it. We were really looking for a cup of coffee. It went pretty good.
Fairly light out. Up at 7:00. Hot cakes for breakfast. Read my Bible.
    Almost hit another peep. He was parked with no blackout lights
on. We moved this p.m. about 8 miles. Are closer to our battery now.
Put my tent up again. Are in a wheat field. Fellows got ahold of some
wine and are feeling good.

After only 1 day of service practice in which the gun crews shot 62
rounds merely to orient the gun crews, the battalion moved into an assembly
area west of Mateur for the attack at Chouigui Pass.
    The battalion survey detail here hit a Teller mine with their quarter-ton
vehicle. It blew Sgt. Prill and Cpl. Staples right out of the vehicle. Though
Prill was burned in the chest, and Staples had a broken eardrum, and others
from the detail were bruised and stunned, they went on with their work and
finished what proved to be a very accurate survey.
    The survey crew had to make positions for the guns before they pulled
in, and there were many things to consider. They were up front more often
than I was, and further up front than I was, as well.
    Charlie Pease of Battery A was seriously wounded here when a shell
burst near his vehicle. Two days of fighting and firing here terminated our
activity in the Tunisian Campaign on the 8th of May.
    There were some real good reports of the Air O.P. with Capt. Constant
and Lt. Feinburg doing some effective counter-battery firing from the Piper
Cub. Otherwise, observed fire was very difficult due to the many rolling
hills that hampered observation.
    B Battery's position was shelled with one round passing through the

camouflage net and landing 18 inches from the ammunition pile of the 4th gun section. There was no damage or casualties, but Jerry once again gave us all he could with his "parting shot."

One thing that was learned in this campaign was the ineffectiveness of the 37 anti-tank guns that I had trained on in Louisiana. They were soon dubbed "the paint-scratchers" and removed from the US Army's use. They had been used a lot around Kasserine Pass, Fondouk and Hill 609, but it was found they didn't pass the required tests in front-line combat.

Monday, May 10, 1943   Up at 6:00. Breakfast. Made a run to the colonel with a special.

Everything is pretty quiet. It's officially "over," though the German Air Force still persists in dropping a few bombs.

We are only about 40 miles from Tunis. Got an ideal tool box. It had been for German ammo. Slept some. Laid around most of the day.

Made one run tonight. The battalion had moved, but not far, and were easy to find. Got rid of Ellis' things; took them to the Supply Sergeant. Mail tonight. I got 10 letters and a *Life* magazine.

Tuesday, May 11, 1943   Slept with pants and shirt off last night. Jack didn't think there would be any specials going out tonight.

Up at 6:00. Picked up some German boxes last night. Mounted them on the peep. Have all my things in order now. One run this morning to Message Center. Dusty, lots of traffic.

The battalion is in assembly area. Seems like the war is over in North Africa, only mopping up left to do. Read *Life*. Got candy rations: a bar of chocolate, the first since March.

A run this p.m. Our battery was hard to find too. Got my peep serviced.

Rettinger is First Sergeant, as Sgt. Deutchens isn't coming back here. I guess his mind just snapped, and they had to take him away. Saw the boys from the kitchen. Wrote home, to bed early. Took off my clothes again. Bright moonlight and cool on the face. This job will be tougher if we go to Sicily and Italy.

Wednesday, May 12, 1943   Up at 7:00. Rigged up my stove from a German ammo box. Works well; have hot water for washing and shaving now.

One run tonight, and one this afternoon. Took Schank along, who wanted a ride. Went to A and B's kitchen, saw Don.

Hot. Flies are thick. Took an outside shower.

Thursday, May 13, 1943   Up at 7:00. Sleep with tent open at both ends and the mosquito bar up. Slept most the forenoon. Two runs this p.m. Hot, but cool breeze. Picked up 3 good chains for the peep on the road. Washed some clothes. Another run before dark. Show tonight, *Call Out the Marines.*

Friday, May 14, 1943   Three runs to the battalion or the battery during the day. I'm never sure what I carry. Some of it comes over the Message Center switchboard; other things come down from the officers' quarters.
   Ellis came back. Don't know if I'll keep this job or not. They moved the Message Center tent closer to the kitchen.

Saturday, May 15, 1943   Slept in the open. Dick and I went back to our old area. Washed our peeps. Went back tonight and took a bath there too.

Sunday, May 16, 1943   Nothing doing this a.m. Went back to the battery on noon. We moved 35 miles. I traveled behind the colonel. Are beside Lake Bizerte, part of the Mediterranean Sea.

   The guns had hardly cooled off, before training schedules made their appearances, and the battalion was engaged in a training program complete with service practice.
   The close of the African Campaign left the battalion with a small casualty list, with only 12 wounded, and one killed. There were good reasons: Our officers had top training, which helped and, of course, we were not infantry, who suffered a much larger list of casualties. There were Silver Stars given for gallantry, and some citations were awarded for meritorious conduct.

Monday, May 17, 1943   Put up my tent. Had my mind going quite a bit today. A lot of running around to the batteries. 3 letters from home.
   Sister Arlene's birthday. She should be 7 years old today. I was harrowing in oats at home with the team the day she was born.

   This was open wind-swept area. Some Arabs were around, and some grain raised. Oxen were the horsepower around here. Days were hot, and nights cool, even cold.

Tuesday, May 18, 1943   Helped the battery police up German equipment this a.m. Went to see Don tonight. Windy and raining a little.

CHAPTER 16

Got a *Life* magazine.

Our job here was to police (clean up) a large area south of Bizerte, and to guard salvage dumps. The men picked up lots of souvenirs during this period. This was the area the Germans had made their last stand in Africa. The colonel's order was to relax and take life easy.

The German Luftwaffe visited Bizerte almost every night during the period of May 16 to June 4. On one of these nights, a stray bomb landed near the battalion area. According to our official 151st F.A. historian, Capt. Grant jumped into bed when he heard the bomb whistling down. Maj. Surdyk tried to crawl under a gas can. They did everything but what they should have done, that is, crawl into a foxhole.

Capt. Grant and Maj. Surdyk were always friendly to me when they were Battery Commanders. I had cooked for them in Ireland, and my face was always around the kitchen, so I suppose they remembered me.

Wednesday, May 19, 1943   Up at 6:00. Breakfast at 7:00. Washed and shaved. Went in swimming in Lake Bizerte. My first time in salt water. Cold, but fun when the waves splash up. Slept this p.m. On duty after 6:00.

Thursday, May 20, 1943   Slept inside the building last night. Up early. Made four runs to all the batteries' C.P.s this morning. Got another peep, a Ford. Runs like new compared to the old one.

Bob and I took off tonight. Went to Bizerte. 60 miles round trip. All bombed out. It's flat, deserted. Back by 9:00.

Friday, May 21, 1943   Up at 7:00. Cleaned up my things. Put some things in the peep. Hot weather, dry. Lake Bizerte is very calm.

Saturday, May 22, 1943   Nothing much doing. Pom and I went to the 133rd Infantry Headquarters. Took a wrong road. Nearly got to Tunis. Nice country. Blacktop road.

Sunday, May 23, 1943   On duty. Dull day. We take turns on the Message Center switchboard when days are dull, so we have something to do.

Went to the salvage dump twice. Got a Jerry bead on, filled it. Went swimming. Made coffee.

Monday, May 24, 1943   Up at 6:30. Nice. Every morning the sun shines in my tent. Went in the lake twice today. Am learning to swim a little. Enjoy myself a lot.

Show tonight. Broadway picture.

I took the operator back to Division Headquarters, about 40 miles each way. The peep has bright lights. Had the windshield down, a little cooler breeze then. Warm, though, and a real enjoyable drive. Didn't get back until 12:00 midnight.

We were all taking old Col. Sly's advice about relaxing and enjoying ourselves. Nobody was pushing us anywhere, and I can't recall any fellows goofing it up for others. All the Battalion Agents were back staying with their own Message Centers.

Tuesday, May 25, 1943   Up, chow, shaved. Cleaned out my tent. Read, wrote.

Put a German rifle rack in my peep. Had to go to Service Battery with it, and have Louie Day bore a few holes in the dash. It holds the rifle in a vertical position next to or between the 2 seats.

Was in the lake 3 times today.

Another show tonight, *Devil and Miss Jones*.

Wednesday, May 26, 1943   On the switchboard for part of the day.

Didn't feel so good. My throat is sore, and I can hardly swallow. I had this one time at home when I was 16, and about this time of year as well.

Thursday, May 27, 1943   High wind all last night. The lake is rough. Went quite a ways towards Tunis on a different road.

Went out with our salvage detail. Hauled back part of a plane and a burned car. Found a good pair of pliers.

Went to ball game, but they didn't have any.

Friday, May 28, 1943   We were bombed last night. So was Ferryville and the docks. The search lights looked pretty, and all the ack-ack and colored tracers.

Felt tough. Didn't sleep well. No report of any damage, but it brings you back to reality in a hurry. I don't think any of our anti-aircraft guns are set up for use and manned. No American aircraft either. They are still using most of or all of it on the Western European Front and against the Japs in the islands and jungle warfare.

Saturday, May 29, 1943   Felt tough. Laid in my tent all day. Ate nothing. Hoping I'll get better and won't have to go on quarters or to a field hospital. I worry about getting back to my outfit again and missing some of my things.

Sunday, May 30, 1943   Rolled all night. Chills and fever. Up at 7:00. Feel somewhat better, at least like moving around. Nobody bothered me; the place is quiet.

I wanted them to take my tonsils out, but they said at the medics, "Probably not; it'll go away on it's own." It finally did, and I still have my tonsils.

Monday, May 31, 1943   Feel better with my throat, but my stomach isn't all OK yet. We moved a short distance to the other side of the lake. The whole battalion is pretty close together now.

No one bothered me to take out the morning report or any other communications. I suppose either Tom or Lynn did it — but the colonel has been true to his word: this is a serious R.R.R. [Rest, Relaxation and Rehabilitation].

Tuesday, June 1, 1943   We have Message Center in a small tent by ourselves. My pup tent is close by. Went swimming this p.m. Mail today. A lot from home.

Wednesday, June 2, 1943   On guard 4:00 - 6:00. Ate some as long as I was up. Got my air mattress fixed yesterday so it holds air again.

Thursday, June 3, 1943   Usual thing. Hardly any driving, and Message Center has more help than is needed. I've been practicing my typing, written a few poems.

Friday, June 4, 1943   Moved this p.m. Are southwest of Mateur in an open field. Have toothache. Are close to the kitchen. Went over there. Bob made coffee for me. It's still nice to see them again, working with them as long as I did — but I'm glad I'm out.

The 3rd Division moved into the Bizerte area around the 1st of June. They needed the space along the lake for amphibious operations, so on June 4, the battalion moved to a wind-swept tundra near Mateur.

We were riddled by details before we had time to settle down in the new area. Capt. Houle and eighty men were sent out to guard a Prisoner of War (P.O.W.) camp near Jefna station. Capt. Vaught took over a P.O.W. camp at Sefanare. C Battery was sent to Tunis on Military Police duty. During the shuffle, Capt. Grant became the Provost Marshall of Tunis.

There weren't enough officers and men left back at Mateur to even pretend we were training.

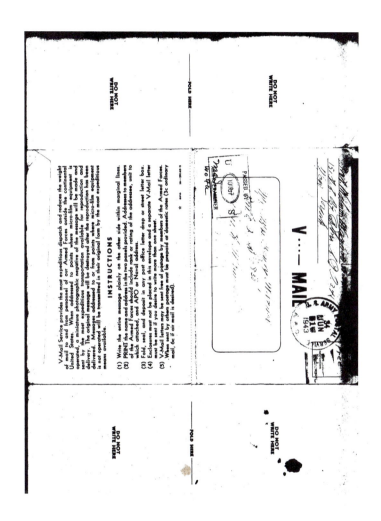

Saturday, June 5, 1943   Up at 5:00. Bacon, eggs for breakfast. Put up my tent, are following a schedule. Didn't do much.
Show tonight. *Blonde Goes to College*. In 125th area. Went all together in a truck. Fairly good, outside. You sit on the ground and watch the show, and run for cover if planes come over — but that's about stopped now.

Sunday, June 6, 1943   Up at 6:30. Cold. Hot cakes for breakfast. Washed, changed to my O.D.s. Feel dressed up. Went to church with Don.
Had my shirt off. Went for a walk. Saw an Arab mosque with graves around it. Other fellows went to a show. Me here alone. Wrote letters, stamped battery mail. Hot and flies.

Monday, June 7, 1943   Up at 6:00. Washed my hair. Dug latrine. Ground is hard and dry, like powder. The Arabs are cutting grain.
Read *Readers' Digest*. Hot. Sat in the sun most the day. A little ice cream tonight. Wasn't a bad show, and band in concert at 175th F.A. *To Be or Not to Be*. One letter from Mom.

Tuesday, June 8, 1943   Up at 6:00. Learned the decoding machine. Read, shaved, cleaned my rifle. Didn't do much else. Hot. Went swimming in the Mediterranean. Am making progress.

Wednesday, June 9, 1943   Up, went to Tunis on a one-day pass. Two truck loads of us went. Kind of a nice town and not shot up too much. Lots of nice-look-

ing French people. Phil and I stayed together. Drank a lot of nectar and ate sandwiches that we brought along. One girl who we talked to on the street could talk some English. Left at 7 a.m. and back at 9:00 tonight. Bought some souvenirs.
Took a picture of a French funeral that was delayed until now as it was a high-ranking French officer. Horses pulling the funeral carriage.

Thursday, June 10, 1943 Slept good, washed all my clothes. Made trip to Division Artillery. Hot. Pom and I are alone here. Louis and Lynn are at school. Wrote 5 letters tonight.

Pom went to a show. I'm all alone with A Battery's agent, who knows Bob's father-in-law. 2 letters, 1 from Ray, and 1 card from the kids. A picture of Mom, Sis, and Rod with roses.

Friday, June 11, 1943 Had the phone in my tent last night. Up at 6:00. Finished the letters. Will send a package home. Bought some bookmarks. Sent them out.

A mine went off close by here. Turned over the weapons carrier. 2 seriously injured. Piece of shrapnel landed real close by here.

Worked on the M209 A. Am learning it OK.

Saturday, June 12, 1943 On all day, nearly by myself. Typed tonight. Pom went to the hospital. Have a bad toothache.

Sunday, June 13, 1943 Slept a little last night. Moved my things to Division Artillery now. My turn this week.

Have my peep in the olive grove. Put my tent up as usual. Slept some. Tooth doesn't ache so much. Had 4 runs to the battery.

Went to Mateur twice tonight.

Monday, June 14, 1943 Not much doing this forenoon. Came back to the battery. To stay this p.m. until further notice — which is hard to say, but I like staying at the battery too.

Went to see Don and Andy. Took them to the show. Was very good. Saw Charlie Jurvelin. He was wounded in February and just got out of the hospital.

Probably one the few times I've ever neglected to mention it was my birthday. I was 24. Personal feelings were sometimes pretty cheap during the war.

Tuesday, June 15, 1943 Up at 5:00. Put my tent up while it was still cool. Went to Division, washed clothes.

Wednesday, June 16, 1943 Not much doing today. Went on a few trips. Was made corporal today, but not a T corporal like before.

My pay was raised, with 20% more for overseas pay.

Thursday, June 17, 1943   Up at 5:00. Fell in for reveille. I went along with B Battery to where they are going to guard prisoners. A medic, Keller, rode with me. Lots of Italian and German prisoners along the road on the way back.

I nearly turned over the peep. Too sharp a curve, too much loose sand and dirt, and too fast. A 6X6 stopped and pulled me out backwards. The peep was none the worse, but both my legs are awful sore. One is skinned, and one is swelled.

Friday June 18, 1943   Very sore and stiff. Lucky I didn't break any bones yesterday. Wrote to Ray. A special to Division Artillery tonight. Stopped to see Don. One letter from Ray.

Saturday, June 19, 1943   Up as usual. Inspection by 1st Sergeant. Cleaned my gun, straightened my rack. Slept this p.m. Got some films developed [through the mail]. Cool wind. Flies worse than ever.

The flies are so thick that when you eat, there's usually some fruit with juice; when they put it on your mess kit cover, the juice runs down your hand and arm, and the flies follow it all the way down.

It's hot as well. Lynn Miller and I have water fights. The water gets so hot in the bead on, that it's too hot for comfort when you throw it at one another. When you drive with the windshield down, the air is so hot it takes your breath away.

Sunday, June 20, 1943   Had to go to Division Headquarters this morning. To the southwest — 40 miles each way. Took most of the day. Stopped several times to look at grapes. They are well taken care of and loaded. Some fields are pretty big, and the vines are staked and pruned. Not ripe enough to eat yet.

Monday, June 21, 1943   Usual day, I guess.

Tuesday, June 22, 1943   Same routine. I am the only agent on several trips to Division Artillery and around to the line batteries. Took mail to S-4.

Tonight I took Tom McGee to Division Artillery, and Pom to a show. Don went along. Got 10 letters and birthday cards. A long letter from Pat. Answered hers, and wrote *A Nerve Center*. Typed quite a bit. Went along with Don to his kitchen. He made coffee.

Wednesday, June 23, 1943   Up a little late. Wrote to Ray. Typed 2 copies of the poems. Sent one to *Stars and Stripes* and one to Pat.

Pom is going to school at Division Artillery for 10 days. Finished my letter. Sent some negatives home. Didn't feel good tonight. Didn't eat any supper.

Thursday, June 24, 1943   Slept good share of the day. Don came over this p.m. Wrote a sentimental poem for Lynn for his girlfriend.

Went to Tunis tonight with a message for Capt. Grant in the center of town. Was nice to see him and be greeted too. Back at 10 p.m. Drove around the main streets.

Capt. Grant was Provost Marshall of Tunis, kind of a military Chief of Police. I'm sure a lot of policing had to be done, as there was a large GI population. Tunis was quite a large city, but I never got lost. It made it easier that there was very little civilian traffic, and also there were quite a lot of rear echelon troops stationed in the city who knew their way around and could help us out.

There were fruits and vegetables for sale in Tunis, but I never stopped at the stands or markets to buy. Our food was pretty good now, and I was starting to stop once in awhile to pick some blue grapes that were starting to get ripe.

Friday, June 25, 1943 Got the oil changed in the peep this morning. Pom and I went to Capt. Vaught's prison camp. All Italians fenced.

This is the prison camp at Sefenare. Capt. Houle's camp for Bat-

tery B is near the Jefna station. They cook a part of their food, or at least have an outside stove belching smoke.

They have a lot of the prisoners on the roads working, leveling off. Hard driving because of it. The prisoners don't look very dangerous — for them, of course, the war is over.

We heard later that prisoners were sent to the United States for the duration, were given good treatment, and that they were even allowed to go to dances. Needless to say, this didn't help our morale the least bit as we were still fighting the war.

Saturday, June 26, 1943   The usual routine. Greased the peep myself. Don came over, and I took him back. We always have a lot to talk about and look forward to — after getting out of this mess.

Sunday, June 27, 1943   Same thing. Hot, don't remember much. Not even church services to strengthen my faith. I guess the chaplain takes turns where he goes.

Monday, June 28, 1943   Laid around most the day. I got 6 snapshots from Ray. My turn to go to Division Artillery for a week.

The Rhythm Majors were here to put on a show.

Made one run to all battalions. Really nice to be back here again for a week. The fellows really treat me nice. Joe and Jack at Message Center switchboard are real good to work with. One or the other is always on duty.

The Rhythm Majors were the official 34th Division band, but this was the first time I'd ever seen or heard them. The band leader was Mickey Levine. His dad came to the Farmer's Market in Duluth to buy vegetables.

All battalions were fairly close together, and most of the traveling here was done during the daytime. No one had to holler at you to put your helmet on either.

Tuesday, June 29, 1943   Up at 5:30. Breakfast is fair to good here. Put my tent up under an olive tree. Washed, shaved. Then had to take Capt. Jones to the 151st and 185th. One run to all battalions this morning.

Took a cold outside shower. One more trip to all 4 battalions tonight. Hot. Division Artillery usually selects better positions to stay than the battalions, especially when in rest areas — more Brass. This place has quite a few olive trees for shade, but the battalions have none.

The ones in command, such as our Capt. Genung, had their own vehicles and drivers, but some captains, 2nd and 1st lieutenants, and master sergeants on down didn't.

While we Battalion Agents were in action, we had to work most of the night, and then haul someone else where they needed to go in the daytime, as well. Most of our passengers weren't hard to get along with.

Wednesday, June 30, 1943   Up at 5:30. Hot cakes, and they were really good.

Took Joe to 175th. Hot. Haven't much ambition anymore.

We went and took a shower this p.m. They have salt tablets. Took quite a few of them today. Feel better.

I washed my mess kit in gas tonight and got some of the black off of it.

Met another fellow from Duluth: Maki.

The ammo dump in Mateur has been blowing up for 2 hours, set off by a mine. Two fellows were killed. Sounds like we are back in action.

Thursday, July 1, 1943   Up at 5:30. Good breakfast. Made 2 trips early, to the 175th. Other usual trips during the day.

Took Jack out tonight. He was looking for wine.

It was always fun to take Jack Salzer out somewhere. Usually, it wasn't for Message Center business. But when someone else was at Message Center to keep things going, Jack and I made many unofficial trips together during the next two years.

Jack's dad owned a seed company in the Twin Cities, and Jack had a good upbringing. He never got angry at anyone, and when we were in action, he really hated to send us agents out in the middle of the night with specials.

Friday, July 2, 1943   Got mail today: 1 from Mom, 1 from Ray and 1 from Alice Reinke. Answered them.

A fellow from the band [authorized] and I went to get wine for the officers.

Mr. Irons and I went to the show, *Crystal Ball*. Not much.

Mr. Irons was a likable fellow and nice to talk to. He was single and was a lot older than the rest of us, probably in his 50's. He went through the entire war with those of us much younger.

He was the overall boss of Message Center and the Personnel Section. We agents had to haul him places often.

When we were in rest areas, speed limits were in place. Mr. Irons would always caution me when I was going over the speed limit, as there were some punishments for speeding. (I held to the idea of "Either drive it, or park it.")

Saturday, July 3, 1943   Usual routine. Not much doing. 2 V-mails from Mom.
French people on stage show at the 175th. Several French girls there.

I always drove to these places. Anyone was welcome to jump on the peep and go along. If enough fellows wanted to go, they'd send a truck.

Sunday, July 4, 1943   Up at 7:00. Parade for all battalions for fellows who received the Silver Star and other decorations. Several runs to all battalions because of the parade.
Read my Bible. Will write to Ray.
Went to a show, *Tortilla Flat*. Saw it before. Took Pom along. In the 185th area.

Monday, July 5, 1943   Had to go to all battalions at 2:30 this morning. Overslept because of that and missed breakfast.
Cut off a pair of pants, hemmed them up. Read, slept.
Came back to the battery tonight with all my things. Dick Johnson's turn to stay at Division Artillery now for a week.

Tuesday, July 6, 1943   Usual run of things, but there have been some personnel changes.

On July 1, Maj. Warner and Capt. Genung received orders to report to Washington, D.C. They were surprised by their sudden good fortune, and lost no time in moving out.
Capt. Genung was the fatherly type, and we both respected each other. I had appreciated him offering me the Mess Sergeant's job, and I got a kick out of his dry, dramatic way of saying, "This is it, Men."
Another thing I'll always remember him by is the joke he used to pull often on Tom McGee. It always went over good in the chow line when the situation was tight. The captain would yell out real loud in the confusion, "Sergeant McGee!! Have you seen that driver?" Tom would stop in his tracks and ask in a real sober way, "What driver, Sir?" Capt. Genung would answer, "The SCREW-driver!!"
Tom would slap his knee and laugh, and all of us would too; because even if we had heard it before and it was silly, it still seemed real funny and always relieved some tension.
Well, that was past history now, and we had to keep on to whatever came next.
Col. Sylvester had been promised a trip home and, on July 5, was relieved of assignment as Battalion Commander. The next day, Maj. Gerald DuBois arrived to take over his duties.

CHAPTER 16

Our long period of inaction following the fall of Tunis was not beneficial to us from the artillery standpoint.

Wednesday, July 7, 1943 Put my tent up. We moved behind the orderly room. In a large tent with Sgt. Molde.

Went to a show tonight. Saw *Pride of the Yanks*. Very good.

Thursday, July 8, 1943 A few runs today. Really this p.m.

Washed out my greens. Don came back for a little while. B Battery is still at the P.O.W. camp. Lynn and I went for a shower tonight.

Friday, July 9, 1943 Up at 5:30. Slept a little more later. A letter from Robert Hamilton in Ireland. Pom and Arky went to the show tonight with me, *In This Our Life*. Starred Bette Davis. Don't like her or Olivia De Haviland, but it was a good picture.

Saturday, July 10, 1943 Usual day and battery runs. One V-mail from home. Got some negatives back from Jerry.

Allied invasion of Sicily this morning.

Lynn and I boxed some this p.m. Went to show tonight with Bob and Lynn, *Born to Sing*. Had seen it before.

Sunday, July 11, 1943 Up at 7:00. Did nothing more than lay around all day. Lonesome as heck. Not many fellows around. Not even church services, but still hot and flies.

Monday, July 12, 1943
Usual routine this forenoon.

This p.m. I drove to where I first got this job over 2 months ago. Tried to find a place to wash the peep. Couldn't, as all the creeks are dry.

There is an American graveyard there now with over 100 crosses on

it. The graves brought home to me something I seldom realize, how many fellows gave their lives, and how fortunate I was.

Show tonight, *Meet John Doe*. Very good.

The attack on Sicily started the night of July 9. The Germans had about 240,000 troops, of which half were demoralized and poorly equipped Italians.

By July 12, we were to have 150,000 ashore on Sicily, and soon to have 400,000, of which half were British.

Gen. Eisenhower was Supreme Commander over Gen. Patton's Seventh Army and Montgomery's Eighth Army.

There was an Allied air bombardment of Sicily. New equipment was being used. LST's and LCT's [see September 3, 1943 commentary] were being used to put armor ashore with the infantry.

Well -- there went our chance to help chase the German and Italian Armies out of Sicily -- someone else was doing the job for us.

From the United States, Churchill and Roosevelt issued a special statement calling for an Italian surrender, and suggesting to the Italian people they get rid of Mussolini. In Italy, some of the Fascist politicians were beginning a plot to accomplish this.

European air operations were going well for the Allies. Hamburg was raided in one of the most effective attacks of the European Campaign. In the Battle of the Atlantic, U-boat activity was at a lower level, though 25 boats were sunk the past month.

Tuesday, July 13, 1943 Pomerleau used the peep last night and cracked the crankcase. All the oil leaked out. Service battery welded it.

Hot. No mail, no ambition. Seems I'll go nuts if we stay here much longer. The usual thing day after day. Am irritable. Can't think with a sentimental attitude anymore like I used to. My only hope is home and salvation.

Am still thankful to God, of course, that everything is as it is, after all.

Wednesday, July 14, 1943 Didn't feel good all day. Laid in my rack. Had fever.

Hot. Flies. You feel like, "Why fight the flies? I'll dump the food and forget it."

The grapes are ripening, though, and I know where some vineyards are.

Thursday, July 15, 1943 Felt tough all day. Went on sick call for the 3rd time in my Army career. Didn't eat yesterday or today. Wanted to have my tonsils out, but they won't listen to me. I can hardly swallow. Laid on my rack all day.

One V-mail from home.

CHAPTER 16

Friday, July 16, 1943   Up as usual at 5:30. Hot cakes and bacon. Feel much better. Back on my job again.

Heard the Arabs' meal-call this morning. Still dark. Wonder what they eat; it can't be much.

Felt pretty good, though no appetite.

Saturday, July 17, 1943   Nothing new. Got a hunting knife and New Testament plus 2 V-mails from home.

Sunday, July 18, 1943   The usual runs. Slept this p.m. Shower tonight. Blue grapes are tasting good again. And they are really good, with no bad ones like in bunches we would buy in stores at home.

Monday, July 19, 1943   Don't remember much. Don't feel at all good. Show tonight. Went to Ferryville and Mateur.

Tuesday, July 20, 1943   Felt tough all day. Hot as heck. Show tonight. Double feature.

Wednesday, July 21, 1943   Up at 5:30. Ate breakfast. I spilled coffee over myself. Had to change. Other batteries are back now. More running for me, but I don't mind.

Thursday, July 22, 1943   Usual thing. The 175th moved out tonight. B Battery is back too, so I went to see Don.

Friday, July 23, 1943   Went to the 133rd Infantry with classified material. In the left rear. Roads are fair, but dusty and hot.

Soon as I got back, I had to go to Tunis with more classified material for Capt. Grant. Really had to roll along to make it.

Showers at Mateur tonight.

This was the first full day I'd had in quite a while. I really had to keep the peep in high gear. I was able to take out some frustration and anxiety with my foot and the gas pedal.

Another thing was obvious to anyone who could read the signs: They said, "A move is in the making."

It was nice to get to Tunis again, and to see Capt. Grant and others.

Saturday, July 24, 1943   Usual routine, except not as much running. Division Artillery has moved to Division Headquarters.

Went to Mateur to the salvage dump. Got a windshield for my

peep from an American staff car, which fits. The whole dump is American vehicles, more smashed up and demolished ones than one would imagine. Some tanks literally blown up inside. Seems impossible that men can ride, drive, and fire the big guns they have on them, all at the same time.

Went to the showers tonight. To bed early with a bad headache.

Sunday, July 25, 1943   Went to see Arky Vaughn, had coffee. Breakfast at 7:00. Didn't do much this forenoon.

This p.m. Jerry and I went back to where we finished in action close to Hill 609. Saw the American graves, about 100, some with dog tags hanging on the crosses, others without. Some marked "Unknown American Soldier." Stumbled on to what might be the Ervin Gulbranson I know. The place is fixed up nice. A fence around the whole cemetery with a gate. Took two pictures. The odor is strong.

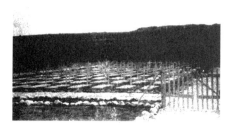

Took a shower tonight. Washed the peep.

Monday, July 26, 1943   I knew it was coming, and it did, first thing this morning. A hot news flash: "Pack up, get ready for an 800 mile trip. We leave 6:30 tomorrow morning."

Where? Back to Oran for amphibious training. I washed my greens, changed oil in the peep. Started loading up. Ready tonight to leave. All tents down. Made a trip to all battalions in the dark.

Well, this trip shouldn't be cold and snowy like the one was in February. I didn't have to worry about where I'd ride, either, as I'd be driving my own vehicle. There were other pluses too: I was better acquainted with the men and the country.

Of course the biggest question was, where would we be going after more training? To a new front, or to train new troops or — what about occupational troops in Northern Ireland? Wagner voted for that one.

CHAPTER 17

To Oran and back to Tunis. 1600 mile round trip.
Waterproofing peep. Getting ready to go.

Tuesday, July 27, 1943   Up at 4:30. The "All present and accounted for" response was at 6:25 a.m., and at 6:30 we rolled west.

I am the 3rd vehicle in the convoy. Maj. Thomas and Sgt. Molde are the first two. I am close up front, as I am road marker when needed in a larger town or fork in the road — I stop, direct the rest of the convoy, about 100 vehicles, and am then expected to pass the whole convoy and do the same thing all over again.

We came 130 miles today, which was good. Through Tabarke where I was road marker, and bought some really good grapes.

With Lynn and Jerry along, it gives us a chance to look around the towns a bit too. It takes a long time for the convoy to get through, because if a vehicle has trouble, they just have to wait for Service Battery's big maintenance truck with the 3 mechanics, Sgt.'s Shurke and Norman, and Cpl. Day to fix it, and then I am the last vehicle until  I can get up some speed and start passing about 100 vehicles.

The lead vehicles travel about 40 mph, the ones towards the last? As fast as you can go, just be sure to keep a 100-yard interval.

Being a road marker was fun. You always had a group of natives around you, and the time went fast. A lot of the way was mountainous. Pretty good road, though some was really dusty.

Wednesday, July 28, 1943   Up at 4:45. Left at 6:00. Good road all day. A lot of blacktop. Road markers again in a town before Constantine.

Went through Bone and Constantine. Beautiful scenery by Constantine. There is a monument on top of the mountain, tunnels carved out of rock and deep drops to the valley below. Took several pictures.

I had almost caught the front of the convoy, but had a flat and had to wait for the service truck to change it. Made 159 miles.

Bought eggs, 33 for 100 francs. Boiled all of them tonight and made coffee. Johnson and Ellis entertained us with their singing. I especially like to hear Jerry Ellis with his southern drawl. They sing all older songs.

Constantine is about 400,000, so road markers are necessary even if there isn't much civilian traffic. We look forward to the evenings.

Thursday, July 29, 1943 Up at 4:45. Breakfast is ready. We eat (the cooks can sleep on the road), get in line, all units report and are accounted for — and the order is given, and we roll at 5:45.

Made 169 miles today. Went through beautiful mountain country this p.m. Good road all day. Went through one good-sized town, Slediff, but no turnoffs, so we didn't have to be road markers.

This is the same road we traveled in February, but there is no way I can remember any of it. Camped in a dusty spot tonight. All vehicles are close together.

Jerry Ellis wouldn't take the messenger's job back for anything. He said, "Get up all hours of the night, drive in blackout with the Krauts shooting at me? And if I turn the peep over again, I may get hurt. They can keep that xxxcensoredxxx job!!"

Well, I was glad in this case that one size didn't fit all.

Friday, July 30, 1943 Up at 4:45. Rolled out almost right away. Traveled along all forenoon. Got in a grape field and got my fill. I had to be the first one in Blidiff to direct traffic through it. The forward party kept on going to better arrange the permanent campsite that we are to have tomorrow. Then to pass the convoy again. It wasn't really necessary, as there was only the one questionable corner all day.

I think it's Mother's birthday. I thought a lot about it, anyway.

It wasn't a real chore to pass the whole convoy on blacktop mountain roads. The 6X6's mostly had a trailer to pull, and there were 16 6X6's pulling guns. They had to take the mountain curves fairly slow, and in a lower gear than we did.

Then too, there was little oncoming traffic, though what little there was served to brighten up my day and make it less lonesome.

Saturday, July 31, 1943   We rolled at 6:00. Tiresome driving when I have to stay in the convoy, but this p.m. I had to go ahead and meet the advanced party at our permanent spot and direct the rest in.

Are close to the Mediterranean. Went there for a swim tonight. Lots of work for me. Had to go to all batteries several times. Got through late. The peep stopped on me.

There were lots of guys in for a swim that night. We could quote the saying of "not seeing all of America, but seeing all of a lot of Americans."

I had to get hold of Louie Day to put points in the peep. The Service Battery was a bunch of really busy boys while on the move, with a lot of maintenance to do. Somehow they also took care of getting enough gas and rations for the whole trip.

Sunday, August 1, 1943   Put my tent up last night. Slept good. Up at 6:00. Am quite a ways from Message Center. The area is rocky and barren and hilly. Had lots of running this forenoon, then left at 10:30 with Mr. Irons for Division Headquarters.

We went through Oran, and it's on the other side. Got back at 5:30. Got lost in Oran. Hard town to find your way through. Mr. Irons wasn't much help either.

12 letters caught up with me. One from Phyllis O'Connor in Minneapolis who I don't know. She got my name from a list of Army names. I didn't answer, at least not yet.

I asked Mr. Irons where he thought we would be going to, and he said, "Wag, even if I knew, I probably couldn't tell you because of security, but look at a map and figure it out for yourself."

So of course, we started thinking and believing we would be a part of the 2nd Front to be landing in France from England. I was thinking maybe there would be the possibility of seeing Peggy again.

None of us liked the thought that there would have to be a "Big Push" that would have to come off sometime to end this war. My personal thoughts were somewhere between I didn't know, or I refused to believe.

Monday, August 2, 1943   Up at 6:00. My peep on the bum again. Louie Day fixed it again.

Washed and cleaned myself, washed my clothes. Started writing letters. Did typing for Sgt. Molde.

Our trip was 834 miles. Lots of running with specials and regulars all day.

Tuesday, August 3, 1943   A very active day for me from 7:00 to 9:00 tonight. Paid, but all I got was 130 francs.
Completely tired out, and nothing really even went wrong. But I'm just tired going steady to all battalions and the batteries with papers and documents.

The official 151st History had this to say about our stay near St. Lou, Algeria: "We were moved to this area for amphibious training, but our efforts during the next week certainly left everyone dizzy."
We had service practices, mockup landing practices using DUKWs (amphibious landing vehicles), and the usual training schedules were thrown at us every day as well. The S-3 Department seemed really disoriented.
The final line for us was just as usual: We did "as told."

Wednesday, August 4, 1943   Up at 6:00 as usual. Still have a few grapes left from the other day for my fresh fruit.
Got the morning reports collected from the batteries, and I wasn't needed until this afternoon. Went around to all the batteries several times this afternoon.
Canteen rations this afternoon. We usually get Lifesaver candy rolls that we give to the French kids, and Burma Shave shaving soap, some cigarettes, and a few cans of beer that I trade for something else or give it away.
Had to haul Gen. Ryder to the 133rd Infantry and didn't get back until after 9:00. Gets dark about 10:00.

Thursday, August 5, 1943   Up as usual at 6:00. Followed the truck to the firing range so I'd know where it was. Took Doc Lyons out there and left him. Always stop for several big bunches of grapes when I don't have anybody riding with me. There must be hundreds of acres of grapes around here.
Washed clothes. Wrote up this. Jerry and I went swimming in the Mediterranean. It's about 5 miles.
Usually takes me until 9:30 at night for all distribution of papers, orders, etc. Played White's guitar a little. White is a 6X6 driver, so he can have room some place for a guitar.

Friday, August 6, 1943   Got to work at 7:00. Had to stamp mail. Off until about noon. Sorted some negatives that I will send to Ray. Read

Life, *Farmer* and the Bible. Ate early. Took Sgt. Johnson to Division Artillery. Dispatch to Division Headquarters and Artillery Headquarters.

Took a new route. Hot. We go through Oran, through the long underground tunnel that we traveled first in Africa.

The air holds tenseness for all of us. Beginning preparedness to move where is anyone's guess. My guess is one of 3 Mediterranean islands.

Thoughts of possible more battle and another boat ride with full field equipment are sore ones.

Back to camp at about 4:00. We stopped and put out a grass fire. Got grapes. Sgt. Johnson didn't mind stopping to get some too.

Tonight Jerry came back with his brother. Made me think of when and if I ever see Ray or Roger again.

The grapes were similar to the blue ones we used to be able to buy in the US in wooden baskets, only these were sweeter, and had no seeds. We could eat them like corn on the cob, instead of just a few at a time, as there were no spoiled ones. All were made into vino — red, sour vino.

Saturday, August 7, 1943   Up as usual. On runs until 10:30, then to Division again with Revels and Bradley. Stopped at Red Cross. Gave a French girl and a fellow a ride to Airel-Teurk. Was nice to have a woman and her friend along, even if we couldn't talk much together. Got back about 3:30. Stopped to get grapes.

Jerry and I went to the beach. Breakers were big. Was fun diving into them. Stayed in the water about an hour.

Sunday, August 8, 1943   Up as usual. Got morning reports. Drained all differential grease and the crank case.

While I was doing it, Leonard Reveness came over. He is with Jerry Ellis' brother in the 907th Ordnance. Was a big surprise to see him. We talked of what news each of us had received from home. He had dinner here with me, and then I took him back as far as the Oran road.

Washed my greens. Getting ready for our move tomorrow.

Went to 133rd Infantry tonight. Picked up our signs. Got some big grapes as big as wild plums, blue.

Took the tent down tonight. Got to bed around 10:00.

I had known Leonard Reveness through school. He lived in Hermantown, but went to school in Duluth. Sometimes he used to visit our

Washington School in Hermantown with a friend, Engman Johnson. Leonard's dad had a farm on Springvale Road that I remembered seeing as we drove to Duluth when I was young.

Leonard heard where I was through Jerry Ellis' brother.

Monday, August 9, 1943   Up at 5:00. Ate. Tore down the Message Center tent. Ready to move by 7:00.

Followed the 133rd Infantry. Went through several towns, largest of which was Sidi-Bel-Abbas. Half hour for dinner.

Arrived at the tour area at 2:00. 92 miles. Helped put up the M.C. tent, also my own. Nicely wooded area with Serub pine trees that afford a little shade.

For once, I didn't mind moving and coming ahead like this.

Kitchen tent is of frame with screen around it. Latrines are already dug, as 36th F.A. had been here at one time. The only objection is dust.

Tuesday, August 10, 1943   Not much to do until this afternoon when the line batteries came in. Then, some running around. Also tonight after dark.

Wrote a few letters, read, took a shower. Don came over.

Our area now was one mile north of Slissen for combat team training under 5th Army leadership.

The battalion engaged in shooting exercises every day. Our batteries spent 2 days shooting rolling barrages for the 133rd Infantry. The doughboys would have to advance under artillery fire as if they were in actual combat. Five infantry men were hit with flying shell fragments, and one of our men was hit. We expended nearly 6,000 rounds of shellfire on this practice.

There were exercises using tanks and infantry on the last day as well.

A lot of Brass were watching, and Capt. Houle was given high marks for directing it all.

Wednesday, August 11, 1943   Up at 6:00. I eat first now in the mornings, and come back while others go. Enjoy getting up a little earlier. Anyway, it's nice and cool nights, almost chilly in the mornings.

Washed clothes, changed to my chinos. Like this spot a lot. The trees make it so.

At 10:00, I got the peep ready, and took Mr. Irons at 11:30 to Division Headquarters. Got there at 2:30. Skipped Oran and Sidi-Bel-Abbas. Left again at 4:00. Back here after 8:00. Stopped several times. Pretty country. Whole trip was 221 miles.

One letter tonight, and canteen rations.

Thursday, August 12, 1943   Up at 5:15. Gassed and serviced the peep.

Followed Maj. Surdyk out to the firing range. Came back and took Col. DuBois out. Fairly easy day, but it's always 9:00 or later when I'm through. At least when not in action, I get 6 or 7 hours of uninterrupted sleep, and I don't have to stand guard when I'm on duty that long either.

Got 5 packages: 2 papers, notebooks, sharpening stone, and gum from Ray.

Friday, August 13, 1943   Up at 5:15. Not so much doing. At 4 p.m. we had to go on a stamina run for about a mile. To bed at 10 p.m.

At 11:15 Mr. Jurgenson called, and the guard got me. I have to take him to Division Headquarters. I got things ready, found some food and coffee.

Left at 5 a.m. and got there about 8:00. Lynn came along. Good road. I knew the way, went 50 mph most of the way.

Jurgenson kept his mouth shut. An Arab gave me a melon. Nearly ran down a chicken. I like to drive on trips like this one.

Mr. Jurgenson was the Master Sergeant in charge of rations, and a down-to-earth fellow. But he always sort of complained when I would bring my peep in for repairs. His remark was, "Wag, you're a hard man on horses."

No one ever told me why these fellows had to go where they did at such times of the night.

Saturday, August 14, 1943   Slept until 11:30. Serviced the peep. Another run to the batteries. To bed early.

Sunday, August 15, 1943   Up at 5:30. No day off for us here. Cool mornings. Left at 7:45 for Division. Got there at 10:45. Alone — the best time I've made so far, but I only stopped when I had to, and rolled right along.

Ate at Division Artillery. Talked to Jack and Joe awhile, and left again at 11:30. Back to camp at 4:00. Took my time on the way back. Had grapes, melons.

Gave a mother and her child a ride. She wanted me to stop and have vino at their house, but I didn't. I had some gum for the little girl. She was real shy.

Didn't seem much like Sunday, but I had a good time. Lynn, Jerry and I went for a stamina run before dark.

Some of the towns that I would go through on my way to Division Headquarters and Division Artillery were Slisson, Detrie, Sidi-Bel-Abbas, Breden, Las-Trembles, Oued-In-Bert, Saint Barbe, and Dutielet. It was about 93 miles. When I went through Oran, it was 110 miles.

Why was Headquarters so far away from the rest of the battalion? It was a good position, and the top Brass could have any place they wanted. R.H.I.P. (Rank Has Its Privileges.)

Monday, August 16, 1943   Not much doing for me today. The batteries are firing live ammo while the infantry advances. One of the infantry officers was killed today, and several wounded. One of our officers.

Tuesday, August 17, 1943   Took Sgt. Revels to the O.P. (Obervation Patrol). Saw Delmer Dunn, a cook who I met at Tynan Abbey in Armagh, Ireland. He is still cooking.

Slept some this afternoon. Running around this p.m. Took a sponge bath. Some mail tonight. 2 from Ray, 1 from Grandma.

Wednesday, August 18, 1943   Nothing unusual that I can remember of. Slept a little. Cajune and Bye were here from the 175th F.A.

Took part in parade tonight.

Thursday, August 19, 1943   Up at 5:00. Real chilly at this time. They are still practicing with live ammo. Usual day. Quite a bit running to the batteries. S-4 started taking over the mail now. No more stamping for us. To bed at 10:00.

Friday, August 20, 1943   Up at 5:00. Ready to roll at 6:15. Just took my blankets and personal belongings. Batteries are firing past Mapeno. Are in pine woods, and I'm sitting in my peep.

Came in at noon myself. We were supposed to bivouac here to-night but — orders are changed, and everybody went back to the battalion.

Tonight after supper we get this shocker: "GET READY FOR A 800 MILE TRIP. LEAVE TOMORROW MORNING." Back to Bizerte. Everything is in turmoil.

I took my tent down, made sure the peep was ready to roll, and helped take down the Message Center tent. No one says yet where to, but my guess now is Sicily.

First thing, I breathed a sigh of relief, thinking that it would probably be Sicily rather than what I had feared the last month: the Second Front in western France. But we soon learned that the campaign in Sicily was officially over on August 17.

I hadn't had much to do with keeping the peep ready for all the long trips I had been making to Division, but it was always ready to go another 800 miles, and the trip would be enjoyed as well.

There were a lot of opinions floating around that night. Some news came in that there was some shelling on the east coast of Italy by destroyers at sea. Then there was the news that the Germans had managed to escape to Italy across the Messina Strait, and there was the feeling that the Allies should have followed them up with an immediate move on the Italian mainland.

Well, we were sure the 34th Division was involved in some kind of a British-American dispute, and we were the military football of some top Brass.

Be that as it may, it seemed ridiculous to be making the same identical trip over again. Not too many of us could understand just what all was involved.

Saturday, August 21, 1943 If Capt. Genung was here this morning, he could say again, "This is it, Men." Who ever thought we would make this same trip back east to Bizerte again?

Up at 4:30, and Message Center was long ready to go before most of the rest were. At 9 a.m. Sgt. McGee with his loud voice said, "Message Center present and accounted for, and ready to roll, Sir." When the other details' sergeants all said the same, we took off, headed east. The captain told us that we were headed for the staging area in Bizerte.

It was 9:00 when we left, and we still made 190 miles. All went well. Our bivouac area is at Orleansville. Warm. Lots of Arabs around.

Sunday, August 22, 1943 Up at 4:35. Left at 6:30. I drove Fred Trompeter's weapons carrier for awhile. We changed off.

Went through Afferville and Blida. Camped in an open spot, full of dust. The place we stayed in on the way to Algeria. Went through

2 ranges of the Atlas Mountains. Real pretty scenery. We are getting to know the road, every bump of it, practically. Haven't even used road markers so far. No chaplains for a long time again.

Monday, August 23, 1943 Up at 5:00. Rolled at 6:26. Through Setiff, a fairly large town. We had to stop awhile. Army French and natives, all marching to the front. Band playing in front of them, every one in step and battle dress. A girl was behind, crying her heart out.

Got to our bivouac area at 2 p.m. Our kitchen is right next to us. Had a chance to see and talk to the old crew again. Washed, shaved, walked into town. Mostly Arabs. Bought a string of beads for Sister. Don came over. My back is bothering me considerably. Made 170 miles today. The driving's not relaxing, dusty. Have to watch the 100 yard interval very closely.

Tuesday, August 24, 1943 Rolled at 6:30. Through Constantine and Bone. Bivouacked at Morris, again the same spot as last month. Made good time.

Afterwards, Sgt. Meagher, Wally Pomerleau and I went to the 105th Station Hospital and got Bill Snyder back. Made an extra 108 miles. The trip was well authorized, with 2 staff sergeants, and not in convoy. It's nice to get Bill back. He was sick, but don't know the details. We moved right along and made good time to be back at 8:00.

Don came over.

Wednesday, August 25, 1943 Left at 7:00. Dusty as heck most of the day. My heart sank when I saw the same old P.O.W. camp and the road I'd hoped I'd never have to drive again.

Camped outside Bizerte. Lots of troops are massed around here. Lots to do, running to the batteries, putting up the Message Center tent. I put mine up in the dark. After that, I had several places to go to for Maj. Surdyk. Up until 3:15.

Thursday, August 26, 1943 Surdyk and Smith opened up a box of US rations and shared it with me. After eating, they said I could go sleep for a while, so I did until 8:30. Took a bath. Changed back to dirty clothes again, and started to service the peep and fix the camouflage net.

Are close to a plane graveyard. French seaplanes, and lots of other smashed up war equipment.

Orders now are pretty sharp: Roll up your things, take your equipment, and start waterproofing the vehicle. Stay in the dock area. OK. I did that.

Then, wash off all parts with gas that salt water would have an effect on. That includes all wiring, exposed metal parts, etc. If in doubt, wash it off with

gas. Got that done pretty much this afternoon.

We are down here at the waterfront. They brought food down, as the drivers have to stay with their vehicles.

Friday, August 27, 1943 Up at 6:00. The cooks came down here this morning and noon with food for us. Flies are real bad. Hot.

Every part has to have cosmolene grease on it, the fan belt has to be off, and there are three tubes sticking out above your head: one large flexible pipe that runs along the side for the exhaust, then a

small pipe up from the gas cap for air, and one up from the carburetor for air.

Saturday, August 28, 1943   Did a few more things to the peep. Quartermaster officers came and checked it over.

Washed a few clothes, cleaned up. Got 2 letters from Ray, also a small package of candy from Mom, *Life* and *Skyways*.

Show tonight, *Aerial Gunner*. Part of the battery is down here as a skeleton crew; the other part is a ways out from here. Few of us understand just what's going on, but are trying to do what we are told to.

Several other officers came through, and one captain asked me, "Is that vehicle going to go through salt water to the top of those tubes?" I sputtered a little and hesitated; then his question was a little sharper, "Well, is it, or isn't it?"

I thought pretty quick, and I answered, "According to instructions, it is, Sir."

He didn't answer me, and another peep driver behind me asked, "Sir, if the water comes over my head, what do I do then?"

The captain answered, "Just keep your mouth shut, and your hands on the steering wheel."

We already had explicit instruction as to how to drive off the LST: "When the ship hits the beach, drops the ramp, and it's your turn, you have your motor running at 2/3 throttle, have it in front-wheel drive, the transfer case in low range, and transmission in first gear. After engaging the clutch, do not under any circumstances touch it again or remove your hands from the steering wheel, until you are on dry land."

Instructions were vague as to what we should do after we got on dry land — we sort of had to find that out for ourselves.

Sunday, August 29, 1943   Up at 6:00. Worked on the camouflage net until noon. Slept in White's 6X6 truck until 4 p.m. We lined them all up as they will go on the boat. This place is a mess. I'd like to get on the boat and get moving.

Monday, August 30, 1943   A long day. Did nothing but lay around.

Lots of my things are in my peep, waiting to load them on the LST.

Tuesday, August 31, 1943   Had another inspection by the Quartermaster.

No smart remarks this time, and I was glad they looked the second time. I didn't want to sink down to the bottom without the ability to keep going. We had done a good job of waterproofing.

Well, it was a fare-thee-well. There were always some C ration cans of hash rolling around in the back of the peep in case of an emergency, and I even had some extra K rations hidden beneath the seat.

CHAPTER 18

Salerno Invasion. Pushing forward. Beginning of rain.

Wednesday, September 1, 1943 Loaded up again, drove the trucks to the dock. We are on with Able Battery. Also have tank destroyers and DUWKs on our ship, an American LST. Tied down my peep. It is on the main deck or 2nd, vehicle #18, and the LST is #356. Baker Battery and Charlie are both on LST #337. Got back at 6:00 to the battalion. We moved a short ways. There still are enough vehicles left to work with, and they will come later — that is, if we secure the beachhead. Back at 6:00. Battalion had moved a short ways. Put up my tent. Bad toothache — to bed early.

This was a crucial time for our whole battalion, especially for those officers who had to figure out the final details. The final word was that we would take 57 vehicles, mine included, all waterproofed, and ready to roll in first-class condition. Maj. Thomas and Mr. Irons labored over changing lists. In the final analysis, though, we took all our officers except those from Service Battery, and approximately 430 men.

Lt.'s Feinberg and Fleming were not sure which LST their observation planes were going on, but they settled on our LST 356. Then they had to build a temporary runway on the top of equipment so they could take off from the width of the ship. This had to be done the last day before we left. The two planes had to be loaded by crane, and were just above my peep.

I was wondering how those planes intended to take off from the width of a LST.

Thursday, September 2, 1943   Up at 6:00, washed a few clothes. Sgt. Molde took me to the hospital. I got my tooth pulled, and 2 filled. Makes me feel better to know they are in good shape again. Back at noon. Talked to Andy and Don. Hot. The spot where my tooth was hurt a lot after the freezing went out of it. Wrote to the folks and to Jack. I get to use almost any vehicle that's idle for my runs now when I have to go somewhere.

Friday, September 3, 1943   Have to pick up morning reports — a little more running, but not much.

Got a haircut from Nelson. Talked with Andy and Don. Wrote to Patsy.

Some running here and there, looking up officers, and to all the batteries.

Read in *Field Artillery Journal* tonight. Wrote to Phyllis, though I don't know her. Bob Vaughn came over tonight. He is made sergeant in the Supply Department. Glad both for him and his wife to see him get out of the kitchen and staff sergeant again.

An air raid tonight.

The Transport Quartermasters, Lt.'s Ciaglo and Colprit, had their LST loaded and ship-shape. Trucks were all complete with rations, gas, water and organizational equipment. The two Observation Patrol Piper Cubs were on their hastily constructed flight deck, and we all wondered how they would be able to take off from a runway less than 50 feet.

Our 105 mm Howitzers were loaded into DUKWs prior to loading on the LST. (A DUKW is a vehicle capable of going in water or on land. They had a fairly big holding space, big enough for a 105 and crew, and these were expected to be driven off the LST about 10 miles out at sea for the invasion on the 8th or 9th of September.)

When the loading was complete, the LSTs were pulled away from the docks at Karoube and anchored out in the middle of Lake Bizerte to await the time for troop loading.

The LSTs, (Landing Ship, Tank), some of the most important ships in the Allied war effort, were built both by Britain and the US. They were 328 feet long with a beam of 50 feet, held 4,080 tons fully loaded, had a crew of 210 men, and could also take 160 troops. An LST was a Navy ship intended to land vehicles directly on a beach during an invasion.

The LST was sometimes dubbed a "Large Slow Target."

Friday, September 4, 1943   Up at the usual. Pick up morning reports. Read, wrote to Rod. We load and move tomorrow. Supposed to pack up this p.m. Went to see Don tonight; had coffee and cake. Stayed late. Some vehicles and rear echelon troops are to stay here until the beachhead is secured.

Sunday, September 5, 1943   Up early. All packed up and ready to go, but we laid around until 1:30, then fell in with full pack and marched to the dock. Ferried out to the 356 in small-craft landing ships, and climbed the side of the LST. Am contented here for now. Have my peep to put all my things in. Blew up my mattress and slept comfortably well across the front seats. Tom McGee and Lynn are to ride in with me, but I don't know where they are sleeping.

This ship is huge when you look at the hold down below and know all the cargo on it. This invasion has got to be pretty big, but we have to be closing in on Adolph. The sooner we take him, the sooner our chances of becoming casualties will end.

Some guys here say death happens to old things first — but the exception is in war.

Monday, September 6, 1943   Up at 6:30. The food is good. It's different — must be good American food under refrigeration. Only thing, you have to stand in line a long time to get it. Good washroom facilities, and nothing to do. Are still in Lake Bizerte. This morning Tom was in the back of the peep sleeping; lots of bedrolls and packs for good mattresses. Boat is rocking quite a bit, but standing still.

Maj. Thomas commanded the group on LST 337, and Col. DuBois the

356 group. On September 7 at 6:20, our two LSTs weighed anchor and moved away from Africa. For 3 days we traveled in convoy, heading generally east and north. The sea was calm and a pleasant one. During this time, we were told of our destination and mission.

We discovered that we, as a part of the Fifth Army under Gen. Clark, were to make a landing on Italy at a point 35 miles south of Naples. For this operation we would be under VI Corps until we hit the beach, when we would come under the control of the 36th Division Artillery. Two British divisions comprising the 10th Corps were to land north of us. "H" hour was to be at 3:30 a.m. September 9th. We were to leave the LSTs in DUKWs at 1:30 on "D" day. The rendezvous point, we were told, would be approximately 10 miles offshore. We hoped the DUKWs could make the distance.

Every officer aboard the 2 LSTs was carefully briefed, and all men on board were given and rehearsed instructions.

Tuesday, September 7, 1943   An air raid last night. All guns of our convoy opened up, including ours and the ship's 3-inch. Two Jerry planes shot down. Quite a spectacular sight — nothing but tracers. Our tracers are supposed to be red, and Jerry's silver, but I'm sure it looked like all colors of the rainbow.

Up at 6:30. Read part of the day. Now that we know we are to make a beachhead south of Naples, it's more relaxing than not knowing. Slept some, read, shaved. Pretty good food. Very few sick on this trip. True to the old saying, the Mediterranean is calm and blue.

Wednesday, September 8, 1943   Up as usual. Air raid early this morning, but nothing happened. Were issued rations this morning. Got my things all rolled up, and another air raid.

British are supposed to have made an invasion on the East Coast of Italy.

The British had started shelling the Italian mainland as early as September 2. By the 6th of September, the Eighth Army had taken Palmi. There wasn't much German resistance, but demolitions caused much delay. The Eighth Army took Locri and landed at Pizzo.

Thursday, September 9, 1943 "D" Day   Our DUKWs left the 356 at 4 a.m. Firing some this morning. Jerry hasn't opposed much yet. At 10 a.m. the coast of Italy is in plain sight; it looks mountainous. Our pontoons are lowered. Nothing but ships around us. I counted 76 from our position. Our gun batteries are reported to have met with some resistance. We were shelled out on the water, one ship being nearly hit. Left the LST about noon. Tom and Lynn rode with me. Though about 2 feet of water came over the hood, she never missed

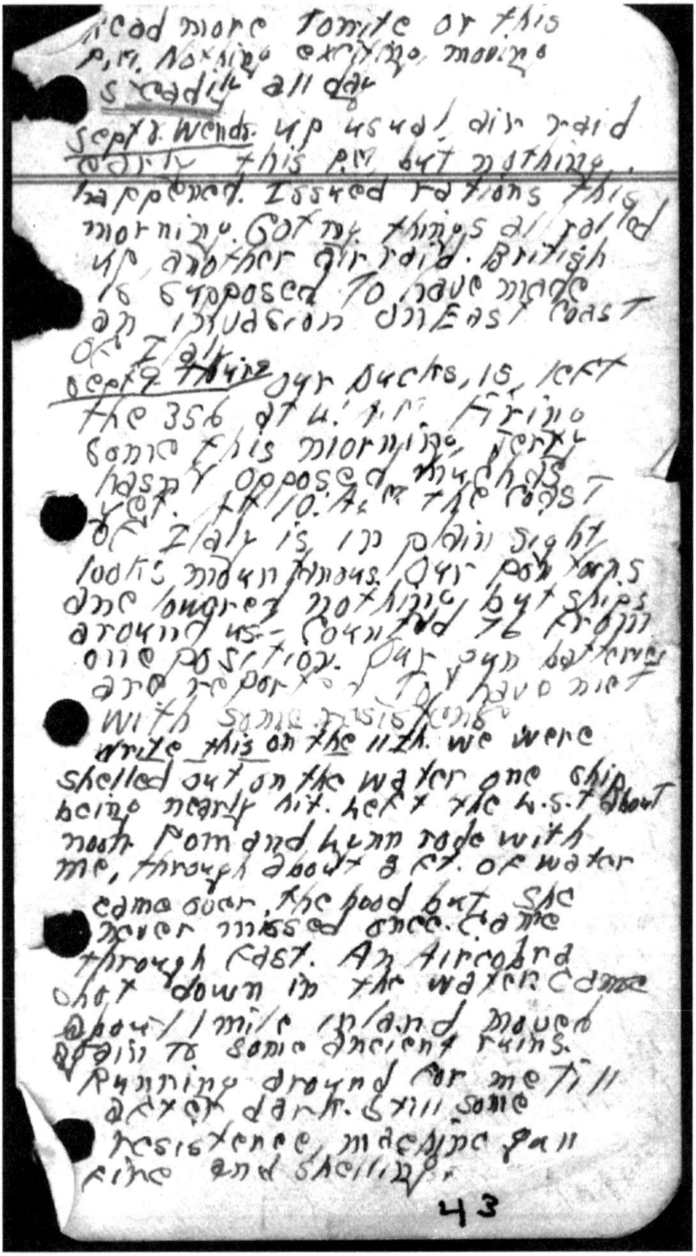

read more tonite or this
P.M. Nothing extra, No moving
steadily all day
Sept 7. Wends. up usual, air raid
early this P.M. but nothing
happened. Issued rations this
morning. Got my things all rolled
up another air raid. British
is supposed to have made
an invasion on East coast
of Italy
Sept 8 Having our ducks, 15, left
the 356 at 4.A.M. firing
some this morning. Jerry
hasn't opposed much as
yet. At 10 A.M. the coast
of Italy is in plain sight
looks mountainous. Our own ships
are around nothing but ships
around us. Counted 76 from
one position. our own batteries
are ready ... they have met
with some resistence
write this on the 11th. we were
shelled out on the water one ship
being nearly hit. Left the L.S.T about
noon Pom and Lynn rode with
me, through about 3 ft. of water
came over the hood but she
never missed once. Came
through fast. An aircraft
shot down in the water came
about 1 mile inland moved
again to some ancient ruins.
Running around for me till
after dark. Still some
resistence, machine gun
fire and shelling.

43

Made a trip to Div. Arty of the 36th. Div. Journal to the gun batteries. C Btry. lost a 105 and Duck in the sea. A Btry knocked out 4 tanks.

Things going fairly well for us. Air activity. Got up at 5:30 and on a steady go till 10:30 Tonite. Hardly had time to eat. Didn't eat breakfast till 11:00. Not so much activity except from the air. Saw the tanks really blowed up. Rebel has photographs of one driver and his girl-he was killed. Shible took his luger. I got papers and soap box out of one tank that was burned. Moved tonite down about 10 miles from pasty m. More running. Jerry has left in a hurry, leaving a lot of equipment behind. Are in spot now with ripe figs and tomatoes. Figs are delicious, ate my fill. Regular ration is class A's. Tom and I got 4 cases today. Lot of sour i sat. An awful lot of air activity last nite. Put to shame all fireworks there ever was. Jerry planes are going all nite. 36th Div. came with us. 45th came in today. We are close to Naples- 20 mi. I like Italy better than Africa, people seem not much better than Arabs tho.

once. Came through fast. Air Cobra shot down in the water.
Came about 1 mile inland; moved again to some ancient ruins.
Running around for me until after dark. Some resistance: machine
gun fire and shelling.
Made a trip to Division Artillery of the 36th Division, and sev-
eral to the gun batteries.
C Battery lost a 105 and a DUKW. A Battery knocked out 4
tanks. Things are going fairly well for us.
Air activity [mostly enemy].

It was quite a sensation to drive the peep off the ramp with only my
hands on the steering wheel. It just sort of sank down to the sand. There was
only 3 - 4 feet of water here. All wheels were driving, in low gear, and at a
pretty good speed. You forgot the immediate danger, and all at once you
were out on the beach. Water came over the hood, but it was gratifying that
the engine didn't miss at all, and I didn't get wet — hardly up to my waist.

We lost one DUWK from Battery C. It got hit by some other equipment
while getting off the LST out at sea. Though all equipment was lost, including a 105 mm and 46 rounds of ammo, all the crew was saved by other
DUKWs in the area. The night was extremely dark, but the general direction
could be told by the glow of fires in the crater of Mount Vesuvius, which we
knew to be southeast of Naples.

This must have been in about the area of the Isle of Capri, as this was
when the 151st Field Artillery Battalion became attached to the 36th Division. Also, at about 2 a.m., a LCVP (Landing Craft Vehicle Personnel) manned
by naval personnel reported to the Battalion Commander to guide the battalion to Green Beach.

In the darkness, an IPCC (Infantry Personnel Carrying Craft) cut through
our column and separated Batteries B and C from the remainder of the battalion.

We heard heavy naval gunfire from the British sector near Naples to the
north of us, and great flashes lit up the sky at 3 a.m. as the naval preparation
was laid down prior to their beaching.

The captain of our LST had informed us that there would be no naval
preparation on our beaches, so we could see or hear nothing from the beaches
in front of us. This was Gen. Clark's order, perhaps to confuse the enemy
into believing that no attempt would be made to land where no softening-up
shellfire had landed first. In view of Italy's surrender (September 8) we were
not sure at all about the amount of resistance that we would encounter.

A little way from the Isle of Capri we attached to the 36th Division.
Riflemen and combat engineers went first in LCVPs. The second wave consisted of more riflemen, mine detector crews and more engineers. The third
wave was heavy weapon Battalion Headquarters, medics, and a Navy beach
party. Later came the bulldozers, anti-aircraft guns, self propelled guns, tanks
and towed field artillery, all in DUKWs unloaded at least 10 miles out at sea

from LSTs.

Paestum Beach was considered the hottest. Confusion on shore delayed some artillery, but all were on Italian soil by mid afternoon. Opposition was stiff. By September 12, Gen. Clark was investigating the possibility of withdrawing the whole American invasion force.

The night of September 13, the US Fifth Army was on the verge of defeat. The 1st Battalion of the 142nd Infantry was reduced to 60 men. The 2nd Battalion of the 143rd Infantry had ceased to exist. Losses of all others were serious. That same night the 3rd Division was called from Sicily.

The British in some cases were considered — too slow — too cautious.

There were many things that happened the day of September 9, 1943 that weren't written down by anyone — or even remembered until long afterward. There was an awful lot of equipment laying around disabled. I really didn't have time to look at much; I was kept on the go.

It seemed we were established on the beach, but really weren't. Several of our gun crews fired pointblank at the German tanks, which was pretty much an unheard-of way to fire 105's.

At 6:30 a.m. the infantry still had not secured Green Beach, which was under very heavy machine gun, mortar and artillery fire that extended a thousand yards to the sea. The column was unable to land through the heavy curtain of fire and was turned back to sea until out of range, and an effort could be made to find and reorganize all elements of the command.

Plans were made to land on Red Beach. Col. DuBois ordered a radio de-waterproofed and a message sent to 36th Division Artillery telling them of our intent, but no answer was received.

Meanwhile naval patrol boats ordered the battalion to land on Red Beach, which was not being shelled as heavily as the others. By this time, many of the DUKWs had run out of gasoline, and some delay resulted in refueling.

The first DUKW carrying Col. DuBois, Maj. Surdyk and 160 rounds of ammo landed on Red Beach at 7:25 a.m. with leading elements of the second wave of infantry which had also been delayed by the heavy hostile fire. Guns were unloaded from the DUKWs and sent to battery positions without any attempt being made at reorganizing by battery, because the situation demanded immediate supporting fire. Three guns of the 36th Division Artillery landed and did not know where to go. Capt. Constant took them and sent them into position with his other guns. They were later sent back to the 36th Division when Capt. Constant had to relocate to an anti-tank position.

Capt. Stewart, the Liaison Officer, continued on with the forward infantry elements and was among the first to reach the crest line on the western extremity of Mount Soprano.

Capt.'s Constant and Vaught were the ones directing fire in support of the infantry with Capt. Stewart, using their own battery's guns and the 3 "strays" from the 36th Division. At 9:30 seven Mark IV tanks attacked the position. The battery destroyed two tanks and drove off the remainder, but the gun crews were forced to evacuate the positions under heavy machine gun fire. Later it was found out that the fire was delivered by some of the tanks that had concealed themselves there to give us again their "parting shot."

At 9:00 Col. DuBois ordered Capt.'s Vaught and Constant to take positions north of Paestum, close to the positions we were to occupy initially. Shortly afterwards, they received a message that a tank attack was coming. At 10:00 they encountered an attack by seven Mark IV's at eight hundred yards. They got two hits on the tanks and broke up the attack, and sent the others north on their way home.

It was in this area and about this time that Tom McGee, Lynn Miller and I came upon the scene. Tom set up a temporary Message Center, and I was starting to be the Liaison Agent.

"Unity of action" between distant fighting forces is maintained by signals or special officers who in the field artillery were known as Battalion Agents. The "unity of action" had not been assumed as yet here, but I remember how thankful I felt, with some of our own officers there right with their gun crews, going more than the 2nd mile required.

Between 10:30 and 13:30 hours a total of fourteen Mark IV's attacked in Capt. Vaught's sector. The battery completely destroyed five of these at ranges varying from two hundred to a thousand yards, and dispersed the others. The guns were hard to fire and handle, as the split trails could not be dug into the hard ground with the time allowed for firing them. The recoil is about 6 feet on a 105. If not properly dug in, the piece will jump all over and has to be manhandled back into position.

A Battery was in the thick of another tank attack. Despite the problems of firing the guns without digging in the split trails, and the lack of any O.P. instructions, they destroyed three tanks. One gun crew member got his ankle broken from the recoil, and at least 6 others were wounded by shrapnel.

During this attack in this vicinity, Gen. Myles Cowles, Commanding General of the 36th Division Artillery, was in the battery area and aided Sgt. Frisk of A Battery in the service of his piece. The general shifted trails and with the efficiency of a professional cannoneer. Frisk had to say that the general was the highest priced number five man that he had ever commanded.

Lt. Robertson left the anti-tank positions and went to a building where he established an Observation Post, wanting to adjust indirect fire on the retreating tanks. He got a battery of the 132 Field Artillery, which was going into position in that area, and arranged to observe for them. Before an adjustment could be started, however, the tanks disappeared around Mount Soprano beyond observation.

Prior to our departure from Bizerte, we were given the responsibility of dispatching ammunition-carrying DUKWs, which were loaded on our convoy, to the battalion position areas of the 36 Division Artillery. Since the 36th carried only twenty rounds per battery on the landing, we knew this mission was sufficiently important to send an officer to guide each ammo train to which it was assigned.

At 3 p.m., permission was given to fly our Piper Cubs off of the LST 356. Lt. Feinberg flew off without incident from the flight deck that had

CHAPTER 18

been especially constructed above my peep and other equipment — that is, if you could call a 50-foot strip a "flight deck."

Lt. Fleming didn't do as well as Lt. Feinberg. As he neared the end of the runway, the LST rolled, and the aircraft struck the Bofors anti-aircraft gun in the bow of the ship. The plane pitched over the bow and fell into the water. Lt. Fleming managed to slip his safety belt and kick his way out of the cabin just before the ship ran directly over the airplane. (This is the way I heard the story, but I believe the ship must have rolled sideways onto the aircraft rather than running directly over it. A ship anchored in a harbor would hardly roll from bow to stern.) Lt. Fleming had some cuts and bruises, but was rescued by a small boat and given medical treatment.

I heard from someone later how the takeoff was done. The pilot had the motor running to full throttle, and he was literally standing on the brakes. At the right moment, he jumped off them, and even with only 50 feet of runway, he had the height of the deck plus the height of the LST to help get him airborne. The Cub plane is really light, and only held the pilot. Though it's really a 2-seater, there were no passengers allowed on this takeoff.

The remainder of "D" day was spent in delivering supporting fire, principally in the sectors of the 142nd and 143rd Infantry regiments, through the forward observers who were on the slopes of Mount Soprano. This was only probably 5 miles, and the beachhead was quite narrow, but anyway it was holding. Mount Soprano was on the other side of the town Capecco which was on the west side of the mountain. We had only really partly secured Paestum at the RR station when Message Center got there.

Between 4 and 8 p.m., Maj. Surdyk was directing fire from the O.P. at Mt. Soprano and did well. By this time at least some of the guns had registered, and German personnel and equipment littered the area. We were strafed twice by low flying bombers who were returning from bombing the beaches.

At 9:00 the battalion reorganized again, and the two batteries that had been on the anti-tank missions were placed in position south of Paestum.

This has been only a partial description of the activity that went on "D" Day, September 9, 1943. Capt. Genung would have said, "This is it, Men," of all it — but he would have been only partially right, as we found out on September 13.

It was late when I got ready to try to get some rest, and this was one night I dug a foxhole for sure and took off no clothes. I was sure I'd be called out for some specials, but the wire crew had got their lines down, and there wasn't much shellfire to disturb them. They were real short lines too, which wasn't all too comforting.

Friday, September 10, 1943   Up at 5:30, and on a steady go until 10:30 tonight. Hardly had time to eat. Didn't eat breakfast [K rations] until 11:00. Not so much activity except from the air.

Saw the tank; really blowed up. Sgt. Revels has photographs of one driver and his girl. He was killed in the tank. Shible took his

Luger. I got papers and the [plastic] soap box out of one tank that was burned.

Moved tonight again, about 10 miles from Paestum. More running. Jerry has left in a hurry, leaving a lot of equipment behind.

Are in a spot with lots of ripe figs and tomatoes. The figs are delicious. I ate my fill. Regular rations are serve-yourself K's. Tom and I got 2 cases today.

I still have the plastic box, the first plastic I'd ever seen — I put it in a display box I made for our 25th wedding anniversary. I also found a small folding pair of scissors, which are also in the display box, and a German gun cleaning kit in a metal box.

Contact with the enemy was sporadic, and even our infantry had a chance to reorganize. From outward appearances it seemed the Germans had retreated, and there were few missions for our observers.

The battalion displaced the guns some distance to support the 141st Infantry Regiment and to help repel any attack from the direction of Rocca d'Aspide Ogliastro or Agropoli. (My memory is a little hazy here, but I think the coastal highway town was named Ogliastro and the town Agropoli right next to the water was probably the RR station.)

Our collection point was to be near some ruins by the town wall, part of an ancient Greek wall surrounding Paestum or a part of it. We were also to be met by another detail of communication ordered to Sgt. McGee, but this didn't materialize.

It was interesting to be here, though I didn't appreciate things at the time. Some of the finest remains of Greek architecture on Italy's mainland were right here. Paestum was originally founded by the Greeks about 600 b.c.

Saturday, September 11, 1943   An awful lot of air activity last night. Put to shame all fireworks there have ever been. Jerry planes were going all night. 36th Division came in with us; the 45th Division came in today. We are close to Naples — 20 miles or so. I like Italy better than Africa. People don't seem much better than Arabs, though.

Running around a lot, most of the day, in fact. Got two German mine boxes for my belongings. There was a whole pile of ammo, etc. Our guns are in position and registered, but that's about all. This afternoon I washed a few clothes. Ate more ripe figs. Italian soldiers everywhere, now that they are through fighting. Wish I could get some information as to where, what and how we are doing.

Three planes were shot down here today — two of our own. Most fellows can't distinguish them. Shot at some Jerry planes myself.

Moved out tonight. Got to new position about 15 miles northeast. A run to A and B Batteries with Andy. It was late or after midnight when I got back. The line batteries should have had agents with our Message Center, but things were in such an unstable condition that I was the only one actually doing the work of 3 agents.

It was fairly quiet September 11, interrupted by daylight bombing of our beaches and some heavier attacks at night and early morning. Much flak and a few unexploded 90 mm ack-ack shells fell into the position area. Until the flak fell, it was hard to keep the men under cover. The spectacle of all the colored tracer ammo and anti-aircraft shells was a great temptation to throw caution to the winds.

Registration of the guns had started, but before the O.P. could even register one battery, the infantry were advancing without hardly any opposition and got into the impact area. Firing had to be stopped.

Motorized patrols passed through Agropoli to the south, and Ogliastro southeast, and advanced thirty miles south of those towns without making contact.

As the 105's were fired, the brass shell casings were thrown in a pile. Rear troops picked them up after we moved up, and they were reused. These casings held up to seven powder bags; seven bags were used for maximum range. Five bags was more common. Sometimes less were used, depending on  the desired range. Powder bags were filled with Cordite pellets. Getting them wet didn't bother them, fortunately. Don Sternke was quite well-versed on the 105 Howitzers, as his battery had 4 of them. Some of this information came from him.

For Don and the others of the kitchen crew, the Italian invasion was an experience in "cooking." The kitchen trucks didn't even arrive in Italy until several weeks later, so Don and the rest of the crew were helpers wherever needed. C and K rations were handed out, and you ate whenever you could.

Sunday, September 12, 1943   Up again at 4:00. Guard until 6:00. Tank attack expected last night. Jerry Panzer brigade is reported close. Are in cow pastures along wooden fence. Have been lucky so far. Eleven casualties, none too serious.

Talked with an Italian yesterday who could speak a little English. Germans have been tough on them. Result: hatred and no cooperation.

This p.m. I took Buck from the Air O.P. to Paestum Airport. The English shot down one of our Mustangs (P-51). Took the squadron leader to where the pilot bailed out; he was burned, but still OK. The Mustang crashed. There was a [report of a] gas attack, but don't know whether it's the real thing or not.

Got ready to move, and we did about 8 p.m. — about 5 miles, the road rough through fields and creeks. Got to position 1000 yards or less from enemy lines.

Went back to Division after the move. Thankfully it was moonlight, or I wouldn't have found my way back. It was 1 a.m. then, and I had to make several more trips back to the main road. Reported back to Message Center at 2:30. An Italian gave me sun-dried figs tonight, which were really good. Laid down by the peep. Up again at 3 a.m. when Tom shot at what he thought was Jerry, but turned out to be Italians.

The battalion again displaced — this time to a position west of Albanella, from where it could again support the 142nd and 143rd Infantry. Albenella is northeast of Paestum, probably 20 miles. Our battalion fired on many targets that had been observed and reported by our own O.P., as well as the O.P. of the 132nd Field Artillery.

An Italian soldier who had escaped from the Germans in the vicinity of Confrane occupied the O.P. of Lt. Zaretsky, B Battery's forward observer, and gave him information which enabled B Battery to fire on and put out of commission several gun positions and vehicles. Some fires were observed, and black smoke was seen in the Confrane area by our O.P. Confrane is somewhat north of Albanella and close to Hill 424, which was very close still to the German 26th Panzer Division.

Sgt. Lunquist was out guiding forward observers to their battalion and had disappeared. He reappeared about midnight — he had been taken prisoner. When asked how he escaped, he replied, "A shell hit the hill, the Krauts hit the ditch, and I hit the road."

There was a displacement again that night to positions 2000 yards south of Altavilla, and observation was sent to the infantry battalions occupying the hills south and east of the town. Dawn was to bring an attack that would secure Altavilla and Hill 424 with observation from those points. This would put us halfway to Salerno, where we could be getting close to British forces.

Monday, September 13, 1943 Guess I slept until almost 8:00. Dead tired. Slept through a hot battle. Sgts. Engstrom and Swanson were killed. Sgt. Murphy was badly wounded; his leg was shot off. Our gun position was not far away.

Had a good breakfast of C ration hash that I mixed with genuine Italian onions, tomatoes and peppers. Boiled some potatoes; made coffee that I got from Division.

A German soldier gave himself up. He got through our infantry and got to us. Talked a little German to him what I could. He is 20 years old, and he could have gone back to his battery and given away our gun positions, but had no desire to go back. Made me homesick to hear him talk. Took him back to the 36th Division P.O.W.

Back here again, then to Division Artillery, and on the way back had to come in under shellfire. One came too close for comfort.

Another German here now who gave himself up.

Quite a lot of artillery shells coming in on our position. Now 4 of our battalion have been killed.

Laid around until dark. About 6 p.m. a P-51 crashed not 150 yards from us, went down in flames and exploded. He was headed right for our position and would have about hit us, but went into a tail spin. We didn't see the pilot bail out.

Heavy artillery fire all day. 36th Division is definitely not as good as the 34th.

Took the other German back to Headquarters tonight. Nearly got hit by a 6X6 truck in the dark blackout.

The battery had moved before I got back — I had to pick up the colonel's trailer and cycle. Lost it and smashed it up. I was the last vehicle still reported "out of position" tonight, which was definitely too close for comfort for me.

Germans were reported coming back in. We were called into an assembly area and had to move again, this time northwest of Division Artillery Hq.

To bed — or laid down at 3:30 a.m.

The battalion delivered barrages on the hills surrounding the town of Altavilla, which lasted from 5:40 a.m. to 7 a.m. At 6:57 wire communications went out between A and B Batteries. Firing orders then went by radio, which wasn't ideal, but necessary.

Shortly after, both A and B Battery commanders reported by radio that their batteries were receiving heavy counter-battery fire, and that they had some casualties. The batteries were ordered to cease fire, and the men to take cover, while Charlie Battery continued to fire missions observed by the forward observers.

A Battery had received about forty rounds in their position area, which killed Pvt. Szewczyk and wounded 1st Sgt. Boyce Murphy. George Moorman, Remington, Mack Cox and Bob Miller were less wounded. Four men were suffering from shock, and a command and reconnaissance car was hit and destroyed by fire.

B Battery received about 50 rounds in their area, which killed 4 men and wounded 16. Sgt. Engstrom, and Pvt.'s Parrish, Meeks and Landry were killed instantly. This was one of the worst of our one-time losses.

Among the seriously wounded were Sgt. Swanson and Pfc. Ted Nelson, who lost a leg. Ted was our barber, and a good friend since Camp Claiborne. He was the one who taught me how to shave with a straight razor while we were in Ireland. He gave me a haircut just before we left Bizerte. He was from LeSeuer Minnesota.

One round had struck the B Battery's ammunition pit when Meeks, Landry, and Parrish were killed. Ammo in the gun pits was exploding at intervals throughout the morning, making it difficult to remove the wounded and dead. Don Sternke, my cook friend, was on the detail of picking up the dead and wounded among the exploding ammunition. These tests and sacrifices we all had to go through that day to hold the beachhead were a real trial for the nerves of every one of us that day. My original diary reported some misinformation as to who was killed and wounded.

The enemy attack on Hill 424 made the laying of wire impossible, and all missions were fired by radio. Capt. Stewart was wounded with the forward O.P. Sgt. Delin of C Battery was killed with the same party, and Sgt. Giovanni was Missing in Action.

The loss of Altavilla and the observation around it made it necessary for the division to fall back to defensive positions. The battalion prepared to occupy a position 2000 yards west of Albanella, but was ordered to move back further to a location just 7000 yards east of the beach. That put us back less than 10 miles into Italy.

The general of the 36th Division ordered us, the 151st Field Artillery Battalion, to be responsible for communication between the 36th Division Infantry and 36th Division Artillery. This, of course, required the services of the Liaison Agent from the 151st, myself.

It's hazy now for me to recall our Message Center's location in connection with the 36th Division Artillery, but I know we still didn't have any agents from the line batteries with us.

In one area the Germans reached within a mile of the beach. Our naval gunfire prevented any more German successes, but unloading of our ships was stopped, and hurried plans were being made for evacuation.

Gen. Eisenhower was very unhappy with it all, and he gave orders and made arrangements for the 82nd Airborne Division to be dropped by evening.

Allied air support and the naval gunfire barely held the Germans at bay. Later reports said the invasion did not turn into another Dunkirk — but was close to being one.

Well, it was quite a day. We had to leave one of our 105's that night, but we didn't leave it for the Krauts to use against us. The gun crew put a shell down the tube and one in the breech, attached a long lanyard, took cover and pulled the lanyard — there wasn't much left of the gun to use.

We moved that night under cover of darkness, and tried to lick our wounds. Considering what every soldier, noncom and officer went through that day, including bending over backwards and risking their lives to help their buddies, we had to say that day, "There were only heroes in this battle: the survivors and the dead."

Tuesday, September 14, 1943   Up at 7:00 — that's 4 hours sleep I had for a change, with not too much activity last night. I repeat that Nelson lost a leg yesterday. I wanted to see him once more, but didn't even see an evacuation hospital. They probably put all casualties and dead back on the LSTs.

I did see Louie Day again from Service Battery, and he hollered at me, "Hey Wag, get that peep in here so I can change the plug gaps." I just waved and kept on going.

What really bothered me was I still have all the waterproofing cosmolene to take off the motor, and several pipes are still sticking above the gas tank and oil breather. Then we had 30 casualties and 6 men killed in our battalion.

Hot, terribly dusty driving. Made a trip to Division Artillery. It was easier for me though, than other days. Got in a little nap later in the day. Don and Jerry came over. Really nice to see them, and they made coffee. Hadn't had much hot coffee since on the LST.

C Battery's guns are real close. So are A's and B's. I had to go and hurry up the ammo supply from the rear. An unusual job for a messenger, but we have fired over 1000 rounds from the 105's, and lost a lot when both A and B's positions were shelled yesterday.

Reports are coming in a little more favorable by tonight. We are retreated now to the southwest and probably will stay here until more reinforcements arrive. No counter-fire on us all day, though we fully expected it.

Have put on 417 miles since landing and that's almost all in low gear, 4-wheel drive and low transfer case engaged, especially at night.

We were firing from the first light of day and before the battalion was registered, which lasted throughout the day. Over 2100 rounds were fired instead of the 1000 I reported in my diary. Small wonder they sent me to the rear to hurry things up a bit. Normally there was always enough ammo for any event, but this was not a normal situation.

Missions throughout the day had been fired by shifts from previous concentrations. At times we were firing two or three missions through Fire Direction Center simultaneously.

The enemy had started his withdrawal to the north, and had left a heavy covering force for their "parting shot." But this time, Lt. Robertson, forward observer, realized a field artillery man's dream and for four days had the chance to fire on those targets with excellent results.

Wednesday, September 15, 1943   Had a real good night's sleep, no guard. Runs to 132 Infantry and the 143rd. Hurley came to stay with me; we have our meals together.

Hot. Not so much action, except air raids, and our battalion firing all day. Several planes gone down again (enemy), guess about all we are doing is holding our own. The fellows are relaxed somewhat after the bloody ordeal we went through, but as of yet just haven't realized how bad it was.

B Battery's kitchen hasn't caught up with them yet, so Hurley and the other cooks haven't much to do.

I'm ready to enlarge this beachhead, get north, and get back with the 34th Division again, though this past week has been an experience I'm glad I didn't miss.

Thursday, September 16, 1943   Hurley slept with me again last night. Some guns of ours firing that are still real close to us. A run to Division Artillery and the 143rd Infantry before I could eat.

The peep and I were gone most the day. Once in a while someone else will use it if Tom gives the OK, but not too often. Knocked the exhaust pipe off it this morning. Haven't had a chance to check anything on it yet, and it's a week today that we landed. It's a wonder I haven't cracked the frame from all the rocks I hit.

Just now I know how close we came to being shot or captured when I went back to get Tom and Lynn the other night, and I sure hope the colonel won't miss the trailer and cycle we tried to get out for him. But I'm sure we won't hear about it as it was a souvenir he had picked up. He still has a sort of camper van — good sized — and was lucky to get out with that.

Friday, September 17, 1943   On guard 3 to 4:30. Moonlight and warm, enjoyed it. Hurley slept with me again. Up early.

Tom got some V rations yesterday. Had some this morning: cereal, milk, coffee, crackers, butter.

Worked quite awhile on the peep. Washed quite a bit of the cosmolene off with gas and finished greasing the universal joints. Took off all the extended air pipes and hoped that was the first and last invasion I'll ever have to go through. Cleaned the battery up, and still have my extra K rations under the seat.

Don and Jerry and I went down to the creek and took a bath. Sure felt good. Washed my wools. Ate. I usually have cold coffee with C biscuits.

Our guns firing some last night and today. We don't seem to be making much progress; all incoming shells are landing on the other side of the hill. I feel pretty swell about everything right now. Thankful most of us are alive and not suffering. My heart goes out to those who were killed and their loved ones back in the States.

Am clean now. Could use lots of rest, but it was pretty easy today — though for the past 5 days I hardly had time to think.

The Stars and Stripes had big headlines of Italian Surrender and our invasion. Wonder what the folks back home think, and what the papers say about it.

The usual run to Division Artillery tonight, but they have moved to within half a mile, so it wasn't much.

Elements of the 50th Paratroop Battalion flanked Altavilla on the 17th and secured the right flank of the sector enabling the 36th Division on our left. During this period Jerry launched 2 counter attacks before the general withdrawal started, but was beaten back by the heavy artillery which was dropped on him.

I can't recall anything about the town Altavilla. When vacated and crumbled up, small towns were just some rubble we had to get through.

Sunday, September 18, 1943   On guard 1:30 - 3:00. Our guns firing. An air raid, but I slept through it. Hurley is still with me; we eat together. I always manage to find something to eat along the way, if I can stop.

Took Capt. Houle to the Air O.P. He says we're not doing too well, but are getting better right along, and closer to the outfits around us.

Laid around this forenoon. This p.m. I drove Mr. Jurgenson to the rear. Saw the graveyard that they already have put up. The infantry lost lots of men. The 3rd Division pulled in today from Sicily as reinforcements. Saw Stark, but was ready to move. Left about 10:00; only came 5 miles. Rear echelons (kitchen and Service Battery trucks) should be catching up to us soon. Actually, we still aren't too far inland, but are considered secure now.

We wondered, and there was much discussion as to why the 3rd Division hadn't been sent sooner.

The enemy batteries could be observed, but were out of range of our guns — so counter-battery missions were fired by the "Long-Toms" of the 36th Field Artillery Regiment through our observers.

A defensive reaction was made north on the 18th in an attempt to get into range, but the Krauts had withdrawn out of our Division sector. The next two days were a chance for most everyone to get cleaned up, and for extra rest, after the almost continuous day and night firing of the past week.

Sunday, September 19, 1943   Up at dawn. Don't like this area. Made one trip back to Division Headquarters. Hauled Lt. Codker around to 45 Division C.P. and 180th Infantry. Another trip to Division again tonight.

Monday, September 20, 1943   Took Mr. Jurgenson to the beach looking for our rear echelons. Moved a short distance to a shadier spot in a grove of trees. Went back to Division tonight in the dark. Lynn came along.

Tuesday, September 21, 1943   Took Jurgenson to the beach again. We found B and C Batteries' rear echelons, but not the rest. I was glad to see Andy. He is B Battery's Mess Sergeant now, and a staff sergeant.

Went back to look again this p.m. but the others still aren't in. Mr. Jurgenson is getting really concerned, as everyone looks to him for supply — you name it: food, mechanical service, mail included. But of course they had little use in the invasion itself, and were not in the original group that left Bizerte on September 5th.

Wednesday, September 22, 1943   Found a broken cot yesterday, fixed it up and used it with my mattress. Slept real good. First time on a cot since Ireland.

Took Jurgenson to the beach again. Still no more of our outfit.

Hot. Don't care too much for Italy as a whole. Back to the beach again this p.m. Still no sign of the 151. Back here about 4:00. Road is always dusty, especially when passing. Washed out my greens.

Pop Bratton was shot and killed by an accidental shot from a Luger. Was quite a blow for me to hear that. The first one from our battery to be killed.

With some of the kitchen and maintenance vehicles in, the others should soon follow. The problem now is for the cooks to camouflage the C rations until our own start coming in. I'm doing fine with what I can pick up, and Italians say the farther north you go, the more grapes, garlic, tomatoes, etc. I will find. Water is no problem, and there are many springs with piped water usually coming out of the animal's mouth. It seems good. It's cold, and it makes great cold, soluble coffee.

Thursday, September 23, 1943   Up at 7:00. Have to stand formation, quite a thing after what our outfit has gone through. Took Sgt. Anderson to the beach again this morning. Still no rear echelon of the 151. Am waiting for mail, also to see the fellows. Found 34th Division Hq. Saw Jack and Joe, also some fellows of the 175th F.A. Stopped where Louie Day has a skeleton auto shop, and he regapped the spark plugs. It does run a little better.

Back at 1:00 and put 5 gallons of water in the gas tank by mistake. What a job to drain it all out again.

Took Mr. Jurgenson to Division Artillery tonight. Their band was playing. Took him back to S-4 tonight.

Everybody resented the training program, even the officers.

A check of ammo reports showed that during the first eight days of action the battalion had expended 10,504 rounds of 105 shells. This amount was about 2,600 rounds more than the battalion's amount for the whole of the Tunisian Campaign.

That was with 16 guns most of the time — one gun was lost and I don't know how long it took to replace it. Then in addition to our 105 mm's, the 155 mm guns of the 185 F.A. also fired many rounds, though not as many as our 105's.

Friday, September 24, 1943   Went to the beach again. No luck. We are now legally back with the 34th Division, so that puts me back with Division Artillery as agent and is where I stay. We are about 10 miles from the 151st. Put up my tent and made one trip back to the 151st tonight. Took Sgt. Revels along. No action.

We found out that it was no mistake on the part of the Brass to have put the 36th Division where they did, and have the 151st along with them.

Saturday, September 25, 1943   Made 2 trips back. Just got back now. Hot. Cleaned out my peep. Straightened up my things. Have quite a few odds and ends of rations saved up. What I need now is some packages from home for more variety. Besides, I'm low on genuine Italian fruit and vegetables.

We were alerted for a move. The destination was not disclosed, but we wanted to get going — north, that is. We were assigned the mission of making a wide enclosure of the Sixth Corp's right flank. Monteorvine was our initial objective, and Avellino our final one.

Sunday, September 26, 1943   [Written on September 29]   On the alert to move, so tonight I had to go back and move with the battery. We finally left at 7:30 and drove all night, but hardly covered 40 miles. Behind the wheel until 9:00 tonight. 35 hours of driving and stopping and waiting. There was no area to pull into, as the infantry was ahead. Our guns hadn't been registered or fired a shot.

Monday the 27th and Tuesday the 28th we were still on the road and moving along very slowly.

Wednesday, September 29 1943   Moved out again last night at about 8:00. Drove until 11:00. Hardest driving I've ever done: bright lightning flashes that would blind you, and then total darkness. Pulled off the road and then the rain came down for an hour in torrents. Got soaked. Spent the night laying on the front seats on the wet camouflage net with the windshield cover and shelter half for blankets. Long, drawn out night, but I managed to sleep a little. Showers all night.

The situation finally jelled on about noon today, and we moved into an area north of Castelvetere. We had been on the road continually since the 26th and not fired a round.

One of our liaison officers, Lt. Bently was killed today, hit by a shell fragment while forward with the infantry battalion commander.

Thursday, September 30, 1943   Pulled out on the road real early. It was nothing but a mudfield that we were in. The sun came out, and we finally dried out. On the road again all day, but mostly stopped, waiting. Lots of Italians along the road offering us fruit.

Went through 2 towns tonight, broken up, dirty, full of dirty people. Came into position about 8:00. Don't like this situation even a little bit; most of our vehicles are on the road close to the infantry. Mountainous country with few narrow roads.

The leading infantry continued their advance on September 30 and October 1. Col. DuBois spent most of his time on reconnaissance. We moved each day and still couldn't find an enemy to fight.

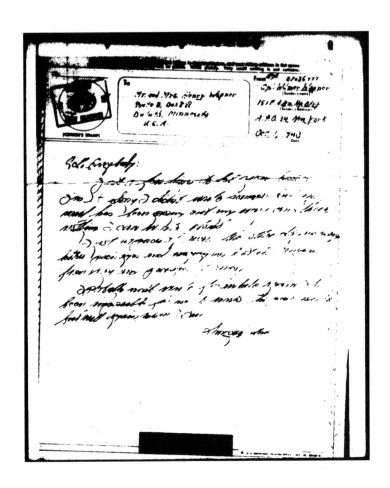

CHAPTER 19

Some mud in Italy.

Friday, October 1, 1943   I stayed by the C.P. truck all last night. Made several short runs, and then to Division through the town and into the next one. Hard driving — dark road, lined with vehicles. Couldn't do much else but stay by the C.P. truck. At least I was where I could be found, and not enough mud to keep me from getting out. Fellows donated me 3 blankets, and I slept on the front seats of the peep. Put a shelter half on each side of the peep and one on top of me. So I slept pretty good until 6:00. Was a little stiff, but rested. Quiet.

The peep stalled last night and again this morning. Had to take it to the maintenance truck and have the 1st Sgt. Pete take me to Division Artillery. Got it fixed again. Moved up about 5 miles.

Got most of my things back from Division Artillery, from Sgt. Revels. Sure am glad of that. We're in a good area: lots of trees, valleys, good ground. Wrote a V-mail home.

Friday, October 1, 1943   Made a mistake somehow — but today is October 1st. Had to make a Division run last night. Back about 11:00. Dark, lots of blown out spots, mostly bridges.

Slept in the peep again. Up at 6:00. Went to all the batteries. Not too hard to find, but nearly went over a mined road that hadn't been cleared. This is beautiful country, and a shame it should be marred by war. Such green, fertile valleys with mountains all around us — indescribable.

Read quite a bit; studied my German. Our batteries fired a few volleys, but for the largest part of the day it was quiet. We hear that Naples has fallen. Some of our bombers flew over us.

Air activities have been relatively light since the Avellino area and first few days. Several runs to all the batteries.

The battalion encountered difficulties in the form of heavy rains and C rations. We moved each day and still could not find an enemy to fight. We were west of Naples close to Benevento.

Saturday, October 2, 1943 Got a good night's sleep. Rained some, but didn't get wet. Went to all batteries twice so far.

Read. It rained this p.m. To Service Battery twice. Went back to our old area. Reported to Division Artillery tonight. Good to be back with them to see all the fellows. Slept in my peep as usual.

By the morning of October 2, the infantry was beyond their assigned objectives, and the next position selected for our battalions was already out of range before we could pull into those positions. At 10 p.m. Col. DuBois came back and led the battalion into position south of Benevento.

Sunday, October 3, 1943 After breakfast I took off looking for the 151; finally found them 21 miles from here. Went through 5 towns, 2 fairly large ones. Lots of people cheering all through. Back at 11:00, cleaned up.

Out there again this p.m. Passed the 185th, looking for the 125th F.A. A high burst had just landed, killing one Yank, and wounded at least one more seriously. The fellow's chest was partly blown off.

Back at 5:30. It rained hard until 7:00; was pitch dark by then.

I had to lead a noncom out to the 151 with officers' bedrolls for those who are staying there. I borrowed a set of chains from Dick, and by a lot of miraculous luck, got them on the rear wheels without any trouble.

The night was black, dangerous road for 6 miles, no light. I was really skeptical, and couldn't help but ask God for guidance. After pulling an ambulance out of the ditch and going for about 5 miles, the sky cleared and we had no more trouble. Back about 12:30.

Monday, October 4, 1943 Slept with all clothes on, including shoes. Cold. Left for the 151st about 9:00. Back at 1:00. Looked for our rear echelon. While looking, I ran across a little out-of-the-way town and saw lots of American-looking people there, dressed nice, and pretty girls. It's amazing the way they cheer us, but I suppose they're thankful they aren't bothered with the Germans anymore. Gave 4 girls some candy. Slept for an hour. Rained again. Have had to put up my top and sides every time it does.

During the next few days we stayed in these positions and fired some rounds. It was here that the Division Artillery forward C.P. moved into our own Fire Direction Center (F.D.C.) We had Liaison Officers from the 178th F.A., the 158th F.A., the 189th F.A. and the 125th F.A.

Tuesday, October 5, 1943   Went out this p.m. to the battalion. On the way back, we went and talked to the pretty girls again. Stopped at our rear echelon. Saw the boys from the kitchen. Meagher is out. Arky is Mess Sergeant.

Wednesday, October 6, 1943   A run this a.m. to the 151st. Saw the same girls again. The family gave us dinner: wine, bread and cheese. Gave some things I had: Lifesaver candy and odds and ends of rations. Rained this p.m.

Tonight Jack and I went to a little out-of-the-way town. People hadn't seen many Americans as yet. Ran into an old fellow who speaks good German. Got along good with him. Better at speaking German than I thought; or really, it's understanding some of the words.

Thursday, October 7, 1943   Made a trip to the battalion. Back by 9:30, but didn't move out until 1:00. Rained. Came about 43 miles on the road until 2:30 a.m. Slow. Had to ford rivers 5 times. Only made it once by myself, have no chains, got pulled and pushed, steep hills and dark.

There was always plenty of traffic at night to help you when you were stuck. Either they helped you, or they couldn't get past, so it was never a problem. Chains would help, but when you were stuck deep enough in mud so all 4 wheels spun freely, only a pull from a bigger vehicle could help.

We passed through Benevento and moved at a snail's pace. There were by-passes at river fords. By midnight, the entire battalion was packed into an assembly area just south of Montesarchio. All through the day our column had been heckled by mud and rain. It was a miserable, wet, muddy bunch by the time we reached our area.

Friday, October 8, 1943   Are in a muddy spot. Had to find the 151st first thing, and the 125th. Several trips out also tonight. Raining. Nothing but mud.

During this move we traveled on the historic Appian Way between Montesarchio and Maddaloni. The FDC crew got into an old concrete building with a leaky roof.

Saturday, October 9, 1943   Still sleep in the peep nights. Wet and raining. Took Doc Lyons to the 151st and 109th Medics, which are in town. A pretty little girl, like Arlene was when I last saw her, came and sat in the peep. Went to the battalion with Dick. Division Artillery moved about 20 miles, are in a farm house. Message Center is in a room of the house. Have my peep alongside the house. One trip to the 151 about 10:00 — wasn't hard to find.

Sunday, October 10, 1943   Up at 6:00. Fairly large family living here. A girl about 15 who reminds me of Evelyn. One trip to the battalion this morning. They have some delicious grapes here, about the best I've ever eaten. A little activity last night, incoming. Aren't far from Mt. Vesuvius. Dick saw it erupt last night.

On the 8th Barney and I went to the top of the hill where the old prison was. Looked inside, was 500 years old. Some shells coming in fairly close this p.m. One trip tonight about 10:00 to the battalion.

We registered our batteries. Company C of the 776 T.D. Battalion was attached to us on October 10, so we spent our time getting them tied to our own battalion system.

We knew the Krauts were holed up on the other side of the Volturno River, so we also knew we would have to cross it if we were to continue advancing.

Monday, October 11, 1943   Rained last night. Was glad I had put up my side curtains. Have a miserable head cold.

Under fire this morning: 88's or 150's. One hit a house close by; another, just below the hill. Slept some. No air activity, but this is devastating enough. Are still in the farm yard, but I've moved my peep by a corn stack.

One of our lieutenants and a private were killed yesterday from a mine. Willie Hall was driving. Demolished the peep and hurt him.

Tuesday, October 12, 1943   The sun came out. I washed a few clothes. Went with Dick to his outfit, about 45 miles.

At 6 p.m. October 12, Message Center delivered a large overlay giving us particulars on an attack which was to start at 2:00 the next morning. The barrage started at 1:40 and ended at 2:00. All battalions were shooting during the same period. The din was terrific.

Following this, the 135th and 168th Infantry jumped off to make their river crossings. By daybreak our troops were well established on the north bank of the Volturno.

Wednesday, October 13, 1943   The heavy barrage was by us early this morning; not much coming in.

One trip to Division and to the 94th Evac Hospital with Doc Lyons. Warm today, but was cool this morning. Took a bath. Washed all my dirty clothes. Feel much better. Made 2 trips tonight. Back by 11 p.m. Bright moonlight like when we first landed here. Got 4 letters: 1 from Ray, 2 from Mom, and 1 from Patsy.

Barney Devine is another Message Center sergeant now. He is older and married. From Kansas originally, but now of Phoenix. He is the life of Division Artillery's Message Center — always has a true story of something in life.

Thursday, October 14, 1943   Up at 5:30. Still dark when the kitchen truck comes. C rations for the infantry and artillery battalions for the duration.

Cleaned up. Cloudy and raining again. Have my side curtains up and motor running. Dry and fairly warm.

We are still forward C.P. Our infantry has crossed the Volturno River in places — the objective in this battle. The 125th moved up last night. Other battalions still firing a little.

Read my Bible. Made one trip tonight at 8:00. Gets dark at 7:00. Wrote 3 letters: to Mom, Ray and Pat.

Friday, October 15, 1943   Took Dick to the 175th this morning, about 40 miles. He had a flat tire.

Moved with the battalion this p.m. Crossed the Volturno on a pontoon bridge. Not too bad, but a little scary the first time. Of course all bridges were blown out by retreating Germans.

Bombing this morning, Jerry Me-109s and FW-190s. Lots of ack-ack. Fellow got scared and left his peep in the middle of the road. I had to move it.

Have a candle lit again. Will read.

We crossed the Volturno at 4:35, October 15. We couldn't move until the crossing point couldn't be reached by enemy small-arms fire.

Saturday, October 16, 1943   Dick took his peep to the Q.M. I took him back to the 151. Have to go way around in order to get back and across the river.

Moved out tonight, came across the river and about 10 miles. Pulled in about 10:00 and hoped it would be the finish for the night.

The battalions' move was close to Cazezzo, and the following day to a position close to Avignano. The infantry advances were such that we were forced to move right up on them each night to be able to support them through the next day.

If we didn't know by this time, we were learning again what infantry soldiers had to go through: steady advancement, full pack, C rations, on foot, in the cold, hot, rain, or in that Axis ally, Italian mud.

They had some stragglers, and I wasn't supposed to pick them up. This was an order I sometimes disobeyed, and I'd give them a ride for awhile.

Sunday, October 17, 1943   Had to go to the 151 at 3:30. Moved again, are closer to my Message Center now. Just got back, and I had to take Jack to Division Hq. Have to go way around to get there.

Germans shot some 10 civilians close to here. Covered the bodies with hay.

Rained some. My legs ache. 151 moved again. One trip tonight, 8:00 to 10:30. Not hard to find, but got caught in a slow-moving convoy on a narrow road. The ammo and supply trucks in the convoys are big 6X6s, and when it's dusty with no moonlight, about all you can do is stay behind and wait until they stop — and then make up for lost time. That's why Mr. Jurgenson always says, "Wag, you're a hard man on horses."

Monday, October 18, 1943   One run at 1 a.m. Didn't take me long, moon light. Division Artillery moved again closer to the battalions.

Slept a little this p.m. Fairly warm at times. Artillery fire still going out, and we can hear small-arms fire in the distance. Blacked out my peep. I read. Dick wrote a letter.

Floyd and I went out to all battalions. He drove, as I had my peep fixed up for the night. We take off a little chill by leaving the motor run. Gasoline is no problem. I always know where the gas dumps are, and we are never short of it.

Other agents usually wouldn't fix up their peeps at night or sleep across the seats. Floyd and Dick were both taller than I, and wouldn't have fit across the 2 seats in front. The seats were flat, and with something jammed in between them, made a good enough bed for me.

We would double up when we could, and take two messages in the same peep. It was nice to have Floyd or Dick in the peep to talk to.

Sometimes we would loaf around Message Center switchboard with Jack,

Joe and Barney. They had a tent, but not always put up; sometimes they used an old building of some sort, or in some cases, a vacant house. Barney's stories and his laugh were always special attractions.

This was different from Headquarters Battery Message Center, operated by Sgt. McGee and Lynn Miller. They were not as outgoing as at Division Artillery — they were more serious, and didn't have time for much besides business.

Tuesday, October 19, 1943 Up at 6:00. Started to service the peep, but had to take Lt. Holmberg several places and didn't get back until 1:00.

We had to move again. I really don't mind. Maybe we will still be home for Christmas. The guys always say to that, "Sure, maybe if we don't stop a bullet — but which Christmas?"

Wednesday, October 20, 1943 The battalion moved again, but I didn't go with. The moves lately aren't far (just to keep behind the infantry), and I'm getting so I can find them. Experience helps, like watching closely for their sign (they always put out a small one) usu-

ally close to the main road. The wire lines are marked, all vehicles have markings on them, and drivers always help one another, especially peep drivers. You're close enough to shake hands with them and talk.

This works, that is, if I'm looking for an outfit in the daytime. At night, it's an entirely different situation and if it's at all possible, you had better move with your Battalion Message Center.

Came back, then had to go out twice more. Went through a town that was really shattered. Germans blew buildings deliberately to block roads.

Got a chance to see Don and Andy at the rear echelon. Left at 5:00 to move with the battalion.

The advance continued without a hitch. The Germans resisted strongly, but our advance kept them off balance all the way.

As a result of the urgent need for artillery support, it was necessary for us to move during daylight hours on many occasions. Nobody liked to move in the daytime as you were going to be observed at times, and there was nothing more helpless than an artillery piece when it was hooked up to a 6X6 traveling on a road.

Thursday, October 21, 1943 Didn't get back until 2:30 this morning with the coordinates. Bad road — got completely lost and turned around. Couldn't remember a thing that I'd seen on the road. Took me from midnight to make 10 miles, but actually I traveled about 80 miles. Slept through breakfast, too tired to get up. Peep runs rotten.

I went out twice this p.m. and got myself oriented with the road.

One trip tonight; also took the 125th's. Another hectic night trying to find them. Floyd had to take an officer somewhere and wasn't back. We never squabble about taking another man's run for almost any reason. Cooperation in that respect is 100%. The 125 wasn't hard to find tonight.

Friday, October 22, 1943 Got back to the battalion about 11:00. Back there this p.m. Moved with them to the other side of Avilino, 4 miles. Are on the foot of the mountain now.

Late for supper. Had a K ration. Out again with overlays at 8:00. It gets pitch dark by 7:00. Had trouble finding the 151; ran smack into a bomb crater. Skinned and bruised my leg getting out of the peep. Had to go to the 133rd. Hard time finding them, another hectic night. Whatever luck I had last night finding Message Centers was bad. Capt. Patterson gave me the wrong map reading. Back at midnight.

The guards always have to know where we are sleeping. As I came in one night, the guard recognized me or the peep. Skipping the password, he hollered, "Wag, get to the C.P. now!" I did, and had to go right back out again.

Many of our "specials" were overlays of map positions, ect.; very important in war, since any position or gun registered wrong could mean shells landing in the wrong place — and this did happen in the 125th F.A. But overall, the officers and noncoms with C.P., Liaison, Survey, Wire, Radio, and Message Center did a beautiful job in many impossible situations.

Firing orders were mostly sent by wire, but sometimes also by radio, and rarely by liaison agents. Map and position overlays were always carried by us liaison agents, though; and of course there was no other way these could be sent. Electronic communications were in their infancy, and graphics could not be transmitted over wire.

I'm not sure what the map coordinates were or how they were used, but I carried many of them.

Saturday, October 23, 1943   Up at 6:00. Took my peep to the 34th Ordnance. By previous arrangement, they put in a new motor assembly.

Had dinner there. Air raid, and it was almost funny to see the rear echelon troops scatter like scared chickens. They did know what they were doing, though, and they had the job finished by 2 p.m. The peep is a pleasure to drive now.

Division Artillery had moved by the time we got back. Find them close to the 151. Clean out my peep, shave, wash, take a sponge bath. Change clothes. Blow up my air mattress, and lay out on my bed. Blackout my peep, and write to Pat. Read a little. Everything quiet tonight.

Sunday, October 24, 1943   A few runs to the battalion today. Got a *Life* magazine and a *Country Gentleman*, read.

Went out tonight to 125th, 151st, and 168 Infantry. Back by 12:00. Warm and nice all day. The infantry Message Centers are always the hardest to find, but I always do.

Monday, October 25, 1943   Slept on the air mattress again last night. Not much doing. The battalion moved. I took Capt. Smith out to new area.

Our move was to get us to a new position near St. Angelo, though not necessarily closer to it. At least our advances were going well. Our artillery support was an integral part of the infantry advances, but of course both were required.

Tuesday, October 26, 1943   As usual, up at 6:00. Breakfast.

Took a lieutenant to Division Artillery and forward O.P. Went through a little town that was all bombed out. A beautiful church ruined, countless other places also. Saw where an American was badly wounded, helmet laying there full of blood, piece of web belt, and 4 morphine vials that I picked up.

Took Mr. Irons to the battalion. Found a steel 30 caliber machine gun shell box (empty), will keep the box.

Wednesday, October 27, 1943   Moved up from Alife this morning. Only about 4 miles, though. Trying to find the Air O.P. tonight, but couldn't.

Thursday, October 28, 1943   Several runs to the battalion today. I go back tonight for the 3rd time, and they are ready to move out. Usually Tom will call Jack and ask or tell him I'm going to move with the battalion. This tells them roughly where I'm at, and I'm not using my own authority. I moved with them.

Had a flat tire — Jerry helped me change it. Lost the chain from it. Got behind. Finally found Headquarters and got the coordinates.

Started back at 11:30. Had a bad draw to go through — soft, muddy road. Pulled Vic Neas off a steep embankment where he was stuck and stalled. Black as ink coming in this road. A nerve-racking and hectic night to say the least.

We were hoping for a break. We didn't get one yet. Most of us, especially the O.P. observers, were crying for rest out of range — but we were again ordered to move. This time the battalion occupied a position just two kilometers southwest of Raviscanina. Here we bogged down for several days.

Friday, October 29, 1943   Couldn't sleep well, or didn't have much time to. Don't remember when I got in, but it was close to morning. The important thing: I didn't have to go out again. Dreamed a lot, sun came out, really feels good. All artillery battalions are close to the front again. Didn't get up for breakfast. Raining off and on.

Wrote 3 letters tonight. Got 8: 4 from Ray and 4 from Mom. Not writing tonight.

Saturday, October 30, 1943   Ate early chow (Cs and Ks), then left for the battalion. Tried to fix the flat, but it was ruined by running flat too long. Went to Ordnance and got a new one and tube.

Read my Bible. Got ready to move again. Rained some. Moved 5 miles up. Shells coming in, but "shorts" for us. Our battalion had some casualties.

Dark before I got my tent up. To bed early, about 6:30 or 7:00. Don't always put up my side curtains. I had a little headache.

Sunday, October 31, 1943   Up at 5:45, still quite dark. V rations again, better than Cs for my taste.

Cleaned up, went to church with Ribelin. First time since Mateur. Don't like this fellow as well as Chaplain Walker.

Camouflaged my peep and tent. Moved with the battalion. Pulled out at 2:00; got there at 4:30. A bad by-pass to go through, worst I've driven in.

Service Battery peep hit a mine. Killed 3 and wounded 3. I saw and heard it go off. Took until 11:30 to get back here. Had to wait to get through.

The first time we had church in our outfit since sometime in August.

I don't get many headaches when I sleep in jumps; it's when I sleep too long or too sound that it bothers me.

Monday, November 1, 1943   Had to go back to the rear echelon with a message from the liaison crew. Woke Don up at 1 a.m. He made coffee, and we talked until 4:15. Back to Division Artillery and to the 151st again. Back at 7:00, slept until 8:30.

Took the chaplain to the 151st. Back at 10:00. Took a bath, changed clothes.

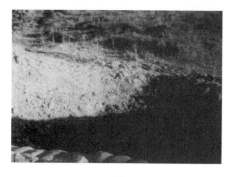

Moved this p.m. ahead of the battalion. A bombing raid just after we pulled in. A 500 pound bomb dropped 300 feet from here; killed Capt. Smith of the 168 Infantry. Wounded 4 seriously. Our Col. DuBois was scratched a little. Lots of other "calls" — close ones, but they didn't count to-day. Demolished a peep; parts of it scattered all around. Capt. Smith was blown up pretty bad around the face and chest. Watched the medics roll him on a stretcher. Others wounded were moaning and crying, a sickening sight. I'm getting used to it and feel I could help, if needed. The whole ground and area shook. Flak falling everywhere.

Four more bombs dropped nearby. More damage, but not to our outfit. Went to bed early, really slept.

Our position was strafed by two FW-190s at 3 p.m. on October 29. Several men in our attached Anti-Aircraft Artillery unit were hit by 20 mm shell fragments. The next day an enemy shell burst in a ravine just rear of the battalion C.P., injuring Sgt Dynon and Pvt. Walker of Headquarters Battery. During the day we saw our own aircraft dive-bomb Pratella.

We stayed in the Raviscanina area for 3 days and fired numerous missions. Our Air O.P. was active. They did good work, despite the increased enemy air activity and small-arms fire from the ground.

CHAPTER 19

We had been in almost continual action now since September 9. I had some breaks, but many did not.

On November 1, our guns were in position just north of Pratella, a small town that had been bombed by our own aircraft. Our area was too small for comfort. Some Me-109s made some passes at the main road during the day, but their bombs carried on over into an area north of us.

Col. DuBois and Capt. Houle had a close call when a bomb dropped so close it threw the 2 of them to the ground. DuBois got scratched up a bit; Capt. Houle did not.

Tuesday, November 2, 1943   Back to the 151st and Division Hq. Caught in another air raid. Left the peep sit, and I headed for a haystack close by. No damage, and the hay brought thoughts of home that were worth the risk. Remember well last night — no damage done, however.

Battalion moved up again; went out there after dinner. Got paid 2,500 lira. Got a nice letter and card from Jean Vaughn.

Slept a little. Went to bed at 7:00. Up a few minutes later when I heard the "Wag!" from the guard. To the battalion again with items. Got in a tank convoy; had to crawl all the way in low gear.

Tanks were almost as dangerous as shells, when you had to pass them at night. They'd go from side to side, and if it was almost dry, they threw up a lot of dirt. I would seldom try to pass at night, and in the daytime only if the road was wide enough and not under observation. Tanks were always a prime target, as the Germans were always happy to get rid of another mobile gun; and they were easy to spot because they make a lot of dust.

During the period November 2 to November 3 the artillery did little shooting. An attack was in the making, so we were limited to registrations shoots. Our infantry moved up and occupied positions which overlooked the Volturno River.

At midnight, November 3 we laid down a barrage in front of the 168th Infantry. The barrage lifted at 00:18 hours, and the infantry jumped off to make their river crossing. Their advance was such that by noon on November 4 we were already working out a move.

Wednesday, November 3, 1943   Up at 6:00. V rations again, my favorite. Went to the battalion, shaved, read in *Green Mantle*. Several more runs.

Took a lieutenant to the Ordnance. Lots of tanks on the road. 1st Armored, 40th Infantry, bringing up some pack mules with them. Supposed to be a heavy attack tonight.

Wrote to Jean. Outgoing artillery fire all day. Only casualty was 1 Italian muleskinner bitten by his ornery mule. These mules and skinners come from Sardinia and Sicily. Are valuable for climbing the areas to O.P.s where the peeps can't go.

Thursday, November 4, 1943   Up at 5:45 as usual. Cold morning. Didn't put up my tent in this spot. Blew up my mattress and laid on a weapons carrier and tarp. Cleaned up my peep this morning. Finished *Green Mantle* by John Boche. A war story, but strangely, I enjoyed it. Two letters: 1 from Mom, and 1 from Uncle Carl in answer to one I wrote in April.

Washed a few clothes. Enemy aircraft around all day, but fortunately, no damage to us. Heavy artillery fire all day.

Are close to an ancient castle. Have no desire to inspect this one.

Barney talked me into going to the castle in the morning if I'm free.

Friday, November 5th, 1943   Up as usual. Barney, Ribelin and I looked over the old castle. Is called something like "Old Podrue." One beautiful room inside, sort of a worship place, altar, crosses, nuns. Below the hill is a tiny city, a part of the castle. Narrow streets, a few stores. Bought some stationery. Quaint and fascinating. One can't really figure out how it was built or planned — approximately 660 years old. Took a picture of it. Wish I had more film.

This p.m. I took the peep to Service Battery. Had the brakes, steering gear and muffler fixed. Runs practically like new again. Got back

to Division Artillery at 4:30. Ate at 5:00.
Went to the battalion, moved with them across the river again.
Water is deep, have to take the fan belt off. Hard getting to it, mud,
rocks. Are within 2,000 yards of Jerry. Back again about 9:30.
175th was moving up; had to zig-zag in between them. Recognized Nelson and a stowaway in the dark. Finally got across. A peep
was stuck that had a 125th medic, and was needing an ambulance.
Took him to the 109th Evac. Hospital.
Division Artillery had already moved. Luckily without much
trouble, I found them. To bed — or to the peep front seats with all
clothes on about 2:30 a.m. My prayer tonight: "Dear Lord, may I not
have to go out again tonight."

We took the fan belt off to prevent the engine's fan from throwing water
onto the wiring and drowning everything out. With the fan belt off, we could
make it through water as deep as the height of the spark plugs.

If the water was deeper than the spark plugs, we were told to try reversing the peep through the water as fast as we could go. The theory was that
the box-like rear end of the peep would create a suction or a "wash" around
the engine, and keep it dry that way.

The trick of taking the fan belt off worked, but I don't recall ever trying
to reverse a vehicle through a river ford.

Saturday, November 6, 1943 My prayer was answered. Up at 5:30.
Tried to find a suitable place to park the peep. The area is flat and
almost all a fertile valley.

Took the Catholic chaplain to our rear. He held services there. I
went to Hq. and B's kitchen. Back about 11:00. Went to Division and
Air O.P. this p.m. Started addressing Christmas cards.

Dick and I went to the battalions after dark. River is still deep, but
road leading to it is improved.

The next several days were almost a normal routine. There wasn't much
shellfire coming in, but still we had a few casualties. Lt. Bauernfeind stepped
on an "S" mine and got a smashed big toe. Then the next day Lt. Gilreath
was killed by a shell that came in close to the C.P. Early in the morning of
November 7, #3 gun of A Battery had a muzzle-burst. Cpl. Eggen, Pfc. Tracey
and Pvt. Walling were hurt. Pfc. Tracey died of his wounds on November 9.

A muzzle-burst was a shell that burst right after or during the time it left
the 105, putting both crew and gun out of commission. These immobile
guns or other broken-down items of equipment were hauled to the rear by
the 109th Ordnance and repaired or used for parts. George and Harvey Olson,
my old schoolmates from Proctor, Minnesota, were still in this group.

Sunday, November 7, 1943 Up at 6:00. Undressed last night for a change, blew up my mattress, had a good night's sleep. Cold this morning. Forgot about going to church. Got 2 *Lifes* last night, looked them through.

Heavy artillery fire all day. Most of the bombs from last night, and other day too, are still burning.

Made one trip this p.m. to the battalion. They made a pontoon bridge last night. The road is still tough getting to it, though. Dick went through while they were shelling it.

Started raining about 5:00. Put up my side curtains. Wrote to Pat, Ray and home. My bed outside got wet, so I slept across the front seats again.

Monday, November 8, 1943 Still raining off and on until 1:00, then cleared up. Left the roads in terrible shape. Took Doc Lyons to all the battalions. Had a devil of a time coming through the by-pass. Ruts a foot deep, and wherever anyone drives becomes another road — dozens of them. To Service Battery twice.

Put up my side curtains again tonight. Got a letter from Pat; answered it. Dick is still with me. Start the motor when my feet get cold. Have my shoes off, dry socks on. Artillery fire still going out. Some coming in, not here. Can hear machine gun fire by the battalion.

The wide areas such as fields or spots where there is standing water are avoided if possible, and another track is made. We usually can get through, unless the frame itself is riding on the mud. Then you have to wait for a bigger vehicle to pull or push you out.

Tuesday, November 9, 1942 Moved the peep a little ways. Some doughboys moved out. Put up my pup tent. Made a floor from an old box to lay on. Dick and I went out this p.m. Back at 2:00. Took a bath, shaved, changed into my long-johns, and to bed early.

Wednesday, November 10, 1943 Was cold last night. Froze a little.

Froze in bed as well.

Charlie and I made a trip across the river in a different spot. Water was really deep. Went to the rear echelon, got my barracks bag, and got some odds and ends of rations. Stayed there until noon; had dinner with Don. Came back at 1:00.

Looked over the contents of my bag. Shells coming in close. Made coffee.

Thursday, November 11, 1943   Made one trip early. Warmed up nicely. Dick and I had a fried egg each for dinner. Took a hot shower this p.m. Wrote some letters and Christmas cards.

A bombing raid; some dropped not far away. Shells coming in close enough. To bed early.

All battalions moved last night. Agents weren't even notified. Positions not hard to find. I think the biggest reason for moving was to get into a better location, as we are not advancing at all now. There is a straw shed where the agents are sleeping; it's dry and smells good. The mud everywhere makes it pretty icky at best. Our kitchen truck is up here now. My source of genuine Italian vegetables has all but dried up.

Friday, November 12, 1943   Dick and I went together this morning. Arden Harris was killed last night, and Emil Ziemer badly hurt. They were repairing wire breaks, when an Army vehicle struck them and didn't stop to help. The driver was not caught — an ironic thing to say. He left the scene of the accident without helping the soldiers he hit. It could have been a vehicle from any outfit in the area, as traffic is heavy at night.

Our battalions moved. Loaded up my things; moved across the river about 2 miles from the 151. Put up my tent and net after finally finding a place to park.

Went to the battalion tonight. Got 2 packages from home: a box of Harvestore cigars from Pa and a box of candy. A pipe from Dick. Passed around the cigars; gave the colonel one, also Lt. Johnson. Beautiful moonlight night. To bed early.

Roland Lindstrom killed today from B Battery. 3 others wounded from a Bouncing Betty mine.

Arden Harris was a good friend. He always had a cheery "Hi, Wag." We saw each other often at night, and I'd sort of look for him when it was possible.

I got to know Emil Ziemer better after he came back to us from being injured, as he was on steady guard in the battalion. He would always know me as I came back in and would many times know where to get me when I had to go out again. He always walked a little stiffly after the injury. He could have been discharged if he had wanted to. Instead he chose to stay, and he took the job as steady guard where he had it a bit easier.

The S-mine was nicknamed the Bouncing Betty. It was a German anti-personnel mine, filled with steel pellets, and had 3 prongs that protruded above ground level. When the prongs were disturbed, either directly or by a trip wire, it was shot about four feet into the air, where it exploded and hurled the pellets for a radius of 50 feet. The theory behind it was that a wounded soldier required four other men to carry him off the battlefield; whereas a larger charge would have killed him, and the rest would continue to attack.

We had been warned about mines, but Roland Lindstrom was the unlucky one to step on one. Roland was from Marshall, Minnesota, and a friend of Don Sternke's. His parents owned a laundry, and Roland's job had been to deliver the laundry to business places in Marshall.

A regular land mine would take a wheel off of almost any vehicle that we had, and throw parts of the vehicle as well. It was always a danger, and you could never be totally sure that the minefields were all marked, or that the minesweepers had found all of them where we had to go.

This was an area where we didn't have to be told to put up our camouflage net or to always wear a helmet. The net was miserable to put over a vehicle unless there were enough trees or other things you could attach the net to and drive in under. It caught on everything. When we were tired, it was an aggravation to put up. When there were natural objects to camouflage us, such as trees, the net did little good. But we always had to carry it rolled up on the front bumper, and this area had nothing in the whole valley to hide anything.

CHAPTER 20

More mud in Italy. Some R.R.R. at Alife.

Saturday, November 13, 1943   Up at 6:00. Fixed my net so I can drive in under it. Heated water, shaved, washed. Message Center is in a building which is an olive press. Schoolhouse upstairs, closed down now though.

Some artillery fire going both ways. One air raid this morning. Took Capt. Lyons to Division Headquarters. Don't remember any more.

Rain was heavy during this time. Some pontoon bridges to the rear were washed away, and fords up ahead were also washed out. We were temporarily grounded.

It's lucky we agents had an old straw shed to sleep in; it had some straw in it, and didn't leak much. Most of the others had some shelter, though some of the men of the battalion were soaked through for days at a time.

Sunday, November 14, 1943   Slept inside the shed last night. Pretty nice. Good thing, too, as I had a tree fall over my tent.

Rained a good share of the day. Went to church.

Went to Division Hq. but the bridge was washed out. Had to ford the river, everything water. Had to take the fan belt off, hardly made it through. Broke the steering gear on the peep. Left it sit.

Monday, November 15, 1943   Got a new steering gear for the peep from 133rd Infantry Service. Fixed it myself. I had borrowed another peep, and the 133rd Infantry was the first place I came to, their Service Battery, and they helped me out. Got soaked several times.

Christmas card from Margaret, but she has little to say about the family or of how things are in Ireland. *Life* magazine, *Farmer*, *Readers' Digest*, letters from Mom and Ray. To bed early.

Everything is mud. Still firing artillery, mostly going out. Feel sorry for the doughboys. I have a dry bed, at least.

Tuesday, November 16, 1943   Still cloudy, raining a little, nothing but mud. Everything I own is soaked except my blankets. Slept in the shed again, straw roof, half filled with dry straw. Put my peep in a new place. Wrote to Ray, Mary Jean, LaVonne and Rod. Am inside the straw shed.

Wednesday, November 17, 1943   Sun came out for awhile, but it rained again. We eat, check with Message Center, head for the straw shed, read. I'm about the only one of the agents that gets magazines, but I don't mind sharing them.

Thursday, November 18, 1943   Floyd has a small Coleman gasoline stove that he shares with us in making coffee. We spend a lot of time in the straw shed.

Friday, November 19, 1943   Still in the same spot, sleep in the straw shed nights. Not much ambition. Everything is still mud. Sun out nearly all day, got most of my things dried out. Cleaned everything out. Threw away a lot of junk, including the set of boxing mitts I carried so long.

To the battalion once. Blacked out my peep tonight. Wrote home and to Pat. Looked over some of my things.

Several air raids. Artillery fire still going out. No incoming shells for several days. Am beginning to realize how tough and long this winter is going to be. We have been in the same spot for 7 days, the battalion for 8.

Saturday, November 20, 1943   Rained last night again, all day today besides.

This p.m. I heated water, went into Message Center, changed clothes and took a bath. 3 letters: from Mom, Ray and LaVonne.

Went with Ribelin to his outfit, tough road. Back before it got very dark.

Sunday, November 21, 1943   No rain since yesterday, but cloudy all day. Went to church at 8:30. Just about a dozen fellows outside the chaplain's tent. Last 2 sermons were of Paul's letter to the Romans.

Read some in my peep. This p.m. I went to the battalion. Bob Vaughn is back from the hospital. Talked quite awhile with him. Read a little this p.m. Went out with Dick after chow. To bed at 7:00.

Monday, November 22, 1943   Sun shining. I heat water in my canteen on the motor. Shave with my straightedge. Whenever I do, I think of Ted Nelson the barber who lost a leg, and I wonder where he is and how he is doing.

Went to the rear echelon. Had the back of the peep welded. Saw Prill. Got a new blanket.

Ate early chow for supper. Went to the battalion and had another supper, only much better. Talked with the boys. Came back about 7:30. Pitch dark, am forgetting how to drive in blackout. Real warm all day.

"Early chow" was to feed part of the men so they could relieve those who would eat later. The system worked good, as someone always had to be on duty on most details all the time. I could always get a little extra food by going to our own battalion kitchen when I had time to stop and talk around mealtime. The boys would always want to feed me if they could, and it was always nice to see Dengler and Snyder, and to hear Bob McKoy ask, "Is she rough as a cob up there, Wag?"

I weighed 169 pounds in Ireland when I was cooking, and was down to 125 pounds now. I missed the vegetables I used to glean from the fields, and I missed meals sometimes, or did up to the lull in the battle the past 2 weeks.

Bob McKoy was from Ames, Iowa; he worked for the city. After the war, we stopped in Ames once. We found his name in the phone book, but it was too hard to find his place. Bill Snyder told me later that Bob died about 1985.

Tuesday, November 23, 1943 Raining again. They moved the kitchen to a drier area. Crawled in my peep and put the side curtains up. Start the motor when I get chilly. Read Revelations, or what I hadn't finished of it, and started on Psalms. Finished reading *Life* this p.m. and started on *Readers' Digest*. Made a run after supper to 175 and 151, about 7:00.

I had to take another prisoner to the rear to the P.O.W. camp at Montekileo. 5 miles each way. Dark and raining — another fellow went along who knew the way.

There was never any danger of being overcome by carbon monoxide from running the peep motor, as there were plenty of air holes all around. There was no heater in the peep, but just running the motor would take the chill out of the area inside, and also felt good on the feet — with my muddy, wet, combat boots off.

I always felt kind of sorry for German prisoners when I'd take them back to a P.O.W. — though they were all done with the war. I had the desire to see it through to the end, was able to, and was glad that I was.

Wednesday, November 24, 1943   Overslept, so didn't eat breakfast. Read some more. Looks like it might clear up today.

Artillery still coming in today, and some landing in back of us. Pontoon bridge was hit the other day. Our battalions are still in the

same spots. V-mail last night from Mom and Mary Jean. Slept a little this p.m. Went to the battalion. To bed early tonight.

Thursday, November 25, 1943   Up at 6:45. Changed the flat I had yesterday. Raining most the day. Barney and I went to Division Hq. Got charcoal. Thanksgiving Day; we have beef steak, rice, coffee. Even in this situation, probably the worst times I've ever been through, I'm still able to count my blessings.

Dick and I went to the battalions about 2 a.m.. Had to find the 69th F.A. and 6th Ar. Ground F.A. Finally found them. Back at 4:30. Raining all the way, mud, a lot of fords to go through. Very difficult driving.

Got a letter from Leonard Archambeau. He is in 601st Tank Destroyer Battalion. To bed, and up within an hour again or so.

Friday, November 26, 1943   Cleared up; hope it stays that way. Washed and shaved. Sewed a piece onto my raincoat. Put permanent sides on the peep using shelter halves.

Dick and I went to Division tonight. Had a flat when we got there. No spare, so had to borrow one. Got back at 9:00.

Had our turkey dinner today. Very good.

Saturday, November 27, 1943   Took the borrowed tire off and used Dick's spare. Cleared up again. Sunshine. 2 V-mails from Mom. They know I'm in Italy.

CHAPTER 20

Took Evens back to the 151. Slept a little. Went to Division to-night after supper. Drove most of it in the dark. To bed early.

The battalion started to move just after dark, and did not get completely moved until morning of the next day. The new area was just across the river, northwest of Colli.

Sunday, November 28, 1943   Up at 5:45. Ate early chow. Took a firing order to the battalion. They moved last night. Division Artillery moved. I went back to the town Colli.

Were in some heavy shellfire this fore-noon. Joe and I nearly got it 3 times. Waited on the road until nearly night.

Agents are in be-neath a water main, which is like a bridge.

This "bridge" was an old water viaduct of some kind, a huge thing that was supported by concrete or stone supports. It must have been for carrying wa-ter by gravity for human or irrigation use. We blocked up some areas on the sides, and it worked very well for us.

It was a sad, memo-rable day. Lt. Fleming was killed in a plane crash. He and Capt. Holleran had taken off for an observation, and had just cleared the strip when the motor coughed. The right wing stalled out, and the Cub crashed and was in flames in seconds. Capt. Holleran broke clear and got out with some burns, but Lt. Fleming didn't have a chance and died in his plane.

Those boys had an important job, and about the most dangerous job there was. I wondered many times how they avoided German machine gun fire, because at times, they were observing real close to enemy lines.

Lt. Fleming was the same pilot who had lost his plane taking off from the LST on September 9, but who had escaped that day with little or no time to spare.

Monday, November 29, 1943   Had to go out twice last night with specials, but for one of the few times in my career, I could walk. It was less than half a mile.

At this point the infantry was ordered to attack west on the morning of November 29, with Attina as the final objective. They were about 5 miles west of Colli.

The artillery fired a preparation barrage from 5:30 to 6:00 on November 29, and the infantry attack moved on at the completion of the preparation. For the infantry, progress was painful. The enemy had observation sewn up tight.

Tuesday, November 30, 1943   Went out last night again (walked). Went to the rear today and brought Barney back.

Don't remember where Barney was, but it was nice to have him back.

Throughout the 29th and 30th, the situation was critical. Our infantry was subjected to accurate mortar fire from nearby positions, but were unable to spot their tormentors. Also, the one road to the rear was harassed by artillery fire, thereby making communication and supply real difficult.

Capt. Stewart was killed by shellfire while enroute to relieve Lt. Young as Liaison Officer of the 2nd battalion, 133rd Infantry. This was his third experience with flying shell fragments. He was a regular fellow and well liked.

Also on November 30th, Lt. DeLisle was reported Missing in Action. He was wounded while attempting to establish an O.P. on Hill 920. Pvt. Fred Humphrey and an infantry medic went to his aid; the medic was killed, and Humphrey driven away by hand grenades and small arms fire.

Later that evening, when men again went to Lt. DeLisle's aid, the lieutenant had been removed by the Germans. Pvt. Humphrey then informed the battalion that the current voice code pad which the lieutenant had on him had been compromised. The lieutenant was listed as Killed in Action.

Our battalion did pretty good these last few days of November. The position we were in was an ideal one for natural camouflage.

The O.P. didn't do so well on November 30. Pfc. Phillips was killed, and Pvt. Savoie wounded when they were hit by shell fragments while on duty at a forward O.P.

However, we were still "in there" all the way — but the immediate future promised only hard fighting.

Wednesday, December 1, 1943   Reb and I went out together last night at 12:00. Charlie and I went back to get charcoal this morning. Raining some; cleared up, though. Got paid today. $265.20. Sent some to Ray, $215.00.

Scotty wasn't the agent from the 185th for long, when Thurmond Ribelin (Reb) took over the job. He was a real inventor, fixer and good driver from the Carolinas. Charlie was from an attached Field Artillery battalion, and from the East as well.

We had found a huge pile of charcoal made by the Italians, and we helped ourselves. Reb made a burner out of an old can, and we had heat all night long, plus a stove we could cook coffee on.

Business was as usual for the battalion on December 1. From all appearances, the German was determined to hold his position at all costs. Every advance by our infantry was quickly fought down. Lt. Robertson, forward observer from 133rd Infantry was wounded in the leg. Lt. Colprit, our O.P. observer, was on Hill 920 and was also wounded. There wasn't much action, but the ceaseless vigilance was almost as bad.

Thursday, December 2, 1943 Raining some today. Didn't do much of anything. Sent a typed letter to Pat. Took Lyons out tonight. Got stuck, had to put on chains.

Chains would help lots of times when the tire treads got filled with mud, and there was no traction. But Louie Day would really scream if we put chains on the front tires, as he would say it caused "undue wear on the front joints." We thought we got better traction with the chains on the front rather than on the back. Anyway…we always carried chains.

Saturday, December 4, 1943 Raining all day. Charlie Durant and I went after charcoal. Got some good stuff this time. Got wet too.

Read *Claudia* by Rose Franhen. Still in our viaduct home, which is nice. Have the charcoal stove going steady, and the coffee pot is on a lot. I can get some coffee from the kitchen once in a while. Letters from Ray and Aunt Anna. Am learning to play cribbage, a good way to pass the time. Breaks up the day when there isn't much to do.

Our artillery shells going out, some in barrages. Some coming in, but not close.

There was a false alarm that some infantry observer reported — he called for supporting fire, but it turned out to be an unfounded report.

Sunday, December 5, 1943 Took Mr. Goodell as far as the 45th, but the bridge was out. Heavy rain at times. Sun came out and was nice. Charlie and I took our laundry out to a place in Colli. A Christmas card from Mrs. Cooke, a V-mail from Mom.

Monday, December 6, 1943 Raining again. Didn't get up for breakfast. Made coffee. Didn't do much of anything.

Three French officers here today looking over our installations. They were the advance party of the 2nd Moroccan Division. They left, and then about midnight, 4 other French officers arrived. They had come to stay, were from the 63rd Regiment African Artillery, 2nd Moroccan Division.

Tuesday, December 7, 1943   Raining most the day. Another flat tire. Took it to Louie Day to fix. To Division once, to battalion several times.

Our Division will be relieved soon. The French are taking over. Our 151 has fired over 33,000 rounds since we've been in Italy.

Played cribbage with Charlie and Reb. Had coffee. A Christmas card from Mrs. Cooke, letter from Mom.

Wednesday, December 8, 1943   Slept through breakfast, up at 8:00. Took an overlay to 151 and 185. Raining a little. Reb and I talked over prewar days.

Our guns are still firing most of the day and part of the night. Are 15 miles north of Venafro, close to Colli, still underneath our water main. Our infantry lost some ground. Jerry is apparently settled for the winter.

Lonely. Not much doing today, very little air activity. Got *Lost Horizon* from Al and Germaine for Christmas. Letter from Mrs. Cooke in Ireland. Went to the 151 tonight — feel down in the blues. Guess 2 years overseas has gotten me down — it's been just about 2 years. Wish I were back in Ireland like a year ago.

Thursday, December 9, 1943   Up in time for breakfast for a change. Went to the outfit. They are packing up. Saw Don and Hurley.

Under heavy artillery fire most of the day. Two killed in the 185th. Quite a few casualties. Two killed here in Division Artillery. One from the band, another T-5, Barry Altadona, hit in the leg. Others wounded. Went through the biggest Jerry barrage up to now. At least 50 to 75 shells. Was thankful we had this spot, although it was nearly hit a little further up the line. Was a little scared and sweating before the second barrage ended. Dick saw 2 others killed along the road.

Our battalion moved back tonight to Alife. I still stay with Division Artillery. Played cribbage, read some insignificant novel. Finished reading *Lost Horizon*.

Few fellows really realize just what happened today. Still don't know how our battalion fared through the barrage. Cloudy, misting a little. The barrage was very devastating, to say the least. Sort of saddens the picture when we are so close to being relieved. The French are already taking over. Sgt. Greg was wounded. One truck was hit.

On the morning of December 9, a battalion quartering party left the area enroute to our rest area.

Unfortunately for our visitors, the French, the Germans elected to shell our area that day. The shelling continued throughout the day, much to our discomfort.

Iver Weckworth and Pfc. Helmar Hendrickson were injured by flying shell fragments. Ironically, these two men had been in action with the battalion for ninety days previous to their being wounded. Had they been able to escape injury that day, they would have been able to accompany us on our long-awaited trip to a rest area.

At about 6 p.m. on December 9 the battalion pulled out of position and moved to the rear. Due to heavy traffic, we didn't arrive at our destination close to Alife until 1 p.m. December 10.

Friday, December 10, 1943   Up at 5:45. Ate early chow. Left at 6:30 for the 151 close to Alife, about 40 miles each way. Had to go around the 45th Division bridge and their area, and came through Venafro on the way back. Back here about noon. No shells came in today.

The French have taken over our positions, did some firing.

It was backwards from the usual case that the 151st moved and I didn't move with them — but this was rest area.

Saturday, December 11, 1943   Up at 6:20. Right after chow, I packed up my things; so did Joe. We came back to Alife to our area, had chow at our 151st. Rest of the battery came in this p.m. Laid ¼ mile of wire with Sgt. Smith. Put my tent up. Have it fairly nice in here. Area is dry so far. Sort of a relief to be away from the front. On the way down we passed French girls driving US ambulances.

Sunday, December 12, 1943   Chow at 7:30 now, woke up by myself. Worked on my peep nearly all forenoon. Changed oil and transmission grease. Moved my tent this p.m. and dug it in.

Show here tonight. I went, but didn't stay as I couldn't hear anything. Package tonight from Aunt Rose and Grandma. Wash cloths, towel, hankies, a can of chicken, soap. Took Don's razor and strap back to him.

Tonite, ends two years overseas, has gotton me down on life, just about that long, wish I were back in Ireland already. And.

Dec 9 Thurs. Up in time for breakfast, for a change. Went to the outfit, they are packing up, saw Don and Hurley. Under heavy artillery fire most of the day, two killed in 185th. Quite a few casualties, two killed here in Div. Arty. one from the band and the - T-5 Berry Alegand hit in the leg, others wounded. Went through biggest Jerry barrage up to now, at least 50-75 shells, was thankfull we had this spot although it was nearly hit a little further up the line. Was really scared and sweating before the second barrage ended. Dirk saw 3 others killed along the road. Our Bn. moved back tonite to AliRc. I still stay with Div. Arty. Played Cribbage. read some insignificant novel. Finished reading "408. horizon" few fellows really realize just what happened today. Still don't know how our Bn. pulled through the barrage. Cloudy misting a little. Barrage was very devastating to say the least. Sort of saddens the picture when we're so close to being relieved. The French are already taking over. Sph

Greg was wounded, one truck
hit.

Dec 10, Fri. Up at 5:45 ate carp
chow, left at 6:30 for the 15th
close to Alife, about 40 mi. each way,
had to go around the 45th Div
bridge and area came through
Venafro on the way back.
Back here about noon, no shells
came in today. The French have
taken over our positions, did
some firing.

Dec 11 Sat. Up at 6:20, right after
chow I packed up my things.
So did Joe. We came back to
Alife to our area, had chow
at the 15th. Rest of the Btry.
came in this P.M. We ed a lot
of wire with Sgt. Smith & put
my tent up. Have it fairly nice
in here. Area is dry so far.
Sort of a relief to be away
from the front. On the
way down we passed French
girls driving U.S. ambulances.

Dec 12 Sun. Chow at 7:30 now, woke
up by myself. Worked on my
jeep nearly all the forenoon.
Changed oil, transmission
grease. Moved my tent this
P.M. dug it in. Show here
tonite, went but didn't stay.
Couldn't hear anything.
Package tonite from Aunt Rose
and Grandma, washclothes,
towel, hankies, can of chicken
soap.

Monday, December 13, 1943   Moved a little ways again — my tent, that is. Don't like having it dug in. Went over my things again. Threw some more away. Warm and nice the last 3 days. Quiet and peaceful; I hope things stay as they are. I mean as long as we are back of the lines, I hope I can stay with Division Artillery.

Went to the battalion tonight. Got mail: 8 letters including Christmas cards from Mom, Rod, Arlene and Jean Vaughn, and a German-English dictionary from Mom. To bed about 8:00.

Tuesday, December 14, 1943   Up at 7:00. Took Jack to Division Hq. Went through a part of Piedmonte. Fairly big town. Washed, took a sponge bath. We took our laundry in today. Took my peep to the maintenance for servicing. They took me back tonight. Wrote 4 letters tonight.

Wednesday, December 15, 1943   Chow at 7:00. Nice today again. We got a pyramidal tent for the 4 agents. We started putting it up tonight.

Thursday, December 16, 1943   Dick, Reb and I finished putting up the tent. Moved in. Jack and I went after our laundry, left some there. Went to Piedmonte twice. Spent $2.00 on oranges, apples and walnuts.

Friday, December 17, 1943   An early trip to all battalions. Reb came with. Cleaned my rifle. A fellow from this battery was born in Piedmonte, lived there 9 years, then went to the States. Jack, Dick and I went to the battalions for a USO show at the 151, and the movie *Top Man*, not so bad. Real black on the way back.

I took Natalie and Jack Salzer in the peep, and we went to Natalie's relatives in the country. It was an experience. The family numbered about 5. They have a large house, mostly concrete and plaster. Nate talks Italian steady. Though I couldn't understand a word, it was worth a lot just to be able to take him there and see his relatives. They may have a farm somewhere; there is lots of garlic and onions hanging in the house. They gave us a lunch too. Haven't had a chance to get to know Natalie too well.

Saturday, December 18, 1943   Up for 7:30 chow, as usual. Barney and I went to Division. Took in some laundry. Washed my peep this p.m. After supper went to the 105th A.A. and then to Alife. Got the clothes. Cloudy all day, rained just a little.

Sunday, December 19, 1943   Usual routine, but nice and quiet.

Monday, December 20, 1943   Got ready for my trip to Naples. A few runs. Rained hard tonight.

Tuesday, December 21, 1943   Went to the battalion early. Jolie takes my place. Got into Naples about 10:00. Took until 4:00 to get organized. Passow and I looked this end of town over. Are staying in an old capitol or school.

Wednesday, December 22, 1943   Up at 7:00. Same variety of chow as at camp. Big lineup of about 1000 men here. We had tops sewn on our shoes. Had my photograph taken. This p.m. went to the center of town. Walked around

a lot. Came back on the trolley about 6:30.

Thursday, December 23, 1943   Up at 6:30. Chow at 7:30. Rose is here cooking; he let me use his watch.

Got a shave this morning, took a shower, spent the rest of the forenoon looking over this part of town close to the rest center. Guess I'm lucky to be spending 5 days in the city of Naples. Wish I could enjoy it more. Cool and cloudy, rained again yesterday. Lots of soldiers here. Went to the Red Cross Theater; saw *Augusta,* and saw a Christmas program.

Somehow our ex-cook Cloyce Rose had ended up here in Naples. It must have been permanent, as I can't remember seeing him again after we left our rest area.

Friday, December 24, 1943   Bob Vaughn and I went to town this morning. Bought some things: rug, horses for Patsy, pillow case for home, another for myself. Ate dinner here.

This p.m. Mellinger and I went to town again. Back at 4:30. A Christmas Eve program in the mess hall. Show afterwards. To bed at 11:00.

Saturday, December 25, Christmas 1943   Up at 7:00. Cleaned up, sent the packages off. Went to church, got a haircut and shave. Ham for dinner.

This p.m. Mellinger and I went to town. Saw the Red Cross show, walked around a little, ran into Chuck — he is in the 3rd Division.

Back at 4:30. Played a game of cribbage. Good supper, turkey. Went to the show, *Rhythm of the Islands*.

Sunday, December 26, 1943   Chow. Got my photographs. Folded my blankets. Went to church at 9:30.

Left at about 1:00. Back to camp at 5:00. Tired. Had supper with Vaughn.

Monday, December 27, 1943   Good to get the old job back again. Cleaned up, changed clothes. Am glad I got to Naples. Don't care to go on pass there again, but hope I get to drive back on business.

Col. DuBois, Maj. Surdyk and the Battery Commanders left the battalion area on December 27 to go forward on reconnaissance. When this had happened before, we always knew it was fact, rather than rumor that we were headed for the front and combat.

The rest period was great. We were issued new clothing where needed. Morale was pretty good, with some reservations.

I still had the 3 olive drab wool blankets that were getting pretty crumby, but they would do until the next break, probably in spring.

CHAPTER 21

Back to the front. Battle of Cassino. Go back to Alife for R.R.R.

Tuesday, December 28, 1943   Had to drive Capt. Patterson to II Corps. We are going to the front again. Back at 2:00. Headache and a bad cold. Started packing my things. Box of candy from Mother. Some Christmas cards.

Our return to action was to effect a relief of the 36th Division, which had taken San Pietro and San Vittorie. The battalion went into general support of the Division, our combat team infantry having been placed in Corps Reserve.

Wednesday, December 29, 1943   Up at 5:45, chow at 6:00. Moved 2 miles, northwest of Venafro. Took Lt. Girth back to II Corps Hq. Back at 9:00. Dark, miserable.

Thursday, December 20, 1943   Went to D.A.O. with Aikers. Back at 11:00, made my tent. After dinner I moved up with Message Center forward. Put up my pup tent. Wrote a few letters tonight. Sent my photograph to Grandma, Aunt Anna and home.

Friday, December 31, 1943   Went to the D.A.O. Again. Cold and windy most of the day. Jack, Joe, Reb, Barney and I had a party with the canned chicken Grandma had sent. We made sandwiches with it and had coffee. The 151 moved up tonight. McGee got lost. Raining a lot, miserable.

One year ago today we were on HMS *Empress of Australia*. Landed in Africa on the 3rd of January. Got into action February 15. Left the kitchen in April. Got the Battalion Agent job then, traveled back to Oran, then to Bizerte, and made the Italian Invasion with the 36th Division September 9th. In action almost continually since then. Our 151st Battalion has had 27 killed, and 200 casualties to this date.

Our battalion moved into positions vacated by the 36th Division on the night of December 31 - January 1.

Because of bad weather, rain, and wind, the positions were the most difficult that we had up to that time. Guns had to be winched into position on the south slopes of Mount Summvero just three km. east of San Pietro. The wind reached velocities of sixty to seventy mph and blew tents far down the valley.

Despite the difficult conditions, the battalion laid down the 3-round New Year's greeting which was fired by the entire Corps on enemy installations. We heard later that Jerry didn't appreciate our New Year's greeting.

Saturday, January 1, 1944   Up at 6:45. Blowing all night, raining and snowing all forenoon. Had to get to II Corps. Most miserable trip I've made, 40 miles. Wet and frozen. Tried to dry out. Changed back to some dirty clothes I had in the back of the peep, but they were dry anyway.

Out this p.m. again. Stopped raining this p.m. Wind died down a little. Moon out for a little while tonight. Sure thankful for that.

Sunday, January 2, 1944   Cleared up. Sun came out. Had a few trips this p.m. I went to the rear echelon. Got a carbine [which was a lot smaller gun for a driver to take care of], another blanket and socks. Fixed my tent over. Went to all battalions after supper. Stopped to see Don. Stayed there several hours. Got a package from Ray.

Whenever I stopped to see Don, if no one was on duty in the kitchen truck, he'd start a stove, heat some coffee, and I got partly dried out and warmed up on the inside as well.

Sgt. Noble, the Mess Sergeant at the time, didn't complain about this; and neither did Andy, who was Mess Sergeant later. I made trips for them whenever I could too.

Monday, January 3, 1944   Fairly nice all day, but I didn't have much ambition. Jerry bombed this p.m. with personnel mines. About 50 casualties, mostly in 185th Service Battery. Capt. Rieser hurt, and Lt. Reef too. To bed early.

Tuesday, January 4, 1944   To the battalion this morning. Wrote Ray a long letter. Cold most the day. Made a trip to the battalion later.

Wednesday, January 5, 1944   Made a trip at 9:00 last night. Flat tire, no spare. Had to call Dick. Waited until 10:30 before he came. Back at 12:00. Raining, foggy around the mountain. Up at 8 a.m. Cold, cloudy.

The battalion was in general support of the Division, and participated

Jan 2 1945 cleared up, sun came
out. Had a few trips. this
P.M. I went to the rear echelon
got a carbine, another blanket
socks. Fixed my tent over.
went to all Bns. after supper,
stopped to see Don, stayed
there several hrs. Got a pkg
from Ray.
Jan 3 1945 Fairly nice all day
but didn't have much ambition.
Jerry bombed this P.M. with
personal mines about 50
casualties, mostly in 185 F. Service
Cpl. Reser hit, Lt. Peet.
to bed early
Jan 4 1945 To the Bn. this
morning. Wrote Ray a long
letter. cold most the day, made
trip to the Bn.
Jan 5 1945 Made a trip at
9 last nite, flat tire, no spare
had to call Dick waited till
10:30 before he came. Back at
12:00 Raining, foggy around
the mountain. up at 8:00
cold, cloudy.
Jan. 6 1945 up at 12:00 last
night to all Bns. back at 1:30
moonlight, cold all day, freezing
a few snow flurries. Froze
more today than when it was 50
below at Pay nc To all Bns tonite.
Had headache. Got a bunch of
over supply candy rations
from I-1. lots of
Artillery fire, constantly

The past 4 days, night and day. Quite a few Italian cavalry with pack mules in this sector. Are supposed to have 35 ans of artillery in around here, some 8in howitzers.

Jan 7. Fri. Had to go to 2/1 Bns at midnite, with F.O. Moonlite didn't mind too much. Slept through breakfast. Were shelled twice here today, my nerves aren't able to take it as well as they have. Some close enough. 151 moved tonite I moved with them. On other side of San Pietro a rubbled mess, battlefield to be sure, back here at 10:00 out again at 1:30 to 2/1 our A's with F.O.

Jan 8. Sat. Slept through breakfast, freezing but sun is out. Cleaned up. Don't remember much more.
Jan 9 Sun. Didn't have to go out last night. Got up for breakfast. Started packing my things. Took an overlay to 2/1 Bn's. Back in time for dinner. Moved out shortly after. Are in 125's old area. Helped put up both C.P. tents. Wen to the 151 after supper

1944

in the preparations which were fired prior to the attack on San Vittorie. This was taken on the 5th of January, after fierce house to house fighting. Our infantry were continuing to take prisoners in the town two days after they entered it.

Thursday, January 6, 1944   Up at 12:00. Went to all battalions. Back at 1:30. Moonlight.

Cold all day, freezing, a few snow flurries. I froze more today than when it was 50 below zero at Payne.

To all battalions again tonight. Had a headache. Got a bunch of oversupply candy rations from 1-1.

Lots of artillery fire constantly going, mostly out, during the past 4 days and nights.

Quite a few Italian Cavalry with pack mules in this sector. There are supposed to be 35 battalions of artillery in around here, some 8-inch Howitzers.

It sounded continually like you were in a bowling alley.

Friday, January 7, 1944   Had to go to all battalions at midnight with firing orders. Moonlight, so I didn't mind too much. Slept through breakfast.

Were shelled twice here today. My nerves aren't able to take it as well as they have. Some shells came close enough.

151 moved tonight; I moved with them to the other side of San Pietro, a rubbled mess, a battlefield, to be sure. Back here at 10:00.

CHAPTER 21

Out again at 11:30 to all outfits with firing orders.

San Pietro and San Vitorrie were two towns literally blown off the face of the earth. There were many trees around that were totally devoid of all branches and were just sticks left from all the shellfire. The towns themselves were piles of concrete rubble. I didn't see life of any kind left any time I drove through.

About this time the II Corps took Mt.'s Porchio and Chiaia, two objectives necessary for our Division to have before our ultimate objective of Cassino.

Saturday, January 8, 1944   Slept through breakfast. Freezing, but sun is out. Cleaned up, but don't remember much more.

We were in with Message Center, where there was good protection, and it was dry and fairly warm.

I missed my breakfast when I didn't get it -- but if I got up after only a few hours' sleep, then that's about all the sleep I got, as someone usually wanted to go someplace and grabbed the first available agent. I got by, but there were no more onions, tomatoes, and very few grapes, as most were frozen. I still saw a bunch of blue grapes once in awhile that was missed in picking, and I'd stop and get it. I still had a few cans of C ration stew and hash that would keep me from starving, anyway. Then the regular chow was not bad, and two meals just about got me through. Also, packages from home helped a lot.

Sunday, January 9, 1944   Didn't have to go out last night. Got up for breakfast, started packing my things. Took an overlay to all battalions. Just back in time for dinner. Moved out shortly after.

Are in 125th's old area. Helped put up both C.P. tents. Went to the 151 after supper. Got caught in a shelling; thankful I don't have to stay there all the time. To bed about 8:00. Reb and Floyd came back from Naples.

Most of the incoming shells lately had been diverted to 185th positions.

Col. DuBois made a reconnaissance and aided Capt. Grant in moving his installations to a safer position in a gully. O.P.s established on Mt. Chiaia gave observation on the town of Cardero, the next objective of the Division.

Monday, January 10, 1944   Had to go out at 2:30. Reb came with. We passed a mule with a broken leg — not by a natural accident. The Italian driver was close-by, killed by the same shell. Mule trains carry ammo and rations to the forward O.P.s where the peeps can't go.

Most of the O.P.s are now in the mountains, or there isn't an O.P. at all.

Tuesday, January 11, 1944   Capt. Crellin gave orders for me to report to him. I shaved, took a sponge bath and reported to him. He wanted me back in the kitchen as First Cook with T-4 or sergeant's rating. I thanked him, but told him I'd rather be the Battalion Agent, so he just let it go at that. Cooking would be now still much the same as when I left the job: opening cans. And then I'd miss out on lots of excitement. Put me to some concentrated thinking, though.
Went to see Andy, Don, and Vaughn tonight and talked to them about it.

Capt. Crellin was a fresh young captain from the East. He was a real health nut; he always took his morning shower out of his helmet with cold water, and did lots of personal exercises. We got along pretty good. The only bad thoughts I had of him was when a new peep came in for the Battalion Agent, and he took it for himself. I got the one he had, which was somewhat better than my old one. He never had a bad word for me, though, as he probably had respect for the job I was doing.
On January 11 Lt. Koobes and Sgt. Casselman reported for duty as Liaison Pilots. Lt. Feinberg was ordered back to the States to attend school, to learn how to fly the combat missions that he had been flying for over 4 months. We hoped he would teach them how to take off from an LST in the face of a real invasion, and how to wait for the enemy to be cleared from a place before being able to land there.

Wednesday, January 12, 1944   Beautiful day, warm. Didn't do a lot.

The US 34th Division got credit for the complete capture of Cervaro on January 12, and was pushing forward to Cassino.

Thursday, January 13, 1944   As usual almost. Took the report to II Corps. Back in an hour and a half. Went 55 — seems terribly fast when you're not used to it. Took the Catholic chaplain to A Battery. Waited for him. Went to B Battery kitchen to wait. Don gave me a haircut and coffee.
To the battalion tonight. Got quite a bit mail that cheered me up a lot. From Margaret, Patsy, Jean Vaughn, Mom and Ray. Christmas cards from Uncle Hank and Aunt Rose. Several *Time* and *Life* magazines.

Friday, January 14, 1944   Got up just in time for breakfast, 7:00.

Haven't heard from Capt. Crellin yet in regards to my going back in the kitchen. I suppose he could order me back, but such orders aren't common. The Brass know they get more out of you if you have a job that you like.

Beautiful day again, clear and still. Not so much artillery fire the last 2 days and nights. Some coming and going, however.

Saturday, January 15, 1944　　Didn't do much of anything.

There were days like this: depressing days, lonesome trying to figure out just what we were doing where we were, not feeling it worthwhile to make a diary entry at all.

Sunday, January 16, 1944　　Letters from Margaret, home and Ray. Took Lt. Holmberg to Division rear. Took a hot shower there and changed into clean used clothing, which we can do if lucky enough to get to the rear once in awhile — otherwise not. Back at 3 p.m. Ate good meal there.

Margaret writes good news from Ireland. Olive's baby, Maureen, is now almost 2 years old and they all enjoy her. Mack, Olives husband from the British Army, is away somewhere.

Ray and Dick are in the woods at Payne.

The battalion continued in general support until January 14, when the 133rd Infantry again came under Division control, and liaison officers were dispatched to battalion headquarters of that unit.

Mount Trochee, the last commanding height before Cassino, was taken on January 15, and O.P.s were established on its crest. The slopes were heavily mined with Schu mines, a small anti-personnel mine which we hadn't encountered before.

Reconnaissance by Col. DuBois and battery commanders was made for position areas west of Cervaro, and the battalion occupied positions 500 yards northeast of Cervaro with only one accident enroute: an anti-aircraft half track drove off a by-pass and overturned. This sort of incident had almost become S.O.P. (Standard Operating Procedure) on all our night marches.

Earlier that afternoon, Lt. Phillips stepped on a Schu mine while going to the O.P. on Mount Trocchio. He sustained a broken leg and other more serious injuries.

Monday, January 17, 1944　　Moved with the battalion last night. Most of my luck was bad. Didn't find back to Division Artillery until 3 a.m. A hellish night. I went through a fair-sized town in total ruins, couldn't believe it without seeing it. A lot bigger than San Vitorrie, but vacant except for the concrete rubble and roads that the engineers made through it with a bulldozer.

The road is full of shell holes, nearly went off the road time and again. Black night and windy and cold. Had to put on my chains in order to get through a by-pass. The road is under Jerry observation part way.

Thirty-some 168th Infantry killed, their first night in action since relieving the 135th. No incoming fire here.

Our Service Battery moved to where our battalion was. Took Barney there this p.m. to see Mr. Irons.

All the other agents are moving with their battalions tonight. Leaves me all alone. Started reading two pocket books; one on history of the world, the other on etiquette. Will read my Bible. Have a charcoal fire. Makes the tent fairly warm. Enjoy being alone. Reminds me of the winters cutting wood at Payne.

Tuesday, January 18, 1944   Got ready to move first thing. Chow an hour earlier. Moved out about 9:00. Division Artillery C.P. is close to our C.P. in Savone, go through San Vittorie. Rough, nearly impassable roadway. #6 is better, but was being shelled and under observation in spots.

Reb and I staying back in the rear echelon this time. Put up our C.P. tent. Had to go back to the front, move our tent. John Berglund from Duluth came in awhile. Played cribbage, read quite a bit. Artillery fire both ways, not too close to here.

Wednesday, January 19, 1944   Reb and I both undressed for a change last night. From 11:30 to 12:30 Jerry threw a barrage of about 15 shells in here. One threw dirt in Reb's face, drew blood. I skinned my nose falling out of the sack and getting in the foxhole. Was glad when it was over and no one was hurt, that I know of. Got up in time for chow. Cold, but will be a clear day.

Had to go to II Corps — back at 1:00. Ate dinner with the M.P.s. Both of us to bed early.

On the 19th, Col. DuBois and Maj. Surdyk attended a conference in which plans were made to deliver a preparation and feint at Cassino from the east to attempt to make the enemy divert his forces to that sector. Meanwhile, the 36th Division was to establish a bridgehead across the Rapido River in the San Angelo area, cut Highway 6 east of Piedmonte and take Cassino from the south; while the 34th Division was to take the enemy from the east and northeast.

The Abbe de Montecassino, a Benedictine Monastery high on the moun-

tain behind Cassino, was placed off limits for all artillery fire, and permission to fire on it could be secured only through the Division Commander. At 11:45 p.m. the S-3 of the 756th Tank Battalion reported to Col. DuBois with orders to attach 6 47s to our battalion to be used to reinforce our fire.
Lt. Giaglo stepped on a Schu mine on the 19th and received a broken leg. The next day Pfc. Francis Crepeau had a foot blown off from a mine. The O.P. was then abandoned in favor of one in a safer location.

Thursday, January 20, 1944   Reb and I up at 5:45. Took down our tent, came to the Division Artillery. B Battery's kitchen is close. Went to see Don tonight. The attack for Cassino starts at 7:00. Some incoming. 125th Message Center was hit — don't know about casualties as yet. Are close to Cervaro.
Bob Vaughn was broke down from Mess Sergeant again. Haven't heard from Capt. Crellin about my going back to the kitchen. Hope he has forgotten about it.

The attack of the 36th Division at 10 p.m. January 20 failed to gain them the much needed bridgehead, and tentative plans were in the process of formulation for the taking of Cassino by the 34th Division.
Preparations were well underway for a spearhead invasion at Anzio Harbor. Some of the previous attacks south and east were meant for the Krauts to take reinforcements from the Anzio area.

Friday, January 21, 1944   Bought Barton's watch for $25.00. It doesn't have a crystal, though.
Went to II Corps again. 60 miles round trip now. 14 miles of unbelievably rough road. Back at noon. Wanted Don to go along, but he couldn't.
Slept this p.m. Had to go out last night at 12:30. Our C.P. is across the road from Division Artillery, so I can walk, and it doesn't take long.
The Cassino attack is still raging; don't know the result as yet.
Don came over tonight. I showed him my pictures. Walked back with him. Have the big light in here, a candle for heat.
Message Center has a position now in an old building — partly blown up, but still lots of protection. They do pretty well for positions, as they have to have some light and dry conditions, since they are always on duty.

The 133rd made the attack at 11:00 on the night of January 24, following a half hour preparation and a seventy minute rolling barrage. Enemy

AND THERE SHALL BE WARS

machine gun, mortar and artillery fire, plus heavily mined areas and barbed wire, proved too great an obstacle to surmount, and that attack was abandoned.

Allied landings at Anzio began on this date. The US 3rd Division and British 1st Division provided most of the assault force of the 36,000 men who landed the first day — only 13 were killed.

Saturday, January 22, 1944   I wake up in time for breakfast now that I have the watch to alert my mind to it. Dug the foxhole deeper and partially covered it. Started reading *The Robe* this p.m. Will quit now at 10:00.

Allied invasion yesterday, just south of Rome. No details as yet. Still heavy artillery fire both ways. No air activity lately. Clear weather, almost hot during the day, cold at night.

The attack or new invasion yesterday was south of Rome at Anzio and Nettuno.

This winter hasn't been a strong defense line like they had predicted it would be. I hope the coldest is past, and that we can keep on going north without that winter offensive holding on until spring.

We feel better about the new invasion. Now we should have a better chance at Rome.

Dick Johnson received news last night that his mother died.

We had to give the Red Cross a pretty low mark. Few of us had even gotten a doughnut from them. Anything they sent was all for the guys in the rear. Now Dick heard of his mother through a letter from home. No credit to the Red Cross who could have notified him much sooner.

Sunday, January 23, 1944   Up at 7:05, but not too late for breakfast. Went to II Corps this forenoon. Sgt. Norman from Service went along. Went to Division rear echelon, back at 12:15.

Cleaned up. Read in *The Robe*. Shells and air bursts coming in not too far away. Turned cloudy this p.m. Rained just a little. In my "heaven" again tonight. Ran the battery down last night — had to crank the peep.

By the end of the day we had 50,000 men ashore at Anzio. Kesselring, the German commander, was bringing in divisions quickly.

Monday, January 24, 1944   A few short runs today. A little cloudy. Went to see Don tonight for a little while. Read.

Tuesday, January 25, 1944   Chow at 6 a.m. Left for II Corps at

354

CHAPTER 21

6:30. Stopped at 109th Ordnance, saw Harvey and George Olson. Stayed for about an hour.

Back here at noon. Slept a little. Finished *The Robe* tonight. The most inspiring, interesting, emotional book I've ever read. Raining a little. Artillery fire still going out. Some coming in, but not in this immediate area.

Wednesday, January 26, 1944   Up at 1:30 a.m. Took a special to the battalion. On the way back I missed the bridge and tumbled 15 feet below. Thankful no bones were broken. I looked the peep over as well as I could and had gone straight down with no upset, so I put it in low range, low gear and 4-wheel drive, and drove it out. Partly stunned me; bruised my knee, face and wrist.

Up at 10:00. Headache from the fall. Lucky. I hardly notice a few more bumps on the peep.

Drizzling until 10:00. The sun came out this p.m. though. Several short trips to Division and the battery. Got 8 letters.

Louie Day checked the peep over, and said I was lucky. I went straight down the embankment, or I know I would have tipped for sure. Nothing wrong with the peep — funny it doesn't happen that way more often.

Twice more in the succeeding two days the infantrymen tried to gain the slopes west of Cassino Cairo road, but each time were driven back east of the Rapido by the intense machine gun and mortar fire from the pill boxes and weapons pits.

During the period 6 p.m., January 24, to January 26, 8 p.m., the 151st Field Artillery Battalion and attached assault guns fired 9457 rounds in their day and night assault.

On the morning of the 27th, the 168th Infantry Regiment passed through the 133rd and continued the attack. The 133rd was put in Division reserve.

Thursday, January 27, 1944   Up at 2 a.m. To our C.P. and to Division Headquarters. Slept through breakfast.

Up at 9:00. Beautiful day. Shaved, cleaned up. Read *The Way of all Flesh*.

Went to Division tonight. Read my testament. Am having battery trouble. I leave the light burning too long, and have to crank the peep.

Lt. John Reid, forward observer with the liaison crew, was shot in the hand by a machine gun bullet.

Friday, January 28, 1944   Went to II Corps this p.m. They have moved and are on this side of Venafro.

355

Pomerleau came over this p.m. 2 letters from Mom.

Saturday, January 29, 1944   Volunteered to go to II Corps. Took my clothes out to be washed, back at 11:00.
   Cleaned up this p.m. Changed clothes, took a sponge bath, shaved. To the Air O.P. this p.m. They are at San Pietro on Number 6. Heavy outgoing barrage tonight. Played cribbage with Reb and Dick until 10:00. Had coffee.

   The battalion continued in general support until the evening of the 29th. At that time, the 133rd Infantry relieved the 135th directly east of Cassino with the mission of containing the enemy from the east, while the 168th continued the attack north of the barracks at Monte Villa. Combined operations with the 756th Tank Battalion enabled the 168th to cross the mine fields and advance, while the supporting fire of the tanks destroyed machine gun positions and pill boxes.

Sunday, January 30, 1944   Overslept until 9:00. Some shells landed in the area last night, although I slept through it all. One landed about 100 feet from my tent and threw shrapnel by Reb's peep 75 feet from here. Ralph Clark from the 175th was killed last night. I knew him well from Camp Claiborne.
   Cleaned up this morning. Traded a new pair of 34 pants to Jack for a used pair of about 30 that fits. Now I have 3 complete uniforms. Got a parka, sweater, scarf, heavy socks and lined pants last night from Supply. Have Sgt. Rettinger to thank.
   Today reminds me for some reason of the Sunday about 3 years ago when I hauled a load of hay home from Floodwood. Probably because I haven't been home for awhile, and I just happened to think about it.

Monday, January 31, 1944   We were paid this forenoon. I got for both last and this month. Sent $100.00 home, kept $45.00.

Tuesday, February 1, 1944   Worked on my peep until almost noon. Changed oil and greased it. Foggy all day and cool. Traded my combat pants with Barney for a Mackinaw; have always wanted one.
   Still a heavy artillery fire going out, practically steady. A few came in tonight not too far away.

   The 133rd Infantry Regiment, after relieving the 135th in the area north of the barracks at Monte Villa and east of Cassino, prepared for an attack from the north and the east to secure the barracks area and the town.

Wednesday, February 2, 1944   Chow at 7:00 instead of 6:00. Went to II Corps. Got my clothes back and took some more into another place. Back at 10:00. Cleaned up, packed over my clothes. Warm and sunshine. The weather is half the war for me.

As yet we haven't taken Cassino. Have been here at Cervaro over two weeks. Steady firing. Hear a lot of screaming meemies coming in, but far enough away. Had a headache all afternoon. Wrote home.

It was always easy to get clothes washed. The country Italian ladies would wash and fold them up for not much money, or sometimes I'd give them some article of clothing, or extra food or candy from home. The main problem was to get back several days later to pick them up again.

Message Center was in an opportune position to drive back to get washed clothes. Jack was real fussy about being clean, as I was also.

Many of the fellows washed their own clothes or went partly dirty. A good way to wash woolens was to slosh them in a pail of gas and they would come out clean. The gas smell disappeared after they hung up to dry. The gas — dump it out. There was no shortage of gas.

Thursday, February 3, 1944   Overslept, missed breakfast. Up at 9:00. Cleaned up, played cribbage. Read *The Way of all Flesh* this p.m.

Steady firing all day and the biggest part of last night. It's upsetting my nerves. Some coming in, but not very close. Our battery's guns are just across the road, battalions all around us. The 995th Field Artillery have 203 mms that shoot a 250 pound projectile with a range of 10,000 feet. There are some big guns in the valley, reported to be 240s that shoot a 340 pound projectile, but I'd like to check those figures further.

Will write to Ray tonight. Cool.

Friday, February 4, 1944   Went to II Corps, got my laundry. Raining most of the afternoon, quite hard tonight. Played cribbage. Went to bed at 11:00.

We spend most of our free time with the Message Center. They have a good spot in a blown-out building that was probably a store, and they have a lot of shelter halves hung up to keep the wind out. There's always a cribbage game going on, and lots of talk.

I usually spend my evenings in the peep, closed in, then sleep in my pup tent. None of the other agents do like I do; most don't read much or write many letters.

Saturday, February 5, 1944 Up at 7:00, but breakfast was at 6:00. Cleaned up. Went to our Message Center. They were shelled, some very close, but no casualties that I know of. Throwing in air bursts this p.m.

Shaved, finished reading *The Way of all Flesh.* Made a trip to the Division. Barney and I went to the water point after water; got caught in an air raid. Took to an old building in Cervaro. It turned out to be an old Post Office or courthouse — in ruins as are all other places in Cervaro area. Found a few stamps and pictures of Italian soldiers all strewn over the floor.

To get water, we'd first go to the kitchen and put on all the empty water bead ons that we could, then exchange them for full ones. This wasn't our regular job, but Barney liked to get away from the Message Center once in awhile too.

By the 5th of February, the 133rd had occupied Hill 175 and the north edge of Cassino. The 1st and 2nd Battalions of the 133rd had been moved into a position abreast of the 3rd Battalion in the north of Cassino, their positions east of Cassino having been occupied by elements of the 36th Division. During the period of 1 February to 5 February, the battalion fired almost continuously throughout the day and night on harassing missions in Cassino and its south exits. The heaviest day's expenditure was February 4, during which the battalion expended 4568 rounds.

Sunday, February 6, 1944 Beautiful out last night. Up at 7:00. Went to church up the hill at the battery. The new chaplain gave a good sermon.

Took a sponge bath. Changed into clean clothes. Warm after the sun came out, but froze last night.

The battle of Cassino still rages; it is nearly in our hands, however.

Wrote to Rod and Ray. Went to bed early.

Monday, February 7, 1944 Slept until 10:00, just lazy. No overlays, firing orders or map co-ordinates going out now, just shells in support of our infantry. This battle is really "rough as a cob," all right, lots of lives lost and casualties. I'm one of the lucky ones the past 2 weeks, mostly

only going back to II Corps. But there are others who don't have that break.

At 5 p.m. 4 of our own American bombers dropped four 500-pound bombs in and around our 34th Division area.

Ken Kramer, my old friend from Ireland, was badly hit while operating a radio and died the next day. Staken and Staples were also wounded, but the 125th Field Artillery suffered greatly; it was during their chow time when the A Battery kitchen truck was hit. There were at least 20 casualties, mostly dead.

Nothing was mentioned of this incident in the official write-up of our battalion's history. Whoever wrote it seemed to glorify the Brass and pull them ahead. Those American bombers were supposed to have been in danger of German fighters behind them, so they dropped their bombs so as to get away faster.

Error is error in war — but even in war, truth is still truth.

II Corps came out with the report that "unidentified aircraft" dropped 3 bombs.

Tuesday, February 8, 1944 Took my clothes off for the first time in 3 weeks. Shells came in at 12:00 and 12:45. Got up to go in foxhole. Went to bed again with my clothes on.

Up at 6:45 in time for breakfast. Went to II Corps with the usual reports. Cold. Froze hardest of any night I've been here. Ice on my water can. Cleaned up, shaved. Finished *Time* magazine. Cool, but bearable to read outside.

The Battle of Cassino still rages on. Our battalion still firing heavily; so are others around us.

Vaughn came to my tent, played cribbage. 3 rolls of film from Ray, 2 *Heralds*, letter from Grandma. I find they are using heavy big guns to break down the town of Cassino. Our 105's are too light for some of the heavy concrete fortifications Jerry has holed up in and holding out from.

By February 7 the situation in Cassino became static, with gains being measured in hundreds of yards and by houses, as our troops attempted to pry the Germans loose from their foothold in the town. Our 105 mm Howitzers proved to be ineffective against the concrete and iron bunkers and heavy stone buildings. We had an 8-inch Howitzer battalion attached to us, which began a systematic leveling of the north sector of the town.

Wednesday, February 9, 1944   Slept until 10:00. Cleaned up. Raining this forenoon; it cleared up after awhile. Read in *Time*. Got 3 in the last several days. Played cribbage this p.m. One letter from Ray tonight. Went to bed early.

Thursday, February 10, 1944   Froze hard last night. Shells coming in from 11:00 to 11:30. I went in the foxhole.

Up at 7:00 this morning. Delicious breakfast: hot cakes, syrup, butter. Changed my tent; moved it about 10 feet. Took all morning.

Shells coming in again. Some close enough. Can hear the German gun that fires them. Started raining about noon and kept on. Read a little. At 8:00 I took 2 fellows to the battery. Foggy and raining. Went to Division. Put the chains on.

Friday, February 11, 1944   Up at 6:30. Chow at the same time.

Went to the outfit. Couldn't start my peep; took Floyd's. Went to the D.A.O. and II Corps. Raining. Wore my parka, but it soaked through on the seat.

Back at 10:00. Heavy attack started at 11:00. Started the peep. Left it run to dry it out and charge the battery. Read some this p.m. After supper read more.

Several lieutenants who are with the O.P. wounded a little.

Saturday, February 12, 1944   Stopped raining. A British Indian outfit pulled in here. Are close to us. Went to II Corps, then to Venafro with some laundry. Very muddy. Took the back road. Under fire from 5 a.m. to noon; some came quite close.

Cleaned up this p.m. Slept a little. Cleared up some, sun shone a little. Played cribbage. Went to bed around 9:00.

On the 12th there were reports of Henry Vaughn being M.I.A., but he was later found wounded in an Evacuation Hospital. On the 12th and 13th there were more casualties, with Pvt. Doyle from Hq. killed.

Sunday, February 13, 1944   Up at 6:30 in time for chow. Reb, Barney and I went to church. Chaplain Temple talked of the Christian faith. Came back from church at 10:30.

Got 7 letters last night from home and the kids. They sent some pictures, mostly of themselves.

Turned warm. The Indians are getting pretty close to me, so I moved my tent further over by the road. The old spot was too muddy to dig, so I dug another foxhole. Took a sponge bath, changed my clothes, wrote 4 letters: 1 to Pat, 1 home, Ray, and Arlene. It's 9:00 now. Will read until 10:30 or 11:00. Warm today, but plenty cool tonight.

Monday, February 14, 1944   Up at 6:00. Cold. Went to II Corps. Got my laundry. Cool and dry. Few shells coming in. Our infantry is starting to be relieved.

One V-mail tonight from Mom. Went to bed early.

Tuesday, February 15, 1944   Slept until 10:00. Our bombers bombed the Benedictine monastery this forenoon. A lot of planes going over, a little Jerry ack-ack. One can see the abbey here from several places. No doubt, a historic event. Some shells coming in.

Cleaned up this p.m. Chopped wood. Read in *Time*. Read after supper.

They had a wood stove in Message Center, so I chopped some wood for it. All peeps had an ax-pick-shovel attached to the driver's side.

Wednesday, February 16, 1944   Shells were coming in and sounding close, so I took two blankets and came into Message Center. Pretty safe here, except for a direct hit. Hot cakes for breakfast. Went to II

Corps, cleaned up, slept some this p.m.

There are varied reports as to whether the abbey was used by the Germans as an O.P. Forward observers reported seeing Germans coming out of the monastery as it was bombed. We watched the Flying Fortresses, Marauders, Bostons and P-40s who did the bombing.

Thursday, February 17, 1944   Slept at Message Center again. Took my clothes off, first time again in a long time. Played some cribbage, cleaned up, slept this p.m.

Artillery still going out. Our planes bombed the monastery again. Fairly nice out today.

The monastery was heavily bombed at the request of the New Zealand Corps. The historic buildings are completely wrecked. Reports now say that the Germans are using the bombed-out monastery for cover, as it gives them more protection from our fire than it did before. Some of us believe that only one, or at least very few Krauts could have used the monastery as a forward O.P. and directed fire on all of the advancing Army from it.

We never thought we were fighting an enemy who was afraid to lie a lot.

The 17 cm gun in the north was still working us over, and Gordon Neel of A Battery was wounded on the 18th.

Friday, February 18, 1944   Burned a lot of worthless junk this morning. At 10:00 I leave for II Corps. Waited until 4 p.m. for Gen. Stanford, but he came back another way. Had blankets along, prepared to stay the night.

Got a *Life* and a *Country Gentleman*.

The Krauts committed 29 Divisions and 26 Panzer Divisions to the attack at Cassino.

Saturday, February 19, 1944   Slept in the Message Center Building again. French toast for breakfast. Cold winds.

Went to the Air O.P. this p.m. On the way back I gave an Italian woman a ride to Cervaro. She had been wounded, and was real thankful to ride.

Read in *Country Gentleman*. To bed at 10:00.

There were further attacks by Indian and New Zealand troops in the hills north of Cassino monastery and over the Rapido against Cassino town. Some gains were made, but couldn't be held in face of fire from dominating

German positions.

Sunday, February 20, 1944   Slept until 8:00. Jack Salzer came back, so I slept in my tent. Cold and clear. Artillery fire going out. Coming in, too, but not just in this area. Can hear firing commands and the brass shell cases coming out of the breech-blocks falling on one another — that's from our 105's, not from the Krauts.

Monday, February 21, 1944   Don't remember much of anything, except that there were rumors floating around that we were heading for the rear for R.R.R.

CHAPTER 22

R.R.R. Orders for Anzio. Landing.
More problems in Italy. Foxholes. Dug in.

Tuesday, February 22, 1944   Got ready and moved out, back to Alife again in our old area. Got back at 2:00. The agents got a pyramidal tent. We put it up and got settled. Nice to be away from the front, and probably won't be so much driving.

The relief of the 133rd Infantry was complete by 3 a.m. on the 22nd of February. The battalion ceased fire on the night harassing missions at 3:15, moved out of position, and started back for the rest area of Alife.

Wednesday, February 23, 1944   Have a bad head cold. Fixed a tire this morning. Rained this p.m. To Division and all the battalions tonight.

This is R.R.R. until the 27th — everybody is taking it mighty seriously!

Thursday, February 24, 1944   Still feel tough. Went over my things. Barney went to the hospital this morning with a bad stomach. Jack and I went to Piedmonte this morning. Got a crystal on my watch — $1.00. Walnuts, $.76 a kilo. Took a shower at the clothing center. Got new pants, but everything else is secondhand, but clean.

Took clothes to the usual place. The girls still knew me. Got my shoes sewed by the shoemaker in Piedmonte.

A letter from Ray tonight. Have a nice charcoal fire in here with a bright light. Wrote to Ray and Mom.

Friday, February 25, 1944   R.R.R.

Saturday, February 26, 1944   R.R.R.

Sunday, February 27, 1944   R.R.R.

Monday, February 28, 1944   Started to clear, but it got cloudy again. Still feel tough. Sinus trouble, I guess, headache. Made a few trips now and then. Still on duty 24 hours a day, but doesn't seem like it. Yesterday I took Hurley Soderlind to see Johnny, but he is at 17th General Hospital. We went to the 9th Evac. Hospital, 21 miles each way.

Johnny and Hurley were brothers who joined the Guards together. Hurley was the older of the 2. I don't think Johnny was in the hospital as a casualty, but stomach trouble was a common ailment. The 17th General Hospital was too far back in the rear for us to go to. Hurley was still a cook in B Battery, and Johnny was with the gun crew in B Battery.

Tuesday, February 29, 1944   Went to the battalion, and to Service Battery to have some things done to the peep. Last night I went to get Don and Jerry. Took them to the 38th Evac. to see Andy. Back at 9:00. Tonight I went to see Barney at the 11th Field Hospital.

The closest hospital to the front was always a "Field Hospital," then the "Evacuation Hospital," and furthest back was the "General Hospital."
Both Andy and Barney were troubled with nervous stomachs.

Wednesday, March 1st, 1944   Still raining mostly every day. Took a fellow to the 38th Evac. I stopped to see Andy.

We started following a real strict training schedule the first week of March. I was lucky again to miss out on that. I was able to keep busy, however, with the special runs morning and night, and hanging around Message Center.

Thursday, March 2, 1944   Raining. Put my top up. Letter from Mom last night. Dick and I went to St. Angelo, after going to Divi-

Casserta

sion Hq. Nothing in particular there, but a chance to see some people again.

Friday, March 3, 1944 Took Doc Lyons to Caserta today. Used Floyd's peep. Tonight Don, Hurley and I went to the 38th Evac. to see Andy.

Saturday, March 4, 1944 Went to Piedmonte with Jack to the showers. Felt tough tonight. Mostly homesick, I guess. Always nice to get a hot shower and clean change of clothes.

Sunday, March 5th, 1944 Missed breakfast. Sun came out for a short time. Rumors out about us moving soon. Cut down the size of my camouflage net. Made my bed over. Cleaned over more of my junk. Went to see Andy at 3rd Convalescent. He seems to be doing pretty good to me, but is on a bland diet.

Monday, March 6, 1944 Packed up more of my junk. Jack and I went after laundry.

Tuesday, March 7, 1944 Up at 2:30. Special to the battalion. Hardly got back and laid down, when up at 4:30. Packed up. Left at 8:00. Came through Benevento and St. Georgia, where I first came to Division Artillery in October. An oil line broke on the peep on the way down here. All the oil ran out. Service Battery had to come and fix it.

Got here to a little town close to St. Georgia at noon. We agents got the upstairs of a shoe repair shop to stay in. The C.P. and Message Center is in town. Battery is close by.

Wednesday, March 8, 1944 Got things better arranged. Got our stove going again, and are quite comfortable. The building didn't seem to have had any bad effects from shellfire or from the Germans.

We treat the old cobbler good, so he brought up some red vino tonight. Never did care for it though. It is hard to say if the cobbler has a family or not, since for us, intelligent conversation among Italians is nonexistent.

This is still part of our R.R.R. It is also a time to bring battalion strength to what some new standards are: Approximately 100 men, 25 vehicles and miscellaneous other equipment was taken from us.

Instructions were received to prepare for a water movement to the Anzio beachhead, utilizing less than half of our organic transportation, and only the personnel necessary to "shoot, move and communicate." This definitely included Message Center, which included me.

Thursday, March 9, 1944   Took Mr. Goodell and Doc Lyons to Caserta. Goodell went to the 43rd Station Hospital on business. 40 miles each way. Good highway.

Friday, March 10, 1944   Went to Benevento. Left my watch there to be cleaned.

Saturday, March 11, 1944   Rained every day previously. Cleared up a little today.

Sunday, March 12, 1944   Raining again. Quite a few trips out.

Monday, March 13, 1944   Floyd and I went to Benevento. Got my watch. $1.00. Cleared up. Sun shining. Saw a USO show in St. Georgia this p.m. Tonight I took Don to the 133rd after we came up here to the shoe shop. I took Don back. Gararto, the Italian kid, came along with us.

This young Italian boy was sort of adopted by the guys. He came along whenever he felt welcome, and he was no problem. The Brass looked the other way, though he ate our food, and the fellows gave him clothes. We asked him how he got along with the Krauts. He answered, "Alles Verboten." (Everything is forbidden.)

Tuesday, March 14, 1944   Rained last night, but cleared up. Wrote home and to Pat.

Wednesday, March 15, 1944   Went to Benevento. Several trips to the battalion. Cleared up.
This is our last night here, I suppose, so we had a party. The old cobbler brought up some real good champagne or white wine, and we all had some extra rations and some goodies from home that we shared. The cobbler doesn't want to see us go. We have been here quite a while.

Thursday, March 16, 1944   Went to the battalion, 185th, and Division Hq. Snowing. Hard driving. Sticky snow, but not turning to rain. About 3 inches on the ground when I came back at 3:00 a.m. Made me homesick to see all the snow, about the first I've really seen in 3 years.

Up at 7:00. My watch still runs. Stopped snowing. A lot of slush and mud. Started packing up and sorting over.

At 2 p.m. Tom called up, and I had to pack up and leave for the battalion. At 3:00 16 peeps from the 151 left for Naples. Budinger lead the convoy. Nice trip, 64 miles. We got into Naples at 5:45.

Couldn't find the Texas Staging Area. We left the peeps in the heart of town. Budinger took off in one direction. An M.P. tried to show me where the area is, and we got caught in an air raid. In Naples they set off smoke bombs during air raids, and the smoke is really heavy. The M.P. hit an elderly Italian woman, and we had to take her to a hospital.

We got her into the back seat of the peep, and I tried to quiet her down, but she was screaming, "Mama mia! Mama mia!" over and over again. The M.P. did know his way around, though, and we took her to an Italian hospital. She was hurt pretty bad in the leg and hip; they carried her into the hospital on a stretcher. What a relief to get her there.

We finally all got to the Texas Staging Area at or after 9:30. We lined up the peeps and spread out on the ground for a few hours' sleep. Shellfire and bombs were the farthest thing from my mind. It is even quieter here than at our rest area at Alife.

Friday, March 17, 1944   Up at 7:00. This staging area is full of equipment, trucks mostly. In a suburban area. I am in charge of Headquarters' 9 peeps. We have rations for 4 days. Laid around all day.

Cpl. Dicky and I took off tonight to look a little at Naples.

We sleep alongside our peeps, waiting to load up and take off.

Lt. Black was really the one in charge of our whole advance detail, but we saw little of him.

Saturday, March 18, 1944   Rolled my bedroll. Ate at the kitchen. Are close to Naples. Waited all day again.

Tonight Dicky and I went to Naples again. We picked up a lieutenant from the 168th Infantry. Was glad to have him along, as the M.P.s like to show their authority when they think it necessary — but think twice if an officer is with. Drove around the town a lot. Two fellows took off with a case of our V rations, so I divided the rest up amongst us.

Sunday, March 19, 1944   Slept in a Diamond T wrecker with Dicky — it looked like rain. The drivers here are those who haul ammo to the beachhead and then come back for more. No rain so far since we have been here.

Floyd, another fellow and I went to Naples and looked around some more. Had something to eat. Back at 9:30.

Monday, March 20, 1944   The usual thing. Waited another day. Some peeps left to load, but not us.

Got picked up by M.P.s. They took us to Headquarters and turned us loose. Back about 8:30. We made coffee.

There was no reason for the Military Police to pick us up. We'd done nothing at all, and it was very humiliating. The M.P.s ran the town of Naples though, and most GIs hated them.

Tuesday, March 21, 1944   Raining and cloudy. Put shelter halves on the sides of my peep. Sat in it most of the day.

This p.m. Floyd and I went to the Service Club and Red Cross. After supper went to the show. Vic Neas and I walked back. Floyd had left us, and got caught in an air raid.

Wednesday, March 22, 1944   Vic and I slept in a Diamond T truck box, covered. Rained. At 8:00 we all left for the docks. I loaded on LST #36, the only peep from the 151. Other T.O.M. trucks. A part of 135 Infantry, and B Battery of the 125th F.A. loaded on late in the p.m. Got chummy with a sergeant from Duluth.

I wasn't really happy about this move. Anzio didn't have a good reputation. From what we had heard, the fighting was about halted for Cassino, and here I was on another LST headed for another hot spot. Well, if this would help us take Rome, I supposed it's what was needed.

Was a bit lonesome too, as I knew no one and the only good connection was that most of 125th's B Battery was from Duluth.

On March 17, 4 officers, our advance party, moved out. By March 21 the battalion was loaded and ready for the trip. The transportation problem was really tough because of restrictions placed on us by higher headquarters. Three hundred and twenty men and officers, fifty-one vehicles, and twelve 105 Howitzers represented our total loading problem on the first wave. The remainder of the battalion remained in a rear echelon in the vicinity of Naples, and was to come forward at a later date.

On March 23 the battalion loaded on LST ships and were ready to sail before dark. The battalion loaded onto 4 different ships, and in many cases, men were not on the same ship as the vehicle they were to ride in. Despite the mixed up feeling caused by this kind of loading, I suppose no single bomb or sinking could get have got all of us.

The trip was quiet and peaceful all the way to Anzio. We expected plenty of air activity because of the nice weather and crowded conditions of the harbor, but no Luftwaffe was in the area.

The following is a letter I received which describes the original invasion at Anzio, January 1944, and the fate of some of the men who participated:

Dear Bud,

My brother, Billy C. Rhoads — Army Service Number 16001304, was in Company C, 83rd Chemical Mortar Battalion and was killed in action off the coast of Anzio on 26 January, 1944. My family has been searching for many years in an attempt to find someone in his unit who knew him or perhaps served with him. If possible, will you please help?

Bill joined the Army in 1940 in Freeport, Illinois, although his hometown was Albia, Iowa. He took training at Ft. Bragg, North Carolina and remained there after being assigned to the 60th Field Artillery, 9th Division. He was with the 9th when they arrived at Casablanca, North Africa in November 1942, and still with the 9th until Sicily was taken in August 1943. The 9th went to England for R and R and to train for the Normandy Invasion. Bill was transferred to the 83rd Chemical Mortar Battalion in September 1943 and was involved with the fighting at Maori, Chuinzi Pass, Fala, Venafro, etc. with the Rangers. The 83rd were pulled off the line in early January 1944 and sent to Pozzouli to conduct amphibious training for the assault from the sea on Anzio.

On 22 January, Companies A & B of the 83rd, plus the 1st, 3rd and 4th Ranger Battalions landed unopposed at Anzio. The Germans were totally taken by surprise. LST 422, after unloading at Anzio, made an uneventful trip back to Naples and, during the night of 25 January, 1944, after being loaded to capacity with tanks, jeeps, half-tracks, ambulances, trucks and various other vehicles, plus tons of ammunition, including the white phos-

phorous shells for the 4.2 mortars, and hundreds of barrels of gasoline, the LST proceeded toward Anzio. The personnel aboard consisted of Companies C, D and Headquarters of the 83rd Chemical Mortar Battalion, and the 68th Field Artillery.

The Germans, after the preliminary appearance of enemy troops on the 22nd, and in anticipation of an assault by sea, dropped floating mines into the water from airplanes. At 0520 in the dark morning hours of 26 January, with dense fog, twenty foot high waves, a mixture of snow and freezing rain, and the water in the Tyrrhenian Sea too cold for human endurance, LST 422 hit a mine resulting in a gaping hole in the bottom and the right side. The intense explosion immediately caused a raging fire, which caused the steel to become extremely hot and ammunition to explode. Some men were blown overboard by the initial explosion. Most of them were in the lower level of the ship where it was much warmer than on the main deck. The ship became a raging inferno, and the men had to abandon it or be consumed.

Relative to information from survivors of the LST 422 tragedy, the number of men in the frigid water of the sea was unbelievable. Some were obviously dead, some injured, and others were struggling to stay afloat in anticipation of being rescued. At 0540, 20 minutes following the LST explosion, LCI 32 (Landing Craft-Infantry) was ordered to pick up survivors. It also struck a mine and sank in less than five minutes with the loss of most of its crew and infantrymen it was hauling. The brass then put out the order to discontinue all rescue operations for fear of jeopardizing more men and ships. Those men in the water were left to the unrelenting and merciless doom of the sea. With the weight of equipment, the immense fatigue, and hypothermia of the icy water, many of the men, including my brother, ultimately drowned. His body was found floating at approximately 10:00 a.m. the same morning of 26 January, 1944. His body was brought aboard a boat long enough for identification (dog tags), then he was returned to the sea.

Unit Journal - aboard LST 422 26 January, 1944		Board of Officers Report Casualties -
479 Enlisted men	83rd C.M.Bn.	53 men survived and returned to duty.
16 Officers		37 recovered dead and buried at sea. (B. Rhoads)
20 Enlisted men	68th F.A.	54 recovered dead and buried at cemetery in Nettuno, Italy
_1 Officer		362 never recovered or identified.
516 - Total		
		506 - Total

The Unit Journal lists two men, Privates Lawless and Kuykendall of

CHAPTER 22

Company B as killed in action on LST 422 on 26 January, 1944.

Kindest regards,

George Rhoads
Iowa City, IA 52240

P.S. If you have any knowledge of Pvt. Wiley Wheeler I would greatly appreciate knowing about it. Wiley was in Company D, 83rd Chemical Mortar Battalion and was never recovered following LST 422 hitting a mine off the coast of Anzio on 26 January, 1944. I'd be most appreciative for any information!

After reading George (Dusty) Rhoad's letter and thinking of the fate of LST 422 and the 506 casualties, among whom was Dusty's brother Billy, I can't help but be thankful even now that our landing was so uneventful in comparison, and remember all those who were Killed in Action that day.

Thursday, March 23, 1944   Slept across the front seats of my peep. Rained and was chilly. Water was pretty smooth all night. Docked at Anzio about 10:30. Two shells came close, one on either side of the ship. If they were going to fire the 3rd shell for effect [in the middle of where the other two had landed], it never came.

Ship run by Greeks. After chow Adler and I looked for the other drivers. We found them in Anzio in an abandoned house.

Friday, March 24, 1944   Slept in under the peep last night. Several air raids. Shells coming in but not close here. I have to go to the docks early and direct the 151 into this area.

Finished up about 1:30. Came to Division Artillery about 2:00. Dug a hole and put the peep over it.

Saturday, March 25, 1944   Up at 7:00. Moved in with Dick and Reb in a grass hut. Dug another hole; some shelling going on all day. Shaved. Got a lot of mail yesterday.

Unloading the vehicles from the LST was much different than at Salerno. Here they had the bow doors open, ramp down, and gently hit the beach. Then we drove off. The immensity of the cargo hold always gets you, though.

When we got away from the town and in position, everybody dug a dugout and covered it with anything that would hold up sandbags — so the only thing that would get to you is a direct hit.

373

Sunday, March 26, 1944 Went to the battalion several times. Once tonight to the front, back at 9:30. Cool and windy.

I think the chaplain is hibernating, as we haven't seen or heard of him again for some time.

We had our dugout pretty well finished, but only really were in it at night. The weather was better here. There was more sun than around Cassino, and it was getting toward spring too. Floyd had his Coleman stove that really came in handy for making coffee or hot water.

Monday, March 27, 1944 Up at 7:00. Cold this forenoon, but sunny. We make coffee several times a day. Reb got a 19 lb. can from his kitchen.

This morning Dick and I went to 6 Corps Hq. in Anzio. Took Lt. Aikers there. This p.m. It warmed up; it's almost hot, but windy.

Heavy air raid last night, some bombs dropped. I was on the road at the time.

The battalion went to the rear echelon area. Just northeast of Nettuno, after orders, the battalion dug in practically out of sight. Even the C.P. and Message Center took up serious defensive positions.

This was unlike Salerno where we were on the move. This place demanded that we have good defensive positions.

The battalion registered on the 27th; the first shot was fired by B Battery at 9:10 p.m.

To the end of the month we were very inactive. During the day, all circulation was discouraged, and resupply was done at night. There was little to do but improve our positions.

Tuesday, March 28, 1944 Reb and I worked all day on a dugout. Practically finished it by tonight. Hard work, but I enjoyed it. Out several times to the 151 tonight. Back at 10:00.

Wednesday, March 29, 1944 We finished our new home and put in a light from my peep.

Went to Anzio this morning. To 6 Corps. Looked through a modern house. The whole city is vacated.

Shaved. Heavy air raid this p.m. 4 Jerry planes shot down. The whole area is fairly flat. Mountains to the northeast. Our C.P. is close to the front. Some shells coming in last night, few close. This place isn't quite as bad as I feared it would be.

Thursday, March 30, 1944   Slept with Reb in the hole last night. Slept until 8:30. Woke up with a sore throat.

Cool and cloudy all day. Went with Dick to 6th Corp's Hq. To the battalion tonight. Back at 8:00. Wrote to Margaret. Feel tough with this cold. Fairly quiet all day. The ground is kind of sandy and damp. The hole is not so nice to sleep in, but a lot safer than anywhere else.

Friday, March 31, 1944   Slept until 8:30. Feel fairly good today. Read some this p.m. Dick and I went to the 194th. Saw Ed Wold; he is 1st Sgt. of 194th Field Artillery Headquarters. He seems the same as when at Camp Claiborne.

To the battalion again tonight. The peep stopped on me again tonight. Can never find out just what's wrong — in due time, it starts again.

Rained this p.m. Wrote to Mr. C'iago of the American Legion. A barrage came in while I was writing this. Several were close; others were over — started a fire.

Saturday, April 1, 1944   Don't remember much. Went to the battalion tonight.

Sunday, April 2, 1944   Stopped to see McGee. Shells coming in, one real close to Division Hq. Message Center. Went to 6 Corps this morning.

Monday, April 3, 1944   Got an Easter card from Mom last night. Got *Life* magazine. Reb and I went to the Division O.P. and got water this morning. Air raids the last 2 nights.

Went to all battalions. Dick came along. Shell hit A Battery Command.Post. Killed 6, including Capt. Houle and Sgt. Ahr. Seriously wounded Lt. Jenks.

Back at 9:00. Read until 11:30.

A heavy concentration of 15 cm fire in the A Battery position area caused the battalion's first casualties on the beachhead. One round landed in the battery C.P. killing Capt. Lucien W. Houle, Battalion S-2 who was acting as Battery Commander in the absence of Capt. Johnson who had been hospitalized.

Staff Sgt. Thomas Ahr, Capt. Donald Vinup, Pvt. Robert Vincent, Pvt. Bill Hicks and Pvt. Charles Mills, who were in the sandbagged shelter, were all killed by the same burst. 1st Lt. William Jenks, who was seriously wounded, and Pvt. William Howitt, lightly wounded, were the only survivors of the group.

These casualties shook everybody pretty badly. A direct hit can be devastating. I started to give our sand pit a pretty low mark, but it was a suit-yourself decision: you could stay on top if you wanted to, or you could go into your sandbagged hole.

Lt. Jenks was always "one of the boys," while still being a topnotch officer. I'd known him since Ireland, when he was the negotiator between us cooks and Col. Sly and the rest of the previous crew of officers. I had come in contact with him several times. After he was wounded, we never saw him again. We later heard that he had recovered, but was permanently disabled.

Tuesday, April 4, 1944   Up at 7:00. Washed, shaved. Read in *Life* and *Time*. Slept some this p.m.

Took Mr. Peterson to 6th Corps. Floyd and I went to all battalions tonight. The 175th and 185th were under fire just before we got there.

Wednesday, April 5, 1944   Slept through breakfast. Played cribbage, cleaned up. Warm, but cloudy. Moonlight nights make for easy driving. To all battalions tonight. Reb came along. Got a package from Mom with a roll of film, some chocolate candy, papers and letters.

Thursday, April, 6, 1944   Germans firing all night. Not so close to us, though they sounded that way. Woke up every once in awhile. Hot cakes for breakfast.

Friday, April 7, 1944   Good Friday, but nothing to remind me of it, not even my conscience. Started reading *Forgive Us Our Trespasses* by Lloyd Douglas.

To the battalions tonight. Floyd came along. A lot of shells coming in, about 4 in our area. Started an ammo dump off — the sky was illuminated, with explosions going off and on for 2 hours.

Saturday, April 8, 1944   Comparatively quiet last night, except for one air raid. 2 Jerry planes downed. Got up for breakfast, but wasn't very good. Took Capt. Raymond to the 36th F.A. where he is now attached. Enjoyed his company.

Finished reading *Forgive Us Our Trespasses*. Played one game of cribbage with Dick for the watch band. I won. Went to the battalions tonight.

Sunday, April 9, 1944   Easter. French toast for breakfast. Attended church services by Chaplain Temple. His topic was, "You shall not die," and he gave reasons to have faith and avoid sin. He also read of the resurrection out of [the book of] John. We all were with helmets and rifles. No one even took his helmet off to use it as a seat, as we do sometimes when the situation is not so tactical. Floyd usually plays on the portable organ.

Slept just a little while before dinner. Washed and shaved. Rained this afternoon.

We played some cribbage. Dick and I went to the battalions. Raining all the way. Went to bed fairly early.

Monday, April 10, 1944   Overslept, didn't get up for breakfast.

Worked on the peep several hours. Cleaned the battery and the air cleaner. Dick and I took a bath before dinner at the creek. Changed into my summer underwear and green denims. Took my camera apart this p.m. and cleaned it.

Part of our home caved in on us. Had to brace up the rafters.

To rear echelons and battalions. Floyd came along. Gets dark by the time we get back. Can't leave any sooner, as no one is allowed to the 151 C.P. during daylight. Reason: is under enemy observation.

About half a dozen horses running loose around here. One gave birth to a colt the other night.

Shells still coming in now and then. One heavy barrage early this morning. No daylight air raids for some time. One last night again, though.

Was really warm today until dinner time. I often get disillusioned and melancholy, but know how thankful I really should be.

Tuesday, April 11, 1944   The usual thing again, not much doing in the day time. To the battalions at dusk, and shells coming in after dark. Went with Reb tonight. Warm sunshine. Got a letter from Mom.

The 133rd Infantry began the relief of the 168th Infantry Regiment and assumed command of the sector on the 13th of April. The 151st Field Artillery Battalion took over the direct support mission from the 175th Field Artillery Battalion when the relief was completed.

Ammunition was restricted to thirty rounds per gun per day. Smoke generators operated almost continuously during hours of daylight on both sides of the line, reducing the targets of opportunity to a small number for the forward observers.

Lt. Fred Ziegler, the Air Observer, found enemy guns and installations on almost every flight. An increased ammo allowance of 65 rounds per gun per day made our artillery fires a bit more brisk, and no doubt made the Krauts no happier.

Wednesday, April 12, 1944   Up at 7:00 in time for breakfast, which was hot cakes. Read some. Lying outside. Warm sun. A little breezy this p.m. Took Col. Peterson to the 151 tonight.

Thursday, April 13, 1944   This afternoon Reb and I remodeled our dugout. We now have a hole 10 feet long, 5 feet wide, and 4 feet deep, completely covered except for a hole big enough to crawl through. Took us until 6:00 tonight to finish.

Jewell came along with me to the C.P. tonight. I got paid $72.70; sent $50.00 to Ray. Wrote him tonight.

We have it pretty nice and comfortable, with little to do. The few runs are routine every day. No map overlays or specials, or not many. Have light, and it's warm enough. Reb is a good partner as well. Has had much more experience in life than I have, and is real sensible and handy at everything.

CHAPTER 23
Dug in, still. Breakout of Anzio. Headed towards Rome.

Friday, April 14, 1944   Slept peacefully last night, although I don't think there was anything coming in. The other day was an air raid, some 40 planes. 2 went down.

Cleaned out my peep. Sharpened my knife, read a little.

Went to the 151. Pomerleau came along. Took him back.

Saturday, April 15, 1944   Didn't do much of anything this forenoon. This p.m. I went to Service Battery. They tightened the front wheels and welded a few broken places. I changed the oil and greased it. Really got dirty.

Came back at 5:00. Changed clothes. Took a bath at the creek.

To the rear echelon again, then to the front. Pom came along, took him back, stayed there, had coffee. Back here at 10:45. Gets pretty dark out now. No moon. Nearly hit an ox.

One letter from home tonight, also some chocolate. B Battery's kitchen is still in Naples on Detached Service. Would like to see Don, but I suppose he's having a great time in Naples without me all this time.

Sunday, April 16, 1944   Up for breakfast. Went to Corps and picked up some junk at the Ordnance. Laid around most the day.

Went out tonight with Floyd. Just about ran into suicide at the Castle. Jerry was throwing them in; we got out. Went to the 151 and came back again. Luckily they stopped during the time we were there. Kim Reed was hit; heard that one fellow supposed to have lost both legs. A hay stack afire by the Bailey bridge.

One letter from Jean, answered it. 2 letters from home.

My forgeterer works much better than my rememberer when it comes to some of my diary entries written 56 years ago, so I don't always remember what I was referring to. At this time we were still operating with a skeleton crew on all details. As far as I can remember, the Castle was the Command

Post of the battalion.

The reason Floyd and I went out together was because our Message Centers were near each other, and whenever we could, we wanted to eliminate one vehicle on the road which was always under observation during daylight hours. Casualties weren't excessive during this period, but there were always some. Many we never heard of until later, unless the person was from your own detail or battalion.

Monday, April 17, 1944   Read some this p.m. I slept. Took Col. Peterson to 6th Corps.
To the rear echelon tonight, and to the front. Pom came along. Road was restricted until 9:15, so we couldn't come back until then. Dark, and hard driving. Tanks still on the road. Round trip is 20 miles. Back by 10:00. Then to bed.

Tuesday, April 18, 1944   Have 3 years of service in now today. Nothing to brag about, but a fact. We don't wonder or worry much about the future anymore. You get sort of numb to life, and the standard, "As told!" answer to the question, "What do you do in the Army?" takes on more meaning all the time.
Raining slightly all day. Finished a letter home. Finished a copy of *Life*. Read *Tortilla Flat* by Steinbeck today. Enjoyed it because I saw the picture twice before I read the book.
The rear echelon tonight. Floyd came along to all battalions. I don't like going to the Castle where the 185 and 175 Message Centers are at, but the other agents seem to get out of going as much as they can.
Cleared up around 2 p.m. Washed a change of clothes before supper.

Wednesday, April 19, 1944   Up for breakfast: oatmeal and coffee. Cleaned up, read.
This p.m. took my peep to Service Battery. They put in a new spring. Back at 3:30.
Read a little more. To the rear echelon and the front.
Wrote to Robert Hamilton, sent a few pictures.

Thursday, April 20, 1944   To 6 Corps. On the way back, I stopped in at 33rd Field Hospital with a note to Helen Richel, a nurse who is a friend of Maj. Surdyk. Four nurses invited me into their tent, gave me wine and fudge. Took notes back from them to Surdyk and Grant. I'd do anything for these two guys. The letters smelled strong of perfume. Was really nice to talk to American nurses again.

Took a bath this p.m. at the creek and changed clothes.

To the rear and all battalions with Floyd. Always take my peep. Had a flat before I left. Had to bring the Catholic chaplain back from B Battery 151. We had to wait for him. A fire mission came down when we were beside a 105 mm. First time I've been that close when a 105 was fired. This particular gun had fired 8,100 rounds in Italy.

Back at 10:00. Started reading *My Friend Flicka* by Mary O'Hara.

Friday, April 21, 1944   Shells came in last night. 3 air attacks. Up at 8:30. Had to take someone to the Air O.P. Gen. Stanford and Capt. Wick left for home today. Nice and warm. Took a Catholic chaplain to 15 Evac. this p.m. 2 letters from Mom last night, 2 from Ray with snapshots. To the battalion as usual.

Saturday, April 22, 1944   To 6 Corps and Air O.P. this morning. Started raining. Put my windshield up. Didn't do much this p.m. To the rear echelon and battalion as usual.

Sunday, April 23, 1944   Took Smith to Division School. Peep conked out once, had to be pushed. Came back here; it stopped again. Took a bath, worked on the peep for 2 hours. Cleaned the plugs and motor. Warm and nice. To the battalions.

There is an open field north of us where there are some shacks with older Italians living in them. We don't see them moving around much.

Monday, April 24, 1944   Don't remember much. The usual, I guess.

Tuesday, April 25, 1944   Cleaned up. To the Air O.P. this p.m. Tonight to the battalion. Took a Lt. Daniels to the 151 C.P. He is a B-36 pilot just seeing how the Air Force runs. He's stationed in Sardinia. Back at 11:00.

Wednesday, April 26, 1944   Raining. Hot cakes for breakfast. Rained on and off all day. To the rear tonight and the battalions. Back at 9:30. Shelling. The ammo dump was exploding again last night too. Finished *Jane Eyre*. Wrote to Aunt Anna and home.

Thursday, April 27, 1944   Up at 7:00. Our photo interpreter was killed last night, and a lieutenant whose name I don't know. A 170 lit on top of their hole. Quite a few shells coming in. Air bursts this

morning.
Carried up a can of water from the creek. Made coffee. Took Col.
Kenniger to Corps this p.m. Went to the rear echelon, but not the
front for a change. Had the first evening off since we've been here.
Got an Easter card from Aunt Anna. Answered it. Also wrote to
Ray and the Cookes. Shells coming in, but not close as yet. Took a
bath at the creek, changed clothes and washed out my shorts. Washed
out socks and shirt.

Friday, April 28, 1944   The usual thing as near as I can remember.

Saturday, April 29, 1944   To the battalions tonight. Just before I got
to the Castle, Jerry had thrown in 186 rounds in 26 minutes. Looked
like 88's. Road was strewn with dirt and grass. One tree knocked
over. I've been lucky around this place as yet.

Sunday, April 30, 1944   Forgot all about it being Sunday until
tonight when Reb mentioned it. Read *The Grapes of Wrath*. To the
rear echelon 3 times, once a special. Not to the front tonight. Letter
from Pat last night. A V-mail from Germaine in answer to a letter I
wrote in January.

During the month of April the front was comparitively quiet, with the
enemy content to be on the defensive here at Anzio, and protect the flanks
and rear of his troops on the Cassino and Garigliano fronts.
We were somewhat more aggressive than that, and had platoon and company raids all along the front every night. These brought in prisoners and
much valuable G-2 information pertaining to the enemy's strength and order
of battle.
The beachhead was approximately fourteen miles wide and eight miles
deep, giving the enemy access to all our occupied area even with light artillery. Rear echelons and hospital areas were subject to harassing fire every
day, and burning ammunition dumps became a nightly occurrence. The Anzio
Express, a heavy railroad gun, was particularly disturbing to occupants of
the rear areas.
The end of the month found us bored with 37 days occupation of the
same position. We were very anxious for an offensive movement of some
sort to commence, which would bring us closer to our goal of Home or
Rome.

Monday, May 1, 1944   To the Air O.P. twice this morning. Harry
Prill is with them now. Took Col. Peterson to 6 Corps again this p.m.
To the battalions tonight. Dick came along. Stopped in to see McGee.

Got a star for the Italian campaign. On the way back something exploded on our right, made a lot of smoke. Don't know what it was. Password is "picture frame."

Tuesday, May 2, 1944   Washed clothes. Took a bath this morning. Wrote to Pat and home. To the battalion tonight. Found C Co. of the 601st Tank Battalion, where Doc Archambeau is. He was on duty with an M-10 tank, though, so I didn't get to see him. Back at 9:00. 2 letters from home.

Leonard (Doc) Archambeau and I went to school together. He was a year behind me at Proctor high school. It would have been nice to see him again, and I always wanted to go inside a tank and look around, though I didn't want to ride in one. I had been inside lots of knocked-out tanks, though, both German and American, and couldn't believe how a crew could stand being inside one as much as they were, and have a good-sized gun mounted on top besides.

Wednesday, May 3, 1944   Up at 6:30. Fried eggs the 3rd day in a row now. Really are good. A heavy air raid early this morning. Lasted on and off through the night until it got light. Personnel bombs dropped in Division Hq. area. To artillery this morning. Read a little. Wrote to Pat and Grandma this p.m. To the battalions, no interference.

Thursday, May 4, 1944   Eggs again for breakfast. After not having fresh eggs for so long, we could easily go on a steady diet of them. Cleaned up, read. Read more this p.m.
To the battalion tonight. Dick came with. To the Air O.P. A beautiful night, moonlight, warm.

Friday, May 5, 1944   Slept until 8:30. Made coffee. Had to go to Anzio and pick up Capt. Temple, but couldn't find him. Back at 12:00, had a headache. Took a nap. Took a bath at the creek, washed out my underclothes.
To the rear echelon and all battalions. Took 4 pigeons to McGee from here. Each Message Center will get 4 of them as couriers. Reb came along. We just got back, when they started to shell across the road.
A letter from Mom tonight. Will write to Ray with money-gram of $70.00. Warm all day. Uncle Hank was supposed to be inducted on the 14th of last month, but is still out.

Saturday, May 6, 1944   Up for breakfast. Cleaned up the peep a bit. It stalled on me last night again. Cleaned out the gas-cleaner, wiped off some mud. Finished *Wuthering Heights*.

To the rear echelon. Took Jim Riley to the 151st Medics, back at 9:00.

2 letters from Mom, one from Ray. Made a $30.00 allotment to Ray, and one $25.00 bond to be sent him monthly out of my pay.

The month of May started out slowly as one of inactivity. However, morale was pretty high, as we could begin to read the signs and the rumors of going after the Krauts. We were still pecking at each other, but without much strength coming from either side.

Our Piper Cub was doing a lot of air observation, and the Krauts tried to knock it down with high air bursts. They found out that was a sad mistake to make — as the Cub picked up their location, adjusted the battalion's guns on them, and soon had some firing for effect.

Sunday, May 7, 1944   Up for breakfast. Hot cakes.

First Sgt. Vessey was made 2nd lieutenant. Took him to the docks. He's going to the rear for awhile. Stopped at 6 Corps. Went past the cemetery. Nothing but white crosses, probably several thousand. Read. To the rear echelon.

A package of candy from Mom. Letter from LaVonne with pictures. 2 letters from Mom.

To all battalions and Division.

Sgt. Vessey was given a field promotion to 2nd lieutenant. He had been the First Sergeant of Division Artillery since I had been associated with them. Gen. Vessey later became the first non-West-Pointer to become Chairman of the Joint Chiefs of Staff, during the Reagan Administration,

We agents were more acquainted with Message Center personnel, however; though we sometimes slept or ate at Division Artillery, where we had more of a "front-row seat" to see how things were going.

Monday, May 8, 1944   Cleaned up, read. Cool and windy. Didn't do much of anything. To the rear tonight. 3 letters from Mom, Ray, an Easter card from Hulda Mehling. Card from Grandma. To all battalions.

Tuesday, May 9, 1944   Up for breakfast, shaved. Read in the *Time* magazine I got last night. Took Mr. Goodell to the Ordnance. Went to 34th Division area in Anzio after dinner and picked up Barney. He had been in the rear all this time.

Wrote to Miss Eliason tonight. To all battalions. Lots of traffic on the road. Terribly dusty.

B Battery was shelled. A fire started in the number three action pit, and the gun was destroyed. Seven men were wounded. The gun was replaced the same night.

The following day A Battery's number four tube became unserviceable, and it too was replaced the same night.

Wednesday, May 10, 1944   Remember nothing more than that I went to the battalions.

Thursday, May 11, 1944   Went to Corps and located B Battery's kitchen crew with 6723 Trucking Co. They have been with them for almost 2 months on Detached Service.

To the battalions. Reb came along.

Friday, May 12, 1944   Had a headache all day. Took a special out at 5:00 to all battalions. Dick came along. Warm. Not much activity.

Had my picture in the paper at home with a short notation.

Saturday, May 13, 1944   Headache all day. Laid around, slept.

Took a special to all battalions at 3:30. Made good time, back in 45 minutes.

To all battalions again tonight. Doc Lyons came along. Back at dark.

Got 5 letters from Mom and Ray. Went to bed at 11:00.

Sunday, May 14, 1944   Had to go to the battalion at 1 a.m. Back at 2:00. Picked up something for Capt. Smith. Dark, but not so much traffic. Could almost go over the road blindfolded, I know it so well. The Bailey bridge is blocked off now, only used for a spare. I guess they have a 2-way then. There's one built alongside it of plank, much better.

An exceptionally heavy barrage went out for about 15 minutes this morning. The ground fairly rocked with its thunder.

Dreamt of Arlene. She is really the one that I want most to see.

Headache is gone today. Hot lazy weather. Lonesome because it is Sunday. Wrote to Ray.

The chaplain must be on vacation again.

Monday, May 15, 1944   Went to the 6th Corps, back to Division

Artillery. Went to the rear echelon, picked up Budinger. Went to the 6723 Trucking Co. Saw Meagher and all the kitchen workers that I know.

Had a good dinner. Stayed until 1 p.m. To the battalions again after that.

Tuesday, May 16, 1944   To the rear echelon this morning. To 3rd Division this p.m. Met Lt.'s Don Nelson and Jimmy Johnson; they are now in the 175 F.A. and Signal.

Took the peep to Service Battery. Had the 2 broken springs replaced, a muffler installed. Fixed the flat tire. Greased and changed oil. Had supper again with the 151 kitchen. Back to Division Artillery. Changed clothes. Really got dirty.

Four letters: 2 from Mom, 1 from Ray and 1 from Ethel Nash. Also 2 books from Book-of-the-Month.

Went twice back to the rear echelon after. Floyd went to the C.P.s. Started reading *The Sign-Post.*

Things were beginning to change now; firing was picking up, and an offensive was in the making. Our ammo on hand had increased to 13,800 rounds for the battalion.

We had a gas attack scare, and everybody had to have his mask handy. It was a scare that had been carried by a rumor.

Lt. Nurnberger was killed on May 25 when an enemy shell landed in his foxhole at a forward O.P.

On May 23 we were attached to the 463rd Field Artillery Battalion. There were other attachments as well.

Two fellows from Service Battery were wounded by shellfire on the road while hauling ammo.

Wednesday, May 17, 1944   Took Lt.'s Holmberg and Granley to the Anzio dock. Holmberg is going to the Air Corp for an official visit. Granley is transferred to 63rd Signal. He is from West Duluth and knows Lucille and Marion Dewsberry. Took a special to all battalions this p.m.

Arlene's birthday today. She must be 8. Remember well 8 years ago today.

Very little incoming fire the last while, especially in our area. Not much going out either, at least not from the large guns by us. One short air raid several nights ago that didn't amount to much. Letter from Ethel. Says George is overseas with a San Francisco address. He's in the Engineers.

CHAPTER 23

George was out in the Pacific Ocean somewhere.

Thursday, May 18, 1944   Read in *The Sign-Post.* Went to 6th Corps. Finished *The Yearling.* Went to the battalions.

Friday, May 19, 1944   Felt down in the blues all day. Slept some, laid around. To 6th Corps this morning, to the battalions tonight. Wrote to Pat.
Cassino has finally fallen several days ago. The Adolph Hitler Line has been broken.
Tremendous barrage has just gone out. Everything was flashes and thundering noise.
B Battery's kitchen has come back to the battalion. I enjoy seeing Don again. He's been a good friend.

Saturday, May 20, 1944   I've been feeling disillusioned the past several days. Remember little as to what was done. Probably the usual battalion runs.

Sunday, May 21, 1944   Again ignorant of today being Sunday, until tonight. To all battalions, as usual.

Monday, May 22, 1944   Took a fellow to the rear echelon, had pork chop dinner there. Back at 1:30. To the rear again, and all battalions. Got back late, 10:00. There were several more specials, but others took them out.
Started reading Betty Smith's *A Tree Grows in Brooklyn.* Got half through. Very enjoyable reading. Makes one feel as though he were leading the life of each character.
Quite a large quantity of shells going out. The Krauts didn't retaliate. Part of Division Artillery's C.P. moved to 125's old area.

Tuesday, May 23, 1944   Up at 6:30, slept with my clean coveralls on. Took a bath yesterday. Cereal and fried eggs.
Went to 6th Corps. They have moved to the vicinity of the Castle. Read more in *The Tree.* Took Mr. Goodell to 11 Evac.
We moved this p.m. to 125's old area. Took time to get settled. To the 151 rear and front. Out again at 11:30 to the 151 with a special.
The long-awaited-for Big Push came off today. We are making big gains. Casualties, of course, are heavy.

I was a real happy boy to leave the sand pit or hole or dugout, whatever

it was we called our home at Anzio. We had been in this place far too long under constant shellfire, and the always-present possibility of a direct hit — that, and then I had to be on the road every day, as well.

There was a lot of regrouping among the field artillery battalions for this push. One 105 of C Battery had to be replaced. The wear and tear was beginning to tell on the guns after 2 years' service. Within a few weeks, several of the tubes had to be replaced when they became defective.

Maj. Surdyk left us to assume duties of Liaison Officer at A.F.H.Q. with the Polish Corps.

Five men were wounded on or about the 25th of May.

Maj. Thomas was beginning to wonder why he had not received the Infantrymen's Badge, as he had been with the infantry in combat for some nine months.

Wednesday, May 24, 1944   We got a ways, at least, and moved. Made me a sleeping place in under the stairway of this house. Blacked it out. A secluded and quiet spot. Radio section in the next room, have nice radio music. Didn't know I was so starved for it. Got mail from Mary Jean, Margaret, home and Ray. Dug in my peep this morning and put up the net — it took until noon.

This place is a farm house typical on the beachhead. The house is well built, cement mostly, barn the same, attached to house. Some farm equipment strewn around. At home this place would be classed with the better ones. Here and now it is vacated, practically in ruins. My heart goes out to the people who own them, and I have more reason than ever to hate this accursed war.

Slept a little this p.m. in the peep. Finished reading *A Tree Grows in Brooklyn*. Liked it really well. Wished the story would not end.

To the rear tonight and front. 133rd Infantry have crossed #7; troops are pressing in from Cassino. The outlook is brighter than last week at this time. Hope it continues again tonight.

I have the privilege and opportunity to be in my little home. A fellow asks little in combat; mainly a place to be alone enough to eat, and of course, protection and comfort from his Maker.

Shells continually going out. They are coming in tonight. They're shelling the Bailey bridge, but shells are going all around.

Thursday, May 25, 1944   Dick and I went to all battalions except mine. Left at 10:15 last night, back at 2:10 this morning. A gruesome, hellish night — most of my luck was bad. The 125th is far up. Had to go cross-country to get there, and back through a minefield.

Slept until 6:30, then Dick and I had to go again to all battalions. Back at 8:00. Then to 6th Corps. Packed up, moved across the Mussolini Canal.

I have a straw shed for my peep and for sleeping, but only got half an hour of sleep today. Took a sponge bath, changed clothes. To my rear echelon, 10 miles now, or more.

Back here, then moved with the 151st.

Friday, May 26, 1944   We crossed #7 yesterday, or the day before. Things are going pretty good, but everyone is tense. This has got to work out, and it is demanding. Didn't get to our new position until 1:30 in the morning. Had to wait around until 3:00 until I could get the coordinates and until the road was clear. Got back at 3:45.

Jerry is definitely on the run. Our troops joined those coming up from Cassino yesterday. I like to gloat on this fact: Cassino is quite a ways south from here, and we were at Anzio, and we finally got to-gether. The Krauts are definitely on the run — we will sure be home for *this* Christmas!

This is no longer a postage-stamp-sized beachhead. It's a great feeling shared by all who are here.

Few shells coming in. The Krauts have more important things now on their minds: that is, they need to head north.

Slept until 7:00. Ate. Slept until 9:00 a.m. when somebody hollered, "Wag, up to the C.P., pronto." This was unusual, as mostly someone from our own Message Center gives me the message or firing order.

But this time, Capt. Smith was waiting with pencil in hand, and map on the wall. He pointed with the pencil to one place on the map and said, "You are here." He moved the pencil and pointed to another spot on the map, and said, "The 151 is here." He handed me 2 enve-lopes and said, "Get these there from here P.D.Q."

I saluted the captain and foolishly asked him, "What does that mean, Sir?"

He snapped back, "Pretty Damned Quick, now move it!"

I moved it, and when I got there to our C.P., the officer told me, "We have 13 minutes left to complete our firing data."

I was lucky that I knew just where our C.P. was, since I had moved with them last night, or this morning … No phone lines were laid yet, and radio couldn't be used — but if German positions are spotted and if we can get the 105's registered in time before they move, we can put a few more Krauts out of commission.

But it is dusty, so dusty I can't describe it. The dust on the road is 2 inches deep like flour. Still, we can't put the windshields up on the peeps, as the sun is shining and would reflect off the glass, making us targets for possible enemy observation. So, just bear it and hope to get through. You come back from driving as white as a ghost, covered with a thick layer of dust, only eyeballs almost shining, and your lungs hurt.

Had a short nap this afternoon. We moved again about 5 miles closer to Cisterno. Haven't had more than 7 hours of sleep in the last 48.

The Krauts moved out not long ago. There is still that unmistakable German smell left behind.

A bunch of rubbled buildings we are in. We agents in a building where one of our shells came in through the window.

To the battalion again, twice. That is twice, but only once since I went to bed.

Our move to Cisterno was via "Purple Path."

I'm not sure how this road was so dubbed, but I began to notice that this road was doubly deep with darker dust, and earned more Purple Hearts than most other stretches of road did.

Saturday, May 27, 1944   Up at 5:30. To the 151 rear with 2 priority messages. Back in time for breakfast.

Went to Cisterno just to look around. It's only been in our hands 2 days. Are some civilians left, but the town is another ruin. Slept a few hours. Out twice to the battalion before supper.

"Purple Path" will always be remembered. It is covered with 6 inches of soft, floury dust. Traffic is heavy — with tanks, half tracks, peeps and 6X6s. Everyone is covered with a mash of crusted dirt all over him. My peep is covered with the stuff inside and out. I wonder which is worse, heat and dust, or cold and mud. Yesterday this area was covered with a blood-colored cloud for miles either way.

Letter from Ray. Haven't much ambition to write, or time or facilities. It's cool and comfortable in this room. Thankful for that, although it's littered with crap of all kinds. Out again before and after supper. My lungs hurt, my kidneys hurt. I'm sore and stiff all over.

We want to clean up this place. Probably won't be here long, but then we want to clean it nice for the noncombatant rear echelon troops to enjoy.

I removed as much sarcasm from the last paragraph as I could.

Sunday, May 28, 1944   Had to go out at 3:30. Back in an hour, not so much traffic. Up at 7:00, hot cakes for breakfast. Out again to the battalion and 6 Corps. Took the main road back to Cisterno. Moved up with the battalion this p.m. Are close to 125 F.A. Tried to take a short cut back to #7. Almost got too far up in territory which isn't ours. Back at 2:30.

One of Division's messenger agents killed last night, his peep blown up. Looked to me like a shell hit him directly, and not a land mine, which some said.

Heavy air raid this morning. Bombing.

Moved with the 151 right after dinner. Back at about 2:00. Made coffee. Out again after supper. Back at 9:00. Our Message Center is in a cave about 30 feet long, 6 feet wide. There are little caves along the long corridor — looks like it might have been a prison years ago.

Monday, May 29, 1944   Hambright and I had to go out at 3 a.m. I drove. We went together, as our outfits are near each other. A very "tangleable" road. [That means crooked as heck and confusing — since any truck's track could have been the road. There were many turns, curves and crossings.] Back to the Castle.

Italian civilians are coming back. The roads are full of them, all kinds, sizes and shapes. Feel sorry for them. Everything they once had is gone.

Had to take Lt. Vessey to the new position. Back in for dinner. We moved out at 1:00. Close to 151 now. Grape fields high with weeds. I'm getting hungry for grapes.

Message Center is in an old dugout cave with radio section. The Krauts had left 70 rounds of 150's packed in there and 30 screaming meemies. Also mines. We had to move it all out. The meemies weigh 200 pounds each crate.

Fairly contented here. I kept everything but my bedroll in the peep. The peep doesn't mind if she sleeps outside or in, but it's safer for me to be inside the cave.

Had to go out twice to the battalion before midnight.

By this time, Hambright (Ham), from one of the Southeastern states, had taken Floyd Johnson's place as agent for the 125th. I believe by this time

Floyd had gotten a better job at the Command Post. He was sharp, and deserved it. We missed his pleasing smile and personality. We would have been even less cheerful than we were if it hadn't been for Floyd.

Tuesday, May 30, 1944   Up at 5:30. Had to go out with a special. Stayed up and had breakfast.

Laid down in my peep for several hours. Took a bath and changed clothes. Washed clothes this p.m.

Had to take a special to Air O.P. Had trouble finding it. Back at 6:30 tonight. To the battalion. To bed at 10:00.

Heavy artillery barrage going out all day, especially this a.m. We can see where the shells are landing.

Wednesday, May 31, 1944   Out at 3:30 with a special. Up at 7:00. Breakfast. Our bombers dropped some bombs on a town just ahead of here this morning.

Washed and shaved. Slept behind my peep for awhile.

Cleaned a few things on the peep. Had my shirt off — sun-burnt just a little.

To the battalion tonight after supper. A *Life* magazine and *Country Gentleman*. Went to bed at 10:30.

Thursday, June 1, 1944   Out to the battalion at 12:15 and 5:00. Slept in between times a little.

Up at 7:00. Read *Life*. Slept outside until dinner. Slept awhile this p.m. as well. Are in a grape vineyard with peach and fig trees.

No shells coming in, but enough going out. Some 8 inchers behind us. They rock the peep when they go off. To the battalion tonight.

Vellitre fell today to the 3rd Division. We are still making good gains.

Wrote home and to Ethel.

Friday, June 2, 1944   One special this morning at 1:30. Beautiful moonlight.

Up at 7:00. Started reading *Blessed Are the Meek*. Overhauled the peep. Regapped and cleaned the plugs, cleaned the air cleaner and motor. Took out the thermostat, adjusted the brakes, and greased it.

Took a bath, changed clothes, read. Started reading *Thunderhead*.

To the battalion. They moved 3 miles, a long, rough and dusty road. Back at 8:30.

Got a paper writing tablet and flat 50 of Lucky Strikes from Jean

Vaughn, and a money belt from Mom. Letter from Ray. Put in a full day. Wrote to Ray. It's after 11:00. I'm finally rested up and ready for more.

We were waiting for June to come around. Actually, things started to move towards the last of May. On about the 28th, the attack and barrage continued, and things seemed to be going along fine. We were all eager to push onwards to Rome — and to get there before the M.P.s did and put everything "Verboten," off-limits for us. Instead of throwing cannonballs and delivering specials, we wanted to see some Italian civilians for a change.

We wondered what kind of dedication and committed troops Hitler had in his Army. They had been retreating now for two years, at least, being encircled and pushed homeward from all corners, and still they continued fighting to the last man. Years later, a lot of younger people asked, and we still wondered, "What kind of a guy was this Hitler, anyhow? How could he get such dedication out of his men?"

With the 6th and II Corps ready to join forces with those who took Cassino, and the Second Front that was expected any day, it was hard to imagine how the Germans could keep on fighting — in the face of bombs of all types and shellfire of all sizes, along with small-arms ammunition, and continually withdrawing forces.

Saturday, June 3, 1944   One special at midnight. Denendorfer came along. Then had to go to Nettuno this p.m. with Mr. Goodell. Had to move along to get back in time for tonight. Goodell is an older warrant officer, and is always afraid I'm going too fast — but he always asks for me when he has to go somewhere. Another agent always takes my runs, so I really don't care.

We get on highway #7 now, good road. Only trouble is, my peep might start flying apart. It's really getting in rough shape — this is either the 3rd or 4th one I've had now.

Sunday, June 4, 1944   Went with the advanced party with the general. Through Albano. Ralph and I looked over some buildings tonight. Found some junk. Albano is not far from the outskirts of Rome.

CHAPTER 24

Rome. Coast Road. Mediterranean R.R.R.
More fighting. Self-inflicted R.R.R

.

Monday, June 5, 1944　　Rome must have fallen several days ago. I've been busy enough anyway, but we moved this p.m. Are only 2 miles from Rome. Had to look up the 151 tonight. 13 miles from here, across the Tiber, and through a part of Rome. On the way back I drove through the city-proper. Streets are 100 yards wide in places, smooth as glass. People stand by the score along the streets and cheer and wave and throw kisses.

I drove into one of the arches of the Coloseum, and wished I'd had my camera. Also wished I could speak Italian and get acquainted with the people. Once in awhile if you make eye contact with someone, they shake a finger and say, "No buono Tedeschi." (Germans are no good.)

There was one whole battery of German 88's put out of the war. They were caught traveling and observed — which proves again that artillery caught moving on the road is helpless.

Tuesday, June 6, 1944　　The long-awaited and talked-of 2nd Front took place today. They're landing troops in Norway and western France — together with us being north of Rome. It makes the picture look pretty good.

I went with the general's advance party again today. Moved through the outskirts of Rome and northwest — we were practically on Jerry's tail. He is scooting along at a good rate. Only some armor of the 1st Division ahead of us.

This p.m. Lt. Vessey and I went 14 miles farther northwest. Our artillery was still firing from behind us, so we would go a little ways, then stop and wait. Finally came west to the sea, where there is a castle just evacuated by the Germans. Lots of their rations left. We took 3 cases of rice and meat along. I also took some of their hardtack. Lots of that there in big cases. Found a German folding cot. The canvas was torn, but Joe gave me another one, so it's like new. Came back at 6:00.

Saw a German prisoner who had just been captured. He was just a scared-looking kid.

Got a ballot for voting in the primary, but tore it up. I'm still mad — in the first place, I know few of the candidates. Also my name was all over the return envelope, and it would have to be censored by an officer before it could be sent.

Wednesday, June 7, 1944   Up at 4:30, but didn't have to go on the usual objectionable detail. Bob Krohn and I went for a long walk. He had been in the CCC's with Ray. Slept for an hour. Went to the battalion at 9:30, came back at 12:00. They are 19 miles away. Was supposed to have been 3 miles. Division Artillery had pulled out when I got back. In the meantime, 151 had moved again, so I went looking for them. They had moved 20 more miles. Back to Division Artillery about 7:00.

Are in a ghost town, right next to the Mediterranean. Dick and I are in a little house. Has holes in the roof, though. The roads are smooth blacktop ones with some by-passes and holes, but a big contrast from driving on the beachhead roads. My peep will still do 60 as it did a year ago. My average speed is 50, and 55 when alone. Made 149 miles today. Took a sponge bath. Set my cot up and went to bed.

Thursday, June 8, 1944   Had to go out about midnight with the battalion. They moved up 6 miles along the Coast Road. Beautiful evening, bright as day. Coming back was like driving along the North Shore of Lake Superior. Waves were coming in to the highway, and there was a good road.

Up at 6:15. Took a special out. Had 2 bacon-toast sandwiches and coffee. Also breakfast here.

Took Nathan Levy back to Service Battery and 151. Slept a little. Cleaned out my junk this p.m. Had the front wheel fixed on the peep. Bearing was loose. To the Air O.P. tonight. A special to the 151 at 11:00.

Friday, June 9, 1944   Had to drive Doc Lyons to the battalion with Rieser this p.m. Message Center moved to another house. We agents did too, to a room next to C.P. Are 15 yards from the Mediterranean; have a window that opens towards the sea. There are boats coming into this harbor. Civitavecchia is the name of this town.

Denendorfer came along. Went to the 976 Field Artillery. Also took a spin into Marinell. Had my blankets out.

This was one of those confusing times for both men and officers. Early on the morning of the 9th we started our rest period. The C.P. was a nice roomy old Italian house overlooking the Mediterranean. We were looking forward to a week or two by the sea, but then we had to move from here again. Here we had some training exercises with the 133rd Infantry.

The same day of these exercises, we were alerted again to move closer to the front. We were ready to move by 8:00 that night, and had the surprise of being able to use our lights.

Looking back at the whole column was like seeing a bunch of cars coming out of a drive-in movie back home. The move was scheduled to take 5 hours. We made it in 3 ½. We hardly got settled, when S-4 grounded us by taking away all our big 6X6s to shuttle infantry.

So we thought we would be here several weeks. Our reasoning was all wrong, though, and the reconnaissance party was soon out again. So we moved twice in several days, dropping split trails and giving the Krauts what they asked for.

Saturday, June 10, 1944   Up at 6:00. Started cleaning my peep and equipment. Took Capt. Smith on a reconnaissance. Washed clothes this p.m. Tonight I went to B Battery. Took Don, Andy and Jerry to the next town, up the line about 10 miles. Then took them to see the 2 big guns here at Civitavecchia. Back at 9:30.

Listened to Dick play the piano until 10:30. This house hasn't been harmed much, and we surely aren't hurting it either.

Sunday, June 11, 1944   Took Barney Devine to 151 and 175 Service. Started to rain; put the top up. Back at noon.

We pulled out shortly after dinner. Came about 10 miles. Are in wooded area close to all battalions. Nate Levy and I put up a wall tent with 6 shelters halves. We really have it nice, both cots and air mattresses. Duck board in between. Went to the battalion tonight. To bed around 10:00.

Monday, June 12, 1944   Up at 6:00, in time for breakfast. Started to fix my tire. Got it apart and ruined the tube, so had to wait for a new one. Took Smith and Ahers to Division and 133 Regiment. Slept a little this p.m. Made a wash stand.

Our whole Division is relieved now — or will be, following a training schedule which doesn't affect me, fortunately.

Joe Hote and I went to Monte Romano tonight. A nice little town. Saw some pretty girls there. Went back to the 151 and saw a movie.

CHAPTER 24

Tuesday, June 13, 1944   To Division most of the forenoon. This p.m. I had to take 2 officers' orderlies to Civitavecchia and Monte Romano — looking for wine.

Wednesday, June 14, 1944   Went early and washed my peep. Worked until 2 p.m. on it: cleaned the motor, changed oil.
Took Barney to A.S.P. Got a flat tire there, no spare. Hambright had to come with his spare.
A V-mail from Miss Eliason.

I missed mentioning my birthday in my diary again. I was 25.

Thursday, June 15, 1944   Took Col. Peterson to the O.P. Watched them fire. Wrote 5 letters.

Friday, June 16, 1944   Don't remember what I did.

Saturday, June 17, 1944   A few trips. Went to Monte Romano, picked up Hank from 133. Took him back.

Hank Amundson was a friend of Don Sternke's, and a farmer from the Marshall, Minnesota area. Hank was in the 133rd Infantry, and both he and Don were working on trying to get him transferred out of the infantry and into the field artillery.
The First Sergeant had told them that the transfer would be done during the next rest, but in the meanwhile, Hank was seriously injured and was returned to the States.
I remember giving Hank a few rides either to or from a visit with Don. Visits with friends were a great boost to a soldier's morale.

Sunday, June 18, 1944   Went to Rome with Division Artillery bunch. Came back with the 151. Looked over St. Peter's Square, part of Vatican City. It's really beautiful. Can't really describe it. Went to the very top of it. Looked over other places of interest, including the Coloseum. Lots of girls on the streets, all kinds of people, really.
Stores are closed, though. Some merchants selling things on the street. Came back with a splitting headache at 10:30. Around 60 miles. Went on #2, and came back on #1.
When we got into St. Peter's, some of the farmer boys came out with the remark, "You could sure stack a lot of hay in here."

Monday, June 19, 1944   Still have my headache. Cleaned up my things. Cool and cloudy. Didn't do much. Wrapped up some packages to send home.

Tuesday, June 20, 1944   Took my peep to 151 Service at 7:30. Worked on it until 5:00. They fixed brakes, steering axles, shocks. Went to Monte Romano to try it out. Loaded up everything before dark. The weather is tops, and the country seems real pretty.

Wednesday, June 21, 1944   We were in line all night. I laid down after midnight with 2 shelter halves.

     Up at 6:00, breakfast at 7:00. Still waiting, pulled out at almost 12:00. Got here close to Grossetto at 3:00. 64 miles.

     Nicely wooded area. Put up my pup tent alone. Raised it about a foot. Have my cot inside. Would be content to stay here.

     Message Center is by itself here. I made one trip to the battalion about 1 mile away, and to Division, about 7 miles.

Thursday, June 22, 1944   A few trips today, but quiet enough. After dinner I took off with water cans and looked for a water point. Found one: the 405 B.E.S. beside a beautiful dammed lake. The dam is huge. Will look at it when I have a chance. Got a bunch of mail tonight. Mom, Ray, LaVonne and Pat. Ray sent some color pictures of the woods at Payne.

     Had a special to take out around 11:00. Guess we will soon be back in the lines. Being close to Grossetto, we are quite a ways from Rome. It's been hectic enough, but moving north at this pace suits all of us just fine.

Friday, June 23, 1944   Rained a little last night. Went to the clothing exchange. Got clean clothes and a shower. Took Don to the 133rd tonight, but couldn't find Hank. A special to go out.

Saturday, June 24, 1944   Up at 7:00, loaded up. Left about 8:30. Came 25 miles, are north of Grossetto, sort of an open spot. I parked alongside of a hedge, have my cot between hedge and peep. The 151st isn't far from here. Hot. Slept a little.

     Three trips to the battalions. To bed around 10:00.

Sunday, June 25, 1944   Up at 5:30, moved with the 151 about 12 miles. Back to Division Artillery, but they had moved too. Found them by 10:00. Put up my net and my cot. Like yesterday, didn't realize it was Sunday until now.

     Moved with the outfit again tonight. A special at 11:30, about 15 miles each way on #1.

Brown and I went back to where the 151 was. I had left laundry with an Italian family there in the woods. Brown had gotten acquainted with their 17-year-old daughter; that's why he wanted to go back with me. I've never had to leave laundry yet, but it's been close sometimes.

Monday, June 26, 1944   We moved up about 6 miles again. It's 27 miles each way to the 151 now. Made a trip back to them this afternoon. Stopped to see the 3 girls: Roseanne, about 14, and her 2 young sisters, Maria, 12, and Vonda, 3 or 4.

Slept some. To the battalion after supper. Had to go again at 10:30; didn't get back until 2:15. The going is bearable though, little or no dust, some blacktop, and when it's not too dark, you can go right along.

Reconnaissance was made for a new position early in the morning. The move was uneventful, but as the infantry was on the move too, another C.P. was picked. For the second time that day the battery positions and the Fire Direction Center were also split.

The forward party moved out, set up, took over, and the balance moved up. Soon it was necessary to move again, and this time two batteries had to move. So that one day we occupied 3 C.P.s and 3 battalion positions, while 2 of the batteries occupied and fired from a 4th position.

We had help that evening from the 91st Division. Their Dipper Battalion joined us in the evening to relieve us of the necessity of leapfrogging gun positions.

We were also joined with the 346 Artillery Battalion from the 91st Division. One of their noncoms was wounded by fire the first day.

The next several days were busy and hectic ones. Observers were calling in targets. The 2 Cubs were in the air continually, and steadily reporting locations. It was a field day. The pressure on the Krauts was too great, and they had to fall back. Many Nazis became "good Germans" in a hurry. The 29th of June brought us within sight of Cecil, a coastal town where I was hoping we could catch some days off.

The fighting was really confused, however. The infantry told us later that more German wounded came through their aid station than Americans.

We couldn't help but wonder just who this madman Hitler was — to keep his armies going like he did. German generals were willing to call it quits, but Hitler wouldn't listen.

During the past month we got in 11 new men and officers. 5 men left for the States on furlough, and there were daily trips for men on one-day passes to Rome. It was reported that prices had risen two hundred percent on souvenirs.

Tuesday, June 27, 1944   Overslept, missed breakfast. Had a "rough as a cob" night.

Loaded up, pulled up about 6 miles again. Capt. Smith and I set out looking for a shortcut to the 151. Found it, only 9 miles of good road.

Several specials to the battalions. Went to the 185 after supper. They are a long way forward, up and around the mountain. Shells came in before I came there.

The most Jerry equipment along the road I've ever seen. Germans are still on the run. Seems to me they are losing unusually heavy on equipment. Some of their artillery is horse-drawn. The end of this Campaign is coming near.

We were a little over-optimistic — not only would it take us almost another year to finish the Campaign, but at what cost, Victory? The landings at Normandy were huge, and losses heavy — and the Battle of the Bulge of December 1944, the last major German offensive which was to result in us losing 8,000 men to the Germans as prisoners, was still to come.

Our local efforts while we were attached to the 91st Division, to break through the German's last defensive line in Italy, the Gothic Line, were not to prove at all easy either.

It must have been a case of old Hitler knowing what was to happen, but not believing it.

We were in the position of not knowing what was going to happen, but we were still free to hope for the best.

Wednesday, June 28, 1944   Quite a few trips to the battalion — but #1 is a good road. Don't mind it. Out on specials until 2:50 this p.m. Battalion moved, but still on #1.

Thursday, June 29, 1944   Made a trip or two to the battalion. 16 miles each way. I go through Suverto and another small town, not touched much by war. Division Artillery moved around noon. Are close to the battalions again. Lt. Moore was killed this morning, and Urban, Bradley and Ashley hurt, when their peep went over a mine.

Near to an orchard of pears, peaches, grapes and sweet corn. The fruit is not quite ripe, but I ate a lot of it anyway. Bill and I talked for quite a while.

Bill Kajikawa's 522nd F.A. Battalion and the 100th Infantry were Japanese-American units firghting the Germans in Italy during World War II.

Bill's family, along with other Japanese-American civilians, many of whom were US citizens who had been in the United States as long as my German family had been, were kept imprisoned during the war in fenced-in and well-guarded "internment camps" on the West Coast. Japanese-Americans were considered "potential security risks" against the

United States. Their property had been taken from them (in many cases never to be returned), they were given shacks or barracks to live in, their sons had been sent to Italy to "prove their worth" by fighting the same Germans I was fighting (and under the same risk of failure), and their daughters and sisters were much sought after as dates by the camp guards and others who had money and power — as the Japanese boys were off fighting the Germans.

Japanese-Americans were not sent to the Pacific side of the war, however. They were considered "too likely to turncoat." I often supposed that, like the rest of us, Bill must have sometimes wondered just what it was he was fighting for in this war.

Friday, June 30, 1944 Had to take a special out, and I hauled some guys back who had been to Rome. Two trips, back by 1:30. #I is getting well shot up, and rough by lots of heavy traffic. Lots of bridges blown out.

Up at 6:00. Moved again. In another orchard. Washed a few clothes. Slept a little. Jerry has paused in his retreat enough to throw in shells around the 151 sector.

The following is a letter I wrote home to my parents, dated June 16, 1944 that they probably received sometime around this time — or later:

Hello Everybody,
Haven't written for awhile but I haven't had much ambition and not too much time.
The weather is fine, maybe a little too hot, but I don't mind it so much; we are in a wooded spot that gives a lot of shade.
It burns me to hear such things about furlough. There hasn't been anything said about them here, and if there was, we wouldn't be able to pick out our time to go. It's a cinch no one has went on any from the 34th, and far too few on rotation. For the time we have been overseas, we should all be back,

according to how other outfits send their men back from 9 months.

I got the money belt about a week ago. Not much mail has been coming in lately though.

There is a "Press Relations" fellow riding with me now. He takes stories from fellows and sends them to the fellow's home town paper. He comes from one of the battalions and they just started this up so he got the job.

I've been through Rome, saw the Coloseum and Kings Palace, also Vatican City, but not close up. I drove around for about half an hour. That was on the 5th. The people were lined along the streets cheering. It's a much better city than Naples; the people are better dressed, and a cleaner town all around. The Pope spoke that night, and some of our fellows heard him, but I didn't get there.

I ran across a big store of German rations, mostly their Knackbrot, which is much better than our biscuits, and canned rice and meat. I also got a cot which comes in pretty handy.

I had a swim in the sea the other day. It seems colder than it was last year at this time.

The package hasn't came yet but I hope it soon does, I'm about out of envelopes.

There hasn't been any night running for awhile now for me and it's fairly easy again.

About all I know for this time.

Sincerely Bud

My family had asked me when I'd be coming home on furlough — evidently, rumors of furloughs were a big morale builder for those at home.

The following is the news release our Press Relations fellow wrote about me:

NEWS RELEASE from
34th INFANTRY DIVISION PUBLIC RELATIONS SECTION
APO 34 Postmaster, New York City, N.Y.

NAZIS HAVE AN ORIGINAL FOOD IDEA AND MINNESOTA CORPORAL PICKS UP SEVERAL CASES OF IT

WITH THE FIFTH ARMY, ITALY—American Quartermaster's imagination has known no bounds in preparing food for the field but an artillery corporal has handed them a dish they hadn't thought of.

Corporal Wilmer Wagner a member of an artillery battalion in the Fifth Army's veteran 34th "Red Bull" Division was sent out on a reconnaissance for a new Headquarters position. He was accompanied by an officer who was in search of a likely forward location. Corporal Wagner drove his superior to a large villa on a beautiful body of water. Entering the deserted home the Minnesotan came upon at least fifteen cases of Nazi canned goods plus large cartons of something else. It is quite unusual for the enemy to leave any considerable amount of food behind and Corporal Wagner eagerly investigated. Opening a can he found it to be a well seasoned combination of cooked rice and beef. Americans soldiers have been served fresh rice, canned rice pudding and a dehydrated rice and raisin pudding but this was a new one. The corporal then found that the cartons contained thin six inch sheets of whole wheat crackers called "knackbrot" and incidentally quite tasty. He loaded a few cases of each on his jeep and returned to his battalion with something new in the way of food.

Corporal Wagner who serves as a motorized messenger ordinarily, is the son of Mr. And Mrs. Henry Wagner, Box 838, Duluth, Minnesota.

DISTRIBUTION: WRITTEN BY:

Duluth Herald   Cpl. Nathan S. Levy
Duluth News Tribune   Hq. Btry. 151 FA Bn.
                                       Field Correspondent
                                       (245 Woodmere Blvd.
                                       Woodmere N.Y.)

Saturday, July 1, 1944   Took Doc Lyons out for about 4 hours. Got a hot shower out of it. 151 F.A. moved again tonight. Moved with them, back at 10:00. We had a feast of corn, fried potatoes and coffee. I had picked up a few potatoes, and Don always saves me some bacon grease.

Whenever I could find corn, I'd stop and pick a few cobs. It was always short field corn, but good with salt and bacon grease. Someone always had a small stove to cook it on.

Sunday, July 2, 1944   Up at 7:00. Ate. Helped Bill fix his tires. Don't remember much more, though busy enough.

I do remember Sgt. Jones and I spent all afternoon riding around. We went to Suverto on the mountain road. Our legitimate reason was to find armor plate for the general's peep. Stopped in a peach orchard and ate peaches, are almost ripe. Came back about 5:00. To the battalion then.

Food must have been on my mind, as the letter I wrote home dated July 2 tells of the peaches almost ripe and of the poor food at the kitchen mess again. They must have been behind in food shipments. I mentioned Floyd Johnson's small Coleman stove being a real lifesaver. I told them of the corn, potatoes and onions that we fried, and of an Italian cow someone had got or bought, which was made into soup which was a lot better than canned.

Monday, July 3, 1944   Moved, as near as I can remember. So did the 151, across the river. Moved again tonight. Saw Hank Amundson; took him to see Don.

Tuesday, July 4, 1944   Had a shell fragment in my newest tire. Ripped both tire and tube while trying to fix. Had another flat. Got a new tire again. Wrote home and to Ray.

Wednesday, July 5, 1944   Fairly quiet nights. We had fried potatoes and corn the last 2 nights. Agents are alone in grape vineyard. We put up our cots in uniform fashion along it.

Thursday, July 6, 1944   Have that dejected feeling last several days. But I try to make myself realize how lucky I am, and how thankful I should be.

Food was still on my mind. I wrote to my brother Roger on July 6 telling him the peaches were now ripe in the orchard I mentioned the other day, but I'd only been able to get there once in awhile lately — and it was the only orchard I'd seen. I mentioned I'd seen a lot of grapes that were still too green, and that our food was a combination of poor canned Army food, and potatoes, corn and onions that we found in already ruined Italian gardens.

In our rear area Staff Sgt.'s Floyd Hanson and Oliver Stivers of Charlie Battery captured nine Germans hiding in a cave in our rear echelon just outside Rome.

Some late bad news we heard was that on June 19th, Lt. Norbert Mott died of wounds he had received in the battle for the beachhead, and Lt. Ralph Moore was killed instantly when the peep he was riding in ran over a mine.

Lt. Mott was a newcomer to the battalion, but left many friends behind. Lt. Moore was beginning to become one of the older officers of the battalion, have come to us in August 1943 while we were still in Africa. He was married, and had a baby he had never seen.

Sgt. Bradley, Joe Urban, and Ashley were injured by the same mine that killed Lt. Moore.

Our casualty list as of this date consisted of 11 officers dead, 23 wounded, 1 captured; and of the enlisted men, 25 dead, 124 wounded, and 2 Prisoners of War.

This may be the place to describe the job of the medics.

The cry of "Medics!" on the battlefield created instant attention, and was repeated over and over again by anyone in the proximity of the need for one, until one or more came running.

Volunteers for the medics were hard to find. Their group varied in size, accordingly. They were united in one desire: to serve, but not to kill.

When the medic first reached a wounded man, he did the briefest exam, put on a tourniquet if necessary, gave a vial of morphine, cleaned up the wound as best he could, sprinkled on sulfa, put on a bandage, and started dragging or carrying the wounded man towards the rear.

Usually by this time some help would have arrived, such as an ambulance, other soldiers to help move the wounded back a ways, or sometimes any vehicle of any kind as long as it was headed toward the rear. Even the hood of a peep has been an "ambulance" many times, especially if the wounded man had been placed on a stretcher.

The medic was under a huge amount of pressure, since if he didn't do his job right and fast, he lost his patient. Sometimes he had to deliver his first aid while under aimed enemy fire. Occasionally, Germans would even fire on a medic at work between the lines. There were many stories — but many were from men who heard about such things, as opposed to having seen them in person.

Generally, if the wounded man could be reached before he died, he had a good chance for survival. His first stop on the way to the rear was the aid station. Some of the men said they were convinced that the Army had a regulation against dying in an aid station, as most of the wounded didn't even remember having been there.

Most patients didn't come back to consciousness, still groggy from the morphine, until they reached the field or evacuation hospital. The first thing many of them saw was a nurse from the Army Nurse Corps (ANC). She would be wearing fatigues, harassed, exhausted and busy. She'd have a smile of assurance, gentle hands and a heaven-sent attitude. Ttrim figures were not as important as these, in this situation.

The Army nurses had to overcome many obstacles. One of the main obstacles was to overcome the taboo of volunteering for the Army, since in the early 1940's women were still considered 2nd class citizens in the United States — and more so if they went into the Army.

Because of a critical shortage of nurses, President Roosevelt proposed that nurses be drafted. A bill to do so passed the House, but lacked one vote in the Senate. To encourage more nurses to volunteer, after 1944 the Army began to give nurses officers' commissions, and extended to them all the retirement privileges, allowances and equal pay male officers had previously enjoyed. During 1944, there were probably fewer than 15,000 nurses serving, but during 1945 this number approximately tripled.

I didn't visit the hospitals often, and except for a few times, not when a lot of wounded were coming in. But if I had time when going by a hospital, I'd stop to see someone in there. Also, several times I would take notes to two of the nurses for Maj. Surdyk and Maj. Grant, and sometimes I would drive them there to visit.

The wounded didn't stay in the hospital long. The boys got in, received emergency treatment, penicillin and sulfa, and were out again.

The medic's worst times probably came during the invasions and during the Battle of the Bulge. During our Italian invasion at Paestum, the medics came in on the 3rd wave, behind the riflemen and combat engineers, but ahead of towed artillery pieces, anti-aircraft guns, self-propelled and tanks.

The infantry was on their own until the medics got there.

The hospitals were very overcrowded at these times also. My school-mate George Olson told me that at Anzio he had to undergo an emergency appendix operation. All the tables were filled, so they had to lay him on a crate. The hospital was in a low spot with water on the floor, and the surgeon and those assisting him had to slosh around in it while performing the operation.

Friday, July 7, 1944   Took a special out to the 522nd and 151. Stopped at Service Btry. Had brakes adjusted. Now I need two new universal joints. Always something.

Slept some this p.m. Moved tonight with the battalion. Up a curving mountain road. Dusty, heavy traffic. Nearly had the choice of sideswiping a 6X6 or rolling over the bank. Got back at 10:30 and went right out again with an overlay. Back about 2 a.m.

Jerry is still on the run; our forces are giving him no rest. During the day, our forward observers and Air O.P. adjust fire on him at every opportunity. At night, harassing fire falls on the roads he is attempting to use as he retreats.

Three men were wounded on July 5th by bomb fragments dropped in Charlie Battery's area. The next day Leonard Majerczyk stepped on an S mine and needed an ambulance. Then the next day we heard the "Medics!" call go out again. This time it came from the No. 1 pit of B Battery's gun. They'd had a muzzle burst, and 5 men were hurt.

Both our infantry and artillery had high praise for our "Midget of the Air," the Piper Cub, that could call for fire on located enemy positions and receive responding fire in a matter of minutes.

On July 7th, Col. DuBois and Maj. Thomas left on reconnaissance to select new positions. Their road led to a small trail where our gun trucks couldn't go, so they had to go back to Collemezzano, then northeast to Riparbella, arriving in position at 11 p.m.

Sunday, July 9, 1944   Bill and I went out for water and made a joy-ride out of it. Dick and I had 2 trips to make tonight. Dark and all, and with the mountain road, tough driving.

We didn't really have to haul water, and could get what we needed for drinking from the kitchen; or else I'd stop at regular water points and fill my 5 gallon water can there.

I was probably hauling water for the ladies who did our laundry. Some of them who lived toward the top of the mountain had to go to the bottom and carry water all the way up on their heads. They used a piece of cloth they rolled up into a rope-like circle. They'd then place their water pots, which were made of clay, inside or slightly on the rolled up cloth. They walked pretty straight when "loaded."

Monday, July 10, 1944   Up for breakfast. Another flat tire. Maintenance exchanged it for another one. Worked a good share of the day, cleaning the motor, greasing.

This p.m. Bill and went and washed the peeps. Took a bath there too.

Several trips to the battalion. Jack and I went to the 10th Evac Hospital to see Reb, but he wasn't there. It's at Grosseto, 65 miles each way.

Tuesday, July 11, 1944   Moved this morning to the 151's old position, or close to it. Dick and I took a little trail that cuts off 13 miles. Saw a big grinding wheel run by water. Took a color picture.

Out again tonight. Battalion moved again.

The old grinding wheel was really huge in size. It was by a small stream and flour mill, covered with green moss in spots, and slowly turning. We stopped and went inside and saw all the machinery. There was a tiny stream of flour coming out. There were several people there, but we weren't able to talk with them.

I took one picture, a color slide. The film got left in my barracks bag in the rear, and when I finally got it again, the two exposed rolls of film I had in it were gone. Another minus mark for the rear echelon boys. I suppose if we could control all the bad things that happened, though, we wouldn't have been fighting this war.

Pvt. Gordon Cashner of Battery C, who was with our O.P. party, was killed on July 9th. Also on this date we welcomed Capt.'s Thomas, Doyle and Lomen. Capt. Prescott came back to us on the 10th.

On the 11th, Col. DuBois was 2500 yards east of Catellina giving good observation from Mt. Maggiere.

Wednesday, July 12, 1944   Had to wait until 11:00 last night for the S-3 report. Finally got back at 1:00 this morning. Very dark. Got behind 2 tanks on the mountain road, and I wasn't entertaining the idea of passing them. It was on this side of Ribabel. The mountain trail was about the worst piece of ground I've traveled on: narrow, rocky, steep grades with sheer drops of hundreds of feet below.

The peep froze on me this morning. Had a hard time loosening it. Bill had a flat; helped him fix it. Shaved, took a bath, packed some things over. Red Cross girls here. Got 3 doughnuts and lemonade.

Dick and I went out together tonight to our outfits, about 20 miles round trip.

A letter home of July 12 mentions that I had passed Secretary of War Henry Stimson the other day. There were a lot of vehicles and big Brass in his party, stopped along the road watching several 105's firing.

Most of my letters home told only of our weather, if I had received a package they had sent me, and that I would write more next time. Everything was censored. Capt. Genung had told us, "You can write home about anything you want, Men. Just don't tell them where you are, or what you are doing." Though my mother saved all my letters, it is only rarely that they said anything to help in the writing of this book.

Thursday, July 13, 1944   Didn't have to go out last night for a change. Slept through breakfast. Had to take the chaplain and assistant to 151. Stayed there for dinner. Pork chops. Back at 4:00. Red Cross was serving doughnuts and coffee in Castella. Had some.

To the battalion and again tonight. Back at 9:00. Then Bill and I had to go to Division — back late.

The Krauts were still moving, and we were right behind them. Lt. Ryan and his O.P. crew had a rough close call when Jerry counterattacked and forced them to destroy their radio.

During the next 8 days we were in 6 different positions.

A 6X6 ammo truck (empty), hit a mine, and the two in the cab were hurt. 185th's medics and those from 100th Infantry helped out.

Friday, July 14, 1944   Up at 6:00. French toast for breakfast.

Jones was made First Sergeant, and Aikers became Chief.

Bill and I took a walk around the hill. Had to take Col.'s Peterson and Kenniger to the battalion. Back at noon. To the battalion again this p.m. They moved quite a ways up. Back in time for supper. Dick and I went out together tonight. Went way around Ribabella, a long ways. Back at 9:00. One letter from Ray. Took Lieberman to Division Hq.

Saturday, July 15, 1944   Up at 6:00. Fried fresh eggs for breakfast. We moved at 11:30. Bill and I put up our tarp for shade in a grape vineyard. To the battalion. They moved again. Back at 5:00. Bill had 2 flats. Had to meet him with my spare.

Roads here are terribly dusty. My lungs hurt from it. Traffic is unusually heavy. A fellow comes back thick with dust all over. Have to drive with windshield down.

To the battalion again after supper. Back about dark.

Sunday, July 16, 1944   Slept late, went to the battalion after dinner and moved with them over one long by-pass. Would never have made it if had been wet weather. Threw some shells in new area. Had a flat, back at 4:30.

Fixed the tire, ate, and to the battalion again. Road is still terribly dusty. Back by dark, or 9:30.

Monday, July 17, 1944   Up at 5:00. Bill and I played a little catch, along with some R.R.R.

CHAPTER 25

More of the same. Bill. Nate. Lorenzano. Cecina rest. Volterra

.

Tuesday, July 18, 1944   Routine runs. Doing as little as possible, not even writing much in my diary here.

Wednesday, July 19, 1944   Same as above.

Thursday, July 20, 1944   Same as above.

Friday, July 21, 1944   Up at 5:30. Bill and I played a little catch and had a few exercises before breakfast. Washed a few clothes, cleaned my mess kit. Bill cut my hair, and I his. Didn't do too bad for my 1st time cutting hair. Meals are very poor again; hope my gardens have been growing along OK as we go north, or at least get growing, so I can get some fresh vegetables and fruit.

We've been getting a lot of almonds several times, and they have a big sack of them in the mess area. I fill my pockets, then fill the one tool box over the back wheel of the peep. I spend lots of time cracking them, and really like them too. Many of the fellows don't take any. I don't have a hammer, but use a pair of pliers.

Saturday, July 22, 1944   We moved this morning. Bill and I are in a barn with 3 horses. Not bad, but not enough room. Several specials to take out.

Bill and I went after our laundry tonight. Went to Lorenzano. I talked with the 2 sisters. One reminds me of Miss Lang, who is really my Aunt Evelyn. She writes to me, Miss Lang does, and has sent packages.

Sunday, July 23, 1944   Went out once last night. Up at 6:00, chow. Started to work on my peep, changed oil.

Had to take out a special, back at 10:30. Took a sponge bath, changed clothes.

Enjoy having Bill here. The 522 F.A. Battalion are all Japanese-

Americans, and are proving their worth. So are the 100th Infantry of the same people.

When I saw Bill Kajikawa in December 1967, he was a football coach at Arizona State University at Tempe, with a beautiful house full of trophies; always easy to get along with, a slow talker. He was heavier than I, but a little shorter, and I am 5-foot-six-and-a-half, about 142 lb.

I hadn't told Bill I was coming to visit him after 22 ½ years, but my son and I walked right up to his door dressed in our raggediest and oldest clothes (clean-washed, however) and knocked. When his wife answered, I asked if the "man of the house" was home. She hollered for Bill, and when he came to the door, I dug in my pocket for a bundle of advertising pencils that had my name on them. I asked Bill if he could help a poor man and his son by buying a bundle of pencils, and I named an outrageous price.

Bill somewhat impatiently started to shut the door. When I stuck my foot in between the door and the jamb, he started to get a little angry, and told me that if I knew what was good for me, I'd take my foot from out of his doorway before he called the cops.

I kept my foot firmly in place, and asked him with a grin, "You don't remember me anymore, do you, Bill?"

He looked at my face, at my son's face, and beyond, at our van with our business name painted on the side. He broke out into a huge grin, said "Bud Wagner," shook my hand, and invited us into his house. We spent a couple days together, and he showed me and my family a lot of the scene in the Tempe area.

The battalion occupied positions 1000 yards east of Colle Salvetti, and orders came to move forward. So we got to the south side of a canal in the vicinity of Vicarelle. This was an area where there were many drainage ditches 3 feet deep, and our trucks had plenty of problems keeping out of them. One 6X6 from C Battery didn't, and a wrecker from 109 Quartermaster had to come up from the rear and take him out.

Monday, July 24, 1944   No entry.

Tuesday, July 25, 1944   Out several times.

Tonight Nate and I went to Lorenzano to this girl's house. She is Nate's cousin, and she speaks German much better than I do.

I was always the one to agree to take someone on an extra trip. Nate was our battalion news correspondent who stayed mostly at Headquarters. He had done a story on me, and was always after me for rides. Sometimes I was a little hesitant to do so for him unless I had authority from higher up.

I still couldn't speak hardly any Italian, but Nate's cousin spoke pretty good German — I secretly wondered if she had been a pretty good friend of some Krauts.

Wednesday, July 26, 1944   Wrote a letter to Ray. Got some Fascist notebooks and made a clipboard out of them.

Had several trips to Division. Dick and I went out together tonight, back about 8:30.

Nate and I went to Lorenzano again. Didn't stay long. I got it over to him that I wasn't really interested in his cousin. But I always appreciate an extra trip for variety.

Took a bath, changed clothes, got a new pair of shoes.

A little 8 year old girl lives here with her parents. Their home is in Pisa. Her name is Leona, and she has made friends with me.

Big news now is people are going home on rotation [to stay in the States] or on furlough [to return after 30 days]. DuBois and Jurgenson are going. At least Pete can't tell me I'm a hard man on horses for 30 days.

DuBois has earned a trip back; he is a fearless, good colonel. Pete Jurgenson never had to be nearer the front than Service Battery, but he has a lot of responsibility on his shoulders. About 20 enlisted men went from the battalion as well.

To bed around 11:00.

None of us knew how the choices were made for rotation or furlough, though in many cases it was obvious enough: R.H.I.P. (Rank Has It's Privileges.)

Besides that, all mail was censored, and if anyone had problems at home, including marital problems, the officers knew about it. No doubt they couldn't help but use their knowledge in picking the men to go.

Thursday, July 27, 1944   Are still in Nolgia. Very nice weather, don't mind this place so much now. Bill and I went for our daily walk. Quite a few people in this town, pretty girls.

Friday, July 28, 1944   No record, but still mostly on R.R.R.

Saturday, July 29, 1944   Took out a special this morning. Went through Faubia, bought some pears and plums. Went out tonight to the battalion.

Dick and I went back to Rosignano to Division Headquarters, 50-some miles. Hq. knows a good spot when they see one. Very nice trip, except we had to leave when it was almost dark. We could drive as far as Leghorn with our lights on, though.

Back to Division Artillery about 11:00.

I took Nate Levy to Lorenzano on way out to the battalion and picked him up later.

Sunday, July 30, 1944   Bill and I went after laundry. Took a bath and changed clothes. Changed into O.D.s.

Went to a Catholic church with Bill here in Nuegla. Enjoyed it somewhat. Our father gave part of the Mass, and the Italian father the rest. Lots of Italians in church. The women are nicely dressed in light-colored dresses.

Then we went to our Protestant services with Floyd. He played the portable organ.

Read a little, also some German.

Nate, Bill and I went to Marjorie's house at Lorenzano. The 151 is moving back tonight. Nate gets to see his cousin quite often. She does seem nice; she's probably Nate's age, a little older than me.

Maj. Surdyk gave us a surprise visit. We had to survey for new positions, and had some picked 1500 yards from the front lines. Even on a road under Jerry observation, we weren't shelled.

Orders were to move back to Rosignano. Dusty road, but who cares, when the road leads back instead of forward. We could use lights too, which was a pleasure.

Monday, July 31, 1944   Up at 6:00, packed up at 7:00. I took an item to the Air O.P., then to Livorno and down to Rosignano. Message Center is in a house; they've got it set up pretty nice.

Vital statistics for July 1944 were 15 men wounded in action, and one killed.

Tuesday, August 1, 1944   Bill and I went to Cecina and washed our peeps. Back by 10:00. Made a trip to the battalion. Some chasing around running errands for M.C.

Bill and I went for a ride tonight. Played catch for awhile.

This house in Rosignano is nice. Could pass for a home in Minnesota. Piano is left not damaged at all. Dick plays, but classical music. Floyd can play gospel, but I don't remember him doing so. Maybe he needs music and doesn't have it.

It's summer by the Mediterranean for us now at least.

Thursday, August 2, 1944   Don't know what happened to Wednesday.

Chow at 6:45 now. Cleaned up, read a little. A trip to the battalion. Nice weather, not too hot. Don and I went for a ride.

Friday, August 3, 1944   Several runs to all battalions. I was the only one here. Slept this p.m.
  To the battalion tonight. Hot. Wrote a letter home.

This was a real luxury, almost nothing to do for us except for a few runs daily. Message Center was operational, but not tactical. We could use our headlights here — but there were no night runs. Most of the battalion were in pup tents in a vineyard with an olive grove for shade. We three agents had a room in a vacant house — with a table, clock and lights. We agents were almost left on our own, so long as one of us was there and knew where all the Message Centers were. We could go swimming in the sea. There was a Red Cross doughnut stand there at least once in awhile.

There was a lot of talk now about being home for Christmas, but it really seemed too far away, and we had to agree we weren't gaining much ground very fast.

There were 105 shoot-out's too, mostly for infantry practice. Officers and men had to be well acquainted with the adjustments of artillery fire. One detail had the chore of keeping watch for any Jerry activity out at sea — no chances were taken. The 109th Engineer Battalion had mines in the harbor to locate and attach flash caps to. Also, there was a school in mine detection.

Despite these training schedules, this place was really "it," for all of us down to the last man. To sum up this period, what we mainly did was to follow the old Indian saying, "Keep your eyes open, and keep your powder dry."

In my letter home, I mentioned ripe tomatoes, almost-ripe grapes, and described our house and situation. I also mentioned that Sgt. Meagher had gone home the past month on furlough, and that he was going to try to either call or see them while he was there. Also, I sent a stamp for the Proctor Post Office for shaving soap. The stamp gave permission to send nonfood items.

Saturday, August 4, 1944   French toast for breakfast.
  Changed oil in my peep, greased it. Took it down to Service Battery. They welded on it until 3:30, then Ordnance gave it a check and decided to keep it another day or two and do more work on it. McGee took me back.
  Changed clothes, showered. Typed a letter to Ray.

Saturday, August 5, 1944   Must have got my dates mixed up somewhere. Today is Saturday.
  Up at 6:30. Chow at 6:45. Started reading *Lost Island* by Hall.
  Had to take Doc Lyons to the battalion. Used Floyd's peep. A little cloudy this morning.

Did some cleaning up this p.m. I've been taking care of Reb's things since he went in the hospital. Packed that over, cleaned my carbine. Read more in *Lost Island*. Have no comment on it.

Another mine blew up here last night. Frenchy was hurt.

We heard the explosion further down the beach. It really disturbs you when you haven't heard it for awhile — then the combined cry of half a dozen guys, "Medics!" and you knew somebody stopped a piece of shrapnel.

Frenchy had been throwing rocks at the exposed part of the mine, when he hit the right part. He came back to us later and was kidded about whether he should get a Purple Heart for it — as it happened in a rest area, rather than on the battlefield.

Sunday, August 6, 1944   Floyd, Dick and I went to church this a.m. Services were held at the theater in Rosignano with Chaplain Temple giving the service. Floyd played the organ. One service for all artillery units.

Did nothing this afternoon. Floyd and I went for a ride and show tonight.

Monday, August 7, 1944   Things at a standstill; didn't get my peep back.

Tuesday, August 8, 1944   Laid around. Bill and I went for a ride tonight. Adjusted his lights.

To Cecina. Buy some fruit every day: pears, plums or grapes. Each are ripe enough now.

This morning Bill and I went to the shoe store, and each bought a handbag and pair of grass shoes. Bill for his sister, mine for Arlene. Both were $1.60.

Wednesday, August 9, 1944   Up at 5:45 again. Now chow is at 6:00.

Bill and I went to the water point. Washed his peep. Read some. Laid around most the day, but did write a letter home.

Floyd and I went out together tonight. My peep is back, but Herb Johnson wanted to give it a spray job first.

Did odd jobs such as washing my mess kit in gas, washing a few clothes, and washing my helmet.

I sent a request for tooth powder with a stamp on it for the West End Station in Duluth, dated there September 2, 1944.

Thursday, August 10, 1944   Rained most of the forenoon. Got the peep back this p.m. They didn't seem to have done much on it, muffler and a few bolts tightened. Bill and I worked most the p.m. on it, put on the bumper guard and a water can rack.

Went to the battalions tonight with Floyd. He introduced me to several fellows from Duluth. One fellow, Oliver Skoog, talked about Ruth Zakowitz. I said, "Yes, she is my cousin, and she's married now." He said, "Yes, I know. I married her."

Floyd, Dick and I went to the show tonight, back at 11:00.

Friday, August 11, 1944   Chow as usual at 5:45. Bill and I went to the shoemakers in Rosignano. Took my knife there to have them make a sheath for it.

Worked some on the peep, cleaning and the like.

Went out tonight with Floyd to the show. Met two fellows from South Africa who are stationed across the street.

Saturday, August 12, 1944   Got a nice photograph of Margaret and her niece Maureen last night. Put it in a cardboard and have it on my stand by my cot.

Took Capt. Smith to a British air strip not far from here. They have Spitfires and Bull fighters there.

After dinner I took a fellow's brother back to Valletro, 64 miles. Hot, dusty road. Got Bob Vaughn, brought him over here. Showered, shaved.

After supper, Bob and I went riding through the high hills on our right. Interesting drive, no traffic or GIs. Went through Piper, Bella and Castellina. Back by 9:00, then to the show at the theater, *Three Men in White*. Back about 11:00.

A letter home mentioned Oliver Skoog, and that Ethel Nash wrote often. George Nash was in New Guinea in the Engineers. I had typed the letter. While in the rear, I got a chance to use Message Center's typewriter once in awhile to keep in practice.

Sunday, August 13, 1944   Woke up with a terrific headache. Ate 4 aspirins, took a little nap. Up at 9:15, showered, changed clothes, went to Division rear.

Got Bob, went to church. Took him back, had dinner there. Got a letter from Ethel Nash, and Arlene's school yearbook.

Nate and I went to Luciano to see Marjie. Back about 10:00.

My mother had to remove the covers off the yearbook, as it was too heavy to mail otherwise.

Monday, August 14, 1944   Up at 6:00.
Lieberman, Jim Love and I went to Volterra right after breakfast. Bought some alabaster trinkets. They have many beautiful things made there. Lester ordered a nude model that they will make for him. I bought some small bookends and little bowls. It's nice to know key fellows and to have the agent's job, or I never would have known about alabaster and Volterra. Back at noon. I spent about $10.00.
To the battalion tonight. Back about 6:00.
Bill's outfit, the 522 F.A., is leaving the 34th Division. He doesn't like to leave, and I hate to see him go as well.

Lester Lieberman was always with the Headquarters C.P., and was the one who knew about alabaster articles made in Volterra. He also knew that there is only one other place in the world where it is found, and that's in South Dakota. Alabaster is a soft, light-colored rock with colored streaks in it, and some is all white. It was cut, ground and polished by hand.
Lester didn't know how to drive. He came from New York City, and had never left it prior to coming in the Army. He was a real intellectual, and nice to know.

Tuesday, August 15, 1944   Packed up the alabaster in between the trips. Bill and I went to one of our positions looking for an ammo box. Finally used the one I had been carrying for a trunk.
Took Capt. Smith to the O.P. where 185th is firing near one of our battalion's former C.P.s, where it was 3 weeks ago, close to Castellina.
To the battalion and to Bill's. Got several *Life* magazines and a Sunday paper.

Wednesday, August 16, 1944   Bill and I went for a ride this morning. Looked at the German ammo, probably hundreds or thousands of rounds there.
Mailed the ammo box with my things.
Bill and I went to the beach. Isn't much good, but it is refreshing.
Bill's outfit has detached themselves from the 34th, and are going to the 85th Division. Bill packed up and left after dinner. Went to see him after supper. I gave him my air mattress as a going-away gift.

Thursday, August 17, 1944   Up at 6:00. Hot cakes for breakfast.
Took Lt. Arps to the Castellina O.P. On the way back I side-

swiped a peep from the 135th. Bent my tie rod arm and cracked the front wheel housing so I couldn't drive it. The fellow went and got Herman, brought him back, and he fixed it. Was lucky and thankful to get out of it that easy.

To the battalion tonight. Took Don over here. Talked awhile, then went to the rest center for coffee and doughnuts.

Friday, August 18, 1944   Got the wheel housing that cracked yesterday fixed on the peep. Read some in *Yankee*. Picked up a lieutenant from Division rear, took him to the 185th F.A. Went to bed fairly early.

Saturday, August 19, 1944   Didn't do much of anything. Was going to have some teeth fixed, but Dr. Legum was too busy.

Took Lyons to the clothing exchange. Took a shower there.

Nate and I went to Luciano and to see Marjie.

Sunday, August 20, 1944   Nate and I got up at 3:00. Went to Luciano. Took Marjie, her mother, friend, and little boy to Livorno. They were going to walk. Just an act of good will, that no doubt was official under Nate's correspondence and writing ability. I'm not sure how he is related to them, but I always have a great time of it. Back at 7:00.

Went to church at the theater again. A new chaplain. Capt. Temple is sick.

Bob Vaughn came this p.m. Took him to the USO show and movie. Division Artillery has a dance tonight. All others went except Dick, Nate and me. I had to go to 109th Engineers for a load of maps. Pretty tired.

Monday, August 21, 1944   Up at 8:00. Had a headache. To Division and all battalions this p.m. Had to haul several USO entertainers around. Took them back to Cecina tonight.

Hot. One letter yesterday, and one today from Mom.

We will be moving into Florence area shortly. Secretly, I would like to go to Southern France.

Tuesday, August 22, 1944   Went to the battalion with a special late last night, and went again early this morning. My peep would hardly run. Took it to Service Battery. They put in new plugs and points; it runs much better.

Changed oil. Slept some this p.m. To the Air O.P. and Division rear.

Tonight took Nate to Luciano. Saw Marjie and her folks for the last time. Wish I would have had film left for a picture.

Wednesday, August 23, 1944   Up at 6:00. One fried egg per man. Bad meals lately. Guess the cooks really aren't to blame, though.

Packed a few things, then went to see Ollie Skoog. Talked quite a bit with him. We went to the Red Cross, had coffee and cookies. Back to Division Artillery with him, and we had had supper together. Took Ollie back about 8:30.

Floyd has taken a job in the Personnel section, so Hambright is back with us again.

Thursday, August 24, 1944   Up at 5:30. Loaded up, pulled out around 8:00. Came 40 miles, close to Montainne. Just an assembly area.

Budinger gave me a siren last night. Put it on the peep. Doesn't make a loud noise, though, as my battery is too small.

Put my cot up alongside of a hay shed. The battalion is one mile from here.

We are expecting to see Gen. Clark in our area. The last time was when we were in Bizerte at the time we were ready to leave for Paestum, Salerno, and all points north in Italy.

Our rest period was concluded on the 24th when we got to the staging area at the town of Montainne. Reconnaissance had previously been made to select gun positions near Firenze (Florence). Positions were prepared while the battalion remained at the staging area.

Friday, August 25, 1944   Up at 6:15. Chow at 6:30.

Fixed the flat, filled up with gas and oil. Had to take Doc Lyons and the "Podry" out until noon. Slept until 4:30.

To the battalions tonight.

Got 8 letters last night, from Patsy, Lavonne, Mom and Ray.

Nate and I had fried eggs and coffee for a lunch tonight. One of the other fellows has a small gasoline stove — unless it's the one that Floyd had, and he left it here when he went to the C.P. One or another of us will get corn whenever we can, and cook it.

Saturday, August 26, 1944   Read my letters over; wrote one home. Put my chair inside a straw shed — windy outside. Slept for half an hour this morning.

Had to take Doc Lyons out this p.m. Took a bath and changed

clothes. Wrote to Patsy and George Nash. Got a V-mail from Ruth Eliason. Roads are dusty around here. Miserable driving.

Battery C's working party received several rounds of Jerry artillery in their area, resulting in wounds to 4 men.

August saw some promotions. One man I knew, Wells Marshall, was promoted to lieutenant. Another selection was made for furlough and rotation.

Sunday, August 27, 1944   Made a trip to Division. Brought back Maj. Williamson.

Slept some. Went to see Don this p.m. He has been to Florence. To bed early.

Monday, August 28, 1944   Washed a few clothes, took a sponge bath. Read *In His Steps,* a book I got from Don about a group that follows Jesus. Still in the same area. No one knows how long we will be here.

Each man got 10 bottles of beer the other night. I let 5 others of Message Center each have two extra.

Took Lt. Ornsbee to our new position this p.m. We were to find a route for the battalions to take. Went close to Florence. Met Bill on his way back.

Back at 6:30, made over 100 miles, tired. Nate and I went to Gaumbassi for a haircut. Ray sent a descriptive folder on the hay rake he bought. To bed at 10:00.

Tuesday, August 29, 1944   Nothing much to do today. Read. Slept a little. Went to Division rear with Girth and Aikers, brought back the money for the fellows. Rough, hot road.

Went to Volterra in the morning with Lester Lieberman.

Wednesday, August 30, 1944   Had to go to Volterra again with Lieberman, and he got his model of the alabaster lady. Real nice; I hope he gets it shipped home OK. I told him I wanted to write my name on her arm or something — like on a plaster cast. He didn't think it was funny.

Stopped to see Bill.

The alabaster lady is really a work of art. It cost a lot too, but is a real souvenir, about half life-size, almost pure white, with a few dark and black streaks throughout.

Thursday, August 31, 1944   Bill came over this morning and stayed until noon. He had dinner with us. Had to take Girth to Division rear again. Back at 5:30. Rough and dusty road. Went to see Don tonight. Back at 10:00.

The rear end went to pieces on my peep last night. Service Battery put in a new one this forenoon.

Friday, September 1, 1944   Started out the month in the right manner with payday. We followed a training schedule after a sloppy manner.

There were also several recons of positions south of Florence, but these positions were never used. We awaited the arrival of Gen. Clark, who did come, and decorated all three men of our Air O.P. who did such a good job under the circumstances.

Saturday, September 2, 1944   Got paid last night. Gen. Clark is supposed to be in the area today. Everyone is supposed to be ready. Washed a few clothes, finished reading *In His Steps*. Two trips tonight to the battalions.

Gen. Clark was here, at least to the Air O.P. and I suppose to Division Artillery and the C.P., but I didn't see him.

Sunday, September 3, 1944   Rained hard this morning 3 a.m. to 7:00. I pulled my cot in the hay shed just as it started. Ham slept in here too, and Dick came crawling in half an hour later soaking wet.

Chow at 7:00. Went back to bed at 8:30. Sun came out, dried out everything. Took Jarbo and Harvey Swanson to Medical Supply. Back at 10:30.

Went to church. One of the better sermons. The text was, "If he will do my will, he shall know."

To the battalion after dinner and saw Don a few minutes. Came back at 1:30.

Looked over my snapshots. I can't make myself believe I have parents, brothers or sister; it's been just too long. War news is favorable, though: the Yanks are on the German border.

CHAPTER 26

Florence. Rest. More mud. Death.
Loiano. Broke down. Pleasure to be here tonight.

Monday, September 4, 1944   Went to show, *Going My Way.* Just got started, when Jerry plane came over. Caused a lot of excitement and dispersion. Some ack-ack, and Jerry dropped two small bombs close by. Didn't see the rest of the show.

Up at 6:30, chow, read, wrote to Ray.

Fall is in the air. Cool all morning. Left my cot in the shed together with the rest of my things.

Tuesday, September 5, 1944   Ready to move. Most of Division Artillery moved out by 2:00. Ham and I were among the last. We left at 6:00.

Are just on northeast side of Florence, still in the city itself. Seems nicer than Rome, much better than Naples. The Arno River has 2 Bailey bridges across the place where we crossed it.

Dick, Ham and I have an old garage to stay in, a family next door. Took a sponge bath before hitting the rack. Couldn't sleep well.

Wednesday, September 6, 1944   Last night the battalions were going right past our door all night. Up at 6:00. Had to go to Division Hq. with Dick. Through Florence (or a part of it), to the battalion twice this morning with specials. 151 is about 2 miles from here.

I came through Florence again, but orders came out that no one is to go through there. Anyway, there is enough to see around here.

Rained about all p.m. Tonight took Col. Kenniger to Division. Took the wrong road 3 times, put my top up.

Ham and I went out together tonight. Made two trips — came via Florence once. Put my peep inside the garage tonight for lights. Wrote to home, Rod and Bill.

The battalion finally had a position north of Florence, having moved in about 11 p.m. on the 6th. The area was heavily mined and booby-trapped.

Three men were wounded by mines.

We still hadn't done any firing — but there were plenty of reasons.

Thursday, September 7, 1944   Not much doing. Wrote to Peggy, or Margaret, as I usually called her.

Battalion was going to move, but fortunately didn't.

Peggy keeps on writing faithfully, and the picture she sent was a photograph — a big item of expense for them. She may be thinking I'm coming back to Ireland, but I didn't say I would.

Friday, September 8, 1944   Took the Catholic father to Firenze to the rest center. Joe came along. On the way back we looked the town over.

To the outfit tonight. Got there in time to move with them. Have to go through Florence to get there. Up a winding, one-way road.

Back before dark. Still put the peep in our house at nights for light.

Saturday, September 9, 1944   Hot cakes for breakfast.

Took Girth to the parade ground. The Division has a parade for presentation of awards to commemorate our 151's landing at Salerno 1 year ago today. I made 15,758 miles on my peep this year in Italy.

Our outfit moved tonight through the northwest part of Florence, back about midnight. Lots of traffic.

The 15,758 miles was driven mostly in low gear, slow traveling in blackout at night, with the top down and windshield down and covered, unless it was raining or snowing. We went through mud fields for miles, and across floating, bobbing pontoon bridges. If there were no bridges, take the fan belt off. Then, put the fan belt back on and ride the brakes awhile to dry them out, as brakes were necessary to stop suddenly — instead of tumbling down an embankment or shell or bomb hole. And then Service Battery would grumble about how in the world could I wear out a set of brake shoes in 3 days!

Sunday, September 10, 1944   Division Artillery moved this morning, northwest of Florence, close to the battalions. Reb came back as agent today. Scott is going home on rotation.

At 3 p.m. Jack and I went up with the forward detail. They shelled not too far away. About a dozen rounds came in. My outfit is not far away. Ham came tonight too.

Are close to a rectory and church; got a pail of water from the family now living there.

The battalion had put out it's signs as of September 9, but there had been no more shooting as yet.

During the occupation of one position, a battery of the 185th F.A. had moved into the position of the A Battery of the 151st F.A. The problem was straightened out peacefully with the 185th moving out.

Monday, September 11, 1944   Up at 7:00. They didn't bring us any breakfast until the battery came up this afternoon. Message Center put up their tent. The agents moved into a vacant room of the rectory. One pretty girl there.

My outfit moved tonight. I got in with the advanced party. Are in a position where the Germans still were this p.m. You make sure you keep a hand on your carbine, if possible.

Back at 10:00, and another special waiting, but managed to catch Maj. Thomas at the old position, and he said he'd save me a trip. Well bless him — he has a heart.

I remembered the Indian quote again to keep my eyes open and my powder dry.

I never wanted to be taken prisoner — if possible, I'd fight it out.

Tuesday, September 12, 1944   Slept well. What a relief when you know what you can save yourself by not having to go out again. The other agents were out practically all night.

Shaved, washed. Ham and I went to get water yesterday. We gave the girls a ride with their water up the mountain this morning, then later I went back and took the two sisters down for another trip.

At 3:00 we loaded up and moved forward about 5 miles. The agents are out in the open under a few scrawny trees. Three trips to the battalion before things settled down. Had one flat, but got an exchange for it. On the way back a Limey scraped my side and tore the top bows off the peep. Some shells coming in not far enough away.

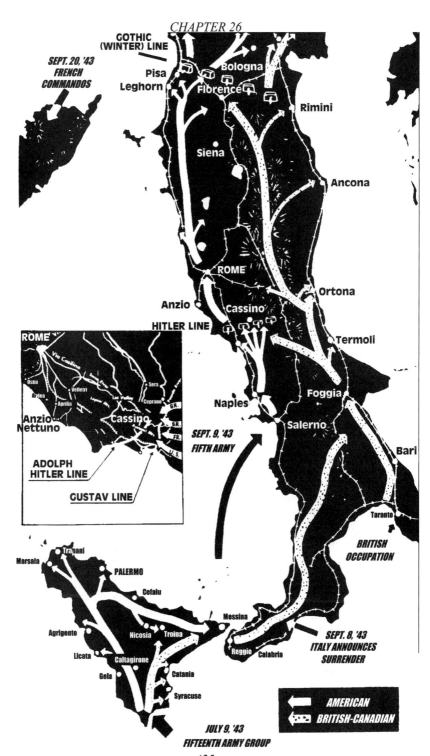

GOTHIC
(WINTER) LINE

SEPT. 20, '43
FRENCH
COMMANDOS

Pisa
Leghorn

Bologna

Florence

Rimini

Siena

Ancona

ROME

Ortona

Anzio

Cassino

HITLER LINE

Termoli

ROME

Ostia

Via Casilina

Sera

Ardea

Velletri

Aprilia

Liri Valley

Ceprano

B.R.

Anzio
Nettuno

Cassino

D.A.

FR.

ADOLPH
HITLER LINE

GUSTAV LINE

U.S.

Naples

SEPT. 9, '43
FIFTH ARMY

Foggia

Salerno

Bari

Taranto

BRITISH
OCCUPATION

Marsala

Trapani

PALERMO

Cefalu

Messina

SEPT. 8, '43
ITALY ANNOUNCES
SURRENDER

Agrigento

Nicosia

Troina

Reggio

Calabria

Licata

Caltagirone

Gela

Catania

Syracuse

JULY 9, '43
FIFTEENTH ARMY GROUP

AMERICAN

BRITISH-CANADIAN

These people in this vicinity really had a chore when it came to getting water. The trail down to the spring was really only for walking, but we went down with the peep, just crawling along. There were lots of sharp turns too. We didn't worry about what we would do if anything went wrong — I always thought that if a horse could go down these mountain paths, so could I with a peep.

There weren't that many English vehicles on the road now, but anyway, one ran into me. I don't remember who got blamed for the broken top bows of the peep. Most likely we blamed it on "wear and tear." After all, the destruction of a few bows from a vehicle top was fairly insignificant in the situation.

Many of these days were full hardworking days. In getting ready to move, we had to pack all our own things, then usually we'd help Message Center load their equipment, and then wait around at times to get started. Just a five-mile move wasn't the worst — but then we had to unload everything again and set it up. Just the three trips to the battalion even without a five-mile move could be rough enough — the sideswipe with the Limey vehicle had to have been in blackout driving at night. And then besides all that, I had a flat tire to change, and another spare to get.

We used to say about going out at night that there was never a good night — just a bad night, a worse night, and only the hope of a better night.

Finally on September 12, after lots of recons and occupying positions, we started firing. There had been a lot of problems in moving here. Charlie Battery overturned a gun, and others had other troubles. All in all, it was a rough trip, but ... we were firing.

The high hills and narrow roads hampered all aspects of war, especially observation and road travel. Due to the problems, we hadn't many observed mission, but there were many time-on targets and harassing fire with missions coming from Division Artillery.

Wednesday, September 13, 1944   Very cool until the sun comes up. Took a sponge bath. Changed clothes.

Joe McDermott and I went back to Florence to get the chaplain. Had some chance to look the town over. The chaplain took us up on a hill from where we could see all of Florence. Also to the gardens,

and another old, beautiful church. Back to camp at 5:30.
Three trips to the battalion. Through after midnight.

Thursday, September 14, 1944   A fellow said a shell landed close in
the morning, but thankful I didn't hear it.

Got the bows straightened on the peep, changed oil, greased it.
It's nice and warm now at 10:00.

I was hoping we wouldn't see any more action, but — here we go
again. They haven't made much of a dent in the Gothic line as yet.
Our planes are bombing a pass in it, and very heavy artillery salvos
are going out continually.

Bill's wife wrote me a letter. Got 3 from home last night. I'm anxious to see Arlene. Mom said she is a good singer for her age. Wrote
home. Finished reading *How Green Was My Valley*.

My letter home of September 14 mentioned we'd had a short Salerno
Day Celebration, and a few fellows did it up good with a remembrance of
those who died.

The grub had been a little better in the past while — we had fried chicken
twice in the past two weeks, and I had robbed a tame beehive the other
morning, early when the bees were still a little stiff from the cold. I didn't get
any stings.

Friday, September 15, 1944   Up at 6:00. Looks like rain; we moved
into an old straw shed — one made of cement, though.

Dreamed of Evelyn Isaacson last night. First time I've thought of
her in a long time.

Made several trips tonight. Have a toothache again. 3 letters from
home, some papers. Reb and I talked awhile after it got dark.

Saturday, September 16, 1944   Up at 7:00. Went to the medics for
a slip, then to the 15th Evac. Hospital. Got two teeth extracted.

Stopped at Service Battery and was going to have a front spring
changed, but they didn't think it was necessary. Back to the battery at
noon. I was packed, but only the forward party left after dinner. I
didn't have to go, so put my cot back up. Slept a little.

We all moved after supper. New position was shelled this p.m.
Agents have a room for themselves in this place. A beautiful estate.
The 151 moved tonight. C.P. is in a farm house. At one time it was a
nice place, only now the house is full of shell holes. The people seemed
to have just walked out — food is still on the table, and furniture is
still there, and pigs and chickens in the yard. Two dead Americans

lying there close by, no doubt our infantry.
We have an electric light in here. I may write a letter.

Sunday, September 17, 1944   Had to go to the Air O.P. this a.m.
Back in time for church, but didn't especially like the service. Chaplain Temple gave the sermon to the battalion tonight.

Monday, September 18, 1944   Went to the battalion this morning.
Then, to the 109 Med for my teeth, but it was too crowded.
    To the battalion again tonight. Back late, really dark out. Got a
letter from Peggy. Started answering it. She has news of Ireland; she's
working at the doctor's home as yet.

Tuesday, September 19, 1944   To the 109th this morning again, but
still crowded, so went to the dentist at Division rear. Got an appointment with him for next week, is the best I could do. Saw Floyd and
Bob. Brought Meyers back here, and took him back to the rear again
at 3 p.m.
    Went to the spring below one of our positions, where I hauled
water for the girls. Saw Ascilia and talked with her for awhile. The
spring water is always my favorite, so I stop when I have a chance
like this, and make a canteen cup of soluble coffee and some hard
biscuits with sliced garlic and onions.
    Went to Division, got *Stars and Stripes*. To the battalion and back
fairly early. To Message Center. Finished writing to Peggy.

Wednesday, September 20, 1944   Ham, Dick, Reb and I played
cribbage until 11:15 last night. Wrote to Bill's wife, Lavonne and

Ruth Eliason. Also to Arlene this a.m.

Some shells landing close again. One came in close enough to throw fragments on our wall, but again, I didn't hear it. Raining this morning. We had to disperse our vehicles, afraid of shellfire. Slept some.

Dick and I went to Division for *Stars and Stripes*. To the battalion. Went with Budinger to A and B Batteries. Got caught in a traffic jam. Back to the C.P. late. Back here at 9:00. Very dark. Knocked a hub cap off the peep as I hit a wall on this one dark stretch of road.

Wrote to Aunt Anna. Read a *Life* of July 24th that I got tonight.

Thursday, September 21, 1944 Up at 6:30. One fried egg for breakfast with 2 pieces of toast and coffee.

My battery was flat. Had to crank. The generator wouldn't charge. Took it to Service Battery this morning. They cleaned the generator brushes. Back at 10:30.

Wrote to Ray and Patsy. Wrote to Bill this p.m.

To the battalion tonight. Went to see Don a few minutes. Back at 8:30, to bed at 9:00.

Fox got wounded the other day.

Friday, September 22, 1944 As usual. Cleaned out my peep a little. Cool, but the sun came out and warmed things up. Took my laundry out this p.m. to Ascilia. We went and got water together again.

The battalion was going to move, but I guess it didn't.

Was sleeping at 10 p.m., when Sgt. Rettinger called me, wanting to know if I wanted to go to Florence on a 5-day pass. I got up again and sewed my stripes on.

Military protocol, such as having our rank insignias (stripes) properly sewn on our uniforms was sometimes neglected in the field.

But in rest areas, instead of shellfire, blackout, mud, dust, death, or drowning to contend with, we had to worry about rear echelon Military Police who often had nothing better to do than to be sure we had our stripes properly sewn on our uniforms. Not a one of them was up towards the front helping with traffic control either; we wrote our own "speeding tickets" up there, and those who couldn't drive, had better park. But it was almost funny how important the M.P.s considered themselves, and they sure looked nice in their uniforms.

Saturday, September 23, 1944 Up at 6:00. Got some things ready.

To the battalion by 8:00. Had to wait around, then went to the Quartermaster, and here to Florence at about 2:30.

The rest center is the railroad station. It's a beautiful place. Large, with entertainment facilities. Red Cross. Small rooms to stay in. 8 in here. The meals are served cafeteria style. Nice restaurant. 6 Italians singing and playing at the Red Cross. Went to a show, *Marriage Is a Private Affair* at the USO. To bed about 10:30.

Sunday, September 24, 1944   Up at 7:00. Breakfast. Is nice to have someone serving it to you instead of eating it out of a mess kit. Met Jack Strong at the show last night. He is driving Capt. Rieser. I came down to the garage this morning to see him.

Everything is so quiet and peaceful: no shells, no dust, no worry. I wish this would last the "duration" that I'm in for. It irritates me to see all the rear echelon troops stationed in town. They have a better job in the Army than they did at home.

Jack and I had the use of his jeep all day. We found a beautiful hotel room this morning for the 2 of us. Twin beds, toilet, everything comfortable.

We went out to see those people where Division Artillery had been. Drove around town, left the car at the garage and walked to our room. Walked the streets for awhile. Up to our room. Jack and I talked for a long while.

Monday, September 25, 1944   The people woke us at 7:00. Slept quite well, but am not used to springs, mattress, or sheets. Came in the rest center to eat.

Jack had to take Rieser somewhere, so I took off alone. Bought some photograph albums and some gloves for Arlene. Went riding around this p.m. Walked quite a bit tonight.

Tuesday, September 26, 1944   Jack and I looked over more of the town. Bought a few things, and walked still more this afternoon. Tonight we listened to music at the Red Cross. We rode on an incline trolley this afternoon about like one they used to have in Duluth; you could see the whole town from the top of it.

Wednesday, September 27, 1944   Slept at the rest center last night. Jack had to go out with Rieser. Good weather while I've been here, and I've enjoyed myself.

We left Florence about 3:00. Got to the Q.M. at 4:00. Got a ride in a 168th truck, but he took us out of the way, and we had to walk quite a ways back.

Finally got back to Cavalina and stayed with the 109th Medics for the night. Raining. Got fairly wet.

Thursday, September 28, 1944 Caught a ride up this morning on 65 and finally got back to the outfit. Rained hard. Roads are nothing but mud. Indescribable.

Friday, September 29, 1944 Mud and more mud. Hell enough for us, but worse for the infantry. Am jealous of all rear echelon troops back in the rear cities.

We are on restricted expenditure of ammo due to transportation difficulties. The roads are in bad shape due to heavy rains, and even a short trip is a big chore if you have to go through a by-pass. Small vehicles rarely get through on their own.

We had 5 men wounded from our battalion, and several deaths from other outfits in our area. Maj. Farrow of the 17th Medium (British) was killed by a mine in C Battery, and Col. Schirdroth, Commander of the 133rd Infantry Regiment, was killed while returning to his Command Post with information.

Towards the end of the month the 105th A.A.A. joined us. We were glad to see them again. The 532nd A.A.A. left us to take infantry training.

Saturday, September 30, 1944 Mud and more rain. The outfit moved a ways, and so did Division Artillery. The roads are jammed with traffic. It took me 4 hours to get 3 miles. Morale is very low. I don't have a dry place to rest my weary body tonight. Laid down across the peep seats covered with shelter halves — was the best I could do.

We talked about what some British soldier was supposed to have said; that if he ever got out of the Army and ever got discontented, he would turn the thermostat down to 40, put on wet socks, start his cigarette lighter to warm his hands, then lay down on the floor and cover up with one dirty blanket and try to go to sleep.

Sunday, October 1, 1944 Things are looking up. Ham and I found a room in the Message Center building that we put our names on. It cleared up somewhat, but I have a bad cold and am miserable.

Outfit moved. Made a trip by 10:00. Fixed a flat.

Monday, October 2, 1944 Raining again. Roads are a sea of mud. Out on a special this a.m. Broke my speedometer, and the generator

went haywire. Out tonight.
Mud, mules and mountains is right.

Tuesday, October 3, 1944   Went to the Air O.P. this morning, still back at Cavalina. Then went to Ascilia's for my laundry. Took her down the mountain and got all her water pots filled again. Back at noon. Barney got my photographs yesterday, didn't turn out too bad. Fixed a tire.

Glad to see Ascilia again, though I suppose this is the last time unless we make our winter line in the area. I kind of like the terrain, but it's heck for moving up, and it's worse for the infantry to be in hills like this.

"Fixing a tire" sounds easy, but we changed on the road and fixed our own flats if we had time. The rims were in two about-equal pieces, held together by about 12 bolts. You took off all the nuts and lifted off half the rim, and could take the tube right out and patch it. Then you didn't have to pound the tire bead in, but just put it between the 2 rim halves, and put the nuts on the bolts and tighten them all around.

Letters home of October 2 and October 9 told of the mud and of the long time it took some nights to get through. I said it was getting colder at nights, and I had to put on extra layers of clothes.

Wednesday, October 4, 1944   Didn't go out until tonight. Fred Ellis came along. The battalion moved. Are about 9 - 10 miles from here. Road is in terrible shape. Back at 10:00. Dark, and had to wait a long time on the road.

Thursday, October 5, 1944   Raining most the day. Ham and I went out this morning. Took a different road. Got stuck, but a much better road than on the mountain.

We were supposed to move, but orders changed again. We were all packed and loaded.

Ham and I went out on a special again this p.m. He got stuck this time, and I had to pull him out.

Friday, October 6, 1944   We moved about 8 miles this a.m. Are in S. Benelletto. Due to our own initiative, we agents have a room. 151 moved. Rained very hard. Terrible road. Got soaked and stuck. Budinger gave me dry clothes — back at 10:00.

Budinger was B Battery's agent. He stayed at 151 Message Center. He was always a nice fellow to know and be around.

Saturday, October 7, 1944 Made a trip to the battalion. Got soaked. Stopped raining, and sun is shining.

Road is terrible. One trip after supper, then out again and back at 4 a.m. on October 8.

There were plenty of problems encountered by all. We were in the vicinity of Fornelli. Then we moved to a cosmetics or perfume factory which was all smashed up — but what a pleasant smell. This was close to Legroci.

Sunday, October 8, 1944 Last night's hecticness practically overcame me; I had one of my worst headaches ever. The other agents covered for me, and I just stayed in bed until 4 p.m.

Gassed up at about 5:00. Had to go to the battalion at 6:00. Back at 9:00. The road is indescribably foggy and awful dark. I couldn't get far; the mud was too deep. A 6X6 had to push me quite a ways. Don't know how the peep can stand such a strain.

Two packages the last two days.

Monday, October 9, 1944 Ate breakfast. Raining, and a heavy fog. The outfit moved up #65, then back across 21 miles. I came back another way, past the 125th. It's only about half as far, but there's bad road most the way.

Had to go back here at noon. It rained hard on the way up. I'm mud from head to foot. Last winter was bad, but this is worse. 91st Division is on Highway 65; wish we were there.

Ham and I went out tonight together. Got stuck on the bad road, waited for over an hour before a 6X6 pulled us out. Back at 10:30.

Our supply road, with the help of the rain, soon became an impassable bog. Although the infantry, with the assistance of the artillery, did all they could to keep it in shape, it was soon obvious we would have to find another home for the battalion.

Maj. Thomas and Capt. Crellin got permission from Division Artillery to recon for positions further east in 91st Division's area. They did so, and after much effort on everyone's part, we started occupying positions close to Monzuno where our one observer of the Forward O.P. was just across the street from our C.P.

The O.P. observer told Command Post that what he could see from his forward Observation Position was about the same as they could see from across the street at their Command Position.

Tuesday, October 10, 1944 Ham and I had to take a special out. We left at 11:30 and didn't get back until 4:30. Most of our luck tonight was again bad. Ham got half way, and his fuel line broke. I took the specials. As I was in Message Center, a shell came in the next building.

I had to pull Ham back — what a job. Had a hard time.

Tom McGee was mad because I wouldn't go out again, but it wasn't a special, and somehow I got out of it.

Tom doesn't always realize what we have to go through. I doubt if we could have made it again, and I also had a flat to fix.

Wednesday, October 11, 1944   Fixed a flat tire, read a little, and wrote to home and Ray.

Ham and I went out again tonight. Took #65 — 22 miles, but it took us 5 hours to get there.

Met Reb, so all three of us came back together. Back at 11:30. Took the bad road on the way back.

Thursday, October 12, 1944   Sun was out yesterday and today. Drying considerably. S. Beneditte. Had to go to Division rear and Air O.P. Brought Lt.'s Hohnburg and Adams back. About 60 miles round trip. Back at 7:15.

Reb took out my items. Just as he got to our 151 Message Center, a shell came in, wounding three: Tom McGee, Sgt. Anderson and Ernie Rose. I was kept from seeing the bloody mess that Reb described to me. Ernie was hit the worst.

In a letter home I mentioned the mud and my rest trip to Florence. I told them we call the furlough plan a "morale joke except for a fortunate few." I mentioned I'd run into Oliver Skoog, Ruth Zakowitz' husband one night. He was hauling ammo to the front, had lots of work, and hadn't had mail in a long time either.

They'd had fried chicken one night last week, but nobody saved any, and I didn't get in until 11:30. The kitchen crew felt bad about forgetting me, so the Mess Sergeant gave me a case of grapefruit juice that they had a lot of.

Friday, October 13, 1944   Still eat at 6:30. Fried eggs. Cleaned the mud from all brake drums and had the maintenance guys tighten the brakes, but it doesn't help much. They wear out so fast from the mud and water, and from drying them out by holding down the brake pedal.

Took a sponge bath and changed clothes this p.m. Feel much better. Had those clothes on day and night a long time.

Still dry weather; hope it lasts.

Got 5 letters several days ago. One from Peggy, one from Ray, and 3 from home.

To the battalion tonight. Took 185th's items along. Back at 9:30. Ernie Rose died today as a result of his wounds yesterday, Sgt. Anderson had a kidney removed and is not expected to be back. Tom McGee wasn't hurt too bad, and will be back.

Ernie was well liked — he always had a smile for me and a welcome word.

Losing a good friend who went through everything you did is hard, when suddenly everything between you and he stops.

I reflected that probably either one of us would have risked his life to save the other — even though I really did not know him that well, or he me.

He died without me knowing anything about his parents, if he had any brothers or sisters, or even the exact Eastern state he came from — or if he had a girlfriend waiting for him, what his home life had been, or where he was buried — or what were his hopes of doing after he got out of the Army had he lived. Any of these questions had no answers.

I always had it in my mind that I wanted to find out the names of the closest survivors of the six closest friends of mine who were killed and write to them after I was discharged. The right time never came, though, and I never did get it done.

The fog finally lifted, and we started to get into position. There was just too much activity in Monzuno, with an O.P., a C.P. and the 151's Message Center all in one place almost. The Krauts spotted us, and the shelling resulted with Ernie's death and the others being wounded.

Then came more rain.

We'd had a 6X6 stalled at a ford through a little creek. Within 6 hours after the heavy rains, the creek had risen 15 feet and washed the 6X6 a hundred yards downstream, with water washing over the top of the cab. Battery B had to move 2 guns in a hurry to save them. Battery C had a ¼ ton car that washed into the stream. When the water went down, it was found upside down in the stream.

So we moved again, this time a short distance of 400 yards for one battery, and 1000 yards for the other — taking 3 days to accomplish the move. No vehicle could get into Headquarters Battery, so rations had to be brought in by man-back.

Later on, the house where our Forward Observer Lt. Dickheiser, his crew and the infantry crew were in was shelled, and practically the whole house fell on and buried the infantry crew. With them at the time was a platoon from C Company. 13 bodies were dug out, all from the infantry.

Saturday, October 14, 1944   Got ready to move, and did so after 11:00. Came close to Loiano on 65, then turned right. Agents set up in a tool shed. My outfit moved, so I left about 4:00. Found them at

5:30. Helped them put up their tent and ate supper with them.

On the way back a 6X6 had gone in the ditch and tied up traffic. A fellow finally came along who knew the way through to B Battery. So I followed, and got back at 11:00. Very dark, but not cloudy until after I got back.

Sunday, October 15, 1944   Up at 6:30. Hot cakes for breakfast. Dick and I went to Division. Came back. Made my bed, and washed. A beautiful day. It hasn't rained for about 4 days now, and I'm really thankful for that. It's warm and like a beautiful fall Sunday at home when I would ride Bird or go for a walk in the woods.

Ernie Rose's death hit everyone hard. He was such a likable guy who went through as much as any of us. He was a little younger than me, from an Eastern state.

Went to the battalion 4 times this p.m. and also tonight. A busy day, but at least I got through it again.

Monday, October 16, 1944   Had to go to the Air O.P. today; it took 7 hours. They are still back at Cavalina, about 75 miles. Rained on the way back. Miserable driving.

Tonight I went out and had a leak in the brake line. Left the peep sit and walked up to here, Message Center.

Tuesday, October 17, 1944   Went all over the country looking for Service Battery. Finally found them 4 miles from here. They put new linings in and repaired the brake line. Good brakes now, thankful for that. Back here about 3:00.

To the battalion's position. Got stuck on the way back. Still using Adler's peep. Terrible road.

Wednesday, October 18, 1944   Up at 6:30. Not raining. Got 3 letters from Mom, one from Ray and one from Ethel. Fixed my chains and cleaned up. Got a haircut. To the battalion once.

Thursday, October 19, 1944   Don't remember.

Friday, October 20, 1944   Took Nate Levy back to 5th Army. He wanted to get his book *Between Barrages* published. I went to 1st Armored Division. Tried to get my clothes, but couldn't find Ham.

Saturday, October 21, 1944   Raining. Put on all 4 chains. Got wet. The peep wouldn't start. Got it towed and going.

Had to make a trip to the battalion after dinner. Roads are worse than terrible. Just a miracle if you can get through. Most people back home never have or will go through anything like this in a lifetime. Wet and muddy, with not a stitch of clothes to change into.

Sunday, October 22, 1944   I went to the 151 last night. Didn't get my peep back until 9:00 this morning. It took a 6X6 to get it out. Reb, Dick, the wire peep and I were all stuck together. Got back at 10:00 tonight after another trip.

Monday, October 23, 1944   Another bad night. Got stuck again, but got out myself.

Tuesday, October 24, 1944   Raining this p.m. Reb and I started to make a tent.
        Had to go out at 3:30. Got to the battalion at 5:00. Had supper there. Tried until 8:30 to get out, but got stuck and had to leave it there. Stayed with the switchboard boys on the floor. Was raining continually.

Wednesday, October 25, 1944   No entry.

Thursday, October 26, 1944   Up at 7:30. Real good hot cakes and bacon for breakfast, the best we've had in a long time.
        It's still raining. Everything is a sea of water, running swiftly down the hill. Got a ride up the hill with Hill in the ration truck. He couldn't pull me out, and the peep wouldn't start either. I walked and found a bulldozer to push me out, but the peep still wouldn't start. Hill couldn't cross the river, so he came back. Left my peep sit, and came back to the battalion with Hill.
        There is no way I can get back to Division Artillery. All lines are out, and can't get ammo or rations in here either. 151st Field Artillery Battalion is a lost and stranded battalion tonight.
        Dengler gave me some of his clothes — dry ones, and what a feeling. Changed, and am in Pomerleau's corner. Got letters from Mom and Peggy last night, answered them.
        The boys have a pretty good secluded spot here. What a pleasure to be here tonight.

CHAPTER 27

Broken down peep. Walking and.thumbing. Almost hit.
Winter quarters.
Some rides and broke down again. Nice weather for Christmas.

Friday, October 27, 1944   Stopped raining a little. I went with Hill. He towed my peep until it finally started.

Back to Division Artillery at 12:00. Had to go out again this p.m. to the battalion. Carried *Stars and Stripes* down the hill. Still raining. My peep wouldn't run, but finally got it back to the main road. Left it sit and walked up to here.

Saturday, October 28, 1944   Slept until 8:30. Still raining. Roads are indescribable.

Walked down to my peep. Dried it out finally and got it running a little, but then it stopped for good. Hill came along and towed me into Service Battery. They found out the frame was broken, so we took it to Ordnance.

Got back to Service Battery with Herb Johnson, then thumbed back to Division Artillery in time for supper. Still misting a little, and it doesn't look like it will stop.

Sunday, October 29, 1944   Division Artillery moved today. We're on the other side of Loiano. I had to load all my things on Reb's peep, and rode with him.

Dick, Reb and I borrowed the medic's wall tent, put it up close to the kitchen. Didn't go out today to the battalion. Raining. Most of the battery is in this house.

Monday, October 30, 1944   Walked to 151 across the hills. Took me two hours to go two miles. I followed the wire, which followed a ravine with high rock walls. Were some small holes in them, which were bird caves.

Got a ride back to Division Artillery with Budinger. Went to Service, still no peep. Saw Dick, so rode back with him. Have to go all the way back to A.P.O. to get through. No raincoat or hat, and no top, so got soaking wet. Didn't get back until 5:00.

Didn't go out tonight. Cold, and roads are practically impassable, except for 65 — and it's very bad.

Some shells came in last night, but thankful I didn't hear them. Part of A Battery's O.P. crew was buried in a house.

Tuesday, October 31, 1944   I had to take Dick's peep. Went to Division. Left at 7:30, back at noon. The sun was shining.

I walked to the battalion this p.m. Came back tonight at 10:00. Still not raining. A letter from Bill.

Wednesday, November 1, 1944   Waited for Reb until 12:30, then went to Service with him. He used a C.R. [command and reconnaissance vehicle]. We hit head-on with a 6X6, but not much damage.

Went back with him to 151, and walked back here at 9:20. Raining, soaking wet, dark and foggy.

Still no peep, but probably wouldn't use one if I did have it.

About the only exciting thing happening around here is that some fellows are going on rotation and furlough. Fred Trompeter is going on rotation. He is older and has a family. And 1st Sgt. Pete Rettinger is going on furlough for 30 days.

Thursday, November 2, 1944   Slept until late. Raining all night and part of today.

Had to go to the 151 this afternoon. Got soaked nearly to my waist. Tiresome walk, muddy and slippery. Three steep hills to climb. Back at 5:00, and nearly had to go out again.

Got a Sunday paper yesterday, and 3 letters from Mom and two from Ray. Sky is clear tonight, but dark, except for a few beams of artificial moonlight.

Dick has been gone since last night — can't get across the river. Reb's 1X1 is 100 yards from here.

In my letter home of November 2, I asked for them to send me a pair of chopper mitts, a used pair I had left at home. I made an official request for them that was stamped on the letter, so they could show it to the Post Office. The gloves the Army issued were almost worthless when driving.

Friday, November 3, 1944   Wrote home last night and read a little.

Left for the 151 at 7:30. Back by 11:00. Walked both ways. Raining on the way back, and still no peep.

Cleaned up and shaved. The sun shined for an hour. Threw out a few of my things. Read *The Farmer* and *Sign of the Times*. Wrote to Ray.

Not much action worth mentioning, just enough juggling around with reports and personnel to remind us we are still in action. Funny they haven't sent out a training schedule yet.

Saturday, November 4, 1944   Reb took me back to Service Battery. Still no peep. Herb let me use a homemade stove.

Most of the battery moved to the top of the hill in other buildings. Reb and I moved in with Nate Levy and Lieberman. Dick and Hambright are here too; it's a fairly big house with a good-sized room. Pretty safe and warm. We expect to be holed up here for awhile. A lady lives in another room, and other people in another part of the house. We have to go through the room where the lady lives to get to our room.

We got the stove hooked up today, and picked up some junk to burn in it.

Sunday, November 5, 1944   Got up at 6:30. Left for 151 at 7:00. Got a ride back with Budinger to here.

Slept a little this p.m. Came here on the mountain at 2:30 to read my Testament and write this up.

Supper at 4:15, and it's 4:45 now. Fried chicken tonight. Steak last night.

Cut some wood for the stove. The Mess Sergeant came in here to write a letter. I wrote to Ethel Nash and Aunt Rose. Cold, but clear tonight. A beautiful day, sunshine and warm. Dried considerably.

Monday, November 6, 1944   Went with Dick to the Air O.P. this morning, but it took until 3:00 before we got back. A cold, miserable ride.

Walked to the outfit and back tonight. It's hard to believe I'm in Italy fighting a war when I have to walk across the hills to the 151 — I might as well be at home walking, for all the good it seems we're accomplishing here.

This Winter Line will be pretty long — I hope nobody on either side wants to do more than just hold it.

Tuesday, November 7, 1944   Election Day at home, but the usual around here. Got 12 letters from Mom and Ray.

Wednesday, November 8, 1944   Roosevelt is voted back as President.

To the outfit twice last night. Stayed there the 2nd time. When I got there, Barney said, "Maj. Thomas wants to talk to you."

I called him on the switchboard and reported, "Cpl. Wagner reporting, Sir."

He said, "Wag, you go to the Supply Sergeant, draw some blankets and stay with Message Center tonight. Go back to Division Artillery in the morning."

I said "Thank you, Sir," and really meant it. I even got some dry socks, got a good night's rest, a good breakfast in the morning, and had a chance to see a lot of old friends again.

Thursday, November 9, 1944   Sick, cold, chills, tired.

Friday, November 10, 1944   It snowed last night. Most of it melted today. Walked to the outfit and back. Not feeling good. Went to bed early.

Saturday, November 11, 1944   In bed until 8:00, probably because of the grapes I ate in the field yesterday. Artillery fire still going out.

On the way back today from the 151, as I was coming up the steepest hill, still finding a few grapes — all at once, BAM! — a shell came in about 170 yards to my right. I dropped and started rolling down the hill, when another one came into my left. I kept on rolling down to the bottom, got behind some rocks and debris and laid there catching my breath. Two more shells came in about in the middle of where I'd been rolling, but farther up the hill.

It wasn't hard to figure out what had happened: I was under observation, and didn't realize it until almost too late.

There weren't many more grapes to glean, so after that whenever I walked to the outfit, I followed the creek and the caves along the bottom of the mountain's edge. One real foggy day when I wasn't worried about being observed, I went to check how close the shells had come to me. One wasn't farther than several hundred feet away, with shrapnel landing probably 10 feet from where I'd been.

The explosion of a shell was frequently followed by the crack of a joke,
and a bullet or a bayonet produced more fun than fear,
yet neither were ever so close that they left no time for a prayer.
Washington Davis

Sunday, November 12, 1944   Walked to the battalion after dinner. Finally got a peep. It's the one the line guards had. It's in better shape than the old one, but wish I could have got the new one that was issued for my position.

Monday, November 13, 1944   Went to the battalion this morning. Didn't do much more of anything. To the outfit 2 times tonight.

I probably drove instead of walking, if the roads were fit to drive on.

Tuesday, November 14, 1944   Got 2 Christmas boxes today, mostly something to eat: cheese, sardines.
Took Joe to the 109th. Ted Shove is taking his place.
To the outfit. Wrote home and to Ray.

My letter home of November 14 told of my stopping at the doughnut machine for 4 doughnuts and all the coffee I wanted. I also thanked them for the packages they'd sent, and said I always kept some of it for occasions when I missed a meal and that I gave some of the candy to the 3 smaller kids living in this house we were staying in.

Wednesday, November 15, 1944   Rained a little last night and this forenoon. The sun came out this p.m. We carried up wood for our stove. Took Maj. Smith to II Corps. Back at 4:30.
Our room is very comfortable. The war is still being fought. We're just south of Bologna on 65.
To the battalion tonight. Back about 7:00. Gets dark at 6:00. Beautiful day.

Thursday, November 16, 1944   Went to the battalion this morning. Cleaned the peep out a bit, and took off the chains.
By this p.m. Reb and I had a gas stove made. [It was all Reb's idea.] Several pipes and a valve welded together. Works fine. More heat and less work than wood.
To the battalion tonight. On the way back, two 91st peeps smashed together head-on. One lieutenant was hurt quite badly, and several others. One fellow stayed behind. I helped him get the peeps off the road. Neither would run, and they were badly damaged.
Back at 7:30. We had a lunch before going to bed. Ham got a case of 10-15.

Friday, November 17, 1944   Up at 7:00. Usually eat inside here.

Shaved, washed.

Went to the 91st. Fixed the horn on my peep. Sewed a blanket to make a seat pad. Beautiful day.

To the battalion tonight. Tony Sermguard came back from school tonight — we kept him here overnight.

November was a very uneventful month as far as 151st war history goes. The 133rd Infantry was relieved by the 135th Infantry, the 133rd going to the Montocatini rest area.

Our battalion was in general support, but we were under the command of the 91st Division.

Officers were going to Rome for rest periods.

Saturday, November 18, 1944   Up at 7:00. Took Tony back to the 151. Cleaned up. Worked a little on my peep this p.m. To the outfit again tonight. Back about 7:00. Warm weather — hope it lasts.

Sunday, November 19, 1944   Another beautiful day, but didn't do much of anything. To the outfit tonight.

A letter from Bill. Answered it, and wrote to his wife and home. Put an electric light in here and are very comfortable.

Monday, November 20, 1944   Went to the outfit this morning, then to 91st Division Artillery. Cleaned the motor on my peep. This p.m. greased it too. Took a shower, changed clothes.

To the outfit after supper. Jerry had just thrown in shells at Headquarters before I got there. One young Italian boy was hurt badly, and not expected to live. On my way back, more shells came in. Pieces fell close to me — I got in under the peep, and took off in a hurry during a lull in the shelling. I stopped at the medics awhile to catch my breath. Fellows from B Battery were coming down. One was hurt, as shells landed in their area. Back here at 7:00.

Thankful I'm still alive after many close ones. Only God's protection has made that possible.

Moonlight. An awful lot of infantry moving up and down. 91st Division, I guess.

Tuesday, November 21, 1944   Went to the battalion this morning, and again tonight. Comparatively quiet to yesterday.

I went back to San Beneddetto today after laundry I had left there over a month ago. The lady still remembered me, and felt sorry because I was going back to the front.

Nov-15 Wends Rained a little
last night and this forenoon.
Sun come out this P.M. We
carried up wood for our stove.
Took Mjr. Smith to IV Corps.
Back at 4:30. Our room is
very comfortable. The war is
still being fought. We are still
just south of Bologna on 65.
Nov 16 Thurs. To the Bn. tonite
back about 7:00 gets dark at 6:00
Nov 16 Thurs Beautifull day.
Went to the Bn. this morning.
Cleaned the peep out a bit, took
off the chains. This P.M. Reb
and I had a gas stove made,
several pipes and a valve
welded together. Works fine,
more heat and less work
than wood. To the Bn. tonite.
On way back 2 91st peeps
smashed together, head on, one
At burnt quite badly, several
others, one fellow stayed
behind, I helped him, got the
peeps off the road, both
wouldn't run and were
badly damaged. Back at 7:30
we had a lunch before going
to bed. Ham got a case of AV
10-15.
Nov 17 Fri up at 7:00 usually
eat inside here. shaved, washed
went to 91st fixed the horn
on my peep. Sewed a blanket
for seat pad. Beautifull day.
To the Bn. Tonite. Tony Scrimguard

came back from school tonite.
kept him here over night.
Nov 18 Sat. up at 7:00. Took Tony back
to the 151. Cleaned up. Worked a
little on my peep this P.M. To the
outfit again tonite. Back about 7:00.
Warm weather hope it lasts.
Nov 19 Sun Another beautifull day but didn't
do much of anything. To the outfit
tonite. A letter from Bill. Answered
it, wrote to his wife and home. Put
an electric like in here. Are very
comfortable.
Nov 20 1902. Went to the outfit this
morning, then to 91st. Div. Arty. Cleaned
the motor on my peep. This P.M.
greased it. Took a shower, changed clothes.
To the outfit after supper. Jerry had
Just thrown in shells at the before
I got there, one Italian hurt badly,
not expected to live. On my back
more came in, pieces fell close
to me I got in under the peep.
Took off in a hurry during a lull
in the shelling. Stopped at
the medics for awhile to get
my breath, fellows from B Btry.
were coming down, one hurt, shells
landed in there area. Back here
about 7:30. Thankful I'm still
alive after many close ones.
Only Gods protection has made that
possible. Moonlite. An awful
lot of Infantry moving up and
down - 91st I guess.
Nov 21 Tues went to the Bn. this
morning and again tonite. Comparitively
quiet in comparison to   1944

Stopped twice at the doughnut machine, and at Service Battery to have the transfer case fixed.

Wednesday, November 22, 1944   Started for the battalion. Got almost to Livergeno when the transmission went to pieces. Left the peep sit and thumbed to the battery. Decker came along with his 6X6 and towed me to Service. No shells, fortunately, while getting it hooked up. Hitchhiked back here.

Cleaned up; luckily I didn't have to go out, as I would have had to walk.

It was the young Italian boy's funeral today. I didn't see it, but fellows said his dad had made a casket, and he was carried on the men's shoulders. Their home was a part of what the 151st took over as C.P. and Message Center.

Our shooting has simmered down to almost nothing. It's 15 rounds per gun per day, plus 10% smoke, so we are not shooting much.

The 133rd Infantry is back in the lines again. We are in direct support, taking over from the 91st Division. Highway 65 is now in our sector, with Bologna at the far end.

Thursday, November 23, 1944   Woke up early with a little headache. Laid in bed and recalled how I spent other Thanksgivings. Probably the happiest, and one that will live long in my memory was at Payne in 1940 when the folks; Pa and Ma, Rod, Arlene and Dick came up there with a dinner Mother had cooked. Took Mom and the kids out to the car when they left, with Bird pulling the sleigh.

Cleaned up this room, carried in water like I do nearly every morning. Shells came in last night, but not in our area.

Got 2 letters, from Mom and Ruth Eliason, and *Time* magazine.

We had our dinner at 2:00, which consisted of turkey, potatoes, dressing and cherry pie. Good, but not exceptionally so, though I am thankful to have had that much. The fellows put up a hospital tent with tables where we ate. Some fellows gave a little entertainment after dinner. A few acts, songs and music.

Didn't go to the battalion. Cloudy and dreary all day, a big contrast from a year ago.

The present offensive in France looks encouraging; French troops have crossed the Rhine and captured Mulhouse.

November 24th to December 2, 1944   [I spent the time at the rest center in Montocatini. It was relaxing, but wasn't very interesing, and I didn't even have a notebook with me for notes. It was in between Florence and Pisa.]

Sunday, December 3, 1944   Had to make 2 trips last night. Back about 11:00. Had a package, a letter from Ray and 2 from Mom. Up at 7:00 this morning. Tried to clean up my peep. It rained while I was gone, and everything is mud again. Cleaned up and shaved.

The old nervous tension grips a fellow as he hits the line again. Quite a few shells coming in while I was at the battery. To the battalion tonight, or late this p.m. actually. Another package from Aunt Myrtle.

Monday, December 4, 1944   Cleaned up our room. Nate came back to stay. Had to take Maj. Lind to the 120th and 151st, where he stayed. Back at 4:00.

Lost the oil plug out of the peep. Had to borrow Dick's and went to the outfit. Back about 8:00.

Tuesday, December 5, 1944   Hitchhiked to Service Battery and got another oil plug. Back at 11:00 and put it in. Crankcase seems OK. A package from Ray last night. Rained a little, and the sun shone.

Got caught in a shelling last night up Highway 65 where I turn off. One fellow still lying there hurt. Three were hurt, and a peep hit.

The fellows came back today who went on furlough in July: Col. DuBois, Sgt. Molde, Hogfuss, G. Sefscik and Meagher. I had to get Col. DuBois from Division. It took about 3 hours. Back here at dark.

Benny Turner stayed here with us. Nate and I had a little lunch. I wrote to Ray and home.

It was kind of nice to get the colonel back. He wasn't very talkative, and I would rarely say anything to him except in answer.

One of the things he did say when we got close up to the front and could hear some shells going out was, "I think I sort of like being back, and I sure like to hear those 105's crack."

Wednesday, December 6, 1944   Up at 7:00. Took the colonel, Nate and Benny to the battalion. Talked to some of the boys. Meagher had lots of excuses for not calling the folks. Back at noon, and out again with another special. Back at 4:00, then out tonight with more "hot stuff." Raining and foggy. Got stuck once. One of the blackest nights I've ever driven in.

Changed clothes, washed. 3 packages today: a 2 lb. box of Fannie Farmers from Alvin and Germaine, a jar of dill pickles, a can of corn and one of chicken from home.

Maj. Everett Thomas went back to the States with 36 months spent overseas. He was one of my favorite officers, a good, smart, fearless soldier officer.

1st Sgt. Barnard moved up to Headquarters Battery from Service to take Sgt. Rettinger's place while he was on furlough to the States.

Thursday, December 7, 1944   Up at 7:00. To the outfit this morning. Foggy and cold enough. Got stuck, drowned out and stalled the peep. Had a hard job to get back, and didn't until noon.

Got the carburetor fixed, and had a few hours off until supper time, then to the outfit again. Back at 8:00.

Got a package from Hulda Mehling: cookies, jam, candy.

Made a lunch from leftover coffee, bread, dill pickles and Limburger cheese.

The Krauts still throw in shells every night after supper. Lucky none have come too close to me lately. The roads are awful bad again, practically impassible. Both vehicles and passengers take terrific beatings.

Remember well Pearl Harbor 3 years ago today at Camp Claiborne on Sunday.

This entry reminds me of how some of the Italian ladies would come to the kitchen and ask for the used coffee grounds. They would bring cooked spaghetti in return.

Friday, December 8, 1944   Rained hard all day. Walked to the outfit tonight. Some real deep mud to go through, and then following the cliff-side of the hill, it wasn't too bad.

Some shells were coming in again, so I got permission to stay the night at Message Center. It's better than walking back to Division Artillery on bad nights. Many nights my legs or feet never dry out.

Tom McGee came back now, after he was wounded at Monzuno. He's healed up again. Tom reports that Sgt. Anderson, who lost a kidney, will be going back to the States. We are glad to hear he is going to be OK and is feeling much better. Tom has written a letter of condolence to Ernie Rose's folks, expressing all our sympathy.

Saturday, December 9, 1944   I started at 7 a.m. Walked to C Battery. Took a C and R from there to Division Artillery. Still raining a little. Had to go to Service Battery from here with a message. Back at noon. Still raining a little.

Got a letter from home last night; answered it.

Had to go out tonight. Left at 5:00. Got stuck at C Battery, left the peep there. Walked to Headquarters. Division Artillery had called and said there was a special waiting, so I borrowed a command car and took it as far as Charlie Battery. Then took my peep back here.

Shells coming in. I crawled under the command car.

Lt. Ryan went out on Command Liaison with 135th Infantry, and Lt. Brandage went over to the 125th Field Artillery Battalion during the first days of the month. This was the start of a great deal of regrouping which went on during the month.

Sunday, December 10, 1944   Up at 6:15. Left at 6:45, to the outfit at 7:00. During this time both the 151st and 185th were shelled. I was in between all of it. One 210 shell killed 4 boys from the 185th, and wounded another seriously. This south of Bologna is as bad as another Anzio — only we could retreat here, if necessary. Got back at 11:00.

Took my peep to Service. Motor mounts are broken, and I had to leave it there. Came back with the ration truck. Reb came in tonight, so I didn't have to go out.

A big air raid tonight. Some bombs dropped, but not close. A big barrage coming in right after dark all through the valley.

Washed, filled up the stoves with gas. Didn't realize it was Sunday until I saw Catholic Mass being held in a field.

Monday, December 11, 1944   Went after my peep. Got a ride with Reb. Had to wait until they fixed it, as a motor mount was broken.

To the battalion tonight. Hard going.

Tuesday, December 12, 1944   Foggy all day. Dave used my peep this p.m. so I had to use his tonight. Got stuck, drowned out, and went off the wooden bridge. Got a weapons carrier to pull me out.

Back at 8:30. It was foggy and dark. I had to drive by instinct. I picked up several fellows who couldn't imagine how I could see to drive. I had to agree with them that I couldn't.

Wrote home and to Peggy.

Wednesday, December 13, 1944   Raining, cloudy, foggy all day. Cleaned up. Put another chain on the peep to replace the one Dave lost.

Germans threw in a tremendous barrage into the valley around supper time.

I didn't go out, as there was nothing really important, but I suppose I should have went anyway.

Zimmerman and I carried up his radio into here today. I enjoy it to a certain extent.

Five years ago today, Ray and I were working on our first log shack at Payne. He is 27 today.

Nate came back. He was at the 151 for about a week.

We still enjoy the same big room here for over a month, still pretty safe and warm with the gas fire. I suppose this gas fire is a little dangerous, but the heat is really something when you are wet and muddy from the knees down. We have the gas spigot just dripping gas into the stove when it is lit. If someone would turn it on too fast, we would soon have quite a blaze in here. There have been quite a few different fellows staying in here too, some just overnight on their ways back to their outfits.

Thursday, December 14, 1944   Rained quite hard. Leaked a lot in here, and I had to move my bed. Up at 7:00. Had to take Maj. Williamson and Lt. Adams to Air O.P.

It snowed around Loiano and farther back last night. Got there to Faizengola at 11:00. Had a flat. Tony helped me fix it. Had another flat before I left. Exchanged spares with Tommy on my way back.

Just missed a shelling at Loiano. I heard it come in. Two were killed; the back of a 6X6 was filled with blood and discarded equipment. A gruesome sight. I wonder how long my nerves will stand up, and my sanity.

Back at 5:00. Didn't go to the battalion as my peep is on the blink. I lost the muffler, and the piston rods are knocking.

Friday, December 15, 1944   Went to Service Battery early this morning. They worked on the peep all day and are still not through.

Shells coming in all over around Highway 65.

To the battalion tonight. Got stuck, and a 6X6 pushed me out. Back at 8:30.

A package from home. Dill pickles, corn on the cob — and a tasty big fruitcake.

Saturday, December 16, 1944   Up at 7:00. Started for Service Battery, but was misting, so came back.

Cleaned up. I am glad for this room. Real comfortable in here.

To the battalion tonight. Got an early start, but got stuck on the way in, so it was almost as late as usual. Made it out by myself this time.

Sunday, December 17, 1944   Went to Service Battery today. They worked on the peep until 1 p.m. Finished the muffler. To the outfit tonight, raining a little.

Five packages, 3 from Mom, 2 from Aunt Rose. Pickled herring, chicken, corn on the cob, honey nuts.

The Mess Sergeant from Division Artillery was in here when I came back. We always have a good snack before we go to bed from packages from home.

Haven't had any sign of a chaplain for some time again.

Monday, December 18, 1944   Cleaned up the room, shaved. Dick and I walked after our laundry below the hill where I used to walk. They seem like they are a nice family; one girl is all the children I've seen there. To the battalion tonight. I managed to drive in and out, but just so.

My letter home of December 18 told them that when I got back the other night, supper was already over. Arky Vaughn, Mess Sergeant again, was in our room, though; so he went to the kitchen and got bread and butter. I used the can of chicken that I had from a package from home, and we had chicken sandwiches.

I said I had lots of clothes now, and that this one lady always washed mine in cold water, and they were as clean as any washed in hot.

Tuesday, December 19, 1944   Cloudy and foggy all day. Took Currie to the 109th Medics. On the way back I rammed into a 6X6 and broke the front tire chain, and bent the muffler, hood and radiator protector.

To the outfit tonight. Only went as far as C Battery. Reb came that far with a command car.

Wednesday, December 20, 1944   Didn't do much of anything until tonight, then went to the battalion. The bulldozer had worked the road. I tried to drive all the way, but got stuck and had to have Hill get me out. While doing it, he wrecked the radiator on my peep. It took 10 gallons of water to get back here.

Thursday, December 21, 1944   Took my peep to Service. Roads are terrible, even #65. Had to leave the peep there and hitchhike back.

Walked to the battalion tonight. Took almost 4 hours both ways. Had a mail bag half full of junk to carry. The trail is very muddy; it was hard walking. I'm completely tired out, or to put it another way, I'm completely out of horsepower tonight.

Friday, December 22, 1944 Cleaned up, shaved, read a little, played some cribbage.

To the outfit again tonight. Walked. A beautiful night, moonlight and crisp. The ground is slightly frozen in spots, so it carries you.

Got a letter from Peggy, several from home. 6 packages, but I couldn't carry them.

A bunch of guys are in here tonight that are rowdy.

Saturday, December 23, 1944 Did nothing much today except read and walk to the battalion tonight.

Sunday, December 24, 1944 It has snowed about 8 inches. Dry snow. The ground is frozen fairly hard. I took Reb's peep and went to the highway. I met Ceedsma; he brought mail for me. I got 12 packages: 9 from home, 2 from Lavonne and 1 from Margaret Kajikawa. Opened them up this p.m. All were something to eat.

Walked to the battalion tonight. Hard walking, but I enjoyed it.

Christmas Eve. I try to realize the significance of it. The war, however, is still going on as usual, though it's quiet on both sides of the line tonight. An attack is planned to come off soon.

Back at 7:30. Had a can of beer, some herring and potato chips, and a little gin. The radio is on, but no carols as yet. A letter from Peggy the other day. Some fellows are in here besides the regulars tonight.

Another thing a lot of us have tonight is that personal, secret nostalgic feeling, which tends to make you clam up, and you just want to go to your sack with the lights out and just think.

All had our annual shots for typhoid and typhus at this time, including the Italians who are living in the battalion C.P. (this is our big building), and including the lady here and others we see every day.

Just a few days ago Col. DuBois was sent to the hospital with high blood pressure and ordered to have rest.

Last week we had another bad Cub Airplane wreck, the 3rd plane we have lost now. On takeoff, they couldn't clear soon enough. The plane was a total wreck, but Lt.'s Kovacs and Ziegler weren't hurt. Many times these Air O.P. pilots really have to push their luck on takeoffs and landings, besides having to fly within range of small arms and mortar fire while they're in the air. Lt. Ziegler told me once, "The only exercise we get now is pushing our luck."

I'm not the only one lately who is "hard on the horses," as Pete Jurgenson always complains I am. They've had a lot of trouble maintaining the ¾ ton weapons carriers and the ¾ ton command cars too, mostly with the differentials and transmissions. They should consider that they're higher than the ¼ ton peeps too, and don't hang up as much in the mud. Even more important than that, most of them don't have to be on the road every day.

Especially here where we stayed several months during the time the Germans were holding the Winter Line, some of the vehicles didn't have to move at all. But even a few years after the war was over when I attended a reunion of the 34th Division in Minneapolis, and I walked up to one of the guys from Service Battery and asked him if he remembered me -- he gave me a short look and said, "Wag, you were a hard man on equipment."

Monday, December 25, 1944   Breakfast at 8:00 this morning. Cleaned up, shaved. Quite cold with 2 or 3 inches of snow on the ground. The guns are almost quiet this morning. Hope they stay that way. I wrote to Peggy and others.

Dinner at 2:00. It was "tops," with everything that we probably would have had at home.

Walked to the battalion tonight. A beautiful crystal-clear night, cool and brisk, with snow still on the ground. For an instant, I was at home tobogganing, or walking to Payne after the mail on similar nights.

George, Greene, Dick and Burt Forstead were in here awhile. All are very good singers; they were singing carols.

My letter home on Christmas told of me walking cross-country once a day to the battalion and of our afternoon big dinner. One of my chopper mitts with liner had arrived. I mentioned the three inches of snow and that we had a radio and Christmas music. Most letter were marked "Free Mail" in the corner where the stamp would usually go.

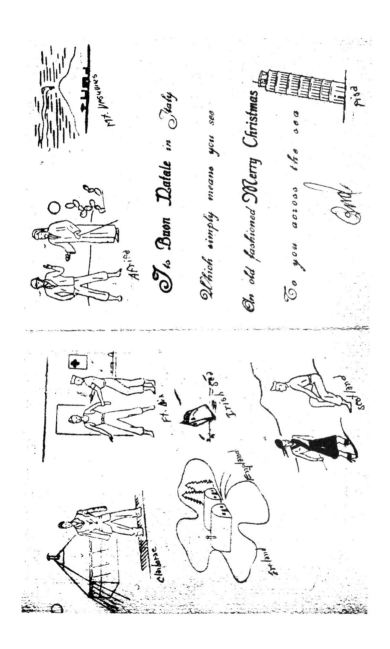

CHAPTER 28

Getting ready to push. Still walking. Borrowed peep.
In "the Hole." Attached to 91st Division and 88th Division.
Peep still broke. Close call on the road.
Chopper mitt arrives in spring. Appropriated peep.

Tuesday, December 26, 1944   All of us overslept until 8:30. Had my teeth cleaned by Capt. Legum. Have to get 5 pulled. Had one pulled. He did a good job, but my jaw has been mighty sore all day.

Didn't go to the outfit today. Reb came in today and took all the hot items with. He also brought 2 more packages, from Uncle Art and Hulda Mehling.

Nate came back tonight from Division rear. We had a lunch together.

Another beautiful night. On a night such as this one in 1938, Al, Germaine, Evelyn and I were sliding on the toboggan.

Wednesday, December 27, 1944   My tooth ached all night and most of the day. Had the dentist clean it out, which helped some.

Walked to the battalion tonight. Got a new combat jacket from Prill. Back at 7:30.

Barney had been drinking and took 18 eggs from the kitchen. I fried them with the bacon we had left. Had a lot of fun.

Thursday, December 28, 1944   My tooth extraction still pains a lot. Legum called it a "dry socket."

Joe and I went below the hill with a weapons carrier and got the trailer up to here. Cleaned up my things again this afternoon. Consolidated a lot of things together, and throwed away. We hear of a push coming up, and I've got to be able to move quick.

Reb went to Florence on pass. A fellow named Nix is taking his place. Shells have been coming in more often of late. Walked to the battalion.

If this walking business doesn't stop pretty soon, I'd be almost better off in the infantry. Well, not really; I can still count my blessings with this job, but I really hired out to be a motor messenger. "Either drive it, or park it," is my motto — it's parked.

Friday, December 29, 1944   Got my peep back from Service tonight. It's still in a mess. To the battalion tonight.

Bob Engelson said, "Hey Wag, why don't they give you agents a weapons carrier or command car?" Well that would have been sensible for the past 2 months, at least, but when it's dry I can and have to run circles around the bigger vehicles. The closer I am to the ground, the better I can see to "move it."

Saturday, December 30, 1944   Took the peep to Service, then to Ordnance. Snowstorm and cold. Difficult driving. Got a ride back with Rieman. Walked to the battalion tonight, borrowed a peep and drove back.

Our stove still keeps the big room warm. Hasn't exploded yet. Nobody thinks it's dangerous. It has a steady drumming, and we never turn if off — only down or up just a hair at a time.

Sunday, December 31, 1944   Good thing I was ready to move. Division Artillery moved back for a rest — all except Dick and I, because the 175th and 151st are now attached to the 91st Division.

Our outfit is in what I call "the Hole." Now they are close together, close to Loiano. I found a vacant spot in this old house in the attic, next to the survey crew. All alone, and it's chilly, but what peace and a pleasure to be here.

They temporarily gave me Adler's peep with only 206 miles on it. Only 206 miles on it, and they got it in for my use several months ago. Well, at least I have it for now.

The white Christmas was nice. A young Italian boy was killed, though, while our battalion was in the Hole. I was there when they were having his funeral. It seemed like it was something like a funeral they would have had during the Gold Rush, or on the covered wagon trips heading West. Very few people could attend; there were no military there, except for me.

Our one casualty of the month was our Capt. Crellin, who was severely burned by scalding water from a water can he was boiling on the stove in his tent. Pvt. Lanquist was burned too, but didn't have to go to the hospital.

Maj. Grant was attached to the 185th F.A. Battalion, but he came to us when Col. DuBois was in the hospital.

Figures showed that in December we expended 4728 rounds, of which 2108 were propaganda. We said that all that white stuff in the Kraut's area was not snow, but paper.

It was really rough to leave our nice quarters where we had been over two months, but I was glad to get rid of my daily walking exercise through the place where I almost had to stop a shell.

The big push to the north was called off due to enemy activities on other fronts. We didn't register until on the last day of the month, when we went under control of the 91st Division. We were in general support of the 916th F.A. Battalion.

Lt. Brundage who had been doing O.P. liaison work with the 125th F.A. Battalion and the 916th F.A. Battalion, was now our Liaison Officer at 91st Division Command Post.

Monday, January 1, 1945 Up at 8:30. Good breakfast. Ate it outside. The fellows are very sociable, but I want to ease into them slowly.

Went to the battalion and Service. Got the brakes adjusted. Back here at 12:30.

The big turkey dinner at 2:30. Very good.

Dick and I went out together tonight. Our outfits are within a mile apart. Back about 6:30. Had coffee and pie. Played 4 handed cribbage until 9:30. Read about half of Best's *Young One.*

A lot of the fellows from the 91st Division Artillery besides the four agents are in this sort of walk-in basement. They seem different than what I'm used to, somehow — then, I'm finding out they haven't been overseas long and haven't seen that much combat. Bernie Mariano is one agent from Michigan. His folks have a tavern there. The fellows are really sociable.

Tuesday, January 2, 1945 Up at 7:30. Eat my chow and spend nearly all my time with Dick and the other agents. They are from the 916th, 346th, 347th and 348th Field Artillery Battalions.

I went back to our last position this p.m. and got my laundry.

Dick and I went out together again tonight. Stopped at the 185th on the way back. Air bursts were coming in at Loiano last night, but quiet tonight.

Wednesday, January 3, 1945 Didn't do much today. Read a little.

Dick and I went out tonight. Everything quiet tonight, but this p.m. a shell landed real close to the C.P. here and threw shrapnel all around.

The Krauts fired a New Year's greeting this year. Their flash was picked up by "now our" 91st Command Post. They registered one of Able Battery's guns of the 348th Field Artillery and had good effect.

The first few days all batteries were registering and changing positions.

The gun crews were getting orders now to shoot the new shell with the adjustable fuse. Baker Battery was the first to shoot with the new fuse, but soon all were using it.

News of the Battle of the Bulge was reaching us. The men there were in much colder winter weather than we were. Germany did take our forces by surprise, but the Allies were regrouping. When the Germans asked some to surrender, the famous answer was "Nuts." Our ground forces and the Allied Air Force were beginning to shake off the offensive.

Thursday, January 4, 1945   Pretty cold last night, but I have enough covering. Beautiful day, though not too warm. Cleaned up, wrote a few letters. To the battalion tonight with Dick.

Friday, January 5, 1945   Had to go to the battalion this morning. Was snowing, so I put the top up. Dick and I had to go out with a special this p.m. Still snowing. Didn't have to go out tonight.

Went in with the survey crew tonight and wrote a letter to Ray and Megs Kajikawa. Four of us played cribbage: Dean, Al, another fellow and me.

The fellows have an Italian boy with them (an orphan). Dean was a school teacher in civilian life, and is teaching him English. The Italian boy was trying to understand the difference between "melt" and "thaw." Dean can speak some Italian, and he told him you can either melt or thaw a piece of ice, but you can only melt a candle, not thaw one. The boy kind of nodded his head in understanding.

Saturday, January 6, 1945   Up at 7:00. French toast for breakfast. Still snowing, and sort of warm, which makes it sloppy. Dick helped me put my chains on. It snowed all day.

Wrote to Art, Germaine, Mary Jean, Lavonne and Hulda. We didn't have to go out tonight, still snowing like heck.

Our position is much higher here and on the side of a mountain. Road is fair — on a bad curve, though. The building we are in could have been an inn or restaurant at one time. My spot up above the whole place wouldn't give me any protection in a direct hit, but then I don't like the bottom part of a concrete building either.

I just like being alone at night. To keep off the chill, I have extra shelter halves in the peep that I use for extra blankets. Am reading through the New Testament.

Sunday, January 7, 1945   Still snowing this morning. My peep was about covered with snow, with about 6 - 7 inches on the ground. I tried to shovel it out, but not much success.

Dick and I went out tonight, or late this p.m. Back in time for supper. No mail.

My peep came back home. Louie Day was fixing it a little bit more.

There were church services tonight in Officers' Mess. Very good. Was on the observance of the Sabbath and on humility.

Wrote to Jean and Bob.

It stopped snowing and started turning colder. A snowplow was on the road today.

Bob Vaughn had been sent to the States on rotation.

Monday, January 8, 1945   Didn't clear up until noon, but then it started to snow again. Wrote to Aunt Anna, Cookes, Arlene and Robert.

Dick and I went out before supper. It started to snow just about when we started, and was really a blizzard before we came back. It has turned quite cold by tonight.

Luckily, few shells have come in since we've been here.

Tuesday, January 9, 1945   Still snowing this morning, but it cleared up a bit. Snow on the ground, about 8 inches.

Dick and I went to our last position after laundry. The wire and radio crew are still there. We started out with my peep, but it stalled, so we took Dick's.

Got a V-mail from Ruth Eliason. Had a bad stomach for the past several days.

Wednesday, January 10, 1945   Snowing just a little, but cleared up. Finally got my peep started after sucking and blowing out the gas lines. It was real cold last night and today.

Two Red Cross girls were here with doughnuts this noon.

Dick and I went out tonight to both battalions. I still have Adler's peep. Mine came back from Ordnance, but it still had a cracked frame, so it went right back there again. This is getting to be ridiculous. Those fellows back there should know a little more than they do about mechanical work by this time.

Thursday, January 11, 1945   Up at 7:30. As usual, Joe couldn't start his peep, so I towed him with mine. Cleaned up in the morning, shaved and washed. Helped chop wood this p.m. and carried it in. I got a new cot-canvas, a pair of gloves and a hood from Dengler.

Dick and I went out again tonight. Two shells came pretty close to Dick and me tonight. Still remains cold.

Friday, January 12, 1945　　As usual this forenoon. Put the new canvas on my cot. Slept a little this p.m.

Dick and I went out tonight. We were surprised to see just how close the shells came to him and me last night. I had stopped to light a cigarette, or otherwise we probably would have run into the fragments. The hand of God has guided us through this war.

Wrote to Bill and home.

The above occurrence was probably my second-closest call of the war. We had dropped off the special at Dick's outfit, and had just left my outfit on our way back, when one of us suggested we stop and roll a cigarette.

I stopped and got out the little sack of rolling tobacco and papers, and I'll never know if I finished rolling my cigarette or not. Just then a shell landed up the road in just about the spot we would have been if we hadn't stopped. Before either one of us had time to think, another shell came in about the same spot. By this time Dick was already hanging on to the peep, and we were taking off under full horsepower. The road was frozen, and when a shell lands on frozen ground it spatters, so I wasn't afraid of that much of a hole. We didn't let any grass grow under our peep that time.

There was no third shell "for effect," as there would have been if we were under observation. Evidently we were almost hit by the common "harassing fire" used by both sides. The only casualty was a sack of roll-your-own tobacco and a package of cigarette papers spilt over the front seats. Some pieces of shrapnel scratched the front of the peep.

After we got out of the Army, whenever Dick would write me, he'd start out his letter with "Hurrah for Cigs!" though both of us quit smoking shortly after getting out.

Ed Dengler, my tent-mate during most of the African Campaign and a steady K.P. for years, was promoted to Supply helper. It was good to see him in there. It was a better job, and he could really be counted on to be fair and to keep things in order. I was never in want for clothing, as I could check out clothes that I needed either at the 151st Field Artillery or at Division Artillery.

Saturday, January 13, 1945　　About the usual thing all day. Still with the 91st Division Artillery.

Sunday, January 14, 1945　　Got a letter from Mary Jean and from Mom.

We went to church here. Another good sermon, "Judgment Day

and the Resurrection." Matthew 25.

Dick and I went out tonight. Snowing and sleeting, and hard driving.

Monday, January 15, 1945   Clear as a bell today. Jerry is throwing in plenty of shells in back of us. Took a sponge bath and changed clothes.

Three years ago last night we loaded on the HMS *Strathaird*, and set sail early in the morning. Little did I realize it would be this long. I will never forget my personal feelings at that time.

Dick and I went out again tonight. No problems.

In my letter to home I thanked them for sending my brother Roger's and sister Arlene's school report cards for me to see, and I told them I'd be sending them back again.

A few years ago, after I'd had a rough draft of my diary typed up, I let Dick Johnson take a copy home with him to Buffalo Lake, Minnesota. His wife Mae read it, and her first question to him was, "Where did you and Bud always go when you 'went out together at night?' Was it to shows or parties?"

Dick told her with his special type of humor, "We enjoyed going out together so much that some nights we'd go out two and three times a night."

Dick was in the 175th Field Artillery when Africa was invaded in November of 1942. Tom McGee was with us both at Salerno, and we were all three together through most of Italy. Whenever we would come to Message Center, we'd kid each other about "invasion tactics," "results," and other things. It was always interesting, sometimes humorous, and it livened up the day or evening.

Tom used to say to me every time I got near him, "Wag, you've been eating garlic again." I really did eat my share of it. One of my favorite snacks was a C ration hard biscuit, some bacon grease, salt and sliced garlic, all washed down with cold soluble coffee.

On January 15th, Able Battery's second section gun blew up. Luckily, no one was injured, due perhaps to the fact that the tube exploded forward on the locking ring. The cause of the explosion wasn't determined, but it couldn't have been a premature burst, something that was always in the soldiers' minds when artillery was firing over them.

Several days later, Col. DuBois came back from the hospital, and Maj. Grant went back to the 185th. Capt. Crellin came back a few days later from the hospital recovered from the hot water burns.

Tuesday, January 16, 1945   Cloudy all day. Did nothing much except to read, write letters, talk and play cribbage. Nothing to go out for tonight.

Wednesday, January 17, 1945   Clear again. Got quite a few letters and Christmas cards from home, Ray and Peggy.

Germans shelled Highway 65 heavily yesterday. The Russians have started their winter offensive and are advancing. Our 5th Army Front remains stagnant.

Dick and I went out tonight to both battalions. No action. I got a paper from home.

Thursday, January 18, 1945   Clear and warmer. Had a headache for the larger part of the day.

Dick and I went out tonight to both battalions almost as usual.

I got a lot of letters from Mom and Ray. Felt much disgusted — or I should say, more lonesome, because I heard they had to sell Eagle, one of my favorite horses. But it's a wonder they could keep him as long as they did.

Friday, January 19, 1945   Raining and cold. Went to the 348th F.A. Battalion and saw the dentist, but he didn't have time to work on me. Didn't have to go to the battalion tonight. Wrote to Uncle Hank, Ray and Peggy.

Saturday, January 20, 1945   Went to the 316 Med this morning and had a tooth pulled. He did a good job; I hardly knew it was out. Back by 11:00. Clear, but cold.

We went out together tonight to both battalions with routine material.

Sunday, January 21, 1945   Greased my peep this p.m. Checked it over all around.

Dick and I went together to both battalions again tonight. Met Don and Tex. Long time since I've seen Don.

Went to church. Another inspiring sermon on St. Matthew 6:32 - 34, "Take No Thought for the Morrow."

Wrote home.

After the 15th, 16th and 17th of January, our area was well covered by enemy shellfire. But luck was with us still, and we had no casualties. But we did have to cancel a USO show that had been scheduled to come on the 19th.

On January 21 we were put into general support under the control of the 88th Division.

I can't recall why I hadn't seen Don in a long time. It seems he should have moved the first days of January when I did.

A letter home of January 21 mentioned we had a foot of snow, and that it was almost fun to drive in it with a 4-wheel-drive peep compared to driving in mud. I commented on their telling me that Bill Kajikawa had written them from France.

I told them that "the Division we are attached to" (it was the 88th, I can say it now), had a sign out by the road saying "Hot Coffee" for anyone who wanted to stop, and that the Red Cross coffee and doughnut machine was quite a ways back. Several days ago 2 Red Cross girls were here at our big building, and one had sung, and the other played the accordion. We'd had ice cream the night before that some of the cooks had made. It was pretty thin, but very good. They'd had to use snow for freezing it, and the snow wasn't really cold enough. I praised this Division's chaplain, said he was very good, always held his services at night, and that I'd heard him three times so far.

Monday, January 22, 1945   The survey crew invited me into their room, so I've been sleeping in there now awhile. They're really nice company, and it's a lot warmer. It was clear and cold outside.

Tuesday, January 23, 1945   Much the same.

Wednesday, January 24, 1945   The 91st Division Artillery moved back to Monte Cetin for a rest. Their artillery battalions and the 175th and 151st are now attached to the 88th Division. Division Artillery finally got settled. We are in Loiano.
Went to the battalion.

A letter home mentioned I'd seen George and Harvey Olson, had heard of George's appendix operation at Anzio, and that both of them were repairing heavy guns in "this outfit."

Thursday, January 25, 1945   Strasser, South and Beechum are the agents from the 88th Division, and then Dick and I. Really a unique group. Seem to fit in here much better than with the 91st Division.
We have a gasoline stove in here as well, and it's fairly comfortable. To the battalion twice, but it's only about a mile. Stopped to see Don. Got a book from him, *Fair are the Meadows* by Ingles.
We are north of Loiano a ways, on the main road in a big building. This building too could have been a rooming house, restaurant, inn, etc. Anyway, the 88th has taken it over.
An Evacuation Hospital just to the rear was reported shelled, either by mistake or on purpose.

Well, this Division is a little different. Joe Beechum is an older fellow from Carolina; I like to hear him talk — he has that slow drawl. He has been around, and "knows his onions." Strasser is just the opposite: he's young and a little naive, but he's not an aggravator — and South, a middle-of-the-road guy who is easy to live with.

I got a light bulb from my old pal, Dengler, and we hooked it up in our room. But the fellow who said he was in charge of the generator said the bulb was too big for "his" generator, and we couldn't use it. Everything he talked about, he used the words "mine" and "I," and everything he was in charge of was "his." So unusual, it was almost funny. But he is almost a newcomer in the Army and has a lot to learn. We still use the light bulb.

This place is an ideal one for agents to live in. It's a big room, the weather is beginning to get warmer, and we have hopes of breaking out of this area soon. Joe keeps us interested most of the time, and Dick has been telling us things he saw when he went to Pompeii.

Dick had gone to Pompeii while on a Naples pass. I could have gone, but Vesuvius was really threatening at the time, and I wasn't entertaining any ideas of being cremated. It had been glowing almost all of the time since we came to Italy in September of '43, and actually did erupt on March 10, 1944. On that date we were beginning to get ready to go to Anzio, and we'd had to go back to Naples on March 16 to get on the LST — that was close enough to Vesuvius for me.

But anyway, Dick told us of all the things he'd seen at Pompeii; the finest example of a Roman town, it's way of life opened by excavation. It was probably built around 300 b.c., and by the first century a.d., was a Roman city of about 20,000. In 63 a.d. much of the town was destroyed by an earthquake, and it was completely covered by ash and pumice stone 6 to 7 yards thick in 79 a.d.

It was thought, and later proven by excavation that the majority of the 20,000 population was able to escape. Those who didn't make it left a hollowed-out shape of their own in the ash and pumice stone. These were filled with plaster of paris, thus preserving true likenesses of the victims.

We five messenger agents agreed that even if a person hadn't seen all of Italy, Pompeii would be a "good place to go and see all of some Italians," at least in the form of plaster casts, statues, pictures and artworks. The victims of Pompeii seemed rather remote to us; they'd probably had their own mourners, while we had our own friends to mourn and our own lives to fear for. Pompeii again had a population of about 20,000.

The location we were in with the 88th Division was really a good place to talk with some new people, and I liked it better than a rest area. We didn't have many specials to take out either.

During one session of talk, Dick told us that his religion was mostly centered on Matthew, Chapter 6, where it says, "Consider the lilies of the field; they toil not, neither do they spin, but Solomon in all his glories was not arrayed like one of these."

I said my religion was centered on Paul's writings in the Epistle to the Romans, and that I'd been really glad I'd been able to visit St. Peter's, and also to have been able to drive my peep into one of the arches of the Coloseum.

Joe and Strasser didn't have their ears tuned our way at all as we were discussing our religion, and South was never one to say much on anything.

I remember Dick telling us too about all the poppies he'd seen in bloom in Africa after a rain. Somehow I missed having seen that, probably because we were in Africa at different times and places.

Then Dick, with his different sense sense of humor, commented that he hoped that this coming year he'd be able to see some trees in Italy with leaves growing on them, as during the past year all we'd seen was trees with all the leaves blown off them by shellfire.

Friday, January 26, 1945   Three years ago today we landed in Belfast. It still is one of the biggest thrills I've experienced so far in the Army.

I got a light bulb and hooked it up again this morning. The chow here isn't as good as at the 91st.

Dick and I made 2 trips to the battalion.

Saturday, January 27, 1945   Nice weather now. We hope this Italian winter is pretty much over, and it seems to be. Made 2 trips to the battalion again. Has turned out to be a routine assignment.

A letter from Bill. They are in action in France.

Sunday, January 28, 1945   Dick and I went to the 34th Division Artillery this morning. Was glad to see them again, but I think I'd rather be attached to another Division.

Went out twice to the 151st.

Got another letter from Bill. His wife had a baby girl on Dec. 31st. Wrote some letters.

Our biggest "shoot" of the month was on the night of the 27th. We fired 370 rounds of harassing fire in support of an infantry raid.

Margaret Bourke White, a well-known photographer who also took pictures at Cassino, was at the front that night taking some shots.

On the last day of the month, the gun of Charlie Battery's third section exploded like the one at Able Battery had recently. Again, fortunately, there were no casualties.

Monday, January 29, 1945   The usual routine, except I had a headache all day. Three times to the battalion, the last one at 9:30 tonight.

Tuesday, January 30, 1945　　Cloudy and dreary day. We had a special to take out this morning. Started to read *Jamaica Inn*. Out again tonight.

Wednesday, January 31, 1945　　Went to Service Battery. Had the broken spring fixed, and they put in a new carburetor. To the battalion twice today. Mail from home tonight.

It was a sluggish, but a not-too-hard month for front-line artillery men. We hoped the Krauts had other places to shoot more shells than on this front, and this seemed to be the fact; the Western Front that Germany had been counting on to win them the war had not been working out for them the way they had planned. The Siegfried Line was about broken, with Canadian, British, French and our US troops making solid advances.

The Eastern Front news was also very welcome. The Russians had taken 100,000 German prisoners in the Budapest area.

Air attacks were massive. The British Royal Air Force sent one night-raid of 737 Lancaster Bombers. This night attack was followed by daylight attacks of the US Eighth Air Force using 600 bombers in two attacks.

With good weather we'd had, along with the prospect of being able to drive in dust instead of mud, the men had a lot higher degree of morale lately, and we all wanted to exercise the 34th Division "Red Bull" motto of "Attack, Attack."

The greatest event for the month was the listing of men to be going home on furlough. This month 21 men and 2 officers were to leave from the battalion. The only two I knew were Pomerleau and Louie Day.

Throughout the month there was some snow on the ground. All the Howitzers were painted white. This was our first experience with winter camouflage.

During this time, passes to Rome or Florence weren't hard to get — if you wanted to go there to fight the Military Police and listen to all the "Fury of War" from the noncombatants and be in places jammed with soldiers. When asked if we wanted to go, lots of us would say, "I want to go home, but let the Romans go to Rome, because I've been there."

Thursday, February 1, 1945　　Up at 7:00. Wrote to Bill. Not much else doing today.

Friday, February 2, 1945　　Joe Beechum and I decided to quit smoking. Read some. Got a *Life* magazine tonight. Dick and I went out twice. Took our laundry to Anna at our last position.

My letter home dated February 2 complained sarcastically that we were being issued all the woolen clothes we needed now that spring is here — they'd given me a heavy wool sweater, a double parka suit with wool-lined pants, and heavy wool socks — but never chopper mitts for those who had to drive.

Saturday, February 3, 1945   Up at 7:00. Has turned much warmer. Raining a little tonight. Dick and I had only one trip tonight.

Sunday, February 4, 1945   Up at 7:00. Strasser, Dick and I went to the clothing exchange. Had a hot shower there and got clean clothes. The weather is much warmer, but still there is snow on the ground. It turned out to be a beautiful day. Went out twice again.

One letter from Mom and one from Ray. It's warm tonight. Ray says Bobby Archambeau was killed in the South Pacific on December 11. He was younger than me. Leonard, his brother, is in the 601 Tank Corps here in Italy.

Jerry hasn't thrown in many shells here lately. Some are going out, but not many either.

Monday, February 5, 1945   I worked all forenoon on my peep, cleaning and greasing. A beautiful day. Dick and I went out twice, as usual. Had 2 letters from Mom, and 3 *Life* magazines.

Tuesday, February 6, 1945   Up at 7:00. Did the chores of the room. Read *Life*. Another beautiful day.

To the battalion this p.m., then went to get out laundry from Anna. Stopped to see Reb; he is with Message Center 185. Scottie is back from furlough and is the Battalion Agent.

Out again tonight. Got a Sunday paper.

Wednesday, February 7, 1945   Toast for breakfast. Washed up. Started writing home, looked over a few of my things. Strasser and I went after *Stars and Stripes*.

Dick and I made 2 trips to the battalion again. I got a letter from Mom and also the chopper mitt that completes the pair. Wrote to Ray and home.

Thursday, February 8, 1945   About the same thing.

Friday, February 9, 1945   Went to the battalion this morning. I had some material for Message Center, so I stopped. First thing Tom

CHAPTER 28

McGee said was, "Wag, they want to see you at Service Battery."

I told him, "I'm having a tooth pulled, but I'll stop before coming back."

So I did, and Sgt. Norman said, "Hey Wag, we got another peep for you. This one is reconditioned."

I was more surprised than thankful, but I took my junk out of the old peep and put it in the new one. It seems like new, with fresh paint, and really clean and nice. This makes the 5th peep I've had.

Back at noon. Raining and snowing this p.m. Out twice this p.m. Shells coming in last night. Letter from Peggy and from Mom. Answered both.

The new peep is sure nice. Not even any rattles in it.

Now I can explain the new peep. I couldn't in my original diary, as I carried it on me constantly. I didn't want anyone to get hold of the story, as it could have gotten some soldiers in trouble.

But as I am writing this commentary over 50 years after the "Peep Incident," I can now give proper credit to the fellows who helped me out.

The morning I got the different peep it seemed to me then that something odd was going on. Sgt. Norman didn't say anything more, and the peep really looked different from being a "reconditioned" one. No one else from the Service Department even greeted me that morning — but sometimes that was normal too.

I did stop at Message Center and told Tom that Service had given me a new peep. He said, holding back a grin, "Now isn't that nice, Wag."

All I knew was that I had gotten a nice, almost new peep. It was days before I found out what really happened. I went into Message Center one time later when Tom was alone. He looked around to see if anyone else was there and whispered, "Wag, do you want to know the story on your peep?"

"Sure thing, Tom, what's the story?"

Well, Bob Engleson and a few others had gone to Rome on a 5-day pass. The most of the time they were there they were pretty much on a liquid diet, and especially so on the last day. So, when it came time for them to get on board the trucks and come back, Bob and the boys didn't feel like going. So, they stayed awhile longer, and started looking around for a peep they could come back with themselves.

There were always a lot of Air Force personnel with peeps in Rome. It didn't take long for the boys to find one. There were no ignition keys in World War II peeps, only on-off switches. Though drivers often tried to theft-proof their vehicle by removing the rotor from under the distributor cap, it wasn't unknown for some soldiers to carry an extra rotor in their pocket. I'm not sure how these fellows got the peep started in this case, but anyway, they climbed in and headed for the front, They even arrived back there before the truckload of other men did.

They drove the peep to Service Battery and woke up Sgt. Norman. He got some fellows together, and they repainted the markings on the bumpers and on the whole peep. All Air Force vehicles had a big white star painted over the entire hood. They painted over that too, of course, but you could always see the outline of the star under the olive drab paint. So that explained why no one at Service Battery greeted me that day. I suppose they just wanted to get the peep out of their sight without making any explanations.

When Bob Engleson first brought the peep in to Service Battery the first thing he said was, "This peep goes to Wag. He's driven enough junk around here."

That's the rest of the story. We didn't consider it stealing, but taking from the rich and giving to the poor.

Several times later I'd have the chance to grin or wink at Bob. He had come in the service about the same time I had, and we were in the same Quonset hut in Ireland. He was a nice guy; heavy, with a big smile and grin, and an unusually musical-sounding voice.

Louie Day had left on furlough the 1st of February, and Pomerleau had too. I guess I was glad Louie was in the States, though I'm sure he wouldn't have spilled the beans, or Sgt Pomerleau (the mailman) either … but still I was glad they weren't there. Anyway, I was just doing what I was supposed to be doing at all times in the Army: "As told."

Saturday, February 10, 1945   Three shells came very close this morning. Shook the building. I'd been shaving by the window with my straightedge razor, and was stropping it on the leather strap to sharpen it, when the shells came in, shaking the entire building. The first blast knocked the razor out of my hand, cut the strap, and landed the razor on the floor. It ruined it, as the edge slivered off. I valued it, as it was the best one I had, and had bought it in Ireland.

Checked over the peep this morning. Strasser and I got *Stars and Stripes*. Dick and I made two trips to the battalion. Got a letter from Bill. Answered it. Cloudy, not freezing. Air bursts over Loiano tonight when we went out.

Sunday, February 11, 1945   Nice day. Strasser and I went after *Stars and Stripes*. Went to the dentist; he filled 3. He reminds me of Lloyd Archambeau. Dick and I went out twice. I was going to go to church, but was a little too late.

Monday, February 12, 1945   Beautiful day. Had 2 specials to go out this a.m. and an appointment with the dentist again, but he didn't have any light to work with.

Dick and I went out again. The 175th was shelled heavily all day, luckily not when we were there. One shell landed close to Message

Center and put a hole in their tent.
Out again tonight. Got stuck with my peep in the parking lot.
Used Chevernoies'. A letter from Miss Eliason.

Chevernoies was the 4th agent from the 88th Division, but my memory doesn't tell me from which battalion.

February was turning out to be a quiet month. We were actually in general support, reinforcing the fires of the 916 F.A. of the 91st Division, which in turn was in direct support of the 351st, 349th, and 350th Infantry Regiments in succession. Towards the end of the month, the 151st and the 346th F.A. battalions formed Groupment A.A. under the control of Lt. Col. Barry of the latter organization. We supported the 1st Battalion of the 349th Infantry Regiment while the 346th provided for the 3rd Battalion.

February brought us good weather. The snow and cold that had plagued us in January was about gone, and a little dust was already in evidence on Highway 65.

My friend Peggy from Ireland had written to tell me she wouldn't be writing any more. Years after the war I wrote to her mother and asked about her. Her mother told me she was married and had several "wee ones." They had moved to southern England, and were in the area that her sister Olive and her husband had been during the war. Both parents had gone with the girls, but said they were sad on leaving Ireland. They had left because of the Troubles in Ireland.

Another pen-pal I'd enjoyed writing to and receiving letters from was Patsy Honstein from Baker, Montana, who I'd been corresponding with since Camp Claiborne. She had been sick with rheumatic fever and confined in bed in a foster or group home of some kind. Her letters stopped coming about this time as well, and I had to assume she had died.

CHAPTER 29
Big Push? Rest.

Tuesday, February 13, 1945   Got my peep out of the mud and didn't do more.

Then, go to the battalion twice.

I'd sent two letters home in one envelope. They told mostly of the mud, that I'd gotten the other chopper mitt and that Christmas mail was still coming in.

Wednesday, February 14, 1945   Broke a brake line on my peep last night. There was some brush on one road that I had to go over, and that's what caught the brake line and broke it. I came in without brakes.

Got letters from Peggy, home and Ray. Also Ray's budget for the year.

Warm and fairly nice.

Peggy still writes and seems her usual quiet self. Ray and Dick are in the woods again, cutting wood at Payne.

Thursday, February 15, 1945   Took the peep to Service Battery. Got the brake line fixed.

Warm. Dick's outfit moved to Barberino with the 185th and Division Artillery. We all miss him.

I made two trips to the battalion this p.m. Wrote home and to Ray.

My letter home for the 15th said the roads were starting to dry up.

I told them that Gen. Marshall was here, but I didn't see him — only a string of vehicles along the road.

I asked for a package again, of dried beef, sardines and cheese, but no candy now, because we were getting 6 bars a week.

I told them the chopper mitts were nice for night driving, but that it had been getting warmer.

Friday, February 16, 1945   Strasser and I went to take a shower, but it wasn't in operation. A shell hit one of the lines last night. Got stuck, but a 6X6 pulled me out. Took a sponge bath, changed clothes, got a haircut.

To the battalion twice, as usual.

No mail. I wrote to Peggy. Warm, but cloudy. Some incoming shells today, but not too close.

Saturday, February 17, 1945   Sort of foggy all day. Made the usual 2 trips.

Got letters from Peggy, Robert and George.

Two years ago we made our first contact with the enemy.

Wrote to George and Peggy. Peggy still writes and tells me news of Tynan Abbey and North Ireland. Her letters are always sort of quaint, timid and shy, and she wonders if I will come back to Ireland.

Robert Hamilton was the Irish boy who I happened to talk to one time while I happened to be out walking, and he happened to be out fishing. We corresponded with each other all the time I was overseas, and he wrote to my younger brother, Roger, as well.

George Nash had gone into the Army much later than I did, and he ended up in the South Pacific around the Philippines. He and his wife Ethel both wrote me, though he wasn't as much of a letter-writer as Ethel was.

Sunday, February 18, 1945   Strasser went on pass to Florence. A Mexican is taking his place. Read some. Went to see Don and Andy awhile.

To the battalion tonight. Foggy. Shells coming in, but not too close.

A lot of men went on furlough at this time again, though the only one I knew was Clarence Ceedsma, an original from Iowa. As I said earlier, we were never told how men were selected for furlough, but evidently the officers had their ways of choosing, probably by looking over our censored mail.

By this time I don't think I would have accepted a furlough anyway — unless I could have gone to Ireland, and it's doubtful if that would have been allowed — and in that case, I was willing to see the war through to the end. It was getting easier now, instead of harder, and the hope for an early victory was as much in the air and as sure as was the hope of spring.

Monday, February 19, 1945   Real cold all day with a strong wind. Cold in the room.

South and I went after *Stars and Stripes*. Two trips to the battalion. Had a flat on the way back. No lug wrench, so came back on the flat. It must be ruined.

Read a book, *Your Life*. The situation has remained untactical so far today.

Corrigedor's fall is immanent. Bataan fell yesterday. Tokyo has been shelled 3 days from sea-based planes and aircraft. It wasn't long ago that we heard of Gen. Doolittle's bombing raid over Tokyo in April of '42.

Tuesday, February 20, 1945   Changed the flat. Took it to Service Battery and exchanged it for a new one. Cold, but clear.

We have lots of time again now to spend in our room, but aren't really satisfied. — we want to start pushing north.

The 10th Mountain Division, Bob Dole's former outfit, made a good beginning in this by capturing Mt. Belvedere to our west in a bitter struggle over very tough terrain. Further west, the 92nd Division drove forward, but was forced to retreat shortly afterwards.

Maj. Surdyk returned to us about the middle of the month in the capacity of S-3. He had been with the Polish Corps and on a 30-day furlough to the States. We heard that Col. DuBois would not be returning to our battalion because of his health.

W. Skains from Able Battery turned his ¾ ton weapons carrier over by trying to turn it around on a narrow mountain road in pitch blackness.

We entertained a lot of Brass — Top Brass, that is, including Gen. Marshall. Dick Johnson commented around this time, "I hope the King and Queen come too. I'd like to see the old girl."

The new Five-Star General insignia was seen for the first time by any of us on Gen. Marshall, who visited us while on his trip from the Big Three Conference in Yalta. He arrived with at least a score of lesser generals, including Gen. Clark, 15th Army Group Commander, and Gen. Truscott, Commander of our 5th Army.

We tried to get a motion picture machine during this period, but met with no success. Truckloads of men were sent to the 88th Division Artillery whenever movies were being shown there.

Wednesday, February 21, 1945   Another cold night, but it turned warm. Played cribbage with Walter for $2.00 again. Broke even.

Fortunately, no shells close for a few days. Went after *Stars and Stripes*. Two trips to the battalion.

Right after I came back tonight, a barrage of shells came in. Thankful I was able to be inside. Several came quite close to this building. A letter and Valentine from Arlene.

Thursday, February 22, 1945   Cleaned on my peep all forenoon. Tried to get a few rattles out of it — but it's not too bad.

To the battalion this p.m. Greased the peep, changed oil. Out again tonight. Turned in my overcoat.

Beautiful day; the snow is nearly all gone, and the roads are drying out fast.

Friday, February 23, 1945   Another beautiful day. Went to the battalion this p.m. They put on a new spring and shock on the peep.

Saw a show here tonight, *To Have or Not to Have.* Humphrey Bogart. A lot of the 151 boys here at the show. I'm glad we got to stay with the 88th this length of time, but thought the big push would have been started by now.

It was on February 23, 1945 that a young photographer named Joe Rosenthal captured on film one of the most moving moments in the Pacific Campaign of World War II, the raising of the flag on Mount Suribachi during the Marine's battle for Iwo Jima. Progress was being made on all fronts, but it was hard-won progress.

Saturday, February 24, 1945   George and I washed our peeps this morning at the 88th. Took showers. Beautiful weather; hope it lasts.

Made 2 trips again. Got 10 letters tonight: from Mom, Ray, Mary Jean and Bob Vaughn. Mary Jean sent some pictures of herself and Lavonne. They have changed and grown. I was going to write letters, but I changed my mind.

Sunday, February 25, 1945   Greased my peep. Wrote to Arlene. A little cloudy.

Out this p.m. Went to church at 2:00. A good sermon by an 88th chaplain. His key words were, "God gave us this world to use, not abuse." Stopped in to see Don and Andy for an hour.

Out again tonight. Two letters, from Ray and Mom. Also a *Life* magazine and *Time.*

Monday, February 26, 1945   Another beautiful day, but colder. Worked on my peep this forenoon. Tightened up some on it, and cleaned it a little more.

Out twice again this p.m. No mail. Wrote to Mom, Mary Jean and Bill.

My letter home of the 26th said I was sorry I wasn't with the bunch that came home on furlough to Duluth, who were all from the 125th Field Artillery.

The 125th F.A. members who got to go home on furlough were all volunteer National Guardsmen from Duluth. As I had been drafted into the

151st from Minneapolis about 3 months later, they all had more time in service than I did. Time in service was considered more important than the fact that the 151 was in the first boatload of soldiers crossing the Atlantic. The fact we had earned a bronze arrowhead for the Italian invasion didn't count either.

Tuesday, February 27, 1945   Beautiful day. George and I played catch for awhile. Put a foolproof ignition switch on my peep. Out twice this p.m.

A letter from Bill with a nice photograph of him.

Got the blues. Wish the war would suddenly end, or we would at least push off. Shells coming in Monzuno and vicinity; several were killed.

Wednesday, February 28, 1945   Another beautiful day. George and I played catch. To the battalion.

Started to reread *Yankee from Olympus*. Packed away some woolens in my boxes.

Two trips to the battalion. Letters from Mom and Ray, and school papers from Arlene.

This had been an odd winter defensive line to hold, as most of us had been in the same position for 4 months, though some outfits had been detached, or were supporting other units, or supporting fire with another battalion.

I had changed locations twice myself; once, by being attached to the 91st Division, and now I had been with the 88th. In my opinion, both of these locations were better than where I had been with the 34th Division.

There was some changing of officers during this period. Some had been sent to special schools — for instance, there was a school on demolition at Caserta.

The infantry had been busier than we had been, in setting up patrols and increasing the tempo.

The Krauts weren't idle either. Their propaganda broadcasts had increased, and the surrender prizes they offered had increased as well. Dick Johnson's comment on this was, "Sorry, Adolph, there's no takers from around here. But have fun — things are slated to change P.D.Q."

Thursday, March 1, 1945   Still good weather. Two trips again. Letters from Mom and Ray.

Friday, March 2, 1945   Turned somewhat colder. George and I played catch.

Two trips again this afternoon. No mail. Went to a show here;

Laura, a murder mystery.

It's funny: You're a murderer if you kill someone in civilian life, unless you're a cop or a strong liar — but a hero if you kill enemy soldiers in war.

Saturday, March 3, 1945   Turned colder and snowed about an inch. Strasser and I went after *Stars and Stripes.*
Sun is out, and practically all the snow is gone. It's still a little cold.
Went out twice this p.m. No mail.

Sunday, March 4, 1945   Had a flat tire. Exchanged it tonight for a new one.
Lt. Kipper is back with the 151st now. He filled 3 teeth for me this p.m.
Made another trip tonight. No mail again. Cold all day.
Units are preparing to shift around again, perhaps the prelude to the immanent punch.

Monday, March 5, 1945   The guard wakes us every morning at 6:45. Chow is from 7 to 7:30.
Changed 2 tires on my peep. I have the new one on the chassis, and the old one for a spare. Shaved and washed.
Kept my appointment with Dr. Kipper. He's a real good worker.
Went to Service Battery this p.m. and had Tim weld one of the fenders.
Read over my diary in part. Am glad I've been keeping it. I might possibly turn it into a book someday.
The 88th, or "Lookouts," have started to move out — they will take over 91st Division Artillery, and go back to their old positions. 34th Division Headquarters will take over legion and be in High Command of this sector.
I dislike leaving this little room. Wish we could all be together again with the 34th. Lots of 34th vehicles on the road again today: Signal, Division Hq. 168th and 133rd.
We had Spam for dinner cooked with pineapple. I got what I wanted, the scrapings of the pan.
To the battalion again. No mail. Quiet, went to bed early.

Tuesday, March 6, 1945   Up at 6:00. Started packing up. Left at 8:00. Dropped off *Stars and Stripes* at the battalion.
Got here at the 91st Division at 9:00. It took until noon to get

settled. Am in the basement with all the agents. Put up my net this p.m. Have the peep parked in back of the building. To the battalion at 4:00.

Sgt. Rettinger has returned from furlough. I didn't recognize him. They have supper here with these boys. Mariani reminds me of Uncle Carl. Scott has a picture of his young girl and boy.

March didn't bring much change to the Italian Front, except the 10th Mountain Division made about 8 miles of advances through rough, mountainous country. Otherwise, positions remained pretty static, and action consisted mostly of patrolling and harassing of enemy positions and supply routes.

The right (eastern) portion of the 5th Army was a mixture of various units, none of which were a part of their original Divisions. For instance, our outfit was supporting infantry regiments of the 34th, 91st and 88th Divisions, and worked under any one of their Division Artillery Headquarters. At one point, the 151st F.A. Battalion, while under the Command of 88th Division Artillery, was supporting two 91st Infantry Division infantry regiments.

These circumstances presented many interesting combinations, and produced a not-too-standard-operating war.

At the beginning of the month, the battalion was still reinforcing the fires of the 346 F.A. Battalion of the 91st Division, which was supporting the 349th Infantry Regiment, 88th Division. On the 5th of March the battalion assumed direct support of the 133rd Infantry Regiment, and the 346th Artillery Battalion went into general support in the same sector.

Activity consisted mostly of patrolling in the Vado, Cavalla and Furcoli areas, with little artillery action because our battalion was limited to 75 rounds a day.

The new time fuse was used frequently, with improved precautions for crest-clearing and airplane control. There were sometimes premature bursts as well, some of which I saw myself, but luckily there were no casualties from them.

Interrogation of German P.O.W.s captured in this area indicated the enemy was aware we were using a new weapon against them, but they hadn't been able to figure out it's nature or operation.

We were also using several American recoilless weapons, the most important of which were the 57 mm rifles which could be fired from the shoulder, and the 4.2 inch mortar which could be fired either as a mortar or as a gun.

We also were using a new British mine-clearing device that operated on a super prima-cord principle — it cleared a path 12 to 18 inches wide for a total distance of 400 feet.

Mine-clearing was never 100% efficient even using the most modern devices.

CHAPTER 29

Wednesday, March 7, 1945   Didn't do much today. Went to the battalion this evening. Warm, nice, summer weather.

Thursday, March 8, 1945   Put up my net again; it had fallen down. To Division Hq. and 151st before dinner.

Worked practically all p.m. on my peep. Took the battery out, cleaned it and the case, cleaned the motor.

To the battalion tonight right after supper.

Got a letter from Aunt Evelyn. Had a distressing dream of home last night. Aunt Evelyn sent some snapshots of herself and Uncle Hank.

To bed about 8:30. Very tired.

Friday, March 9, 1945   Up at 6:40 as usual. I eat down in the cellar where I sleep.

Bernie Mariani and I walked over to where a peep crashed over a bank last night. The driver and passenger had jumped clear, but the peep rolled over and down. It was probably 200 feet down — completely smashed. I got a lug-wrench and several smaller wrenches out of it.

Beautiful weather we are having. Thankful for it. Shells came in last night, but I didn't hear them. Jerry usually throws in high bursts in the early mornings — keep your helmets on.

Reports say the Russians have crossed the Oder River in the vicinity of Frankfurt, and the 1st, 3rd and 9th Armies are across the Rhine at Cologne and Coblenze.

Nothing had to go out tonight, so I didn't go. To bed early.

Saturday, March 10, 1945   Took Mariani to 180 Signal this morning. They are south of the doughnut stand. Still nice weather.

To the battalion this p.m. Saw Mr. Irons; he had been home on furlough. The roads are almost as dusty as they were last summer, but I enjoyed it.

Dad's birthday, and Uncle Hank's. Probably 63 and 35.

Sunday, March 10, 1945   Someone used my peep last night. Tore my net and parked it wrong.

Read *Sign of the Times* in my peep. It's warm enough to sit out here, hot and coatless.

Comparatively quiet, but still lots of shells going out. The Americans have an established beachhead east of the Rhine.

Did little except go to the battalion tonight.

Monday, March 11, 1945   Still warm and dry. Cleaned a little more on my peep. It's something to do, and it adds to the appearance somewhat.

To the battalion. 7 letters from Mom and Ray.

Tuesday, March 12, 1945   Warm, almost hot. The doc had his shirt off today getting a sun tan. I went to the dentist, but couldn't locate him. Back at 11:00. Read the *Readers' Digest* out in my peep.

Out this p.m. just before supper. Took Strasser's distribution along. He went to Florence with Mariani.

Wednesday, March 15, 1945   Left at 8:00 for the 346th. Went to Capt. Oneguard, the dentist. He pulled my tooth, but I had to wait until 11:00. Back here at noon. The easiest tooth I've ever had pulled. Hardly any aftereffects.

Painted the motor of my peep this p.m. Took until 4:00.

Then went to the battalion. No mail. Comparatively quiet. Dean Johnston is back with this Division Artillery. Rumor has it that 151 is scheduled to move.

Thursday, March 15, 1945   Painted the bumper numbers over on my peep this forenoon. Went to the battalion around 2 p.m. We may be going back for a rest. At least I hope.

Made two more trips to the battalion before dark. One was an overlay, the other a special movement order. The most trips we've made, and the first special in a long time.

Played cribbage with Walter.

I never knew exactly what the "specials" were, as they were sealed, and none of my business except to sign for them, be sure to deliver them, and get a signed receipt that they had been delivered. My peep had a canvas zippered seat-pad I either sat on or leaned my back against when I drove. We were supposed to keep all our sealed deliveries inside it so they wouldn't get lost, but many times I would just put the common things under it, instead of inside. This was to save the zipper, which usually broke soon enough anyhow.

It was important that gun crews aim their artillery fire above our own infantry's heads and down towards the Germans. As infantry was always on the move, the specials told the gun crews where not to aim, just as much as they told them where to aim.

Friday, March 16, 1945   Scott, Russell and Long played poker until

1:30 — inconsiderate of us who were all in bed. Read through *Life* that I got last night. Warm today.

Packed up about 3:30 this p.m. and left the 91st. Had supper at the battalion and waited there until 10:30, when we pulled out, heading south for rest. At 10:00, Jerry started shelling us. Approximately 15 shells landed in our area, one close to the Orderly Room. Lt.'s Tague and Ryan were hit, but not seriously.

Tom McGee rode with me. When we got to Mongnudore, a guard almost machine-gunned us for putting lights on a half mile too soon. Was odd to travel with lights.

We were just getting out of this little town, when Sgt. McGee said, "Wag, put your lights on."

I knew it was too soon, but Tom had a belly-full of cognac, and said it again louder, "Wag, put your lights on!"

So I obeyed, and very shortly the guard of the town was in the middle of the road with his machine gun aimed at us. He really chewed me out, but I didn't say anything. Tom didn't admit ordering me to do it, either, so alcohol chalked up another low mark.

Saturday, March 17, 1945   We arrived almost in Florence at about 1:30. Put up my cot outside, and slept until 6:30. Helped Message Center set up.

Came to Division Artillery this p.m. We are set up in an old shed. Glad to see all the old boys again, and be welcomed back as well.

Tom McGee sobered up today — he's always pretty sober-faced for a while afterwards.

Tom was older than me. He came from Illinois. After the war, the State of Illinois gave each veteran a new car, so Tom drove his to Duluth to visit my wife Evelyn and I not long before we got married. I also got to see him at a reunion of the 34th Division in Minneapolis a few years later. He passed away about 1960 from a heart attack.

Sunday, March 18, 1945   This was really a day. I forgot the 4 months up north and the Winter Line in a hurry. Had a wonderful night's sleep, and my stomach didn't bother me anymore either — it's a great feeling to be away from shellfire and mud.

Joe Staniger and I went to take a shower. Changed clothes, shaved.

All the agents are together again: Scottie from the 185th, Dick from the 175th, Dave Holt from the 125th, and myself from the 151st.

Beautiful weather, as warm as summer. Not a bad position here, though it looks like this rest period won't be as good as at Rosignano

6 months ago.

Went to church tonight. Partook of communion. Chaplain Temple preached.

Went with Dick to his battalion tonight around 8:00. To bed early.

Most all the fellows in Division called me "Bud," and in my own outfit, they called me "Wag." I answered to either, but it was good to hear the familiar "Wag" again.

Monday, March 19, 1945   Dick moved in with me. Glad to have his company again. This place reminds me of Ireland. Another beautiful day.

There was some hurry around Message Center for awhile though, as batteries are on training schedule. Those who haven't been doing much still have their teaching mission to fulfill.

One agent makes all battalions on one trip to minimize the number of vehicles on the road. We go along with this to a certain extent. If I have a place to go, though, I go — just as long as Jack Salzer knows about it.

Tuesday, March 20, 1945   A few trips and lots of talking with Dick. Also, just relaxing and enjoying ourselves.

The night we left the front, March 16, an estimated 40 rounds of artillery fell in the vicinity of Calenzeno. Lt.'s Tague and Ryan both stopped some shrapnel, but nothing really serious.

We had been in the front line for 6 months and 11 days. We had to admit that morale and health were excellent, as a whole, and that for most of the time we had lived rather comfortably — except for the times my peep was always broke down, and I had to walk 2 miles each way to the battalion each day, plodding and climbing through the mud and the mountains without the benefit of having a mule. Rear echelon troops were hogging the mules almost to the death of me, until Bob Engleson went and got me one.

Wednesday, March 21, 1945   Worked all forenoon on the peep. Greased it, changed the oil. Went to Service Battery this p.m. but they were too busy.

I went to all battalions tonight. Back at 8:30. Ice cream from the kitchen, really a treat.

Thursday, March 22, 1945   Up at 6:45. Chow at 7:00. Went to Service Battery. They put in a new spring and universal joint. Tim did some welding. Back by noon. Beautiful weather.

Friday, March 23, 1945   Dick and I went to Division rear with the morning run. Saw Floyd Johnson. Back at 10:30.

They had a USO show here this p.m. Pretty poor. Red Cross girls here with doughnuts.

To the battalion this p.m. Stopped to see Don. Andy is going home soon. Scottie and I went out tonight to all battalions.

Went to bed at 8:30. Little else to do, and no ambition to do anything anyway. Got a letter from Bill the other day.

Saturday, March 24, 1945   Cleaned up my peep this morning. Took Lt. Adams to the Air O.P. Beautiful weather.

To the Air O.P. again this p.m. To the 125th, and after 7:00, to all battalions.

Lester Lieberman came along; did some extra driving. Back at 10:00. Lester said his alabaster statue got home alright without any breakage, and everyone thought it was a beautiful work.

Sunday, March 25, 1945   Went to Divison Rear this morning. Lt. Hamilton came along with. A likable fellow. My starter button went haywire, and had to push the peep instead of the button.

Took a bath, got the starter fixed, wrote to Ray and to Bill. A little cloudy, but still warm. To all the battalions.

Monday, March 26, 1945   Like Dick says, my forgeterer is working better than my rememberer. Probably not much happened today anyway.

Tuesday, March 27, 1945   Raining about all day. Got ready to leave. I went back to the 151st tonight at 8:00 to move with them. Maj. Surdyk rode with me, and we brought up the rear of the convoy. We were in, or went through Futapass.

Maj. Surdyk was talkative. He asked me if I'd been on furlough. He maybe would have had something to say about me getting one, but I really didn't want one at the time. I wanted to see Northern Italy, and I told him I'd rather stick it out until the end of the war.

Maj. Surdyk had been home for a month, and had also been on detached S-3 service for a long while. He owned a liquor store in Minneapolis. I heard he had died around 1978.

I remember this trip was hard traveling. It was always hard keeping up when you were at the end of a convoy, as the vehicles ahead of you were either churning up dust or mud.

We'd had 10 days of R.R.R. and were now heading north again to re-lieve the 913th Field Artillery Battalion (88th Division) in the Idice Valley, and to assume direct support of the 361st Infantry Regiment of the 91st Division.

Wednesday, March 28, 1945   Got to our position on the river bank at 3:15 a.m. I had to come back then to 88th Division Artillery; it was about 4:00 then, so I just went to sleep on the front seats of the peep. Woke up at 6:15, cold, stiff and damp. Dick came here at 9:00. The 88th's agents have moved out, so Dick and I are taking their place. It's in a barn, but I am comfortable. One fellow gave me a good light, a fancy bed-lamp, so I am well contented.

Went to the battalion right after supper. It just takes 15 minutes, and a good road. Back at 6:00.

Am very tired, but will write home and read awhile. No shells coming in, and very few going out.

Our armies on the Western Front are making spectacular drives into the heart of Germany. Again — who does that guy Hitler think he is? Doesn't he know, or does he just refuse to believe?

I hope our American government never gets the same idea that it can fanaticize its own people, and dictate to the world by force of arms.

Thursday, March 29, 1945   Took Lt. Aikers to 34th Division. He is a likable fellow. He insists on talking German to me — I usually give him no more satisfaction than to answer "Ja!" ("Yes") or "Ja wohl!" ("Yes indeed") and sometimes for added emphasis, I'll throw in a "Du haben Sie recht gesagt!" ("You, sir, have spoken correctly.")

To the battalion twice. Nate Levy came along tonight. Had a ter-rific headache. Went to bed early.

The weather remained dry and sunny, and there was much speculation about the time, place, and extent of the spring push that the Army Com-mander had promised a few days earlier in the *Stars and Stripes*.

Some recon had been made of a position area that the battalion had occupied the previous fall, but specific instructions were still lacking at the close of the month.

My letter home of March 28 is really dull reading, and short. "Weather is good," is about what I told them. The paper I used looks like the recycled paper we now have in 2000. I had picked up a bunch of it in what must have been a storage place for school supplies. Anyway, I hadn't been short of paper.

It seemed odd to me that in many places where the Germans could have done a lot of vandalism, they hadn't. The place where I found the paper hadn't been hurt much at all. They were only after buildings, bridges, soldiers and sometimes civilians — but had left the paper alone.

Friday, March 30, 1945   Overslept a bit. George bawled us out, but we got fed anyway.

A beautiful day. Good Friday. Am reading *The Man Nobody Knows,* a fitting book in memory of the day's significance.

Took Maj. Smith to II Corps Artillery this p.m.

To the battalion tonight. Came back late.

Saturday, March 31, 1945   Cleaned up. Put my blankets out to air. Took Adams to 109th. Took out a special to 151st and 185th. Back at 3:00.

Took a sponge bath and changed clothes all around.

To the battalion tonight. Got 8 letters, from Bob Vaughn, home, and from Ray. Bob and Jean Vaughn are at Camp Hood, Texas. Jean is expecting a child. Wrote to them.

This was Bob and Jean's first child and one of the first of the "Baby-boomer Generation."

CHAPTER 30

Big Push. Premature shell bursts. German prisoners. FDR dies.
End of Hitler and Goebels. Finito Benito.
End of the war in Europe.

Sunday, April 1, 1945 Easter. Two fried eggs for breakfast. Wrote home and to Ray.
Out several times. Beautiful day.
No church services that I knew of. Read my Bible, which I usually do.

My letter home mentioned I could hear church bells in every town I went through. I said we were feeling optimistic, and that I was going to send my chopper mitts back home. I told them I'd heard Bill Kajikawa was back in Italy again, so not to send him a package.

Monday, April 2, 1945 Scott and I washed our peeps this morning. To the battalion twice. Cooler and windy.

Tuesday, April 3, 1945 Greased my peep this morning. Cool and windy. Slept this p.m. To the battalion several times.

Wednesday, April 4, 1945 Nothing much. Went to see Don tonight. Read a lot today, and sat around in the peep.

Thursday, April 5, 1945 Made one trip after supper. Stays light until almost 8:30. Went with Nate to take a shower. To bed at 9:00.

Friday, April 6, 1945 Did a little work on my peep. Clear weather, but cool wind. To the battalion several times.

Saturday, April 7, 1945 Took a special out right after dinner. Out again tonight. Had to take Capt. Fisher to Division. Back at 9:00.

Sunday, April 8, 1945 There was church at 9:00, but I found out too late about it.

Took Prine to Annes, one of our previous positions. A little girl there about Arlene's age. Remember her from before.

To the battalion tonight. Two letters from Mom and Ray.

Gains are still being made on Western and Eastern Fronts, though limited.

Monday, April 9, 1945   Nothing.

Tuesday, April 10, 1945   Turned warm again. Went to the clothing exchange this p.m.

To the battalion tonight, twice. A special came out at 7:30 for all battalions and 77th Group. Back at 9:30.

Another special for all battalions, but Duke took mine out.

Wednesday, April 11, 1945   A beautiful day, warm and sunny. Washed and shaved. Started reading *My Return to Religion,* by Link.

To the battalion before supper on the routine run. At 9:30 I went to all battalions with specials. Back at 11:30. Dark, but warm, and good roads, so I didn't mind it. A letter from Mom.

Tuesday, April 12, 1945   Up at 6:00. Packed up, got ready to move.

Took Lloyd Dahl to the Ordnance. Cooler and windy. We (Division Artillery) moved up to where C Battery of 151 was last winter. I am in a pup tent.

To the outfit after supper. Raining just a little. The roads are highways compared to what they were last winter when I had to come here.

Friday, April 13, 1945   Didn't sleep well. A terrific barrage went out a 4 a.m. Many premature V-T fuse bursts, as dangerous as incoming enemy fire. Guns of all sizes and descriptions around us.

Went to the battalion after breakfast. Cleaned up. Slept a little.

To the battalion at 6:30 with *Stars and Stripes*. President Roosevelt died last night. The paper carried full account of it. He was a great man. He did a lot for our country, and distinguished himself by being President for 12 years.

I couldn't understand the premature shell bursts. We were in as much danger from them as from enemy fire. Why did the Brass allow it to happen? Where were our brainy officers when this was happening? It seemed they were testing the new weaponry on us as well as on the enemy. All the other fellows felt the same, yet there was no safe place to go. There was no explanation, no apology — just the fact that some of the 105 shells with the new V-T fuses were exploding in the air before they reached their targets. We'd all seen it happen.

The 168th Infantry Headquarters and Staff relieved the 133rd in preparation for the attack which was to be made with only one regiment, the other two regiments being held in reserve. Based on patrol intelligence, it was thought that the enemy had withdrawn by April 12.

Daylight patrols were sent out, and heavy small arms and mortar fire were encountered all along the front. One twelve-man patrol from the 133rd was captured in the vicinity of the church at Gorgonano.

Firing was done each day over a seven day period, but the enemy showed little reaction other than flare activity and some machine gun fire.

My letter home of April 13 told them that now we could get all the tooth powder and brushes we wanted, and I mentioned that the leaves were all greened out on the trees by this time.

Saturday, April 14, 1945   Stopped to see Don last night. Took papers to the battalion. Another hectic night. Premature bursts until about 1:00, when I finally fell asleep. After that, I don't remember.

Up at 7:00. Henderson was killed here last night. His dugout caved in on him. Little emotion shown about it.

I had my shirt off for an hour and got sunburned. Packed over my box. Slept a little this p.m., but it's really too warm in the pup tent.

Progress is still being made on the Western and Eastern Fronts. Leipzig has fallen, or is almost encircled.

To the battalion before supper. Roast chicken here.

Sunday, April 15, 1945   I found some shell fragments not too far from my tent yesterday morning. Duke and I vowed we would sleep under cover tonight — no if's, and's or but's. We took our bed rolls and went in the farm house, found a corner, and had a good night's sleep.

Went to church at 9:00. Chaplain Temple gave the sermon. Text was the 10th chapter of St. Matthew, that one shouldn't be ashamed or apologetic because one is a Christian. Services were outside by the Medic's Center.

Another warm day, almost hot at 9:30 p.m.

To the battalion 3 times tonight. The last trip back was 10:30. Went to the Italian home again tonight.

Duke was the agent from the 185th for awhile. He was a good driver, and not afraid to call a "spade" a "spade."

The problem of the premature exploding shells must have been fixed after a few days, because I don't remember it happening after about this time.

On the 15th of April, the battalion displaced to its battle positions, and at 2 a.m. on the 16th, the attack was started.

Sgt. Dion was wounded when he stepped on an antipersonnel mine as he was laying wire.

Monday, April 16, 1945   Another beautiful day, though not quite as warm as yesterday. Worked until 11:00 on my peep. Changed oil, greased it, tightened some things.

Took Fischer and Grant to the 151 for dinner. Back at 1:00. Went to 804th. This p.m. took #65 to the battalion again.

Got a book, *The Bible for the Common Reader,* by Mary Chase.

The long-awaited attack came off this morning and most of the day. Little gain, if any. Tremendous artillery barrage going out since 2 a.m.

The 168th Infantry passed through the position of the 133rd and launched the attack. The 133rd withdrew, reassembled in the rear, and stayed in Division reserve. The 175th Field Artillery Battalion assumed direct support of the Division sector, and then the 151st reverted to general support.

Progress was very slow; the infantry encountered heavy mortar and machine gun fire, but little artillery fire. For the next three days, the Division artillery delivered heavier concentrations of fire than for any previous engagement in Italy. Ammo trains were on the roads night and day, and frequent reliefs of drivers had to be made to keep the trucks rolling.

The Germans were leaving a lot of equipment behind, including ancient wooden-wheeled artillery pieces, showing how far the Nazis had stretched the resources of Germany.

The full horror of the

Nazis' crimes began to become clear to the West, with the liberation of Belsen and Buchenwald by British and American forces respectively.

The 5th and 8th Armies were in major offensive operations at this time. The 5th Army attacks were sent in on either side of the roads to Bologna from Florence and Pistoia. In this latter sector, Vergato was taken.

Tuesday, April 17, 1945   Some ground was gained by us, but by painful, costly effort. The attack continues. The 175th fired 6000 rounds. How long are those stupid stubborn xxxcensoredsxxx going to be able to stand such punishment?

Wednesday, April 18, 1945   Slept at the house again. Still tremendous artillery fire on our part. To the battalion twice. Read in *Life* and *Time* magazines. Ernie Pyle, the correspondent who wrote *Brave Men* about the Italian Campaign, was killed today in the Pacific. Wrote to Ray tonight. Hot during the daytime. Usually have my shirt off for an hour or two.

By this time we had been capturing a lot of German prisoners. Division P.O.W. was located about two miles behind the lines in a stable adjoining a farm house. I had been there before, but my only business was to see that the P.O.W. got in the hands of an M.P. guard. They'd ask him what Division he was from, which battalion, which company, and sometimes there were some personal questions as well — but there was little in it that was any of a messenger agent's business, so I'd just drop off the prisoner and head back to where I had come from.

One of the first prisoners I'd brought to the rear was in or around Salerno at the beginning of the Italian Campaign. I had asked him in German if I could see what German money looked like. He had dug in his pocket and tried to give me his entire wallet. I refused, as I couldn't have taken it without some serious consequences, though actually, he had no use for it anyway. I had wanted something small as a souvenir.

None of the P.O.W.s I had experience with had a belligerent attitude — just the opposite, in fact. They seemed to be glad to be away from the front. I found out later that it wasn't the real Nazi soldiers who would walk back to us waving a white flag. The real Nazi's were the ones who had been with the Party since the early 1930's, who had been indoctrinated in the Hitler Youth Movement.

By 1945, most of the prisoners knew the war was coming to an end. As German defeat neared, incoming prisoners were more likely to be old men and young kids, a sign that Germany was stretching its manpower to the very limit. One prisoner said it was obvious to him that Germany would lose, but there were still those who wouldn't believe it.

German P.O.W.s were treated well enough in the States. There were at one time or another 20 P.O.W. camps in Minnesota under the jurisdiction of a base camp in Algona, Iowa. The number of prisoners in Minnesota peaked in September 1945, when there were 3,480 Germans housed in 13 camps.

During the war, the prisoners were used to help ease manpower shortages in America caused by the large amount of our men fighting overseas. Paid 80 cents a day, the prisoners in Minnesota helped with harvests on farms and worked in canning factories, brickyards and the logging industry. Some of us calculated that the 80 cents a day was about 10 cents a day more than we were paid for the first 4 months we were in the Army at $21 a month, though our pay was raised to $30 a month after the 4th month.

*[Present day American prisoners (now called "residents") in a local work-farm type correctional facility in this county are paid $1.50 a day for hard farm labor. Some are in for assault against other human beings, but the biggest category of the residents there are for traffic crimes -- many for drinking and driving, and some for driving without license and insurance. They are billed for their own medical care, unless injured while working for the facility. Local youths (under age 18) are made to do free labor for some local businesses, institutions, individuals and farms for crimes such as skipping school, exhibiting a poor attitude, drinking and smoking cigarettes. Many times their parents are billed for their kids' "treatment," and the kids are forcibly "medicated" (drugged) to improve their behavior.

Though the German soldier P.O.W.s had comparatively longer sentences to serve than do our present-day American young people, it seems their treatment was comparatively good as well. Most of them left the US with a very good attitude toward the American system. As my Grandma, Elsie Wagner used to say, "You can generally catch more flies with honey than with vinegar."]*

Conditions for German prisoners actually got worse after the war, as the Army started feeding them poorer food, possibly in retaliation for reports of how poorly American prisoners were treated in Germany.

Alfred Mueller was one P.O.W. who was kept in Minnesota. He arrived back in Germany in June of 1946, but his folks had been killed in the bombing, and he discovered that his home corner of Berlin had been devastated. He emigrated to the US and ended up working for General Mills. Like many veterans, he attended Division reunions. He went to those of our 34th Division, the unit he fought against in Tunisia.

Tuesday, April 19, 1945   Dick and I moved forward tonight. Got shelled. Dusty. Moved up 65. Pianora is literally demolished. Are just southeast of Bologna.

The 168th had made advances of 1500 to 2000 yards by the 19th, and was bolstered by the 133rd which was committed on that day on the left. The Division sector had been widened to the west by a shift of units of the 91st Division. Lt. Grahn, forward observer from C Battery, was wounded by a sniper and evacuated shortly after he established an O.P. in front of the 133rd.

Division Artillery Headquarters ordered a harassing program of 100 rounds per hour during daylight, and 60 rounds per hour at night. The infantry had pushed beyond Pianoro now, and flat country gave attached armor more maneuverability.

Recon parties pushed out close behind the infantry over roads as yet unswept for mines, and littered with dead Germans, horses and mules.

[...] *Editor's comments.*

My letter home of April 19 didn't have much war news; I only mentioned that the dried beef they had sent in the last package was completely spoiled by the time I got it. I said I hadn't been getting much mail in lately, and that my driving tasks had increased recently.

Friday, April 20, 1945   Somewhere in between here is April 20th. We went to Bologna today. The Italians are happy people to get rid of the Krauts. People stand close to the vehicles and want to hold your hand; they throw flowers and kisses. I feel like the President when he goes along shaking hands.

I sent a letter to my sister Arlene to wish her a happy birthday. It was her 9th, and I enclosed $5.00. I'd received her report card and also my brother Roger's, and I said they were very good. I told her the weather is like summer where we were in Northern Italy (this wasn't censored), and that everything was green and warm.

Saturday, April 21, 1945   Division Artillery is within half a mile of Bologna, and our battalion not far away.

Really the 3rd Battalion of the 133rd entered Bologna from the south, as the II Polish came in from the east on April 21.

Writing in this diary and keeping the days straight isn't easy when moving up and in a hurry.

No resistance was offered in the city of Bologna itself, and Italian Partisans were making a roundup of all known Fascists, while American, Polish and Italian troops of the 5th and 8th Armies streamed through the city. Civilians jammed the streets all day long shouting "Viva!" and throwing flowers at the victorious troops.

I didn't see any damage at all in Bologna. It was a large city, approximately 400,000. It was built largely of the finest of Italian brick. It had been a Roman colony several hundred years before Christ. I would really have liked to have spent some time here, but I knew this wasn't likely to happen with the end of the war approaching so quickly.

Sunday, April 22, 1945   To the battalion 4 times. Hot and dusty. Much traffic on the side of the road.

The enthusiasm and greetings of the civilians was as heady as champagne, and greatly inspired the soldiers of our armies who had been stalemated throughout the long winter in the mountains of the South.

As soon as the town was entered, the Division Commander detailed Maj. Surdyk to establish liaison with the Polish Corps where he stayed throughout the days.

Monday, April 23, 1945   Have had no chance to write since the 18th, so have been filling in. We are in Bologna, but ready to move again. I moved with the battalion at 2:30, back at 3:30, out again at 6:00, out again at 7:30. All specials.

We moved at 10:00, through Bologna and 30 miles northwest. This p.m. Lt. Adams and I went to the 151st as liaison between here and there.

We moved up with the battalion through Modena. We were some of the first troops to go through. People lined the streets in droves to greet us, throwing flowers and waving. We were ahead of everything at times; Modena wasn't actually in our hands when the 151 went through — only a few tanks had gone through before us. I saw 4 Germans killed laying on the side of the road. There was still sniping going on.

This is the Po Valley. Hot, very beautiful country. Level. Many fruit trees, usually with grain planted between. Fairly modern buildings. The farmers are all making hay. All cattle are in the barns for safety's sake against shellfire. Some tractors and also horses. The farms are similar, in a way, but different from those at home.

I'm very thankful to be out of the Appenines. We are on Hwy 9. Am very tired; I've only had about 3 hours sleep since the night before last. Then I had about 4 hours.

The 34th Division had been detailed to garrison Bologna, but the rapid withdrawal of the Krauts changed this, and the Division was ordered to move out the following day. We had thought that this one would be our prize, instead of seeing the M.P.s take over, but again, no luck.

Large pockets of Germans had to be by-passed, and the Division was given the mission of destroying or capturing these enemy troops. A march was made through Modena to Reggio, forty miles west of Bologna, before any substantial resistance was met.

On April 12, the Air O.P.s observed a considerable amount of movement and destroyed a great amount of enemy motor transport, guns, horses and troops. During this action, Pvt. Robbins of Headquarters Battery was wounded and evacuated while with a liaison party.

Several thousand prisoners and much equipment were taken in this area. When the infantry reached a point just south of the Po River in the vicinity of Piacenza, the Brazilian Expeditionary Force took over, and the Division went on another long end run back through Modena and north across the Po to the vicinity of Bergamo. From Bergamo, the infantry regiments fanned out westward, taking prisoners and mopping up without resistance.

Tuesday, April 24, 1945   Moved through Ruberia and Reggio. Lots of chasing around, but don't mind it. Still sniper fire in Reggio.

To make this rapid advance, the artillery battalions furnished transport to shuttle the infantry. The doughboys were utilizing all captured transport that was capable of rolling. With the addition of truckloads of heavily armed, red-bandanaed Italian Partisans, the long columns of vehicles took on the aspect of gypsy caravans.

Long convoys of German vehicles towing ack-ack and field guns, and still being driven by their Kraut drivers, streamed down the roads to the P.O.W. compounds in what seemed an endless column. Many of the P.O.W.s were nurses and women auxiliaries. By the end of the period, the total of prisoners taken by the 5th Army reached 160,000.

The battalion was preparing to displace again from the vicinity of Bergamo to an area northwest of Milan, where the German 75th Corps was reported to be dug in and awaiting a fight.

Wednesday, April 25, 1945 Took a side road; actually it was today that we went through Reggio, and not yesterday. Moved this morning and tonight. Went back to Division Artillery tonight about 10:30.

Thursday, April 26, 1945 Scott and I went looking for the Air O.P. this morning. We made 71 miles in less than 1 ½ hours. Could go 62 m.p.h. The road is perfect.

Stopped at Reggio. Division Artillery moved again through Prava. A small-arms battle between Jerry snipers and Partisans. One bullet knocked out glass above me.

Lt. Smith and I are liaison with 151 now. Still rapidly advancing up Highway 9. Much German equipment litters the highway. Most dead are quickly removed, though I saw one this morning.

Rained a little and made the highway slippery, but still fine weather.

Took off north from #9 on another good blacktop road. We are in a beautiful building, a farm house that must be the landlord's. Our guns are still firing a little, but we are still advancing. Made 2 trips to Division Artillery with Lt. Smith. Are sleeping in a tool room with Tom McGee.

I liked being with Lt. Smith, as I didn't feel as if I was his driver, but rather that both of us were working on it.

Only one dead German was one too many at this part of the war — most we saw were the helpless who had gotten sucked into the Nazi war machine.

On April 23, Goering sent a message to Hitler offering to take over the leadership of the Reich, if Hitler should become unable to continue with that task by becoming surrounded and harassed in Berlin. Hitler was furious at

Goering's presumption and ordered his arrest.

Dessau on the Elbe was taken by the 1st Army, and British forces began attacks near Bremen. To the south, Ulm was taken on the Danube, and the French 1st Army continued its advance in the Black Forest region.

Friday, April 27, 1945   Had to make one trip to Division Artillery last night around 1 a.m. Took less than an hour. Raining this morning, rained quite a bit during the night.

Moved again, raining most of the day. Several more trips to Division Artillery.

Both 5th and 8th Army units have been pouring across the Po and into the valley for 3 days; there's little or nothing now the Germans can do. I'm thinking now when I see hay being made, that with luck, I'll be home even this summer helping make some more of it.

On April 25, the US 1st Army met up with the Soviet forces at Torgau on the Elbe. The US 3rd Army crossed the Danube near Regensburg, and was attacked there. Berlin had been entered in the south and the east.

Saturday, April 28, 1945   We moved on to #9 again today; are in kind of an assembly area. Nice place alongside the road.

Several trips to Division Artillery. A pretty girl came up to talk — she could speak German. Always nice to talk a little to them.

As far as I can tell, we came through Modena and Parma, maybe farther.

It was nice to go through Modena, a city of over 150,000. There were no old, narrow streets here, and there was a really tall 290 foot cathedral. Parma was another city worth forfeiting a furlough in order to see. It looked modern, with straight streets. The people were wild for the Americans. Both Modena and Parma were Roman colonies before Christ.

Seeing these cities had to have been a part of the glory of war — there wasn't much glory in the shooting, killing, seeing the wounded and the dead, slogging through the mud, or slowly advancing toward the front. That's where the fear, and the sickly feeling and the wondering of "Why are we doing this?" come in instead of glory. As Desiderius Erasmus said a few hundred years ago, "War is delightful to those who have had no experience of it."

I was also happy to be out of the mountains. I'd seen enough of mountains to last me a lifetime, and I still prefer the valleys. The hills in Duluth are more than I want to climb nowadays.

An ersatz surrender ceremony affecting all troops fighting in Italy took place at 2 p.m. on April 28. The ceremony was kept somewhat secret; the German officers were dressed in civilian clothes, and were acting on their own. A German major and lieutenant colonel appeared at the peace table before Gen. Morgan and many other high-ranking American and British officers. Their muscles were taut, their hands were clenched fiercely together behind their backs, and they had an "I hate you" expression on their face, just opposite of most of the low-ranking prisoners I had hauled to the rear.

The German lieutenant colonel said for the record that he had received only limited powers from his Commander in Chief, and that he was being forced to overstep those limits. He assumed his Commander would approve his action, but said he could not be sure if this was the case.

Gen. Morgan just told him casually, "We accept those conditions."

The Germans sat and signed 5 copies of the surrender documents, and Gen. Morgan signed them last. The Germans left swiftly, and the ceremony was over at 2:17.

Sunday, April 29, 1945   A day I won't forget for awhile. Up at 7:00. Pulled out at 8:30. Made 172 miles. Cold and windy. Really enjoyed it, though. Thick droves of people lined the road all the way. Many beautiful girls, and well-dressed adults and younger people, all waving and cheering. Some close enough to you hold out their hands to touch yours.

Saw thousands of German prisoners. I counted 35 heavily loaded vehicles with Jerry prisoners, some high ranking officers, also nurses, all standing in their trucks, with Kraut drivers heading north.

We just crossed the Po again today, as wide as the Missouri River. We're at the foot of the Alps; they tower high in the distance, capped with snow. Am sure glad we don't have to chase Jerry through the

Brenner Pass. We've heard about that place.

We parked in a courtyard for the night. Was a hard day, but nice driving on a good road, and made good time. Tom McGee rode with me.

Monday, April 30, 1945   Laid around most of the day, but went to Division Artillery several times. They are in a large town. It seems we were supposed to get to Bergamo, but I'm not sure. I don't think the Krauts who we heard were waiting there to ambush us are going to — after all, the Germans are heading homewards.

We are close to, or in the outskirts of Milan.

All the Italians are chanting "Finito, Benito!" and he is pretty well finished, all right. He and his mistress Clare Petacci are hanging by their heels in the main square of Milan for all to see. Dick and I were going to go, but we changed our minds. Some of our fellows went to see Benito and his girlfriend, and said it was a pretty gory sight. It seems this couple was almost in Switzerland on vacation when they were intercepted.

The Soviets were a mile from Hitler's bunker in the east and south. On April 29, Hitler married Eva Braun in his bunker and prepared his political testament. He appointed Admiral Doenitz as his successor, and described how Germany had failed him in the struggle against Bolshevism. The next day he and Eva committed suicide. Their bodies were carried outside, doused with gasoline and burned.

Hitler had said back in 1933, "I am insulted by the persistent assertion that I want war. Am I a fool? War! It would settle nothing."

President Roosevelt had said during discussions of what the Allies were going to do with Germany after the war was over, that the US had no intent to destroy the German people or ruin their nation — but we did intend to teach them that they are not a "Master Race." I guess the war did settle that, and it definitely settled that Hitler was a fool.

The concentration camp at Dachau was liberated along with 30,000 surviving inmates by troops from the US 3rd Army. The sight of Dachau was far worse than anything the American infantrymen had seen even on the battlefield. Forty railroad cars with 2,000 corpses in them were parked at a railroad siding, with thousands more corpses stacked like cordwood near the crematorium. The SS troops had run out of fuel and out of time to burn them. Emaciated survivors could hardly make their way out of the filthy, crowded barracks to greet their liberators, and some died as they made the effort.

Tuesday, May 1, 1945   Rained most of the day. We finally pulled out at 6 p.m. and came about 47 miles to a little town. I believe we are east of Milan, but everything is sketchy now.

20,000 Germans surrendered this A.M. to the 135th. This about winds up the Campaign for Italy. I am very Thankful. Hitler is supposed to be dead. Munich has fallen. Troops in Austria have surrendered. Our prayers to God have been answered.

May 3 Thurs. slept very soundly but awoke with a headache. Fixed the tire that went flat, it too was ruined so got two new ones. Changed oil, cleaned out my jeep. Washed and shaved. Wrote home. Slept a little this AM. to the BN. Noose came along. Was cold close to the Alps. They tower in the fore ground. Had to load all my things and was supposed to go out with Lt. Smith again but was called off. I waited around till 12:00 then finally slept in Message Center.
May 4 Fri. up at 6:00 Smith [and] I rolled at 6:45 got to the 151 arty. in time to move with them. Moved 47 miles, went to one place but Bn. didn't stay. Lempke and I went looking around, found a house or room where mother and beautiful daughter lived, they gave us coffee. Smith and I had dinner then went 66 miles back to Div Arty. Got here at 3:30. Smith is going home on rotation tomorrow, so I'm staying here again tonite. Are on outskirts of fairly large town. Am staying with Dick in an office, has 2 desks, electric heater and lights.
May 5 Sat. W. Grueber and I went back to the 151 this morning. Got back around noon. Sat up my

1945

etc, read a little. Tonite we went
to Callarche. Drank wine. Found a fellow
that could speak German. Also went to
Busto Arizico. Saw a carnival there
Just like at the fairs

May 5th. Grueber and I made the
round trip to Div. Arty. again. Tried
to take a short cut back, went through
lots of towns, many beautiful women.
Back at 4:30. 130 miles round trip. Went
to Busto Arezio again Tonite. Met a
pretty girl but she was only 16. Back
about 10:30 a half hr. late
May 7 1902. Grueber and I made the
trip again. Went to Vicenese where
Div Arty. will move. Beautifull weather
and country. Can see Mt. Rosa from
here. Switzerland is very close. We
have strict orders to keep away.
On the way back we passed through
a little village. The whistles were
blowing and people cheering — The war
in Europe is over".
May 8 9th. We made the trip again

May 9. Went came to Vinese where
Div. Arty. will be.
May 10 there overslept till 8:00. Greased
my peep and washed it. Beautifull
weather but a little too warm.
Div Arty is in Vinese, a town of about
40.000. The 151 is in Malnate 5 miles
away. We are about 4 miles from
the Swiss border. I had a terrific
headache all day. Scott and I put up a
wall tent, in a back garden, puts us
by ourselves where its quiet.
Nate and I went after my laundry
tonite, in another little town

We were already receiving notices of a type that would arise with the cessation of hostilities. The Commanding Officer of the 133rd Infantry Regiment stated that any man found firing a round of ammunition after hostilities ceased would be court-martialed. Hearing this sort of order was morale-raising.

Wednesday, May 2, 1945   We pulled into a cotton factory at 10:30. Tom and I had to place the line batteries. To bed by 11:30.

Up again at 2:00 and to Division Artillery. Lynn came along. It was hard to find — we had to get a Partisan to help us. The rain was coming down in sheets.

Back at 4:00, and we moved out at 5:00. Came another 30 miles. Really cold and raining. We parked at a farm house. A really pretty girl was there. Smith and I had to go to Division Artillery 4 times, 14 miles each way. It cleared up, but it's still cold.

Tonight I reported back to Division Artillery. We're in a small town, probably Busto Arsizio. Dick and I walked around town a bit, but not much was going on. Nate, Barney, Dick, Les and I are staying in an Italian home, nicely furnished, very pleasant and comfortable. We have our cots set up in a front room. One woman speaks perfect English. Reminds me so much of being home.

40,000 Germans surrendered this p.m. to the 135th. This about winds up the campaign for Italy. I'm very thankful. Hitler is supposed to be dead. Munich has fallen. Troops in Austria have surrendered. Our prayers to God have been answered.

On May 2nd, word of surrender came from the entire German 75th Corps to a unit of the 34th Division. This was the same Corps that we had expected to engage, since word had been received that they were dug in and waiting for a fight. Later on the same day came news of the unconditional surrender of all German troops in Italy.

I hadn't been able to see much of Milan, as I had been busy driving Lt. Smith. Actually, my interest in seeing Italian cities was at a low ebb at the time anyway, and I enjoyed hearing about the larger picture of what was going on in the war from the lieutenant.

Milan was a large city. There were modern sections with really wide streets, and also old narrow streets. The cathedrals, amphitheaters, universities and palaces took my breath away.

Thursday, May 3, 1945   The shooting has finally stopped. We didn't register any 105's yesterday. I got a too-good night's sleep, and woke up with a headache.

CHAPTER 30

Took the tire apart that went flat yesterday, but it too was ruined, so I got 2 new ones. Changed oil, cleaned out my peep, washed and shaved. Wrote home. Slept a little this p.m. Moose came along when I went to the battalion.

Is cold. We're close to the Alps. They tower in the foreground. I loaded all my things and was ready to go out with Lt. Smith, but it was called off. I waited around until 12:00, then finally slept in Message Center.

The nearby mountains were high, with snow on top. I wasn't anxious to ever get closer to them. This was country that tourists would love to see, but I hoped my forgeterer worked good just as soon as I could head out.

My diary was getting a little bulky in my shirt pocket after 4 years, and I wished I could have written more, but I was just glad I had as much as I had. "Don't spoil what you have by dreaming about what you have not."

I supposed any other accounts of soldiers' activities had maybe been kept by personnel in Division Headquarters, or somewhere else where there would be an official safe place to transport it while enroute. I figured that even if I was ever to see my barracks bag again, I didn't expect to find many of my personal things left in it, after it had spent all this time with the non-combatants in the rear.

We couldn't expect too much of the forward echelon now either, because we were it as much as anyone else was, and it took a little time to get it sorted out.

A letter sent home dated May 3rd said we were thankful to be through with this campaign, but that they shouldn't expect me home for awhile. Headquarters was only giving us encouragement about increasing the furlough quota. I told of how beautiful the Po valley was, and of the wide Po River where the bridges weren't blasted away. I told them of the house where we 4 messengers were staying where the lady spoke perfect English, and I said I'd had my first full night's sleep since April 20th.

Friday, May 4, 1945   Up at 6:00. Smith and I rolled at 6:45. Got to the 151st just in time to move with them. Moved 47 miles. We went to one place, but the battalion didn't stay there.

Jemke and I went looking around. Found a house where a mother and beautiful daughter lived. They gave us coffee and a dinner there, then we went 66 miles back to Division Artillery. Got here at 3:30. Smith is going home on rotation tomorrow, so I'm staying here again tonight. Are on outskirts of a fairly large town. Am staying with Dick in an office; it has 2 desks, electric heater and lights.

Smith and I were a sort of reconnaissance party looking out for those who wanted a good area to stay in.

We were close to the town of Vicolungo. This position was not approved by our Upper Classmen, however, so after more reconnaissance we moved just south to Rocetto.

Mail delivery was scarce during this period. I was really feeling bad at the time that I had no more film, but I'd made a few special trips and stops and got quite a few good postcard pictures.

Just about any time we were served food by the Italians, it was spaghetti with tomato sauce. Cheese seemed to be plentiful too. When I was younger, I had different tastes in food than I do now, and I didn't really appreciate the spaghetti.

Saturday, May 5, 1945   Lt. Grueber and I went back to the 151 this morning. Got back about noon. Set up my cot. Read a little. Tonight we went to Collerate. Drank wine, and found a fellow who could speak German. Also went to Busto Arsizio and saw a carnival there, just like the fairs at home.

Sunday, May 6, 1945   Grueber and I made the round trip to Division Artillery again. Tried to take a shortcut back. Went through lots of towns, were many beautiful women. Back at 4:30. 130 miles round trip.

Went to Busto Arsizio again tonight. Met a pretty girl but she was only 16. Back at 10:30 — a half hour late.

There was little or no traffic, except for military, and in some of the out-of-the-way towns, none of that either.

We must have had a 10:00 curfew, though I'm not sure, as my memory is still good, but getting shorter. At this time I couldn't hide behind the excuse of taking out specials or coordinates in order to be on the roads and in the towns anymore — but going with Lt.'s Smith and Grueber was even better, as nobody questioned you if an officer was in the peep.

In Berlin, Goebbels and his wife committed suicide after poisoning their six children. News was trickling in to us about the horrors of the "Final Solution" to the Jewish problem in Germany: the concentration camps, and the "extermination" in the gas chambers. We heard that German Brass were being arrested, but many were escaping.

Monday, May 7, 1945   Lt. Grueber and I made the trip again. Went to Varese, where Division Artillery will be moving. Beautiful weather and country. Can see Mt. Rosa from here. Switzerland is very close, but we have strict orders to keep away.

On the way back as we were passing through a little village, the whistles were blowing and people were cheering. The war in Europe is over!

502

I started blowing my horn.

We'd been expecting this, but didn't know exactly when it was coming. This was the final full surrender of Germany, and officially it. Admiral Freideburg and Gen. Jodl signed the unconditional German surrender at Gen. Eisenhower's Headquarters. British, French, Soviet and American representatives were all present. Military operations were to cease at 23:01 on 8 May, 1945. Two merchant ships sunk by U-2326 at the Firth of Forth in Scotland were the last U-boat victims of World War II.

We had been feeling as if we were at a basketball game with the score 40 to 65, with 3 minutes left to play. The full benefit of the victory doesn't come until the game is really over. But now it was over.

CHAPTER 31

Out-processing and the trip home.

Tuesday, May 8, 1945   Grueber and I made the trip again.

We had many good experiences this time of the war that I just didn't take the time or effort to put in print. It was beginning soak "in," and our top priority was to get "out."

Prime Minister Winston Churchill made the announcement on the radio that "Hostilities have ceased one minute after midnight, Tuesday, May 8." So came the end of the war in Europe. There was no hilarious celebrating, but the feeling of contentment and relaxation was predominant.

The 151st received word that we would have the mission of guarding prisoners, so Maj. Francis and Maj. Surdyk took working parties out to prepare the P.O.W. cage near Sesto Calende.

Wednesday, May 9, 1945   Came to Varese, where Division Artillery will be.

Thursday, May 10, 1945   Overslept until 8:00. Greased my peep and washed it. Beautiful weather, but a little too warm. Division Artillery is in Varese, a town of about 40,000. The 151st is in Malnate, 5 miles away. We are about 4 miles from the Swiss border. I had a terrific headache all day.

Scott and I put up a wall tent in the back garden. Puts us by ourselves where it's quiet. Nate and I went after my laundry tonight in another little town where no GIs are. The Italians make much of us. It's hard to believe the war is actually over. We have waited so long.

The point system came out from the War Department. I will have 104.

Friday, May 11, 1945   Up at 7:00. Another beautiful day. Cleaned up. Made several trips to Malnate where the battalion is. Dick and I went to Division rear, got *Stars and Stripes* and brought them to Dick's battalion. They are at Somma Lombardo. Nate and I went driving around a bit tonight.

Saturday, May 12, 1945   It was my turn to go to Division by [Piper] Cub today, but the battalion moved to Sesto Calendo, so I moved with them. About 20 miles away now, but beautiful roads.

Went out again after dinner. Dick and I made another trip to Division rear, and to the battalion before supper. Talked with Barney awhile. Took a sponge bath.

Sunday, May 13, 1945   Breakfast at 8:00. Shaved and cleaned up as usual. A little girl came and got my laundry. Beautiful weather and surroundings make one very thankful to be alive. Several trips to the battalion. Dick and I go together.

We began moving to the new area at 9:30 on the 13th of May. The town is situated on a river which runs into Lake Maggiore. The stockade was further up at a place which was used as a school for the training of torpedo men in the Italian Navy. Even though the place had been pretty well damaged by bombings, it served our purpose perfectly. Excellent work was done by the work details in preparing the cage, and on the 14th, the prisoners began arriving.

Our mission of guarding prisoners came to a sudden end on the 17th when we moved to an area about 10 miles west of Torino (Turin) near the town of Villardon. The battalion settled down to what was hoped to be an extended stay. Orders were issued that an inspection would take place the next afternoon, but the schedule was interrupted with an order from Division Artillery to make a reconnaissance and move artillery battalions into one area.

Monday, May 14, 1945   Usual thing. Beautiful weather.

Tuesday, May 15, 1945   We moved 162 miles today. Barney and Nate rode with me. Part of the way was hot and dusty. We came through Turin, and are close to the French-Italian border, south of Turin. French and Italian Patriots are having trouble; the 34th was brought up here for arbitration.

Am tired out with a headache. We are in a large Italian garrison room for thousands of soldiers.

Wednesday, May 16, 1945   Didn't sleep well in here. Too hot, and too many soldiers. Up at 7:00. Washed and shaved. The flies are thick, like they were at Lake Bizerte. I took a sponge bath this p.m. and changed clothes. Wrote to Ray, Rod and Arlene.

Nate and I went for a ride into Fossana. Had some fried eggs.

A letter home of this date said I would expect to be home in about 6 months. I told them the wheat here was already over a foot tall, and that we all really admired the Po Valley. I said the conditions in the large Italian Army camp we were in were not ideal, and that we hoped the rumor of moving out soon was true.

Thursday, May 17, 1945   We moved to Raconigi this p.m. Set up in pup tents. Dick and I are together. I had to go to the battalion. I left at 7:30, and got back at 11:30. They are 80 miles west of Turin, and hard to find. I took Nate up there and left him. I had a really hard time getting out of Turin. It's a very large city, and damaged a lot on the outside.

Turin's population is over a million, laid out in that Roman style of straight, wide streets. The hugeness of the architecture is too much for me to grasp; no wonder I've got a hard time finding my way through these places. I'm better at it than some are, but it's still too big and strange.

Friday, May 18, 1945   Took my peep into Ordnance this morning. They put in a new transmission. Came back in a 6X6 with Prine. Dick took me to the battalion this p.m. They moved after we were there.

Saturday, May 19, 1945   Dick took me down to get my peep this morning. It runs fine. No trouble in shifting. We took a shower at the clothing exchange. Got a new pair of pants.

I went to the 185th by Cub this p.m. Left here at 12:30, back at 4:30. My first ride in a plane, and I enjoyed it. We landed and took off 4 times [or vice versa]. I'd like to be able to pilot a small plane. We went 2700 feet up at 90 m.p.h.

Ted and I went to the battalion. They are about 5 miles away. Dick and I walked around a little tonight.

The pilot showed off a few things to me; some more German vehicles were coming up the road, and he sort of "dive-bombed" at them, then landed twice in small fields. I guess he didn't have the authority to just fly any-where, but as we were now taking turns going to Division, he liked the chance to go too.

I did finally take flying lessons during the mid-1980's, but I never got my license. It was very expensive, I had a hard time to hear the radio instructions as my hearing was never too keen after the war, and I also lost my nerve. A motorcycle was more to my liking at that stage of my life.

Sunday, May 20, 1945   Up at 8:00. Beautiful morning. This reminds me of Tynan or Enniskillen in Ireland. We are all put up on one of the many little roads that run through this estate. I keep the peep close by.

Went to church at 9:30. The text of Chaplain Temple's sermon was Matthew, Chapter 4.

Got a letter from Mom. Read some, and sent a letter home and a package to Ray.

Barney, Ham and I went to my outfit tonight, then took off to another town and found a laundress. Were lots of people on the streets. We never cease to be the liberators.

Back about 9:00. Lester Lieberman was promoted to Staff Sergeant, and bought drinks for us. Ham and I got 9 eggs for $1.00, and we fried them tonight.

As soon as there is a rating available, that is, whenever someone leaves for home, someone else gets the rating, just to keep the ratings used up, so to speak. I haven't been that lucky, but I still consider myself lucky to have had this job all the time I did.

A letter to home of this date says we were in pup tents and were under some discipline, but I was still exempt from that as the battalions still had daily reports to send out.

This was a large estate we were at — lots of woods, and a castle, which was out of bounds for us. A young boy from one of the families had gotten chummy, and I took his picture.

This was the last picture I took with the Kodak 828 Vest-Pocket camera I had carried hidden in my back pocket thoughout the war. I had been out of film for awhile, but had received a few rolls recently from my brother Ray. I had kept the camera wrapped up in my handkerchief, and several times when I pulled out my handkerchief, the camera fell out, one time landing on the steel deck of one of the ships I was being transported on. It was pretty well cracked up by the end of the war, but I taped it to hold it shut, and it still worked.

Monday, May 21, 1945   Up at 7:00. Took Brown to the Air O.P. Had cramps and wasn't feeling so good. Laid around. Two trips to the battalion. Wrote a few letters and cards tonight. Rained just a little. Are still at the estate.

Some guys are leaving every day, some being transferred to the 88th Division. Major Surdyk left for another assignment. I'm just waiting for transfers to be completed and papers to be made out. We have our choice to fly home in converted bombers or transports, or to go by boats. I chose the plane. Will probably leave early next month.

I got a commendation or a citation (both words are on the paper). It says some nice things about me having done my duty as a battery agent for Headquarters Battery, 151st Field Artillery Battalion, and is signed by Charles L. Bolte, Major General, US Army.

I had never had a chance to explore the grounds here or to see the castle. Whenever I had a chance, I'd go driving, but I wished I'd written down or remembered more.

Tuesday, May 22, 1945   Hot all day. Have that lazy feeling, but it's different than when we were in combat. Got 2 letters from home, and from Ray and Bill. We all had a physical this p.m. Dick and I went to our battalions together. Barney and I talked together for awhile. Had a few drinks of wine with him.

Wednesday, May 23, 1945   Cloudy all day. To the battalion this p.m. Brought Don up here; we had supper together. We went to Murello, and went back there at 9:30. Were supposed to have a date, but it was raining too much and we got soaked. We met the girls, but didn't stay. Back about 11:30, still raining.

Thursday, May 24, 1945   Barney gave a class on English and vocabulary. I attended — interesting. Barney taught school for awhile in Kansas. Took a shower at the clothing exchange. I took out laundry tonight. Did some driving around. Got 3 more dozen eggs. We cooked 15, and ate all but 4 by ourselves.

Friday, May 25, 1945   Attended Barney's class again. Slept a little. Had cooked eggs for dinner. Dick and I went to all battalions tonight. Back around 9:30, had a few more eggs, then to bed.

Why all the eggs? They're readily available, easy to cook, and it will be awhile before any of us gets tired of eggs. The food is pretty good, but it's surprising how much more you can eat and still enjoy it

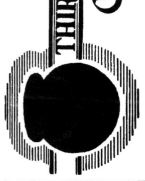

Headquarters
THIRTY FOURTH INFANTRY DIVISION

Commendation

To All Whom It May Concern

CORPORAL WILMER A. WAGNER

is hereby cited for outstanding performance of duty.

CITATION

WILMER A. WAGNER (37026777), Corporal, Field Artillery, Headquarters Battery, 151st Field Artillery Battalion. For exceptionally meritorious conduct from 9 May 1943 to 2 May 1945, in North Africa and Italy. During this period Cpl Wagner served as battery agent for Headquarters Battery, 151st Field Artillery Battalion. Cpl Wagner continuously drove blackout over unfamiliar roads that were often almost impassable due to rainfall. Cpl Wagner furnished valuable information as to the condition of the roads and the location and use of short cuts. Frequently the roads traversed by Cpl Wagner were subjected to heavy enemy harassing fires and information regarding minefields was lacking, but Cpl Wagner never failed to reach his destination in time for operational changes and new plans to be effected. Cpl Wagner's courage and devotion to duty reflect great credit upon himself and the military service. Home address: Duluth, Minnesota.

Charles Bolte

CHARLES L. BOLTE,
Major General, U. S. Army,
Commanding.

when you are relaxed.

My letter home of May 25 was the first one I've noticed that wasn't censored. I told the folks I probably wouldn't be home for awhile, though we were doing practically nothing except making a few short trips. We were still close to Turin. I told them we ate a lot of eggs; we went to farms and bought them pretty cheap, or traded with C rations or a little gasoline.

Saturday, May 26, 1945 Raining, so stayed in bed until 9:30. Cleared up later. Took Harvey Swanson to the 175th. Dick and I took a shower at the clothing exchange. Cool all day. Don Prill left from the battery today, flying home. I have hopes of being home by fall. Wrapped up some things to send home.

Harvey was one of the original medics who I first knew. We never became fast friends, but we always exchanged greetings. Bob Vaughn told me he became a traffic cop in Minneapolis after the war, and he would see him often.

Sunday, May 27, 1945 Attended Memorial Day services this morning at Division Headquarters. We all had to move into pyramidal tents. Got ready, and went out with Don. Picked him up in Casalgrasso. We went to Murello to the dance, and then to Cavaller-maggiori. Met some girls and had ice cream with them. Back about 12:30.

Monday, May 28, 1945 Had a bad headache. Slept until 8:30. Raining tonight, or this p.m. Went riding tonight with the same girls. They really enjoy it. Back about 11:30. Don is going home day after tomorrow. Stopped in to see him.

Tuesday, May 29, 1945 Raining most the day. Slept some. Several trips to the battalion. Ham and I went to Murello again tonight.

Wednesday, May 30, 1945 Fair weather, usual thing. I read a lot, rest, talk, and wait for my day to leave. Northern Italy doesn't hold much attraction for me anymore.

News from the War Department is that about 400,000 men will remain in Germany to form the occupation force. 2,000,000 will be discharged from the armed forces, and 6,000,000 will be left serving in the war against Japan.

Thursday, May 31, 1945 Got paid. Made 4 trips to the battalion. Sun came out today. Warm. Ham and I went riding again tonight.

Headquarters promises me I should either be going home soon or get a promotion — I'm one of the old-timers now.

Friday, June 1, 1945   Clear again today. I could almost write this a week ahead of time.

Saturday, June 2, 1945   Several trips today. The sun came out. Dick and Floyd are leaving for home. We three went to Savigliano. Had Muscato. Back by 11:00.

We were a little sad to be parting, I guess, as we three messengers had been together the most, especially Dick and I. We used the old quote, "Focus on a brighter future helps to get rid of a gloomy past."

We had a feeling that the Army could get along OK without us anyway, even as good as we were in delivering specials, firing orders, map overlays, etc.

We used to tell each other when the weather was bad to "Never judge a day by its weather," and that was pretty much true — but if the day was rainy, snowy, or especially muddy, we knew for pretty sure what the night driving would have in store for us.

But all in all, we were pretty lucky and happy to part as we could — alive. It's a good thing they didn't give Purple Hearts for nervous stomachs or close calls, or we would all have had a full row of them on our uniforms.

I tried to explain to the folks at home how the point system worked, since they, as farmers, just thought that since I'd been gone so long, I should be among the first to come home.

The point system was a little more complicated, though, as it had been devised by Army intelligence rather than farmer intelligence. The point system ran this way: any outfit which had men with at least 85 points got to send the same amount of men home as outfits who had men with more than 85 points. Though I had 104 points, Army intelligence did not consider that to be any more than 85 points, or, to put it another way, they considered 104 to be equal to 85. It was hard to explain that to the folks back home, as I could hardly figure it out myself.

Besides that, there were still far more soldiers left in Italy than a lot of people imagined, and the clerical work involved in mustering us out, and the arranging of transportation for us were huge jobs. They wouldn't let me drive my own peep home, or I might have gotten there sooner.

Sunday, June 3, 1945   Made a trip to the battalion. Rained this p.m. Am kind of lonesome without Dick to talk to. Ham wanted to go to Murello again, so we did. Took the 4 girls, Albina, Jeanie, a friend, and Piente for a ride. There are very few civilian vehicles on the road. Back at 11:00.

Monday, June 4, 1945   Up at 7:00. Sun is out again, but a little cool. Two trips to the battalion. I found out I'm not leaving the 6th, but probably the 9th. Time drags by very slowly.

Tuesday, June 5, 1945   7:00 breakfast. Greased the peep, went to Division rear. I took the top down — beautiful weather again.

Wednesday, June 6, 1945   Staniger and Berglund left from here this a.m. Went to the battalion and find out I am leaving on the 9th. Not much doing. Hot and quiet.

Thursday, June 7, 1945   Overslept a little. To the battalion. On the way down I reflected back on the first trip I made alone as an agent. It was in Africa, May 9, 1943. This was my last trip alone. I picked up Henry Vaughn who will be my replacement when I leave.

Came back here. Time drags heavily. I have just a very little conception as to what things will be like in the States, how I will react to it, or how conditions will be at home.

Friday, June 8, 1945   A trip to the Air O.P. this morning with Barney. Packed all my things. Went to the battalion this p.m. Sat around and talked with the boys.

At 7:30 we all left and went to Division rear. It's hard to realize that after more than 4 years I am actually leaving the 151st. Am sure glad I kept this diary. Even though I think it's so incomplete, I'm one of the very few who has this much.

Barney gave me some good tips on what to say to the pro-Germans I might still run into in Minnesota: "Mostly nothing. The war is water over the dam now," he told me.

There had been more than a fair amount of pro-Hitler people in Minnesota before the war, as Minnesota had quite a large German-born or first- or second-generation German population. I myself learned to speak German before I learned to speak English. After my older brother Ray had a hard time during his first year in school because of his tangled English, my mother insisted that she and my dad start speaking only English at home, though as she told my son once, they "weren't no experts at it neither." I remember at Camp Claiborne being kidded because I pronounced the word "sink" as "Zink."

Though more than once I remember pro-Hitler and anti-Jewish comments floating around my home area during the 1930's spoken in both German and English, no one at home, and including the great majority of Germans in Germany itself, could even start to realize just how far anti-Semitism (which started as simply being against those who didn't believe in the same Christ that we did, or didn't believe in any Jesus Christ at all, but only in One nameless God who rules over all his own Creation) could ever go as wrong to the extent that it did in Hitler's Germany, where they tried to rule over God, His whole world and all common sense put together.

This poison too soon grew beyond the power of the common people to halt it. All they could do was watch and wonder how they could have been so taken in by Hitler's pseudo-religious "God will only bless those who look, believe and talk exactly as we do" Ayran rant-and-rave which resulted in the murder of millions.

When all of us guys who had been together for quite some time and had spent a lot of life and emotions together finally parted, there were a lot of handshakes and good-byes — and then we just left.

I did see Barney Devine again in 1968 in Tempe, Arizona. He had a small orange orchard, and my son and I applied for a job picking oranges.

Barney kept saying he knew me from somewhere, but I kept denying it, and kept asking him for a job. He insisted he knew that he knew me from somewhere.

Finally I asked him where he had been 23 years ago that day. At first he said he had been right there in Tempe, but when I told him, "No you weren't. Think again, Mister," he suddenly figured out who I was.

"Bud Wagner, you son of a ..." he exclaimed with a big wide grin, and shook my hand for close to a full minute.

He was a little embarassed when I noticed he was driving a Mercedes, but when I told him that the car I drove to work was a Volkswagen, we had to shake our heads at the irony. The war was really water over the dam.

Besides his orange orchard, Barney was working in a lumberyard and at the American Legion.

We spent a couple of days visiting with him and his wife, and kept in touch afterwards, until he passed away in 1969 from a heart attack.

Saturday, June 9, 1945   We had good accommodations last night. Up at 3:30. They took us in a 6X6 to Milan. We got there by 10:00, boarded a C-47 transport, and got to Naples in 2 ½ hours. Enjoyed the ride at 6,000 feet. We came about 500 miles. My ears hurt a lot coming down, though. Finally came down to the 7th Replacement Depot in Naples, close to the Texas Staging Area from where we left going to Anzio about 15 months ago. We ate in a plywood barracks. The place hasn't changed much. We had good service and food. The people, all military, are doing the best they can.

The C-47 seemed awful big — there were seats fashioned along each side of this converted transport, with the plane itself serving as a backrest for us. You can see a lot of an airplane from an inside view.

Sunday, June 10, 1945   Up at 6:00, and went through part of the out-processing. Very disagreeable, but necessary, as they're not going to let me go home without it. Roller-skated for several hours. Dengler and I are keeping close company. There are about 25 here from the 151st.

Monday, June 11, 1945   Drew more clothes: summer cottons and shoes. Went roller-skating for about 4 hours. Really tired tonight.

Tuesday, June 12, 1945   Laid around.

Wednesday, June 13, 1945   On guard duty, but only stood one post.

Thursday, June 14, 1945   On guard until 10:30. Took a shower and shaved. It's hot out here.

I sent a short letter to my sister Arlene thanking her for the birthday card I had received in time for my birthday today. I was 26.

Friday, June 15, 1945   Still at the Replacement Depot.

Saturday, June 16, 1945   On guard today. We wait.

Sunday, June 17, 1945   Went to the show, *A Tree Grows in Brooklyn* last night. Up at 6:00 as usual. A little cooler, perhaps, than before.

Monday, June 18, 1945   Went to the race track. Saw some of the other boys, including Dick and Hambright.

Tuesday, June 19, 1945   Waiting at the Medical Center in Naples. Am not going to keep this diary anymore, as I am tired of writing the same thing day after day — nothing — and it will take several weeks yet.

From what I've heard, the military service hasn't changed much at all since I was in. There are the men who have to do all the fighting, there are many people who keep themselves very busy feeling important doing nothing, and there is a whole lot of "Hurry up and wait."

Wednesday, July 4, 1945, Independence Day   We are put on the alert now. We left the Medical Center for the "Block House." One step nearer to home.

Thursday, July 5, 1945   Just laid around waiting. We were given a briefing tonight preparatory to our flight tomorrow.

Friday, July 6, 1945   Up at 4:30; left the Block House at 6:45. To the airport at 8:00. Boarded the B-17 Flying Fortress and flew to Casablanca, Africa. The trip took 7 hours.

A "Fort" is really some plane for power and hugeness, but only could be converted to haul 16 men at a time. We flew about 1,350 miles at 8,000 feet. Could see the clouds below us. The Mediterranean is as calm as ever. Cold in the plane. Can see all the pipes, tubes, and wires. Really something to get a ride in a B-17. Could see the wing flaps moving as we landed.

We are at a large airfield run by the Navy.

Saturday, July 7, 1945   Just waiting at Casablanca. Really can't go far, and aren't supposed to anyway. Eat and sleep and rest.

Sunday, July 8, 1945   The same.

Monday, July 9, 1945   Was put on the alert. Turned in my baggage. Will leave in the a.m.

Tuesday, July 10, 1945   Turned in blankets, etc., and etc. Got aboard the C-54 about 6:15. Took off shortly after. Landed at Dakar at 1:00. Chow and refueling. Off again at 2:00. Crossed the Atlantic. Arrived at Natal, Brazil at 11 p.m. — or 8:00 South American time. Had chow. Were assigned to beds. Enjoyed the trip all right, except I have a miserable head cold, and the difference in altitude is hard on my ears. There was nothing but sand and wasteland desert all the way from Casablanca to Dakar. Flew high. Many times could see nothing but clouds below.

I was continually comparing the air flight to the boat-ride I took across the Big Pond from New York to the British Isles in January of '42. This time I had a book along, the title lost in memory, and I read most of it over the Atlantic. There were about 50 of us on the plane, sitting on small bucket seats lined along both sides. It was a chilly and noisy ride, but smooth enough for me.

When we got to South America we all had to stay on the plane until some fellows came in and sprayed us and the whole area down with some chemical to get rid of any foreign bugs we might have still had on us.

We were at a regular Army or Air Force base. There were a lot of barracks, and we got a good meal. There was a Post Exchange there, and I bought a pair of sunglasses that I still have. We could go anywhere on the base, but weren't allowed to go off the base.

It was a real feeling of relaxation as we waited to get off the plane in the Western Hemisphere for the first time in years. The engines had been cut, and it was quiet. I think all of us on board shared the same feeling.

Wednesday, July 11, 1945   Had one white sheet and a pillow last night, a novelty.

Raining slightly. It reminds me of Louisiana. Can see but little of the country. Roamed around the camp area all day. Drank Coke. To bed at 8:00. Good meals and treatment.

Thursday, July 12, 1945   Up at 1 a.m. Ate. Waited, then boarded the C-46 at 2:30. Stopped at Berlin, Brazil at 9:00. Ate again. In the air at 10:00. Landed at 2:00 in British Guiana. Off again at 2:30. Landed at 6:00 in Puerto Rico. Ate. Off again at 7:00. Landed in Miami, Florida at 12:30 a.m. Made 3,960 miles in 19 hours.

Fitzgerald and I showered and shaved.

Went to the Red Cross and called home. Mom was asleep, but she answered the phone. Arlene said hello too. It was about 2:30 a.m. here before I finally got the call through. I'm really thankful to hear their voices again.

We each had an ice cream dish and tried to soak up as much of the USA that we could. This too is a large-sized base.

When we flew over the Amazon River, one of the crew members came back to tell us. We were pretty high up, and the whole area looked like a lush, green lawn with a silver strip, the Amazon running through it. I remember thinking of all the life that must have been going on in those lush, green forests and in the water, and I was glad I was up above all of it and heading for home.

We went through a bad rainstorm on one of the legs of the trip. The ride was getting a little rough, and some of our stomachs were getting a little uneasy. One of the flight crew told us to lay on the floor and to inhale and exhale with the ups and downs. I did that, and when we got through the rainstorm, I felt fine again.

During World War II times, if you'd flown for over 20 hours, you could become a member of what they called the "Short Snorter Club." The pilot gave each of us a printed card signed by him, stating we were members.

This printed card was only one version of the Short Snorter membership card. Many club members carried Short Snorter dollar bills which were signed by other passengers on the same cross-Atlantic flight. Passengers caught without their Short Snorter bill on them could be fined a dollar by the person who caught them.

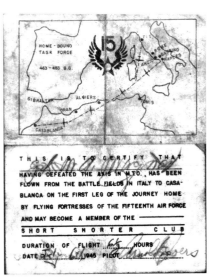

Friday, July 13, 1945   I didn't get to sleep until after 6:00 this morning. Bought more food, stuff we hadn't seen for 4 years. Up again at 7:00. Bought a few things at the canteen. Had a haircut. We boarded the train at about 6:30. Came here to Camp Blanding, Florida.

I'd always wanted to see Florida, and now I could say that I had, though I haven't been back there since. We had more Army food that day, and a good night's sleep.

My last letter home I mailed from Miami. I told them we were leaving for Camp Blanding, and were then heading for Fort McKoy in Wisconsin. Actually, we went to Fort Snelling in Minneapolis instead, and I was glad for that.

Saturday, July 14, 1945   Got to Fort Blanding at 4:30 this morning.

Up at 6:30. Ate. Had to stand a formation. Washed my cotton clothes. Not too much to do. They haven't started the deactivation process yet.

Sunday, July 15, 1945   Had to stand one more formation. Went to church. Boarded the train about 5 p.m. and took off. Stopped at a little Georgia town for two hours sometime after midnight. Everybody got out, and Roy and I met two pretty girls. Bought a watermelon and ate most of it. We're riding on Pullman cars.

When the train stopped that night, all the boys got out, and Roy and I walked around a bit and started talking to these 2 girls. We walked back towards the train and noticed that there was a gas station nearby that had cold watermelons for sale. They were in a shed filled with sawdust and ice chunks. I bought a nice one and came out with it. All 4 of us asked the other, "Who has a knife?" None of us did, but I had noticed a pile of railroad ties close to where we'd gotten off the train, so I said, "Come on, I'll get it cut."

I carried it back to the train, climbed up the pile of ties, and dropped the melon with force onto the ties. It broke into a beautiful, most tasty mess. Roy and I gorged ourselves on it, and even the girls thought it was a good way to have a little party. Roy and I, of course, were the celebrities, with all our chest-lettuce, corporal stripes, and 7 overseas stripes.

The party soon ended, though, and we had to get on board the train headed north. I don't think either one of us had girls much on our mind. What we wanted was to get going for home.

Monday, July 16, 1945   Went through Atlanta, Georgia this morning, and into Tennessee and Kentucky. Traveling all day. It's tiring, but I walk around a lot. It's beautiful country, what we can see of it.

Tuesday, July 17, 1945   Into Chicago about 8:00. We were fed on the train, then spent until 11:00 tonight here. Budinger, Fitzgerald and I looked over the town. Went to the USO and through the main part of town.

We left here about 11 p.m. still in the Pullman sleepers. I'm glad of that.

I'm starting to think about the day I'm actually going to walk in the door at home.

Wednesday, July 18, 1945   Got into St. Paul about 9:00. To Fort Snelling at 10:00. Started processing. It will take a few days. Called home again tonight, talked to Mom, Arlene and Ray. Was good to hear Ray again. Fort Snelling has changed considerably since I was last here 4 years ago.

Thursday, July 19, 1945   Had a physical this morning. Processing all day. Food is good, morale is high, and I remember nothing more.

Friday, July 20, 1945   Out of the Army today. Called Hurley, and I went to Bob and Jean Vaughn's by taxi. They took me back to the bus station, and I used that as my headquarters for the afternoon. Put my things in a locker and walked around town some. Had my stripes and medals sewn on my uniform by a tailor. Took a taxi to the train depot tonight, and left for Duluth at midnight.

Saturday, July 21, 1945   My head was full of thoughts all the way. Got to Duluth at 6 a.m. this morning, and walked to the Farmer's Market. Ray, Roger and Arlene were there. I took the truck home and saw the folks. Went back to the Market and talked to a lot of people.

Home at last. All the relatives came tonight and sort of celebrated my birthday with my homecoming.

The walk from the Soo Depot to the Market was an emotional one. I'd had thoughts I might not be able to find the Market after 4 years, but of course it is still there as if I had left yesterday.

Every time I walk by or go into the place I'll think of the morning I came in at 6:00, of being just discharged from the service, and of those who I know full well won't be coming back.

> There is no flock, however watched and tended,
> But one dead lamb is there;
> There is no fireside, howsoe'er defended,
> But has one vacant chair.

Bob and Jean Vaughn are staying at his folk's place, a big house in Robbinsdale; their baby was born not too long ago. Hurley just got out a few days before I did, too, but I didn't get to see him.

I had my jacket off as I was walking around Minneapolis yesterday, as it was a hot, July, Minneapolis day. Someone yelled, "Hey soldier!" It was an M.P. who told me, "Put your jacket on."

I sputtered a bit, and told him it was hot, and that I was discharged.

He snapped back at me and said, "You're out of uniform, now put that jacket on."

I put the jacket on.

At the St. Paul depot waiting for the midnight train, though, a fellow came up to me and remarked at my 7 overseas stripes. He told me he was from Hibbing, had not been drafted before for some valid reason, and he wanted to give me some money. I refused, but we talked quite a bit, and it left me feeling better after my encounter with the M.P. yesterday afternoon.

Six overseas stripes were common, but seven were not. The 151st Field Artillery was one of the first to leave the US January 16, 1942, and returned to US soil on July 13, 1945. One stripe was authorized for every 6 months overseas. Though we were 3 days shy of 42 months, the War Department was big about it and authorized us to wear the seven stripes. The 151st also had a bronze arrowhead for being attached to the 36th Division during the Italian Invasion at Salerno, and 5 battle stars for combat service from Tunisia to Milan.

My discharge paper says six stripes, but we were authorized to wear seven. The days of departure and return are stated on the discharge.

After I got home, one of my uncles asked me if I thought Army life bettered a person. I hadn't really thought this one out ahead of time, but I told him that I felt that if a person went in with a good attitude, he'd come out with a better one, but if he went in with a chip on his shoulder, he'd come out with a little more hate in him. I told him that I placed myself in the first category. My uncle was glad to hear that. I think he had been in favor of Hitler in the beginning, but changed his mind when the entire picture started to come out.

One thing I learned during the war was to be able to distinguish between a coincidence, and a situation that God had His hand in. Another thing I learned is that all heroes didn't make it into the history books or receive medals. My definition of "hero" has nothing to do with who killed the most Germans.

There was real sacrifice at home, as well. All the packages my family and others sent me had to be packed with contents, wrapped, driven to the Post Office and mailed. Postage was not free or even cheap for them. They sent many letters as well, as did many other friends.

As I said before, there is little or no glory in war; none at all in the combat zone. As someone once said, "War is a jigsaw puzzle of fighting men, bewildered and terrified civilians, unfinished conversations, fear, pain, fatigue, high explosives, and blood."

Nearly 3,000 years ago the prophet Isaiah prophesied a time when "Nation shall not lift up sword against nation, neither shall they learn war any more."

Since then, countless millions of lives have been lost in war, and vast resources have been used to aid man in killing his fellow man.

The Norwegian Academy of Science and the World Organization for the Protection of Humanity have calculated that in the last 5,000 years since man's written history has begun, there have been 14,531 wars, leaving only 292 years of peace. The same organizations figured that deaths caused by wars have totaled 3.4 billion.

Between the time England and France declared war on Germany on September 3, 1939, and the end of the war with Japan on August 8, 1945, there were no less than 27 declarations of war. There have been many more since then.

Most countries are prepared for war, or at least partially so. The United States heads the list with more strategic warheads than Russia, China, France, Israel, Britain, India, Pakistan, Korea, and Iran — but they all have them, and so may Iraq.

The world is in as much danger today as it ever has been. Terry Hawkins, director of nuclear security for the National Laboratory, said that during the Cold War, it was difficult for nations to obtain nuclear materials, but now, he said, "The barrier is no longer as strong as before. If a terrorist group or an unstable government obtains this nuclear material which is transported by illegal salesmen, they have solved the most difficult part of building a nuclear bomb."

Nowhere has man ever been promised that he will find lasting peace by his own efforts. He will keep on trying, but not by God's way, but by his own hypocritical way, turning plowshares into swords and dirt into nuclear bombs, and calling this a "quest for peace." Man's nature has not changed, and he is destined to fail for that reason. Nor have most humans even tried to live by truly applying God's word. But the good news is that there is a loving God who has determined He will save man from himself. The Bible predicts that human nature eventually will be changed, but only on the final Judgment day when every person shall be judged by his Maker, and many people will be rebuked. "Then nation shall not lift up the sword against nation, neither shall they learn war any more."

This book ends with the words of Jesus, the man who was crucified for expressing his faith and beliefs: "These things I have spoken to you that in me ye might have peace. In the world ye shall have tribulation; but be of good cheer. I have overcome the world."

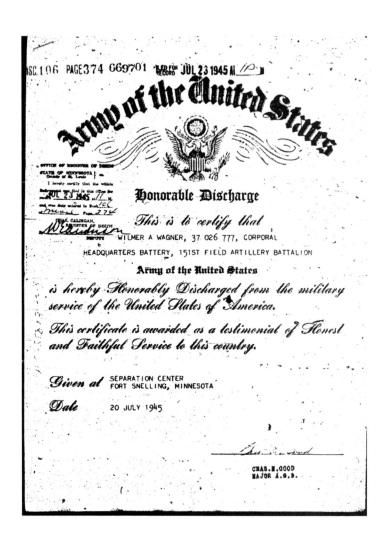

ENLISTED RECORD AND REPORT OF SEPARATION
HONORABLE DISCHARGE   MSC 1706 REC375

1. LAST NAME - FIRST NAME - MIDDLE INITIAL	2. ARMY SERIAL NO.	3. GRADE	4. ARM OR SERVICE	5. COMPONENT
WAGNER WILMER A	37 026 777	CPL	FA	AUS
6. ORGANIZATION	7. DATE OF SEPARATION	8. SEPARATION CENTER		
HQ BTRY 151ST FA BN	20 JUL 45	FORT SNELLING, MINNESOTA		
9. PERMANENT ADDRESS FOR MAILING PURPOSES	10. DATE OF BIRTH	11. PLACE OF BIRTH		
RT 2 BOX 838 DULUTH MINN	14 JUN 19	DULUTH MINN		
12. ADDRESS FROM WHICH EMPLOYMENT WILL BE SOUGHT	13. COLOR EYES	14. COLOR HAIR	15. HEIGHT	16. WEIGHT	17. NO DEPEND
SEE 9	BLUE	BROWN	5-6½	138 LBS	O

18. RACE	19. MARITAL STATUS	20. U.S. CITIZEN	21. CIVILIAN OCCUPATION AND NO.
WHITE X	SINGLE X	YES X	TRUCK DRIVER HEAVY 7-36.250

MILITARY HISTORY

22. DATE OF INDUCTION	23. DATE OF ENLISTMENT	24. DATE OF ENTRY INTO ACTIVE SERVICE	25. PLACE OF ENTRY INTO SERVICE
18 APR 41	18 APR 41		FORT SNELLING, MINNESOTA
SELECTIVE SERVICE	26. REGISTERED 27. LOCAL S.S. BOARD NO.	28. COUNTY AND STATE	29. HOME ADDRESS AT TIME OF ENTRY INTO SERVICE
YES X	5	ST. LOUIS MINN	SEE 9

30. MILITARY OCCUPATIONAL SPECIALTY AND NO.	31. MILITARY QUALIFICATION AND DATE
LIAISON AGENT 761	DRIVERS BADGE

32. BATTLES AND CAMPAIGNS
TUNISIA, NAPLES-FOGGIA, ROME-ARNO, NORTH APENNINES, PO VALLEY

33. DECORATIONS AND CITATIONS
GOOD CONDUCT MEDAL SO 22 151ST FA BN 44
BRONZE SERVICE ARROWHEAD 45

34. WOUNDS RECEIVED IN ACTION
NONE

35. LATEST IMMUNIZATION DATES				36. SERVICE OUTSIDE CONTINENTAL U.S. AND RETURN		
SMALLPOX	TYPHOID	TETANUS	OTHER (specify)	DATE OF DEPARTURE	DESTINATION	DATE OF ARRIVAL
10JUN45	17DEC44	3FEB43	TYPHUS10JUN45	15 JAN 42	E T O	26 JAN 42
				22 DEC 42	M A T O	3 JAN 43
37. TOTAL LENGTH OF SERVICE		38. HIGHEST GRADE HELD		6 SEP 43	M T O	9 SEP 43
CONTINENTAL SERVICE	FOREIGN SERVICE			5 JUL 45	U S	12 JUL 45
YEARS MONTHS DAYS	YEARS MONTHS DAYS					
0 9 5	3 5 28	CPL				

39. PRIOR SERVICE
NONE

40. REASON AND AUTHORITY FOR SEPARATION
CONVENIENCE OF GOVT, RR1-1 (DEMOBILIZATION), AR 615-365, 15 DEC 44

41. SERVICE SCHOOLS ATTENDED	42. EDUCATION (Years)		
NONE	Grammar	High School	College
	8	1	0

PAY DATA

43. LONGEVITY FOR PAY PURPOSES	44. MUSTERING OUT PAY		45. SOLDIER DEPOSITS	46. TRAVEL PAY	47. TOTAL AMOUNT, NAME OF DISBURSING OFFICER	
YEARS MONTHS DAYS	TOTAL	THIS PAYMENT				
4 3 3	$300	$100	$32.28		AUS-24 W J MCCORMACK 1ST LT FD

INSURANCE NOTICE
IMPORTANT IF PREMIUM IS NOT PAID WHEN DUE OR WITHIN THIRTY-ONE DAYS THEREAFTER, INSURANCE WILL LAPSE. MAKE CHECKS OR MONEY ORDERS PAYABLE TO THE TREASURER OF THE U. S. AND FORWARD TO COLLECTIONS SUBDIVISION, VETERANS ADMINISTRATION, WASHINGTON 25, D. C.

48. KIND OF INSURANCE	49. HOW PAID	50. Effective Date of Allotment Discontinuance	51. Date of Next Premium Due (One month after 50)	52. PREMIUM DUE EACH MONTH	53. INTENTION OF VETERAN TO
U.S. Govt. X	Allotment	31 JUL 45	31 AUG 45	$6.60	Continue X

54. REMARKS (This space for completion of above items or entry of other items specified in W.D. Directives)
EUROPEAN-AFRICAN-MIDDLE EASTERN THEATER SERVICE MEDAL
AMERICAN DEFENSE SERVICE MEDAL
SIX (6) OVERSEAS SERVICE BARS
NO TIME LOST UNDER AW 107
LAPEL BUTTON ISSUED
FOUR (4) DISCHARGE EMBLEMS ISSUED

55. SIGNATURE OF PERSON BEING SEPARATED	57. PERSONNEL OFFICER (Type name, grade and organization - signature)
[signature]	*[signature]* L A RIKANSRUD CAPT AUS ASSISTANT ADJUTANT

WD AGO FORM 53-55
November 1944   This form supersedes all previous editions of WD AGO Forms 53 and 55 for enlisted persons entitled to an Honorable Discharge, which will not be used after receipt of this revision.

DEDICATED BY THE WORLD WAR II MEMBERS OF THE 151st FIELD ARTILLERY BATTALION, TO THE MEMORY OF THEIR COMRADES WHO SACRIFICED THEIR LIVES IN THE SERVICE OF THEIR COUNTRY DURING THE GREAT CONFLICT 7 DECEMBER 1941 - 2 SEPTEMBER 1945

HQ & HQ BTRY

LT.	ROBERT B. BENTLEY
PFC.	ROBERT J. BRATTON
LT.	WILBUR DICKHEISER
PVT.	JOHN DOLASH
PFC.	DANIEL T. DOYLE
LT.	ROSS T. FLEMING
CPL.	ARDEN HARRIS
CAPT.	LUCIEN W. HOULE
T/5	KENNETH W. KRAMER
LT.	NORBERT F. MOTT JR.
CAPT.	EDWARD STEWART
T/5	JOSEPH URBAN

A BTRY

SSGT.	THOMAS J. AHR
CPL.	JOSEPH G. BANWARTH
PVT.	DANIEL J. CASEY
PVT.	JOHN ESPINOZA
PVT.	BILLIE F. HICKS
CAPT.	HAROLD HOLLERAN
PVT.	CHARLES R. MILLS
PFC.	GEORGE W. MILTON
1SGT.	BOYCE P. MURPHY
LT.	MARVIN E. NURNBERGER
PFC.	MILO A. PHILLIPS
PFC.	CHESTER C. SZEWCZYK
PFC.	JOSEPH T. TRACEY
PVT.	ROBERT T. VINCENT
CPL.	DONALD H. VINUP

B BTRY

PVT.	HOYTE L. ASHE
SSGT.	EUGENE R. ENGSTROM
PVT.	CLAUDE J. LANDRY
T/5	ROLAND M. LINDSTROM
PVT.	JAMES A. MEEKS
PFC.	EARL L. MEISTER
PVT.	JOHN G. PARRISH
T/5	ERNEST R. ROSE

C BTRY

PVT.	GORDON N. CASHNER
SSGT.	VERNON L. DELIN
LT.	JOHN P. GILREATH

SVC BTRY

LT.	EUGENE L. DELISLE
PVT.	GEORGE A. HERR
LT.	RALPH J. MOORE
PFC.	CLAIR W. MOSER
PVT.	FERDINAND E. RUBEN
CPL.	ARTHUR A. WEST

MED DET

T/3	JOHN W. KELLER

"they gave the last full measure of devotion"

Plaque erected by members of the 151st to commemorate the memory of those who died in combat.

APPENDIX A

SOME ITEMS OF INTEREST IN THE HISTORY OF THE 151ST FIELD ARTILLERY BATTALION

1.   The 151st Field Artillery Battalion, as such, was formed on 30 January 1942, by the redesignation of the 1st Battalion, 151st Field Artillery Regiment, Minnesota National Guard. A brief history of the Battalion follows.

The 151st Field Artillery Regiment was originally organized in 1864 as the 1st Regiment, Minnesota Heavy Artillery. After the Civil War the Regiment commenced its reorganization, and in 1893 the 1st Battalion, Field Artillery, was organized. In 1900 it was redesignated as the 1st Field Artillery, and three years later was expanded to six batteries. The 1st Field Artillery served on the Mexican Border, 1916-1917. It was drafted into Federal service 5 August, 1917, and subsequently redesignated the 151st Field Artillery, a unit of the 42nd Division of World War I.

The 151st Field Artillery served in France and participated in the Champagne-Marne, Aisne-Marne, St. Mihiel, and Meus-Argonne operations and in defensive sectors in Lorraine and Champagne. It returned to the United States and was demobilized in 1919 and reorganized as the 1st Field Artillery, which, in 1921, was redesignated the 151st Field Artillery. On 30 January, 1942, the 151st was split into two battalions. The 1st Battalion kept the designation of the 151st Field Artillery Battalion; the 2nd Battalion of the Regiment was redesignated as the 175th Field Artillery Battalion.

The 151st Field Artillery Battalion is entitled to Streamers as indicated:

CIVIL WAR

               (Gettysburg)   Without inscription

WORLD WAR I

Lorraine	Aisne-Marne
Champagne	St. Mihiel
Champagne-Marne	Meuse-Argonne

WORLD WAR II

Tunisian Campaign
Naples-Foggia Campaign
Rome-Arno Campaign
Po Valley Campaign

Members who actually participated in the Salerno Landing are entitled to the Bronze Arrowhead.

2. The 151st Field Artillery Battalion was the only unit of the 34th Division to hit the beaches at Salerno on D Day. They were attached to the 36th Division. In this crucial battle the 151st was credited with playing a major part in saving the beachhead.

3. The 34th Division Artillery probably holds a record for the US Army in World War II in the amount of artillery thrown at the Axis forces.

Below is shown the number of rounds fired by each battalion in the various campaigns:

UNIT	TUNISIAN	NAPLES-FOGGIA	ROME-ARNO	NO. APPENINES	PO VALLEY	TOTAL
125	30,328	30,938	147,620	54,993	38,368	302,247
151	10,430	51,573	132,670	87,915	38,393	320,981
175	45,000	42,706	94,580	92,894	40,496	315,676
185	16,100	29,162	60,139	49,150	18,549	173,460
	101,858	154,379	435,009	285,312	135,809	1,112,364

On April 16, 1945, the 151st Field Artillery Battalion reported 7,213 rounds expended, and on the following day the 175th Field Artillery reported expending 7,215 rounds. It is believed that these were the biggest expenditures ever made in a like period by one battalion. During the period April 15 to 19 inclusive, the Division artillery expended 70,655 rounds.

APPENDIX B

ANATOMY OF A DIVISION

The 34th Infantry Division — Approximately 30,000 troops were in training during our stay at Camp Claiborne, Louisiana.

The following units were each a part of the 34th Infantry Division in 1941:

59th Field Artillery Brigade
    A. 125th Field Artillery Battalion
    B. 151st Field Artillery Battalion (Later separated, becoming the 151st Field Artillery Battalion, and the 175th Field Artillery Battalion.)

67th Infantry Brigade
    A. 133rd Infantry
    B. 168th Infantry

68th Infantry Brigade
    A. 135th Infantry
    B. 164th Infantry

34th Division Headquarters

34th Division Artillery Headquarters

136th Medical Detachment

109th Special Engineer Troops

109th Quarter Master

28th Quarter Master

367th Infantry

5th Signal Battalion

151st Engineers

Station Hospital

Camp Headquarters

Post Troops

Warehouses

Stockade

Service Club

     All mess halls, latrines, warehouses, hospital buildings, and the large two story Service Club were of frame construction built on concrete posts. Otherwise, Camp Claiborne was strictly a tent city, with five men to a 16' X 16' tent.

APPENDIX C

ARMY RANKS AND INSIGNIA

ENLISTED

Private	Pvt.	No stripes
Private First Class	Pfc.	One stripe
Corporal	Cpl.	Two stripes
Sergeant	Sgt.	Three stripes
Staff Sergeant	Staff Sgt.	Four stripes, three on the top and one on the bottom.
Technical Sergeant	Tech Sgt.	Five stripes, three on the top and two on the bottom.
First Sergeant	1st Sgt.	Three stripes on the top, a diamond in the middle and two stripes on the bottom.

WARRANT OFFICERS

Were between enlisted men and commissioned officers. Were called "Mr." or the "Master Sergeant."

COMMISSIONED OFFICERS

Second Lieutenant	2nd Lt.	One gold bar
First Lieutenant	1st Lt.	One silver bar

Captain	Capt.	Double silver bars
Major	Maj.	Gold Oak Leaf
Lieutenant Colonel	Lt. Col.	Silver Oak Leaf
Colonel	Col.	Silver Eagle
Brigadier General	Brig. Gen.	One Silver Star
Major General	Maj. Gen.	Two Silver Stars
Lieutenant General	Lt. Gen.	Three Silver Stars
General	Gen.	Four Silver Stars
General of the Army	Gen.	Five Silver Stars

"General of the Army" or "Five-Star General" was a new rank created during World War II, and first awarded to General Dwight D. Eisenhower.

There was other Army insignia besides that of rank. We were awarded one "overseas stripe" for each six months we were overseas. Bronze and silver arrowheads were awarded to those who participated in D-day invasions; the bronze was for participation in one invasion, and the silver for participation in more than one. I was awarded the bronze. Though I was at Anzio as well as at Salerno, I was not a participant in the actual invasion.

APPENDIX D

The following was taken from the current 34th Division's Web page:

WELCOME TO THE 34TH INFANTRY DIVISION'S (RED BULL) HOMEPAGE

GERALD A. MILLER
MAJOR GENERAL, COMMANDING

CHARLES J. BENDA
COMMAND SERGEANT MAJOR

34th Infantry Division (RED BULL)
"ATTACK! ATTACK! ATTACK!"

RED BULL HISTORY

The 34th Infantry Division was created from National Guard troops from Minnesota, Iowa, the Dakotas and Nebraska in the late summer of 1917. It arrived in France in October of 1918 but was too late to see action in World War I as the war ended the following month.

The 34th Infantry Division was activated during World War (WW) II on February 10, 1941. The Division made a good showing at the Louisiana Maneuvers. As the first Division to be shipped overseas, Pvt. Henke of Hutchinson, Minnesota was credited as being the 1st American soldier to step off the boat in support of the war effort.

The Division participated in five major Army campaigns in North Africa, Sicily, and Italy. The Division is credited with amassing 517 days of continuous front line combat, more than any other division in the European theater. Portions of the 34th Division are credited with over 600 days of front line combat. The Division suffered 21,362 casualties, of which 3,737 were killed. Members of the Division were awarded 11 Medals of Honor and 98 Distinguished Service Crosses.

The US Rangers trace their lineage through the 34th Infantry Division. During WW II, the 1st Ranger Battalion was formed under the command of one of the Division's officers, CPT William Darby. 80% of the 1st Ranger Battalion's volunteers were drawn from the 34th, and they soon became famous as "Darby's Rangers."

ABOUT THE RED BULL PATCH

The RED BULL insignia of the 34th Infantry Division was based on a design by Marvin Cone of Cedar Rapids, IA who drew it for a contest while training with the Division at Camp Cody in 1917. A steer skull imposed on the shape of a Mexican water jar (called an "olla") recalled the Division's desert home not far from the Mexican border.

During WW II, German soldiers in Italy referred to the American soldiers who wore the familiar patch as "Red Devils" or "Red Bulls." The latter name stuck, and the Division soon adopted it officially, replacing its WW I name of the "Sandstorm Division."

CURRENT STRUCTURE

The current 34th Infantry Division (Medium) was reactivated into active National Guard status on February 10, 1991, exactly 50 years after the Division's mobilization for WW II. Currently transitioning into a Medium Division, the 34th Infantry Division has a required strength of 16,906 soldiers.

The Division's force structure is currently spread across three states (Minnesota, Iowa and Illinois). Changes in the command plan will increase the Division's span to seven states (Minnesota, Iowa, Wisconsin, North Dakota, Illinois, Colorado, and Michigan) and includes a modernization plan for a majority of the units in the Division.

For additional information about the Division such as, Opportunities, Organizations and News Stories, click on one of the "Hot" buttons to find out more about us.

ACKNOWLEDGMENTS

When I first began to seriously talk about writing up my World War II diary in the early 1990's, I was impressed and surprised at how many people showed genuine interest in reading it. I expected my own family to be interested, of course, but everyone else who heard about it was genuinely interested as well.

During the early 1990's, Carol Bly, a Minnesota author, writer, and teacher of writing, invited would-be writers to send her questions about writing.

I responded with a copy of an original diary page with the question, "Do you think I should attempt to write this into a journal or possibly a book?" I gave her a few more details about the diary I had kept.

Her answer was definite and positive. She said, "Of course you should write it. Certainly you should write it. Who else could write it for you?" She pointed out to me that there were those whose voices had been stilled and who couldn't speak for themselves, and that I had the opportunity of telling their stories as I told my own. She continued by saying that in the not too distant future, all the World War II veterans would be gone, along with the many personal stories that were theirs during the war.

The diary page I had sent to Carol Bly had a simple sentence saying, "Bombers were over this afternoon."

In her reply she pointed out to me that the answers to the questions, "Whose bombers? Were they enemy or friendly? What kind, and how many were there? Did they drop bombs? What was your reaction?" would all add details that would interest and inform the general reader much more than the original diary entry alone.

I appreciated Carol Bly's comments and encouragement very much, and I always kept her advice in mind as I wrote this book.

My son-in-law Ed Newman gave me similar advice and encouragement. He had a constant desire to see my diary written up at least into the form of a journal for the family's benefit, as Ed had relatives who had fought in the Civil War, but no record had been kept of their experiences.

It was Ed's vision of my diary being written into a book he expressed to me many years ago, as well as a booklet about my war experiences he put together and printed himself a few years ago, that finally got me started writing. I owe him a heartfelt "Thank you" not only for his vision and his goading me onward, but for all his work in helping getting this book published.

I'd like to thank my daughter, Susie Newman for helping greatly in the proof-reading.

My son, Lloyd was also interested in seeing this book written, as he has always been an avid reader and student of history. From the time he was very young, he had always shown a lot of interest in my photographs and asked a lot of questions about the war. There were some incidents I had told him of nearly 40 years ago and didn't realize he had remembered — until they mysteriously showed up in this book during his typing of the first draft. I had nearly forgotten them myself.

I'd like to thank Lloyd for all the work he did in working over the manuscript, making some deletions and additions, typing and retyping, retrieving lost information after a bad computer crash, scanning and enhancing more of my old faded photographs than I had ever dared to hope could be salvaged and putting this book into its present form.

Both Ed and Lloyd made clear to me an adage I had heard before: "No writer works alone."

Much of the commentary in this book was written from memory. During the war itself, however, I didn't have a very large overview of what was going on in the greater world situation, so of course I have had to take information from other sources besides my memory. I have credited those sources in the text whenever possible.

Some information on our troop movements, and statistics of casualties, Killed in Action, numbers of rounds of ammunition expended, etc., was taken from a "Narrative History of the 151st Field Artillery Battalion." This was a brief, month-by-month officially-approved record of the battalion's history from its induction into Federal Service on February 10, 1941, to its deactivation on November 3, 1945. There could have been more than one official battalion historian who wrote up these monthly accounts. I would like to acknowledge each one of them, as when I worked on the commentary, I borrowed liberally and sometimes literally from the official history.

I would like to extend my thanks to Don Sternke, both for the pleasure of having known him as a friend for so many years, and for the fact that so many times during my writing of this book when my rememberer would fail me, it was Don on the other end of the telephone line giving me needed advice and information.

"Old Dick" Johnson, as we called him, isn't with us anymore, but his memory always will be. I would acknowledge him for his unusual type of humor, his good company and his friendship, all of which I could always count on when we made our many night trips together with specials, overlays and firing orders.

Even when we were totally exhausted from being kept going for days and nights on end, and many times when we were the most tired and crying for rest, and even when the "close ones" were still coming close to leaving us as no more than little grease-spots in the Italian mud, rain, fog, snow, dust, or cold, "Old Dick" and I could still say that there wasn't enough darkness in all of Italy to overcome the one small candle-beam of light that we always had between us as friends.

Thanks go as well to Bob "Arky" Vaughn and to Hurley Soderlind who were excellent friends and fellow workers in the kitchen during the war. Annual summer visits back and forth between our families after the war are among my happiest memories.

I would like to again give thanks to my family, friends and relatives for the many packages, letters, prayers and greetings they sent me while I was away. They made mail-call always something for me to look forward to as a reminder of Home.

I would like to give thanks and acknowledgment to all those who fought in other campaigns than I did. To a neighbor in Hermantown, Wilfred Pehl, whose children I drove to school after the war. He had gone through the Normandy Invasion on Omaha Beach, and he once told me there was so much war equipment assembled in England in June 1944 for the coming Invasion, it was a wonder the whole Island didn't sink into the sea.

Over 37,000 men were Killed in Action at Normandy during this "Greatest military operation the world has ever known." And these 37,000 dead were still only a small part of the huge and terrible price paid for Victory. Without all of them, this book would probably never have been written.

Nor could it have been written without the thousands of millions of people from coast to coast in this country and from the entire round world over, who were the **Allies against the Axis Powers** during World War II. No matter what their particular jobs or sacrifices were, or their age, sex, color, or creed — all pulled together for the long haul, and we won, and may God preserve the peace.

Wilmer (Bud) Wagner
Hermantown, Minnesota
Sunday, June 18, 2000

Bud Wagner resides in Hermantown, Minnesota, where he and his wife, Evelyn, raised three children, Lloyd, Nancy and Susan. They have six grandchildren and two great-grandchildren, with two more on the way.

Bud and Evelyn operated a truck farm and greenhouse until 1991. Bud retired from driving school bus (another job, he says, that required more nerve than brains) for the Hermantown School District in 1982. He is currently working on his second book.

Mr. Wagner completed 9th grade at Proctor High School in 1934, and is presently continuing his education in the school of hard knocks.

To order a copy of this book
send $24.95 plus $3.50 S/H to:

Contact Robert Wagner

218-269-4444